Hugh Johnson   Jancis Robinson

THE WORLD ATLAS OF
WINE

7th EDITION

MITCHELL BEAZLEY

This edition was first published in Great Britain in 2013 by
Mitchell Beazley, an imprint of Octopus Publishing Group
Ltd, Carmelite House, 50 Victoria Embankment, London
EC4Y 0DZ
www.octopusbooks.co.uk | www.octopusbooksusa.com

An Hachette UK Company
www.hachette.co.uk

Distributed in the US by Hachette Book Group, 1290 Avenue
of the Americas, 4th and 5th Floors, New York, NY 10020

Distributed in Canada by Canadian Manda Group,
664 Annette Street, Toronto, Ontario, Canada M6S 2C8

ISBN 978 1 84533 689 9

Printed and bound in Malaysia

10 9 8 7 6 5

Managing Editor **Gill Pitts**

Assistant Editor **Julia Harding MW**

Research Assistant **Priscilla Reby**

Art Director **Jonathan Christie**

Deputy Art Director **Yasia Williams-Leedham**

Design concept **Peter Dawson, Louise Evans,
Grade Design**

Designers **Lizzie Ballantyne, Peter Dawson,
Louise Evans**

Senior Production Manager **Peter Hunt**

Cartographic Editor **Alison Ewington**

Gazetteer **Andrew Johnson**

Index **Jane Parker**

Proofreader **Jamie Ambrose**

Picture Research Manager **Giulia Hetherington**

Picture Research **Emma O'Neil**

Revisions and new cartography for the seventh edition
Cosmographics

Original cartography **Clyde Surveys Ltd**

HOW THE MAPS WORK

The maps in this Atlas vary considerably in scale, the level
of detail depending on the complexity of the area mapped.
There is a scale bar with each map. Contour intervals vary
from map to map and are shown in each map key.

Serif type (eg MEURSAULT) on the maps indicates
names and places connected with wine; sans serif type
(eg Meursault) mainly shows other information.

Each map page has a grid with letters down the side and
numbers across the bottom. To locate a château, winery,
etc, look up the name in the Gazetteer (pages 385–399),
which gives the page number followed by the grid reference.

Every effort has been made to make the maps in this Atlas
as complete and up to date as possible. In order that future
editions may be kept up to this standard, the publishers
would be grateful for any information that will help to keep
the maps up to date.

Previous page: O Fournier's futuristic winery,
Mendoza, Argentina

Right: Merlot vines in winter, Fanagoria vineyard,
Taman Peninsula, Russia

Contents

Foreword

Seven editions in 42 years. A strike rate of one every six years. Does this reflect the rate of change in the world of wine? Pretty well, I think. Other arts and industries evolve quicker. Planting a vineyard and processing the results involves an inevitable time lag – five years at least – and evaluating those results is a business that can't be rushed either. But anyone who has, or can remember, one of the early Atlas editions must be amazed at the scope of this one.

Who would have dreamed, even two or three editions ago – in, say, the 1990s – that we would need detailed contour maps of what were then bare mountainsides in the Andes or New Zealand's Southern Alps? Still less, though admittedly in less detail so far, that we would be plotting the wine producers of China. What is driving this seemingly ineluctable expansion of the wine world? We are: by our thirst, by our curiosity, and by the quest for better that is almost the definition of a fast-developing world.

Once there seemed to be logical cultural limits. Wine is, after all, a European phenomenon. Where Europeans settled, wine would follow; the only question was (and is no longer) whether it could match up to its originals. But Asia? The world conquered by Islam, perhaps the first place where wine was made, aeons ago, has tragically ruled itself out. Further east there seemed little chance, whether for cultural reasons or agricultural ones. Far Eastern peoples, we thought, often have problems metabolizing alcohol – and great vintages are not associated with monsoons.

How little we knew. The big news of the past few years is that China has very much got the point of wine, and is not only buying it, sometimes regardless of price, but producing a very great deal in the heart of the Middle Kingdom. India, Thailand, one eastern Asian country after another are following suit.

True, when you compare the agricultural world of wine with the science-driven worlds of communication or transport its progress seems more stately. But there is another variable to add in: that of fashion. It seems odd for fashion to so profoundly affect something as personal as taste in food and drink. But not so odd, perhaps, when you think that all of us need guidance through the maze of labels and prices, qualities and styles.

When the previous (sixth) edition went to print there were two major trends in evidence (climate change had already emerged as a major force by the fifth edition). The first was differentiation. It was no longer enough to name a broad region;

premium prices were going to smaller and smaller units of land that could claim to be distinct and different. Winemakers who formerly mocked the gospel of terroir started looking hopefully and hard at their own.

At the same time, the market was demanding difference in grape varieties, too. "Anything But Cabernet/Chardonnay" was the catchphrase. So grape-growers who had a choice were studying not only where their Cabernet was ripening best, but whether a different grape altogether wouldn't give them a better result. The rise and rise of varietalism, or grape-consciousness, or the desire to taste different fruits, has been evident since California stopped calling its wines Claret or Burgundy 60 years ago. In the past five or 10 it has become the overruling factor.

You will see the results in this Atlas. My colleague Jancis was one of the first writers to spot (or did she help to create?) the trend. Her book *Vines, Grapes & Wines*, published in 1986, was the first popular work to describe the vast variety of the planet's wine grapes. Nearly 30 years later, having surveyed every other aspect of wine in her *Oxford Companion to Wine*, she and two colleagues published *Wine Grapes*, a detailed review of 1,368 grape varieties in commercial use for winemaking today.

THE LANDSCAPE OF THE VINE

The landscape of the vine the Atlas portrays is many times the size it was. Its population, too, is becoming far more varied and its ethnic variety much more appreciated. Yet the essential connection, the unique link, between fruit and soil becomes only more intense. There is no other product on earth, agricultural or industrial, where value is as directly and precisely related to where it grows and is made. Only wine goes to market with the name of a field, a farm, or at least a county, as its business card. Tracing the meaning of these cards, and the consequent value of their bottles, is the business of this book.

It was the smartest move I ever made when, with four editions of this work behind me, I

invited Jancis to share the load. She is younger than I, and (being a Master of Wine) far better qualified. She now travels and tastes much more than I do, and through her website, her books and articles, and her efficient team of co-workers is as well-informed and well-connected as anyone in the world of wine has ever been.

My role? Supervisory in a distant sense. Critical, sometimes, in a stylistic one. Questioning about some of the more amazing revelations that continually occur in compiling this book. Admiring – as you can imagine. Founder, of course – I don't forget that. And grateful for the huge efforts and intense cooperation of everyone involved, from Julia Harding, Jancis's closest co-worker; Allison Walls and Alison Ewington who, respectively, compute and supervise the maps; Priscilla Reby, who collects the labels and undertakes many other editorial tasks; and, above all, to Gill Pitts, who never leaves her command post at Mitchell Beazley, keeps track of every detail, every development, subs our copy and makes it fit, tactfully drives us on, and keeps the utmost good humour through a pretty taxing schedule.

Authors routinely thank their collaborators, genuflect to their publishers, claim responsibility for the mistakes, and take their bow. I make a supplementary claim: to be the luckiest wine-atlas-maker ever in my partner, our helpers, and you, our readers. It is your curiosity, enthusiasm, passion for wine, and eagle eyes for detail that makes our efforts so rewarding.

"Hugh Johnson and Jancis Robinson are the Bordeaux and Burgundy of wine writers"

Introduction

One of the very few frustrating responses I get from the swelling army of wine lovers around the globe is: *"The World Atlas of Wine*? I've got a copy of that."* It almost always turns out that the copy they are referring to dates from another decade. Don't they realize how much this book changes with each edition? The third edition just will not do!* This seventh edition, for example, has been the prime project for Hugh, me, my hard-working associate Julia Harding MW, and the book's doughty managing editor Gill Pitts for two long years. As we progressed along the route from shaping it to doing it, our party of workers ballooned to include a battalion of cartographers, designers, artists, researchers, indexers, and the all-important local consultants. Every word, symbol, and comma has been reviewed and, typically, revised so as to offer in this book a true and up-to-date representation of the world of wine in 2013.

This world is very different even from the wine world of 2007, when the last (sixth) edition was published, and is completely unrecognizable compared with the size, let alone state, of the world of wine in, say, 1985, when the third edition was published. In that edition just two pages were devoted to South America, one to New Zealand. There was no hint that Asia would become the major force in wine that it is today, and so on.

What is fun with each edition is to join the dots, to chronicle the changes reported from each wine region and, often, realize that they are surprisingly similar. The wine world, too, is a village, it would seem: one that reflects in stark detail the effects of climate change.

Hugh has already remarked on the dramatic broadening of the range of grape varieties put to commercial use. It was not that long ago when it seemed as though the world's winemakers, wherever they were, were making wine to a handful of global recipes using quite remarkably few international grape varieties. Today, real joy is taken in recuperating, exploiting, and celebrating local vine varieties in traditional regions, and in experimenting with novel varieties in newer ones. The producer is much more entertained and the consumer is surely considerably more titillated.

But we have noticed another, more recent, global trend, even if it tends to have been reported from each region as though it were a strictly local phenomenon. Virtually everywhere there is a distinct movement away from mass and concentration for their own sake, a realization that wines are more interesting if they express a vineyard's natural characteristics rather than winemaking technique. An increasing proportion of the wine made today is lighter, fresher, and more transparently the product of geography than it was a decade ago. We are delighted by this, not just because it suits our own taste in wine more, but also because it adds further justification for a detailed geographical guide to wine such as this.

Thus, even in California, home of the blockbuster, we can also choose from delicate Pinots and racy Chardonnays grown on the Sonoma Coast or in the equally fog-cooled Sta. Rita Hills of the Central Coast much further south. Meanwhile, in Australia, where only yesterday surely all Chardies were rich and oaky

and Shirazes tarry essences, there has been a comprehensive volte-face. Most Chardonnays are now so lissom they can almost be accused of being anorexic, while a completely new style of Shiraz, sometimes even called Syrah, has emerged, one in which elegance is a virtue. In Spain, the most revered reds were once the densest and most obviously oaked, but today, the focus has been moving northwest to vineyards cooled by the Atlantic and those at particularly high elevations inland. In Italy, too, less is more, with the transparent wines grown on the slopes of Mount Etna and those on the subalpine slopes of the Aosta Valley enjoying newfound respect.

We have tried to reflect new areas of interest in what we have introduced in this new edition. Texts have been thoroughly updated and sometimes completely rewritten and we present no fewer than 25 new maps. France remains the country mapped in the most detail because it is, of the two most significant wine producers in the world by far, that with the longest history of celebrating geographical precision. But even in France, the winescape has changed noticeably since 2007, and not just in how its wines are denominated. The Languedoc *vignoble*, in particular, has shrunk while average quality has soared. We have introduced for this edition a detailed map of Richebourg to illustrate the parcellation of even some of the most famous vineyards of the Côte d'Or, and a particularly detailed map of the many different soil types of Châteauneuf-du-Pape. On the other hand, we no longer devote a map to Vins

---

No, not a château in Bordeaux, but Chateau Changyu AFIP Global in China's Hebei province. France provides the templates for both wine styles and winery architecture. In the past 10 years, China has established itself as hugely important in the wine world – not just as a consumer, but also as a grape-grower and wine producer.

de Pays now that they are being replaced by IGPs (see p.46). New maps of Etna and northwest Spain are a response to the trend outlined above in Italy and Spain, respectively, while we have introduced a map of Vinho Verde and extended that of the Douro in northern Portugal, as well as adding new maps of parts of Austria, Croatia, Slovenia, and, for the first time, Georgia. The emergent wine industry of Turkey gets its own treatment, while the shrinking one of North Africa has been mothballed (perhaps to re-emerge as Morocco beefs up its tourist industry).

Hugh and I could not be more aware of the huge changes there have been in the wines produced in Germany. As a result, we offer you a completely new map of the Ahr plus detailed maps of Wonnegau in Rheinhessen, Monzingen in the Nahe, and Kaiserstuhl in Baden – all in the name of greater geographical precision.

But we know, too, that much of the recent development in the world of wine has been far from Europe and are keen to have this Atlas reflect that. The number of pages devoted to North America has grown from 34 to 40, thanks in part to much deeper coverage of Canada (with Germany and England, one of the prime beneficiaries of climate change) and of Mexico, which now has its own burgeoning wine culture in Baja California. The maps of Northern Sonoma and Washington State's Columbia Valley have been extended, while Virginia, the Finger Lakes, and Santa Ynez Valley all have their own new detailed maps now.

Both Chile and Argentina have new maps, and Australia's Mornington Peninsula and part of Tasmania have detailed map treatments for the first time in this edition. The maps of the Awatere Valley in Marlborough and Canterbury are innovations for our coverage of New Zealand, while new maps for Swartland and Cape South Coast in South Africa and Ningxia in China are symptomatic of recent developments in those countries – all of them unthinkable when we were preparing the last edition.

HOW THIS ATLAS WORKS

The maps have been put together with the consumer, not the wine bureaucrat, in mind. If an appellation – AOC, DOC, DO, AVA, GI, or South African ward, for example – exists but is of no practical interest to the wine drinker, our policy is to omit it. If the name of a region, area, or district is in common wine parlance, even if it has not yet been granted an official designation, we have tended to include it.

We have marked those wineries we think are of particular interest to the world's wine lovers, whether on the basis of the quality of their wine or their local importance. It can be difficult in some parts of the world, however, to pinpoint exactly where a winemaking enterprise is based. Many operations, particularly but by no means exclusively in California and Australia, have a "cellar door", sales outlet, or tasting room in a quite different location from where they actually produce the wine (which in some cases may even be in a contract winery or custom crush facility). In such cases we have marked the former location as being where they choose to present themselves to wine lovers. Wine producers are not marked on the exceptionally detailed Côte d'Or maps, however, since these concentrate on vineyards rather than cellars – which tend to be huddled together in the same village backstreets anyway.

Note that in order to make it easier to distinguish between wine-related names and place names, all wine names, whether appellations or wineries, are in type with serifs (for example, the appellation of MEURSAULT) whereas geographical names are in sans serif type (for example, the village of Meursault).

In deciding the order of different regions within countries, we have tried very roughly to go from west to east and from north to south, although like all rules this has its exceptions. While choosing which labels to feature on these pages (a wine-publishing innovation when it was introduced in the first edition), I have tried as far as possible to make the labels shown reflect my personal choice of the best wines made in that particular country, region, or district. The vintage shown on the label has no particular relevance, although at the time of publication they are generally current and eminently respectable. These choices should have a track record over many vintages, or at least several in the most embryonic wine regions. The number of labels shown on each page is often determined far more by page design than by qualitative considerations. Nor should anything qualitative be read into the order in which the labels are shown on the page. Aesthetics, geography, grape varieties, and ease of caption-writing have all variously played their part in this.

PERSONAL THANKS

Hugh Johnson could not be a more generous, supportive, good-humoured, not to mention talented, collaborator. He has been particularly closely involved with this edition, scrutinizing every image and map, reading every word, and often rewriting mine, sprinkling Johnson gold dust throughout the extensively revised texts that illuminate the maps. The book is all the better for this.

As so often over the past two years, we have relied extremely heavily on the knowledge, diligence, and memory of my associate and fellow Master of Wine Julia Harding, who took particular charge of revising the maps and has herself developed a network of extremely generous informants in vineyards, wineries, and laboratories around the world. And Hugh, Julia, and I, not to mention publisher and originator Mitchell Beazley, continue to depend heavily – probably too heavily – on our managing editor Gill Pitts who, as usual has managed to achieve what on paper looked to be impossible in the time allowed. A veteran of three editions of this work, she quite literally bears the scars, and has been pure pleasure to work with. I have been keenly aware of an unparalleled level of efficiency in cartographic editor Alison Ewington and Alan Grimwade and Allison Walls of Cosmographics. I have been delightedly and directly aware of the hard work and tenacity that has been displayed by the multi-talented Priscilla Reby over the past months. Her unenviable job has been to track down often the most obscure labels from all over the world. I have also had the pleasure of working with art director Yasia Williams, who has been unfailingly good-humoured and accommodating, as has the publisher Denise Bates, who has tactfully consulted Hugh and me on all important points. Hugh and I are enormously grateful to all those specified on p.2, who have managed to get this book from our furrowed brows to crisp, beautiful, physical reality. And, as always, I owe much to my wine-loving literary agent of more than 30 years, Caradoc King.

Particular thanks are also due to everyone cited in (and especially those inadvertently missed off) the list of Acknowledgments on p.400. We have prevailed upon the goodwill of a vast array of informants all over the world and can only bless them and the way improved technology has allowed us all to communicate with such satisfying, almost dangerous (in terms of meeting deadlines), speed. Any faults in this book are much more likely to be mine than theirs. They cannot be held responsible for the many opinions expressed in this book, and certainly not for such tendentious issues as the choice of labels.

As ever, however, I owe most to Nick and our expanding family Julia, Will, Rose, Charlie, and Jake. I am deeply grateful for the fact that those of them who are old enough to drink seem increasingly tolerant of the time I devote to my other great love, the magical liquid that is fermented grape juice.

ABBREVIATIONS

The following most common abbreviations are used throughout the text:

AOC Appellation d'Origine Contrôlée
AOP Appellation d'Origine Protégée
AVA American Viticultural Area
DO Denominación de Origen
EU European Union
GI Geographic Indication
IGP Indication Géographique Protégée
INAO Institut National de l'Origine et de la Qualité
OIV Organisation International de la Vigne et du Vin
PDO Protected Designation of Origin
PGI Protected Geographical Indication

The Ancient World and Middle Ages

Wine is far older than recorded history. It emerges with civilization itself from the East. The evidence from tablets and papyri and Egyptian tombs fills volumes. Mankind, as we recognize ourselves – working, quarrelling, loving, and worrying – comes on the scene with the support of a jug of wine. Pharaonic wine, however vividly painted for us to see, is too remote to have any meaning. Our age of wine, with still-traceable roots, begins with the Phoenicians and Greeks who colonized the Mediterranean, the Phoenicians starting about 1100 BC, the Greeks 350 years later. It was then that wine began to arrive where it was to make its real home: Italy, France, and Spain. The Greeks called Italy the Land of Staked Vines (see p.148), just as the Vikings called America Vínland for the profusion of native vines they found circa AD 1000.

ANCIENT GREECE

The wines of Greece herself, no great matter for much of modern times, were lavishly praised and documented by her poets. There was even a fashionable after-dinner game in Athens that consisted of throwing the last few mouthfuls of wine in your cup into the air to hit a delicately balanced dish on a pole. Smart young things took coaching in the finer points of *kottabos*. But such treatment of the wine, and the knowledge that it was almost invariably drunk as what we would call "a wine cup", flavoured with herbs, spices, and honey and diluted with water (sometimes even seawater), seems to question its innate quality. That the wines of different islands of the Aegean were highly prized for their distinct characters is indisputable. Chios in particular was a supplier in constant demand. Whether the wines would appeal to us today we have no way of knowing, but the Greek term "symposium" for a conversation over wine hints at how much they appreciated it.

Greeks industrialized wine-growing in southern Italy, Etruscans in Tuscany and further north, and Romans followed. So much was written about wine and winemaking in ancient Rome that it is possible to make a rough map of the wines of the early Roman Empire (see right). The greatest writers, even Virgil, wrote instructions to wine-growers. One sentence of his – "Vines love an open hill" – is perhaps the best single piece of advice that can be given to a wine-grower. Others were much more calculating, discussing how much work a slave could do for how little food and sleep without losing condition. Roman wine-growing was on a very large scale, and business calculation was at the heart of it. It spread right across the Empire, so that Rome was eventually importing countless shiploads of amphoras from her colonies in Spain, North Africa – the entire Mediterranean. Since Pompeii was a tourist resort and considerable entrepôt for the wine trade, its remarkable survival gives us a great deal of detailed evidence.

How good was Roman wine? Some of it apparently had extraordinary powers of keeping, which in itself suggests that it was well-made. The must was frequently concentrated by heating, and wine was stored over hearths to be exposed to smoke to achieve what must have been a madeira-like effect.

ROME'S GREAT VINTAGES

Rome's great vintages were discussed and even drunk for longer than seems possible; the famous Opimian – from the year of the consulship of Opimius, 121 BC – was being drunk when it was 125 years old.

The Romans had all that is necessary for ageing wine, although they did not use the same materials as we do. Glass, for example, was not used for wine storage. Wooden barrels were used only in Gaul (which included Germany). Like the Greeks, the Romans used earthenware amphoras. An amphora holds about 7.5 gallons (35 litres).

Most Italians of 2,000 years ago probably drank wine very like some of their less sophisticated descendants today: young, rather roughly made, sharp or strong, according to the vintage. Even the Roman method of cultivation of the vine on trees, the festoons which became the friezes on classical buildings, was still practised until recently in parts of the south of Italy and northern Portugal.

The Greeks took wine north to southern Gaul. The Romans domesticated it there. By the time they withdrew from what is now France in the 5th century AD, the Romans had laid the foundations for almost all of the most famous vineyards of modern Europe.

The Roman army veterans who established Mérida in Extremadura, western Spain, in 25 BC were quick to exploit the region's suitability for wine-growing. This mosaic, which depicts the enthusiastic treading of grapes in a stone trough, was created in the 2nd century AD.

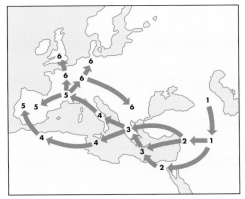

Starting in Caucasia or Mesopotamia **1** in perhaps 6000 BC, the vine was cultivated in Egypt and Phoenicia **2** in about 3000 BC. By 2000 BC it was in Greece **3** and by 1000 BC it was in Italy, Sicily, and North Africa **4**. In the next 500 years it reached at least Spain, Portugal, and the south of France **5**, and probably southern Russia as well. Finally (see map below) it spread with the Romans into northern Europe **6**, getting as far as Britain.

Roman vineyards and wines in AD 100
The middle map shows the approximate distribution of the grapevine *Vitis vinifera* throughout the Roman Empire in AD 100. It displays a remarkably close correspondence with the vineyards of the 21st century, although there is much less in Spain and Portugal, and less in France but vastly more in Eastern Europe (and apparently also in Britain). The map on the left is a reconstruction of wine-growing in Italy in the same year. Names of modern cities are shown in bold; wine names in non-bold type.

Starting in Provence, which had had Greek-planted vineyards already for centuries, they moved up the Rhône Valley and into the Languedoc, the Provincia Narbonensis, but we still have no clear evidence of exactly when viticulture started in Bordeaux. The earliest mention is in the works of the poet Ausonius in the 4th century AD (Ausonius lived in St-Emilion, perhaps even at Château Ausone), but it probably began long before this.

All the early developments were in the river valleys, the natural lines of communication, which the Romans cleared of forest and cultivated, at first as a precaution against ambushes. Besides, boats were the best way of moving anything so heavy as wine. Bordeaux, Burgundy, and Trier on the Mosel (where the museum preserves a fully laden and manned Roman wine-boat in stone) probably all started as merchant centres for imported Italian or Greek wine, and then planted their own vines.

By the 1st century AD there were vines on the Loire and the Rhine; by the second in Burgundy, and by the fourth in Paris (not such a good idea), in Champagne, and on the Mosel. Burgundy's Côte d'Or remains the least easy vineyard to account for, having no convenient navigable river. It lay where the main road north (to Trier, the "northern Rome") skirted the rich province of Autun. Presumably the Autunois saw the commercial opportunity, then found they had chosen a golden slope. The foundations had been dug for the French wine industry we still know.

THE MIDDLE AGES

Out of the Dark Ages that followed the fall of the Roman Empire we gradually emerge into the illumination of the medieval period, to see in its painted pages an entirely familiar scene: grape-picking and pressing, barrels in cellars and merry drinkers. Winemaking methods were not to change in their essentials until the 20th century. The Church was the repository of the skills of civilization in the Dark Ages – indeed the continuation of Rome's imperial administration under a new guise. The Emperor Charlemagne recreated an Imperial system – and took great and famous pains to legislate in favour of better wine.

As expansionist monasteries cleared hillsides and built walls around fields of cuttings, and as dying wine-growers and departing crusaders bequeathed it their land, the Church became the greatest vineyard-owner. It was indeed identified with wine – not only as the "Blood of Christ", but as luxury and comfort in this world. Cathedrals and churches, but above all the multiplying monasteries, owned or created most of the greatest vineyards of Europe.

The Benedictines, from their great motherhouses of Monte Cassino in Italy and Cluny in Burgundy, went out and cultivated the finest vineyards, until their way of life became notorious: "Rising from the table with their veins swollen with wine and their heads on fire." Their great monasteries included Fulda, near Frankfurt, Lorsch, near Mainz, and major establishments in Alsace, Switzerland, Bavaria, and Austria.

Reaction came in 1098, when Saint Robert of Molesme split from the Benedictines and founded the ascetic order of the Cistercians, named for their new abbey of Cîteaux, within walking distance of the Côte d'Or. The Cistercian order was explosively successful, founding not only the great walled vineyards of the Clos de Vougeot in Burgundy and Steinberg in the Rheingau, beside their abbey of Kloster Eberbach, but magnificent monasteries all over Europe – and eventually, of course, becoming as notorious for their gluttony as the Benedictines. Alcobaça in Portugal seems to have been their Michelin 3-star establishment.

The one important exception to domination by the Church was the thriving vineyard of Bordeaux, where development was simply commercial, with a single market in view. From 1152 to 1453, the great Duchy of Aquitaine, most of western France, was united by marriage to the crown of England and bent its efforts to filling great annual wine fleets with hogsheads of light claret: the *vin nouveau* the English loved. The Vintners Company in London was granted its first Royal Charter (virtually a monopoly over this thriving trade) in 1363.

But it was within the stable framework of the Church and the monasteries, in which tools and terms and techniques seemed to stand still, that the styles of wine and even some of the grape varieties now familiar to us slowly came into being. Few things in the medieval world were so strictly regulated. Wine and wool were the two great luxuries of northern Europe in the Middle Ages. Trade in cloth and wine made fortunes – most notably in Flanders and the great annual fairs that took place in Champagne, attracting merchants even over the Alps. No region became more obsessed with wine than Germany, where vast barrels known as "tuns" were built for great vintages. The Heidelberg tun held the equivalent of 19,000-dozen bottles. Connoisseurship may have been rudimentary, but in 1224 the King of France held an international tasting. "The Battle of Wines" included 70 entries: from Spain, Germany, and Cyprus as well as all over France. The judges were the king and an English priest. Cyprus won.

The Evolution of Modern Wine

Up to the start of the 17th century wine was in the unique position of being the one and only wholesome and – up to a point – storable beverage. It had no challengers. Water was normally unsafe to drink, at least in cities. Ale without hops very quickly went bad. There were no spirits, nor any of the caffeine-containing drinks that appear essential to life today.

Europe drank wine on a scale of which it is difficult to conceive; our ancestors must have been in a perpetual fuddle. It is hard to have confidence in the descriptions of wine that survive from before about 1700. With the exception of Shakespeare's graphic tasting note from *Henry IV, Act II*, "a marvellous searching wine, and it perfumes the blood ere one can say 'What's this?'," they tend to refer to royal recommendations or miraculous cures rather than to taste and style.

In the 17th century all this changed, starting with chocolate from Central America, then coffee from Arabia, and finally tea from China. At the same time the Dutch developed the art and commerce of distilling, turning huge tracts of western France into suppliers of cheap white wine for their stills; hops turned ale into more stable beer and great cities began to pipe the clean water they had lacked since Roman times. The wine industry was threatened with catastrophe unless it developed new ideas.

It is no coincidence that we date the creation of most of the wines we consider classics today from the second half of the 17th century. But these developments would never have succeeded without the timely invention of the glass wine bottle. Since Roman times wine had spent all its life in a barrel. Bottles, or rather jugs, usually of pottery or leather, were used simply for bringing it to table. The early 17th century saw changes in glassmaking technology that made bottles stronger and cheaper to blow. At about the same time some unknown thinker brought together the bottle, the cork, and the corkscrew.

Bit by bit it became clear that wine kept in a tightly corked bottle lasted far longer than wine in a barrel, which was likely to go off rapidly after the barrel was broached. It also aged differently, acquiring a "bouquet". The *vin de garde* was created and with it the chance to double and treble the price of wines capable of ageing.

It was the owner of Château Haut-Brion who first hit on the idea of what we might call "reserve" wines: selected, later-picked, stronger, carefully made, and matured. In the 1660s he opened London's first restaurant, under his own name, Pontac's Head, to publicize his produce.

In the early 18th century, burgundy changed its nature, too. The most delicate wines, Volnay and Savigny, were once the most fashionable.

Now these *vins de primeur* began to give way to the demand for long-fermented, dark-coloured *vins de garde*, especially from the Côte de Nuits. In Burgundy at least, though, the master-grape, Pinot Noir, had been identified and made mandatory. Champagne, too, adopted Pinot Noir in emulation. Germany's best vineyards were being replanted to Riesling. But most other regions were still experimenting.

The wine that benefited most from the development of the bottle was the fiery port the English had started to drink in the late 17th century – not out of choice, but because the duty on their preferred French wine was raised to prohibitive levels by an almost uninterrupted state of war. They had doubts about it at first, but as the century, and their bottles, grew older, their opinion of it rose sharply. The trend is graphically illustrated by the way the port bottle changed shape within a century from a globe with a neck to a near-cylinder.

In 1866, André Jullien published the figures for the alcoholic strengths of recent vintages. By today's standards the burgundies are formidable: Corton 1858, 15.6%; Montrachet 1858, 14.3%; Volnay 1859, 14.9%; Richebourg 1859, 14.3%. In contrast, Bordeaux wines of the same two years ranged from 11.3% (St-Emilion Supérieur) to a mere 8.9% (Château Lafite).

The low natural strength of the Bordeaux wines explains what seems today a curious habit of the old wine trade. Up to the mid-19th century the wines for England – which was most of the best of Bordeaux – were subjected to what was known as *le travail à l'anglaise*. One recipe called for the addition of 30 litres of Spanish wine (Alicante or Benicarlo), two litres of unfermented white must, and a bottle of brandy to each barrel of claret. The summer after the vintage the wine was set to ferment again with these additives, then treated as other wines and kept for several years in wood before shipping. The result was strong wine with a good flavour, but "heady and not suitable for all stomachs". It fetched more than natural wine.

Today's preoccupation with authenticity, even at the expense of quality, makes these practices seem abusive. But it is as if someone revealed as a shocking practice the addition of brandy to port. We like Douro wine with brandy in it; our ancestors liked Lafite laced with Alicante. (And tastes change; today we like Douro wine without brandy as well.)

In the 19th century, champagne was sweeter and fuller in colour and flavour – although otherwise very like it is today. Port and sherry had both been perfected. There was more strong sweet wine: Málaga and Marsala were in their heydays. Madeira, Constantia, and Tokay (as it was then called) were as highly regarded as Germany's Trockenbeerenauslesen.

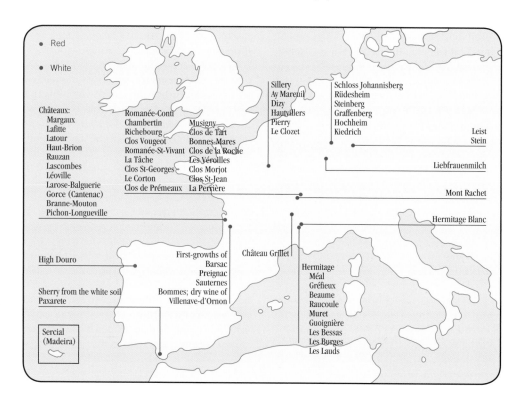

- Red
- White

Châteaux:
Margaux
Lafitte
Latour
Haut-Brion
Rauzan
Lascombes
Léoville
Larose-Balguerie
Gorce (Cantenac)
Branne-Mouton
Pichon-Longueville

Romanée-Conti
Chambertin
Richebourg
Clos Vougeot
Romanée-St-Vivant
La Tâche
Clos St-Georges
Le Corton
Clos de Prémeaux

Musigny
Clos de Tart
Bonnes-Mares
Clos de la Roche
Les Vérolles
Clos Morjot
Clos St-Jean
La Perrière

Sillery
Ay Mareuil
Dizy
Hautvillers
Pierry
Le Clozet

Schloss Johannisberg
Rüdesheim
Steinberg
Graffenberg
Hochheim
Kiedrich

Leist
Stein

Liebfrauenmilch

Mont Rachet

Hermitage Blanc

High Douro

Sherry from the white soil
Paxarete

First-growths of
Barsac
Preignac
Sauternes
Bommes; dry wine of
Villenave-d'Ornon

Château Grillet

Hermitage
Méal
Gréfieux
Beaume
Raucoule
Muret
Guoignière
Les Bessas
Les Burges
Les Lauds

Sercial
(Madeira)

It is fascinating to compare A Jullien's 1866 classification of the world's great wines with our modern ideas. In his *Topographie de Tous les Vignobles Connus* he listed the vineyards shown on this map (in their original spelling).

When it opened in Australia in 1888, Seppeltsfield's gravity-flow winery was the largest and most modern of its type in the world. It was built into a Barossa Valley hillside on a series of terraces.

The wine trade was booming. In the wine-growing countries an unhealthy amount of the economy rested on wine: in Italy in 1880, it was calculated that no less than 80% of the population more or less relied on it for a living. Both Italy (in Tuscany and Piemonte) and Spain (in Rioja) were creating their first modern export wines. California was in the midst of its first wine rush. This was the world phylloxera struck (see p.15). At the time, when it caused the pulling up of almost every vine, it seemed like the end of the world of wine.

In retrospect, the rationalization of planting, the introduction of grafting, and the enforced selection of the most desirable grape varieties together made a chance for a great new beginning. But it was a slow and tortuous start, with every sort of setback in glut, fraud, Prohibition, Depression, World War – and bad weather. In 40 years (to take Bordeaux as the sample), only 11 vintages could be described as good. It was against this depressing background that the French government made the first moves towards regulation in the fledgling regime of Appellations d'Origine Contrôlées (see p.46). The notion of terroir was codified for the first time.

SCIENCE AND INDUSTRY

The 20th century saw two revolutions in the world of wine: the first scientific, the second industrial. As it began, the practical significance of Pasteur's science was just sinking in; fermentation was no longer a mystery but a process that could be controlled. Bordeaux had opened the first university department dedicated to oenology, at the same time as Montpellier, Geisenheim, UC Davis in California, and Roseworthy in Australia opened departments for the study of viticulture. The established wine world had enough problems to solve; the emerging one had every decision to take, starting with which varieties to plant.

But it was not until the 1950s, as America struggled out of the chaotic legacy of Prohibition, and Europe began to recover from World War II, that anything like prosperity returned to châteaux, wineries, and domaines.

For the warm countries of the New World the true revolution came with refrigeration and the ability to cool the fermenting must. Almost the only aromatic, balanced, and profitably ageable table wines therefore came from northern Europe. Once that nut was cracked, California took to varietal wines like a religion. Not many varieties: Zinfandel was California's own grape, but Chardonnay was "the sole source of the great French white burgundies", Cabernet "the premier red grape of the Bordeaux area of France". Their names became incantations, their wines categories that no winery could be without. Australia, whose founding wine-growers planted Shiraz, Semillon, and Riesling, had to hurry to introduce the grapes the whole world started to want.

The modern world of wine started in the 1960s, with the almost simultaneous appearance of new wineries with high ambitions in California and Australia, and perhaps more significantly the launch by E & J Gallo of cheap palatable table wines (even if they were labelled "Chablis" and "Hearty Burgundy") to cater to a completely new public.

OAK AS MAKE-UP

Armed with the science to improve quality, and with technology that accelerated with demand, ambitious winemakers felt there were no heights they could not scale. The great discovery of the 1960s was that French oak barrels, used judiciously, could give wines from very different terroirs more than a passing resemblance to the "classics" of France. No single factor did more to close the gap between French wine and its imitators.

Sadly, it was a trick that soon got out of control, as novices confused the taste of oak with the taste of good wine. Overuse of oak as flavouring, making wines that refresh no one, is still a widespread problem, not only in the New World, but among French, Italian, and Spanish producers who have lost confidence in their own taste and bend to the wind of fashion.

The 21st century started with the greatest supplies (indeed, a potentially embarrassing glut) of good wine from more sources than the world has ever known. Added to all the scientific and technological advances, the great leap at the end of the 20th century was in communication, hence in worldwide competition.

There are few, if any, secrets today in a world which used to play its cards close to the chest. The "flying winemaker" was an invention of the 1980s: a high-tech professional, usually Australian, originally commissioned to make wine in Europe in Australia's winter, now often making many wines at the same time all over the world. Winemakers, flying or earthbound, sometimes seem to be in constant confessional, spewing out every detail of their doings on back-labels. The ever-present danger of a global village, of course, is that marketing takes over from the people with wine-stained hands. Marketeers play safe. Their advice will flood the market with what sold last year rather than what a vineyard is best capable of.

The danger of sameness, of every producer aiming at the global market with a "me-too" wine, has been well aired. To most consumers, it must be said, it is not a danger at all. Base-level wine drinkers make up the majority, and what they want is continuity. Variety equals confusion and loss of confidence. To Anglo-Saxons, the reassurance of labels in English has been another big factor in the success of New World wines.

On the other hand, the world's wine drinkers are slowly but measurably trading up and taking more interest in what they are drinking. Quality wine is gaining at the expense of table wine – a trend that a future surplus at all levels will only accelerate.

The days are passing when, for example, branded Chardonnays can slug it out in the marketplace on the basis of low price and lots of advertising. As consumers learn more about wine, and about their own tastes, they are prepared to spend more. It became clear in the last decades of the 20th century that the days of the nondescript are numbered. The vineyards of the Midi that once produced *vin ordinaire* are now the home of Vins de Pays (IGPs). Few grudge the premium, and success spurs the producers.

There are many reasons to believe in the survival of variety –indeed in its revival, as ambitious New World growers replace Cabernet and Merlot with Sangiovese, Nebbiolo, Tempranillo, Touriga Nacional, and vast tracts of Syrah or, more likely thanks to Australia's increasing influence, Shiraz. But there are heartening signs that wine producers all over the world are taking new interest and delight in what they and they alone have to offer today's increasingly discerning consumer, whether it be very special local conditions or an almost extinct indigenous grape variety. This does not make learning about wine any easier, but wine is naturally complex – and all the better for it.

The Vine

It is an extraordinary fact that this wonderfully varied and evocative drink we call wine is the fermented juice of a single fruit, the grape. Every drop of wine we drink is made from rain (and in hotter regions irrigation water) recovered from the ground by the mechanism of the plant that bears grapes, the vine, and in the presence of sunlight converted by photosynthesis into fermentable sugar, with a little help from nutrients in the soil.

For the first two or three years of its life, a young vine is too busy creating a root system and building a strong woody trunk to bear more than a few grapes. Thereafter, left to nature, it would rampage away, bearing some fruit but spending much more of its energy on making new shoots and putting out long, wandering branches of leafy wood, ideally seeking out a tree to climb, until it covered as much as an acre (nearly half a hectare) of ground, with new root systems forming wherever the branches touched the soil.

This natural form of reproduction, known in French as *provignage*, was used to make a vineyard in ancient times. To prevent the grapes rotting or the mice getting them, since they lay on the ground, little props were pushed under the stems to support each bunch. If the vine grew near trees, it used its tendrils to climb them to dizzy heights. The Romans planted elms especially for the purpose. Freelance labour was hired for the vintage; it was too dangerous to risk your own slaves.

Modern vines, of course, are not allowed to waste their precious energy on being "vigorous" – making long, leafy branches – however much they may try (see p.25). Better-quality grapes grow in moderately fertile soil on a vine that is pruned in winter and regularly cut back to a very limited number of buds.

Like most other plants, vines will reproduce from seed, but the seeds rarely turn out like their parents. Instead, viticulturists propagate vines asexually by taking cuttings so that they can be sure that the offspring are the same as the mother vine. Pips are used only for experimenting with new crosses between different varieties.

For planting a new vineyard, cuttings are either planted to take root on their own or grafted onto a rootstock: a rooted cutting of another species specially selected for the soil type or resistance to drought or nematodes (tiny worms), for instance.

Nurserymen should try to take cuttings only from plants that are healthy and free of virus. The little grafted "slips" are planted out for a season until they form roots. If there is any danger of virus infection, tissue-cultured vines, grown from only the virus-free growing-tip, have to be nurtured in a laboratory to become a rooted plant.

As a vine grows older, its principal roots penetrate deeper into the ground in search of water and nutrients. In very general terms, the younger the vine, the lighter and less subtle the wine – although vines can produce delicious fruit in their first year or two, when yields are naturally low and the available flavour is concentrated into relatively few grapes. Somewhere between three and six years after being planted, the vine stabilizes, filling the space allotted to it above ground. It produces increasingly flavourful grapes and therefore more and more concentrated wine. This is presumably thanks to an increasingly complex root system that regulates the supply of water and nutrients.

Yields typically start to decline after 25 or 30 years (or the vine succumbs to disease or is of an unfashionable grape variety), when vines tend to be pulled out as uneconomic. Wine from vines older than this generally command a premium and may be labelled the produce of old vines – *vieilles vignes* in French.

The best soils (see pp.22-23) drain quickly and often deeply, sometimes drawing the roots down to great depths to find a stable but not-too-generous water supply. At the same time, the vine constantly grows new feeder roots near the surface.

THE VINE THROUGH THE GROWING SEASON

BUDS DEVELOP

As early as March in Northern Europe and September in the southern hemisphere, the buds left after winter pruning start to swell and the first signs of green can be seen emerging from the gnarled wood. This happens when temperatures reach about 50°F (10°C).

LEAVES SEPARATE

Within 10 days of budbreak, leaves start to separate from the bud and embryonic tendrils begin to be visible, and are all too vulnerable to frost, which can strike as late as mid-May or mid-November in cooler districts of the northern and southern hemispheres, respectively. Late pruning of the vine can delay budbreak.

FLOWERING BEGINS

Between 6 and 13 weeks after budbreak, the crucial flowering of the vine begins with the emergence of tiny caps of fused petals. These look very like miniature versions of the grapes that will be formed here once the caps fall, exposing the stigmas so that they can be fertilized by pollen to create the berries.

FULL RIPENESS

Measuring ripeness – and in particular deciding what constitutes perfect ripeness – has been the focus of much recent research. Dark-skinned varieties should certainly have uniformly deep-coloured skins, but stems and stalks should start to lignify (turn woody) and grape seeds should show no sign of greenness.

VERAISON

The place of such buds as escape frost and rain is taken by hard, green baby grapes in June/December. These grapes swell during the summer, and in August/February undergo veraison, whereby they soften and turn reddish or yellow. The ripening process begins and sugars start to build rapidly inside the grape.

FLOWERING EFFECTS

The size of the eventual crop depends on the success of pollination. Poor weather during the 10- to 14-day flowering can result in coulure, whereby the stalks of an excessive number of very small berries shrivel, causing them to drop off, and also millerandage: different-sized berries on the same bunch.

PESTS, DISEASES, AND THEIR EFFECTS ON THE VINE

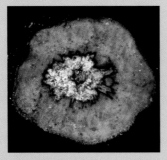

The phylloxera louse eats vine leaves and tendrils as well as roots. Native to North America, it reached Europe on the botanical specimens collected by Victorians, on steamships able to cross the Atlantic fast enough for it to survive the journey. American vines are resistant to it, and grafting European vines onto American roots is the only effective defence.

Trunk diseases are increasingly affecting vines all over the world. A range of diseases such as esca, eutypa dieback, and black dead arm (BDA) can fatally damage the wood of the vine trunk (see esca-affected trunk above). The first symptoms are strange colours and patterns on vine leaves and wood. Vines can die soon after. Research into the causes and a cure is a top priority.

Leafroll virus is a complex of different viruses which turns vine leaves a deep red and causes them to curl downwards. While the vines are often gloriously photogenic, the wines are seriously lean because the disease slows the whole ripening process, and it tends to reduce yields by up to 50%. Leafroll virus is present all over the world but has been a particular problem in South Africa.

Fungal diseases such as downy and powdery mildew as well as various sorts of rot are the vine's chief enemies except in the most arid climates. The most effective weapon in the vigneron's armoury is spraying vines with fungicides based on copper, traditionally copper sulphate, which is known as Bordeaux mixture. The copper can leave the vines this alarming bright-blue colour.

PESTS AND DISEASES

The European vine family, called *vinifera*, or "wine-bearing", has countless enemies, the worst of them diseases and pests introduced far too recently (mostly from America) for it to have developed any natural resistance. In the 19th century, first powdery mildew (oidium) and then downy mildew (peronospera) attacked Europe's vines – and vinifera vines planted in the New World. Laborious remedies were discovered for these two fungal diseases, though both still need treatment by regular spraying. Another common reason for the persistent drone of tractors spraying vineyards in the growing season is rot, specifically the malign form of botrytis fungus (as opposed to the benevolent form, which can produce such exceptional sweet white wines as those described on p.96). This botrytis bunch rot, also called grey rot, can impart a fatally mouldy taste to grapes, and is increasingly resistant to anti-rot chemicals (see pp.24–25 for alternative strategies). Fungal diseases are a particular problem in damp climates or where the vine's leaves are particularly dense.

Towards the end of the 19th century, soon after a cure for the two mildews had been developed, a far more dangerous scourge was observed and, eventually, identified. The phylloxera louse feasts on the roots of the vine and eventually kills it. It almost destroyed the entire European vineyard, until it was discovered that native American vines (phylloxera came from America) are immune. Virtually every vine in Europe had to be replaced with a vinifera cutting grafted onto a rooted cutting from an American vine, a phylloxera-resistant rootstock.

Some of the world's newer wine regions (Chile and parts of Australia being the most obvious examples) have yet to experience this predatory aphid, and so happily plant their vinifera vines directly as ungrafted cuttings. In Oregon and New Zealand, however, this has proved a short-term stratagem, and in the 1980s vine-growers in northern California learnt to their cost that rootstocks have to be very carefully chosen if they are to offer reliable resistance to phylloxera. Hundreds of thousands of acres there had to be replanted with more suitable, truly phylloxera-resistant rootstocks, and strict quarantine rules are in force in many wine regions to keep phylloxera out.

The parts of the vine that grow above ground are on the menu for a whole menagerie, too. Red spiders, the grubs of the cochylis and eudemis moths, various sorts of beetles, bugs, and mites find vines nutritious. The latest enemy to viticulture is the Asian lady beetle, which releases a body fluid that even in tiny amounts taints the wine. Most of these pests can be controlled by the various chemical sprays to which so many vines are subjected throughout the summer. Meanwhile, the growing band of organic and biodynamic vine-growers are experimenting with more natural methods such as predators, pheromones, and biopesticides. Teas made from plants such as horsetail may be used prophylactically against fungal diseases.

Pierce's Disease is spread by a leafhopper, the glassy-winged sharpshooter, whose ability to fly long distances has put a wide range of American vineyards at risk. Vines die within five years of first succumbing to this bacterial disease, showing first as dead spots on the leaves, which eventually fall off. No grape varieties are resistant and there is no known cure.

THE SPREAD OF PHYLLOXERA

1863	Phylloxera louse discovered in southern England.
1866	Found in the southern Rhône Valley and the Languedoc, France.
1869	Phylloxera reaches Bordeaux.
1871	Discovered in Portugal and Turkey.
1872	Phylloxera found in Austria.
1874	The louse spreads to Switzerland.
1875	Phylloxera found in Italy and also as far afield as Victoria, Australia, in late 1875 or early 1876.
1878	Phylloxera reaches Spain. Grafting of vines onto resistant American rootstocks begins in France.
1881	Presence of phylloxera confirmed in German vineyards.
1885	The louse is discovered in Algeria.
1897	Phylloxera found in Dalmatia (Croatia).
1898	Spreads to Greece.
1980s	Phylloxera-affected vines found in northern California.
1990s	Diseased vines discovered in Oregon and in New Zealand.
2006	Phylloxera found in Victoria's Yarra Valley, Australia.

International Grapes

If geography determines the nuances of how a wine tastes, the raw material is the grape variety or varieties that go into the wine. Since the mid-20th century, varieties have played an increasingly important role in the language of wine. Today far fewer wine drinkers know the name Chablis, for instance, than know the name of the grape from which wines in this northern French appellation are made: Chardonnay. It is much easier to get to grips with a handful of well-known grape names than to know all the possible place names that could be found on wine labels, which is why "varietal labelling" has become so popular. That said, blends of two or more varieties are becoming increasingly common at the expense of monovarietal wines.

A passing acquaintance with the particularly well-travelled varieties described on these pages would provide a good start to anyone's wine education. At least some of the most obvious characteristics outlined below each grape name should be more or less guaranteed in any varietally labelled bottle – which includes the great majority of wine produced outside Europe and an increasing proportion of European, even French, wine.

But to progress in terms of wine knowledge, to start to understand most of the good and great wines of Europe and to understand the subtleties of wines made elsewhere, you need to satisfy some geographical curiosity. A book like this can help to explain more than any other why Hermitage tastes different from another wine made from the same grape, Syrah, grown 30 miles (48km) upstream on the differently angled slopes of Côte-Rôtie.

CROSS-SECTION OF A PINOT NOIR GRAPE TOWARDS THE END OF THE RIPENING PROCESS

Stem (or stalk) As grapes reach full physiological ripeness, stems turn from green and fleshy to brown and woody. Stems can make a wine taste tart and astringent.

Brush What remains attached to the stem when grapes are destemmed at the winery, or knocked off the bunch during mechanical harvesting.

Pip (or seed) The number, size, and shape of pips is different for different grape varieties. All pips release bitter tannins if crushed.

Pulp (or flesh) This is wine's main ingredient by volume, containing grape sugars, acids, and, mainly, water. The flesh of almost all wine grapes is this grey colour.

Skin The most important ingredient in red wines, containing a high concentration of tannins, colouring matter, and compounds which determine the eventual wine's flavour.

CABERNET SAUVIGNON
Blackcurrant, cedar, high tannin

Synonymous with serious red wine capable of ageing into subtle splendour. For this reason Cabernet Sauvignon is also the best-travelled red wine variety, but since it is a relatively late ripener it is viable only in warmish climates. Some years it may not ripen fully even in its homeland, the Médoc/Graves. But when it does, the colour, flavour, and tannins packed into the thick skins of its tiny, dark-blue berries can be remarkable. With careful winemaking and barrel-ageing, it can produce some of the longest-living and most intriguing reds of all. In Bordeaux, and increasingly elsewhere, it is blended with Merlot and Cabernet Franc, although it can make delicious unblended wine if grown somewhere as warm as Chile or northern California, its second home.

CHARDONNAY
Broad, versatile, inoffensive – unless over-oaked

The white burgundy grape, but so much more versatile than Pinot Noir. Chardonnay can be grown and ripened without difficulty almost everywhere except at the extremes of the wine world (its early budding can put it at risk of spring frost damage). It became the world's best-known white wine grape, perhaps because (unlike Riesling, for example) it does not have a particularly strong flavour of its own, which is one reason why it responds so well to barrel fermentation and/or oak-ageing. It routinely takes on whatever character the winemaker desires: vivacious and sparkling, refreshingly unoaked, rich and buttery, or even sweet. It can make steely, crisp wine like Chablis and is particularly valued as an ingredient in champagne and other similar wines.

PINOT NOIR
Cherry, raspberry, violets, game, mid-ruby

This most elusive grape is relatively early-ripening and extremely sensitive to terroir. Planted somewhere hot, it will ripen too fast and fail to develop any of the many fascinating flavour compounds its relatively thin skins can harbour. Pinot Noir's perfect place on earth is Burgundy's Côte d'Or where, if the clones, vine-growing, and winemaking techniques are right, it can convey intricate differences of terroir. So haunting are great red burgundy's charms that growers all over the world try to emulate them, with the greatest success so far in Germany, New Zealand, Oregon, and the coolest corners of California and Australia. Pinot Noir is rarely blended for still wine, but with Chardonnay and its cousin Pinot Meunier it is part of the standard recipe for champagne.

SYRAH/SHIRAZ
Black pepper, dark chocolate, notable tannin

In its northern Rhône Valley home, Syrah most famously makes great dark, long-lived Hermitage and Côte-Rôtie (where it is traditionally perfumed with a little Viognier). It is now planted all over southern France, where it is commonly used in blends. Syrah tastes quite different in Australia, where, called Shiraz, it is the country's most planted red grape, making dense, rich, potent wines in places as warm as Barossa, though it can still have a hint of black pepper in the cooler reaches of Victoria. Today growers all over the world are experimenting with this easy-to-love grape whose wines, however ripe, always have a savoury kick at the end. It is increasingly important and revered in Chile, South Africa, New Zealand, and Washington State, and is widely planted in Argentina, too.

MERLOT
Plump, soft, and plummy

Cabernet Sauvignon's traditional, slightly paler, fleshier blending partner, especially in Bordeaux, where its earlier ripening makes Merlot so much easier to grow that it is the most planted grape there. Easier to ripen than Cabernet Sauvignon in cooler vintages, it is more alcoholic in warmer ones. Its bigger berries and thinner skins mean generally less tannic, more opulent wines that can be enjoyed sooner. Merlot also has an independent existence as a varietal, particularly in the USA, where it is regarded as easier to drink (if more difficult to admire) than Cabernet, and in northeast Italy, where it is easier to ripen. It reaches its apogee in Pomerol, where it can result in voluptuous, velvety essences. It is widely grown in Chile, where it was long confused with Carmenère.

SAUVIGNON BLANC
Grass, green fruits, razor-sharp, rarely oaked

Piercingly aromatic, extremely refreshing, and, unlike most of the grapes on these pages, best drunk relatively young. Sauvignon Blanc's original home in France is the Loire, particularly in and around Sancerre and Pouilly-sur-Loire for Pouilly-Fumé, where it can vary considerably according to vintage. Grown in too warm a climate it can lose its characteristic aroma and acidity and can be too heavy in much of California and Australia. Provided the vine's tendency to excessive vigour is tamed by canopy management, Sauvignon Blanc does particularly well in New Zealand, notably Marlborough, as well as in cooler parts of South Africa. In Bordeaux it is traditionally blended with Sémillon for both dry and luscious sweet wines.

RIESLING
Aromatic, delicate, racy, expressive, rarely oaked

Riesling is to white wine what Cabernet Sauvignon is to red – it can make entirely different wines in different places and can age magnificently. Mispronounced (it is "Reessling"), underrated, and underpriced for most of the late 20th century, Riesling is slowly becoming more fashionable. The wine tends to be powerfully scented, reflecting minerals, flowers, lime, and honey depending on its provenance, sweetness, and age. Riesling makes great botrytised wines in its homeland, Germany, but thanks to global warming it now makes fine, firm dry wines there, too, as well as lighter, sweeter styles in between these two extremes. Riesling is still the noblest grape of Germany and Alsace and does particularly well in Australia, Austria, New York State, and Michigan.

SEMILLON
Figs, citrus, lanolin, full-bodied, rich

Sémillon is included here on the strength of the exceptional quality of the sweet wine produced from it, particularly in Sauternes and Barsac, where it is traditionally blended 4:1 with Sauvignon Blanc, together with a little Muscadelle. Its relatively thin skins make Sémillon (Semillon outside France) highly susceptible to the botrytis mould that can in the right conditions concentrate the grapes miraculously with noble rot. It is the most planted white grape in Bordeaux, where it is also responsible for some fine oaked, dry wines, especially in Graves. Australia's Hunter Valley also has a special affinity with it, making long-lived, complex, unusually light-bodied dry wines from early-picked grapes. South Africa has some venerable Semillon vines.

Regional Grapes

The grape varieties featured here and on the previous page are some of the best-known varieties of the European *vinifera* species of the *Vitis* genus, which also includes American and Asian vine species, and Virginia creeper.

In parts of the USA, wine is made from American vines, which are usefully resistant to many of the fungal diseases that commonly attack vines (outlined on p.15), but species such as *labrusca* have a particularly strong "foxy" flavour (characteristic of Concord grape jelly) which non-locals find off-putting. American and Asian vines can, however, be extremely useful for breeding new varieties for particular conditions. Hundreds of hybrids have been bred by crossing them with European vinifera varieties, notably so that they will ripen in regions with short growing seasons and/or withstand arctic winters. Some Mongolian species, for example, can be used to breed vines resistant to cold.

Because many (though by no means all) hybrids produce inferior wine they have at times been scorned, and in Europe are officially outlawed. Many European vine breeders have concentrated on crossing various vinifera varieties to respond to a particular need or environment. Müller-Thurgau, for example, was an early crossing developed specifically to ripen in sites where Riesling would not.

Growers need to decide more than which variety and rootstock to plant. The life of a vine is usually about 30 years (although in fashion-conscious regions the variety is sometimes changed by simply lopping off the plant above ground and grafting on a new, more desirable variety). Just as important can be the choice of clone(s) of the favoured variety. Nurserymen have long observed, selected, and propagated particular plants with special characteristics: high or consistent yield; good resistance to various pests, diseases, and environmental extremes; early ripening, and so on. Growers may choose a particular clone or mix of clones, or may make a mass selection of cuttings from many different plants.

Not all vines come with labels attached. The science of vine identification by observation of precise variations in grape and leaf shape, colour, and so on, is known as ampelography. It has revealed various fascinating relationships between varieties, but none quite so radical as the recent discoveries enabled by DNA analysis. This exact science has shown that Cabernet Franc and Sauvignon Blanc, for example, are the parents of Cabernet Sauvignon, and that Chardonnay, Aligoté, the Beaujolais grape Gamay, the Muscadet grape Melon de Bourgogne, Auxerrois, and many others are all the progeny of Pinot Noir and the obscure but historic grape Gouais Blanc. Pinot seems to be a great-grandparent of Syrah, and Merlot is closely related to Malbec (Côt).

GRENACHE NOIR

Pale, sweet, ripe, useful for rosé

Grenache is widely planted round the Mediterranean and is the most planted grape of the southern Rhône, where it is often blended with Mourvèdre, Syrah, and Cinsault. It is also widely grown in Roussillon where, with Grenache Blanc and Grenache Gris, its high alcohol levels are useful for the region's Vins Doux Naturels (see p.138). As Garnacha it is the most planted red grape in Spain, often as old bush-vines offering great value. As Cannonau in Corsica, and as Grenache in California or Australia, it is increasingly revered.

SANGIOVESE

Tangy, lively, variable: from prunes to farmyard

Italy's most planted grape, in its many forms, and particularly common in Central Italy, most gloriously in Chianti Classico, Montalcino (as Brunello), and Montepulciano (as Prugnolo Gentile). The least noble Sangiovese clones, overproduced, make light, tart red wine – oceans of it in Emilia-Romagna. The traditional Chianti recipe diminished it with the white grape Trebbiano as well as the local Canaiolo and a bit of deep Colorino. Today, Tuscany's many ambitious producers coax maximum colour and flavour from it. Sangiovese is increasingly planted elsewhere in the world.

CABERNET FRANC

Leafily aromatic, refreshing, rarely heavy

The less intense, softer progenitor of Cabernet Sauvignon. Because it ripens earlier, Cabernet Franc is widely planted in the Loire and on the cooler, damper soils of St-Emilion, where it is often blended with Merlot. In the Médoc/Graves it is planted as an insurance against Cabernet Sauvignon's failure to ripen. Much more resistant to cold winters than Merlot, it can make appetizing wines in New Zealand, Long Island, and Washington State. In northeast Italy it can taste positively grassy, and reaches its silky apogee in Chinon.

TEMPRANILLO

Tobacco leaves, spice, leather

Spain's most famous grape. As Tinto Fino or Tinto del País it provides the backbone of Ribera del Duero's dark, deep-flavoured reds. In Rioja, it is blended with Garnacha. In Catalunya, it is known as Ull de Llebre; in Valdepeñas, Cencibel. In Navarra, it is often blended with Bordeaux grapes. As Tinta Roriz it has long been used for port and is increasingly respected as a table wine grape in Portugal, where in the Alentejo it is known as Aragonês. Its early budding makes it vulnerable to spring frosts, its thin skins to rot, but it is valued internationally for fine wine.

MOURVEDRE

Animal, blackberries, alcoholic, tannic

This is a grape that needs considerable sunshine to ripen and is by far the most important grape in Bandol, Provence's most noble wine, although it has to be aged with care. Throughout southern France, and South Australia, it adds flesh to Grenache and Syrah blends in particular. In Spain, as Monastrell, it is the country's second most planted red grape and is associated more with heft than quality. It was known, and somewhat overlooked, as Mataro in both California and Australia until being renamed Mourvèdre and enjoying a new lease of life with glamorously Gallic associations.

NEBBIOLO

Tar, roses, violets, orange with black tints

Piemonte's answer to Pinot Noir. In Barolo and Barbaresco, it responds to every nuance of aspect and elevation. It will ripen only on the most favoured of sites. When fully ripe it is exceptionally high in tannins and acids, if not pigments, but long cask- and bottle-ageing can result in hauntingly seductive wines. Nebbiolo makes a wide range of other, usually lesser, wines in northwest Italy (in Valtellina and Gattinara, for example), but like Pinot Noir it has shown a reluctance to travel. Some Americans and Australians keep trying to prove otherwise.

ZINFANDEL
Warm berry flavours, alcohol, sweetness

Zinfandel was regarded as California's own grape for a century, until it was established that, as Primitivo, it was known on the heel of Italy at least as early as the 18th century. DNA analysis has now established its origins as Croatian. The vine ripens unevenly but some berries build almost unparalleled sugars so that "Zin" can be as strong as 17% alcohol. Old vines can make great reds but it is more commonly grown to produce much less intense wine in California's Central Valley, much of it stripped of colour, flavoured with aromatic Muscat or Riesling, and sold as (pale-pink) "White Zinfandel".

GEWURZTRAMINER
Lychees, roses, heady, high alcohol, deep-coloured

Gewürztraminer is a devil to spell – and often loses its Umlaut – but is a dream to recognize. Its distinctive aroma, so strong that it earned the grape the prefix Gewürz, or "spiced", in German, can easily be tiring, especially if combined with high residual sugar in the wine. But the best examples of Gewürztraminer from Alsace, where it is most revered, have an undertow of body and nerve, as well as a savoury finish, which stops them from cloying. Sufficient acidity is the key. Some fine examples have also emerged from New Zealand's east coast, Chile, British Columbia, Oregon, and Alto Adige.

MALBEC
Spicy and rich in Argentina, gamey in Cahors

Malbec is a conundrum. It has long been a blending grape all over Southwest France, including Bordeaux, but is the dominant grape only in Cahors, where, known as Côt or Auxerrois, it has typically made rustic, sometimes rather animal wines suitable for only medium-term ageing. Emigrés took it to Argentina, where in Mendoza it was so clearly at home that it has become the country's most popular red grape and makes gloriously velvety, concentrated, lively wines, high in alcohol and extract. Ambitious Cahors producers take Mendoza's best Malbecs as their model.

CHENIN BLANC
Extremely versatile; honey, damp straw

Chenin Blanc is the grape of the middle Loire, sandwiched between the Melon de Bourgogne of Muscadet and the Sauvignon Blanc of the Upper Loire. Much misunderstood, it makes sometimes ordinary dry wine in both California and South Africa, where it is widely planted, but Cape Chenin from old bush-vines can be marvellous. In the Loire, too, it can make nervy, age-worthy, distinctive wines of all stages of sweetness. Botrytised Chenins such as Vouvray can be great, long-lived, sweet whites, but in the Loire, Chenin also makes lightly honeyed, dry, still wines, and some characterful sparkling Saumur and Vouvray.

TOURIGA NACIONAL
Tannic, fireworks, occasionally porty

Portugal's most famous port grape, although just one of a wide range of distinctive grapes grown in the Douro Valley, such as the unrelated Touriga Franca, Tinta Barroca, Tinto Cão, and Tinto Roriz (Tempranillo). Floral in youth, it is increasingly bottled as a varietal wine throughout Portugal, and is an increasingly important ingredient in Dão. It is also likely to be planted much more widely throughout the wine world for it is by no means short of class and personality. Touriga Nacional is always extremely high in tannin, alcohol, and colour, not least because it is naturally unproductive.

VIOGNIER
Heady, full-bodied, hawthorn blossom, apricots

Fashionable, distinctive variety that has now travelled from its home in the northern Rhône to virtually all corners of the wine world. Unless fully ripe, its distinctively seductive aroma does not develop, which means that most memorable examples are relatively alcoholic; the trick is to keep the acidity, too. California and Australia have managed it. Best drunk young, it is increasingly blended with the other Rhône white grapes: nervy but aromatic Roussanne and big, almondy Marsanne – especially in southern France. Viognier is sometimes fermented with Syrah/Shiraz to stabilize it.

CARMENERE
Firm, Bordeaux-like, can be slightly green

Historic, very late-ripening Bordeaux variety which is rare in Bordeaux today, but is common in Chile where pre-phylloxera cuttings were introduced in the 1850s. For long, Carmenère was confused with Merlot but it has now been distinguished in the vineyard. The grapes have to be fully ripe if the resulting wines, which are very deep in colour, are to avoid a green, tomato-leaf character, and many growers think Carmenère is best blended with other Bordeaux varieties. It is also found in northeastern Italy and, as Cabernet Gernischt, in China.

MUSCAT BLANC
Grapey, relatively simple, often sweet

This is the finest sort of Muscat and has small berries (*petits grains* in French) that are round rather than oval like those of the less noble Muscat of Alexandria (Gordo Blanco or Lexia in Australia, where this lesser variety is grown for the table). As Moscato Bianco in Italy, the finer Muscat is responsible for Asti and many fine, light fizzes. It also makes great sweet wines in southern France and Greece. Australia's strong, sweet, sticky Muscats are made from a dark-skinned version, Brown Muscat. Spain's Moscatel is usually Muscat of Alexandria. Muscat Ottonel is different and lighter.

PINOT GRIS
Full, golden, smoky, pungent

This fashionable grape has its power base in Alsace where, with Riesling, Gewurztraminer, and Muscat, it is regarded as a noble grape, responsible for some of the region's most powerful, if quite soft, wines. This pink-skinned mutation of Pinot Noir is a cousin of Chardonnay. In Italy, it is known as Pinot Grigio and can produce both characterful and decidedly dull dry whites. Growers elsewhere dither between calling it Gris or Grigio without any significance for style. It is a speciality in Oregon, New Zealand, and Australia.

MARSANNE
Almond, marzipan aromas, very full-bodied

Along with Roussanne, this is the characteristic grape variety of white Hermitage in the northern Rhône. It is now planted throughout the southern Rhône as well as in Australia, especially in Victoria. In southern France and in California, particularly the Central Coast, Marsanne is often blended with varieties such as Roussanne, Rolle/Vermentino, Grenache Blanc, and Viognier. Its wines tend to be deep golden, heady, and alcoholic. Marsanne is also grown to a limited extent in Switzerland.

Wine and Weather

After the vine comes the weather, the second-most important ingredient in wine and the great variable. Growing grapes to make wine is highly dependent on both the seasonal and the long-term climate, which puts the overall limits on what types of grapes can be grown where and how well, and the day-to-day weather, which can make or break a vintage.

Many weather and climate factors influence the grapevine and its ability to produce good-quality fruit and wine, including sunlight, temperature, precipitation, humidity, and wind. But because grapevines grow best in specific regions in the mid-latitudes (see map, pp.42–43), temperature tends to be more critical, especially in cool climates. Cool-climate wines are typically lower in alcohol and higher in acidity than those made in hot climates, whose flavours may be less refined but more emphatic.

Different weather and climate factors play different roles during the year. During the winter, when vines are dormant, extreme cold can severely damage the vine. While winters need to be sufficiently cool to allow the vine its revitalizing winter sleep, if temperatures regularly fall below about 5°F (-15°C) in winter, the risk of even dormant vines fatally freezing may be uneconomically high and some winter protection may be needed (see Russia, p.271, for example).

During the spring, when the vines bud, frost poses a serious threat and can severely reduce the year's crop. During the growing season, which generally lasts 150–190 days, sunlight is critical for photosynthesis but without sufficient warmth or rainfall during this period, grapes will not ripen properly.

Average growing season temperatures in wine regions vary from cool (55°F/13°C) to hot (70°F/21°C), largely determining which varieties are likely to ripen consistently (see panel, right). Mean temperatures in the final month of ripening need to be 60–70°F (15–21°C) to produce fine table wines. Hotter climates, such as those of, Andalucía, Madeira, and northeast Victoria in Australia, can make good table wines, and extremely good fortified wines.

Broad differences between wine regions are also seen in contrasting winter and summer temperatures. In continental climates, such as those of New York State's Finger Lakes, Ontario in Canada, or Germany, the seasonal contrast is great due to the effect of the land mass. In these regions, temperatures fall so rapidly in autumn that there is a risk that grapes will simply not ripen fully. In maritime climates, moderated by a nearby sea or ocean, seasonal temperature contrasts are much less. In warmer maritime climates, winters may not always be cold enough for the vines to fall dormant, and organic viticulture may be difficult because pests and diseases are not always killed off in the winter. In cooler maritime climates, such as Bordeaux in France and Long Island in New

An early autumn frost dessicated these bush-vines in Rueda, whose leaves were verdant just the day before. Fortunately for the vineyard owner, the grapes had already been harvested.

KEY FACTS PANELS

Many of the maps are augmented by summary panels of each region's vital statistics: location; the principal grape varieties grown; viticultural challenges; and, most importantly, climate data.

The climate facts, based on data kindly supplied in 2012 by US wine climatologist Dr Gregory Jones, are derived from the most recent 30-year period available for each location (mostly 1981–2010, with a few locations indicated by a * based on 1971–2000). The weather stations (WS) that are the source of the climate averages, denoted by an inverted red triangle on the maps, are chosen to best represent the wine region. However, some are located on the edge of towns rather than in vineyards themselves, which means that because of urban development and different elevations, they may experience slightly different, often warmer, temperatures than the vineyards themselves.

Compare the very different sets of statistics shown here for the hot, dry climate of Mendoza and the much cooler, wetter one of Bordeaux. The Mendoza data runs from July through to June, that for Bordeaux from January to December.

Latitude / Altitude

In general, the lower the latitude, or the nearer the equator, the warmer the climate. But this can be offset by altitude, an important factor also determining likely diurnal temperature variability: the higher the vineyard, the greater the likely difference between day (maximum) and night (minimum) temperatures.

Average growing season temperature

The growing season is taken to be 1 April to 31 October in the northern hemisphere and 1 October to 30 April in the southern hemisphere. The average temperature during that period gives a simple and reliable measure of climate in wine regions worldwide. These temperatures, calculated by taking the average of the seven months of the growing season, are classified by Dr Gregory Jones into four climate groups: cool (55–60°F/ 13–15°C), intermediate (60–62°F/15–17°C), warm (62–66°F/17—19°C), and hot (66–70°F/19–21°C). These groups correlate broadly to the maturity potential for wine-grape varieties grown across many wine regions worldwide, giving a good indication of whether a particular variety is likely to ripen in a particular region. The known cool limit for viticulture is an average growing season temperature of 55°F (13°C), while the upper limit is approximately 70°F (21°C), although table grapes can be grown up to 75°F (24°C) or higher.

Annual rainfall

Average total precipitation indicating the likely availability of water.

Harvest month rainfall

Average rainfall during the final month of ripening and harvest (although this can vary according to variety and individual year); the higher the rainfall, the greater the risk of berries becoming diluted, splitting, or being affected by rot.

Principal viticultural hazards

These are generalizations and may include climate-related challenges such as spring frost or autumn rain as well as endemic pests or vine diseases.

Principal grape varieties

A by-no-means-exhaustive list of the varieties most commonly grown for wine in the region, usually in declining order of importance.

BORDEAUX: MERIGNAC ▼
Latitude / Altitude of WS **44.83° / 154ft (47m)**
Average growing season temperature at WS **63.8°F (17.7°C)**
Average annual rainfall at WS **37.2in (944mm)**
Harvest month rainfall at WS **September 3.3in (84.3mm)**
Principal viticultural hazards **Autumn rain, fungal diseases**
Principal grape varieties **Merlot, Cabernet Sauvignon, Cabernet Franc, Sémillon, Sauvignon Blanc, Muscadelle**

*Climate data from 1971 to 2000

ARGENTINA: MENDOZA ▼
Latitude / Altitude of WS **-32.83° / 2,312ft (705m)**
Average growing season temperature at WS **71.6°F (22°C)**
Average annual rainfall at WS **8in (207mm)**
Harvest month rainfall at WS **March: 1in (26mm)**
Principal viticultural hazards **Summer hail, zonda, nematodes**
Principal grape varieties **Bonarda, Malbec, Criolla Grande, Cereza, Cabernet Sauvignon, Barbera, Sangiovese, Torrontés, Chardonnay**

York, the weather during flowering can often be unsettled or cool, which can influence fruit set. But diurnal temperature variation is also important. Warm days followed by cool nights is an (under-researched) combination valued by wine producers.

WATER INTO WINE

The vine needs water as well as warmth. An average annual rainfall of at least 20in (500mm) is generally required to promote sufficient photosynthesis to ripen grapes; this rises to 30in (750mm) or more in hotter climates, where evaporation from the soil and transpiration from the leaves are much greater. Many wine regions have much less rainfall than this, but growers with access to irrigation water can make up for the shortage. Some varieties, such as La Mancha's Airén, grown as bush-vines are particularly tolerant of near-drought conditions.

If a vine runs short of water, it is said to suffer water stress and is likely to produce smaller grapes with thicker skins. Although this tends to reduce total yields, it can, up to a certain point, result in wines with greater concentration of flavour and colour. Severe drought, however, stops the ripening process completely as the vine goes into survival rather than reproductive mode and can result in unbalanced wines (see p.22). Availability of irrigation water rather than any climatic aspect is what limits the spread of the vine in many regions with hot summers, notably in the southern hemisphere and California. In theory there is no upper limit on annual rainfall. Even flooded vineyards can recover quickly, especially in winter, and parts of Galicia in northern Spain and the Minho in northern Portugal, for example, can receive an average of more than 60in (1,500mm) of rain a year.

Weather extremes such as untimely or heavy rainfall, hail, and very high temperatures during the growing season can have a major impact on the crop. If the weather during flowering in early summer is unsettled or cool, this can prejudice both how much fruit is set and how even is the setting. Prolonged wet weather during the second half of the growing season also tends to encourage the fungal diseases to which vines are prone (see p.15). If there is very heavy rainfall just before harvest, especially after a period of relatively dry weather, grapes can swell quickly and sugar, acids, and flavours may rapidly become diluted (see p.26 for details of how winemakers can try to compensate). Hail, while generally rare in most wine regions, can be extremely detrimental to the crop, damaging the vine's shoots and often splitting the grapes. Fortunately hail tends to be localized. On the other hand, heat extremes (temperatures greater than 95°F/35°C) can be widespread, leading to vine stress, a slow-down in photosynthesis, or the fruit simply dropping off the vine.

THE WIND EFFECT

Wind can play an important part, too. During the early stages of vine growth, high winds can break off shoots and delay or critically affect flowering. Winds can be beneficial by cooling hot vineyards and drying out damp ones – in Corsica or southern Uruguay, for example – but constant wind stress, as in the Salinas Valley of Monterey in California, can stop photosynthesis and severely delay the ripening process. Vine-growers in more exposed parts of the southern Rhône Valley have to install windbreaks to minimize the effects of the notorious mistral, and the hot, dry zonda of Argentina is feared rather than welcomed by wine producers.

Terroir

There is no precise translation for the French word _terroir_. Perhaps this is why many Anglo-Saxons long mistrusted it as a Gallic fancy: a conveniently mystical way of asserting the superiority of French soil and landscape and the unknowable peculiarities that give French wines special qualities. Yet there is no mystery about terroir. Everyone – or at least every place – has one. Your garden and mine have terroirs, probably several. Total natural growing environment is all that terroir means.

At its most restrictive, the word means soil. By extension, and in common use, it embraces the soil itself, the subsoil and rocks beneath it, its physical and chemical properties and how they interact with the local climate, or macroclimate, to determine both the mesoclimate of a particular vineyard and the microclimate of a particular vine. This includes, for example, how quickly a patch of land drains; whether it reflects sunlight or absorbs the heat; its elevation; its degree of slope; its orientation to the sun; and whether it is close to a cooling or sheltering forest or a warming lake, river, or the sea.

Thus, if the foot of a slope is frost-prone, it will have a different terroir from that of the hillside down which the cold air drains, even if the soil is the same (which is why, for instance, vines are not planted in the Willamette Valley in Oregon at altitudes below 200ft/60m). In general, the higher the altitude, the cooler the average temperature, especially at night (which explains why viticulture is possible as close to the equator as, say, Salta in Argentina), although some hillside vineyards in northern California can be warmer than the valley floor because they lie above the fog line.

Similarly, an east-facing slope that catches the morning sun may have identical soil to a west-facing slope that warms up later and holds the evening rays, but its terroir is different and the wine it produces will be subtly different, too. In the case of the meandering Mosel in Germany, even the precise orientation of a slope can determine whether great wine or no wine can be produced from it.

The single most important aspect of terroir, however, given that the vines have been planted somewhere with summers that are warm and dry enough for them to stand a chance of ripening, is the extent to which water and nutrients are available. If a vine is planted on fertile soils with a high water table, such as those of some of the least-favoured sites on the floor of the Napa Valley in California, or the Wairau Valley in Marlborough, New Zealand, vines will have almost constant access to water. The vine's natural instinct will be to become "vigorous", growing shoots and leaves at such a rate that there is danger they will shade any fruit, producing unripe grapes and wines that actually taste leafy and green because they have put all their energy into vegetative growth rather than ripening grapes.

However, if a vine is planted in very infertile soil with access to barely any water, so that supplies are severely restricted, such as in many of the traditional vineyards of southern Spain or southern Italy, photosynthesis virtually stops for a significant part of the summer. The vine suffers such water stress it "shuts down" and, in order to survive, the vine has to use up, or respire, some of the energy that should have gone into ripening. The only reason sugar concentration increases in the grapes under these circumstances is from the gradual evaporation of water from the berries. Few interesting flavour compounds are formed, tannins do not ripen and the result can be extremely unbalanced wines that are high in alcohol but have harsh, unripe tannins, less intense flavours, and dangerously unstable colours.

All sorts of viticultural tricks are used to compensate for these natural disadvantages (canopy management and controlled irrigation are respectively the most obvious for the extreme environments described above) and the result can be some extremely good wine. Some growers and winemakers choose to manage their vineyards in such a way as to override or minimize the effect of terroir characteristics, by blending from diverse or distant regions or by manipulating the wine in the winery; others wish to express environmental effects in their wines as eloquently as possible. Some producers might suggest that the traditional winemaking practices of their own region have themselves become part of the terroir.

So what sort of terroir naturally produces great wine? Research into the crucial interaction between soil and water and vine nutrition has developed considerably over the last 50 years,

PRECISION VITICULTURE: UNDERSTANDING VINEYARD VARIABILITY

The tools of precision viticulture allow a grower to understand, and so better manage, vineyard variability. In this example, yield mapping has been used in conjunction with a high-resolution electromagnetic soil survey and elevation mapping to identify "zones of characteristic performance" within the block. Yields can vary tenfold (between 2 and 20 tonnes/ha, for example) within vineyards managed in exactly the same way throughout. In this example, an 18-acre (7.3ha) vineyard in Coonawarra, Australia, the variation in topography leads to variation in soil depth and therefore the availability of water, which controls the variation in yield. Even though the block is essentially flat with a mere 4ft (1.2m) difference in elevation from the lowest to the highest point, the variation in the land underlying the vineyard clearly exerts enormous influence on its productivity.

Zones of characteristic performance

Yield over three vintages

Plant-available water (PAW)

Soil depth

Electromagnetic field (EM38): soil conductivity indicates soil moisture levels

1 The lowest-yielding areas characteristically occur on ridges where the soil is shallowest.

2 Higher-yielding areas characteristically occur in hollows where the soil is deeper and the most moisture is available.

3 This zone is intermediate between the other two and has yields that are similar to the average for the block.

	Low						High
Yield							
PAW							
Depth							
EM38							

Maps created by Rob Bramley, CSIRO Ecosystem Sciences, Adelaide

and in the last 15 years, sophisticated technology (see panel, below left) has allowed a far greater understanding of very localized terroir effects.

In Burgundy, the vineyards that have over time proved to produce the finest wines tend to be those in the middle of the famous Côte d'Or, where the combination of marl, silt, and limestone that has ended up there (see p.51) seems most propitious for adequate but restricted water supply and therefore wine quality. The panel on the right illustrates the use of soil analysis to maximize the potential quality from a vineyard and produce wines that best express their place of origin.

It should be said, however, that superior terroirs have a way of perpetuating themselves that is not entirely natural. The owner of Grand Cru land can afford to maintain it to perfection with drainage ditches, the precise amount and quality of fertilizer, and ideal cultivation techniques, while such cosseting is uneconomic for a less glorified plot. Terroirs depend on man and his money for their expression, as witness the dip in Château Margaux's performance between 1966 and 1978, when the owner could no longer afford to maintain his first growth in the style it merited.

Some organic and biodynamic wine-growers suggest that the term terroir should also apply to all the flora and fauna of the land, visible or microscopic (such as yeast), and that terroir is inevitably changed by chemical fertilizers and other soil additions that have been imported from outside the ecosystem of the local vineyard. And you could also argue that centuries of monoculture and such wholesome practices as ploughing and planting cover crops have almost certainly altered the land. But the interesting thing is just how much different, even adjacent, plots of land can vary in their effect on the resultant wine, even when they have been nurtured in exactly the same way.

VINEYARD ZONING

This has become an exact and exacting science, harnessing geology (the underlying rocks), geomorphology (how the land is shaped by the geology), and pedology (study of soils). Growers with deep pockets can now acquire soil maps at very high resolution to help them decide which plot of land to buy, how to modify various parts of it, and exactly which variety to plant where. In existing vineyards, especially larger ones where yield and ripening may vary greatly from one part of the vineyard to another, vine vigour can be measured using similarly sophisticated methods such as remote sensing via aerial imagery, and yields can be monitored and mapped (see panel).

Approaches to such "zoning" vary, but increased geographical and viticultural precision allows growers the luxury of, for example, picking each plot within a vineyard at just the right moment or reducing chemical intervention in certain blocks – but it is an option only where the potential quality and price of the wine are high enough to justify the costs. Zoning on a larger scale is also a critical tool in delimiting areas in newer wine regions.

SOIL PROFILING

In Bordeaux in the 1960s and 1970s, Gérard Seguin's studies of the Médoc showed that the very best soils were not particularly fertile and drained quickly and deeply, drawing the roots down to great depths, up to 23ft (7m) in Margaux, to find a stable water supply. Subsequent research by Bordeaux's Cornelis van Leeuwen and others has shown that it is not so much soil depth as water availability that matters for wine quality – so much so that the water-holding capacity of richer soils can be too great if roots go deep. On heavy clay in Pomerol (for example, Petrus), roots may penetrate no deeper than about 4.3ft (1.3m) and on the limestone soils of St-Emilion (for example, Château Ausone), roots range from 6.6ft (2m) on the slopes to 1.3ft (0.4m) on the plateau (see map on p.105). However, in clay soils there must be enough organic matter to allow water to move freely. It seems, based on such research, that drainage and water availability, rather than precise chemical composition, are the key to the perfect soil for great wine.

Soil pits are proliferating. Here, consultant Xavier Choné wields his pick in a Beckstoffer-owned vineyard in St Helena, California. He analyses soil type and depth and water availability in conjunction with every other aspect of the "vineyard architecture" (rootstock, vine, planting density, vigour, and so on) to advise on the timing and minimum levels of irrigation for wine quality.

His work has shown that detailed soil analysis and appropriate vineyard practices may obviate the need for irrigation altogether, or that a late-ripening variety such as Cabernet Sauvignon can be harvested earlier yet with riper tannins.

Chilean consultant and soil-pit proponent Pedro Parra takes a more "geological approach" – investigating not just the type of rock and the way it fractures – important for root penetration – but also its water-holding capacity – particularly with regard to the rock's influence on tannins: granite soils often produce wines with dry tannins, volcanic soils may be associated with bitter tannins. With older terroirs, he starts by defining the mother rock (examples include limestone in Burgundy, schist in Spain's Priorat or granite in Chile's Cauquenes) and then takes into account geomorphology (the way, for instance, layers of hard and soft rock create plateaux and slopes) and finally he looks at the actual soil, including texture and porosity. Younger soils such as those in Crozes-Hermitage in the Rhône, Maipo in Chile, or Ribera del Duero in Spain are not generally shaped by their geology, although gravelly alluvial terraces often produce wines that show the complexity of a "geological terroir", according to Para. For all this to be relevant to the wine-grower, the profiler has to dig enough pits to reflect the diversity of the whole vineyard and correlate vine performance with the soil analysis.

Making Wine in the Vineyard

We now know something about which grape variety to plant and the likely effect of weather, climate, and local environment on the vine. But how about choosing exactly where and how to plant vines? Vineyard site selection, while virtually unknown in the traditional wine regions of Europe, where inheritance, appellation laws, and planting rights tend to dictate vineyard location, is becoming an increasingly important and exact science.

A prospective vineyard investor needs to know that a commercially viable quantity of healthy grapes is likely to be ripened on that site every year. Close analysis of topography, climate, and soil data is safer (see p.23) than acting on a hunch.

Crude statistics on temperature, rainfall, and sunshine hours can help, but need careful interpretation. High average summer temperatures, for instance, may look good on paper, but photosynthesis effectively stops above a certain temperature (between about 85 and 95°F, or 30 and 35°C) depending on the location, so ripening could be adversely affected if there are too many very hot days. Wind, excluded from many sets of meteorological statistics, can also stop photosynthesis by closing the stomata, the tiny openings on leaves and berries that regulate the process.

In cooler areas, the critical aspect of temperature evaluation is whether grapes will ripen reliably. If average summer and autumn temperatures are relatively low for viticulture (as in England), or if autumn usually arrives early with either anticipated rains (as in Oregon) or a substantial drop in temperature (as in British Columbia), then relatively early-ripening varieties may have to be planted. Chardonnay and Pinot Noir are fine for the Pacific Northwest, but even they ripen too late for vineyards furthest from the equator. Riesling will ripen on the most favoured sites in the Mosel in western Germany, but would be marginal for much of England (even if climate change is making this less predictable). Seriously early-ripening varieties such as Seyval Blanc and Müller-Thurgau may be safer choices – for still wines anyway.

The average summer rainfall and its timing gives a useful indication of the likelihood of fungal diseases (see p.15). Monthly rainfall totals, likely evaporation, and soil analysis, should help assess the need for irrigation (see p.20). Even if the site is in an area where supplementing natural rainfall is allowed, a suitable source of water must be found. Precise control of timing and rates of irrigation is an increasingly important way of shaping the quality as well as quantity of the wine produced. Lack of water is likely to be the most significant brake on vineyard expansion in California, Argentina, and, especially, Australia, where water may be unavailable, expensive, or too saline, thanks to excessive deforestation.

Water may be needed for other purposes, too. At the coolest limits of viticulture, in Ontario and the northeastern states of the USA, for example, the total number of frost-free days governs the length of the growing season and therefore which grape varieties are likely to ripen. In Chablis and Chile's cool Casablanca Valley, water is needed for sprinkler systems to protect young vines from frost, but in Casablanca there is a shortage of available water – frost having proved an unforeseen hazard.

The soil, or more likely soils, of any prospective vineyard site needs careful analysis (see p.23). The diagram on p.22 maps the results of soil and water information gathered using more sophisticated techniques and equipment. The fertility of the soil is key to the likely quality of wine produced there and the choice of vine-training system. Too much nitrogen (a common ingredient in fertilizers and manure) can result in excessively vigorous vines that put all their energy into growing leaves rather than ripening grapes, so that the bunches are dangerously shaded by a dark, heavy canopy of leaves and shoots. The phenomenon is particularly common on very fertile soils, typically relatively young soils such as those in New Zealand and on the floor of the Napa Valley. Vigour also varies with the variety of vine and rootstock. The soil should be neither too acid nor too alkaline and have a suitable degree of organic matter (the remains of other plants, animals, and insects) and minerals such as phosphorus, potassium, and nitrogen. Phosphorus is vital for photosynthesis and is rarely lacking in the soil. Too much potassium can result in wines dangerously high in pH and low in acidity.

DESIGNING A VINEYARD

Once a vine-grower has selected a site or cleared a vineyard for replanting, he or she must design the vineyard. The orientation of the rows, how best to train the vines, the height of the posts (and, later, wires), and the number of buds to keep when pruning must all be taken into consideration. Will it be necessary to create terraces on a hillside site – more expensive to design and maintain – so that rows of vines follow contour lines, allowing tractors and people to move easily along them?

Then comes one of the most important decisions of all: how close to plant the vines, both between and within rows, based on the sort of yields the vine-grower is aiming for (see p.78 for more on yields) and the vigour of the site. In Mediterranean climates, where it is frequently too hot and dry, a restricted water supply in low-latitude vineyards can dictate widely spaced traditional bushes with a vine density of less than 1,000 vines per hectare and naturally low yields.

ANALYSING GRAPE JUICE

A portable refractometer is used to analyse the sugar content of a drop of grape juice in the vineyard. During ripening, the levels of acidity (mainly tartaric and malic acids) fall, while the fermentable sugars (mainly fructose and glucose) rise. As harvest approaches, vine-growers pay close attention to the weather forecasts and monitor these measurable aspects of maturation alongside a more subjective assessment of flavour and phenolic changes, particularly the ripeness of the tannins in dark-skinned berries, in order to decide when to pick. Even if the refractometer suggests a sufficient sugar level has been reached (see right), some winemakers prefer to wait for "physiological ripeness", when the skins start to shrivel slightly, the stalks turn brown and the grape may be pulled easily off the stalk. Others prefer to pick earlier to retain greater freshness in the wine and avoid excessive alcohol levels.

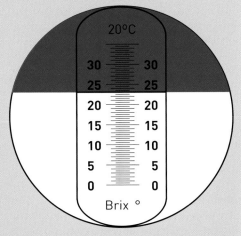

Measurements of sugar content

Specific gravity	1.060	1.065	1.070	1.075	1.080	1.085	1.090	1.095	1.100	1.105	1.110	1.115	1.120	1.125
Oechsle	60	65	70	75	80	85	90	95	100	105	110	115	120	125
Baumé	8.2	8.8	9.4	10.1	10.7	11.3	11.9	12.5	13.1	13.7	14.3	14.9	15.5	16.0
Brix	14.7	15.8	17.0	18.1	19.3	20.4	21.5	22.5	23.7	24.8	25.8	26.9	28.0	29.0
% Potential alcohol V/V	7.5	8.1	8.8	9.4	10.0	10.6	11.3	11.9	12.5	13.1	13.8	14.4	15.0	15.6

VIGOUR AND CANOPY MANAGEMENT

Low-vigour vines

Bordeaux vineyards such as this one at Château Haut-Brion in Pessac-Léognan tend to be densely planted, up to 10,000 vines per ha, and trained low on a simple vertical trellis such as the single or double Guyot since the soils are not particularly fertile and the climate is generally temperate. With careful pruning and shoot and leaf removal, the grower can maintain the ratio of fruit to leaves that is needed to ripen the berries fully before the temperatures drop.

High-vigour vines

In more fertile soils, vines can produce a slightly larger crop without loss of quality as long as the training system provides sufficient foliage to ripen the crop without shading the fruit. The lyre system, shown here at Kumeu River in New Zealand, splits the canopy in two to maximize photosynthesis, but it must be carefully managed to avoid excessive shading. Vine density is relatively low, which suits higher-vigour soils. Expensive netting may also be needed to keep birds off.

New World vineyards were once typically planted in warm or hot regions, often on fertile virgin soil, which threatened to oversupply the vine with nutrients. Growers left wide spacing for vineyard machinery between the rows, and often between vines, resulting again in a vine density of just over 1,000 vines per hectare, though for very different reasons. This economized on plants, posts, wires and labour and made cultivation and mechanical harvesting easy. But all too often the price paid was excessive vigour, sprawling canopies burying their own fruit and most of the leaves needed for photosynthesis in deep shade. Not only do such grapes not ripen properly, resulting in wines that belie the climate with unattractively high acidity and unripe tannins, but the wood destined to carry the next year's crop does not ripen either. The embryo buds on the cane need exposure to the sun to make them fruitful. A dense canopy thus starts a vicious spiral of smaller crops and more foliage year by year. Liberal irrigation could result in economically viable yields per hectare, but each vine would be required to ripen too heavy a charge of grapes.

This stereotype, now much modified, contrasts markedly with the traditional vineyards of Bordeaux and Burgundy, where yields per hectare are generally much lower, and yields per vine lower still. Here vines are planted as densely as 10,000 vines per hectare at intervals of 3ft (1m) along rows just 3ft (1m) apart (worked by *tracteurs-enjambeurs* that straddle the vines). Each vine is kept deliberately small, typically trained according to the single or double Guyot system (see above left). Planting and labour costs are much higher, but the grapes are given the maximum chance to ripen with beneficial effects on the quality of the wine. Over the last few decades there has been considerable progress in what is known as canopy management, based on a wider range of vine-training systems, designed

to spread out and control the canopy of even the most vigorous vines (see the lyre system, for example, above right).

Other important decisions throughout the year include which form of fungal or pest control to use, if any, whether to cultivate between the rows or leave grass or other cover crops to grow, whether to ignore the sprawling shoots of summer or to trim them off, and whether to "green harvest" to reduce the number of bunches before or during ripening. Over centuries of sometimes unconscious experimentation in Europe, solutions have evolved that are appropriate to the local conditions of some of the world's most precious vineyards and most universally admired wines.

These choices may well be influenced, or reduced, by the grower's overall philosophy of farming. More and more growers are adopting organic or biodynamic viticulture. Both

approaches prohibit the use of all agrochemicals and synthetic fertilizers, which may leave residues, although limited amounts of sulphur-based sprays are used to control mildew. Biodynamic growers rely on homeopathic doses of preparations based mainly on specially treated manure or wild plants to stimulate the health of the soil and the vine, and, even more controversially, plan their work in the vineyard and cellar according to the lunar calendar. Results can be impressive, even if the science behind it remains a mystery – even to those who practise it.

Vine-growing is, after all, like all farming, utterly dependent on nature and local practicalities. Of all aspects of wine production it is rightly recognized as the single most important, and demanding, factor determining exactly how wine tastes.

Viña Falernia's Huanta vineyard in Chile's Elqui Valley is at an altitude of 5,185–6,320ft (1,700–2,070m). This is a desolate landscape where very little grows, except these carefully irrigated vines.

Making Wine in the Cellar

If in the vineyard nature is ultimately in charge, man takes over in the winery or cellar. Winemaking consists of a series of decisions dictated by the grapes and their condition, and by the style of wine the winemaker has set his or her heart on or has been asked to produce. Occasionally these conflict. The diagrams opposite and overleaf respectively show the steps involved in making a relatively inexpensive unoaked white and a high-quality, traditionally made, barrel-aged red wine.

HARVESTING THE GRAPES

The winemaker's first and possibly most important decision is when to pick. He or she should have been monitoring the sugar and acid levels in the grapes and their general health, appearance and flavour in the weeks leading up to harvest.

Decisions on harvest date need to be taken in conjunction with the weather forecast. If, for example, the grapes are not quite ripe enough but rain is predicted, the decision is whether to leave the grapes on the vine and hope that there will be sufficient warm, dry weather afterwards for them to ripen fully. Some varieties are much more sensitive than others to the exact date of harvest. Merlot, for example, can easily lose a certain liveliness if kept too long on the vine, whereas Cabernet Sauvignon is much more tolerant of a few extra days. If the grapes are already suffering from fungal disease (see p.15), the rain will exacerbate this so it may be best to pick the grapes just slightly less ripe than ideal. White wine is much more forgiving of a few rotten grapes than red, in which the colour is rapidly lost and the wine tainted by a mouldy taste.

The winemaker, in conjunction with whomever is in charge of labour, also has to decide at what time of day to pick. In hot climates grapes are generally picked either at night (easier by machine, with big spotlights) or very early in the morning in order to deliver the grapes to the winery as cool as possible, typically – if the winemaker aspires to quality – in shallow, stackable crates so that the grapes are not crushed before arriving at the winery. All the greatest wines in the world are still picked by hand, no matter how expensive and elusive the pickers, because they can both snip whole bunches off the vine (machines shake off the berries) and also make intelligent decisions about which fruit to pick.

Once the grapes arrive at the winery, they may be deliberately chilled – some hot-climate wineries even have cold rooms where grapes may be kept for hours or days (in rare cases even weeks) until a fermentation vat is available. Even more likely at a top-quality winery in any climate is that the grapes are subject to further selection. One of the most obvious winery innovations in the 1990s was the installation of sorting tables, typically a slow-moving belt onto which grapes are tipped to be minutely examined by human eye before arriving at the destemmer and/or crusher. Mechanical crushing releases the juice, which is 70-80% water, and replaces the human foot – still used for some high-quality port. The latest time-saving and quality-oriented technology for well-funded producers is an optical sorter comprising a computerized camera plus air jets that blow away debris and unripe berries after destemming.

PREPARING WHITE WINE GRAPES

Most white wine grapes are destemmed before they are pressed because stems can be astringent and would spoil a light, aromatic wine. For some full-bodied white wines, however, and most top-quality sparkling and sweet white wine, the winemaker may choose to put whole bunches into the press. This is because the stems can help drainage – and in any case only the first portion of it, the "free-run" juice, may be used.

For white wines, winemakers must decide whether they are going to protect the juice as much as possible from oxygen, preserving every ounce of fresh fruit flavour (preventing oxidation and stunning ambient yeasts at the start with added sulphur dioxide; complete destemming; low temperatures throughout, and so on), or to adopt deliberately oxidative techniques, exposing the grapes to oxygen and aiming for secondary, more complex flavours.

Riesling, Sauvignon Blanc, and other aromatic varieties tend to be vinified protectively, while most top-quality Chardonnay, including white burgundy, is made oxidatively. Oxidative handling may include a period of deliberate "skin contact": not as exciting as it sounds, but a few hours either in the press before it is turned on or in a holding tank, during which further flavour will be leached into the "must" (the pulpy mixture between grape juice and wine) from the skins. If the skins are allowed contact with juice for white wine for too long, however, they tend to impart astringency – which is why grapes for most white wine, unlike red wine grapes whose skins are needed for colour and tannin, are pressed before fermentation. However, wines fermented with the skins in clay amphorae or in Georgian *qvevri* buried underground have deliberately prolonged the skin contact throughout and beyond fermentation to produce "orange wines" that are deliberately astringent and highly distinctive.

Over the years, presses used for the vast majority of white wines have been designed with increasing ingenuity to squeeze out the juice as gently as possible, without breaking the pips or extracting astringency from the grape skins. Pneumatic presses, some of them completely insulated from oxygen for protective juice handling, are the gentlest and the most common. Winemakers are increasingly careful to separate different portions of juice from the press, the earliest being the least astringent.

At this stage, particularly protectively made white wines may be clarified: cleared of all the little grapey fragments still in suspension, usually by letting the solids settle to the bottom of a holding tank and then running off the clear juice into the fermentation tank. It is important at this stage that fermentation still hasn't started, which is why low temperatures and sulphur additions are crucial. Oxidatively made whites, however, are treated more like reds.

Red wine grapes are usually destemmed and crushed, although winemakers are experimenting more and more with fermenting whole bunches, as has been traditional in Burgundy. This works only in climates with growing seasons long enough to ripen the stems as well as the fruit, otherwise the stems would make the wine taste horribly tough. Some winemakers deliberately sulphur the grapes and chill them for up to a week to delay fermentation, extracting colour and primary fruit flavours.

THE FERMENTATION PROCESS

The winemaker then has to make decisions about fermentation, the miraculous transformation of sweet grape juice into much drier, more complex-flavoured wine. If yeast (naturally present or added) is put into contact with grape sugars, it converts them into alcohol, heat, and carbon dioxide. The riper the grapes, the higher the sugar level, the stronger the resulting wine. Fermentation vats naturally warm up as the process gets under way, so in warmer climates they may well need cooling jackets or internal cooling elements to keep the must, below the temperature at which precious flavour compounds may be boiled off. The gas that is generated can make a winery a heady – and dangerous – place at harvest time, where the smell is an intoxicating mixture of carbon dioxide, grapes, and alcohol, especially if the fermentation vats are open-topped, as for many traditionally made red wines. Although white wines are fermented in sealed vats so as to protect the must from damaging oxidation and avoid browning, a vat full of red must has its own protection: the thick "cap" of skins that floats on the surface.

Yeasts and their behaviour continue to provoke scrutiny and heated debate. The winemaker's initial choice is whether to use specially selected and prepared yeast, so-called cultured yeast, as opposed to relying on the strains of yeast that are naturally in the atmosphere of the vineyard and winery.

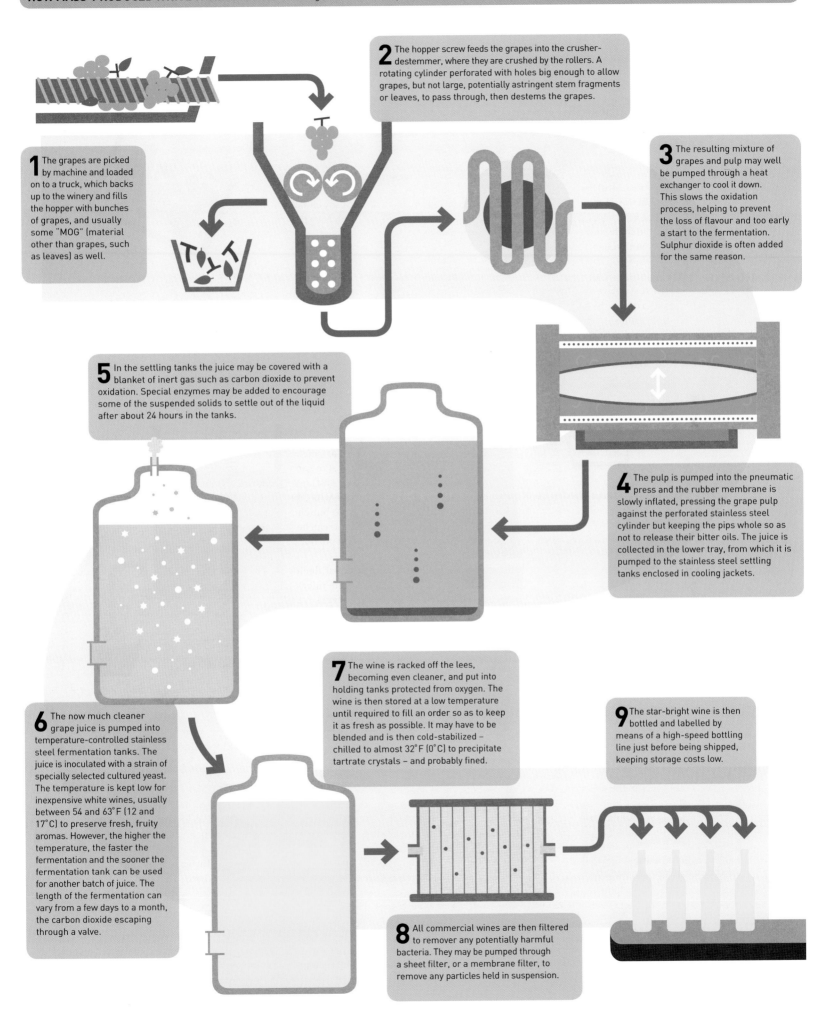

HOW MASS-PRODUCED WHITE WINE IS MADE

This diagram shows an inexpensive white wine made in a well-equipped winery in a warm region.

2 The hopper screw feeds the grapes into the crusher-destemmer, where they are crushed by the rollers. A rotating cylinder perforated with holes big enough to allow grapes, but not large, potentially astringent stem fragments or leaves, to pass through, then destems the grapes.

1 The grapes are picked by machine and loaded on to a truck, which backs up to the winery and fills the hopper with bunches of grapes, and usually some "MOG" (material other than grapes, such as leaves) as well.

3 The resulting mixture of grapes and pulp may well be pumped through a heat exchanger to cool it down. This slows the oxidation process, helping to prevent the loss of flavour and too early a start to the fermentation. Sulphur dioxide is often added for the same reason.

5 In the settling tanks the juice may be covered with a blanket of inert gas such as carbon dioxide to prevent oxidation. Special enzymes may be added to encourage some of the suspended solids to settle out of the liquid after about 24 hours in the tanks.

4 The pulp is pumped into the pneumatic press and the rubber membrane is slowly inflated, pressing the grape pulp against the perforated stainless steel cylinder but keeping the pips whole so as not to release their bitter oils. The juice is collected in the lower tray, from which it is pumped to the stainless steel settling tanks enclosed in cooling jackets.

6 The now much cleaner grape juice is pumped into temperature-controlled stainless steel fermentation tanks. The juice is inoculated with a strain of specially selected cultured yeast. The temperature is kept low for inexpensive white wines, usually between 54 and 63°F (12 and 17°C) to preserve fresh, fruity aromas. However, the higher the temperature, the faster the fermentation and the sooner the fermentation tank can be used for another batch of juice. The length of the fermentation can vary from a few days to a month, the carbon dioxide escaping through a valve.

7 The wine is racked off the lees, becoming even cleaner, and put into holding tanks protected from oxygen. The wine is then stored at a low temperature until required to fill an order so as to keep it as fresh as possible. It may have to be blended and is then cold-stabilized – chilled to almost 32°F (0°C) to precipitate tartrate crystals – and probably fined.

9 The star-bright wine is then bottled and labelled by means of a high-speed bottling line just before being shipped, keeping storage costs low.

8 All commercial wines are then filtered to remover any potentially harmful bacteria. They may be pumped through a sheet filter, or a membrane filter, to remove any particles held in suspension.

HOW TOP-QUALITY RED WINE IS MADE
This diagram shows how a typical fine red wine is made in the most traditional way possible.

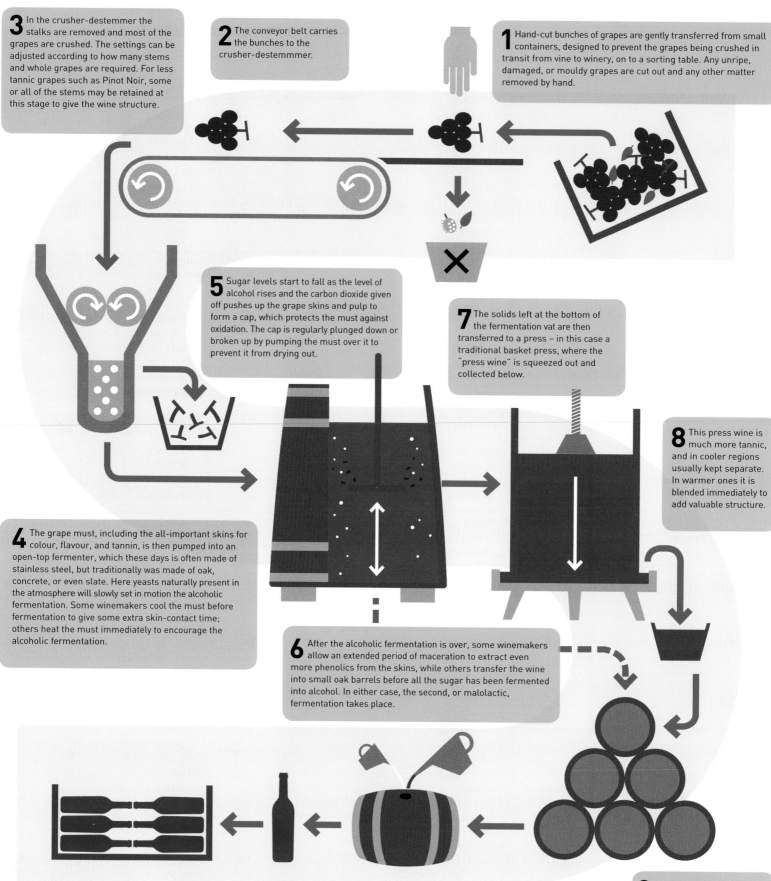

3 In the crusher-destemmer the stalks are removed and most of the grapes are crushed. The settings can be adjusted according to how many stems and whole grapes are required. For less tannic grapes such as Pinot Noir, some or all of the stems may be retained at this stage to give the wine structure.

2 The conveyor belt carries the bunches to the crusher-destemmmer.

1 Hand-cut bunches of grapes are gently transferred from small containers, designed to prevent the grapes being crushed in transit from vine to winery, on to a sorting table. Any unripe, damaged, or mouldy grapes are cut out and any other matter removed by hand.

5 Sugar levels start to fall as the level of alcohol rises and the carbon dioxide given off pushes up the grape skins and pulp to form a cap, which protects the must against oxidation. The cap is regularly plunged down or broken up by pumping the must over it to prevent it from drying out.

7 The solids left at the bottom of the fermentation vat are then transferred to a press – in this case a traditional basket press, where the "press wine" is squeezed out and collected below.

8 This press wine is much more tannic, and in cooler regions usually kept separate. In warmer ones it is blended immediately to add valuable structure.

4 The grape must, including the all-important skins for colour, flavour, and tannin, is then pumped into an open-top fermenter, which these days is often made of stainless steel, but traditionally was made of oak, concrete, or even slate. Here yeasts naturally present in the atmosphere will slowly set in motion the alcoholic fermentation. Some winemakers cool the must before fermentation to give some extra skin-contact time; others heat the must immediately to encourage the alcoholic fermentation.

6 After the alcoholic fermentation is over, some winemakers allow an extended period of maceration to extract even more phenolics from the skins, while others transfer the wine into small oak barrels before all the sugar has been fermented into alcohol. In either case, the second, or malolactic, fermentation takes place.

9 The wine is then aged in oak barrels for up to 18 months.

12 After careful bottling the wine is laid down in bins and stored for bottle ageing; it is labelled and capsuled just before despatch.

11 The wine will also probably be fined – clarified by adding a fining agent that attracts any suspended solids – and lightly filtered to ensure that it is microbiologically stable. Before bottling, a final blend may be made.

10 Evaporation means that these barrels will have to be topped up, and the wine will occasionally be "racked" off its sediment into a new barrel to aerate it and prevent the build-up of harmful compounds.

In new wine regions there may be no choice; wine yeasts need time to build up a population and in the early years the only ambient strains available are more likely to be harmful than benevolent. With admittedly an increasing number of exceptions, most wines are therefore made by adding specially cultured yeast to the must. (Once one vat has started, the addition of fermenting must from it will kick-start a second.)

Cultured yeasts behave predictably. Particularly powerful strains can be chosen for high-sugar musts, those which encourage coagulation of sediment may be useful for sparkling wines. The choice of cultured yeasts can also have a significant influence on the flavour of the wine: for example, enhancing particular aromas. Traditionalists, however, prefer to leave everything to ambient yeasts in the belief that they add more interest to the wine's flavour, even if they are less predictable. It is not going too far to regard them as an aspect of terroir, and indeed proprietors can be very proprietorial about them.

HELPING FERMENTATION

The winemaker's nightmare is a "stuck fermentation", when fermentation stops before all the sugar has been converted into alcohol, leaving a dangerously vulnerable mixture that can all too easily fall prey to oxidation and nasty bacteria. The level of alcohol in a finished wine is an effective weapon against many bacteria.

The exact pace of a red-wine fermentation is critical to the sort of wine that results. The warmer the fermentation (up to the dangerous flavour-evaporation limit), the more flavour and colour will be extracted. Long, cool fermentations tend to result in light, fruity wines, but if a fermentation is too short and hot, the wine will also be low in body and flavour. The temperature rises during fermentation, but is generally between about 72 and 86°F (22 and 30°C) for full-bodied red wines, and cooler, sometimes as low as 54°F (12°C), for aromatic white wines.

To extract tannins, flavour, and colour from the grape skins during red-wine fermentation, the cap and the must need to be encouraged to commune with each other. This is generally done by either pumping the must over the cap or by physically punching it down into the liquid, although there is an array of mechanical and computerized ways of submerging the cap. The science of this process, and any post-fermentation maceration designed to extract and soften tannins, has become extremely exact, and is a key factor in how much more palatable many young red wines are today.

Fashions in fermentation vessels come and go. Stainless steel is easy to clean and control but some winemakers currently prefer wood or a return to cement.

Gentle handling of the grapes, must, and wine is generally, though not universally, considered to be a factor in ultimate wine quality. Where money is no object, or if a winery is conveniently built into a hillside, winery design and equipment harness the force of gravity to avoid the use of pumps (as shown on p.35).

It is at the fermentation stage, red or white, that the winemaker decides whether or not to add or remove acid or add sugar, or concentrated grape must. French winemakers, apart from those in the far south, have been adding sugar to fermentation vats to increase the alcohol content (not sweetness) of the final wine for 200 years, ever since this process, "chaptalization", was proposed by the agriculture minister Jean-Antoine Chaptal. The AOC laws generally restrict such "enrichment" to the equivalent of no more than an additional 2% of alcohol. In practice, thanks to warmer summers, better canopy management (see p.25) and anti-rot strategies, growers are now able to pick grapes riper and riper so that less and less additional sugar is needed.

Winemakers may also decide to exclude a portion of juice from the red-wine fermentation vat so as to improve the all-important ratio of flavour- and colour-filled skins to juice. This traditional practice, known as *saignée* in France, is sometimes replaced by more mechanical manipulation: concentration based on evaporation under vacuum or reverse osmosis.

Winemakers in warm climates, on the other hand, routinely add (or "adjust") acidity to musts from grapes that have ripened to sugar levels only dreamt of in northern France, but whose natural acidity has dropped to an unappetizingly low level on the way. Tartaric acid, grapes' natural acid, is the acid of choice. There is another, arguably more natural, way in which winemakers can influence the acidity of a wine. Alcoholic fermentation of any wine is often followed by malolactic fermentation, in which the grapes' harsher malic (appley) acids are naturally converted into softer, lactic (milky) acids and carbon dioxide. Understanding and mastery of this process, sometimes warming the wine and/or adding cultured lactic acid bacteria, was the key factor in the mid-20th century in making red wines drinkable younger by lowering the overall acidity and adding some extra flavours as well.

But those extra flavours may not be desirable in an aromatic, protectively made white wine, and if the malolactic conversion is deliberately suppressed (by temperature control, sulphur addition, or filtering or fining the necessary yeasts and proteins out of the wine), the effect is to make the wine taste crisper. In practice, malolactic fermentation is generally encouraged in most good-quality Chardonnay to add texture and flavour, and in warmer climates it is compensated for by added acidity.

Malolactic fermentation is invariably good for red wine, and in recent years a fashion has emerged for conducting it not in large tanks, but in individual barrels. This is much more labour-intensive and is warranted only for high-quality wines, but the short-term result at least is a perceptibly smoother, more seductive texture, a characteristic that some wine tasters have come to associate with quality. Increasingly, therefore, winemakers who wish their wines to show well in youth run red wine out of the fermentation vat just before the end of fermentation into barrels, where the wine will finish its alcoholic and then its malolactic fermentation.

A controversial issue, particularly in warmer climates such as California and parts of Australia, is high alcohol levels in wine, generally the result of picking grapes later to get more flavour and riper tannins. As with must concentration, various mechanical methods, again based on evaporation or reverse osmosis, may be used to reduce the alcohol level of the finished wine. However, some producers prefer to find alternative strategies in the vineyard so that the raw material is in better balance to begin with.

While some top-end red wines finish their alcoholic fermentation in barrel, full alcoholic fermentation in barrel has become de rigueur for many full-bodied whites with aspirations to a high price. By the end of the 20th century, oak had become The Other Ingredient in wine, such a high proportion of good to great wine both red and white being matured if not fermented in oak barrels. Indeed, practically all serious red wine undergoes the smoothing process of maturation in oak, and all but the most aromatic and lively whites are both fermented and matured in oak barrels. A more recent trend is towards using larger barrels, or barrels that are not new, so that the wines benefit from aeration through the wood but are not marked by oak flavour.

BOTTLING AND THE BUILD-UP

However a wine is matured after fermentation, it will have to be bottled. Before a wine is subjected to this often rather brutal process, the winemaker has to be sure it is stable: that it does not contain any potentially dangerous bacteria and will not do anything inconvenient if subjected to extreme temperatures. It must be clarified, for the wine is still likely to be cloudier than the consumer has come to expect. Inexpensive white wines are often therefore put into a tank and fiercely chilled so that any tartaric acid that remains in solution is precipitated before bottling and won't reappear as (completely harmless but worrying-looking) crystals in the bottle later on. Many wines are filtered in some way so as to remove any danger of refermentation, and fined so that any remaining particles drop out of the wine. Although there is a growing interest in so-called "natural wines" with minimal or no additions, most wines contain small amounts of sulphur to keep them fresh. "Contains sulphites" must be declared on the wine label. Such is the no-risk culture.

Filtration is a heavily political subject among wine folk. Overdone, it can remove flavour and the potential for ageing; underdone, it can leave the wine prey to harmful bacteria and refermentation, particularly if the bottle gets too warm. Wines that spend a long time in oak barrels are likely to become clear by the natural settling process and are less likely to need further processing.

Oak and its uses

Oak is not the only wood used for storing wine, but for centuries it has been the most popular because it is both watertight and easy to work. Its more recently appreciated attributes, however, are that oak flavours have a natural affinity for those of wine, adding more complex compounds, and, more importantly, its physical properties are unparalleled for gently clarifying and stabilizing, while deepening the colour of a red and softening the texture of any well-made wine.

Fermenting a white wine in barrel, provided it has not been stripped of all of its solids and left defenceless against the assault of all the tannins and pigments in the oak, makes the wine smoother in texture yet deeper in flavour. Another white winemaking ploy to give the wine a more creamy texture, whether it was fermented in barrel or tank, is to stir the lees of the fermentation. However, this may also impart some of their often rather milky flavour to the wine and the extra aeration may reduce a wine's finesse or longevity.

White wines may be barrel-aged for as few as three months to take up just a little oak flavour (the older the barrel, the less flavour and oak tannins). Serious red wines are usually matured for longer: up to 18 months, or possibly more in older or larger oak casks. To separate the new wine from the larger particles of the lees (the so-called gross lees), the wine is generally racked into a clean barrel quite soon after fermentation and several times thereafter. Racking aerates the wine, softening its tannins and minimizing the risk of nasty odours building up in the barrel. Some wine is always lost by evaporation, however, and the barrels need regular topping up, another process that beneficially exposes the wine to a little air and softens its rough edges. The winemaker's job during barrel maturation is regularly to taste the contents of each barrel, and to judge not just when the wine should be racked, but also when it is ready for bottling.

An alternative, occasionally a supplement, to barrel-ageing, is to add tiny, measured doses of oxygen to a wine in tank or barrel. This technique of micro-oxygenation has become increasingly popular, but its application is still more of an art than a science.

While micro-oxygenation is a way of imitating the way barrels aerate wine, oak chips, staves, and oak fragments of various shapes and sizes can be used to replicate the flavour effect of oak barrels without their considerable cost. They may also improve texture and make the colour more stable. The use of such alternatives is not free of controversy, but it does have a history: French agronomist Olivier de Serres refers to *"vin de coipeau"* (*copeaux*, that is "wood chips", in modern French) in his book *Théâtre d'Agriculture*

published in 1600. He explains how they should be prepared and suggests that they will help clarify the wine, making it drinkable younger, and add an attractive aroma.

A 500-litre oak barrel under construction at Fanagoria Estate, the only Russian winery to have its own cooperage. Pressure from metal hoops in conjunction with heat is used to bend the long oak staves into shape to create a watertight barrel.

WHERE OAK COMES FROM

The important factors in barrel maturation (and fermentation) are the size and age of the cask (the older or fashionably larger the barrel, the less oak flavour imparted), length of time in cask, how the barrel was toasted (a heavily toasted barrel will impart fewer wood tannins, but more spicy or roasted flavours), how well or long the oak was seasoned (stacked outside to lose its harshness) or even – less propitiously – kiln-dried, before being made into a barrel, and the provenance of the oak.

American oak can be attractively sweet with a vanilla note. Baltic oak was admired at the end of the 19th century. Eastern European oaks are enjoying a revival, but French oak is still generally revered above all others – not least because the forests in the regions mapped here have been so well managed.

Limousin is wide-grained, tannic, and generally more suitable for brandy than wine. The oaks of Tronçais, a single, large government-owned forest in the Allier département, grow so slowly that the wood is tight-grained and excellent for wine. Vosges oak is similar, light in colour and preferred by some winemakers. Others simply ask for oak from *"le Centre"*. However, there may be different species and growing conditions within each forest. Winemakers tend to have a range of favourite coopers rather than sticking to one source.

Major French oak regions

Stoppering Wine

Wine can be stored only if there is an effective and appropriate stopper. The three corks of varying quality and age pictured below are all susceptible to cork taint – especially the cheap agglomerate version made of cork chips glued together. (The old champagne cork shows the effect of years of compression; the long cork has been in a bottle of Bordeaux for several decades.) A cork that has come into contact with both chlorine and mould will develop the thoroughly off-putting mustiness associated with trichloroanisole, or TCA which, when transmitted to the liquid, results in unpleasantly "corked" or "corky" wine. But cork producers have recently invested heavily in upgrading their production techniques and quality control. As a result, the incidence of cork taint has been significantly reduced. However, many wine producers have become so exasperated by the proportion of tainted wine that they have adopted alternative stoppers.

Synthetic corks, usually made of plastic, have been popular, particularly with New World producers, and their quality has improved. They come in a wide range of styles and quality levels, allowing wine drinkers to continue the cork-pulling ritual without any risk of cork taint, although they are not always easy to get back in the bottle, and are not generally suited to wines made for extended ageing in bottle.

Producers at all quality levels, and particularly those in Australia and New Zealand, are increasingly adopting or experimenting with screw caps. They were used initially for aromatic wines such as Riesling, and simple fruity reds for early drinking, for which no oxygen ingress is thought necessary for ageing, but are now increasingly widely used. Concerns that in the long term wine would age differently, and very possibly less gracefully, under stoppers other than natural cork, or that the potentially airtight seal of a screw cap or glass Vino-Lok stopper might cause other unwanted flavours, are being addressed.

Research has enabled winemakers to adapt winemaking practices to avoid such issues, and manufacturers to fine-tune the amount of oxygen allowed in by the liner inside the screw cap.

This mature cork oak in the Algarve, Portugal, had its bark stripped in 2000 by the Amorim cork company, the world's largest cork producer. By the time you read this, it will have been harvested again.

STOPPERS

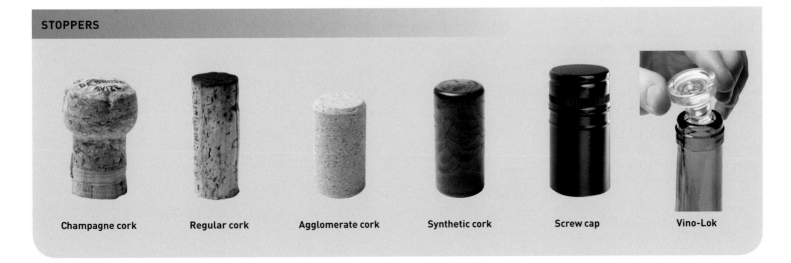

| Champagne cork | Regular cork | Agglomerate cork | Synthetic cork | Screw cap | Vino-Lok |

Anatomy of a Winery

In 1870, Don Maximiano Errázuriz Valdivieso established the original Errázuriz winery and estate at Panquehue in the Aconcagua Valley, 60 miles (100km) north of Chile's capital Santiago (see map, p.324). Fifth-generation scion Eduardo Chadwick celebrated the 140th anniversary of Viña Errázuriz by constructing a brand-new building nearby, which he grandly named the Don Maximiano Icon winery. The scheme may have been inspired by a certain sentimentality, and Eduardo's cousin, architect Samuel Claro's

design is certainly eye-catchingly futuristic, but functionality is the key. The over-arching aim was to have a winery for Viña Errázuriz's flagship Don Maximiano Founder's Reserve equipped so as to maximize the quality of the grapes that go into this Cabernet-based blend, as well as the company's other top wines. No winemaker would be allowed to complain of being under-equipped.

In tune with prevailing sensibilities, and because the Errázuriz family have long been leaders in Chile, the winery was also designed

with sustainability in mind. Harnessing gravity to transport grapes and wine is by no means unique. It was traditional in the days before pumps (see photo, p.13) and is increasingly common in modern wineries that can afford to handle grapes with kid gloves. But gravity flow has been taken to an extreme degree, while ducts buried up to 13ft (4m) below the ground use the prevailing underground temperature to regulate that in the winery. And the special low-emissivity glass windows, cooled by fountains in what is effectively a moat around the winery, also help temperature control, and reflect sunlight into the cellar. See overleaf for the detail of how all this is achieved.

Note that, since this is an auxiliary, albeit luxurious, winery on an established wine estate, it concentrates on winemaking. It is able to take advantage of many of the features already in place for other operations such as the barrel room, where the wine is stored in barrel during *élevage*; the bottling line; the bottle storage cellar prior to shipment; and the quarters for individual personnel, on the roof of which solar panels help to keep energy use at the Don Maximiano Icon winery at what its owner and designers calculate is 20% below that of a conventional winery. See the diagram below for a plan of the principal winemaking buildings on the Errázuriz estate.

The new Icon winery where, from 2011, the Kai, Don Maximiano Founder's Reserve, La Cumbre Syrah, and Seña wines have been made. The Max Reserva winery is in the background.

THE ERRAZURIZ ESTATE WINERY BUILDINGS

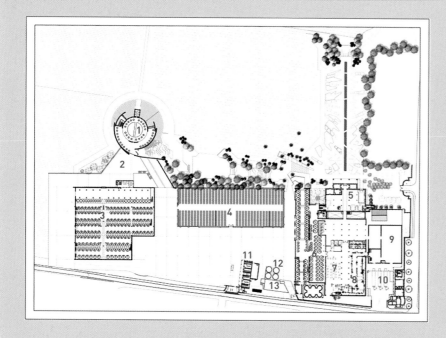

1 Don Maximiano Icon winery

2 Icon winery grape reception area

3 Max Reserva winery (built in 2008 for the Reserva line of wines)

4 Barrel room (Reservas and other wines)

5 The original 1870 winery

6 Blending and ageing (Reservas and other wines)

7 Elaboration (pre-bottling)

8 Bottling line

9 Storage cellar before bottles are dispatched to port for shipping

10 Parking for trucks

11 Dining and changing rooms (solar panels located on the roof above these rooms)

12 Other blending vats

13 Biomass heating system provides hot water for cleaning vats and pipes during the winemaking processes

The glass in the low-emissivity windows (above) is specially insulated and coated so that heat radiation from the Sun during summer is reflected, keeping it cooler inside, and radiant heat from indoors in winter is kept inside. Fountains in the foreground also help to control temperatures in the winery. Errázuriz is particularly proud of its 10 11,000-litre French oak fermentation vats, three of which can be seen through the windows to the left of the door. They help oxygenation of the must and need much less energy for temperature control than the stainless steel tanks that supplement them.

On the left can be seen clearly the three levels in the interior with, on the top level, openings into the top of the fermentation vessels into which grapes can be emptied; the oak and stainless steel fermentation vats, with room for 300 tonnes of grapes each year, on the middle level; and the bottom level, where barrels are filled by gravity from the middle level before they are transferred to the barrel room. There is room for 272 barriques in all. Perforated metal walkways are easy to keep clean and allow maximum visibility.

SUSTAINABLE WINE PRODUCTION

There are almost as many theories about what constitutes sustainable viticulture as there are vine-growers, but it must be agreed that certified organic and biodynamic practices are generally better at protecting the environment and vineyard workers, and yielding a long-term future for the land and state of the planet than continued systematic additions of agrochemicals. Sustainability schemes of varying rigour are increasingly prevalent and have already been devised for wine producers in California, Oregon, Chile, South Africa, and New Zealand.

Some of those in the wine business have been doing their individual bit to reduce their consumption of the planet's precious resources. Water is the most obvious one used in profusion by wine producers, particularly those in drier parts of the world where irrigation has become a habit. These tend to coincide with regions where a preoccupation with hygiene requires considerable amounts of water inside the winery, too. (Some wine-growers calculate that in some areas more than 100 litres of water are needed in total to produce one litre of wine.) Those wineries practising effective water reuse are to be congratulated, as are those questioning their methods of temperature control, many of which use enormous amounts of water and/or energy.

Wine unfortunately needs to be kept relatively cool at all stages of its life, whether in tank, barrel, or bottle, and this can involve heavy energy consumption. Praise is due, for instance, to all those who have excavated caves in the hills of the Napa Valley and are now self-sufficient in natural cooling rather than having to rely on the constant energy input that above-ground storage requires.

Another distinguishing mark of wine production is the huge amount of carbon dioxide that is given off by alcoholic fermentation. Eco-conscious wine producers such as Torres in Spain have instituted special schemes involving CO_2-guzzling algae to absorb this by-product instead of seeing it contribute to the dangerously high levels of CO_2 in the Earth's atmosphere. They have undertaken a full audit of all their operations with sustainability in mind and, for example, create their own biofuel for their vehicles.

And there is no shortage of ways in which consumers can help to reduce wine's carbon footprint. Recycling bottles is the most obvious step, but discouraging producers from using unnecessarily heavy bottles that use up so many raw materials and are expensive to transport would also help. In the long term, we should probably reconsider whether glass is really the most ecologically sensible material for packaging everyday wines.

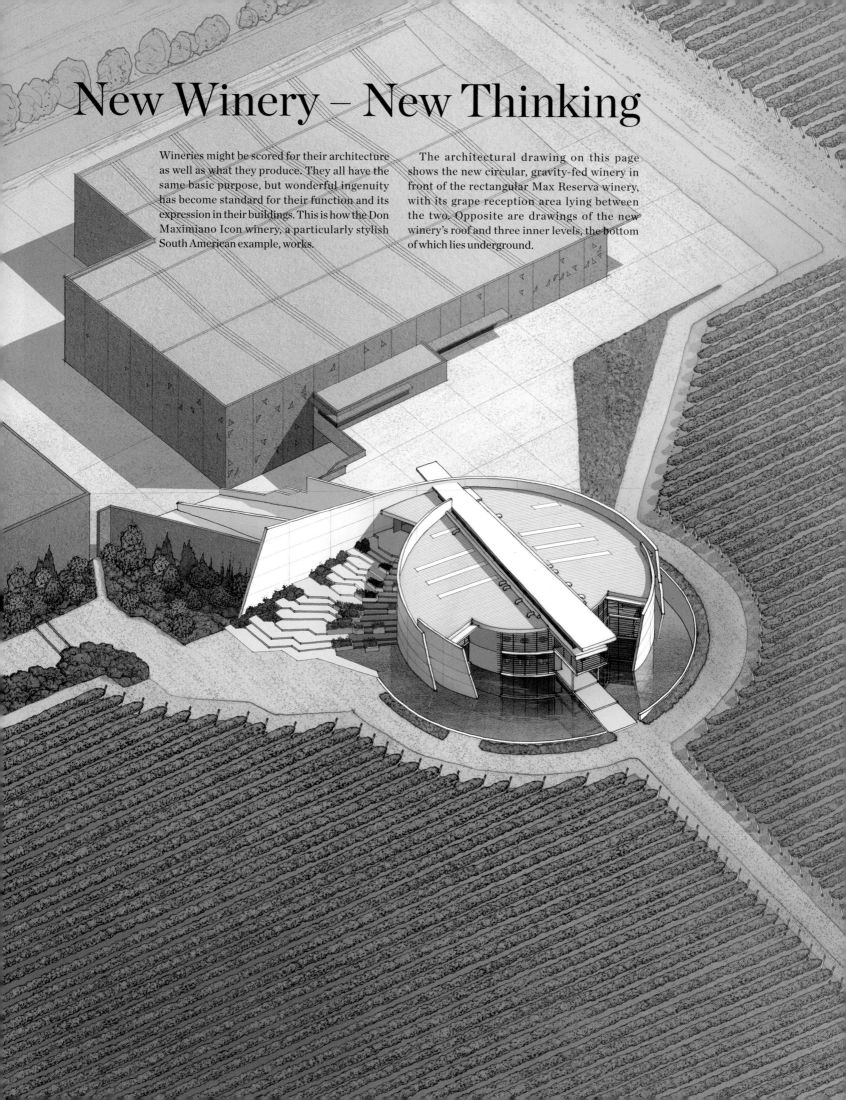

New Winery – New Thinking

Wineries might be scored for their architecture as well as what they produce. They all have the same basic purpose, but wonderful ingenuity has become standard for their function and its expression in their buildings. This is how the Don Maximiano Icon winery, a particularly stylish South American example, works.

The architectural drawing on this page shows the new circular, gravity-fed winery in front of the rectangular Max Reserva winery, with its grape reception area lying between the two. Opposite are drawings of the new winery's roof and three inner levels, the bottom of which lies underground.

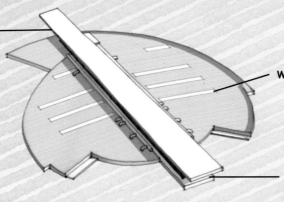

Grape reception area Hidden by the overhang of the roof, the grape reception area delivers grapes in hygienic shallow plastic trays, ensuring that they are not split nor exposed to oxidation. These are taken inside to vibrating grape sorting tables installed on the upper level during the harvest.

Windows

Natural light Skylights and windows in the roof enable natural light to flood the interior of the winery.

Grape sorting and gravity flow At a first sorting table leaves and obviously damaged grapes are removed. After the destemmer, a second sorting table eliminates any rogue stem fragments, small leaves and green berries. Healthy whole berries then fall directly into the fermentation vessels below – some oak and some stainless steel – through openings in the floor. Gravity does it all, leaving berries as whole and fresh as possible, retaining maximum primary fruit flavours.

Tasting room This is accessed by the gangway above the fermentation hall.

Ventilation system The temperature in the winery is maintained between 57 and 68°F (14 and 20°C) by a geothermic system of air injection. All round the winery, a total of 558ft (170m) of ducts that reach 13ft (4m) below the ground carry air – cooler in summer, warmer in winter – up and blow it into the winery, sheltering the wine from dramatic temperature fluctuations.

Transportation ramp After fermentation is complete the grape skins are removed from the vats and taken to the press room in the Max Reserva winery; the stems are discarded.

Fermentation hall 18 of the stainless steel vats can hold up to 10,000 litres; nine of them contain 7,500 litres, while the 10 French oak vats have a capacity of 11,000 litres each. This enables each parcel of grapes to be vinified separately. Temperature control is automatic. The circular design and natural lighting help to save energy and reduce the amount of electricity needed.

Reflective pools

Underground ventilation duct

West-facing windows Pools surrounding the winery and special low-emissivity glass windows help to regulate the temperature inside the winery.

Barrel ramp Once filled, the barrels are taken by a forklift to the barrel room. Eventually the wine is blended then piped to the bottling line, after which it is stored prior to shipment.

Barrel filling cellar Once fermented, the wine is transferred from the vat through a pipe, again by gravity, to fill one of the 225-litre barriques in the underground cellar below the fermentation hall.

Wine and Time

There is a myth about wine that refuses to wither, let alone die, which is that all wine improves with age. One of wine's most magical properties is that some of it is capable of evolving and improving for decades, and very occasionally centuries. The great majority of wine made today, however, is ready to drink within a year or less of being bottled, and some wines are best drunk straight off the bottling line.

Almost any inexpensive wine, especially whites and rosés, as well as such light-bodied, low-tannin reds as those made from Gamay (Beaujolais, for example), Grignolino, Dornfelder, Lambrusco, Portugieser, the Australian crossing Tarrango, and some of the simpler Pinot Noirs, are at their best young. And very few rosés are designed to age more than a couple of years in bottle. The pleasure in them is a matter of freshness and youthful fruitiness before it starts to fade. As a general rule, the more expensive a wine, even when quite young, the longer it is designed to be aged – with the possible exception of Condrieu and other fine Viogniers. Champagne and other top-quality sparkling wines are the only other highly priced unfortified wines that are generally ready to drink straight off the shelf, although many people find a year or two more in bottle deepens their flavour, and some vintage and de luxe champagnes can reach perfection after as much as 20 or 30 years.

Most of the great white wines and practically all the best reds, however, are sold long before they are ready to drink. Such wines are grown to be aged. When young, they contain an unresolved complex of acids and sugars, minerals and pigments, tannins, and all sorts of flavour compounds. Good wines have more of these things than ordinary wines, and great wines more than good wines. Which is why, in the end, they have more flavour and character. But it takes time for these elements, the primary grape-derived aromas and the secondary ones of fermentation and in many cases oak, to interact, to resolve themselves into a harmonious whole, and for the distinct scent of maturity, called (by analogy with flowers) the bouquet, to form. Time, and the action of small amounts of oxygen, gradually make wine mature. There is enough oxygen in the headspace between the liquid and the cork (or screw cap sophisticated enough to allow a tiny amount of oxygen ingress) and dissolved in a bottle of wine to account for an ageing process lasting for years.

A youthful fine red wine goes into bottle containing a mix of tannins, pigments, flavour compounds (these three known collectively as phenolics), and the more complex compounds formed by them. In the bottle, tannins continue to interact with pigments and acids to form new compounds and larger molecules which are eventually precipitated. This means that, as it ages, a fine red wine loses colour and astringency,

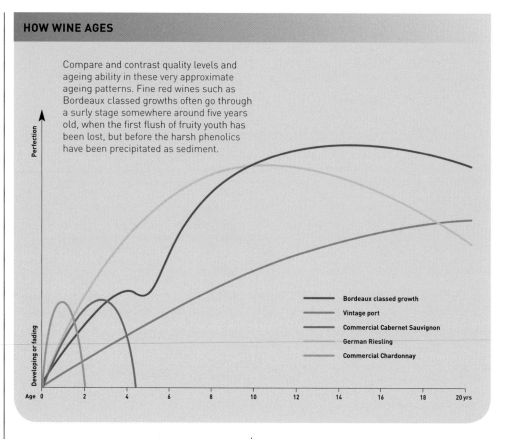

HOW WINE AGES

Compare and contrast quality levels and ageing ability in these very approximate ageing patterns. Fine red wines such as Bordeaux classed growths often go through a surly stage somewhere around five years old, when the first flush of fruity youth has been lost, but before the harsh phenolics have been precipitated as sediment.

Perfection

Developing or fading

Age 0   2   4   6   8   10   12   14   16   18   20 yrs

— Bordeaux classed growth
— Vintage port
— Commercial Cabernet Sauvignon
— German Riesling
— Commercial Chardonnay

but gains complexity and sediment. In fact, holding a bottle of fine wine up to the light to examine how much sediment there is gives a good clue as to how mature it is – although the more heavily a wine has been filtered before bottling, the less sediment will form.

The equivalent process in white wines, which have a much lower charge of phenolics, is less well understood, but gradual oxidation turns the phenolics gold and eventually brown as primary and secondary fruity and "winey" aromas and crisp acids mellow into honeyed, nutty, or savoury complexities. If the principal preservative of red wine is tannin, of white it is acidity. White wines with sufficient acidity (and sufficient substance to balance it) will mature as long as reds – or in the case of some botrytised sweet whites, top-quality Sauternes, German Rieslings, Tokajis, and Loire Chenin Blancs (all high in acidity), even longer.

REACHING A PEAK

The most frequently asked question about any specific wine is "When will it be at its best?" The inconvenient truth is that even a wine's maker can only guess, and often the answer is clear only after a wine has started to decline, to lose fruit and flavour at such a rate that the acidity, or sometimes tannins, starts to dominate. All that is predictable about fine wine is its unpredictability.

Those who buy wine by the case of a dozen bottles and monitor the wine's progress bottle by bottle frequently find that a wine seems wonderfully opulent in youth, then goes through a sullen, dumb stage (when many of the complex compounds are busy forming) before emerging as an even more magnificent wine afterwards.

Bottle variation, even of different bottles from the same case, is another common phenomenon. The case may have been filled with bottles from different lots (many bottles nowadays have lot numbers marked on the glass), which were stored in different conditions. Bottles often vary because the corks have allowed varying amounts of oxygen in, or because they are affected to different degrees by some sort of taint, most commonly TCA (see p.31). An unstained, uniform cork in a mature wine is the best sign; one stained red, where the wine has crept up the side to stain it, can mean trouble. But often there is no rational explanation: just further proof that wine is a living, capricious entity. Different vintages of the same wine vary enormously in their ageing ability. Red grapes with thick skins, typically the product of a dry year, are likely to age longer than those from wet years, whose skin-to-pulp ratio is much lower. Similarly, white wines made from grapes grown in a cool year are likely to need longer before their acidity mellows to an acceptable level.

Another factor – quite apart from storage conditions, which are discussed opposite – is the size of bottle in which a wine is stored. The amount of headspace is usually constant no matter what the size of the bottle, which means that there is twice as much oxygen per volume of wine in a half-bottle as in a bottle, and only half as much in a magnum (two bottles in one). The ageing effect of that oxygen is therefore much faster in a half-bottle and much slower in larger bottles. This is why halves seem to deteriorate so rapidly and why collectors will pay a premium for the large bottle sizes (although the damage inflicted by a poor-quality cork of course increases with the size of the bottle). Stately ageing is deemed the best.

But, in very general terms, it is possible to say which sorts of wine are most worthy of ageing, or "laying down" as English parlance has it. In very approximately descending order of potential life in bottle for red wines, to take some obvious candidates for the cellar, are well-made examples of vintage port, Hermitage, classed-growth claret, Bairrada, Madiran, Barolo, Barbaresco, Aglianico, Brunello di Montalcino, Côte-Rôtie, fine red burgundy, Dão, Châteauneuf-du-Pape, Chianti Classico Riserva, Georgian Saperavi, Ribera del Duero, Australian Cabernet and Shiraz, California Cabernet, Rioja, Argentine Malbec, Zinfandel, New World Merlot, and New World Pinot Noir – although this can vary enormously according to the producer's capability and ambitions.

This cellar was purpose-built for a wine collector in California's Silicon Valley. Wines ready or nearly ready for drinking are stored here (along with his humidor), while younger vintages are stored in a professional warehouse prior to being moved here.

By far the most important body of wines that positively demand to be kept are the Crus Classés of Bordeaux. A generation ago such wines were made to endure, on the assumption that they would be kept a minimum of seven or eight years, and more likely 15 or more. Today's wine drinker is less patient. Modern taste looks for softer tannins (the all-important flattering "mouthfeel") and riper flavours that mean the wine can be drunk after a mere five years or so, sometimes earlier. California can manage this style virtually every year, but Bordeaux still depends on nature; the 2005 and 2010 Bordeaux vintages, for example, produced great wines, for the patient. Red burgundy poses fewer problems because its tannins are rarely obtrusive enough to demand extreme patience, although some Grands Crus are so obviously stuffed with substance in youth that it would be a shame, and a great waste of money, to drink them at less than 10 years old. All but the very finest white burgundies mature much faster, and recent evidence of premature oxidation in too many of them has shaken faith in their ageing ability. Chablis increasingly seems a safer bet for ageing than Côte d'Or white burgundy but, in general, Chardonnay is not a particularly long-lived grape variety.

All things being equal, the white wines that most obviously benefit from bottle-age, in declining order of longevity, are fine examples of Tokaji, Sauternes, Loire Chenin Blanc, German Riesling, Chablis, Hunter Valley Semillon, sweet Jurançon, white burgundy from the Côte d'Or,

and dry white Bordeaux. Like most fortified wines, wood-aged port such as tawnies, sherry, madeira, and many sparkling wines are ready to drink as soon as they are bottled.

STORING WINE

If good wine is worth paying extra for (which in the majority of cases it is), it is worth keeping and serving (see overleaf) in good condition.

Storing wine badly can turn nectar into sludge. Wine asks only to be kept lying quietly in a dark, cool, ideally slightly damp place. Strong light can harm wine, particularly sparkling wine, over an extended period. Warmth speeds up reactions, so the warmer any wine is kept, the faster and less subtly it will mature.

Wine storage is a problem for almost everyone. Few houses today come with underground cellars: the perfect place for keeping a collection. One solution, particularly for those in hot climates, are special, temperature-controlled wine storage cabinets, but they are hardly economical in terms of either investment, space, or energy use. You can also pay someone else to store your wine for you in ideal conditions. This has the obvious disadvantages of continuous expense and loss of spontaneity, but it does shift the responsibility on to a professional's shoulders. Many fine wine merchants offer this service. The best truly monitor your wine collection and advise you when to drink what. The worst have been known to abscond with their clients' wine. Most are delighted to act as brokers in a fine wine market owned by their clients. Any professional wine warehouse should be able to offer a sound tracking and retrieval system and a guarantee of ideal temperature and humidity.

Wine is not over-fussy about temperature; anything from 45–64°F (7–18°C) will do, although 50–55°F (10–13°C) would be ideal. What matters more is that it varies as little as possible (in an outdoor shed or next to an uninsulated boiler or water heater will not do). No wine will stand alternate boiling and freezing. In high temperatures wine will not only age faster, but there is also the danger of the cork expanding and contracting so rapidly that it stops being a perfect seal and lets far too much oxygen in. If there is any sign of seepage, drink the wine as soon as possible. But if coolness is impracticable, steady moderate warmth will do. Just beware very high temperatures, above 95°F (35°C). This is why fine wine should be shipped either in temperature-controlled containers or only at cool times of year.

Traditionally, bottles have always been kept lying horizontally so as to prevent the cork from drying, shrinking, and letting in air, but screw capped bottles may be stored upright, or however will best protect the screw caps from being damaged and breaking the seal. There are several good arguments for buying certain wines young, at their opening price, and storing them until they reach perfect maturity, but remember that not all fine wine will appreciate in value, alas.

Enjoying Wine

Wine is not a solitary drink. It is essentially sociable, and one of the greatest pleasures it has to offer is the sharing of it. The more thought that goes into the process of sharing, the more pleasure it can give. It is worth working out in advance how many bottles and types of wines you are likely to need, and what order to serve them in. A young wine served first tends to show off the qualities of an older one; a white wine is usually good at ushering in a red one; a light wine a massive one; a dry wine a sweet one. Many of these combinations played the other way round can be disastrous for the second wine.

The question of how much to serve is more difficult. In a normal 75cl bottle, there are six to eight glasses (which means generous glasses filled one-third full, not small ones filled to the brim). At a light lunch, one glass per person might be enough, whereas at a long dinner, five or six might not be too much. There is a golden rule for hosts: be generous but never pressing, and be sure to pour water, too.

If the number of wine drinkers at the table calls for more than one bottle with each course, consider serving two slightly different wines together – perhaps different vintages of the same wine/producer, or the same grape but of different provenance. (To avoid confusion, the wines can be served in different glasses.) Once likely quantities have been decided, bottles containing sediment can be stood up in time for it to fall to the bottom of the bottle – which can take a day or two. Even more importantly, this preparation allows time for all bottles to be brought to their ideal temperature.

Nothing makes more difference to enjoying wine than its temperature. Stone-cold Cabernet and lukewarm Rieslings are abominations – not because they offend any rule of etiquette, but simply because the wines taste so far from their best. And there are several good reasons why this should be so. Our sense of smell (and hence the greater part of our sense of taste) is susceptible only to vapours. Red wine generally has a higher molecular weight – and is thus less volatile, or smelly, than white. The object of serving red wine at "room temperature" (conventionally about 65°F/18°C), is to warm it to the point where its aromatic elements begin to vaporize – which is at a progressively higher temperature for more solid and substantial wines. An aromatic light red such as Beaujolais or cool-climate Pinot Noir can be treated as a white wine; even cold, its volatility is almost overwhelming. On the other hand, a full-scale red wine such as a Brunello or a Shiraz may need the warmth of the room, of the cupped hand around the glass, and possibly of the mouth itself to volatilize its complex constituents.

Tannins are much more obvious at low temperatures. Thus, the warmer a tannic young red wine is served, the softer, more generous, and more evolved it will taste. The illusion of maturity can be created for a young Cabernet or red Bordeaux, for example, by judiciously serving it on the warm side, which will increase the apparent flavour and decrease its astringency. Pinot Noir or red burgundy, however, tends to be lower in tannin and more naturally aromatic. This explains the long tradition of serving red burgundy cooler than red Bordeaux, almost straight out of the cellar.

Cold is also necessary to counterbalance the richness of very sweet wines, as suggested by the chart on the right. Like tannin, acidity tastes more pronounced at lower temperatures, so whites whose acidity needs to be emphasized, whether because they are high in sugar, over-aged, or from particularly hot climates, can be given apparent zip by serving them particularly cool.

A wine served too hot lacks refreshment value and is in practice very difficult to cool down, whereas a wine served too cool will naturally approach room temperature and can easily be warmed by cupping the glass in a hand.

It is easier to serve white wine at the right temperature than red as it can be put in a refrigerator. But the fastest way to cool a bottle is to put it in a bucket of ice and water (not ice alone, which will not touch much of the bottle), or a special cooling jacket. Always keep bottles out of direct sunshine.

Persuading a red wine to reach the right temperature is harder. If it starts at cellar temperature, it can take several hours in a normal

DECANTING WINE

Cut the foil, possibly taking it off completely if you want to see all of the bottleneck. Take the cork out gently, keeping the bottle (and sediment) as still as possible.

Having wiped the lip of the bottle to clean it, hold the bottle in one hand and the decanter in the other. Pour steadily, ideally with the bottleneck against a strong source of light such as a naked lightbulb or a candle. If you store wine with the label on top, the sediment is in the right place.

Continue to pour until you see the sediment (if any) moving into the lower neck of the bottle. Then stop when the dregs start to move dangerously close to the rim. If there is much more sediment than this, stand the wine for longer, stopper the decanter, and try again later, although some wines throw a "bottle deposit" which sticks irrevocably to the sides. Pour the dregs into a glass to settle; this is for after washing up.

room to raise it 10 or 12 degrees. The kitchen is the logical place – but many kitchens are well over 68°F (20°C), especially while dinner is cooking. At this sort of temperature red wines may be thrown out of balance; the alcohol starts to vaporize and produces a heady smell, which masks the wine's character. Some of its flavour may even be lost forever.

One practical way of warming red wine in a hurry is first to decant it, then to stand the decanter in water at about 70°F (21°C). It does no harm to heat the decanter (within reason) first. Microwave ovens also come into their own for heating wine bottles in a hurry. The danger, however, is being too impatient and heating the wine beyond the point of no return. A little experimentation with a bottle of water would be prudent.

It may be difficult to get a red wine to the optimum temperature, but there are also times when it is necessary to make an effort to keep it there. Vacuum bottle coolers, or even ice buckets, may be needed when serving red wine in hot climates or high temperatures. In a restaurant, do not hesitate to ask for an ice bucket if your red wine has been served too warm. You will be continuing a long and noble tradition of connoisseurship.

PULLING THE CORK

The next, rather obvious, step is opening the bottle(s). Except for screw-capped bottles this means removing the foil, or capsule, and pulling the cork. Foils are usually cut neatly just below the rim of the bottle so as to keep the look of the bottle intact, but this is just convention. Special foil cutters are an optional boon. A good corkscrew has a hollow helix rather than a solid shaft, which could pierce the cork straight through and give no leverage. It should end in a good, sharp point.

Opening bottles of sparkling wine requires a special technique. Well-chilled bottles that have not recently been agitated make the least fuss when opened (warm, shaken fizz can spume alarmingly, and wastefully). It is worth remembering that the pressure inside a champagne bottle is not dissimilar to that inside the tyre of a truck, so an unguarded cork pushed out of a bottle can do a great deal of damage. After taking off the foil and untwisting the wire muzzle, hold the cork down into the bottleneck while gently twisting the bottle off it, ideally at an angle. The cork should pop out discreetly with minimum loss of liquid. Seriously recalcitrant champagne corks can be persuaded to turn by a "champagne star" that fits into the four grooves in the top of the cork to give more torque.

Very old corks can pose problems. They can easily disintegrate under the pressure of a corkscrew, particularly one of the more powerful modern designs. The two-pronged sort, the so-called butler's friend (because it theoretically enabled him to replace the contents of a bottle with inferior wine without having pierced the cork), can be useful for such bottles. Old vintage port can be the devil to open; the cork breaks;

finally you have to let part of it fall in. Filter the wine; no harm is done.

Decanting is much discussed but little understood, largely because its effect on a given wine is unpredictable. There is a mistaken idea that it is something you only do to ancient bottles with lots of sediment – a mere precautionary measure to get a clean glass of wine. But experience shows that it is usually young wines that benefit most. The oxygen they contain has had little chance to take effect. But the air in the decanter works rapidly and effectively. In a matter of a few hours it can often induce the opening of what was a closed bud. Some strong young wines – Barolo springs to mind – can benefit from even as much as 24 hours in a decanter. An hour makes all the difference to others. A good rule of thumb is that young, tannic, alcoholic wines need, and can withstand, much earlier decanting than old, lighter-bodied wines. But full white wines such as white burgundies can benefit from decanting, too – and will look even more beguiling in a decanter than reds.

Those who feel most passionately opposed to decanting argue that there is a danger of losing some fruit and flavour to the decanter. Better, they feel, to pour straight from the bottle, taste and evaluate the wine's state of maturity, and aerate in the glass if necessary by swirling the wine around. This is debatable, and is often debated, but trial and individual taste are the only real guides.

It was once widely believed that pulling the cork from a bottle of wine and leaving it unstoppered to "breathe" would have a marked effect. In reality the area of wine in a bottle's neck is too small to make much difference.

The wine drinker requires one more vital piece of equipment: glasses. Wonderfully complicated experiments and blind tastings have shown that a slight modification to the basic shape can accentuate what certain types of wine have to offer. But there is no absolute need to have different glasses for different wines.

It may seem too obvious to mention, but wine glasses should be clean – that is, polished and untainted with smells of detergents or cupboards. Some can withstand modern dishwashers, but most are best rinsed with hot water and polished by hand with a linen cloth, ideally when still hot. Cupboard or cardboard smells usually come from keeping glasses upside down, on a shelf or in a box. This may be necessary on open shelves, but it is better to keep them right way up in a clean, dry, airy cupboard. Sniff them before putting them on the table. It is good practice for the nose.

WINE AND TEMPERATURE

This chart suggests the ideal temperature for serving a wide range of wines. "Room temperature" is low by modern standards: all the better for fine wine. White and pink wines are shown in yellow; reds and fortifieds in purple. The top (°C) and bottom (°F) lines give the more general guidance on ideal serving temperatures.

Domestic fridge temperature						Ideal cellar temperature								Room temperature
SWEET WINES			DRY WHITES				LIGHT REDS					FULL-SCALE REDS		
°C 4 — 5 — 6 — 7 — 8 — 9 — 10 — 11 — 12 — 13 — 14 — 15 — 16 — 17 — 18

(Chart of wines plotted by serving temperature, °C 4 to 18 / °F 39 to 64)

- MUSCADET — CHABLIS — GRAND CRU CHABLIS
- MACON — CHINON — BEST WHITE — RED BURGUNDY
- GEWURZTRAMINER & PINOT GRIS — BURGUNDIES & GRAVES
- BEAUJOLAIS NOUVEAU — BEAUJOLAIS CRUS
- SANCERRE/POUILLY — SAUTERNES — COTES DU RHONE (RED) — TOP RED RHONE
- ALSACE RIESLING — VINTAGE PORT
- JURANCON — WHITE RHONE — LANGUEDOC-ROUSSILLON REDS
- FINO & MANZANILLA — ORDINARY RED BORDEAUX
- ALIGOTE — TAWNY PORT
- TOKAJI — NON-VINTAGE CHAMPAGNE — AMONTILLADO — MADEIRA — FINE RED BORDEAUX
- MONTILLA — MADIRAN
- SPARKLING WINE (eg SEKT, CAVA) — BANDOL
- BEST CHAMPAGNE
- EISWEIN — GOOD GERMAN & AUSTRIAN WINE — BEST DRY GERMAN WINE — BEST SWEET GERMAN WINE
- SWEET LOIRE/CHENIN BLANC — CHIANTI CLASSICO RISERVAS — BEST PORTUGUESE REDS
- VALPOLICELLA — CHIANTI
- ASTI — SICILIAN REDS — SUPER TUSCANS
- SOAVE — BARBERA/DOLCETTO — BAROLO
- VINHO VERDE & RIAS BAIXAS — VERDICCHIO — PUGLIAN REDS — RIBERA DEL DUERO & PRIORAT
- NAVARRA & PENEDES
- TOKAJI ASZU — RIOJA
- MOSCATO & MOSCATEL — FENDANT — CHILEAN REDS
- LAMBRUSCO — LIGHT ZINFANDELS — ARGENTINE REDS
- PINOTAGE
- CHENIN BLANC — CALIFORNIA/AUSTRALIAN/OREGON PINOT NOIR
- MOST CHARDONNAYS — TOP CALIFORNIA/AUSTRALIAN CHARDONNAYS — NZ PINOT NOIR
- MOST MUSCATS — BEST CALIFORNIA CABERNETS & ZINFANDELS
- NZ SAUVIGNON — CALIFORNIA
- NEW WORLD RIESLING — SAUVIGNON BLANC — OLD HUNTER VALLEY SEMILLON
- LIQUEUR MUSCAT — TOP AUSTRALIAN CABERNET/SHIRAZ
- PINK WINES — URUGUAYAN TANNAT

°F 39 — 41 — 43 — 45 — 46 — 48 — 50 — 52 — 54 — 55 — 57 — 59 — 61 — 63 — 64

Tasting and Talking about Wine

A great deal of wine, even good or great wine, flows over tongues and down throats of people who drink it but don't actively taste it. Nothing the winemaker can do dispenses with the need for a sensitive and interested drinker. If the sense of taste were located in the mouth (where our impulses tell us it is), anyone swallowing a mouthful of wine would get all the sensations it has to offer. But all that the hundreds of taste buds on the tongue can sense are the basic tastes: sweet, sour, salt, bitter, and the savour of umami. The nerves that receive more distinctive sensations such as the complex flavours of wine, are located at the top of our noses.

The most sensitive bit of what we call our sense of taste is actually our sense of smell. The real organ of discrimination is the olfactory bulb in the upper nasal cavity. When the vapours of wine are inhaled (either through the nose or,

less effectively, the back of the mouth) they are sensed by a thousand different receptors, each sensitive to a particular group of related aromas. Amazingly, we humans are apparently able to distinguish up to 10,000 different smells.

It is often remarked how these smells stir memories far more rapidly and vividly than other sensations. From the position of the olfactory bulb, nearest neighbour to the temporal lobe where memories are stored, it seems that smell, the most primitive of our senses, may have a privileged position of instant access to the memory bank.

Experienced tasters often rely on the immediate reaction of their memory to the first sniff of a wine. If they cannot relate it straight away to wines they have tasted in the past they must fall back on their powers of analysis. The range of reference available is the great difference between an experienced taster and a

beginner. There is little meaning in an isolated sensation, though it may be very pleasant. Where the real pleasures of wine tasting lie are in the cross-references, the stirring of memories, the comparisons between similar and yet subtly different products of the same or neighbouring vineyard. Wines differ from one another in terms of colour, texture, strength, structure, body, and length, as well as their complex of flavours. A taster takes all these into account.

Tastings come in many different forms, from the simple act of enjoyment around a friendly table to the professional blind tasting tests involved in qualifying as a Master of Wine. One that puzzles many wine neophytes is the tasting ritual acted out in so many restaurants whereby the wine waiter pours a small sample of the chosen wine for you to taste. The purpose of this is for you to check that firstly, the wine is at the right temperature, and secondly, that it is not obviously faulty, most usually tainted by some degree of TCA (see p.31). You cannot send it back just because you don't like it.

What is much harder than appreciating wine is communicating its sensations. There is no notation of taste as there is of sound or colour; apart from the words used for its basic dimensions such as "strong", "tart", "tough", "sweet", and "bitter", every word in the language of taste is borrowed from the other senses. And

HOW TO TASTE AND APPRECIATE WINE

Eyes

Pour a tasting sample into the glass so that it is no more than a quarter full. First, check the wine is clear (cloudiness or fizziness in still wines indicate a fault) and look straight down at it to see how intense the colour is (the deeper a red, the younger the wine and/or thicker-skinned the grapes: a valuable clue if tasting a mystery wine "blind"). Red wines become paler with age, white wines deeper. Tilt the glass away from you against a white background and observe the colour in the middle of the liquid and at the rim. All wines turn slowly brown with age and the rim is the first place where any brick colour is noticeable in a red. Young reds are more purplish-blue than brick. Old reds lose colour completely at the rim. The glossier the colour and the more subtly shaded its different colour gradations, the better the wine.

Nose

Take one sniff with all your concentration, then swirl the wine around and sniff once more. The stronger the impression, the more intense the aroma or bouquet. A subtle, maturing wine may need the swirl before it gives off much smell. If you are tasting blind, this is the moment when you are hoping for a massive intuitive clue: some relationship to something from your tasting memory bank. If you are tasting to assess the wine, note whether it smells clean (most wines do nowadays), intense, and what the smell reminds you of. It is much easier to remember a smell if you can attach words to it. As you taste or drink the wine (and these two activities can feel very different) notice how the smell changes. With time good wines tend to become more interesting, inexpensive commercial wines often less so.

Mouth

This stage involves taking a good mouthful of wine and exposing all of the taste buds distributed over the tongue and insides of the cheeks to it. If the nose is best at sensing the subtle flavours in a wine, the mouth is best at measuring its constituents: tip of the tongue often for sweetness, upper edges for the all-important acidity, back of the tongue for bitterness, insides of the cheeks for drying tannins, and the entrance to the throat for any burning excess of alcohol. Once a mouthful has been swallowed or spat out, a judgement can be made as to whether all these elements are in balance (young reds are often deliberately high in tannins) and how persistent the wine is on the palate – a good indicator of quality. At this stage the wine can be judged, possibly even identified, in its entirety.

yet words, by giving an identity to sensations, help to clarify them. Assembling a vocabulary is a crucial element in becoming a wine connoisseur.

From talking about wine to writing about it is but a step – one that few wine drinkers ever take. Yet there is a strong case for keeping notes on what you drink or taste in a more or less organized way. In the first place, having to commit something to paper makes you concentrate: the prime requirement for being able to taste wine properly at all. In the second, it makes you analyse and pin labels on the sensations passing across your palate. In the third, it is an *aide-mémoire*; when somebody asks you what a wine is like, you can look it up and say something definite. In the fourth, it allows you to extend comparison between wines over time – either the same wine a year later, or different but related wines on different occasions.

In short, keeping tasting notes is like keeping a diary: obviously a good idea, but hard to get off the ground. A little guidance may help. Professional tasting sheets are often divided into three, simply to remind tasters to make a note of the appearance of the wine, how it smells, and the impact of the wine on the palate. There may even be a fourth space for overall impressions. Different tasters evolve their own tasting language and shorthand and there is no point in being too prescriptive. The single most important note to be made is the full name of every wine tasted. A date can be useful on tasting notes, too, in case you ever have the chance to monitor the same wine later in its life and make comparisons. And a note of the place and/or fellow tasters may help to jog your memory when you come to read these (usually increasingly illegible) notes again.

KEEPING SCORE

Are scores appropriate for judging wine? Under some professional circumstances, such as competitions or judging panels, they are unavoidable – either as symbols, or the numbers that have become such a powerful weapon in wine retailing in some countries. The habit of applying points out of 100 to wines has been seized on with delight by a new generation of wine buyers around the world, for it offers an international scoreboard (reflected often by a similarly calibrated international marketplace), and can be understood no matter what your native language.

But, despite the apparent accuracy and precision of a score out of 100, let no one forget that wine tasting is an essentially subjective process. A score that is the average of a panel can be deeply suspect, an average that tends to exclude any wine with real individuality (which is bound to displease someone). And even the pronouncements of a single palate can be misleading. We all have our own likes and dislikes among wine flavours and styles. We all begin with one set of preferences and then our taste evolves and continues to change throughout our wine-drinking lives. The best judge of the right styles of wine for your palate is you. There are no absolutes of right and wrong in wine appreciation.

OLD AND NEW

The red on the left is a four-year-old South Australian Shiraz, still very deep in hue with some suggestion of purple and its deep tint right out to the rim. On the right is another New World wine from a deeply coloured grape, an eight-year-old California Cabernet. See how the colour is less intense, much less blue, and more orange with a much paler rim – the effects of bottle-age.

The white on the left is a two-year-old California Chardonnay but it could be almost any young white wine. A Riesling would be greener, a Muscadet almost water-white. The wine on the right is a 15-year-old Grand Cru white burgundy. Notice how white wines also acquire a brown tinge with age but gain rather than lose intensity of colour.

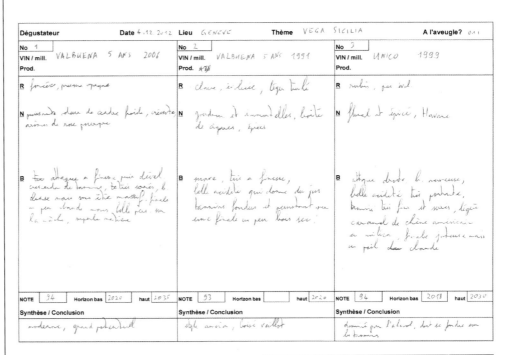

Recording impressions

Above is a relatively traditional tasting sheet with notes for appearance (R for *robe*), nose (N for *nez*) and palate (B for *bouche*, or mouth). The date is always particularly helpful on a tasting note as wines can change so much over time. On this sheet a suggested score and drinking window are given below the tasting notes and above the overall conclusion. On the right is how tasting notes are increasingly recorded, in this case on a BlackBerry, but many tasters now use their iPads and other electronic toys.

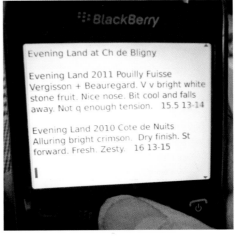

The World of Wine

The world's wine map is no longer composed of two neat bands through the temperate zones of each hemisphere. Climate change, bravado, and the increasingly sophisticated art of tropical viticulture are extending the reach of the vine as you read this.

Europe may still dominate the list of the world's most important vine-growers, based on the most recent set of OIV statistics, but South America and Asia in general, China in particular, have been moving up the ranks at extraordinary speed, even if it is difficult to verify the true extent of Chinese vineyards dedicated to wine production. Turkey may be the world's fourth-most important vine-grower but its wine production, of increasing interest, is relatively modest. Throughout the Middle East, the Central Asian Republics, and North Africa, grapes are more likely to be dried or eaten fresh than turned into wine. Such countries are marked † on the right.

The European Union's determined programme of subsidies and other encouragements to reduce Europe's wine surplus in the current era of plummeting wine consumption in the continent's major wine-producing countries seems to have been successful, judging from these 2010 figures. Within Europe, with the sole exception of Moldova, every single country's vineyard total either shrank considerably between 2004 and 2010 or, in a few cases, remained the same.

Outside Europe, Argentina, Chile, and especially Brazil have been planting vines with unbridled enthusiasm, just as Australia did in the 1990s. According to these OIV figures, Australia's total vineyard has continued to grow this century, but the Australians' own figures show a rather different story. New Zealand's much smaller total, on the other hand, has grown faster than that of any country in the world other than India.

Per capita wine consumption continues to decline in all of the world's most prolific wine-producing countries, with the exception of China, Australia, Germany, and the United States, which recently overtook all European countries to become the world's biggest market for wine.

DISTRIBUTION OF THE WORLD'S VINEYARDS
(in 1,000s hectares)

Rank	Country	2010	2004	% change
1	Spain	1,082	1,200	-9.8
2	France	818	889	-7.9
3	Italy	795	849	-6.3
4	China †	539	438	23
5	Turkey †	514	559	-8
6	USA	404	398	1.5
7	Iran †	300	329	-8.8
8	Portugal	243	247	-1.6
9	Argentina	228	213	7
10	Romania	204	222	-8.1
11	Chile	200	189	5.8
12	Australia	170	164	3.6
13	Moldova	148	146	1.3
14	South Africa	132	133	0.7
15	India	114	62	83.8
16	Greece	112	112	0
17	Uzbekistan †	107	104	2.8
18	Germany	102	102	0
19	Ukraine	95	97	-2
20	Brazil	92	76	21
21	Bulgaria	83	97	-14.4
22	Algeria †	74	67	10.4
23	Serbia & Montenegro	71	75	-5.3
24	Egypt †	70	63	11.1
25	Hungary	68	87	-21.8
26	Russia	62	73	-15
27	Afghanistan †	61	50	22
28	Syria †	60	52	15.3
29	Georgia	53	64	-17.1
30	Morocco †	48	50	-4
31	Austria	46	49	-6.1
32	Slovakia & Czech Rep	37	38	-2.6
33	New Zealand	37	21	76.1
34	Croatia	36	54	-33.3
35	Tajikistan †	36	34	5.8
36	Tunisia †	30	24	25
37	Turkmenistan †	29	29	0
38	Mexico	28	35	-20
39	Peru	21	14	50
40	Macedonia	20	27	-25.9
41	Japan	20	21	-4.7
42	Pakistan †	17	13	21.4
43	Slovenia	16	18	-11.1
44	Switzerland	15	15	0
45	Cyprus	10	16	-37.5
	World total	**7,447**	**7,690**	**-3.1**

† Country in which a significant proportion of vineyards are devoted to products other than wine.

The hectare (100 ares) is the equivalent of 2.47 acres.

HECTOLITRES The hectolitre (100 litres) is the commonest measure for wine production. It equals 22 imperial gallons (26.4 US gallons).

- · - International boundary

Vineyards (not to scale)

WINE CONSUMPTION BY COUNTRY 2010
(Litres per head)

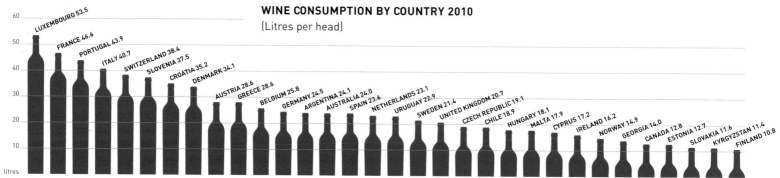

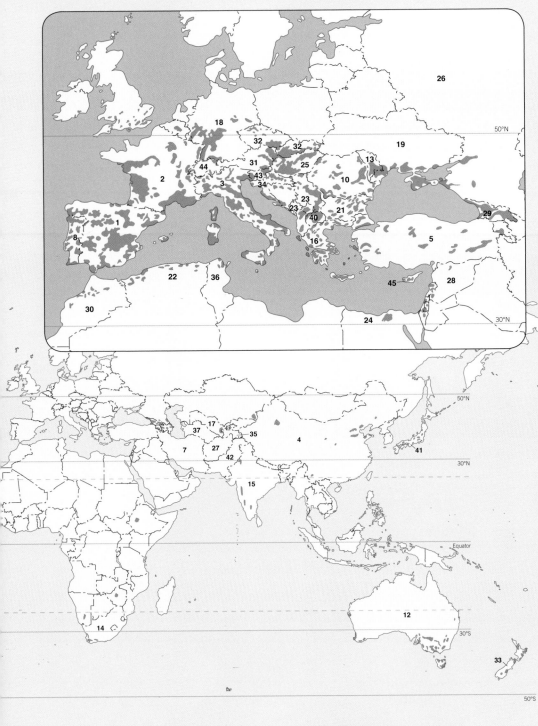

WORLD WINE PRODUCTION
(in 1,000s hectolitres)

Country	2010	2004	Average Yield 2010 hl/ha
North America			
USA	20,887	20,109	51
Canada	550	522	45
Latin America			
Argentina	16,250	15,464	71
Chile	8,844	6,301	44
Brazil	2,459	3,925	26
Uruguay	793	1,126	88
Mexico	303	730	10
Peru	727	480	34
Bolivia	81	71	13
Europe			
France	44,470	57,386	54
Italy	48,525	49,935	61
Spain	35,353	42,988	32
Germany	6,907	10,007	67
Portugal	7,133	7,481	29
Russia	7,640	5,120	123
Romania	3,287	6,166	16
Moldova	1,270	3,026	8
Hungary	1,762	4,340	25
Greece	2,950	4,248	26
Austria	1,737	2,735	37
Ukraine	3,002	2,012	31
Bulgaria	1,224	1,949	14
Serbia & Montenegro	2,562	2,446	36
Switzerland	1,030	1,159	68
Slovakia & Czech Rep	771	949	20
Slovenia	587	506	36
Luxembourg	110	156	–
Albania	181	140	18
Armenia	51	68	3
Azerbaijan	91	31	5
Malta	40	70	–
UK	28	17	–
Belgium	5	2	–
Africa			
South Africa	9,327	9,279	70
Algeria [†]	745	850	10
Tunisia [†]	222	375	7
Morocco [†]	333	326	6
Europe/Middle East			
Cyprus	118	404	11
Turkey.[†]	580	309	1
Lebanon	65	150	4
Israel	230	240	38
Far East			
China [†]	13,000	11,700	24
Japan	843	909	42
Australasia			
Australia	11,339	14,679	66
New Zealand	1,900	1,192	51
World total	**260,312**	**292,078**	

Based on the 2010 statistics gathered by the Organisation Internationale de la Vigne et du Vin (OIV).

BULGARIA 10.0 MACEDONIA 9.7 UNITED STATES 8.9 RUSSIA 8.5 BELARUS 7.6 ROMANIA 7.6 PARAGUAY 6.9 SOUTH AFRICA 6.9 ALBANIA 6.2 UKRAINE 5.5 TURKMENISTAN 3.4 LATVIA 3.0 LEBANON 3.0 PERU 2.6 POLAND 2.3 JAPAN 2.3 TUNISIA 2.2 NEW ZEALAND 2.1 MOLDOVA 1.9 BRAZIL 1.9 ARMENIA 1.7 ALGERIA 1.7 KAZAKHSTAN 1.3 CHINA 1.1 ISRAEL 1.0 MOROCCO 0.9 AZERBAIJAN 0.8 TURKEY 0.8 BOLIVIA 0.8 LITHUANIA 0.7 UZBEKISTAN 0.7 AFGHANISTAN 0.6 MEXICO 0.5 MADAGASCAR 0.4

litres

FRANCE

The fortified city of Carcassonne, a UNESCO World Heritage Site, Western Languedoc

France

It would be as impossible to think of France without wine as it is to think of wine without France. The map shows France's administrative départements and, more important to national pride and international pleasure, her many and varied wine regions. Names such as Burgundy and Champagne have long been so redolent of greatness in wine that, much to the disgust of the French, they have in their time been liberally borrowed without apology.

The vine was once grown much more widely in France, but the total vineyard area has shrunk considerably. In the Languedoc it has been only in the last decade or so that vignerons were persuaded by sweeteners designed to drain Europe's wine lake to pull up vines in the less favoured flatlands, often replacing them with other crops. The green triangles show the total area of vines per département or, as in the case of cognac country in and around the Charentes, for all four départements that grow grapes for France's most famous spirit.

France still supplies more great wine, and in greater variety, than any other country. Geography is the key. France, washed by the Atlantic and lapped by the Mediterranean, is uniquely well-situated with the influence of the continent to the east and a rich variety of soils, including more of the precious calcaire (limestone), so propitious to wine quality, than any other country. Climate change, so far, has been largely beneficial.

But France not only has good vineyards; she defines, classifies, and controls them in more detail and has a longer history of this, and producing fine wine, than any other country – the original templates for many of the wines in the rest of the book are found on these French pages. It started with the Appellation d'Origine Contrôlée, born in the 1920s, which broke new ground by restricting the use of a geographical name to wines made in a precisely specified area. The law also stipulates which grape varieties may be grown, the maximum crop per hectare (yield), minimum grape ripeness, how the vines are grown, and to a certain extent how the wine is made. AOCs, which in 2011 constituted around 45% of all French wine, are administered by the Institut National des Appellations de l'Origine et de la Qualité (INAO). Today there is much discussion about whether the much-imitated AOC regulations are a national treasure or an unnecessarily restrictive straitjacket, stifling experimentation and handicapping France in its rivalry with the products of the much more liberal New World.

Two new, less demanding categories, chiming with changes in EU regulation, are designed to allow French wines to compete more directly with them. Below the AOC category, equivalent to the EU's Appellation d'Origine Protégée (AOP), is France's second-biggest wine category, previously known as Vins de Pays and now generally rebadged as Indication Géographique Protégée (IGP). We show all of them on this map other than the 25 that coincide exactly with départements. At the bottom of the ladder of quality is the shrivelling underbelly of wines sold as Vin de France (previously Vin de Table).

— · —	International boundary
— - —	Département boundary
D'OC	Regional IGP/Vin de Pays
Agenais	IGP/Vin de Pays
○	Chief town of département
Marcillac	Appellation not mapped elsewhere
•	Centre of appellation area
	Champagne (*pp.72–75*)
	Loire Valley (*pp.110–117*)
	Burgundy (*pp.48–71*)
	Jura and Savoie (*pp.144–145*)
	Rhône (*pp.122–133*)
	Southwest (*pp.106–109*)
	Bordeaux (*pp.76–105*)
	Languedoc (*pp.134–137*)
	Roussillon (*pp.138–139*)
	Provence (*pp.140–141*)
	Alsace (*pp.118–121*)
	Corsica (*p.143*)

Proportional symbols

▼ 40 Area of vineyard per département in thousands of hectares (no figure given if area <1,000 hectares)

THE LANGUAGE OF THE LABEL

QUALITY DESIGNATIONS

Appellation d'Origine Contrôlée (AOC) wines whose geographical origins, varietal make-up, and production methods are precisely regulated – generally the best and certainly the most traditional; equivalent to the EU's Appellation d'Origine Protégée (AOP)

Indication Géographique Protégée (IGP) the EU denomination gradually replacing Vin de Pays, often from areas larger than AOC zones, in which non-traditional varieties and higher yields are allowed

Vin or Vin de France the basic EU denomination replacing Vin de Table; variety and vintage may be stated on the label

OTHER COMMON EXPRESSIONS

Blanc white

Cave (coopérative) co-operative winery

Château wine estate or even farm, typically in Bordeaux

Coteaux de, Côtes de typically hillsides

Cru literally a "growth": a specified superior plot of land

Cru classé cru that has been distinguished by an important classification such as the 1855 in Bordeaux (discussed on p.76)

Domaine vineyard holding, Burgundy's generally smaller-scale answer to château

Grand Cru literally "great growth": in Burgundy, the finest vineyards; in St-Emilion, nothing special

Méthode classique, méthode traditionnelle sparkling wine made using the same method as for champagne

Millésime vintage year

Mis (en bouteille) au château/domaine/à la propriété estate-bottled wine made by the same enterprise as that which grew the grapes

Négociant merchant bottler, an enterprise that buys in wine or grapes (cf domaine)

Premier Cru literally "first growth": in Burgundy, a notch down from Grand Cru; in the Médoc, one of the top four châteaux

Propriétaire-récoltant owner-vine-grower

Récoltant vine-grower

Récolte harvest or vintage

Rosé pink

Rouge red

Supérieur usually just slightly higher in alcohol

Vieilles vignes old vines and therefore in theory denser wine, though the "old" is unregulated

Vigneron vine-grower

Villages suffix denoting selected communes, or parishes, within an appellation

Vin wine

Viticulteur vine-grower

1:3,625,000
Km 0   50   100   150 Km
Miles 0   50   100 Miles

BELGIQUE

LUXEMBOURG

DEUTSCHLAND

Calais

PAS-DE-CALAIS

Lille

NORD

Arras

SOMME

Amiens

Charleville-Mézières

ARDENNES

MEUSE

Metz

MOSELLE

BAS-RHIN

Cherbourg

SEINE-MARITIME

le Havre

Rouen

OISE

Beauvais

Laon

AISNE

MARNE

Reims

Châlons-en-Champagne

Bar-le-Duc

Toul

Côtes de Meuse

MEURTHE-ET-MOSELLE

Nancy

Côtes de Toul

Strasbourg

RHIN

MANCHE

St-Lô

Caen

CALVADOS

EURE

Evreux

Pontoise

VAL-D'OISE

SEINE-ST-DENIS

HAUTE-DE-SEINE

Versailles

PARIS

ET-MARNE

SEINE-

Melun

VAL-DE-MARNE

Evry

YVELINES

ESSONNE

Troyes

AUBE

Chaumont

HAUTE-MARNE

Vesoul

HAUTE-SAÔNE

Belfort

Colmar

HAUT-RHIN

ORNE

Alençon

EURE-ET-LOIR

Chartres

LOIRET

Orléans

YONNE

Auxerre

Chablis

Coteaux de Coiffy

Franche-Comté

ILLE-ET-VILAINE

MAYENNE

Laval

SARTHE

le Mans

Montoire-sur-le-Loir

LOIR-ET-CHER

Blois

Tours

INDRE-ET-LOIRE

CHER

Bourges

Côtes de la Charité

Coteaux de Tannay

Coteaux de l'Auxois

Beaune

Dijon

CÔTE-D'OR

DOUBS

Besançon

Doubs

Rennes

Angers

MAINE-ET-LOIRE

LOIRE-ATLANTIQUE

Ancenis

Nantes

Thouars

LOIRE

VAL DE LOIRE

INDRE

Châteauroux

Coteaux du Cher et de l'Arnon

NIÈVRE

Nevers

Ste-Marie-la-Blanche

le Creusot

SAÔNE-ET-LOIRE

Mâcon

JURA

Lons-le-Saunier

Franche-Comté

SCHWEIZ

VENDÉE

le Roche-sur-Yon

DEUX-SÈVRES

Niort

Haut-Poitou

Poitiers

VIENNE

Châteaumeillant

Châteaumeillant

ALLIER

Moulins

St-Pourçain-sur-Sioule

St-Pourçain

AIN

Bourg-en-Bresse

Vin des Allobroges

HAUTE-SAVOIE

Annecy

la Rochelle

CHARENTE-MARITIME

Charentais

Angoulême

CHARENTE

Guéret

CREUSE

HAUTE-VIENNE

Limoges

PUY-DE-DÔME

Clermont-Ferrand

Boën-sur-Lignon

Roanne

Côte Roannaise

Urfé

LOIRE

RHÔNE

Lyon

St-Étienne

Côtes du Forez

Belley

ISÈRE

Chambéry

COMTÉS RHODANIENS

SAVOIE

ITALIA

ATLANTIQUE

Périgord

Périgueux

CORRÈZE

Tulle

HAUTE-LOIRE

le Puy

Tournon

Collines Rhodaniennes

Valence

Die

Clairette de Die
Châtillon en Diois

HAUTES-ALPES

Gap

Bordeaux

Libourne

Dordogne

GIRONDE

DORDOGNE

Coteaux de Glanes

Entraygues

Entraygues le Fel

CANTAL

Aurillac

Mende

LOZÈRE

ARDÈCHE

Privas

Côtes du Vivarais

DRÔME

Coteaux des Baronnies

ALPES-DE-HAUTE-PROVENCE

Digne

Coteaux de Pierrevert

Pierrevert

ALPES-MARITIMES

Nice

LOT-ET-GARONNE

Buzet

Agen

Estaing

Marcillac-Vallon

Estaing

Marcillac

Rodez

AVEYRON

Côtes de Millau

Duché d'Uzès

VAUCLUSE

Avignon

Alpilles

LOT

Cahors

Thézac-Perricard

TARN-ET-GARONNE

Montauban

GARD

Cévennes

Coteaux du Pont du Gard

Nîmes

Sable de Camargue

BOUCHES-DU-RHÔNE

Draguignan

VAR

Maures

LANDES

Mont-de-Marsan

Agenais

la Villedieu-du-Temple

Larrillédieu

GERS

St-Mont

Auch

Côtes de Gascogne

Gaillac

Albi

Côtes du Tarn

TARN

Haute Vallée de l'Orb

HÉRAULT

Montpellier

Côtes de Thau

D'OC

Marseille

Toulon

Mont Caume

COMTÉ TOLOSAN

Toulouse

HAUTE-GARONNE

PYRÉNÉES-ATLANTIQUES

Pau

Tarbes

HAUTES-PYRÉNÉES

Geaune

Adour

Haute Vallée de l'Aude

Foix

ARIÈGE

Le Pays Cathare

Carcassonne

Narbonne

AUDE

Perpignan

PYRÉNÉES-ORIENTALES

Côtes Catalanes

Côte Vermeille

ESPAÑA

Languedoc IGPs/Vins de Pays

1   St-Guilhem-le-Désert
2   Vicomté d'Aumelas
3   Côtes de Thongue
4   Coteaux du Libron
5   Coteaux d'Ensérune
6   Coteaux de Peyriac
7   Coteaux de Narbonne
8   Cité de Carcassonne
9   Vallée du Paradis
10   Vallée du Torgan

Burgundy

The very name of Burgundy has a sonorous ring. Is it the chapel or the dinner bell? Let Paris be France's head, Champagne her soul; Burgundy is her stomach. It is a land of long meals, well-supplied with the best materials (Charolais beef to the west, Bresse chickens to the east, and such super-creamy cheeses as Chaource and Epoisses). It was the richest of the ancient duchies of France. But even before France became Christian it was famous for its wine.

Burgundy is not one big vineyard, but the name of a province that contains several distinct and eminent wine regions. By far the richest and most important is the **Côte d'Or**, Burgundy's heart and ancestral home of Chardonnay and Pinot Noir, composed of the **Côte de Beaune** to the south and the **Côte de Nuits** to the north. In any other context the Chardonnays of **Chablis**, the reds and

whites of the **Côte Chalonnaise**, and the whites of the **Mâconnais** (all equally part of Burgundy) would in themselves be the stars. Immediately south of the Mâconnais is **Beaujolais**, quite different from Burgundy in scale, style, soil, and grape (see pp.66–68).

For all its ancient fame and riches, Burgundy still feels simple and rustic. There is hardly a grand house from one end of the Côte d'Or to the other – none of the elegant country estates that stamp the Médoc as a creation of leisure and wealth in the 18th and 19th centuries. Most of the few big holdings of land, those of the Church, were broken up by Napoleon. Burgundy is still one of the most fragmented of France's important wine-growing districts. The average domaine, as a grower's various vineyards are called, may be bigger than it used to be, but is still a mere 18.5 acres (7.5ha).

The fragmentation of Burgundy is the cause of the single great drawback of its wine: its unpredictability. From the geographer's point of view the human factor is unmappable, and in

Tucked away behind the hill of Corton, some of the east-facing vineyards to the left of the village of Pernand-Vergelesses (above) once struggled to ripen. But rising temperatures have tended to benefit many of Burgundy's cooler communes.

Burgundy, more than in most places, it needs to be given the limelight. For even having pinned down a wine to one particular *climat* (plot of vines) in one particular commune in one particular year, it could still, in many cases, have been made by any one of six or seven people owning small parcels of the land, and reared in any one of six or seven cellars. Monopoles, or whole vineyards in the hands of one owner, are rare exceptions (see p.53). Even the smallest grower has parcels in two or three vineyards. Bigger ones may own a total of 50–100 acres (20–40ha) spread in small lots in a score of vineyards throughout the Côte d'Or. Clos de Vougeot's 125 acres (50ha) are divided among as many as 80 growers.

For this very reason about 60% of burgundy is still bought in barrel from the grower when it is new by négociants (or shippers), who blend it with other wines from the same appellation to achieve marketable quantities of a standard wine. This is offered to the world not as the product of a specific grower, whose production of that particular wine may be only a cask or two, but as the wine of a given district (be it as specific as a vineyard or as vague as a village) *élevé* – literally, reared – by the shipper.

Reputations of the larger négociants vary enormously but Bouchard Père et Fils, Joseph Drouhin, Faiveley, Louis Jadot, and Louis Latour (for its best whites) have long been reliable, while Bichot, Boisset, Chanson, and Pierre André have all improved enormously recently and are all significant vineyard owners themselves. The end of the 20th century saw the emergence of a number of ambitious young négociants making some of Burgundy's best wines, with Dominique Laurent and Verget leading the field in red and white wine-rearing respectively. Today an increasing number of respected growers also run their own négociant business in parallel.

Burgundy's appellations

There are nearly 100 AOCs in Burgundy. Most refer to geographical areas and appear in detail on the following pages. Built into these geographical appellations is a quality classification that is practically a work of art in itself (explained in detail on p.52). However, the following appellations can be applied to wine made from grapes grown in any part of Burgundy, including vineyards within famous communes whose soil and situation are below par: **Bourgogne** (for Pinot Noir or Chardonnay), including such recondite mini-appellations as **Bourgogne Vézelay**, an obeisance to a single village south of Chablis blessed by gastronomy as well as by the Church; **Bourgogne Passetoutgrains** (for a mixture of Gamay with at least a third Pinot Noir), and **Bourgogne Aligoté** (for the relatively tart white wine that is made from Burgundy's other white grape). The 2011 **Coteaux Bourguignons** appellation encompasses all vineyards mapped here plus, controversially, declassified Beaujolais and/or blends thereof.

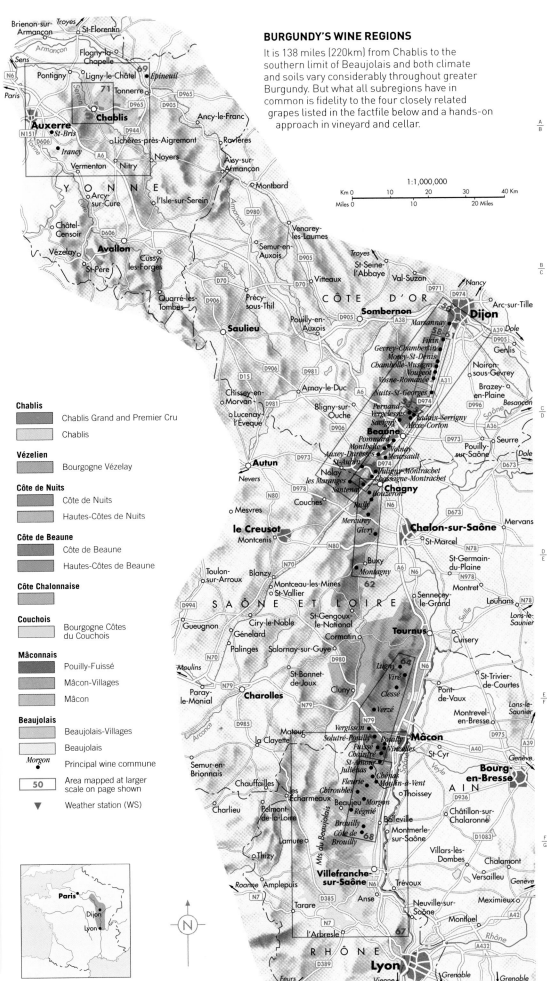

BURGUNDY'S WINE REGIONS

It is 138 miles (220km) from Chablis to the southern limit of Beaujolais and both climate and soils vary considerably throughout greater Burgundy. But what all subregions have in common is fidelity to the four closely related grapes listed in the factfile below and a hands-on approach in vineyard and cellar.

1:1,000,000

Chablis
- Chablis Grand and Premier Cru
- Chablis

Vézelien
- Bourgogne Vézelay

Côte de Nuits
- Côte de Nuits
- Hautes-Côtes de Nuits

Côte de Beaune
- Côte de Beaune
- Hautes-Côtes de Beaune

Côte Chalonnaise

Couchois
- Bourgogne Côtes du Couchois

Mâconnais
- Pouilly-Fuissé
- Mâcon-Villages
- Mâcon

Beaujolais
- Beaujolais-Villages
- Beaujolais
- *Morgon* Principal wine commune

50 Area mapped at larger scale on page shown

▼ Weather station (WS)

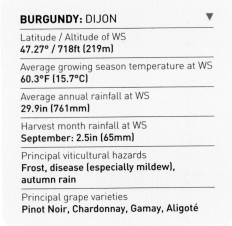

BURGUNDY: DIJON ▼

Latitude / Altitude of WS	**47.27° / 718ft (219m)**
Average growing season temperature at WS	**60.3°F (15.7°C)**
Average annual rainfall at WS	**29.9in (761mm)**
Harvest month rainfall at WS	**September: 2.5in (65mm)**
Principal viticultural hazards	**Frost, disease (especially mildew), autumn rain**
Principal grape varieties	**Pinot Noir, Chardonnay, Gamay, Aligoté**

Côte d'Or

A Burgundian understandably feels a certain reverence towards the rather commonplace-looking ridge of the Côte d'Or – like the Athenians towards an unknown god. One is bound to wonder at the fact that a few small parcels of land on this hill give superlative wines, each with its own positive personality, and that others do not. Surely one can discover the factors that distinguish one parcel from another – giving to some grapes more sugar, thicker skins, or generally more character and distinction.

One can. And one cannot. Soil and subsoil have been analysed time and again. Temperature and humidity and wind direction have been recorded; wines have been minutely analysed… yet the central mystery remains. One can only put down certain physical facts, and place beside them the reputations of the great wines. No one has yet proved conclusively how the two are connected (even if wine-loving geologists are attracted to the Côte d'Or like moths to a flame).

The Côte lies along an important geological fault line where the sea-bed deposits of several different geological epochs, each rich in calcium from defunct shellfish, are exposed like a sliced layer cake (see opposite). Exposure has weathered their rocks into soils of different ages and textures; the varying degrees of slope have mixed them in different proportions. The small valleys, locally called *combes*, which lie at right angles to the Côte add variations to the mix. The altitude of the mid-slope is roughly constant at about 820ft (250m). Higher, on the thinly soiled hard rock cap of the hill, the climate is harsher; grapes ripen later. Lower, where the soil is more alluvial, deeper, and moister, the risk of frost and disease is greater.

The Côte faces east with a bias to the south, locally skewed (especially in the southern half, the Côte de Beaune) to full south and even west exposure. Along its lower part, generally about a third of the way up, runs a narrow outcrop of marlstone, making calcareous clay soil. Marl by itself would be too rich a soil

for the highest-quality wine, but in combination with the stones and scree washed down from the hard limestone higher up it is perfect. Erosion continues the blending below the actual outcrop, the distance depending on the angle of incline.

In the Côte de Beaune the marly outcrop, or Argovien, is wider and higher on the hill; instead of a narrow strip of vineyard under a beetling brow of limestone there is a broad and gentle slope vineyards can climb. The vines almost reach the scrubby peak in places, and in these warmer times some higher land is being (re?)converted to the vine. Indeed, some villages – St-Aubin springs most readily to mind – once thought too cool for top-quality white wine production are coming into their own.

Burgundy was the northernmost area in Europe to produce great red wine. It is vital that the Pinot Noir vines ripen before the cold and damp of autumn set in. The climate peculiar to each vineyard, the so-called mesoclimate (see p.22), in combination with the physical structure of the land, has the most decisive effect. The other, unmappable, quality factor is the grower's choice of vines and the way they are pruned and

THE CÔTES AND HAUTES-CÔTES

Just below the Hautes-Côtes, or high slopes, the Côte d'Or is a golden slope indeed, not least because so many wine lovers are now keen to buy the little that is produced there. The black lines A, B, C, and D show the locations of the four cross-sections opposite in the panel.

- - - Département boundary

Côte d'Or

Hautes-Côtes

53   Area mapped at larger scale on page shown

A——A   Cross-section (see opposite page)

1:220,000

Km 0   1   2   3   4   5 Km

Miles 0   1   2   3 Miles

trained. There are more or less vigorous clones of the classic varieties, and a grower who chooses the most productive, prunes inadequately, or over-fertilizes the soil, compromises quality. Today, however, the pursuit of quality has the upper hand over greed, and growers are increasingly aware of the need to revitalize the soil after years of the overuse of agrochemicals. Burgundy was one of France's first bastions of biodynamic viticulture.

Mapping the Côte

The Côte d'Or is mapped in more detail here than any other wine region partly because of its singular pattern of varying mesoclimates and soils but also because of its unique history. Of all regions this is the one where wine quality has been studied the longest – certainly since the 12th century, when Cistercian and Benedictine monks were already eager to distinguish one cru from another and explore their potential.

In the 14th and 15th centuries the dukes of Burgundy of the house of Valois did everything possible to encourage and profit by the region's wines. Every generation since has added to the sum of local knowledge that is expressed in the *climats* and crus of the hills that stretch from Dijon to Chagny.

The map opposite gives the essential overview. At the top of the not-very-impressive hills, the pale mauve patches on the left/west of the map, is a broken plateau with abrupt scarps (steep hills) where geological fault lines protrude. This is the **Hautes-Côtes**, divided into those of Beaune and those of Nuits, rising to over 1,300ft (400m) and subject to lower temperatures and exposure that puts their harvest a good week behind the Côtes below.

This is not to say that in their more sheltered east- and south-facing combes the Pinot Noir and Chardonnay vines cannot produce generally lightish but sometimes fine wines of true Côte d'Or character. In exceptionally hot years, such as 2005 and 2009, the Hautes-Côtes, like the cooler corners of the Côte d'Or itself, can produce exceptional wine. The best communes in the Hautes-Côtes de Beaune include Nantoux, Echévronne, La Rochepot, and Meloisey; in

VARIATIONS IN SURFACE SOIL IN THE COTE D'OR

These cross-sections through four great vineyards serve as illustrations of the Côte d'Or's variability. The surface soil derives from the rock both under it and higher up the hill. In Gevrey-Chambertin immature soil or rendzinas persists low down until the layer of marlstone. On and below the marlstone is good calcareous brown earth on limestone in a well-sheltered position (Chambertin). A mixture of

soils continues into the valley, giving good vineyard land but not of Grand or Premier Cru class. At Vougeot the marlstone outcrops twice. Below the top outcrop is Grands Echézeaux; on and below the second is Clos de Vougeot.

The hill of Corton has a broad band of marlstone almost to the top; the best vineyards are on it. But

on this steep gradient growers constantly have to collect soil from the bottom and carry it back up the slope. Where limestone debris falls from above, white wine is grown (Corton-Charlemagne). At Meursault the marlstone is again high and broad but its benefit is felt lower, where it forms stony soil on a limestone outcrop. The best vineyards are on this convex ramp.

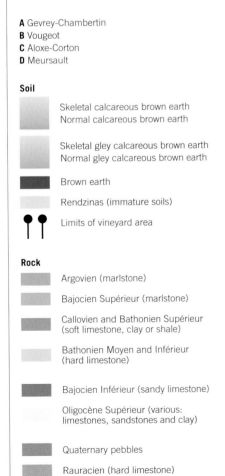

A Gevrey-Chambertin
B Vougeot
C Aloxe-Corton
D Meursault

Soil

Skeletal calcareous brown earth
Normal calcareous brown earth

Skeletal gley calcareous brown earth
Normal gley calcareous brown earth

Brown earth

Rendzinas (immature soils)

Limits of vineyard area

Rock

Argovien (marlstone)

Bajocien Supérieur (marlstone)

Callovien and Bathonien Supérieur (soft limestone, clay or shale)

Bathonien Moyen and Inférieur (hard limestone)

Bajocien Inférieur (sandy limestone)

Oligocène Supérieur (various: limestones, sandstones and clay)

Quaternary pebbles

Rauracien (hard limestone)

Loess

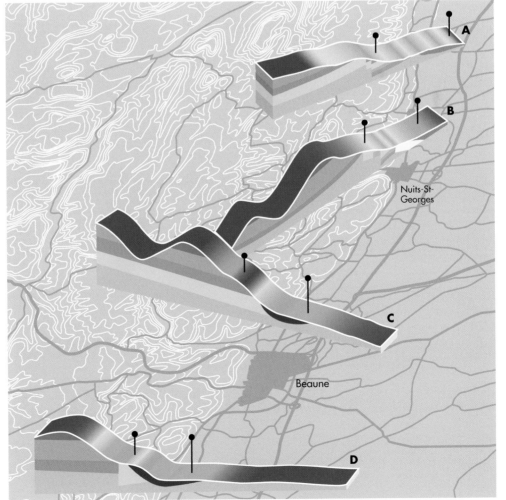

the Hautes-Côtes de Nuits, where red wines dominate, Marey-lès-Fussey, Magny-lès-Villers, Villars-Fontaine, and Bévy.

At the southern tip of the Côte de Beaune is **Maranges**, responsible for delicate reds from the three communes just west of Santenay bearing the suffix -lès-Maranges.

Vineyard classification

The classification of the qualities of the land in the Côte d'Or is the most elaborate on earth, further complicated by slight differences in nomenclature and spelling among different producers. Based on classifications going back to the mid-19th century, it divides the vineyards into four classes and stipulates the precise labelling of each wine accordingly.

Grands Crus are the first class, of which 31 are effectively in operation today, mainly in the Côte de Nuits (see pp.58–61). Each Grand Cru has its own appellation. The single, simple vineyard name – Musigny, Corton, Montrachet,

or Chambertin (sometimes prefixed by "Le") – is the patent of Burgundy's highest nobility.

Premiers Crus, the next rank, use the name of their commune, followed by the name of the vineyard (or, if the wine comes from more than one Premier Cru vineyard, the commune name plus the words "Premier Cru"). Examples would be, respectively, "Chambolle-Musigny, (Les) Charmes" or, if the wine were a blend between Charmes and another Premier Cru vineyard or two, then the name would be "Chambolle-Musigny Premier Cru". Some Premiers Crus are better than others, which is hardly surprising since Burgundy has 635 in all. Perrières in Meursault and Rugiens in Pommard, as well as Les Amoureuses in Chambolle-Musigny and Clos St-Jacques in Gevrey-Chambertin, can command prices in excess of lesser Grands Crus such as Clos de Vougeot and Corton.

Appellation Communale is the third rank: that is, with the right to use a commune name such as Meursault. These wines are often referred to as

"village" wines. The name of a specific vineyard, or *lieu-dit*, is permitted – and increasingly used – on the label of these wines but it must be printed in smaller type than the commune name. A few such vineyards, while not officially Premiers Crus, can be considered to be in the same class.

Fourth, there are less propitiously sited vineyards even within some famous communes (typically on lower-lying land east of the main road, the D974), which have only the right to call their wine Bourgogne. Their produce may be clearly inferior, but not by any means always. There are growers here who offer some of the Côte d'Or's rare bargains.

The consumer must remember to distinguish the name of a vineyard from that of a commune. Many villages (Vosne, Chassagne, Gevrey, etc.) have affixed their name to that of their best vineyard. The difference between Chevalier-Montrachet (from one famous vineyard) and a Chassagne-Montrachet (from anywhere in a big commune) is not obvious, but it is vital.

RICHEBOURG VINEYARD OWNERSHIP

Côte d'Or vine holdings tend to be long and narrow, sometimes just a few rows of vines. As on all our Burgundy maps we give the full, original names of each parcel. The coolest, highest Verroilles parcel of vines was incorporated into Richebourg in 1936, the Veroillistes presumably not being averse to being allowed to use the smarter, more valuable name.

Typically "The Domaine" (de la Romanée-Conti) has the lion's share of this Grand Cru, with the most interestingly divided of the extraordinary wealth of Grands Crus to the west and north of the little village of Vosne-Romanée. The Domaine's various parcels were acquired in several separate transactions.

Domaine Leroy's holdings were acquired when Madame Lalou Bize-Leroy took over the Domaine Charles Noëllat in 1988. See p.59 for the Richebourg labels of Leroy and Anne Gros.

The three Gros mentioned below are by no means the only vine-growing members of this extended family. Such is Burgundy.

Domaines

- Clos Frantin
- Méo-Camuzet
- Gros Frère et Soeur
- AF Gros
- Anne Gros
- Domaine de la Romanée-Conti
- Leroy
- Mongeard-Mugneret
- Grivot
- Hudelot-Noëllat
- Thibault Liger-Belair

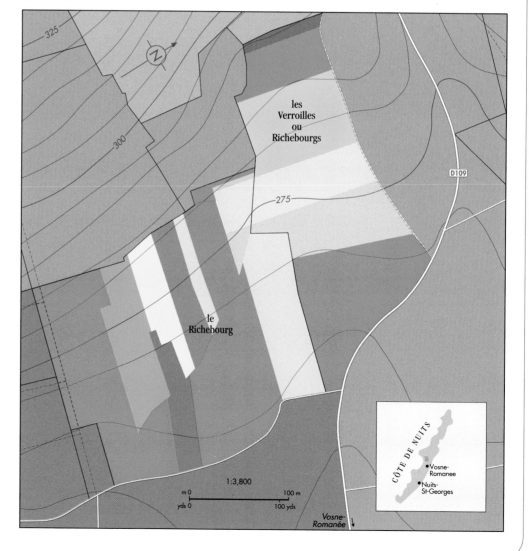

Côte de Beaune: Santenay

The maps on this and the following eight pages trace the vineyards of the Côte d'Or from south to north. Unusually for this Atlas the orientation of the maps has been turned through between 45 and 90 degrees so that in each section the intricacies of the Côte lie across the page. The sections are named after the most important village or town in the middle of the area mapped.

The Côte de Beaune starts without a great explosion of famous names. It leads in gradually to the increasingly celebrated commune of **Santenay**. After the hamlet of Haut-Santenay and the little town of Bas-Santenay (a spa frequented by local bons viveurs), the Côte half-turns to take up its characteristic slope to the east.

This southern end of the Côte de Beaune is the most confused geologically and in many ways is atypical of the Côte as a whole. Complex faults in the structure of the hills make radical changes of soil and subsoil in Santenay. Part of the commune is analogous to parts of the Côte de Nuits, giving deep-flavoured, if not exquisitely fine, red wine with a long life. Other parts give light wine more typical of the Côte de Beaune. Les Gravières (the name draws attention to the stony ground, as the name Graves does in Bordeaux), Clos de Tavannes, and La Comme are the best *climats* of Santenay.

As we move into **Chassagne-Montrachet** the quality of these excellent red wine vineyards is confirmed. The name of Montrachet is so firmly associated with white wine that few people expect to find red here at all. But most vineyards on the south side of Chassagne grow at least some red wine: Morgeot, La Boudriotte, and (overleaf) Clos St-Jean are the most famous. These red wines are naturally tough, tasting more like a rustic Gevrey-Chambertin than, say, a Volnay, although the tendency nowadays is to vinify them in a way that prioritizes suppleness over structure.

Visiting at around the time of the French Revolution, Thomas Jefferson reported that white wine growers here had to eat hard rye bread while red wine growers could afford it soft and white. But Le Montrachet (mapped overleaf) had been famous for white wine since the 16th century, and at least part of the village's soil is much better suited to Chardonnay than to Pinot Noir.

White wine growing really took over in the second half of the 20th century when the world fell in love with Chardonnay. Nowadays Chassagne-Montrachet is known to the world chiefly for its dry but succulent, golden white wine scented with flowers or sometimes hazelnuts.

Soils vary enormously in Santenay, and Passetemps' red soils actually have more in common with the Côte de Nuits. Pierre-Yves Colin-Morey, run by one of Marc Colin's sons, exemplifies the new wave of small negociants depending on intimate knowledge of superior growers.

SANTENAY AND CHASSAGNE-MONTRACHET

In marked contrast to most of the Côte d'Or, many of Santenay's vineyards face due south and some even face west. Like the southern end of Chassagne-Montrachet, they can produce both red and white wines, but today Chassagne is one of the prime hunting grounds for white burgundy at its finest.

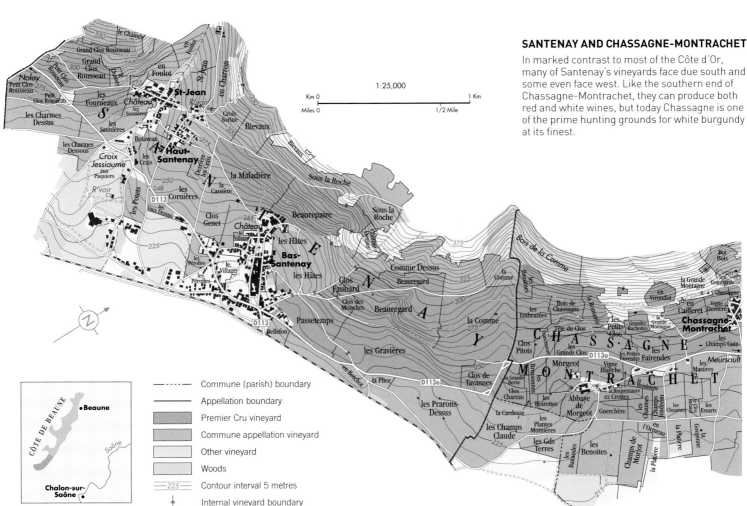

1:25,000

Km 0 ———————————— 1 Km

Miles 0 ———————————— 1/2 Mile

Commune (parish) boundary

Appellation boundary

Premier Cru vineyard

Commune appellation vineyard

Other vineyard

Woods

—225— Contour interval 5 metres

Internal vineyard boundary

Côte de Beaune: Meursault

This is the heartland of white burgundy. Although some earthy red is made south of Chassagne-Montrachet, and north of Meursault are the red wine villages of Volnay and Pommard, the vineyards between the two are the source of the best white wine in Burgundy, if not the whole world.

The Grand Cru Montrachet earns its fame by an incredible concentration of the qualities of white burgundy. At its incomparable best it has (given 10 years) more scent, a brighter gold, a longer flavour, more succulence and yet more density than any Chardonnay on Earth; everything about it is intensified – the mark of truly great wine. Perfect exposure to the east, yet an angle that means the sun is still flooding down the rows at nine on a summer evening, and a sudden streak of limestone soil are factors giving it an edge over its neighbours. So much greater is demand for than supply of this illustrious wine, however, that expensive disappointments are not unknown.

Chevalier-Montrachet, grown on a steeper, higher slope, tends to have less depth but thrillingly crystalline precision. Bâtard-Montrachet lies on heavier ground and often fails to achieve quite the same finesse (though it can take as long to age). Les Criots (in Chassagne) and Bienvenues belong in the same class – as at their best do the Puligny Premiers Crus Les Pucelles, Les Combettes, Les Folatières, and Le Cailleret (and the best of Meursault's Les Perrières).

There is a real distinction between **Puligny-Montrachet** and **Meursault**, even though the vineyards of the one flow without a break into the other. In fact, the hamlet of Blagny – which makes excellent wine high up on stony soil – is in both, and boasts a typically complicated appellation; depending on colour and location, the vineyards can be Puligny-Montrachet, Meursault-Blagny, or (for reds) plain Blagny, almost all at Premier Cru level in each case.

Puligny tends to be rather more delicate and refined than Meursault, not least because the water table here is higher and it is more difficult to dig cellars deep enough for the wines to be intensified by a

second winter in cask. Overall, Meursault has less brilliant distinction (and no Grand Cru) but a very high and generally even standard over a large area. Les Perrières, the upper parts of Les Genevrières, and Les Charmes offer the sternest challenge to Puligny's best Premiers Crus; Porusot and Gouttes d'Or a nuttier, broader, mainstream Meursault experience. Narvaux and Tillets, which are even higher *climats*, while not Premiers Crus, can also make intense, age-worthy wines.

The busy village of Meursault itself lies across another dip in the hills where roads lead up to **Auxey-Duresses** and **Monthelie**, both sources of a little white wine and plenty of good red which is less highly valued (being shorter-lived) than Volnay, and therefore often a bargain. Behind Auxey lies **St-Romain**, a promoted former Hautes-Côtes village producing light but refreshing red and white. Meursault in turn flows into **Volnay**. Much red wine is grown on this side of the commune, but it is called Volnay-Santenots rather than Meursault. Volnay and Meursault sometimes draw as near together as red and white

CHASSAGNE-MONTRACHET TO POMMARD

This stretch of east-facing vineyards as far north as Volnay is white burgundy's powerhouse. The villages of Chassagne, Puligny, and Meursault are increasingly complemented by the well-priced wines of St-Aubin which, like Auxey-Duresses and St-Romain, also makes quite delicate reds on vineyards higher than the Côte de Beaune's prime red appellations Volnay and Pommard.

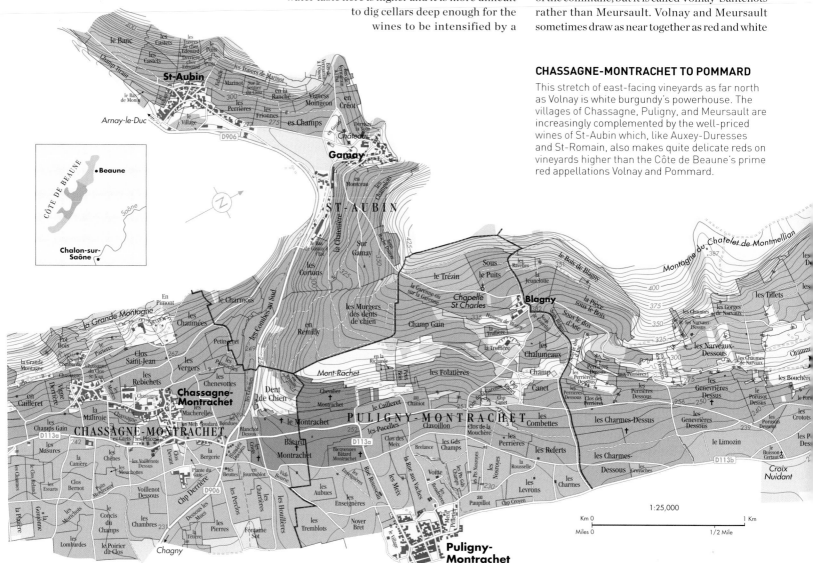

can without being rosé: both soft, very fragrant, the red rather pale yet with great personality and a long, perfumed aftertaste.

If Volnay makes one of the Côte's lighter reds it can also produce some of the most brilliant. Longest-lived are the Clos des Chênes and Caillerets, the great names here. Champans, Bousse d'Or, and Taille Pieds are close behind, while the steep little Clos des Ducs is the best *climat* on the north side of the village. For the riches of neighbouring Pommard, see overleaf.

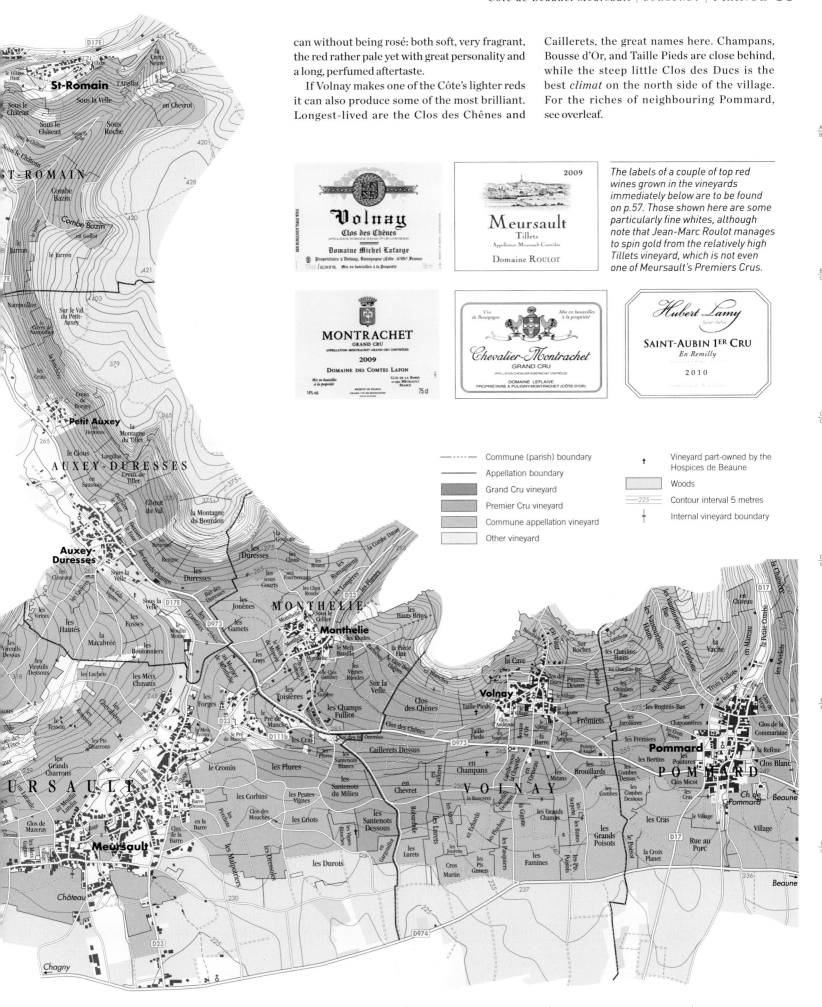

The labels of a couple of top red wines grown in the vineyards immediately below are to be found on p.57. Those shown here are some particularly fine whites, although note that Jean-Marc Roulot manages to spin gold from the relatively high Tillets vineyard, which is not even one of Meursault's Premiers Crus.

Commune (parish) boundary
Appellation boundary
Grand Cru vineyard
Premier Cru vineyard
Commune appellation vineyard
Other vineyard

† Vineyard part-owned by the Hospices de Beaune
Woods
225 Contour interval 5 metres
Internal vineyard boundary

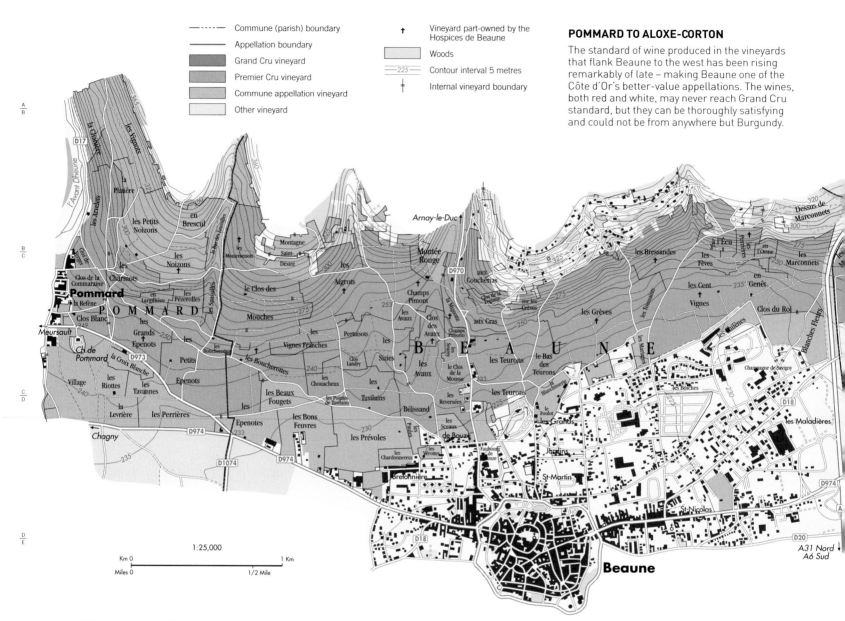

Commune (parish) boundary
Appellation boundary
Grand Cru vineyard
Premier Cru vineyard
Commune appellation vineyard
Other vineyard

† Vineyard part-owned by the Hospices de Beaune
Woods
—225— Contour interval 5 metres
† Internal vineyard boundary

POMMARD TO ALOXE-CORTON
The standard of wine produced in the vineyards that flank Beaune to the west has been rising remarkably of late – making Beaune one of the Côte d'Or's better-value appellations. The wines, both red and white, may never reach Grand Cru standard, but they can be thoroughly satisfying and could not be from anywhere but Burgundy.

1:25,000

Km 0 ———— 1 Km
Miles 0 ———— 1/2 Mile

Côte de Beaune: Beaune

You might expect the Pommard vineyards bordering Volnay (mapped on p.55) to give the most Volnay-like, fragrant, and ethereal wines. But Burgundy, as ever, foxes expectations. The commune boundary marks a soil change that makes Les Rugiens (ruddy, as its name suggests, with iron-rich earth) Pommard's standard-bearer for a different style entirely: dark, heady, tannic in youth, and surprisingly long-lived. Many vineyards entitled to the simple **Pommard** village appellation, which make up about a third of the commune, produce wines in this style that can lack grace and distinction. But there are two or three exceptional Premiers Crus – above all Rugiens and Epenots – and four or five fine growers. It is worth remembering that in Burgundy the grower counts as much as the vineyard, and the saying goes, "There are no great wines; only great bottles of wine."

Pommard's most prestigious vineyard is the lower part of Les Rugiens (Les Rugiens-Bas on the map on p.55), just above the western side of the village. Dames de la Charité, one of the best *cuvées* of Beaune's annual auction (see below), is made mainly from Rugiens and Epenots combined. The Clos de la Commaraine and the wines of the growers de Courcel, Comte Armand, and de Montille are some of Pommard's finest: sturdy wines that need 10 years to develop the lovely savoury character of the best burgundy.

The focus of the vineyards mapped on these pages, indeed arguably of the whole Côte d'Or, is the lively, wine-centric, ramparted medieval town of **Beaune**, home to the famous Hospices de Beaune charity wine auction each November. In the string of famous vineyards that occupy what the Burgundians call "the kidney of the slope", at about the 800ft (250m) line above the town, a large proportion belongs to the town's négociants: Bouchard Père et Fils, Chanson, Drouhin, Jadot, and Louis Latour among them. Drouhin's part of the Clos des Mouches is celebrated for both red and its exquisite white, while a part of Les Grèves belonging to Bouchard Père et Fils is known as the Vigne de l'Enfant Jésus and makes another marvellous wine. No Beaune is a Grand Cru; the best is usually gentle wine, lasting well but not demanding to be kept the 10 years or more that a Romanée or Chambertin would.

Travelling north from Beaune, the hill of Corton looms with its dark cap of woods. Corton breaks the spell that prevents the Côte de Beaune from having a red Grand Cru. The imposing hill presents faces to the east, south, and west and is home to a Grand Cru of each colour. A small amount of white Corton is made, but most is Corton-Charlemagne, grown on the western and southwestern flanks of the hill, and in a very different ribbon of Chardonnay vineyards round the top of the east flank, where debris from the limestone top is washed down, whitening the brown marly soil. Chardonnay,

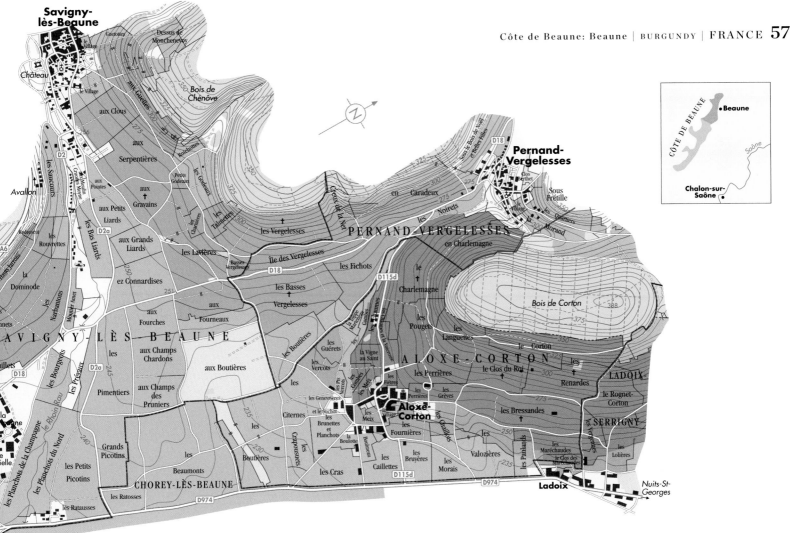

incidentally, did not replace the Pinot Blanc that was long grown on the hill of Corton until the late 19th century. Corton-Charlemagne can occasionally rival Montrachet.

The big, often fruity, sometimes tannic Corton red is grown mostly on the east- and south-facing slopes, but the lower vineyards produce much simpler wine and should not have been classified Grand Cru. Top red Cortons come only from Le Corton itself, Les Bressandes, Le Clos du Roi, and Les Renardes.

Aloxe-Corton is the appellation of the lesser wines (mainly red) grown below the hill to the south, while **Pernand-Vergelesses** round the back has some notably cooler east-facing Premier Cru vineyards (red and white) as well as some of the hill's west-facing Grand Cru slopes.

If **Savigny** and Pernand are slightly in the background it is only because the foreground is so imposing. The best growers of both make wines up to the highest Beaune standard, now fully reflected in their price. Up a side valley, Savigny, producing wines that are *"Nourrissants, Théologiques, et Morbifuges"* according to local publicity, can be a marvel of finesse. **Chorey** lies on flat ground across the main road, but is nonetheless a useful source of approachable red burgundy.

Some of the most reliable representatives of the prime red wine appellations on p.55, plus solid names from the northern Côte de Beaune mapped here. Jadot and Drouhin may be négociants but these wines come from their own vineyards.

Bonneau du Martray is one of many historic, family-owned domaines now following biodynamic rituals in the vineyard, as here in Corton-Charlemagne.

Côte de Nuits: Nuits-St-Georges

More "stuffing", longer life, and deeper colour are the signs of a Côte de Nuits wine compared with a Volnay or a Beaune. This is red wine country; white is a rarity.

The line of Premiers Crus, wending its way along the hills of the Côte de Nuits, is threaded with clutches of Grands Crus. These are the wines that express with most intensity the inimitable sappy richness of Pinot Noir. The line follows the outcrop of marlstone below the hard limestone hilltop, but it is where the soil has a mixture of silt and scree over the marl that the quality really peaks. Happily, this corresponds time and again with areas that enjoy the best shelter and most sun.

The wines of Prémeaux go to market under the name of **Nuits-St-Georges**. They are finer boned than the rest of the appellation, especially such *monopole* vineyards as Clos de l'Arlot and Clos de la Maréchale. Les St-Georges and Vaucrains vineyards just over the commune boundary produce tannic wines with tense, positive flavours that demand long bottle age – something that cannot be said of most Côte de Nuits-Villages, a junior appellation for the extreme northern and southern ends of the Côte de Nuits.

Beaune bustles; Nuits is quiet, but it is home to a number of négociants, and the Nuits Premiers Crus leading north into **Vosne-Romanée** are a worthy introduction to that extraordinary parish. Vosne-Romanée is a modest little village with only its uncommon concentration of famous names on the backstreet nameplates to suggest that the world's most expensive wine lies beneath your feet. The village stands below a long incline of reddish earth, with the Romanée-St-Vivant vineyard nearest the village. The soil is deep, rich in clay and lime. Mid-slope is La Romanée-Conti, with poorer, shallower soil. Higher up, La Romanée tilts more steeply; it seems drier and less clayey. For about 30 years in the late 20th century the wine produced in La Romanée Grand Cru was made by the négociant Bouchard Père et Fils of Beaune, but from the 2002 vintage it has been restored to the owner, the Vicomte Liger-Belair.

On the right the big vineyard of Le Richebourg (mapped in detail on p.52) curves around to face east-northeast. Up the left flank runs the narrow strip of La Grande Rue, and beside it the long slope of La Tâche. These produce some of the most highly prized of all burgundies, the most expensive wines in the world.

Romanée-Conti and La Tâche are both *monopoles* of the Domaine de la Romanée-Conti, which also has substantial holdings in both Richebourg and Romanée-St-Vivant (and Echézeaux, Grands Echézeaux – and Corton –for good measure). For the finesse, the velvety warmth combined with a suggestion of spice, the almost oriental opulence of their wines, the market will seemingly stand any price. Romanée-Conti is the most perfect of all, but the entire group has a family likeness: the result of vineyard location, small crops, old vines, late picking, and inordinate care.

Clearly one can look among their neighbours for wines of similar character at less stupendous prices (though all too similar in the case of Domaine Leroy). All the other named vineyards of Vosne-Romanée are splendid. Indeed, one of the old textbooks on Burgundy remarks drily: "There are no common wines in Vosne." The Premier Cru Malconsorts just south of La Tâche deserves special mention.

The big, some would say too big, 90-acre (37.5ha) Echézeaux Grand Cru – which includes most of the violet *climats* around that marked Echézeaux du Dessus on the map – and the

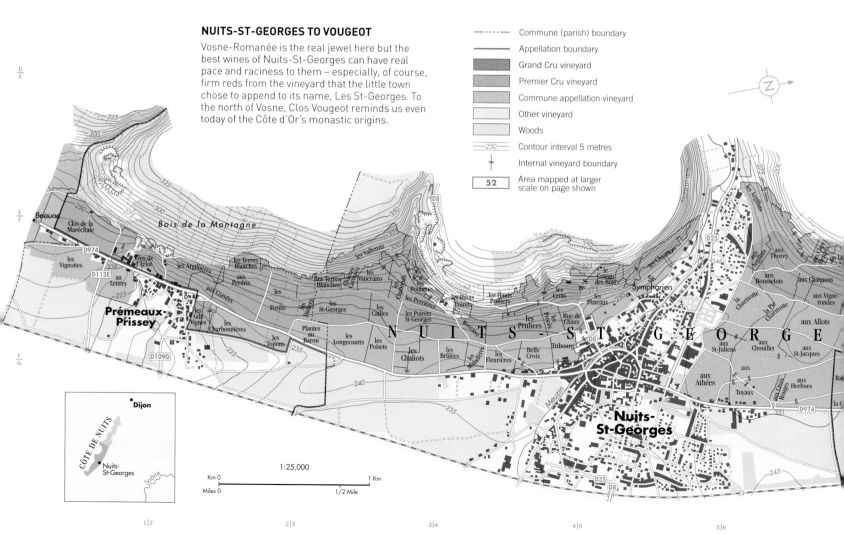

NUITS-ST-GEORGES TO VOUGEOT

Vosne-Romanée is the real jewel here but the best wines of Nuits-St-Georges can have real pace and raciness to them – especially, of course, firm reds from the vineyard that the little town chose to append to its name, Les St-Georges. To the north of Vosne, Clos Vougeot reminds us even today of the Côte d'Or's monastic origins.

----- Commune (parish) boundary
——— Appellation boundary
Grand Cru vineyard
Premier Cru vineyard
Commune appellation vineyard
Other vineyard
Woods
—250— Contour interval 5 metres
+ Internal vineyard boundary
52 Area mapped at larger scale on page shown

1:25,000

Km 0   1 Km
Miles 0   1/2 Mile

smaller Grands Echézeaux are really in the commune of Flagey, a village too far east to feature on our map and which has been absorbed (at least oenologically) into Vosne. Grands Echézeaux has more regularity, more of the lingering intensity that marks the very great burgundies, and certainly higher prices.

One high stone wall surrounds the 125 acres (50ha) of the **Clos de Vougeot**: the sure sign of a monastic vineyard. Today it is so subdivided that it is anything but a reliable label on a bottle. But it is the *climat* as a whole that is a Grand Cru. The Cistercians used to blend wine of the top, middle, and sometimes bottom slopes to make what we must believe was one of the best burgundies of all and one of the most consistent, since in dry years the wine from lower down would have an advantage, in wet years the top slopes. It is generally accepted, however, that the middle and especially top of the slope tend to produce the best wine today. There are wines from near the top in particular that can be almost as great as their northern neighbour Musigny. The name of the grower, as ever, must be your guide.

No one (yet) has attempted to use machines to harvest the steeper Côte d'Or vineyards, such as these above Nuits-St-Georges. The grapes are so valuable that it is *de rigueur* to harvest them in particularly small containers so that the skins are not broken by the weight of grapes above.

Four of Vosne's famous Grands Crus. Domaine de la Romanée-Conti's most famous, La Tâche, and Romanée-Conti itself are such targets for counterfeiters that the domaine is reluctant to part with labels of these wines. A fine Premier Cru, next to Les St-Georges, from one of Nuits-St-Georges' finest practitioners is also represented above.

CÔTE DE NUITS

• Dijon

• Nuits-St-Georges

Saône

1:25,000

Km 0 — 1 Km
Miles 0 — 1/2 Mile

Map labels (selected): la Taupe, la Combe, D122h, Chambolle-Musigny, les Véroilles, Montagne de la Combe Grisard, MOREY-ST-DENIS, GEVREY-C, la Combe d'Orveaux, les Cras, les Fuées, Bonnes Mares, Clos de Tart, Chambertin Clos de Bèze, Bel-Air, Château, CHAMBOLLE-MUSIGNY, les Charmes, les Baudes, les Sentiers, Clos St-Denis, Clos de la Roche, Latricières-Chambertin, Chambertin, Clos de Vougeot, VOUGEOT, les Amoureuses, les Bussières, Morey-St-Denis, Clos des Ormes, Mazoyères-Chambertin, Charmes-Chambertin, aux Ételois, Champs Chenys, Vignes Belles, Vougeot, Nuits-St-Georges, D974, les Herbues, Clos Solon, D25, D122g, D122h

Côte de Nuits: Gevrey-Chambertin

The finest, longest-living, and eventually most velvety red burgundies are made at this northern end of the Côte d'Or. Nature adds rich soil to the perfect combination of shelter and exposure provided by the hills. The narrow marlstone outcrop, overlaid with silt and scree, follows the lower slopes. From it Chambertin and the Grands Crus of Morey and **Chambolle-Musigny** draw their power: wines of weight and muscle, unyielding when young, but the best will offer unmatched complexity and depth of flavour when mature.

The Grand Cru Musigny stands apart, squeezed in under the tree-capped limestone crest, obviously more closely related to the top of the Clos de Vougeot and Grands Echézeaux than to the vineyards north of Chambolle such as Bonnes-Mares. The slope is steep enough to oblige the vignerons to carry the brown limy clay, heavy with pebbles, back up the hill after prolonged rainy weather. This and the permeable limestone subsoil allow excellent drainage. Conditions are just right for a wine with plenty of body.

The glory of Musigny is that it covers its undoubted power with a lovely, haunting delicacy of perfume; a uniquely sensuous savour. A great Musigny makes what is so well described as a "peacock's tail" in your mouth, opening to reveal ever more ravishing patterns of flavour. It is not as strong as Chambertin, not as spicy as Romanée-Conti – but it fully warrants ten to 20 years' ageing. Bonnes-Mares is the other Grand Cru of Chambolle. It starts as a tougher wine than Musigny, and never quite achieves the tender grace of its neighbour. Les Amoureuses and Les Charmes – their names perfectly expressive of their wine – are among the best Premiers Crus of Burgundy – honorary Grands Crus, in effect. But any Chambolle is likely to be very good. In this age of warming, quality seems to be migrating uphill, with many a Cras and Fuées as sought after as Charmes.

The commune of **Morey-St-Denis** is overshadowed in renown by its five Grands Crus. Clos de la Roche, with little Clos St-Denis (which gave its name to the village), are wines of great staying power, strength, and depth, fed by soil rich in limestone. The Clos des Lambrays is a *monopole* promoted to Grand Cru rank in 1981 that makes seductive wines, and Clos de Tart, the *monopole* of the Mommessin family, is realizing

its full glorious potential. Morey has more than 20 tiny Premiers Crus, few of whose names are well known but whose general standard is very high. The vineyards climb the hill, finding soil higher than anywhere else in the area. The lofty, stony Monts Luisants even produces some fine white wine.

Gevrey-Chambertin has a vast amount of good land. Suitable vineyard soil stretches further from the hill here than elsewhere; some east of the main road is still, justifiably, appellation Gevrey-Chambertin rather than the more usual plain Bourgogne. Its two greatest vineyards, Chambertin and Clos de Bèze, acknowledged leaders across the centuries, face east on a gentle slope just under the woods. The constellation of adjoining vineyards – Charmes, Mazoyères, Griotte, Chapelle, Mazis, Ruchottes, and Latricières have the right to add Chambertin after their names, but not (like Clos de Bèze) before. Burgundian wine law can be more subtle than theology.

The commune also has a slope 160ft (50m) higher with a superb southeast exposure. Its Premiers Crus –Cazetiers, Lavaut St-Jacques, Varoilles, and especially Clos St-Jacques –

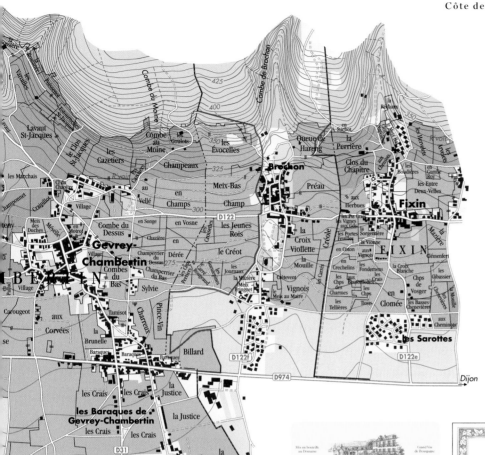

VOUGEOT TO FIXIN

Note how unusually far east the vineyards of interest stretch from the well-endowed village of Gevrey-Chambertin. Growers such as Denis Bachelet can produce hauntingly beautiful village Gevrey from old vines here, whereas in other communes most vineyards to the east of the D974 main road may produce only Bourgogne.

---------- Commune (parish) boundary

————— Appellation boundary

▮ Grand Cru vineyard

▮ Premier Cru vineyard

▮ Commune appellation vineyard

▮ Other vineyard

▮ Woods

══ 275 ══ Contour interval 5 metres

╬ Internal vineyard boundary

It is almost impossible to pick just five representatives of the great wines produced in this stretch of vineyards, yet it sometimes seems that each grower not only has a unique collection of vineyards, but also a unique way of vinifying his or her produce.

are arguably peers of the Grands Crus. There are more famous individual vineyards in this village than in any other in Burgundy. The slopes to the north, once called the Côte de Dijon, were until the 18th century considered to be among the best. But growers were tempted to grow bulk wine for the city and planted the "disloyal" Gamay. Brochon became known as a "well of wine". Today its southern edge is included in Gevrey-Chambertin; the rest of its vineyards have the right only to the appellation Côte de Nuits-Villages.

Fixin, however, has some tradition of quality with the Premiers Crus La Perrière, Les Hervelets, and Clos du Chapître potentially up to the standards of Gevrey-Chambertin. **Marsannay**, which is situated just off the map to the right, specializes in some delicious Pinot Noir rosé, plenty of increasingly interesting red, and a little ordinary white.

The Clos des Lambrays is based in a house that is unusually grand for Burgundy. This Grand Cru, seen here under the snow that is common during the Côte d'Or winter, reaches right up as far as the woods behind the house.

Côte Chalonnaise

So close is the north of the Côte Chalonnaise to the southern tip of the Côte d'Or that it is surprising that most of its wines taste so perceptibly different, like slightly undernourished country cousins. The rolling, pastoral hills south of Chagny are in many ways a continuation of the Côte de Beaune, although the regular ridge is replaced here by a jumble of limestone slopes on which vineyards appear among orchards and pasture. Some of these vineyards rise to a markedly higher altitude than those of the Côte de Beaune, resulting in a slightly later harvest and a more precarious ripening process. The Côte Chalonnaise, once called the "Région de Mercurey", was named for its (relative) proximity to Chalon-sur-Saône to the east.

In the north, **Rully** makes more white wine than red. The white is brisk, high in acid: in poor vintages ideal material for sparkling Crémant de Bourgogne, and in the increasing proportion of warmer vintages lively, apple-fresh, appetizing white burgundy that can be exceptional value. Rully reds tend to leanness – but are not without class.

Mercurey is much the best-known appellation, accounting for nearly two in every three bottles of Côte Chalonnaise red (if you include Bourgogne-Côte Chalonnaise; see below). Pinot Noir here is on a par with a minor Côte de Beaune: firm, solid, almost rough when young, but ageing well. The négociants Antonin Rodet and Faiveley are among the important producers.

There has been rampant Premier Cru inflation here, the total number in Mercurey alone rising from five in the 1980s to over 30 on more than 380 acres (154ha) of vineyard today. This significantly higher proportion of Premiers Crus than in the Côte d'Or to the north is characteristic of the Côte Chalonnaise, but the resulting modest premium is worth paying.

Mercurey's neighbour **Givry** is the smallest of the five major appellations and is almost as dedicated to red wine. It is often lighter, easier, and more enjoyable young than Mercurey, although the Clos Jus, recovered from scrubland in the late 1980s, is producing solidly powerful wine that is well worth ageing. Premiers Crus are multiplying here, too.

Montagny to the south is the one all-white appellation and includes neighbouring Buxy, whose co-operative is probably the most successful in southern Burgundy. The whites here are fuller and the best are more like minor Côte de Beaune wines than the leaner Rullys. The firm of Louis Latour long ago discovered what good value they can be and is responsible for a significant proportion of total production.

Bouzeron, the village just north of Rully, has its own appellation exclusively for the wines of one grape. Indeed, it is the only appellation for a single-village Aligoté white in Burgundy: a reward for the perfectionism of Domaine A and P de Villaine perhaps.

The whole region, Bouzeron included, is a good source of both generic red and white burgundy sold under the appellation Bourgogne-Côte Chalonnaise.

THE CENTRAL STRIP
This map shows only the most celebrated, central strip of the Côte Chalonnaise, specifically the five major communes that give their names to the appellations Bouzeron, Rully, Mercurey, Givry, and Montagny, and some of their better-known vineyards situated on mainly east- and south-facing slopes.

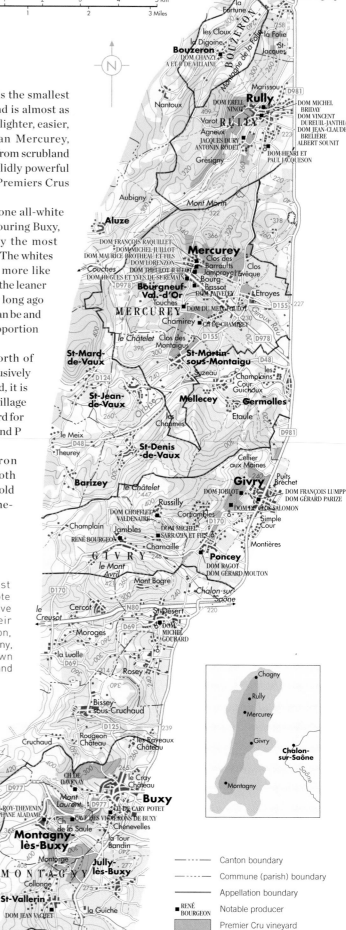

On the left are wines from two of the region's top producers, who offer fine white burgundies for those who can't afford to shop in the Côte d'Or, while Domaine Joblot's Clos de la Servoisine (above) has joined Givry's growing number of Premiers Crus.

Mâconnais

The city of Mâcon on the Saône, 35 miles (55km) south of Chalon, gives its name to a wide, hilly, and profoundly rural area that is increasingly recognized as producing extremely interesting whites on its own account. With its characteristic limestone subsoil, overlaid either with clay or alluvial topsoil, this is definitively white wine country. The slightly warmer climate than that of the Côte d'Or suits the Chardonnay grape, which

seems gloriously at home in the Mâconnais and now accounts for almost 90% of all its wine. This means that there is almost as much Mâcon Blanc made as there is Chablis and yet the international reputation of the latter is very much greater than that of the former. What helps is that a considerable proportion of the white wine made in the Mâconnais is sold, quite legally, as Bourgogne Blanc – not least from the co-ops such as that at Buxy that are so active there.

The Beaujolais vine Gamay is still the mainstay of Mâcon Rouge. When grown on limestone as opposed to the granite of Beaujolais to the south, Gamay can take on a hard, rustic edge, so

Chardonnay vines, some planted as long ago as the 1930s, sprout spikes of frost in the Pouilly-Vinzelles vineyard Les Quarts, cultivated biodynamically by the Bret Brothers (see label below).

Mâcon Rouge is rarely thrilling. An increasing proportion of land, however, is devoted to Pinot Noir, which is sold as the rather more valuable Bourgogne Rouge.

The locater map overleaf shows which section of the greater Mâconnais region is mapped in detail. The pale mauve area to the north and west of this section is responsible for the most basic

It was quite a feather in the Mâconnais cap to have attracted Dominique Lafon, the king of Meursault, and Anne-Claude Leflaive, the queen of Puligny-Montrachet, to invest so far south of the Côte d'Or. Lafon makes a range of highly distinctive, single-vineyard white Mâconnais wines, while Leflaive's more reticent wine is – so far – a blend from five different parcels of vines.

Mâcon Blanc, Rouge, and a little Rosé. Mâcon-Villages should in theory guarantee superior quality from the region's best villages, but in practice this applies to virtually all white Mâcon. A surer guide to white wine quality is to seek out wines sold under the name of one of the 26 villages allowed on wine labels, some of which are marked on the map. Of these, some also have the right to the red Beaujolais-Villages appellation that extends into the southern end of the Mâconnais at the bottom of the map.

In this buffer zone, the villages of Chasselas, Leynes, St-Vérand, and Chânes also qualify for the strange appellation of convenience, **St-Véran**. It applies to Chardonnay grown on the southern and northern fringes of the Pouilly-Fuissé appellation mapped in detail opposite. Soils in southern St-Véran tend to be red, acidic, and sandy, producing very different and generally much simpler, leaner wines than the luscious ones made on the limestone of Prissé and Davayé to the north of Pouilly-Fuissé.

Pouilly-Vinzelles and **Pouilly-Loché**, lying just to the east of the central Pouilly-Fuissé zone, are theoretical alternatives to the real thing, but are in very short supply.

Mâcon-Prissé, also grown on limestone, can be good value, and Lugny, Uchizy, Chardonnay (the lucky village with the name of the grape), and Loché all have their fans as providers of keenly priced, plump burgundian Chardonnay. Two of the best villages, however, are Viré and Clessé, both on the strip of limestone that threads its way north through the region vaguely parallel to the main north–south A6 *autoroute* from the Pouilly-Fuissé cluster of excellence and then even further north to form the backbone of the Côte d'Or. A special AC, **Viré-Clessé**, applies to the wines of these villages and several more (see map).

You will not find the brilliance of Montrachet or Corton-Charlemagne in the Mâconnais but there is no shortage of strong, stylish, well-made answers to the Chardonnays of the New World, wines with a perceptibly French accent whose ranks swell with every vintage.

EASTERN MACONNAIS

The 26 villages whose wines are regarded as distinctive enough for their names to be allowed on labels as a suffix to the word "Mâcon" can be divided into those in the deep south on land that overlaps with Beaujolais; those such as Milly-Lamartine, Verzé, and Cruzille that are tucked away in the folds of the hills and whose grapes ripen relatively late; and those whose grapes ripen early because, like Prissé, they overlook the road to Cluny or because, like Charnay, Uchizy, and Chardonnay, the vineyards face east towards the morning sun across the plain of the River Saône. The area bounded in red as Viré-Clessé is distinguished geologically.

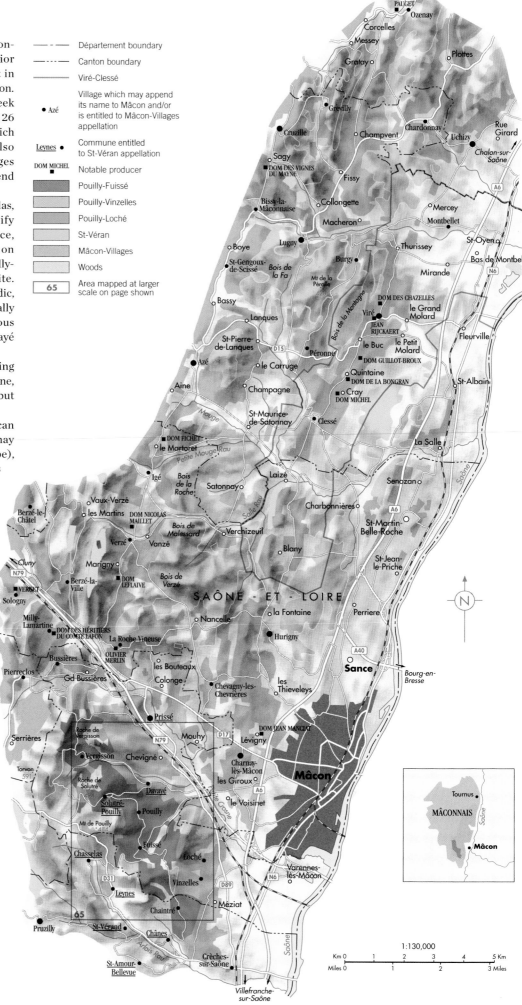

Département boundary
Canton boundary
Viré-Clessé

● Azé
Village which may append its name to Mâcon and/or is entitled to Mâcon-Villages appellation

Leynes ●
Commune entitled to St-Véran appellation

DOM MICHEL ■
Notable producer

Pouilly-Fuissé
Pouilly-Vinzelles
Pouilly-Loché
St-Véran
Mâcon-Villages
Woods

65
Area mapped at larger scale on page shown

MÂCONNAIS

1:130,000
Km 0   1   2   3   4   5 Km
Miles 0   1   2   3 Miles

Pouilly-Fuissé

Close to the Mâconnais border with Beaujolais is a pocket of white wine-growing with distinction of a different order. The Pouilly-Fuissé district is a sudden tempest of wave-shaped limestone hills, rich in the alkaline clay the Chardonnay vine loves.

The map shows how the four very varied Pouilly-Fuissé communes shelter on the lower slopes; the contour lines alone are enough to suggest just how irregular the topography is, and how varied the vineyards. Vines on the south-facing, open slopes of Chaintré may ripen a full two weeks before those on the north-facing slopes of Vergisson, whose wines can be some of the most full-bodied in a long, late vintage. The commune of Solutré-Pouilly shelters under the pale pink rock of Solutré, with its northern end similar to Vergisson and the Pouilly terrain being broadly similar to that around Fuissé. The twin villages of Pouilly and Fuissé are relatively low-lying and peaceful, but for the constant prowl of wine-loving tourists.

The best Pouilly-Fuissé is full to the point of richness and capable of sumptuous succulence with time. Perhaps a dozen small growers make wines that frequently reach these heights, applying wildly varying policies on oak, lees-stirring, and the occasional addition of second-crop berries to add acidity to what can be a too-fat wine. Others may be bland in comparison, virtually indistinguishable from Mâcon-Villages, their producers leaning heavily on Pouilly-Fuissé's international fame.

Ambitious producers

After a period of stagnation in the 1980s, the appellation can boast a host of over-achievers such as Guffens-Heynen, the Bret Brothers, J-A Ferret, Robert-Denogent, Daniel Barraud, and Olivier Merlin (based just to the north of this zone on excellent land on the west-facing slopes of La Roche Vineuse). For some years ambitious producers such as the above have been encouraged to offer single vineyard bottlings as the precursor to the current campaign to appoint some Premiers Crus. This movement alone has been a significant drive towards quality, as well as enabling growers to earn more through higher pricing for their best cuvées. The idea is not universally popular locally, though, and as usual there will certainly be squabbles when the final decisions on what's in and what's out are made. The most obvious candidates for elevation to Premier Cru status are marked on this map.

In 2008 the Beaune négociant Louis Jadot acquired J-A Ferret. It would not be surprising if more of its rivals moved into the Mâconnais as they have already done in Beaujolais.

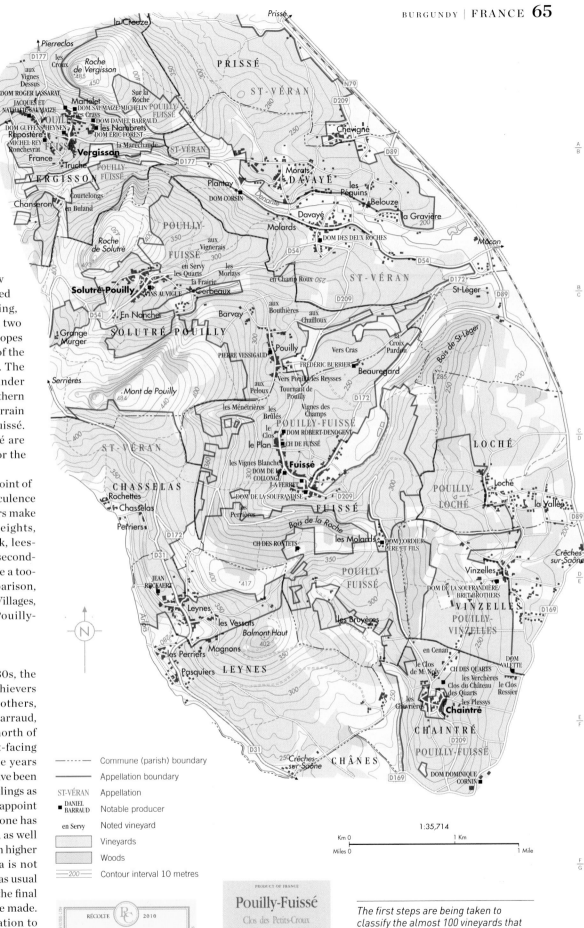

Commune (parish) boundary
Appellation boundary
ST-VÉRAN — Appellation
■ DANIEL BARRAUD — Notable producer
en Servy — Noted vineyard
Vineyards
Woods
—200— Contour interval 10 metres

1:35,714
Km 0 — 1 Km
Miles 0 — 1 Mile

The first steps are being taken to classify the almost 100 vineyards that have been specified on the labels of Pouilly-Fuissé for many years. Some of the most obviously outstanding are expected to be accorded Premier Cru status before long. Many of these are mapped above.

Beaujolais

In one of the marriages of grape and ground the French regard as mystical, in Beaujolais' sandy clay over granite the Gamay grape, undistinguished virtually everywhere else, can produce uniquely fresh, vivid, fruity, light but infinitely swallowable wine. *Gouleyant* is the French word for the way fine Beaujolais slips ineffably down the throat.

Lightness is not (yet) a fashionable virtue, and even committed wine drinkers may overlook Beaujolais, not least because the popularity of Beaujolais Nouveau every late November in the late 1970s and 1980s, and the associated rapid cash flow, conferred a dangerous complacency on the region. Today, however, there are serious efforts to make much more serious wine, though very rarely with a serious price tag. The rushed, banana-flavoured ferments that once characterized the region have largely been abandoned.

The Beaujolais region stretches 34 miles (55km) from the granite-based hills immediately south of Mâcon, the southern end of Burgundy, to the much flatter land northwest of Lyon. Beaujolais in total produces almost as much wine as the rest of the Burgundy wine regions put together and, as one would expect, the region's 50,000 acres (20,000ha) of vineyards are far from homogeneous. Its soil divides it sharply, just north of Villefranche, the region's capital. South of here in "Bas" Beaujolais the soil is clay over granite and limestone, notably in the area of the Pierres Dorées, the golden stones, which add lustre to some of the prettiest villages in France. Wine made on this flatter land is plain Beaujolais. Very fresh and new (and natural), it can be the ultimate bistro wine, served by the pot in Lyon's famously authentic *bouchons* (small brasseries). Plain "Bas" Beaujolais rarely keeps well. Even in a good vintage its clay soil is too cold to ripen really full flavours in the Gamay grapes – although there are notable exceptions.

Juliénas, named after Julius Caesar, can trace its wine-growing history back more than 2,000 years to when France was that part of the Roman empire known as Gaul.

The northern part of the region, "Haut" Beaujolais, is granite-based, with a variously sandy topsoil that drains, warms, and ripens the Gamay, often to perfection. Thirty-eight of its communes, marked in the areas coloured blue and mauve on the map, have the right to the appellation **Beaujolais-Villages**. Their vineyards climb the wooded mountains to the west to heights above 1,480ft (450m).

It is almost always worth paying more for a Villages wine for its extra concentration. Only individual growers who bottle (very much the minority) tend to use the names of the Beaujolais-Villages communes. Merchants still dominate production and are much more likely to blend the produce of different communes to make a wine labelled simply Beaujolais-Villages.

The 10 places marked in magenta within the mauve area on the map have the right to use their own names on labels and are expected to show distinct characteristics of their own. These are the Beaujolais Crus, mapped in detail overleaf and lying just south of the Mâconnais, close to Pouilly-Fuissé. In this northern region a small and growing amount of Beaujolais Blanc is also made (red wines having been so difficult to sell) – indeed, some villages can sell their red wine as Beaujolais-Villages and their white as Mâcon-Villages.

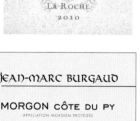

All of these wines come from individual growers in the Crus Beaujolais communes, and their locations are mapped overleaf. The Côte du Py in Morgon is a lieu-dit *on the slopes of an extinct volcano; the wines are firm and tannic, becoming meaty with age. Moulin-à-Vents can also be long-lived, while Fleurie and Brouilly wines tend to be lighter.*

The Gamay grape is in its element here. Each Gamay vine in Beaujolais was traditionally staked individually (although trellising is now allowed in the better vineyards). Its plants are almost like people, leading independent lives: after 10 years they are no longer trained, but merely tied up in summer, standing free. A Gamay vine can live longer than a human, and has to be harvested by one.

The great majority of Beaujolais today is made by semi-carbonic maceration, in which whole bunches of grapes go into a subsequently sealed vat uncrushed, and the grapes – at least at the top of the vat – begin fermenting internally: a high-speed fermentation that emphasizes the characteristic smell and flavour of the fruit and minimizes tannins and malic acid. But there are significant signs of a return to the old, more burgundian methods of vinification, some producers even willingly reintroducing oak casks to make much more age-worthy, rather burgundian wines.

Gamay in the Upper Loire

Well off the map to the west, over a mountain ridge and in the Upper Loire basin in fact, are three much smaller regions similarly devoted to the Gamay grape (see the map of France on p.47). The **Côte Roannaise**, on south- and southeast-facing slopes of the Loire near Roanne, also enjoys a granite base, and several individual domaines here can produce wines that have the same refreshing integrity as Beaujolais in its purest form. Further south, growing Gamay on similar soils, the **Côtes du Forez** is dominated by a single, superior co-op. **Côtes d'Auvergne**, near Clermont-Ferrand, is even more extensive, and makes light reds and rosés from Gamay, and a little light white.

BEAUJOLAIS VILLAGES AND CRUS

The full extent of the Beaujolais appellation is mapped here, including the overlap with the Mâconnais region in the north. The Beaujolais Crus, which provide just under a third of the region's total production, are mapped in detail overleaf.

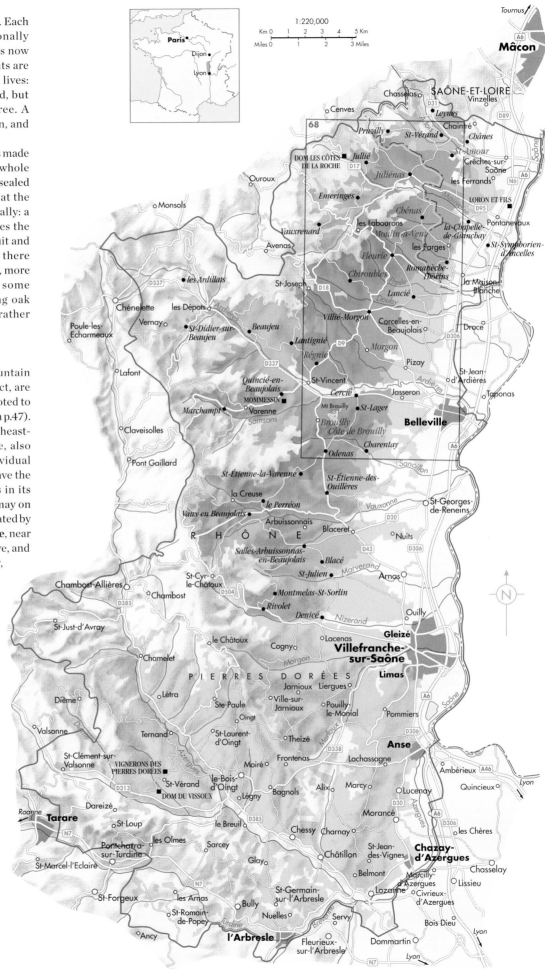

— · — · — Département boundary

———— Limit of Mâconnais region

———— Limit of Beaujolais region

Fleurie Beaujolais Cru

•*Pruzilly* Beaujolais-Villages commune

MOMMESSIN ■ Notable producer

Crus Beaujolais

Beaujolais-Villages

Beaujolais

68 Area mapped at larger scale on page shown

The Crus of Beaujolais

The hazy blue hills mapped here, often crowned with woods but densely planted with vines below, are home to the 10 individual Crus of Beaujolais, where the wines at their best display to perfection the effects of terroir on a single grape, Gamay.

Recent geological studies have demonstrated that the underlying rock is the same volcanic schist or sandy granite as is found 60 miles (100km) south in Côte-Rôtie. But constant erosion has left a mosaic of different topsoils, aspects, and gradients so that wines can vary enormously even within a single Cru. However, some generalizations are possible.

The northernmost Cru, **St-Amour,** shares some limestone with its northern neighbours St-Véran and Pouilly-Fuissé. Its best wines combine minerality with fruit that is almost as seductive as its name. **Juliénas** is usually fuller-bodied and can be a little rustic, although Les Mouilles and Les Capitans are superior *lieux-dits*. **Chénas** lives in the shadow of **Moulin-à-Vent** and, similarly, needs time to blossom. Examples from the lower, flatter land in the far south of the Cru lack the complexity, ageability, and nobility of those grown on the best two sub-areas. One is near the windmill itself and consists of the *lieux-dits* Le Clos, Le Carquelin, Champ de Cour, and Les Thorins. The second is slightly above them and comprises La Rochelle, Rochegrès, and Les Vérillats.

Perhaps because of the name, a certain femininity is generally associated with **Fleurie**; rightly in the case of the sandy Chapelle des Bois, La Madone, and Les Quatre Vents. But Fleuries grown in more clayey vineyards such as La Roilette and Les Moriers, and in the particularly warm, south-facing Les Garrants and Poncié, can equal the best Moulin-à-Vent in body and longevity. **Chiroubles**, with very light, sandy soils, is the highest Cru. Its wines can be a little too tart in cooler vintages but can have enormous charm in sunny ones.

Morgon is the second-largest Cru, associated with its famous, volcanic Côte du Py, whose wines are particularly strong, warm, and spicy. Les Charmes, Les Grands Cras, Corcelette, and Château Gaillard vineyards give lighter and rounder wines. South of Morgon, in the very large **Brouilly** Cru, wines can vary enormously. Only those grown on the volcanic slopes of Mont Brouilly in the much smaller **Côte de Brouilly** Cru are really worth ageing. **Regnié** in the far west is rather like a Brouilly, or a superior Beaujolais-Villages. Prices reflect this.

—— —— ——		Département boundary
— — — —		Canton boundary
— · — · —		Commune (parish) boundary
MORGON		Limits of Beaujolais crus
■ CH THIVIN		Notable producer
		Vineyards
		Woods
═200═		Contour interval 20 metres

1:75,000

Km 0   1   2 Km
Miles 0   1   2 Miles

Chablis

For all its fame, Chablis is one of the wine world's most underestimated treasures. It is almost the sole survivor of what was once a vast wine-growing region: the main supplier to Paris, only 110 miles (180km) away to the northwest.

In the late 19th century its département, the Yonne, had 100,000 acres (40,000ha) of vines – many of them red – and fulfilled what was to become the role of the Midi. Chablis' waterways flowing into the River Seine were once thronged with wine-barges.

First phylloxera crushed, then the railways bypassed the wine-growers of the Yonne, leaving it one of France's poorest agricultural regions. The second half of the 20th century saw a great renaissance and a fresh justification for its renown, for Chablis is one of the great inimitable originals. Chardonnay responds to its cold terroir of limestone clay with flavours no one can reproduce in easier (or any other) wine-growing conditions – quite different even from those of the rest of Burgundy to the south. Chablis is hard but not harsh, reminiscent of stones and minerals, but at the same time of green hay; when it is young it actually looks green, which many wines are supposed to do.

Grand Cru Chablis, and even some of the best Premier Cru Chablis, tastes important, strong, almost immortal. And indeed, it does last a remarkably long time; a strange and delicious sort of sour taste enters into it when it reaches about 10 years of age, and its golden-green eye flashes meaningfully. Chablis fanatics know it can go through a less exciting wet-wool phase in middle age that can put others off. So much the worse for them.

Oysters and Chablis

Cool-climate vineyards need exceptional conditions to succeed. Chablis lies 100 miles (160km) north of Beaune – and is therefore nearer to Champagne than to the rest of Burgundy. Geology is its secret: the outcrop of the rim of a wide submerged basin of limestone and clay. The far rim, across the English Channel in Dorset, gives its name, Kimmeridge, to this unique pudding of prehistoric oyster-shells. Oysters and Chablis, it seems, have been related since creation. The hardy Chardonnay variety (sometimes known here as the Beaunois – the vine from Beaune) is Chablis' only vine. Where the slopes face the sun it ripens excellently.

Chablis and **Petit Chablis**, the much-expanded outlying area, are not the only appellations of the Yonne. **Irancy** and the village of Coulanges-la-Vineuse (Bourgogne Coulanges-la-Vineuse AOC) have long grown Pinot Noir to make light red burgundy. The Sauvignon Blanc grown around St-Bris-le-Vineux, unusual for this part of France, has its own appellation, **St-Bris**, while the

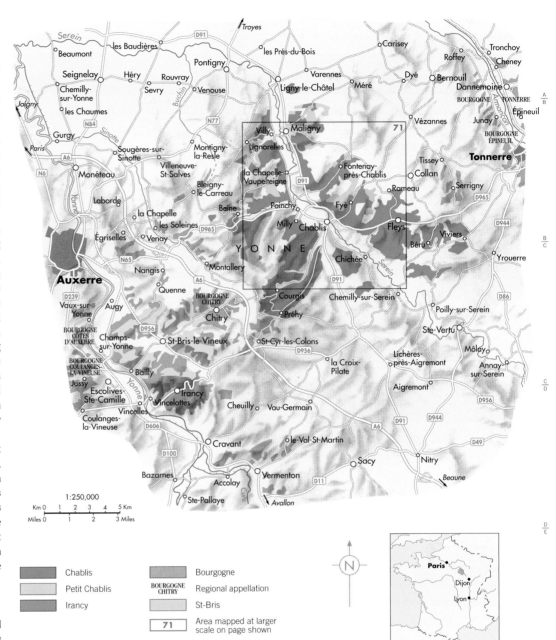

Chardonnay and Pinot Noir grown there is sold as **Bourgogne Côte d'Auxerre**, except for that around Chitry, which is labelled **Bourgogne Chitry**. The red wine grown west of Tonnerre is called **Bourgogne Epineuil**, while **Bourgogne Tonnerre** is white. Are such distinctions worthwhile? They do no harm.

THE YONNE

The département responsible for Chablis and the lesser, more recent appellations carries the name of the River Yonne in the west of the area mapped here, but it is the valley of the River Serein and its tributaries that define the Chablis vineyards. The fortunes of Chablis have always fluctuated enormously.

Map legend:
- Chablis
- Petit Chablis
- Irancy
- Bourgogne
- **BOURGOGNE CHITRY** Regional appellation
- St-Bris
- **71** Area mapped at larger scale on page shown

1:250,000

Wines such as these carrying the simple Chablis appellation are grown on land coloured dark green above, but outside the terroirs deemed propitious enough to produce Premier and Grand Cru Chablis that are mapped in detail overleaf.

Cold air drains reliably from most Grand Cru vines, but many Premier Cru vineyards are less propitiously sited. Spring frosts can seriously prejudice the crop of such an early-budding variety as Chardonnay. The calor gas in the cylinder on the left waits in readiness.

The Heart of Chablis

The classification of Chablis into four grades is one of the clearest demonstrations anywhere in the northern hemisphere of the importance of southern slopes. Grand Cru wines always taste richer than Premiers Crus, Premiers Crus than plain Chablis, and Chablis than Petit Chablis.

All seven Grands Crus lie in a single block looking south and west over the village and the river, their 257 acres (104ha) representing only 2% of the total Chablis vineyard area. In theory each of the seven has its own style. Many regard Les Clos and Vaudésir as best of all; certainly they tend to be the biggest in flavour. But more important is what all have in common: intense, highly charged flavour on the scale of the best whites of the Côte de Beaune but with more of a nervy edge – which, with age, leads to noble complexity. Grand Cru Chablis must be aged, ideally for 10 years, and many examples are still majestic at 20, 30, or even 40.

Les Clos is the biggest, with 64 acres (26ha), and best known; often also first in flavour, strength, and lasting power. Fine vintages of Les Clos can develop an almost Sauternes-like perfume in time. Les Preuses should be very ripe, round, and perhaps the least stony in character, while Blanchot and Grenouilles are usually highly aromatic. Valmur is some critics' ideal: rich and fragrant. Others prefer the definition and finesse of Vaudésir.

La Moutonne, a small plot straddling Vaudésir and Les Preuses, is not officially classified as a Grand Cru, although it certainly deserves to be, and the name can be found on labels. Bougros comes last in most accounts – but the hallmark of the producer is often more distinctive than that of the precise plot on this relatively homogeneous slope.

Chablis Premiers Crus

The number of named Premiers Crus has shrunk to 40, with the lesser-known ones having long since been discarded or permitted to go to market under the names of the dozen or so best known. The map opposite shows both the old names and the new ones that are now in common use. These Premiers Crus vary considerably in exposure and gradient; certainly those on the north bank of the River Serein, flanking the Grands Crus to the northwest (La Fourchaume, for example) and east (Montée de Tonnerre and Mont de Milieu), have the advantage. A Premier Cru Chablis will generally have at least half a degree of alcohol less than a Grand Cru, and be correspondingly less impressive and intense in scent and flavour. Nonetheless, it should still be a highly stylish wine and can last at least as long as a Premier Cru white from the Côte d'Or. Its principal fault these days is likely to be dilution as a result of over-production. It is, after all, an easy sell.

Conservatives credit the Chablis heartland's Kimmeridgian marl with unique properties; their opponents claim the same for the closely related Portlandian bedrock and clay that crops up much more widely in the area. The INAO has favoured the latter, allowing expansion of the Chablis vineyard to a total of more than 12,464 acres (5,044ha) by 2010. In 1960, there was more land dedicated to Premier Cru Chablis than straight Chablis. Today, although Premier Cru land has expanded considerably, more than four times as much vineyard is allowed to produce unqualified Chablis. The quantity made each year can vary enormously; Chablis vineyards are still perilously subject to frost damage.

Some say that quality has suffered as a result of this huge expansion. It remains, as it always will this far north, very uneven from year to year as well as variable (particularly in style) from grower to grower. Most growers today favour tank-fermented, unoaked wines. Some producers have shown that oak, especially well-used oak, can have special properties to offer some of their better wines.

Grand Cru Chablis, largely ignored by the world's fine-wine traders, remains even now half the price of Corton-Charlemagne. Parity would be closer to justice.

The vintage featured may be 2009 but Chablis is the one Burgundian appellation not flattered by such a ripe year. High natural acidity is a distinct advantage in white wines capable of such long ageing. Top Chablis Grand Cru such as the one from Les Clos can last decades.

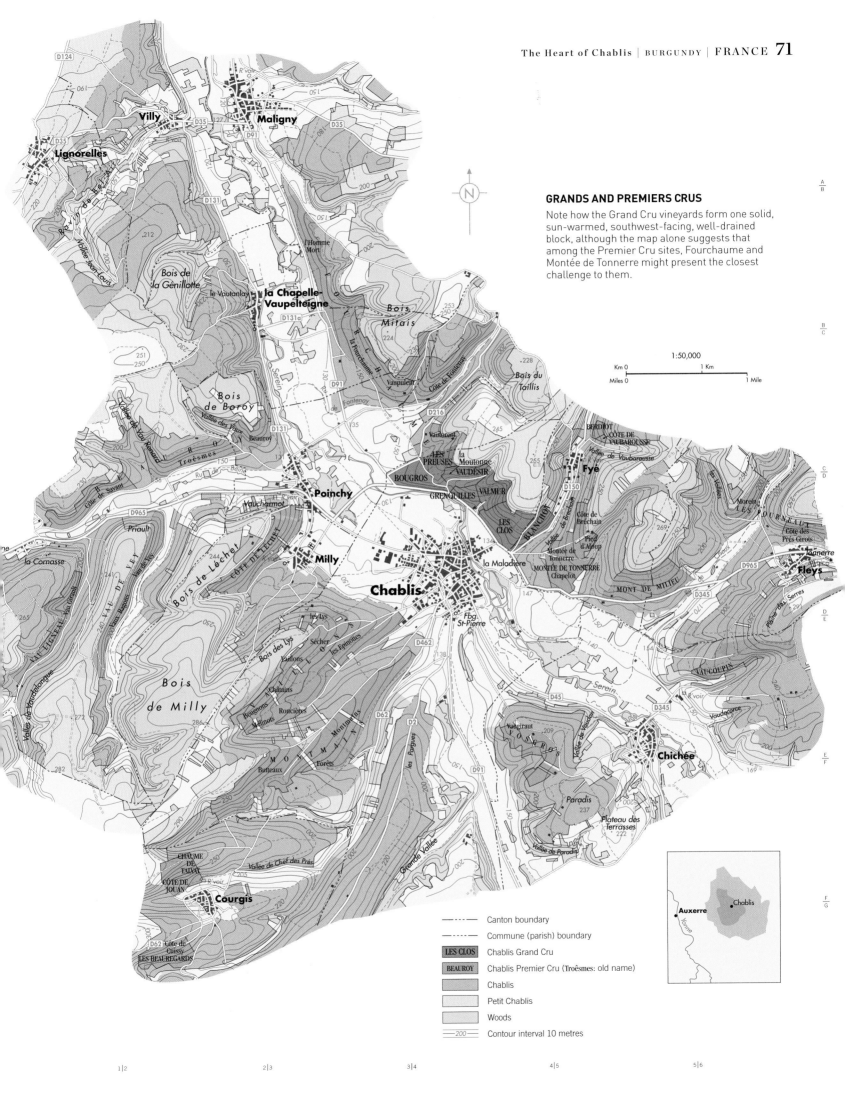

GRANDS AND PREMIERS CRUS

Note how the Grand Cru vineyards form one solid, sun-warmed, southwest-facing, well-drained block, although the map alone suggests that among the Premier Cru sites, Fourchaume and Montée de Tonnerre might present the closest challenge to them.

1:50,000

| Km 0 | | 1 Km |
| Miles 0 | | 1 Mile |

D124

Villy

Maligny

Lignorelles

Bois de la Génillotte

l'Homme Mort

la Chapelle-Vaupelteigne

Bois Mitais

Bois du Taillis

Bois de Boroy

Beauroy

Vallée des Vaux

Vaupulent

Côte de Fontenay

BERDIOT

CÔTE DE VAUBAROUSSE

Vallée de Vaubarousse

Vaubvent

LES PREUSES

la Moutonne

VAUDÉSIR

BOUGROS

GRENOUILLES

VALMUR

Fyé

Poinchy

Vaucharmot

Priault

la Cornasse

Côte de Savant

LES CLOS

BLANCHOT

Côte de Bréchain

Pied d'Aloup

MONTÉE DE TONNERRE

Chapelot

Tonnerre

Fleys

Milly

Bois de Léchet

CÔTE DE LÉCHET

la Maladière

Fbg. St-Pierre

MONT DE MILIEU

Chablis

les Lys

Bois des Lys

Sécher

les Epinottes

Vaillons

Châtains

Beagnons

Roncières

Mélinots

Bois de Milly

MONTMAINS

Forêts

Butteaux

les Pargues

Serein

VAUCOUPIN

Vaudecorce

Vaugiraut

VOSGROS

Chichée

Paradis

Plateau des Terrasses

Vallée de Paradis

CHAUME DE TALVAT

CÔTE DE JOUAN

Vallée de Chef des Prés

Grande Vallée

Courgis

Côte de Cuissy

LES BEAUREGARDS

Auxerre

Chablis

Yonne

–·–·–·–		Canton boundary
– – – –		Commune (parish) boundary
LES CLOS		Chablis Grand Cru
BEAUROY		Chablis Premier Cru (Troêsmes: old name)
		Chablis
		Petit Chablis
		Woods
—200—		Contour interval 10 metres

Champagne

To be champagne, a wine must do more than sparkle. It must come from the Champagne region in northeast France. This is a basic tenet of wine law in France, throughout Europe and now, thanks to tenacious negotiation, in much of the rest of the world.

It would be claiming far too much to say that all champagne is better than any other sparkling wine. But the best champagne has a combination of freshness, richness, delicacy, and raciness, and a gently stimulating nuance that no sparkling wine from anywhere else has yet achieved.

Part of Champagne's secret lies in its combination of latitude and precise position. The latitude in the key facts panel opposite is higher than for any other wine region in this Atlas (except for England – whose best sparkling wines are fair copies of champagne). Even before global warming brought a not – always – welcome decrease in average acidity, Champagne's proximity to the sea has always helped to ripen grapes this far from the equator.

Champagne, whose soil and climate have so much to offer, is only 90 miles (145km) northeast of Paris, centred on a small range of hills rising from a plain of chalk and carved in two by the River Marne. The map overleaf shows Champagne's heart, but the whole region is much more extensive. The Marne département still produces more than two-thirds of all champagne, but there are vineyards in the Aube to the south that specialize in vigorous, fruity, distinctive Pinot Noir (about 22% of the region's total), and the mainly Pinot Meunier vineyards on the banks of the River Marne extend westwards well into the Aisne département (about 9%).

Planned extension

Demand for champagne is higher than ever and, as all of Champagne's 84,000 acres (34,000ha) are planted, the authorities are examining a proposal to include 40 new villages in the appellation, although new areas would not be planted until at least 2017. Among existing plantings, only 10% of this precious vineyard belongs to the large exporting houses responsible for the worldwide reputation of champagne; they tend to blend ingredients from all over the region to produce their wines. The rest is owned by more than 19,000 owner-growers, many of whom are part-time.

More and more of these growers, well over 2,000 at the last count, are making and selling their own wine rather than selling grapes to the "maisons", although they sometimes do that as well. The growers' champagnes, which are increasingly highly regarded, now account for almost a quarter of all sales. Just over a tenth of all champagne is put on the market by one of the co-operatives established in Champagne's dog days in the early 20th century. But the champagne market is still dominated by the famous names, the big houses of Reims and Epernay – together with a few, such as Bollinger of Aÿ, based outside the two Champagne towns.

Because it is obviously so successful here, the champagne recipe has been much copied. Take Pinot Noir, Pinot Meunier, and Chardonnay grapes and apply a kid-glove process now called the "traditional method" (the Champenois having objected even to the world's admiring use of the old term "champagne method").

The grapes are pressed, in four-ton lots, so gently that the juice is very pale, even from the dark-skinned Pinots Noir and Meunier, and only a precisely prescribed amount of juice from each lot may be used for champagne. (Most of the increasingly popular rosé champagne is made by deliberately adding some red wine to the white.)

The juice ferments lustily at first. In the past it slowed down, the doors would be thrown open to let in the autumnal chill and fermentation stopped. The wine spent a chilly winter, still with the potential of more fermentation latent in it.

So it used to be shipped. England in the 17th century was an eager customer for barrels of this delicate, rather sharp wine. The English bottled it on arrival, in bottles that were stronger than any known in France. It re-fermented in spring, the corks went pop and the *beau monde* found that they had created a sparkling wine. Whether or not it was the English who did it first (and the inhabitants of Limoux claim to have made the first brut sparkling wine in the 16th century), premature bottling was vital to the process that changed Paris's favourite local wine into a prima donna.

For the wine continued to ferment in the bottle and the gas given off by the fermentation dissolved in the wine. If the natural effect was

Champagne styles vary from the challenging concentration of a Krug or a Bollinger to the seductive creaminess of a Dom Pérignon, with Pol Roger and Louis Roederer as models of classical balance. Among growers, Egly-Ouriet, Jacques Selosse, and Larmandier-Bernier are leading a movement towards champagnes with more vinous and vintage expression, and even Krug now admits publicly that consistency is not the point of its flagship multi-vintage Grande Cuvée blend.

encouraged by adding a little sugar and a little more yeast, what had been a pretty but very light wine was found to improve immeasurably, gaining strength and character over a period of two years or more. Above all, the inexhaustible bubbles gave it a miraculous liveliness. Today, sugar and yeast are added to the fully fermented dry wine so that a second fermentation takes place in the bottle.

The chief difference between champagne brands lies in the making of the cuvée, as the blend of dry base wines is called. Everything depends on experience in assembling the young wines – which are sometimes deepened by a dose of older, reserve wine – and on how much the house is prepared to spend on raw materials. As described overleaf, the quality and character of vineyards even in the heart of Champagne vary considerably.

Another crucial ingredient in champagne quality is the length of time the producer leaves the wine on the lees of the second fermentation in bottle. The longer the better, and certainly longer than the mandatory minimum of 15 months for non-vintage and three years for vintage champagne, for it is contact with this sediment as much as anything that gives champagne its subtle flavour. The reputation of an established house is based on its non-vintage wines, most blended so that no difference is noticeable from year to year.

The industrialization of champagne began with the widow Clicquot in the early 19th century. Her achievement was a way of cleaning the wine of its sediment without losing the bubbles, which involved *remuage*, literally shaking by hand the sediment on to the cork in gradually upended bottles. Today this is done mechanically in large computer-controlled pallets. The neck of the bottle is then frozen, a plug of murky ice shoots out when the bottle is opened, leaving perfectly clear wine behind to be topped up by wine with varying dosages of sweetness. The trend in the region today, however, is for wines of lower dosage, and sometimes even none at all.

— - — Département boundary

——— Limit of Champagne appellation

Wine-producing areas

75 Area mapped at larger scale on page shown

▼ Weather station (WS)

1:1,000,000

Km 0   10   20   30   40 Km
Miles 0   10   20 Miles

THE CHAMPAGNE APPELLATION

The contrast between the limit of the Champagne appellation and the area currently planted shows just what theoretical possibilities there are for extending the valuable right to own some of the most expensive vineyard land in the world. Up to 40 villages may eventually be added to the roster.

A crucial part of the champagne-making process is the delicacy with which the juice is squeezed out of the grapes, preferably with a traditional wooden basket press. Juice, pale and untinted even by black skins, runs out between the slats into a tray below.

CHAMPAGNE: REIMS ▼

Latitude / Altitude of WS
49.31° / 298ft (91m)

Average growing season temperature at WS
58.4°F (14.7°C)

Average annual rainfall at WS
24.7in (628mm)

Harvest month rainfall at WS
September: 1.9in (49mm)

Chief viticultural hazards
Spring frost, fungal disease

Principal grapes
Pinot Noir, Pinot Meunier, Chardonnay

It is safe to assume that these colourful spring crops are planted on land not classified for champagne production on the slopes around the evocatively named village of Bouzy on the "Montagne" de Reims.

The Heart of Champagne

What lies beneath the vines is Champagne's trump card. Chalk is a soft rock that can easily be hewn into cellars. It also retains moisture and acts as a perfectly regulated vine humidifier while actually warming the soil. And it produces grapes rich in nitrogen – which in turn encourages the activity of yeasts. Today three grapes dominate. Meaty Pinot Noir is most planted (39% of the vineyards), having overtaken Pinot Meunier, a sort of country cousin that is easier to grow and ripen, obviously fruity but not so fine. Plantings of fresh-flavoured, potentially creamy Chardonnay have also increased, to 28% of the total.

Slight variations of slope and aspect are crucial. The Montagne de Reims, the wooded "mountain" of the city where France's kings were crowned, is planted with Pinot Noir and, to a lesser extent, Pinot Meunier. Pinot vines planted on such north-facing slopes as those of Verzenay and Verzy produce base wines notably more acidic and less powerful than those grown on the warmer, more propitious southern flanks of the "mountain" at Aÿ, but can bring a refined, laser-etched delicacy to a blend. Montagne wines contribute to the bouquet, the headiness, and, with their firm acidity, the backbone of the blend.

The village of Bouzy, whose lower slopes can be too productive for top-quality champagne, is famous with English-speakers for obvious reasons, but also because a small quantity of still red wine is made there. Red is essential for tinting champagne rosé (and magically increasing its perceived value). The comparatively tart still wines of the Champagne region – mostly light reds but occasionally whites – are sold under the appellation Coteaux Champenois.

The Vallée de la Marne in the west has a succession of south-facing slopes that catch the sun and make these the fullest, roundest, and ripest wines, with plenty of aroma. These too are predominantly black-grape vineyards, famous for Pinot Noir in the best-exposed sites but with Pinot Meunier and, increasingly, Chardonnay planted elsewhere.

The east-facing slope south of Epernay (topographically not unlike the Côte de Beaune) is the Côte des Blancs, planted with Chardonnay that gives freshness and finesse to a blend. Cramant, Avize, and Le Mesnil are three villages with long-respected names for their wines. (The Côte de Sézanne is effectively a slightly less distinguished extension of the Côte des Blancs.)

Champagne's classification system
These (and all Champagne-appellation) villages are classified in a ranking known as the *échelle* (ladder) *des crus*, which gives the grapes of every commune a percentage rating. Until this century an indicative grape price was agreed for the harvest as a whole. A grower in one of the Grand Cru communes would be paid 100% of the price. Premiers Crus would receive between 99% and 90%, according to their place on the ladder, and so on down to 80% for some of the outlying areas. Now the grape price is agreed on an individual basis between the grower and the producer, although the vineyard ratings may still apply – and some would like to see the ratings revised to distinguish more precisely between different vineyards' potential.

Among champagnes made from region-wide blends, super-luxury "prestige" brands such as Dom Pérignon, Roederer Cristal, Krug, Salon, Perrier-Jouët's Belle Epoque, and Taittinger's Comtes de Champagne naturally have the highest average *échelle* rating in their constituent wines. Growers' champagnes, on the other hand, can often be blended exclusively from several Grand and Premier Cru villages, or can even come from a single village or vineyard. Krug and Bollinger have long been exponents of fermenting their base wines in oak. An increasing number of other producers, including many of the more ambitious growers, are following suit. The resulting wines invariably need bottle-age. Of all wines top champagnes are aged longest before release – up to 10 years. It is a crime to chill them and swill them. The cheapest champagnes have little to offer at any stage.

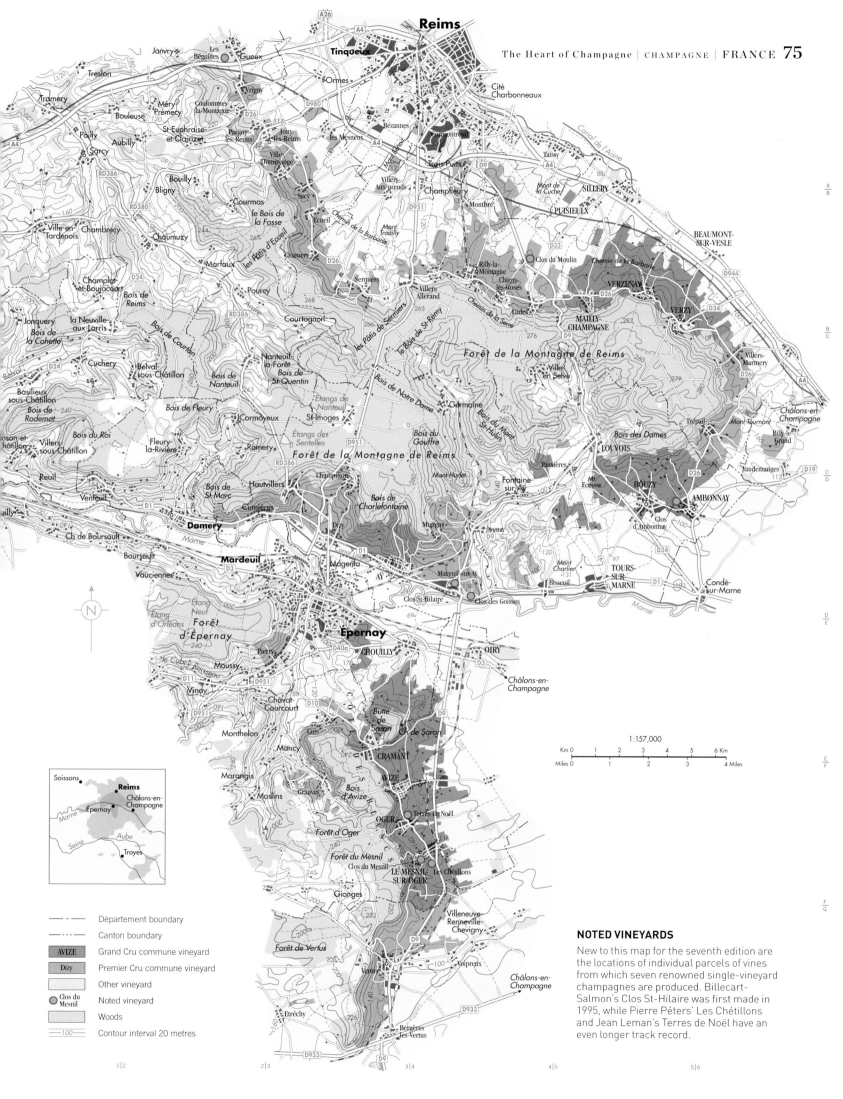

NOTED VINEYARDS

New to this map for the seventh edition are the locations of individual parcels of vines from which seven renowned single-vineyard champagnes are produced. Billecart-Salmon's Clos St-Hilaire was first made in 1995, while Pierre Péters' Les Chétillons and Jean Leman's Terres de Noël have an even longer track record.

Legend

- - - - Département boundary
- - - - Canton boundary
AVIZE — Grand Cru commune vineyard
Dizy — Premier Cru commune vineyard
□ — Other vineyard
○ Clos du Mesnil — Noted vineyard
— Woods
≈100≈ — Contour interval 20 metres

Scale 1:157,000
Km 0 1 2 3 4 5 6 Km
Miles 0 1 2 3 4 Miles

Bordeaux

If Burgundy's appeal is unashamedly sensual, Bordeaux's is more cerebral and, increasingly, financial. On the one hand is the nature of the wine itself: at its best indescribably subtle in nuance and complexity. On the other is the sheer intellectual challenge of so many estates, or châteaux as they are called here, in so many regions and subregions – and the way in which fine Bordeaux has, regrettably but inescapably, become a trading commodity. It has always been a status symbol; suddenly a whole new market is seeking status. The result? An alarming increase in the premium on the most famous names – which tend to come from the most favoured spots on the maps that follow. Nowhere else in the wine world is the link between geography and finance so evident.

Bordeaux is the largest fine-wine district on earth. The whole département of the Gironde, named after its most important estuary, is dedicated to wine-growing. All of its wine has the right to the name of Bordeaux. Its production, about 6 million hectolitres a year, dwarfs that of all French regions except for the vast Languedoc-Roussillon. Red wines outnumber white by nine to one.

The great red wine areas are the Médoc, north of the city of Bordeaux, and to the south the best of the Graves, Pessac-Léognan, on the west bank of the Garonne. These are the so-called "left bank" wines. The "right bank" consists of St-Emilion and Pomerol and their immediate neighbours along the north bank of the Dordogne. The country between the two rivers is called Entre-Deux-Mers, a name found only on bottles of its dry white wines, although this region also makes three-quarters of all the red wine sold as AC Bordeaux and Bordeaux Supérieur. In the far south of the map opposite lies Bordeaux's centre of sweet white wine production.

In 2008 Cadillac Côtes de Bordeaux replaced Premières Côtes de Bordeaux as the denomination for red wines produced in the narrow, river-hugging zone on the right bank of the Garonne, southeast of the city. Three other right bank appellations also had a change of name (see p.92). Some of the fringe appellations mapped, such as Ste-Foy-Bordeaux and Côtes de Bordeaux-St-Macaire, are rarely seen, but fine wines carrying the northern right bank appellations Côtes de Bourg and Blaye Côtes de Bordeaux (some good whites) are increasingly common, with the simple appellation Blaye usually signifying particularly ambitious reds.

Bordeaux's great glories are its finest red wines (the world's archetypes for blends of Cabernet and Merlot), the tiny production of very sweet, golden Sauternes which can live even longer, and some unique dry whites made in the Graves. But not all Bordeaux is glorious; the vineyard is still too big (272,300 acres/110,200ha). Vines have been pulled out since the optimistic years at the beginning of the 21st century, but not nearly enough. The most favoured areas, for the reasons outlined overleaf, produce some of the world's greatest wines and command some of the world's highest prices. In less glamorous areas, however, are far too many vine-growers without the means, incentive, will or, in some cases, the physical ability to produce interesting wine.

The marginality of Bordeaux's climate means that in some years basic red Bordeaux looks a very puny thing alongside the Cabernets so reliably ripened in much of the New World. The straight Bordeaux appellation, which is applied to more red wine than the total South African or German vintage each year, too rarely upholds the glory of this world-famous region. After much debate on how to solve this problem, including the uprooting of less favoured vineyards, a Vin de Pays de l'Atlantique (now IGP) was created in 2006 for wine in all three colours. Another solution, which in the long term could have greater appeal, is the declassification of wines to Vin de France (formerly Vin de Table) status with no more than a mention of grape variety and/or vintage. Unsurprisingly, farmers would still rather call their wine Bordeaux.

Bordeaux's appellations

Compared with Burgundy the system of appellations in Bordeaux is simple. The map opposite shows them all. Within them it is the wine châteaux (sometimes grand estates, sometimes no more than a smallholding with cellar attached) that look after their own identification problem. On the other hand there is a form of vineyard classification by quality built into the system in Burgundy that is missing in Bordeaux. Here, in its place, is a variety of local château classifications, unfortunately without a common standard.

By far the most famous is the classification of the wines of the châteaux of the Médoc – plus Château Haut-Brion of Graves and Sauternes – which was finalized in 1855, based on their value as assessed by Bordeaux brokers at the time. Its first, second, third, fourth, and fifth "growths", or crus, represent the most ambitious grading of agricultural produce ever attempted.

It succeeded in identifying the soils with the highest potential, as the following pages detail. Where present standards depart from it there is

Silvio Denz bought Château Faugères in 2005 and commissioned this decidedly unusual winery by his fellow countryman, the Swiss architect Mario Botta.

usually an explanation (an industrious proprietor in 1855 and a lazy one now, or, much more likely nowadays, vice versa). Even more to the point, in most cases land has been added or exchanged; the vineyard is not precisely the same. The vineyards of a château rarely surround it in a neat plot. More often by now they are scattered and intermingled with those of their neighbours. They can produce annually anything from 10 to 1,000 barrels of wine, each holding the rough equivalent of 300 bottles, or 25 cases. The best vineyards make a maximum of 5,000 litres from each hectare of vines, the less good ones considerably more (see panel overleaf).

The super-luxury first-growths, which can easily make as many as 150,000 bottles of their principal wine, or *grand vin*, as opposed to a second or even third wine, traditionally fetch at least twice the price of the second growths – and three times as much was asked for the lauded 2009 and 2010 vintages. But thereafter a fifth growth may fetch more, for example, than a second if it is better run. The system adopted on the maps that appear on the following pages is simply to distinguish between classed growths (in areas where they exist) and the vineyards that surround them.

One notable development at the end of the 20th century was the emergence, particularly on the right bank, of *microcuvées* – wines made by *garagistes*, so-called because their production of a few hundred cases a year is small enough to be vinified in a garage. With the exception of the prototypes Le Pin of Pomerol and Château Valandraud of St-Emilion, few of these *microcuvées* have established a durable market and reputation – a fact that does not seem to have discouraged anyone from trying.

Of greater long-term significance for the region is the vast improvement in viticultural practices that has been effected since the mid-1990s. Far more producers nowadays are able to harvest fully ripe grapes, not just because of climate change, but thanks to stricter pruning throughout the year, higher trellising, more careful canopy management, and much more cautious use of agrochemicals.

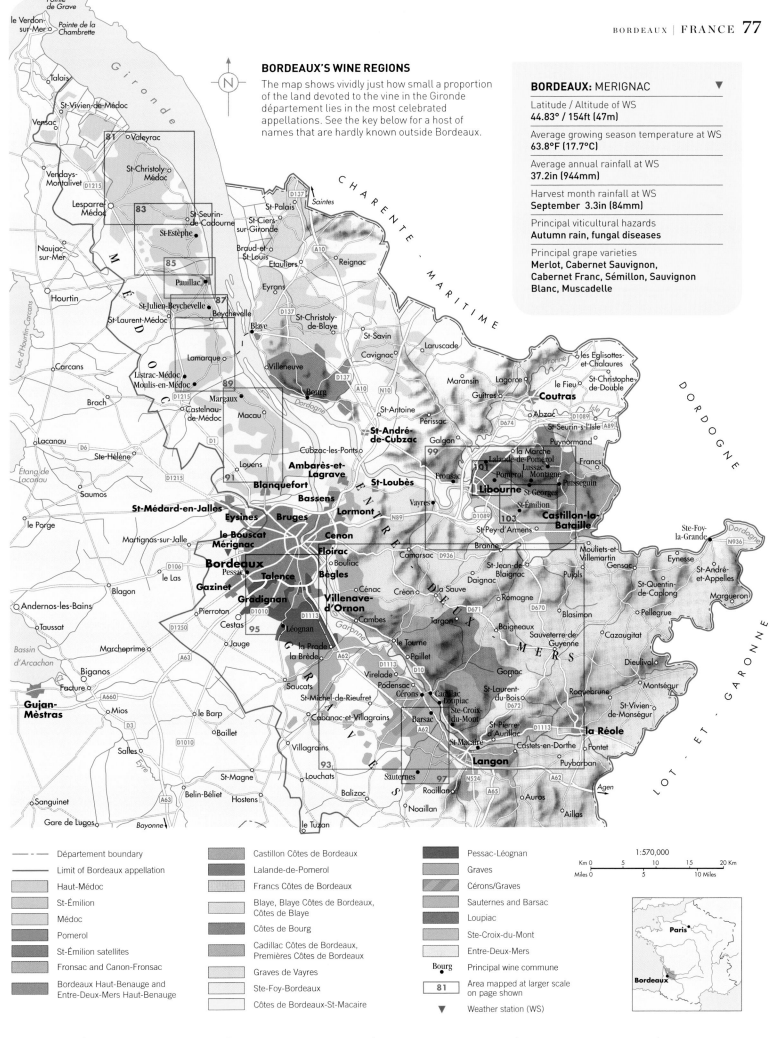

BORDEAUX'S WINE REGIONS

The map shows vividly just how small a proportion of the land devoted to the vine in the Gironde département lies in the most celebrated appellations. See the key below for a host of names that are hardly known outside Bordeaux.

BORDEAUX: MERIGNAC ▼

Latitude / Altitude of WS
44.83° / 154ft (47m)

Average growing season temperature at WS
63.8°F (17.7°C)

Average annual rainfall at WS
37.2in (944mm)

Harvest month rainfall at WS
September 3.3in (84mm)

Principal viticultural hazards
Autumn rain, fungal diseases

Principal grape varieties
Merlot, Cabernet Sauvignon, Cabernet Franc, Sémillon, Sauvignon Blanc, Muscadelle

---

Key:

- – · – · – Département boundary
- ——— Limit of Bordeaux appellation
- Haut-Médoc
- St-Émilion
- Médoc
- Pomerol
- St-Émilion satellites
- Fronsac and Canon-Fronsac
- Bordeaux Haut-Benauge and Entre-Deux-Mers Haut-Benauge
- Castillon Côtes de Bordeaux
- Lalande-de-Pomerol
- Francs Côtes de Bordeaux
- Blaye, Blaye Côtes de Bordeaux, Côtes de Blaye
- Côtes de Bourg
- Cadillac Côtes de Bordeaux, Premières Côtes de Bordeaux
- Graves de Vayres
- Ste-Foy-Bordeaux
- Côtes de Bordeaux-St-Macaire
- Pessac-Léognan
- Graves
- Cérons/Graves
- Sauternes and Barsac
- Loupiac
- Ste-Croix-du-Mont
- Entre-Deux-Mers
- **Bourg** Principal wine commune
- 81 Area mapped at larger scale on page shown
- ▼ Weather station (WS)

1:570,000
Km 0 — 5 — 10 — 15 — 20 Km
Miles 0 — 5 — 10 Miles

Bordeaux: The Quality Factors

The quality and quantity of wine the Bordeaux region produces each year may vary quite markedly, but as the world's biggest resource of fine wine, it clearly has some geographical advantages, outlined on the map opposite. The weather during flowering in June is variable, which is why the crop size varies too, but summers (and particularly autumns) are usually reliably warm and sunny. Average temperature is higher than in Burgundy – compare the statistics on p.77 and p.49 – which means that Bordeaux can successfully grow later-ripening grape varieties, as shown on p.77.

Because these grapes all flower at slightly different times, growing a mix of them provides château owners with some insurance against a few days of bad weather at the critical time in June – as in 2012 – and against a particularly cool autumn which may fail to coax Cabernet Sauvignon to its full ripeness.

It is a right bank tradition to favour the early ripening Merlot over Cabernet Sauvignon, which predominates in the warmer Médoc and Graves – one of the reasons that the two banks tend to produce such very different styles of wine.

But there are clearly marked differences in soil structure and soil type all over the Bordeaux region, however difficult it can be to identify a precise soil type with, say, first-growth quality (see the notes on the left of the map opposite). Even within one part of Bordeaux, the Médoc being perhaps the most intriguing example, the soil is said to "change at every step". And a look at the map on p.89 shows how one portion of it, between St-Julien and Margaux, is an exception to the streak of superlative wine quality that is the Haut-Médoc. The map on p.77 also suggests that there is something very special about the plateau of Pomerol and St-Emilion.

In very general terms Bordeaux soils have developed on either Tertiary or Quaternary geological deposits, the former generally giving way to clay or limestone soils, the latter made up of alluvial sandy gravels left in gentle mounds hundreds of thousands of years ago by melted glaciers from the Massif Central and the Pyrenees. These gravels, still fully exposed unlike the other gravels deposited in most of the rest of Southwest France, are most marked in the Graves (hence the name), Sauternes, which is effectively a continuation of it, and the Médoc.

Dr Gérard Séguin of the University of Bordeaux undertook some of the first key studies of how Bordeaux soils relate to wine quality. He studied the gravelly soils of the Médoc, where deep-rooted vines produce great wine because the gravels so carefully regulate the water supply. His most notable discovery was that a supply of moisture to the vine that was no more than moderate was much more important than the exact composition of the soil.

His successor, Cornelis van Leeuwen, has probed further and discovered that there is no absolute correlation between how deep the roots go and how good the wine is. Old vines plus deep gravels happen to be the perfect recipe in some parts of the Médoc – in Margaux for instance, where some vine roots penetrate as deep as 23ft (7m) – but in Pomerol vines seem perfectly capable of making great wine from vines that go less than 5ft (1.5m) into Petrus's heavy clays. The key factor for quality is the regulation of water supply: just slightly less than the vine wants.

One general observation about the relationship between soil and wine quality, especially marked in Bordeaux, is that the best sites stand out most clearly in lesser vintages and are able to maintain consistent quality.

PRODUCTION COSTS

The table below gives the most recent (2011) estimates of production costs in euros for a typical AOC Bordeaux (A), a typical Médoc château (B), and a classed growth (C). Much more new oak, for example, is used for C than B, and none for A. While A and B are machine-harvested (as nearly 90% of Bordeaux is these days), C's grapes are hand-picked and many more vineyard operations are undertaken, by hand, throughout the year. First growths may cost even more to run, but the rewards are even greater than for a so-called "super second".

Most Bordeaux properties are run on bank borrowings, typically a value of around €1.8 million per hectare for a top classed growth, which would be amortized over 15 years, with a fixed interest rate of about 4.5%. (It is often said, with justification, that the Crédit Agricole bank owns France's entire *vignoble*). This would add at least €100,000 per hectare each year to costs, and therefore almost €20 per bottle to the figure at the bottom of column C. And, of course, the costs in the table leave the wine unbottled, unmarketed, and untransported. Production costs look incredibly low compared with the selling price of a *grand vin*, even though this represents only a (generally diminishing) proportion of the wine sold by the château.

	A	B	C
Number of vines per ha	3,330	5,000	10,000
Harvest costs per ha	468	754	1,529
Total viticultural costs per ha	4,401	6,536	36,000
Average yield (hl per ha)	58	58	40
Total viticultural costs per hl	76	116	950
Barrel ageing	–	200	350
Total costs per hl	76	313	1,300
Total costs per bottle	0.57	2.35	9.8

Source: Cornelis van Leeuwen and Christian Seely

EVOLUTION OF WINE PRODUCTION IN BORDEAUX

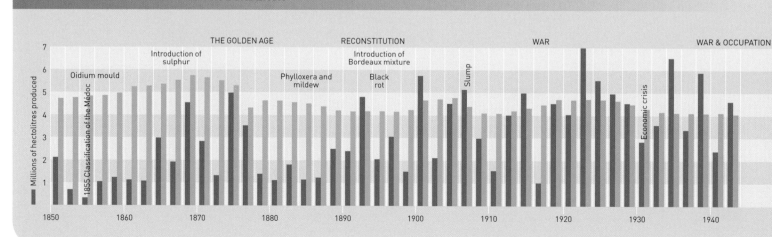

WHAT MAKES THE WINE

Some of the factors affecting the varying qualities and character of Bordeaux wine are shown in this diagram of the Gironde basin.

More clay further from river and downriver: coarser wines

Banks of gravel provide warm, well-drained soil for vines

First growths do not all share the same soil type: some have deep gravelly soils, others stony clay soils (Latour, Lafite), and even limestone soils (Margaux, Haut-Brion, Lafite)

Pine forests provide protection from strong salt winds and moderates rainfall

Soils of Pessac-Léognan are highly variable. Beside gravel, there are also various limestone soils and sandy soils. Good red and white wines. Highest rainfall in the Bordeaux area

Atlantic Ocean; influence means mild winters and warm summers, a moderate and stable climate with relatively few frosts severe enough to kill vines in winter or harm buds in spring

Drainage by river and stream: best growths have good drainage

River; helps to keep even temperature by day and night. This helps in reducing frost damage (as was shown in 1991)

Islands in the Gironde; more silt than gravel. Marginal wine production

Clay with limestone: average to good reds and average whites. Also a lot of sandy soil in Blaye on which good white wines are made

Flat river-silt land, locally called palus, no longer used for vineyards

Various gravelly soils, including clay, in Pomerol and the western part of St-Emilion

St-Emilion Côtes; limestone and clay on slopes: strong wines

Sandy ground by the river produces generally lighter wines

Mainly loamy soils with some gravelly soils and some limestone. Most wines produced in the Entre-Deux-Mers region are now red, sold as AOC Bordeaux

Bordeaux exports 1.77 million hectolitres of wine a year. It is increasingly surrounded by storage for maturing fine wine

Cadillac Côtes de Bordeaux, Premières Côtes de Bordeaux; clay on limestone subsoil: good white and red wines

Soils are markedly different in Sauternes and Barsac. In Barsac the soil is mostly shallow limestone; in Sauternes mostly gravelly soils, but also heavy clay soils, sometimes with a little limestone. Excellent sweet white wines with noble rot encouraged by mists off the Ciron

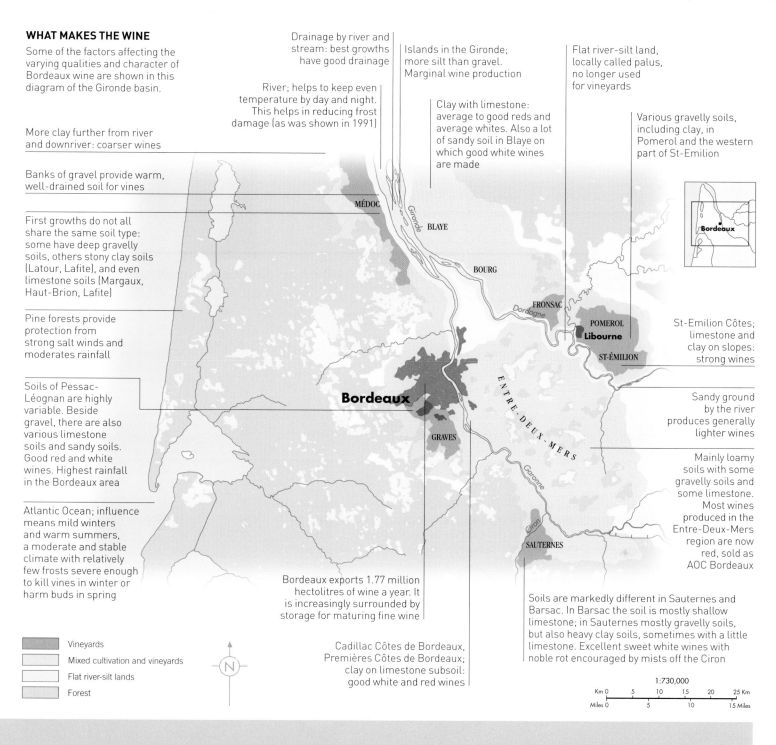

MÉDOC
Gironde
BLAYE
BOURG
FRONSAC
Dordogne
POMEROL
Libourne
ST-ÉMILION
Bordeaux
GRAVES
ENTRE-DEUX-MERS
Garonne
Ciron
SAUTERNES

Bordeaux

Vineyards
Mixed cultivation and vineyards
Flat river-silt lands
Forest

N

1:730,000
Km 0   5   10   15   20   25 Km
Miles 0   5   10   15 Miles

A|B B|C C|D D|E E|F F|G

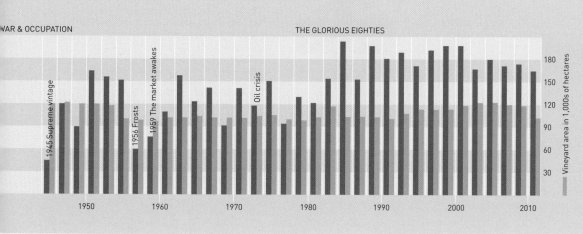

WAR & OCCUPATION

THE GLORIOUS EIGHTIES

1945 Supreme vintage
1956 Frosts
1959 The market awakes
Oil crisis

180
150
120
90
60
30

Vineyard area in 1,000s of hectares

1950   1960   1970   1980   1990   2000   2010

Bordeaux's vineyard area and wine production in relation to wars, pests, diseases, slumps, booms, and the weather are plotted here for every other (odd) year until 1987 by Philippe Roudié of Bordeaux University and since then using figures from the CIVB. Two great chemical aids, sulphur (against oidium mould) and Bordeaux mixture (copper sulphate and lime), against mildew had immediate effect. The 21st century has seen increasingly extreme weather but ever more skill in combating it.

Northern Médoc

Geographically, the Médoc is a great tongue of flat or barely undulating land isolated from the body of Aquitaine by the broad, brown estuary of the Gironde. In common usage its name is given to more fine wine than any other name in the world: Margaux, St-Julien, Pauillac, St-Estèphe, and their surrounding villages are all "Médoc" in location and in style.

But the appellation Médoc is both more limited and less prestigious. It is more clearly understood under its former name of Bas- (meaning lower) Médoc. The term *Bas* was dropped for reasons of – shall we say? – delicacy. But the fact remains. The lower Médoc, the tip of the tongue, the farthest reaches of the region, has none of the high points, either physically or gastronomically, of the Haut-Médoc to its south.

The well-drained dunes of gravel give way to lower, heavier, cooler, and more clay-dominated land north of St-Estèphe, with St-Seurin, the last commune of the Haut-Médoc, riding a characteristic hump between areas of channel-drained marsh. North and west of here is fertile, long-settled land, with the bustling market town of Lesparre as its capital since the days of English rule six centuries ago.

Until recently, vineyards took their place here with pasture, orchard, and woodland, but after an orgy of planting they have spread to cover almost all the higher ground where gravel lightens the clay, centring on the villages of St-Yzans, St-Christoly, Couquèques, By, and Valeyrac along the banks of the Gironde Estuary, and covering much of the interior in St-Germain-d'Esteuil, Ordonnac, Blaignan (Caussac), and (the biggest) Bégadan. Their vineyards total around 13,600 acres (5,500ha). In and around these villages are some of the Bordeaux producers who have been hardest-pressed, encouraged to invest in both vineyard and cellar by what seemed to be a buoyant market in the late 1990s, only to find that the market was really only interested in the more famous châteaux to the south.

There are no classed growths here, but there is the greatest concentration of the best of the rest and, in ripe vintages, some of the best value Bordeaux has to offer. Many of them are labelled Crus Bourgeois, a title awarded each year on the basis of tastings (see panel). Château Potensac, classified Cru Bourgeois Exceptionnel in 2003 but no longer part of the system, has the same perfectionist owners as Château Léoville Las Cases in St-Julien and is situated on the same slight plateau as La Cardonne and the well-run Tour Haut-Caussan. Other notable properties temporarily classified Crus Bourgeois Supérieurs in 2003 were the following Châteaux: Castéra at St-Germain; Loudenne, overlooking the Gironde near St-Yzans-de-Médoc; the well-distributed Greysac; reliable if light Patache d'Aux; generous Rolland de By; beguiling and consistent La Tour de By; enterprising Vieux Robin of Bégadan; Bournac and d'Escurac of Civrac-en-Médoc; Les Ormes Sorbet of Couquèques; and Les Grands Chênes of St-Christoly-Médoc.

But there are many other wines of note, such as Châteaux Preuillac, Haut-Condissas, and Laulan Ducos (one of the first Médoc properties to be Chinese-owned), and the defiantly modern Goulée blend developed by the team at Château Cos d'Estournel in St-Estèphe.

The clearest way to see the difference between Médocs Haut and Bas is to compare the career of a notable bourgeois château mapped here with one from one of the pages that follow. When young, there may be little to distinguish them: both are vigorous (like the vines on the rich soils of the Bas-Médoc), tannic, dry, and "très Bordeaux". At five years, though, the Haut-Médoc wine is finding that clean transparency of flavour that will go on developing. The Bas-Médoc has begun to soften, but remains a sturdy, rather rustic wine, often deep-coloured, satisfying and savoury rather than enlightening and inspiring. At 10 years of age there has been more softening, but usually at the expense of "structure": rarely the refining of character that we find further south.

Even a property as relatively lowly as Château Potensac benefits from a proportion of brand-new barrels each year. Bordeaux as a region is one of the best and most faithful customers for the world's coopers, so felicitous is the union between new French oak and young Cabernet and Merlot.

Some of the names that have managed to rise above the tide of anonymity and overproduction in the far north of the Médoc – a very long way from the glamour and commercial cut and thrust of the Bordeaux Place, the system on which all the most valuable deals are done.

CRU BOURGEOIS

In 2003 the Crus Bourgeois of the Médoc were officially reclassified, with 247 out of 490 candidates making the grade. These were accorded a hierarchy: Crus Bourgeois Exceptionnels (9), Crus Bourgeois Supérieurs (87), and Crus Bourgeois (151). However, a number of the excluded châteaux contested the decision (which was due to stand for 10 years) and after a lengthy wrangle through the French courts the classification was annulled. In its place a yearly certificate or label has since been adopted, administered by an independent body, Bureau Véritas. Producers from any of the Médoc appellations may apply and the wine evaluated by blind tasting roughly two years after the harvest. Failure to obtain the label one year does not compromise applications for subsequent vintages. The first vintage to be adjudged in this fashion was the 2008 (in 2010) with 243 châteaux awarded the Cru Bourgeois label. A number of well-known names were unattracted by the new system (which presently has no hierarchy) and withdrew from the selection process. These include the nine châteaux temporarily designated Crus Bourgeois Exceptionnels in 2003.

Canton boundary
Commune (parish) boundary
Ch Preuillac   Notable château or producer
Vineyards
Woods
20   Contour interval 10 metres

1:65,000

Km 0   1   2   3   4 Km
Miles 0   1   2 Miles

St-Vivien-de-Médoc
Janton
Cantelaude
Valeyrac
le Pointon
Sipian
Ch Sipian
l'Ardiley
Villoneuve
la Rivière
VALEYRAC
la Verdasse
le Moulin de la Verdasse
Troussas
Ch le Bourdieu
la Clède
Ch Loustenneuf
l'Oustau Neuf
Ch le Temple
Bois de Troussas
la Lagune
Ch Greysac
Ch la Clare
la Tour de By
Condissas
Ch Haut-Condissas
Port de By
le Peyrat
Courbian
Lassus
les Berlins
By
Ch Rollan de By
la Caussade
Ch Vieux Robin
BÉGADAN
Ch Bégadanet
Laujac
Canissac
les Cabans
Ch Laujac
St-Jean Cave Co-op
Ch la Tour St-Bonnet
Meillan
Mabouzat
Ch Patache d'Aux
la Lande
le Breuil
le Fourneau
le Basca
St-Christoly-Médoc
Nouret
le Bourdieu
Bégadan
Ch les Grands Chênes
ST-CHRISTOLY
le Sablona
Bois de Gombeau
les Bernedes
Ch Tour Blanche
le Sablonat
Castillon
Vivien-Médoc
Biars
Vieux Château Landon
la Tour
Ch les Ormes Sorbet
Basse Terre
Escurac (Haras)
Cazot
Trembleaux
la Lande
Couquèques
Mazails
la Pouyade
Déguenon
Cantérane
COUQUÈQUES
Lamena
CIVRAC
la Métairie
Civrac-en-Médoc
Ch Bournac
les Petites Granges
Queyzans
Andron
Ch d'Escurac
le Fourneau
ST-YZANS
Montignac
Co-op Agricole
Ch la Gorce
St-Brice Cave Vinic.
le Moulin
Taillanet
Badet
Prignac-en-Médoc
Bessan
la Pigotte
la Colonne
Uch
la Landette
Cantemerle
la Hourqueyre
St-Yzans-de-Médoc
St-Vivien-de-Médoc
Ch la Tour Prignac
BLAIGNAN
Ch Loudenne
Gelade
le Moulin d'Uch
Ch Tour Haut-Caussan
Caussan
Ch Grivière
Moulin de Courrian
Ch Blaignan
PRIGNAC
Co-op Vinic.
Peyressan
Centre Comm.
la Gravette
Ch Chantelys
l'Inclassable
Romefort
ORDONNAC
Coulon
Gautheys
Ch la Cardonne
Fontaine
l'Abbaye de l'Île
St-Seurin-de-Cadourne
Lesparre-Médoc
Ch Preuillac
Ch Potensac
Ordonnac
St-Trélody
Potensac
Plautignan
Ch Vernons
Cave Co-op. Vinic. Bellevue
Lussan
Palus de tussac
urtin Petit Bosq
les Marceaux
l'Hôpital
Barbehère
Raynaud
Fangrouse
le Gay
Marque
Ste-Marie
Ch d'Escot
Hourbit
Loquey
Couloumey
Ch Castéra
Boyentran
St-Seurin-de-Cadourne
Planque
Canquillac
Garraméy
St-Germain-d'Esteuil
Senillac
Caillou
Roque
ST-SEURIN
Bénet
Laguneaussan
Barbannes
Bayron
Ch Livran
Cassan
Doyac
Plassan
Brion
le Trale
Lucbeit
Miqueu
Palus de Doyac
LESPARRE
AU-DIGNAC-ET-LOIRAC
la Matte de Valeyrac
Chenal de Guy
Petit Chenal de Guy
Chenal de Troussas
Grand Chenal de By
Grande Palu de By
Petite Palu de By
Gironde
la Banche
Brie
Rillet
Lagunas
Artiguillon
Liard
St-Laurent-Médoc
ST-GERMAIN-D'ESTEUIL
Peyres
Chenal de la Calupeyré
VERTHEUIL
Chenal de la Maréchale
Estey d'Un

A/B
B/C
C/D
D/E
E/F
F/G

Lesparre-Médoc
MÉDOC
Blaye
Bordeaux

St-Estèphe

The gravel banks that give the Haut-Médoc and its wines their character and quality, stretching along the shore of the Gironde, sheltered from the ocean to the west by forest, begin to peter out at St-Estèphe. It is the northernmost of the four famous communes that are the heart of the Médoc. A *jalle* – the Médoc word for a stream – divides it from Pauillac, draining on the one hand the vineyards of Château Lafite, on the other three of the five classed growths of St-Estèphe: Châteaux Cos d'Estournel, Cos Labory, and Lafon-Rochet.

There is a distinction between the soils of St-Estèphe and Pauillac to the south; as the gravel washed down the Gironde diminishes, there is more clay. Higher up in Margaux there is very little. In St-Estèphe the soil is heavier and it drains more slowly. This is why vines grown in St-Estèphe seem to withstand particularly hot, dry summers, such as those of 2003 and 2010, better than those in the well-drained gravels to the south. Even in less extreme weather the wines tend to have more acidity, are fuller and more solid, and often have less perfume – but they fill your mouth with flavour. They have traditionally been sturdy clarets which can become venerable without losing vigour. In recent years, however, the general tendency to make red Bordeaux to the same bigger, bolder model has had the effect of blurring some of the differences between St-Estèphe and wines from other communes.

Strong, dark, and long-lived

Cos d'Estournel is the most spectacular of the classed growths, crowning the steep slope up from the Pauillac boundary, overlooking the meadows of Château Lafite. It has an eccentric Chinese-pagoda'd edifice, now home to a cutting-edge, high-tech winery and tasting hall reminiscent of a particularly luxurious Asian hotel lobby. Together with Château Montrose, Cos d'Estournel makes the biggest and best of the St-Estèphes: strong wines with a dark colour and a long life. "Cos", as it is nearly always called (with the S pronounced), has particular power and succulence, partly perhaps because of a high proportion of Merlot in the vineyard but also because of marked determination at its helm. The situation of Montrose on its gravel mound overlooking the Gironde anticipates that of Latour in Pauillac to the south. Some find a similar echo in its intense, tannic, deeply flavoured wine. Classic Montrose vintages take 20 years to mature, although since 2006 new ownership, new management, and vineyard expansion are making their presence felt.

Of the other two classed growths near Cos d'Estournel, Château Cos Labory often seems content to be full of fruity flavour at a fairly young age. Lafon-Rochet, revamped in the 1960s by Guy Tesseron, a cognac merchant, was the first of many Médoc châteaux to be rebuilt in the 20th century and now makes particularly reliable wines. Calon Ségur, north of the village of St-Estèphe and the northernmost classed-growth of the Médoc, is as solid as any St-Estèphe, but has gained in purity, consistency, and finesse in the new millennium. Some 250 years ago the Marquis de Ségur, owner of both Lafite and Latour, reputedly said his heart was at Calon. It still is, on the label (see below). The property was sold to a French insurance company in 2012.

Above all, St-Estèphe has been known for its Crus Bourgeois (see panel on p.80), which were temporarily reclassified as Exceptionnels, Supérieurs, and straight Crus Bourgeois in 2003. No fewer than four of the nine Exceptionnels are on the plateau south and west of the village. Châteaux Phélan Ségur and de Pez are both outstanding producers of very fine wine. Pez, now owned by the same champagne house as Pichon-Lalande in Pauillac (see p.84), has an extraordinary historical record: as the property of the Pontacs of Haut-Brion, its wine was sold as Pontac in London in the 17th century – possibly before any other growth of the Médoc. Neighbour Château Les Ormes de Pez, far from the only Bordeaux château to double as a small hotel, benefits from the same strong management as Château Lynch-Bages in Pauillac, while Château Haut-Marbuzet to the southeast between Montrose and Cos d'Estournel is known for seductive and oaky wine.

Among the dozen properties classified in 2003 as Crus Bourgeois Supérieurs (more than any other commune), Château Meyney is unusual in the Médoc for having monastic origins. Its situation by the river, neighbour to Montrose, might make one look for finer wine with more potential for development. In practice it is sturdy and often good value, just like châteaux Beau-Site, Le Boscq, Chambert-Marbuzet (under the same ownership as Haut-Marbuzet), Clauzet, Le Crock, La Haye, Lilian Ladouys, Petit Bocq, Tour de Marbuzet, Tour de Pez, and Tronquoy-Lalande (now part of the Montrose stable) – all making wines that demonstrate the commune's solid virtues but are usually ready to drink much sooner than the classed growths.

To the north of St-Estèphe the gravel bank diminishes to a promontory sticking out of the palus – the flat, river-silted land beside the estuary on which no wine of quality grows.

On top of the promontory, in the little village of St-Seurin-de-Cadourne, a cluster of notable wines are made: the gentle, Merlot-based Château Coufran, the more tannic Château Verdignan, the sometimes admirable Château Bel Orme Tronquoy de Lalande, and, most notable of all, on a classic mound near the river, Château Sociando-Mallet, whose flamboyantly ambitious wines have been known to beat first growths in blind tastings. The owner has always operated outside the Cru Bourgeois system.

North of St-Seurin is the end of the Haut-Médoc. Any wine grown beyond that point qualifies for the appellation Médoc, plain and simple (see p.80).

West of St-Estèphe, further from the river, Cissac and Vertheuil lie on stronger and less gravelly soil at the forest's edge. Château Cissac is the outstanding growth: for long vigorous enough to be a Pauillac, although, like so many red Bordeaux, especially here, it has been deliberately softened since the early 1990s.

There were changes in ownership and direction in each of the top three St-Estèphe properties, Châteaux Montrose, Calon Ségur, and Cos d'Estournel, in the early years of the 21st century, while little changed at Jean Gautreau's honorary St-Estèphe Château Sociando-Mallet.

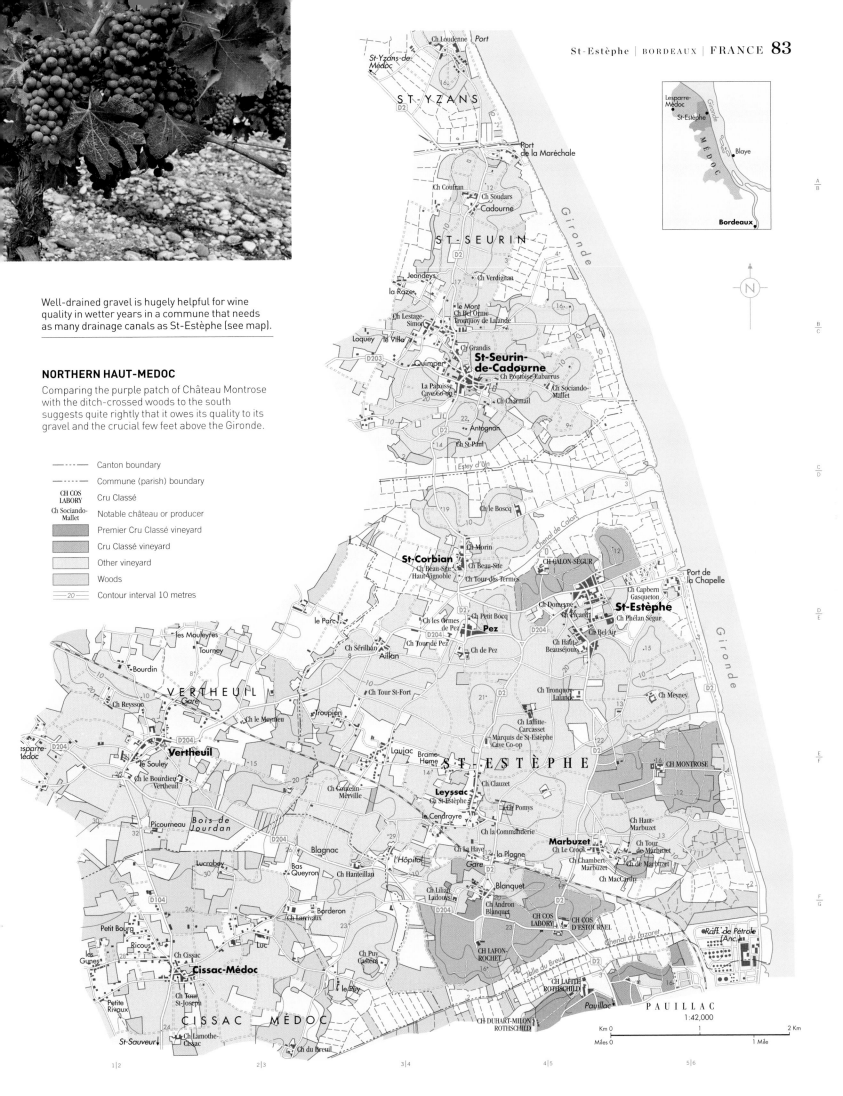

Well-drained gravel is hugely helpful for wine
quality in wetter years in a commune that needs
as many drainage canals as St-Estèphe (see map).

NORTHERN HAUT-MÉDOC

Comparing the purple patch of Château Montrose
with the ditch-crossed woods to the south
suggests quite rightly that it owes its quality to its
gravel and the crucial few feet above the Gironde.

–·–·–	Canton boundary
–·–·–	Commune (parish) boundary
CH COS LABORY	Cru Classé
Ch Sociando-Mallet	Notable château or producer
▧	Premier Cru Classé vineyard
▧	Cru Classé vineyard
▧	Other vineyard
▧	Woods
—20—	Contour interval 10 metres

Map labels

Ch Loudenne
Port
St-Yzans-de-Médoc
ST-YZANS
D2
Port de la Maréchale
Ch Coufran
Ch Soudars
Cadourne
ST-SEURIN
D2
Jeandeys
Ch Verdignan
la Roze
le Mont
Ch Bel Orme
Tronquoy de Lalande
Ch Lestage-Simon
Loquey
le Villa
Quimper
Ch Grandis
St-Seurin-de-Cadourne
Ch Pontoise-Cabarrus
La Paroisse Cave Co-op
Ch Sociando-Mallet
Ch Charmail
Antognan
Ch St-Paul
Estey d'Un
Ch le Boscq
Ch Morin
St-Corbian
Ch Beau-Site
Ch Beau-Site Haut-Vignoble
Ch Tour des Termes
CH CALON-SÉGUR
Port de la Chapelle
Ch les Ormes de Pez
Ch Petit Bocq
Ch Capbern Gasqueton
Pez
Ch Tour de Pez
Ch Domeyne
Ch Picard
St-Estèphe
Ch Phélan Ségur
le Parc
Ch Sérilhan
Aillan
Ch de Pez
Ch Bel Air
Ch Haut-Beauséjour
les Mouleyres
Tourney
Bourdin
Ch Tour St-Fort
Ch Tronquoy-Lalande
Ch Meyney
VERTHEUIL
Gare
Ch Reysson
Ch le Meynieu
Troupian
Ch Laffitte-Carcasset
Marquis de St-Estèphe Cave Co-op
Vertheuil
le Souley
Laujac
Brame-Hame
ST-ESTÈPHE
CH MONTROSE
Ch le Bourdieu Vertheuil
Ch Goudelin-Merville
Leyssac
Ch Clauzet
Ch St-Estèphe
Ch Pomys
Picourneau
Bois de Jourdan
le Cendrayre
Ch la Commanderie
Ch Haut-Marbuzet
Blagnac
l'Hôpital
Ch la Haye
la Plagne
Marbuzet
Ch Le Crock
Ch Tour de Marbuzet
Lucrabey
Bas Queyron
Ch Hanteillan
Gare
Blanquet
Ch Chambert-Marbuzet
Ch de Marbuzet
Ch MacCarthy
Ch Lilian Ladouys
Ch Andron Blanquet
Petit Bourg
Borderon
Ch Larrivaux
CH COS LABORY
CH COS D'ESTOURNEL
Raff. de Pétrole (Anc.)
Ricous
Ch Cissac
Luc
Ch Puy Castéra
CH LAFON-ROCHET
les Gunes
Petite Rivaux
Ch Tour St-Joseph
le Puy
Cissac-Médoc
CH LAFITE ROTHSCHILD
Pauillac
PAUILLAC
St-Sauveur
Ch Lamothe-Cissac
CISSAC MÉDOC
Ch du Breuil
CH DUHART-MILON ROTHSCHILD
Chenal de Calon
Chenal du Lazaret
Gironde

Lesparre-Médoc
St-Estèphe
MÉDOC
Blaye
Bordeaux

1:42,000
Km 0 · · · 1 · · · 2 Km
Miles 0 · · 1 Mile

Pauillac

If one had to single out one Bordeaux commune to head the list, there would be no argument. It would be Pauillac. Châteaux Lafite, Latour, and Mouton Rothschild, three of the five superstar first growths, are its obvious claim. But many red Bordeaux enthusiasts would tell you that the wines of Pauillac have the quintessential flavour they look for – a combination of fresh soft fruit, oak, dryness, subtlety combined with substance, a touch of cigar box, a suggestion of sweetness, and, above all, vigour and longevity. Even the lesser growths approach the enthusiasts' ideal.

At Pauillac the gravel mounds, or *croupes*, of the Médoc get as near as they ever do to being hills. The highest part, with Châteaux Mouton Rothschild and Pontet-Canet on its summit, reaches 100ft (30m) – quite an achievement in this coastal area, where a mere swelling of the ground provides a lookout point.

The town of Pauillac is the biggest of the Médoc. Happily, its long-established oil refinery has ceased operation and become a mere (though colossal) depot. Its old quay has become a marina; a few restaurants have opened. The Cazes family of Château Lynch-Bages has endowed the sleepy hamlet of Bages with a Michelin-starred restaurant, Château Cordeillan-Bages, an all-day brasserie, and two or three rather smart shops. So far, that's it. Pauillac could scarcely be called animated – except for one weekend in September when thousands of runners compete in the Marathon du Médoc.

The vineyards of the châteaux of Pauillac are on the whole less subdivided than in most of the Médoc. Whereas in Margaux (for example) the châteaux are bunched together in the town and their holdings in the surrounding countryside are inextricably mixed up – a row here, a couple of rows there – in Pauillac whole slopes, mounds, and plateaus belong to a single proprietor. One would therefore expect greater variations in style derived from terroir. One is not disappointed.

The three great wines of Pauillac are all dramatically different. Châteaux Lafite Rothschild and Latour stand at opposite ends of the parish: the first almost in St-Estèphe, the second almost in St-Julien. Oddly enough, though, their characters tend in quite the opposite direction: Lafite more towards the smoothness and finesse of a St-Julien, Latour more towards the emphatic firmness of a St-Estèphe.

In a typical year Lafite, which with 250 acres (100ha) is one of the biggest vineyards in the Médoc, makes about 700 barrels of its top wine, or *grand vin* – a perfumed, polished, and quintessentially elegant production in a unique circular subterranean *chai* – and even more of its second label, Carruades.

The firmer and more solid Latour, with its vast stocks of maturing vintages, seems to spurn elegance, expressing its supremely privileged situation on the hill nearest the river in robust depths that can take decades to reveal their complexity. Latour has the great merit of evenness over uneven vintages. Even the château's second wine, Les Forts de Latour, mainly from separate parcels of land shaded on the map as for a Cru Classé to the west and northwest of the château, is considered and priced as a second growth. A junior selection, still identifiable in taste, is sold simply as Pauillac.

Mouton Rothschild is a third kind of Pauillac: strong, dark, full of the savour of ripe blackcurrants, some say exotic. No visitor to Pauillac should miss the museum of works of art connected with wine – old glass, paintings, tapestries – as well as the new *chais*, which make Château Mouton Rothschild the showplace of the whole Médoc. A second wine, Le Petit Mouton, was introduced in 1997. Mouton-Cadet is a big pan-Bordeaux brand.

Smelling the richness and feeling the force of Cabernet Sauvignon in these wines, it is strange to think that it is a mere 150 years since it was recognized as the best vine for the Médoc. Up to that time even the first growths had established the superiority of their terroirs with a mixture of less distinguished grape varieties – above all

Malbec. But the best Cabernet Sauvignon is famously slow to mature. Given the 10 or often even 20 years they need (depending on the quality of the vintage), these wines reach into realms of perfection where they are rarely followed. But millionaires are impatient: too much is drunk far too young.

Second-growth rivals

The southern approach to Pauillac, the D2, is flanked by the two rival second-growth halves of the historic Pichon estate. For years Pichon-Lalande (as Château Pichon Longueville Comtesse de Lalande is known) had the better name, but Château Pichon-Longueville, as the property once known as Pichon-Baron now styles itself, is now challenging even the first growths. The key ingredient here has been investment on a massive scale (see photo). Not to be outdone, the Champagne house Louis Roederer, which bought Pichon-Lalande across the road in 2007, has restructured the vineyard, is building new cellars, and renovated that château, too.

Château Lynch-Bages, though "only" a fifth growth, has long been loved, particularly in Britain, for its richly spicy wine – a sort of Mouton for not-quite-millionaires. The recent over-performer to the north of the town has been biodynamic pioneer Pontet-Canet: the biggest Cru Classé of all. Superbly sited as a neighbour to Mouton, it is, however, utterly different: solid and reserved, where Mouton is open and opulent. Recent vintages have been so good that it is now recognized as a "super second".

Château Duhart-Milon belongs to the Rothschilds of Lafite, and Châteaux d'Armailhac and Clerc Milon to Mouton. All three clearly benefit from the wealth and technical knowledge of their proprietors and managers – witness the new cellars at Clerc Milon. Châteaux Batailley and the usually finer Haut-Batailley, both archetypal Pauillacs, lie back from the river in the fringe of the woods. Like Haut-Batailley, the renovated and dependable Grand-Puy-Lacoste is managed by François-Xavier Borie, whose brother Bruno runs Ducru-Beaucaillou in St-Julien. Grand-Puy-Ducasse also expresses itself in the firm, energetic tones of a fine Pauillac. Lacoste is one continuous vineyard on high ground, surrounding its château,

In the burgeoning Chinese market, Château Lafite carried such cachet that fake labels – from crass to cunning – abounded to the extent that most of the top Bordeaux growths now take special measures to thwart counterfeiters. For decades Mouton has commissioned a new artist to design each year's label.

After the insurance group AXA bought Château Pichon-Longueville in 1987, it restored the distinctively turreted château and erected a dramatic visitors' centre and winery. It is one of relatively few Pauillac properties to actively encourage tourists.

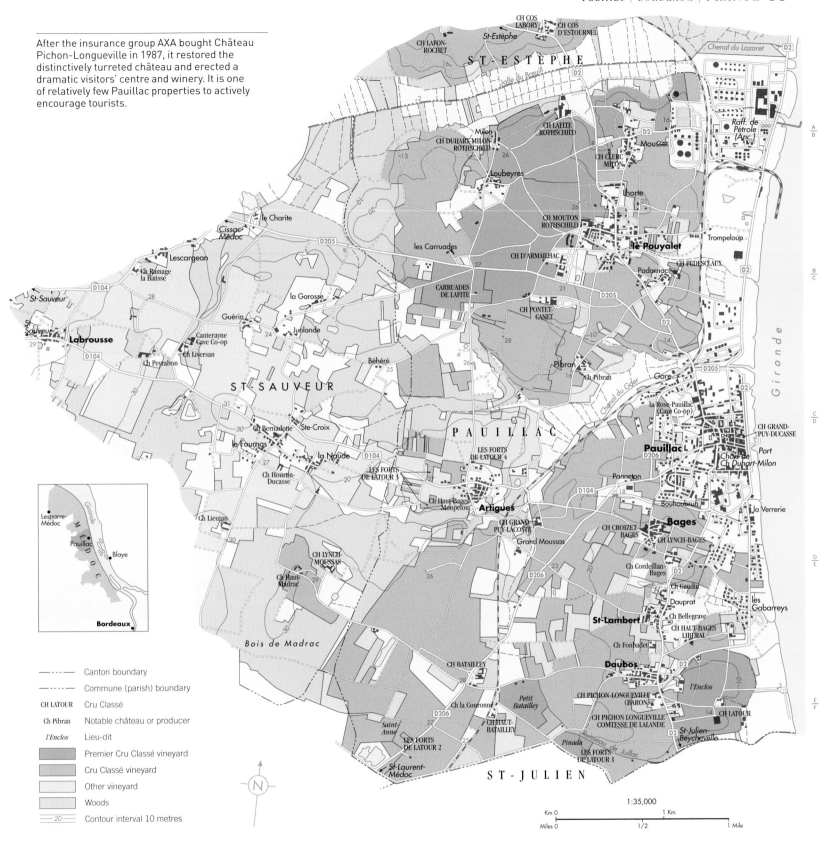

Map legend:

- – · – · – Canton boundary
- – - – - – Commune (parish) boundary
- CH LATOUR — Cru Classé
- Ch Pibran — Notable château or producer
- *l'Enclos* — Lieu-dit
- Premier Cru Classé vineyard
- Cru Classé vineyard
- Other vineyard
- Woods
- — 20 — Contour interval 10 metres

1:35,000

Km 0 — 1 Km
Miles 0 — 1/2 — 1 Mile

while the Ducasse property is scattered in three separate parcels to the north and west of Pauillac and its old château is situated right on the quay in the town itself.

Château Haut-Bages Libéral, its vineyards propitiously sited in St-Lambert, has acquired new premises and a new lease of life. Château Lynch-Moussas, run in conjunction with Château Batailley, sells consistent wine at modest prices.

Châteaux Croizet-Bages and Pedesclaux are fifth growths that have true rivals in wines deemed Crus Bourgeois Supérieurs in 2003: Fonbadet in St-Lambert, with old vines and serious wine; Haut-Bages Monpelou (under the same ownership as Batailley); and the AXA-owned and cosseted Pibran. The local co-operative, under the name of La Rose-Pauillac, also makes creditable wine, though in diminishing quantities.

PAUILLAC AND ST-SAUVEUR

As the local saying goes, all the finest wine is made within sight of the Gironde – although see the southern half of the map for the extent to which Château Latour has been adding vineyards inland for its second wine, Les Forts de Latour, now made up of four parcels.
The parish of St-Saveur, even further inland, is Cru Bourgeois territory.

St-Julien

No other commune in Bordeaux has so high a proportion – 80% of the total vineyard – of classed growths as St-Julien. It is a small commune, with the smallest production of the famous four of the Médoc. Yet almost all of St-Julien is superlative wine-growing land: typical mounds of gravel, not as deep as in Pauillac, but all are either close to the river or sloping south to the considerable valley (considerable by Médoc standards, that is) drained by the Jalle du Nord and the Chenal du Milieu.

Thus the great châteaux of St-Julien divide into two groups. The riverside estates are epitomized by the three Léovilles, situated around the village of St-Julien itself. The southern group is centred on the village of Beychevelle, led by Châteaux Beychevelle, Branaire-Ducru, and Ducru-Beaucaillou, and reaches back inland with Châteaux Gruaud Larose and Lagrange. Around Beychevelle there is a cluster of superior but unclassified châteaux, including the reliable Gloria.

If Pauillac makes the most striking and brilliant wine of the Médoc, and Margaux the most refined and exquisite, St-Julien forms the transition between the two. With comparatively few exceptions its châteaux make rather round and gentle wine – gentle, that is, when it is mature; it starts as tough and tannic in a good year as any.

The three Léovilles

The principal glory of the commune is the vast estate of Léoville, on the boundary with Pauillac, once the biggest in the Médoc, now divided into three. Château Léoville Las Cases has the most extensive vineyards of the three, with 240 acres (almost 100ha), although the heart of the estate is the 131-acre (53ha) Grand Enclos. Its dense, almost austere, long-lived wine is so obviously "classic", and the Delon family who runs it so astute, that Léoville Las Cases is sometimes priced almost at first-growth levels. Léoville Barton runs it a close race, and belongs to the old Irish merchant family of Barton, who moved to Bordeaux early in the 18th century. Anthony Barton lives in the beautiful 18th-century Château Langoa Barton next door, and makes his two wines side by side in the same chai. Langoa

is usually reckoned the slightly lesser wine of the two, but both are among the finest of clarets in a traditional manner and are never less than good value, even in tricky years. Léoville Poyferré has perhaps more obvious stuffing, and now more than merits second-growth status.

To the south of the Léovilles, Bruno Borie's Château Ducru-Beaucaillou, with its Italianate mansion, has established a style of its own, distinct in emphasizing finesse at a very high level, while its neighbour Branaire-Ducru is often somewhat a little less polished. On form, Château Beychevelle and its neighbour St-Pierre with stablemate Gloria convey finesse and elegance with an easy plumpness that is intensely seductive.

Château Gruaud Larose marks the beginning of the "inland" section of St-Julien, with wines whose richness and drive puts them in the very top rank. Château Talbot, which occupies the central high ground of the commune, may be a shade less fine, but is consistently dense, smooth,

Pruning is cold work but vital to maintain low yields and high quality. Léoville Barton's Cabernet Sauvignon canes are burnt in early January, while blending decisions are taken inside.

ST-JULIEN AND ST-LAURENT

St-Julien is so close to Pauillac that this map overlaps the one on p.85, and the church of St-Julien-Beychevelle dominates the view from Château Latour's tasting room. Note the drainage canals separating the classed-growth vineyards from the Gironde.

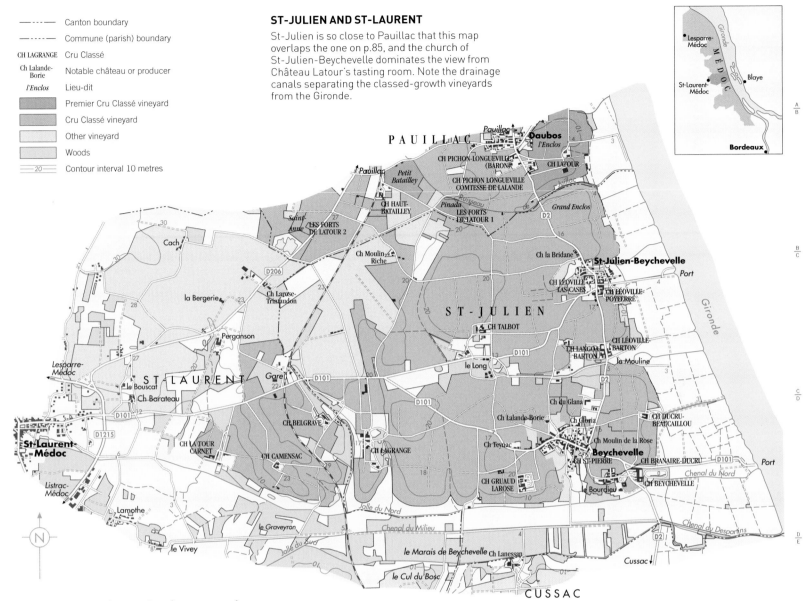

Canton boundary
Commune (parish) boundary
CH LAGRANGE Cru Classé
Ch Lalande-Borie Notable château or producer
l'Enclos Lieu-dit
Premier Cru Classé vineyard
Cru Classé vineyard
Other vineyard
Woods
20 Contour interval 10 metres

and savoury – perhaps owing almost as much to winemaking skill as to its site.

The last of the classed growths, Château Lagrange, used to be very highly regarded for its rich, substantial wine. Suntory of Japan acquired it in 1984 and has brought it back into focus. It lies far back in the country in the sleepy hinterland on the border of St-Laurent (whose appellation is Haut-Médoc, like that of the vast and improving Larose-Trintaudon estate). Here is a group of three more classed growths, all in different stages of resurrection. La Tour Carnet is most advanced and nowadays makes alluring wine. Camensac, now owned by the Merlaut family of Gruaud Larose, was replanted a few years later. Château Belgrave has also, like so much in the Médoc since the early 1980s, been restored, in this case by the négociant Dourthe – but this hinterland never manages to produce quite the class of the vineyards closer to the Gironde.

St-Julien is not prime bourgeois country but Châteaux du Glana and Moulin de la Rose were both ranked Crus Bourgeois Supérieurs in 2003 (see p.80), and Châteaux La Bridane and Teynac can provide good value.

The three Léovilles were once a single estate. The label for that with the most restrained pricing policy (Léoville Barton) depicts its sister property Château Langoa Barton, home to Anthony Barton, one of the few famous Médoc proprietors to live in the region.

Central Médoc

This is the bridge passage of the Médoc, the mezzo forte between the andante of St-Julien and the allegro of Margaux. Four villages pass without a single classed growth; their appellation simply Haut-Médoc. Here the gravel mounds rise less proudly above the river and the water table is much higher, leaving vines watered more readily and the wines they produce generally less complex. The commune of Cussac maintains some of the momentum of St-Julien – indeed, there is the rather forlorn local hope of having some of its land reclassified as such. But this is the stretch of the drive up the Haut-Médoc during which the dedicated wine tourist (if a passenger) can enjoy a little snooze.

This, even more than St-Estèphe, is bourgeois country, with, in the 2003 classification, a significant proportion of the Crus Bourgeois Supérieurs, and no fewer than two of the nine Crus Bourgeois Exceptionnels in Moulis: châteaux Chasse-Spleen and Poujeaux. Both lie on the outskirts of the little hamlet with the grand name of Grand Poujeaux well west of Arcins, where the gravel ridges rise and fan out inland, culminating at Grand Poujeaux and at Listrac. These two communes are dignified with appellations of their own instead of the portmanteau "Haut-Médoc". In recent years Listrac and Moulis have risen steadily in reputation.

Quality rises with the gravel and its water-metering effects. Chasse-Spleen can be viewed almost as an honorary St-Julien for its smoothness, its accessibility, and yet it does not lack structure. Château Poujeaux, showing increased polish recently, can be just as impressive, if usually rather more robust and less subtle. Between these two properties, the village of Grand Poujeaux is surrounded by a knot of properties with "Grand Poujeaux" in their names: Gressier, Dutruch, La Closerie, and Branas, all reliable for stout-hearted, long-lived reds with the flavour that makes the Médoc unique. Just north of here, Château Maucaillou can sometimes offer exceptional value and is, unusually for this less glamorous stretch of the Haut-Médoc, open to casual visitors.

Listrac even further inland has a higher plateau, limestone beneath its gravel, and, although producers have recently tried to change it by planting more Merlot to soften them, a name for tough, tannic wines. The name here is Fourcas; of the four châteaux that bear it, Hosten and Dupré are those to watch.

Today's thoroughly modernized Château Clarke, with 130 acres (53ha) of vines and lying just within Listrac, was the creation of the late Baron Edmond de Rothschild. Every luxury has been lavished on it, but the contrast between its wines and those of the two Rothschild estates in Pauillac provides a vivid illustration of terroir's superiority over investment. The twin châteaux Fonréaud and Lestage south of the village of Listrac have 182 acres (74ha) between them. These redeveloped estates temper the Listrac austerity and make rounder wines, which may help to make the appellation better known.

Closer to the river

In the north of the area mapped, the Haut-Médoc Château Lanessan faces St-Julien across the canal that separates the parishes. Lanessan and its neighbour Caronne Ste-Gemme (largely in St-Laurent) are well-run estates whose owners can afford high standards. Otherwise Cussac has little of the all-important gravel. The forest here comes close to the river. Château Beaumont occupies its best outcrop. Its wine is easy, fragrant, quick to mature – and correspondingly popular. Oddly,

This middle stretch is so relatively unfavoured that machine harvesting is common. Machines may be quicker than humans, and not necessarily inferior, but first growths are unlikely to adopt them soon. Noblesse oblige...

Château Tour du Haut-Moulin in Vieux Cussac is just the opposite: dark, old-fashioned, needing years – but worth the wait.

The riverside here is worth a visit to see the 17th-century battlements of the Fort Médoc – an anti-English precaution now turned to peaceful uses. At Lamarque an earlier fortress, the splendid Château de Lamarque, has established a name for carefully made, satisfyingly full-bodied wine with the true stamp of the Médoc on it. Lamarque is the Médoc's link with Blaye on the other side of the Gironde: a regular car-ferry service runs from the pier. It is also notable for being the base of Jacques Boissenot and his son, Eric, the Médoc's most admired professional oenologists.

A good deal of replanting has given the area a more purposeful look in recent years. Château Malescasse was one of the first to be restored. And in the next commune south, Arcins, the big old properties of Château Barreyres and Château d'Arcins have been hugely replanted by the Castel family, whose empire stretches from Morocco to Patriarche in Burgundy. The Castels and their well-managed neighbour Château Arnauld are steadily making Arcins better known. The village's chief claim to fame, however, is still the little Lion d'Or, the Médoc's wine trade canteen.

Beyond the Estey de Tayac, in the southeast corner of the area, we enter the sphere of Margaux. The extensive Château Citran is owned by the Merlaut family. It and the smaller Villegeorge (off this map to the south, but a name to watch) lie in the commune of Avensan. Both are well known and approach Margaux in style.

Soussans is among the communes whose appellation is not merely Haut-Médoc but Margaux, a name some proprietors just north of here would like to appropriate. Châteaux La Tour de Mons and Paveil de Luze continue to be certified as Crus Bourgeois, the latter being for a century the stylish country resort of one of the great merchant families of Bordeaux, making the kind of easy, elegant wines the family liked.

Some of the best of not a bad lot, but they can sometimes lack the finesse, definition, and longevity of the best wines from the better-drained vineyards in more favoured communes further north and south.

BETWEEN ST-JULIEN AND MARGAUX

See how far inland the drainage ditches are needed in the communes of Arcins and Soussans in the south of the area mapped. Some vineyards in this stretch can find themselves underwater for prolonged periods after heavy rain.

Lesparre-Médoc

MÉDOC

Blaye

Lamarque

Bordeaux

———————	Canton boundary
——·——·——	Commune (parish) boundary
CH BRANAIRE	Cru Classé
Ch Lanessan	Notable château or producer
	Premier Cru Classé vineyard
	Cru Classé vineyard
	Other vineyard
	Woods
——20——	Contour interval 10 metres

St-Julien

Pauillac
Beychevelle
CH ST-PIERRE
CH BEYCHEVELLE
Ch Moulin de la Rose
le Bourdieu
CH GRUAUD LAROSE
CH BRANAIRE-DUCRU
Port

le Marais de Beychevelle
Chenal du Milieu
Chenal du Despartins

St-Laurent
le Cul du Bosc
Ch Ste-Gemme
Ch Lachesnaye
Ch Lanessan
les Valets
le Pré de Madame

Labat
Ch Caronne Ste-Gemme
le Marais du Merich
les Maragnes
le Grand Pré Neuf

le Parc Neuf
la Rue
Gaston
CUSSAC
Ch du Moulin Rouge
Ch Lamothe-Bergeron
Bernones
Payat

Cussac-Fort-Médoc
Ch du Raux
Fort Médoc

Lalande
Ch Aney
Ch Beaumont
D2

Ch Tour du Haut-Moulin
les Martins
Talle
Port de Lamarque
Ch de Lamarque
Ch Cap de Haut
Vieux Cussac
Ch du Retout
Milous
Lamarque
le Retou
Cartillon
Fossé de Monchuguet du
Plantey
Martinon
Couhenne
Cap l'Ousteau
les Calinottes
Ruisseau
la Planche du Roi
LAMARQUE

Lesparre-Médoc
St-Laurent-Médoc
Ch Fourcas-Loubaney
les Marcreux
Ch Malescasse

Ch Fourcas Dupré
le Fourcas
Ch Peyredon-Lagravette
Ch Maucaillou
Ch Barreyres
D1215
Gare
Médrac
le Tris
Ch Poujeaux
le Beyan
la Potence
le Petit Bourdieu
ARCINS
Ch Saransot-Dupré
Ch Gressier Grand-Poujeaux
Ch Fourcas-Borie
Ch Peyre-Lehade
Grand Poujeaux
Ch Duluc Grand-Poujeaux
Ch Chasse-Spleen
Ch Tour-du-Roc
Listrac-Médoc
Ch Fourcas Hosten
Ch la Closerie du Grand-Poujeaux
Ch Brans Grand Poujeaux
Ch Arnauld
Arcins
Cave-Co-op
Ch Semeillan-Mazeau
le Bourdieu
Cagnac
Cave-Co-op
Ch d'Arcins
Berniquet
LISTRAC-MÉDOC
D208
Ch Clarke
MOULIS-EN-MÉDOC
Queue de Boeuf
SOUSSANS
Ch Anthonic
le Malinay
Ch Lestage
Seguin
Grand Soussans
Ch la Tour de Mons
Ch Fonréaud
Peyvignau
Ch Bellevue de Tayac
Bourriche
Ch Brillette
Ch Tayac
la Tamponnette
Moulis-en-Médoc
Ch Paveil de Luze
Soussans
Ch Fonréaud
Ch Ruat Petit-Poujeaux
le Petit-Poujeaux
Ch Biston-Brillette
Ch Haut-Breton-Larigaudière
Margaux
Piquey
Ch Duplessis Fabre
AVENSAN
la Mouline
le Mayne
Ch Citran
Chaux
Ch de Villegeorge
Ch Moulin-à-Vent
Bouqueyran
Lauderie

1:42,000

Km 0   1 Km
Miles 0   1 Mile

Margaux and the Southern Médoc

Margaux and Cantenac, the village just south of it, are considered to make the Médoc's most polished and fragrant wine. Their historical record says so, and contemporary reality is catching up. There are more second and third growths here than anywhere, and a new broom has been sweeping through the southern Médoc.

The map shows a rather different picture from Pauillac or St-Julien. Instead of the châteaux being spread out evenly over the land, they are huddled together in the villages. An examination of the almost unliftable volumes of commune maps in the *mairie* shows a degree of intermingling of one estate with another that is far greater than in, say, Pauillac. One would therefore look to differences in grape varieties, technique, and tradition more than changes of soil to try to explain the differences between the châteaux.

In fact the soil of Margaux is the thinnest and most gravelly in the Médoc, so that vines may root as deep as 23ft (7m) for their steady but meagre supply of water. The result is wines that start life comparatively supple, although in poor years they can turn out thin. In good and great years, however, all the stories about the virtues of gravel are justified: there is a delicacy about archetypal Margaux, and a sweet, haunting perfume, that can make it the most exquisite claret of all.

The wines of Châteaux Margaux and Palmer are the ones that most often reach such heights. Château Margaux is not only a first growth of the Médoc, it is the one that most looks the part: a pediment at the end of an avenue; the air of a palace with *chais* to match. The Mentzelopoulos family acquired it in 1978 and has been making superlative wine ever since. The seminal oaked white Pavillon Blanc du Château Margaux, grown on the western limit of the map opposite, being white, qualifies only as a humble Bordeaux AOC. The third-growth Château Palmer, however, with its higher proportion of Merlot, can present a formidable challenge. Château Lascombes (owned successively by American wine writer Alexis Lichine, English brewer Bass, an American investment syndicate, and now a French insurance group) is a case where buying more land diluted second-growth quality in the 1970s and '80s. Nearby, the recently revived third-growth Château Ferrière is producing convincing Margaux with characteristic finesse.

Of the famous pair which used to be the big Rauzan estate, as famous in the 18th century as Léoville was in St-Julien, Rauzan-Ségla (once Rausan-Ségla) is today much the better, having been reformed in the 1980s and taken firmly in hand from 1994 by the family behind the fashion house Chanel. The smaller Rauzan-Gassies has lagged far behind second-growth standards but is now showing some inclination to narrow the gap.

There are several distinguished pairs of châteaux in Margaux. The two second growths, Brane-Cantenac and Durfort-Vivens, are owned by different members of the ubiquitous Lurton family, yet make distinctly different wine: the Brane fragrant and almost melting, the Durfort much less generous. A tiny vestige of the third-growth Desmirail has been resurrected to join them as a third bowstring.

Fourth-growth Pouget is the often forceful brother of third-growth Boyd-Cantenac. Malescot St-Exupéry has hit high notes under the ownership of the Zuger family, while the small third-growth Château Marquis d'Alesme-Becker is being restored by the Perrodo family, which has also taken unclassified Château Labégorce, now incorporating Labégorce-Zédé, in hand.

Still in Margaux proper, fourth-growth Château Marquis de Terme, although rarely seen abroad, now makes rather good wine, and beautiful and improving third-growth Château d'Issan has one of the best situations in Margaux, with its vineyard sloping gently towards the river.

In Cantenac itself, Château Prieuré-Lichine was deservedly famous for making some of Margaux's most consistent claret when it was owned by Alexis Lichine – and also for being the first to admit passers-by in a way which has, remarkably, only just become accepted practice.

Having been owned far more often in recent years by a consortium than by an individual, Château Lascombes has not lacked for investment, as these smart cellars suggest.

Château Kirwan is once more showing Margaux finesse after a flirtation with heft. Yet another tale of restoration and renewed quality has been the lonely Château du Tertre, isolated on high ground well inland in Arsac, under the same dynamic Dutch ownership as Château Giscours. Château Cantenac-Brown, which competes for the prize of ugliest Médoc château (it looks like a Victorian boarding school), flanks Brane-Cantenac and makes some of Margaux's most solid wine.

There are three more important classed growths before the Haut-Médoc vineyards give way to the northern suburbs of Bordeaux: Giscours, whose half-timbered farm buildings face a most impressive sweep of vines and harbour a particularly flattering style of wine (the 1970 was superb); Cantemerle, a perfect "Sleeping Beauty" château, deep in a wood of huge trees and quiet pools, whose wine is more known for elegance; and the top-flight La Lagune, a neat 18th-century building under the same ownership as Paul Jaboulet Aîné of the Rhône Valley.

Dauzac, the fourth classed growth of this southern area and managed by the Lurton family, has raised its sights. Its neighbour Siran was classified a Cru Bourgeois Exceptionnel in 2003. Both Siran and Château d'Angludet, owned and inhabited by the Sichel family, can make wine of classed-growth quality.

The neighbouring pinnacles of Margaux, châteaux Margaux and Palmer, could not be accused of irregularity, even if their styles are very different. The hand-drawn label by Karl Lagerfeld for Rauzan-Ségla's 2009 vintage reflects its close links to the world of fashion.

Canton boundary

Commune (parish) boundary

CH MARGAUX Cru Classé

Ch Martinens Notable château or producer

Ch Marojallia Microcuvée or part of one

Premier Cru Classé vineyard

Cru Classé vineyard

Other vineyard

Woods

—25— Contour interval 5 metres

SOUTHERN HAUT-MEDOC

Margaux is the most southerly of the famous Médoc communes, but the Haut-Médoc appellation reaches as far south as the city of Bordeaux.

1:42,000

Km 0   1   2 Km

Miles 0   1 Mile

Graves and Entre-Deux-Mers

There is much more to the Graves region than its most famous communes of Pessac and Léognan, conjoined in a single appellation (mapped overleaf). The southern end of this zone of scattered vines has been coming to life, too – notably thanks to a new wave of reds with deep, sappy fruit and ripe tannins.

Langon should now be a regular resort of buyers looking for flavour and value. In central and southern Graves a number of the old properties, particularly in the once-famous parishes of Portets, Landiras, and St-Pierre-de-Mons, have new owners and new philosophies.

The ability of Graves soil to make red and white wine equally well is seen at Châteaux de Chantegrive in Podensac and Rahoul and Crabitey in Portets, and in properties dotted around Arbanats and Castres-Gironde. Clos Floridène at Pujols-sur-Ciron and Château du Seuil, like so many successful properties situated close to the Garonne, excel at understated, oak-aged dry whites from the Sauvignon Blanc and Sémillon grapes that seem so at home in this quiet southern corner of the Gironde, even if fewer than one bottle of Graves in four contains white wine.

Entre-Deux-Mers

The extent of this map northwards and eastwards is testament to the efforts being made in some of Bordeaux's even less glamorous wine areas. Most of the red wine sold as lowly Bordeaux AOC is made in the Entre-Deux-Mers, the wedge of pretty farmland between the Garonne and Dordogne rivers, with the name Entre-Deux-Mers itself reserved on wine labels for the harmless dry white produced there, in much smaller quantity.

An increasing number of producers of red wines that qualify for no grander an appellation than Bordeaux or the slightly stronger Bordeaux Supérieur are seriously trying to make wines of note, by tending their vineyards much more carefully and reducing yields. Many of them are marked on this map, which includes the most interesting part of Entre-Deux-Mers.

A number of substantial châteaux, and the odd exceptional co-op, have changed the aspect of the region, especially of the parishes in the north of this map towards the Dordogne and St-Emilion, from one of mixed farm and orchard to vinous monoculture. Some of the most successful flag-bearers were the Lurton family's excellent Château Bonnet south of Grézillac, the Despagne family's versatile Château Tour de Mirambeau south of Branne, the Courselle family's Château Thieuley near Créon, and the négociant-owned Château Pey La Tour at Salleboeuf just off this map. Many of these make even more successful dry whites (from Sémillon and Sauvignon grapes) than reds. Château de Sours of St-Quentin-de-Baron has even managed to sell its Bordeaux rosé *en primeur*.

But there are signs of even more exciting wine-craft in Entre-Deux-Mers, as well there might be in the far north, where limestone soils can be uncannily similar to parts of the St-Emilion appellation. The Despagnes have created Girolate, a handmade Merlot garage wine, out of one of the most densely planted vineyards in all Bordeaux. Northwest of this map, Château de Reignac near St-Loubès, has achieved similarly dizzy prices, thanks to the single-mindedness of owner Yves Vatelot. While Pierre Lurton, winemaker at Châteaux Cheval Blanc and d'Yquem no less, brings a certain glamour by association to the region via his own property, Château Marjosse, near Grézillac.

Since 2008 the name **Premières Côtes de Bordeaux** has been used exclusively for the semi-sweet white produced in this narrow, river-hugging zone on the right bank of the Garonne, with its often toothsome reds now using the appellation **Cadillac Côtes de Bordeaux**. At the same time, three other right bank appellations were given new designations: **Castillon Côtes de Bordeaux** is for red wine only, whereas both **Blaye Côtes de Bordeaux** and **Francs Côtes de Bordeaux** can produce reds and whites (see map, p.77). An umbrella appellation, **Côtes de Bordeaux**, permits cross-blending of red wines among the four.

Since the Premières Côtes de Bordeaux encircle the sweet white appellations of Cadillac, Loupiac, and Ste-Croix-du-Mont, it is no surprise that good sweet wines are produced here, too. Those made in the south of the zone are sold as **Cadillac**, while the dry whites are sold as straightforward Bordeaux. One of Bordeaux's leading oenologists, Denis Dubourdieu, at Château Reynon at Béguey near the town of Cadillac, has succeeded with a fresh Sauvignon white and a particularly reliable red. Château Fayau at Cadillac is keeping up the local tradition of sweet, fruity whites.

It is too much to claim that the liquorous **Ste-Croix-du-Mont** has become a money-making proposition, as it once used to be, but three châteaux – Loubens, du Mont, and La Rame – make great efforts, and in neighbouring

Villa Bel-Air, owned by the Cazes family of Pauillac, is one of Graves' most reliable wines. Château du Seuil is owned by a Welsh couple whose daughter and son-in-law are in charge of winemaking.

VILLA BEL AIR Notable producer

Barsac

Cadillac Côtes de Bordeaux, Cadillac, and Premières Côtes de Bordeaux

Cérons

Côtes de Bordeaux-St-Macaire

Entre-Deux-Mers

Bordeaux Haut-Benauge and Entre-Deux-Mers Haut-Benauge

Graves

Loupiac

Pessac-Léognan

Cadillac Côtes de Bordeaux and Premières Côtes de Bordeaux

Ste-Croix-du-Mont

Sauternes

95 Area mapped at larger scale on page shown

Loupiac both châteaux Loupiac-Gaudiet and de Ricaud are ready to run the risks inherent in making truly sweet, rather than just semi-sweet, wine (see p.96).

Just across the River Garonne, to the north of Barsac in the Graves, lies **Cérons**, a separate appellation long forgotten (it includes Illats and Podensac), which has found new prosperity (at Château d'Archambeau, for example) by making mainstream white and red under the Graves

appellation, largely abandoning its tradition of a style midway between Graves Supérieures (the sweetish white of Graves) and Barsac that was softly rather than stickily sweet. Château de Cérons and Grand Enclos du Château de Cérons produce superior examples. On the other hand Château Haura (see label opposite), made by white wine genius and academic Denis Dubourdieu of Château Doisy-Daëne, can be fine and sweet enough to challenge many a Sauternes.

BORDEAUX'S HINTERLAND

The vast Entre-Deux-Mers region may not be home to many superstars in terms of wine but it is undoubtedly the prettiest of all the many wine regions in the Gironde département. Its name, "between two seas" (the Garonne and Dordogne) is seen only on a minority of white wine labels.

Pessac-Léognan

It was here, in the southern outskirts of the city of Bordeaux, that the whole concept of fine red Bordeaux was launched, in the 1660s, by the owner of Château Haut-Brion.

Its arid sand and gravel had already supplied the region and its export market with its best red wine since at least 1300, when the archbishop who became Pope Clement V (of Avignon) planted what is now Château Pape Clément.

Pessac-Léognan is the modern name for the heartland of the Graves, mapped in its entirety on the previous two pages. Pine trees have always been the main crop of this sandy soil. The vineyards are clearings, often isolated from one another in heavily forested country crossed by shallow river valleys. The map opposite shows how the city and its oldest vineyards reach out into the forest.

Now the city has swallowed all the vineyards in its path except the superlative group on the deep gravel soils of Pessac: Haut-Brion and its neighbour and stablemate La Mission Haut-Brion, Les Carmes Haut-Brion and Picque Caillou (north and west of Haut-Brion, respectively, and off this map) and, a little further out of town, the archiepiscopal Pape Clément.

Châteaux Haut-Brion and La Mission are found with difficulty, deep in the suburbs, on opposite sides of the old Arcachon road which runs through Pessac. Haut-Brion is every inch a first growth, a suave equilibrium of force and finesse with the singularity of great Graves: hints of earth and fern, tobacco and caramel. La Mission tastes denser, riper, wilder – and often just as splendid. In 1983 the American owners of Haut-Brion bought its old rival, including Château La Tour Haut-Brion now incorporated into La Mission itself – not to unite the vineyards

but to continue the match. The game is played out each year, not just between the two famous reds, but between their incomparably rich white sisters, too, Châteaux Haut-Brion Blanc and Laville Haut-Brion, tidily renamed La Mission Haut-Brion Blanc from 2009. There are few more vivid examples of what terroir, the uniqueness of each piece of ground, means on this Bordeaux soil.

Although the majority of wine produced in the vineyards mapped here is red, with much the same grape recipe as in the Médoc, most Pessac-Léognan properties also produce some white of sometimes superlative quality within the same appellation. The commune of Léognan, well into the forest, is the hub of this map. Domaine de Chevalier is its outstanding property, despite its modest appearance. The domaine has never had a château. Although its *chai* and *cuvier* have been impeccably rebuilt and its vineyard considerably expanded in the late 1980s and early 1990s, it retains the air of a farm in a clearing in the pines. Its reds and especially whites are easy to underestimate in youth. Château Haut-Bailly is the

A quick glance at Château La Mission Haut-Brion's label, below, reveals which is the newer wing of this recently restored monastic building.

other leading classed growth of Léognan: unusual in these parts for making only red wine, but deeply and persuasively. Château de Fieuzal's red, apart from a wobble at the turn of the millennium, provides a serious challenge – and its white is also very fine. Malartic-Lagravière is similar, and has been thoroughly modernized since being acquired by the Belgian Bonnie family in 1997.

Château Carbonnieux is different. This old Benedictine establishment was for a long time much more famous for its reliable white than for its light red, although the red has gained weight recently. Château Olivier, surely Bordeaux's oldest and most haunting château building, produces wine of both colours and is also the subject of long-term renewal.

Since 1990 no Graves property has had a more obvious face-lift than Château Smith Haut Lafitte in the commune of Martillac, which marks the southern limit of Pessac-Léognan. Not only does it make a very successful red and white, the property boasts in Les Sources de Caudalie a hotel, restaurants, and a pioneering grape-based spa. Improvements at Château Latour-Martillac to the south have been on a more modest scale but the wines represent excellent value.

The prophet and prime mover in the region is octogenarian André Lurton: founder of the local growers' organization; owner of châteaux La Louvière, de Rochemorin, the classified Couhins-Lurton (virtually all the properties mentioned here were classified in 1959), and de Cruzeau (south of Latour-Martillac and mapped on p.92); and the driving force behind much of the recent renewal. Château Bouscaut, also classified, and increasingly worthy, is owned by his niece Sophie Lurton.

Although the wines of the two leading Pessac-Léognan properties, Haut-Brion, and La Mission Haut-Brion, tend to be more concentrated than the rest, all the reds made here have a particular fresh sappiness. All except Haut-Bailly make fine whites, too.

NORTHERN GRAVES

The map suggests it is almost a miracle that vineyards survive surrounded by suburbs in the far north of this area – but what vineyards, at Haut-Brion and La Mission! Those just west of St-Bris belong to the official viticultural research station.

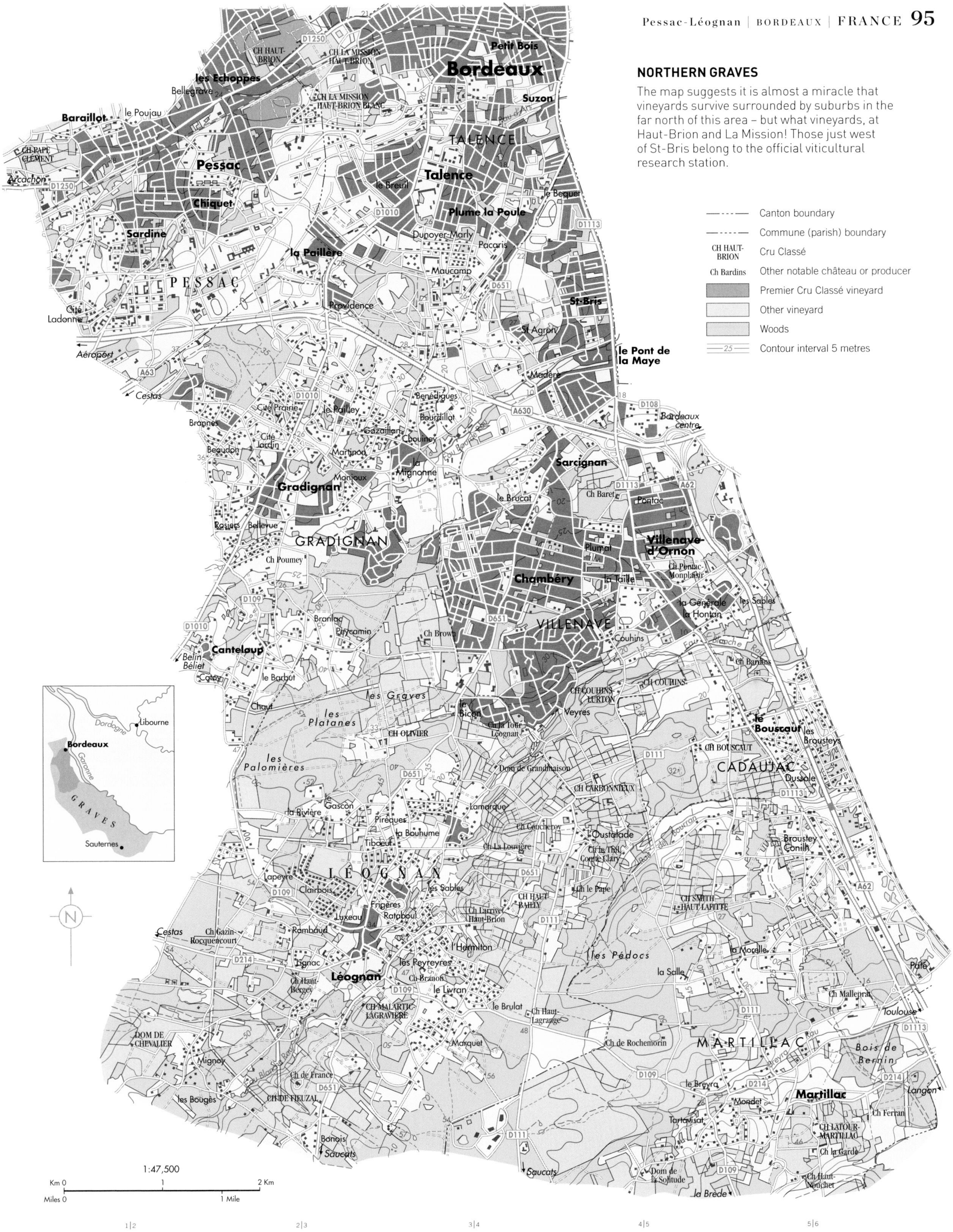
Canton boundary
Commune (parish) boundary
CH HAUT-BRION Cru Classé
Ch Bardins Other notable château or producer
Premier Cru Classé vineyard
Other vineyard
Woods
25 Contour interval 5 metres
1:47,500
Km 0 1 2 Km
Miles 0 1 Mile
Bordeaux
Petit Bois
CH HAUT-BRION
CH LA MISSION HAUT-BRION
CH LA MISSION HAUT-BRION BLANC
les Echoppes
Bellegrave
Suzon
Baraillot
le Poujau
CH PAPE CLÉMENT
TALENCE
Talence
Pessac
Arcachon
Chiquet
le Breuil
le Bequet
Plume la Poule
Sardine
la Paillère
Dunoyer-Marly
Pacaris
Maucamp
PESSAC
Providence
St-Bris
Cité Ladonne
St Agrep
Aéroport
le Pont de la Maye
Madère
Cestas
Bénédigues
Bourdillot
Cité Prairie
le Pailley
Brannes
Gazaillan
Chouiney
Bordeaux centre
Cité Jardin
Beaudon
Martinon
la Mignonne
Sarcignan
Monjoux
Gradignan
Ch Baret
Pontac
le Brucat
Rosiers
Bellevue
GRADIGNAN
Plumat
Villenave-d'Ornon
Ch Poumey
Chambéry
la Taille
Ch Pontac-Monplaisir
la Générale
la Hontan
les Sables
Branlac
Peycamin
Ch Brown
VILLENAVE
Couhins
Canteloup
Belin-Béliet
Ch Bardins
Catoy
le Barbut
CH COUHINS-LURTON
CH COUHINS
les Graves
Chaut
le Bicon
Veyres
les Platanes
Ch la Tour Léognan
le Bouscaut
les Brousteys
CH OLIVIER
CH BOUSCAUT
les Palomières
Dom de Grandmaison
CADAUJAC
Dussole
CH CARBONNIEUX
le Gascon
la Rivière
Lamarque
Pirèques
Ch Coucheroy
la Bouhume
Tiboeuf
Ch La Louvière
l'Oustalade
Ch le Thil Comte Clary
Brousteys Conilh
LÉOGNAN
Lapeyre
Clairbois
les Sables
Ch le Pape
Frigères
Ratabouil
Luxeau
CH HAUT-BAILLY
CH SMITH HAUT LAFITTE
Ch Larrivet Haut-Brion
Cestas
Rambaud
Ch Gazin-Rocquencourt
l'Hermitton
les Pédocs
la Morelle
Lignac
les Peyreyres
la Salle
Pâté
Léognan
Ch Branon
Ch Haut-Bergey
le Livran
Ch Mallenrat
le Brulat
CH MALARTIC-LAGRAVIÈRE
Ch Haut-Lagrange
Toulouse
DOM DE CHEVALIER
Marquet
Ch de Rochemorin
MARTILLAC
Bois de Bernin
Mignoy
Ch de France
le Breyra
Langon
les Bouges
CH DE FIEUZAL
Mondet
Martillac
Ch Ferran
Tartavisat
CH LATOUR-MARTILLAC
Bonois
Saucats
Ch la Garde
Saucats
Dom de la Solitude
Ch Haut-Nouchet
La Brède
Libourne
Dordogne
Bordeaux
Garonne
GRAVES
Sauternes
N

Sauternes and Barsac

All the other districts of Bordeaux mapped in this Atlas make wines that can be compared with, and preferred to, one another. Sauternes is different: lamentably underappreciated but incomparable, it is a speciality that finds few real rivals. Potentially one of the world's longest-living wines, it depends on local conditions and on a very unusual fungus and winemaking technique. In great vintages the results can be sublime: a very sweet, rich-textured, flower-scented, glittering golden liquid. In some years it can frankly fail to be Sauternes (properly so-called) at all.

Above all it is only the best-situated and best-run châteaux of Sauternes – and in this we include Barsac – that make such nectar. Ordinary Sauternes is just sweet white wine.

Noble rot

The local conditions in this warm and fertile corner of Aquitaine include the mists that form along the little River Ciron on autumn evenings, lasting till after dawn. The special technique that only the well-financed châteaux can afford to employ is to pick over the vineyard as many as eight or nine times, typically beginning in September and sometimes continuing until November. This is to take full advantage of the peculiar form of mould (known as *Botrytis cinerea* to the scientist, or *pourriture noble* – "noble rot" – to the poet) which forms, capriciously, on the Sémillon, Sauvignon Blanc, and Muscadelle grapes during the mild, misty nights, then multiplies in the heat of the day to reduce the grape skins to brown pulp. Instead of affecting the blighted grapes with a flavour of rot, this botrytis engineers the escape of the greater part of the water in them, leaving the sugar, acids, and the flavouring elements in the juice more concentrated, but far from easy to ferment. After ageing in small oak barrels, the resulting wine has an intensity of flavour, a smooth, unctuous texture, and the potential to be exceptionally long-lived.

Grapes should ideally be picked as they shrivel, sometimes berry by berry – but the proprietors of little-known châteaux can afford only to pick the entire crop at once, and hope for botrytis to be as concentrated on that date as possible.

Production is absurdly low, since evaporation is actually encouraged. From each one of its 250-odd acres (roughly 100ha) Château d'Yquem, the greatest of the Sauternes producers and now owned by the deep-pocketed but commercially astute LVMH, makes fewer than a thousand bottles of wine. A first-class Médoc vineyard makes five or six times as much.

The risk element is appalling, since humid weather in October can turn the mould into the noxious fungus known as grey rot and rob the grower of all chance of making sweet wine, and sometimes of making any wine at all. Costs are correspondingly high and the price of even the finest Sauternes (with the exception of Yquem), makes it one of the least profitable wines to the grower. Prices have been rising gradually but few wine drinkers realize just how underpriced great sweet white Bordeaux is compared with its red counterpart.

The 1855 classification

Sauternes was the only area outside the Médoc to be classed in 1855. Château d'Yquem was made a Premier Cru Supérieur (First Great Growth) – a rank created for it alone in all Bordeaux. Strangely, for its dominant hilltop position, it has a "perched", therefore unusually high, water-table that necessitates drainage but keeps its vines growing well even in drought. Eleven other châteaux were made first growths and 12 more were classed seconds.

Five communes, including Sauternes itself, are entitled to use the name. **Barsac**, the biggest of them, has the alternative of calling its wine either Sauternes or Barsac.

Styles of Sauternes vary almost as much as standards, even if most of the finest properties cluster around Yquem. Château Lafaurie-Peyraguey can taste as floral as it sounds; AXA's Château Suduiraut in Preignac is typically lush and sumptuous; Château Rieussec (owned by the Rothschilds of Lafite) is often deep-coloured and rich. Other current top performers include Clos Haut-Peyraguey and Châteaux de Fargues (run by the Lur-Saluces family which used to own Yquem), Raymond-Lafon, and La Tour Blanche, which doubles as a winemaking school. A quite different but long-living style of unoaked wine is made at Château Gilette. In Barsac, Châteaux Climens, Coutet, and Doisy-Daëne lead the field with wines slightly fresher than Sauternes. The increasing proportion of diligently made nectar from this part of the wine world deserves a far more appreciative following.

Botrytis cinerea, pourriture noble, or noble rot is far from pretty, but it does miraculous things to the composition of ripe Sémillon grapes in Bordeaux's prime sweet white wine district, somehow managing to encourage sweetness, freshness, and longevity.

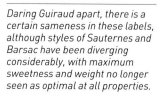

Daring Guiraud apart, there is a certain sameness in these labels, although styles of Sauternes and Barsac have been diverging considerably, with maximum sweetness and weight no longer seen as optimal at all properties.

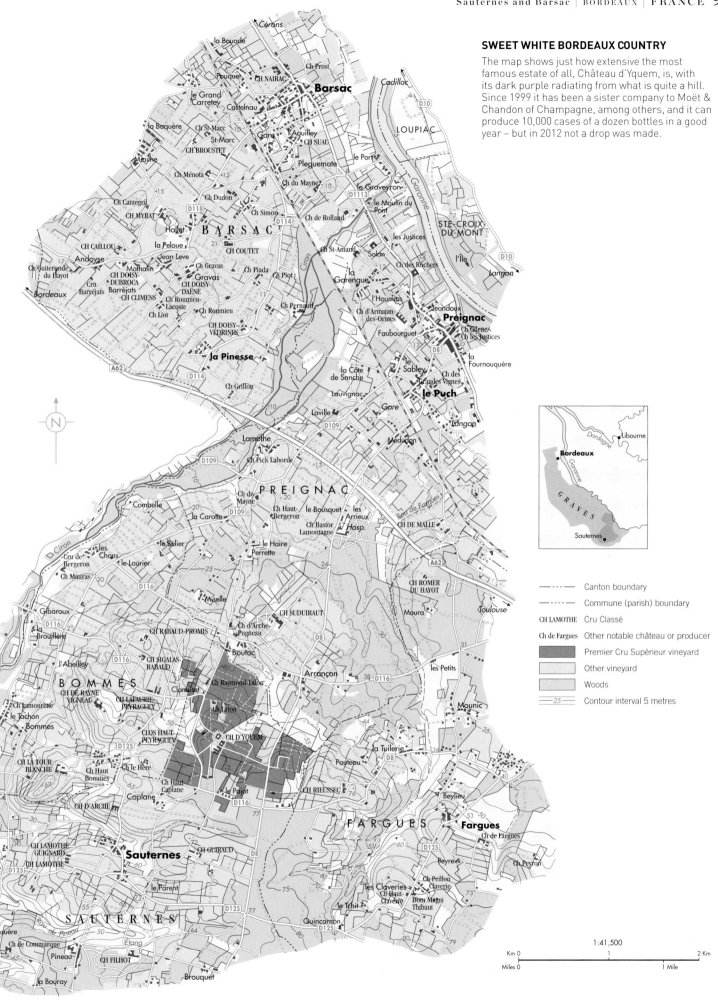

SWEET WHITE BORDEAUX COUNTRY

The map shows just how extensive the most famous estate of all, Château d'Yquem, is, with its dark purple radiating from what is quite a hill. Since 1999 it has been a sister company to Moët & Chandon of Champagne, among others, and it can produce 10,000 cases of a dozen bottles in a good year – but in 2012 not a drop was made.

Canton boundary
Commune (parish) boundary
CH LAMOTHE Cru Classé
Ch de Fargues Other notable château or producer
Premier Cru Supérieur vineyard
Other vineyard
Woods
25 Contour interval 5 metres

1:41,500

Km 0   1   2 Km
Miles 0   1 Mile

The Right Bank

This map provides an overview of Bordeaux's most dynamic region, named "right bank" by Anglo-Saxons in contrast to the Médoc and Graves on the "left bank" of the Gironde. The French call it the Libournais after its ancient capital, Libourne, Bordeaux's second centre of wine commerce. Historically Libourne supplied northern Europe with simple and satisfying wines from its neighbouring vineyards, Fronsac, St-Emilion, and Pomerol. Belgium was Libourne's chief market.

Today, two of these names are as famous as any and more expensive than most. Pomerol and St-Emilion are described in detail on succeeding pages, but what we can see here is how dynamic are the wine areas that surround them. The most distinctive are the twin appellations of **Fronsac** and **Canon-Fronsac**, west of Libourne. This gentle wooded district of sudden hills has recently benefited from several well-heeled outsiders supplying the will and means to give Fronsac a vigour it has lacked for centuries.

There was a time when Fronsac was widely admired as an historic region in its own right and it is certainly true that its best wines are distinguished by being not just splendidly fruity in typical right bank manner, but also more characterfully rigorous, more tannic when young. They are rustic in style compared with the high gloss of, say, the finest Pomerol, but they are improving year by year with investment in modernization. The limestone slopes along the river are known as Canon-Fronsac, although even locals can sometimes be at a loss to describe what differentiates the two appellations. Some of Bordeaux's best-value wines are grown here.

The outlying vineyards of Pomerol are clustered around the villages of Néac and **Lalande-de-Pomerol** and qualify for the appellation named after the latter. They are generally less vivid than wines from the plateau of Pomerol itself but the key to quality as in much of the area mapped on these two pages is often investment by the owner of a grander property. Thus, for example, La Fleur de Boüard in Lalande-de-Pomerol benefits from the equipment and expertise of the family that owns Château Angélus in St-Emilion, just as Château Les Cruzelles does from its association with Château L'Eglise-Clinet in Pomerol.

A similar phenomenon is evident in the easternmost appellations of the right bank, **Castillon Côtes de Bordeaux** and (off the map to the east) **Francs Côtes de Bordeaux**. Both Château Les Charmes Godard and Château Puygueraud are part of the many holdings of the Belgian Thienpont family (others include Vieux Château Certan and Le Pin). In Castillon, only the western sector of which is mapped here, Château d'Aiguilhe shares an owner with Château Canon-la-Gaffelière in St-Emilion, Château Joanin Bécot is part of a major conglomeration of smarter right bank properties, while Domaine de l'A is the home base of a famous international oenologist, Stéphane Derenoncourt. In geological terms Castillon is very similar to St Emilion.

St-Emilion's so-called "satellites" are four villages north of the town, **Montagne**, **Lussac**, **Puisseguin**, and **St-Georges**, which are all allowed to append St-Emilion's name to their

These are just some of the more notable wines made, generally from Merlot with Cabernet Franc, in the area mapped here but outside our Pomerol and St-Emilion maps. The two immediately above are the personal properties of winemakers well-known on both left and right banks.

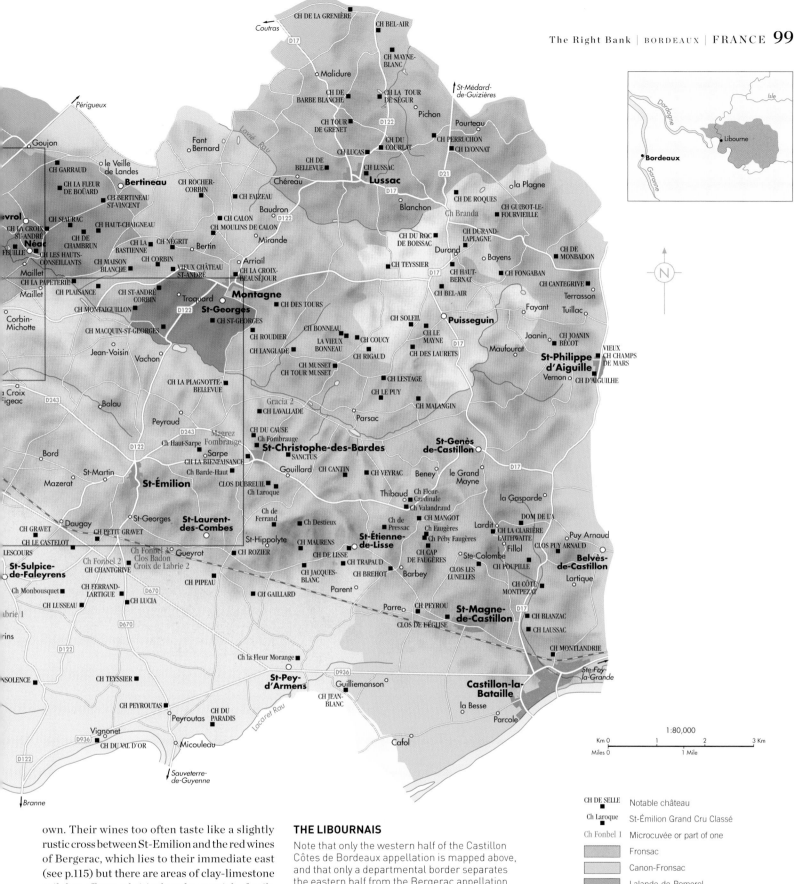

own. Their wines too often taste like a slightly rustic cross between St-Emilion and the red wines of Bergerac, which lies to their immediate east (see p.115) but there are areas of clay-limestone soil that offer good viticultural potential – fertile ground for investment and improvement?

But most interesting of all is how many well-known chateaux are plotted on the pale purple zone of St-Emilion but way outside its classic heartland, mapped on pp.102–103. Nowhere in Bordeaux has so much effort been expended recently in pushing the limits, geographical and stylistic, of what is regarded as great red Bordeaux. For more details see pp.102–105.

THE LIBOURNAIS

Note that only the western half of the Castillon Côtes de Bordeaux appellation is mapped above, and that only a departmental border separates the eastern half from the Bergerac appellation in the Dordogne. The vineyards marked in magenta go into some of the better known small-production wines that sprouted on the right bank in the late 20th century. The market seems to be falling out of love with them now however.

CH DE SELLE — Notable château

Ch Laroque — St-Émilion Grand Cru Classé

Ch Fonbel 1 — Microcuvée or part of one

Fronsac
Canon-Fronsac
Lalande-de-Pomerol
Pomerol
St-Émilion
Castillon Côtes de Bordeaux
Montagne-St-Émilion
Lussac-St-Émilion
Puisseguin-St-Émilion
St-Georges-St-Émilion

101 — Area mapped at larger scale on page shown

Pomerol

Although Pomerol is, relatively speaking, a new star in the firmament of Bordeaux, its most sought-after wines can fetch a higher price than the much larger first growths of the Médoc. And an astonishing number of small properties, for an area no bigger than St-Julien, are generally agreed to be among the best in the whole of Bordeaux.

Pomerol is such a curious corner of the world that it is hard to get your bearings. There is no real village centre. Almost identical small roads criss-cross the plateau apparently at random. Every family seems to make wine, and every house stands apart among its vines. The landscape is evenly dotted with modest houses – each rejoicing in the name of château. The church stands oddly isolated, too, like yet another little wine estate. And that is Pomerol; there is nothing more to see.

Geologically it is another big gravel bank, slightly rising and falling but remarkably flat overall. Towards Libourne the soil tends to be sandy while to the east and north, where it meets St-Emilion, it is often enriched with clay. What grows here is the gentlest, richest, most velvety, and instantly appealing form of red Bordeaux.

Pomerol is a democracy. It has no classification, and indeed it would be very hard to devise one. Some of the most glamorous names are only a few decades old, or less. Châteaux are small family affairs and subject to change as individuals come and go. Nor is the complexity of the soil, as it switches from gravel to gravelly clay to clay with gravel, or from sandy gravel to gravelly sand, exactly reflected in vineyard boundaries.

There is a good deal of agreement, however, about which are Pomerol's outstanding vineyards. Petrus was for years allowed by all to come first, with perhaps Trotanoy as runner-up – though Vieux Château Certan ("VCC") would contest this. Then along came Le Pin, microscopic even

by Pomerol standards (hardly 5 acres/3ha), the creation of Jacques Thienpont, a member of the Belgian family that also owns VCC.

Wine made in such tiny quantity can be hand-reared, resulting in an "ultra-wine", with an excess of everything, including charm (and of course scarcity), and this has been reflected in prices sometimes higher than those of Petrus. Impressive new cellars at both properties demonstrate how easy it has been to sell these super-luxurious wines.

Jewels in the crown

The map opposite distinguishes in capitals the growths whose wines currently fetch the highest prices. Clos l'Eglise and Châteaux

Le Pin's new *cuverie* could hardly be in greater contrast to the original cellar below the decidedly ordinary house that once stood here. The pine tree may remain but visitors no longer have to navigate a domestic washing machine.

Clinet, L'Eglise-Clinet (how confusing these names are!), La Fleur de Gay, and La Violette are relatively recent jewels in the Pomerol crown. Châteaux La Fleur-Pétrus, La Conseillante, L'Evangile, Lafleur, and Latour à Pomerol all have much longer track records of excellence.

The tight grouping of these châteaux on the clay soil is an indication of their character as well as their quality. These properties generally make the densest, fleshiest, and most opulent wines. Rather than being overwhelmed by the complications of Pomerol, it is worth knowing that the average standard here is very high. The village has a name for reliability. Bargains, on the other hand, are not often found.

One of the most potent influences in the district is the family firm of Jean-Pierre Moueix, the Libourne merchant which either owns or manages a high proportion of the finest properties. They renamed and rebuilt Hosanna (once Château Certan Guiraud) next to Petrus, and nearby Providence (formerly Château La Providence) was relaunched by the Moueixes with the 2005 vintage.

One advantage that has certainly helped the popularity of this little region is the fact that its wines are ready relatively soon for Bordeaux. The chief grape here is not the tough-skinned Cabernet Sauvignon, whose wine has to live through a tannic youth; in Pomerol Merlot is king. Great growths have about 70–80% Merlot,

The most famous Pomerol of all, Petrus, once managed by Christian Moueix, is now the property of his older brother, Jean-François, with Olivier Berrouet, the son of the previous winemaker Jean-Claude Berrouet, in charge of the cellar.

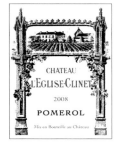

LALANDE-DE-POMEROL AND POMEROL

Our map shows how Pomerol merges into the gravelly western boundary of St-Emilion, where Châteaux Cheval Blanc and Figeac are to be found. The greatest concentration of leading Pomerol properties is easy to see, although their modest size surprises many visitors.

1:25,000

| Km 0 | 1 Km |
| Miles 0 | 1/2 Mile |

with perhaps 20% Cabernet Franc, known here as Bouchet. The greatest Pomerol, Petrus, is 100% Merlot (since 2010), growing in almost pure clay – with astonishing results.

Even the best Pomerol has produced much of its perfume and achieved its dazzling finesse within a dozen years or so, and many are already attractive at five years old.

- – – – – – Canton boundary
- – · – · – Commune (parish) boundary
- **CH LAFLEUR** Leading château
- Ch Guillot Other notable château
- La Fleur de Gay Microcuvée or part of one
- St-Émilion Premier Grand Cru Classé (A) vineyard
- Other vineyard
- Woods
- —50— Contour interval 5 metres

St-Emilion

The ancient and beautiful town of St-Emilion, epicentre of what has recently been Bordeaux's most seismic wine region, is propped in the corner of an escarpment above the Dordogne. Behind the town, on the sand and gravel plateau, vines flow steadily on into Pomerol. Beside it, along the ridge, they swoop down steep limestone slopes (the Côtes) into the plain.

The town is the tiny but much-visited rural gem of the Bordeaux region – a UNESCO World Heritage Site since 1999 – inland and upland in spirit, Roman in origin, hollow with cellars, and heady with wine. Even the church at St-Emilion is a cellar: cut, like them all, out of solid rock. The Michelin-starred Hostellerie de Plaisance in the town square is actually on the church roof, and you sit beside the belfry to eat your foie gras and lamb.

St-Emilion makes rich red wine. Before many people can really come to terms with the dryness and slight asperity of Médoc wines, they love the solid tastiness of St-Emilion. The best, made in ripe and sunny seasons, grow almost sweet as they mature.

The grapes of St-Emilion are the plump Merlot and the Cabernet Franc. Cabernet Sauvignon can have problems ripening in this climate, less tempered by the ocean, especially in its damper, cooler soils.

St-Emilion's classification system

The classification of St-Emilion is much more rigorously topical than that of the Médoc. Every 10 years or so (most recently in 2012) it revises its candidates for Premiers Grands Crus Classés and Grands Crus Classés. Other St-Emilions may be described as Grand Cru without the Classé (careful label inspection is needed). There are currently 18 of the first, with Cheval Blanc and Ausone now joined by Angélus and Pavie in a separate super-category of four, and 64 of the second. The plain Grands Crus run into hundreds. The most recent promotions to Premier Grand Cru Classé were Châteaux Larcis Ducasse, La Mondotte, and Valandraud (see below), and even quite famous properties may be demoted.

But many properties operate outside the classification system, some of them very successfully. In the early 1980s Château Tertre Roteboeuf was one of the first to be taken under new, fanatical management and pushed to the limits of quality and desirability without seeking official rank. Since then, dozens if not hundreds of the 800-odd châteaux to be found within this appellation have been modernized, and their wines made generally smoother, less rustic, and more concentrated.

Another new, arguably less benevolent, wave began in the early 1990s with the emergence of Château Valandraud, a fiercely unfiltered, concentrated wine conjured up by local négociant Jean-Luc Thunevin from a few tiny parcels of vines. This was the first of St-Emilion's "*microcuvées*" or "garage wines" (so-called because they tend to be made in such small quantities they can be made in a garage) and is now recognized as part of the establishment. But it spawned an army of imitators, appearing as if from nowhere. Those *microcuvées*, which seem to have established at least some reputation, are marked in magenta on the map here and on p.99 but many came and went without reaping the expected financial rewards. The formula is to produce attention-grabbing wines in quantities minute enough (generally fewer than 1,000 cases) to create demand. It sometimes works.

Meanwhile, the extensive St-Emilion appellation has also attracted more than its fair share of newcomer investors who have typically bought vineyards, invested heavily in new cellars and winemaking equipment, and hired one of several high-profile oenologists who specialize in this area, such as Gilles Pauquet, Michel Rolland, Stéphane Derenoncourt, and Stéphane Toutoundji. In this respect, and even in the style of some of its more deliberately modernist wines, St-Emilion has a certain unexpected similarity with California's Napa Valley. The hand of man and mammon can seem particularly powerful here.

The plateau and the Côtes

There are two distinct districts of St-Emilion, not counting the lesser vineyards of the river plain and the parishes to the east and northeast that are allowed to use the name (they are described and mapped on pp.98–99). See overleaf for more detail on the particularly varied soil types of the St-Emilion appellation.

One group of the finest châteaux lies on the border of Pomerol, on the western edge of St-Emilion's sandy and gravelly plateau. The most famous is Cheval Blanc, its new eye-catching, environmentally friendly winery (see overleaf) as impressive as the beautifully balanced wine that its predominantly Cabernet Franc vines can produce. Of Cheval Blanc's

---

Map legend:

- – – – – – Canton boundary
- ———— Commune (parish) boundary
- **CH AUSONE** Premier Grand Cru Classé (2012)
- **Ch Laroze** Grand Cru Classé
- *Ch la Fleur* Other notable château
- Ch Rol Valentin Microcuvée or part of one
- Premier Grand Cru Classé (A) vineyard
- Other vineyard
- Woods
- —25— Contour interval 5 metres

CHÂTEAU AUSONE
SAINT-ÉMILION
1ᵉʳ GRAND CRU CLASSÉ "A"
→ 2009 ←
FAMILLE VAUTHIER
Propriétaire

1ᵉʳ GRAND CRU CLASSÉ
Château Pavie
SAINT-ÉMILION GRAND CRU
2009
C. & G. PERSE - VITICULTEURS

CHÂTEAU CHEVAL BLANC
2009
St Émilion
1ᵉʳ GRAND CRU CLASSÉ "A"
Mis en bouteille au Château

Châteaux Angélus and Pavie were promoted to the same elevated status as Ausone and Cheval Blanc in 2012 – not without controversy. Meanwhile, the Moueix family absorbed the vineyards of the old Château Magdelaine into Bélair Monange (once simply Belair).

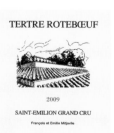

THE HEART OF ST-EMILION

All 18 of the Premier Grand Cru Classé châteaux are located on this map, as are the majority of the Grands Crus Classés. The remainder are mapped on pp.98–99, where the full extent of the St-Emilion appellation is revealed.

neighbours, it is the big Château Figeac which comes nearest to its level, from even more gravelly soil and with, unusually, a significant proportion of Cabernet Sauvignon.

The other, larger, group, the Côtes St-Emilion, occupies the escarpment around and to the east of the town towards St-Laurent-des-Combes. A particularly propitious, south-facing slope flanks the southern tip of the town from Tertre Daugay via the Pavies to Tertre Roteboeuf. The plateau ends so abruptly that it is easy to see just how thin a layer of soil covers the soft but solid limestone in which the cellars are hewn. At the revitalized Château Ausone, the jewel of the Côtes, in one of the finest situations in all Bordeaux overlooking the Dordogne Valley, you can walk into a cellar with vines growing above you.

THE TERROIRS OF ST-EMILION

The soil map of the St-Emilion appellation below, based on extensive research undertaken by Cornelis Van Leeuwen at the University of Bordeaux for the Syndicat Viticole de St-Emilion, shows just how dramatic are the variations in terroir within this complex appellation.

Much of the land south of the main road to Bergerac looks distinctly unpromising, with its recent alluvial deposits from the Dordogne, which are gravelly closer to the river's flood plain, sandy further away. Moving uphill towards St-Emilion itself we encounter sandy soils which

we would expect to produce relatively light wine (there are exceptions), but this soon gives way to the limestone base that is so obvious to visitors to the town. Soft *molasses du Fronsadais* (the same soil type as is found in Fronsac) forms the lower slopes and the much harder *calcaire à Asteries* plateau, with clay-rich topsoil. It is hardly surprising that such good wine can be made from grapes grown on the so-called Côtes. These slopes around the town are the result of the work of the Dordogne, Isle, and then Barbanne rivers on Tertiary deposits in the Quaternary period.

Note, too, the islands that are richer in loam than clay, particularly the one north of St-Hippolyte.

But northwest of the town is an extensive swathe of quite different shallow sandy soils that is relieved most dramatically by the mound of gravel on the Pomerol border where châteaux Figeac and Cheval Blanc are to be found.

This map explains very clearly why Figeac and Cheval Blanc can taste so similar, and why Cheval Blanc is so very different in style to the other three Premiers Grands Crus Classés (A).

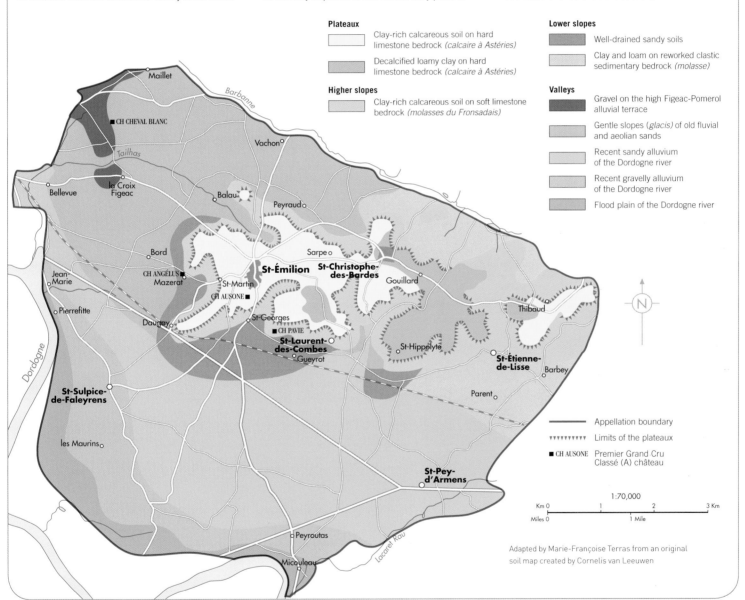

Plateaux

Clay-rich calcareous soil on hard limestone bedrock (*calcaire à Astéries*)

Decalcified loamy clay on hard limestone bedrock (*calcaire à Astéries*)

Higher slopes

Clay-rich calcareous soil on soft limestone bedrock (*molasses du Fronsadais*)

Lower slopes

Well-drained sandy soils

Clay and loam on reworked clastic sedimentary bedrock (*molasse*)

Valleys

Gravel on the high Figeac-Pomerol alluvial terrace

Gentle slopes (*glacis*) of old fluvial and aeolian sands

Recent sandy alluvium of the Dordogne river

Recent gravelly alluvium of the Dordogne river

Flood plain of the Dordogne river

Appellation boundary

ᐅᐅᐅᐅᐅᐅᐅᐅ Limits of the plateaux

■ CH AUSONE Premier Grand Cru Classé (A) château

1:70,000

Adapted by Marie-Françoise Terras from an original soil map created by Cornelis van Leeuwen

The Côtes wines may not be quite so fruity as the "Graves" wines from the plateau (the name Graves is confusingly applied to them

because of their gravel soil), but at their best they are some of the most perfumed and generous wines of Bordeaux. They are typically more alcoholic than wine from the Médoc, often more than 14% nowadays, but the best can live as long. The Côtes provide shelter from the north and west, an incline towards the sun, and relative immunity to frost. On the plateau around Château Cheval Blanc, on the other hand, a slight dip in the

ground acts as a sump in which freezing air can collect on cloudless winter nights.

In a remarkably short time St-Emilion has been transformed from a sleepy backwater into a hotbed of ambition and heavily touted new labels, but the comfort of St-Emilion to the ordinary wine-lover is the number of other châteaux of moderate fame and consistently high standards which can provide relatively early-maturing, utterly enjoyable, reasonably affordable wine.

Château Cheval Blanc's defiantly modern new winery was officially operational in time for the 2011 harvest, gathered in to fill up to 52 different, unusually potbellied concrete fermentation vats. The modern fashion is to appoint one vat per discernibly distinct plot of vines.

Wines of the Southwest

South of the great vineyard of Bordeaux, west of the Midi, and sheltered from the Atlantic by the forests of the Landes, the vine flourishes in scattered areas that still have strong local gastronomic traditions, each by a river – the vine's old link to distant markets. This was the "High Country" that the jealous merchants of Bordeaux excluded from the port until their own wine was sold (sometimes, to compound the injury, beefed up with sturdier stuff made upstream). The Bordeaux grape varieties may dominate the areas on the fringes of the Gironde département where Bordeaux wine is made (including the Dordogne wines discussed overleaf), but elsewhere in this southwestern corner is France's most varied collection of indigenous wine grapes, many peculiar to their own small appellation. Ancient vine variety recuperation is a popular sport here.

Cahors, famous for the depth and longevity of its wines since the Middle Ages, is typical. Although some lesser wines are softened by Merlot, it depends for its soul and flavour on a grape known here as Côt, in Argentina and Bordeaux as Malbec. Thanks to this grape, and to summers that are generally warmer than Bordeaux's, Cahors tends to be fuller and more vigorous, if a little more rustic, than typical red Bordeaux. Vines are planted on the three alluvial terraces above the River Lot with the highest most highly regarded. Since Argentina recently put Malbec on the international wine map, there has been a certain amount of emulation, with some winemakers chasing ripeness and making a much more daring use of oak. A few dozen wines are designated by a panel as Cahors Excellence each vintage.

As far again upstream from Cahors as Cahors is from the Gironde département boundary (and therefore marked on the map of France on p.47 rather than here) are the vineyards of the Aveyron département. Up in wild country are the last vestiges of the Massif Central's once-flourishing vignoble. **Marcillac** is the most important wine, a much-improved, peppery light red made from Fer Servadou, potentially hard as iron but increasingly ripe, thanks to global warming. Its multihued neighbours, **Entraygues – Le Fel** and **Estaing** are rare and becoming rarer, in contrast to the **Côtes de Millau** to the south, whose mountain reds are made from a thoroughly southwestern cocktail of grapes.

The hill country around the River Tarn, west of Albi, and downstream of the magnificent gorge cut by the river into the Cévennes, seems tame by comparison. Its rolling green pastureland is gentle in both aspect and climate, studded with beautiful towns and villages, of which 73 are contained within the appellation **Gaillac**. Wine was probably made here long before vines were cultivated downstream in Bordeaux but, as in Cahors, the phylloxera vine louse crippled the wine trade. It has been revived with real enthusiasm only in the last decade or two. Much of this is because of increased sophistication in matching the varied terroirs of Gaillac to its decidedly various vine varieties. The most characteristic red wine ingredients are the peppery local Braucol (Fer Servadou), now making some convincing wine, and much lighter Duras. Syrah is a welcome intruder, Gamay less so for early-drinking Gaillac Primeur, and

SOUTHWEST FRANCE'S WINE REGIONS

You have only to look at the key to this map to see how complex official wine geography is in this corner of France. Cahors and Jurançon are two of the few appellations to have any reputation outside France.

The wines whose labels are shown here vary enormously in grape varieties used, colour, and sweetness level (the Renaissance Gaillac is very sweet indeed). But they all echo the sort of structure to be found in their counterparts made in Bordeaux to the northwest.

CH PINERAIE — Notable producer
— - — International boundary
— - — Département boundary

AOP/AOC
- Armagnac
- Béarn
- Brulhois
- Buzet
- Cahors
- Coteaux du Quercy
- Côtes de Duras
- Côtes du Marmandais
- Fronton
- Gaillac
- Irouléguy
- Jurançon
- Madiran et Pacherenc du Vic-Bilh
- St-Mont
- St-Sardos
- Tursan

IGP/Vin de Pays
- Côtes de Gascogne
- Lavilledieu
- 109 — Area mapped at larger scale on page shown

Bordeaux red grapes are tolerated. Darker-skinned grapes now predominate and work best on the gravelly clay soils south of the Tarn. Those around Cunac (off the map to the east of Albi) are rather wasted on the Gamay currently grown for the local co-op. The southeast-facing Premières Côtes, which rise on the river's right bank, are particularly well-suited to the sweet and sweetish whites for which Gaillac, with its long, dry autumns, was once famous. They are made from such local specialities as Mauzac (whose apple peel flavours are also common in Limoux), Len de l'El, the relatively rare Ondenc, together with Muscadelle and Sauvignon Blanc. Modern white

wines are typically off-dry and made with varying degrees of sparkle, including the gently fizzing Perlé, and are a speciality of the limestone vineyards to the north, notably around the hill town of Cordes. Outsiders can find this proliferation of grapes and wine styles confusing, but for innovators such as Robert Plageoles – his standard range of still reds, pinks, and whites is supplemented not only by a sweet, cloudy, low-alcohol fizz made by the traditional *méthode gaillacoise* but also by a Gaillac variant on a dry sherry – it serves only as inspiration.

Immediately to the west between the Tarn and the Garonne, **Fronton** is the local red and rosé

wine of Toulouse based on the florally scented native Négrette grapes, mixed with sundry others of the southwest (and sometimes Syrah or Gamay). **Lavilledieu** and **Brulhois** are similar wines made downstream, the latter stiffened by Tannat.

A vast sweep of vineyards east of Mont-de-Marsan is devoted to Armagnac, in many eyes a brandy that surpasses even Cognac, although its grapes are increasingly diverted into inexpensive crisp white IGP Côtes de Gascogne. Just to its north, on the left bank of the Garonne, lies **Buzet**, with vineyards scattered over 27 communes of orchards and farms. Production is largely in the

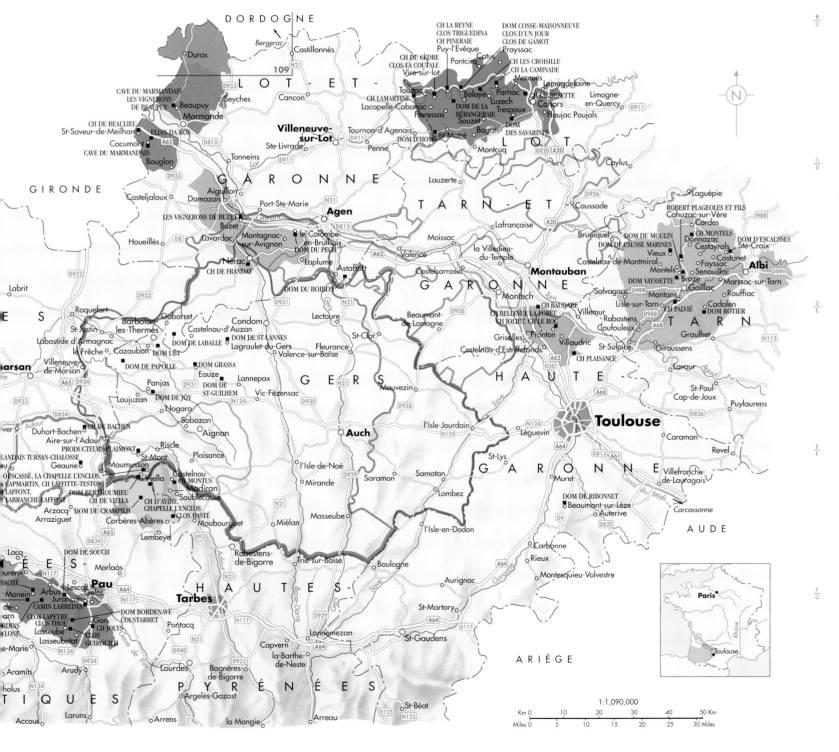

1:1,090,000

hands of one well-organized co-op, whose red could be described as "country claret". The **Côtes du Marmandais**, even further north, has been revolutionized by local winemaker Elian da Ros. Abouriou grapes spice up the Bordeaux blend that characterizes these parts.

The remaining wine regions on this map historically depended on the port of Bayonne rather than Bordeaux. The general **Béarn** appellation and its **Béarn-Bellocq** enclave encompass the red, white, and rosé wines made outside the celebrated wine zones of Madiran and Jurançon, the two true jewels of the southwest.

Madiran is Gascony's great red wine, grown on clay and limestone hills along the left bank of the River Adour. The local red grape, Tannat, is well-named for its dark and tannic, tough and vigorous wines, often blended with some Cabernet and Pinenc (Fer Servadou). The region's dynamic winemakers differ on whether and how to tame these monsters, using varying degrees of new oak and even deliberate (micro-) oxygenation. Some of these wines can be drunk earlier but, after seven or eight years, fine Madiran is truly admirable: aromatic, full of

flavour, fluid, and lively, well able to withstand both comparison with classed-growth Bordeaux and an accompanying *confit de canard*.

The winemaking talent of this region has been turning its attention to the local whites, too, not least the Plaimont co-operative union, which dominates production of **St-Mont** and has done much to rescue local vine varieties from extinction. Sweet and dry white **Pacherenc du Vic-Bilh** is made within the Madiran zone from Arrufiac, Petit Courbu, and Gros and Petit Manseng grapes, and is more exciting every year, but tends to be overshadowed by its counterpart south of Pau, Jurançon.

Jurançon is one of France's most distinctive white wines, a tangy, green-tinged essence made in a wide range of sweetness levels on the steep Pyrenean foothills of Béarn. Gros Manseng grapes are responsible for the dry, earlier-picked Jurançon Sec, while the smaller, thicker-skinned Petit Manseng berries are much more suitable for leaving on the vine into November, and sometimes even December, to shrivel and concentrate both sugars and acidity (noble rot is not a feature of Jurançon). These sweet *moelleux*

All vineyards are photogenic in autumn, but the mix of soil types and the varieties planted in Cahors adds to the already colourful mosaic. The leading variety, Malbec, has been given a new lease of life by its popularity in Argentine form.

wines are lively enough to drink, as the French do, at the beginning of a meal, with the local foie gras for instance, and are perhaps closer to Vouvray in style than to the weight of a good Sauternes. Wines labelled Vendange Tardive are richer, made from even more shrivelled grapes picked during at least two passages through the vineyard.

Tursan, downstream of Madiran, is being revitalized by several ambitious producers, among them the super-chef Michel Guérard, although red wines outnumber the interesting whites made from Baroque grapes.

The tiny appellation of **Irouléguy** makes France's only Basque wine: firm, refreshing rosé, red, and white wines of the local grapes, including Tannat, Petit Courbu, and the Mansengs, grown on south-facing terraces as high as 1,300ft (400m) above the Atlantic, their labels heavily adorned with Xs.

Dordogne

The Bordeaux right bank's beautiful hinterland, the bastide country of the Dordogne leading back into the maze of green valleys cut into the stony upland of Périgueux, has long been a favourite with tourists. And now they can buy IGP wines labelled Périgord Dordogne, made anywhere in the département, and Périgord Vin de Domme, made around that particular village (see p.47).

The small **Côtes de Duras** appellation is effectively a bridge between Entre-Deux-Mers and Bergerac and produces a number of thoroughly respectable reds and whites from Bordeaux grapes. Traditionally, the wines of **Bergerac** were seen as country bumpkins beside the sophisticates of Bordeaux. The most ordinary red and dry white wines of the Dordogne département's catch-all appellation still resemble the most basic AOC Bordeaux, with the same shortcomings, but there is now a critical mass of producers who produce far more serious wines of all three hues and, in whites, all sweetness levels. Luc de Conti of Château Tour des Gendres, a biodynamic convert, deserves considerable, although not exclusive, credit.

The grapes are the same as Bordeaux's. The climate is a little more extreme than that of the Atlantic-influenced Gironde, and there is limestone on higher ground. The range of whites is wide, if confusing, and worth exploring. Bergerac Sec can be a forceful dry white made from any combination of Sémillon and Sauvignon Blanc (although some serious sweet white is also produced, mainly for local consumption). Côtes de Bergerac distinguishes superior reds. Within the greater Bergerac region are many individual appellations – so many that some are virtually ignored. Only a handful of growers choose to sell their delicate, slightly sweet whites as **Rosette**, for example. In the same area the **Pécharmant** appellation is celebrated almost exclusively locally for its full-bodied, sometimes-oaked reds.

Just over the departmental boundary from the Côtes de Castillon (see pp.98–99) is the complex **Montravel** wine zone in which **Côtes de Montravel** and **Haut-Montravel** are sweeter whites coming from, respectively, the north and east of the area. Straight Montravel white is a dry wine produced all over the zone, made with increasing confidence and often using both Sauvignon Blanc and oak, while Sémillon is king

of the sweet wines, which are remarkably like the best sweet whites made over the border in Bordeaux's Côtes de Francs. Muscadelle is allowed here, too. Merlot-dominated Montravel red now has its own appellation but the wine may be declassified to Bergerac if it does not pass muster with the local tasting committee.

The most distinctive, most glamorous wines of this part of France are sumptuously sweet, white, and made in dispiritingly small quantities in two zones southwest of the town of Bergerac. Indeed, the total production of **Saussignac**, Monbazillac's western neighbour and home to some extraordinarily determined producers, is only a few thousand cases.

The total output of Bergerac's most famous wine, **Monbazillac**, is 30 times greater and average quality has improved considerably since 1993, when machine-picking was abandoned in favour of several selective harvests by hand. Much lighter doses of sulphur dioxide have become the norm. Like the Sauternes region, Monbazillac lies just east of where a tributary flows into the left bank of a major river (in this case the Gardonette and the Dordogne) but the terrain is much hillier. The permitted grapes are also the same, but the wines are not – one reason perhaps being Muscadelle's particular aptitude in Monbazillac.

Botrytis may sweep through the vineyards of Monbazillac when there is none in Sauternes, but multiple picking sorties through the vineyard are usually necessary, just as in Sauternes. The best young Monbazillacs, such as those of Château Tirecul La Gravière, are more exuberant, more sprightly than the best young Sauternes, whereas mature Monbazillac takes on an amber nuttiness that is decidedly uncharacteristic of Bordeaux's most famous sweet white wine.

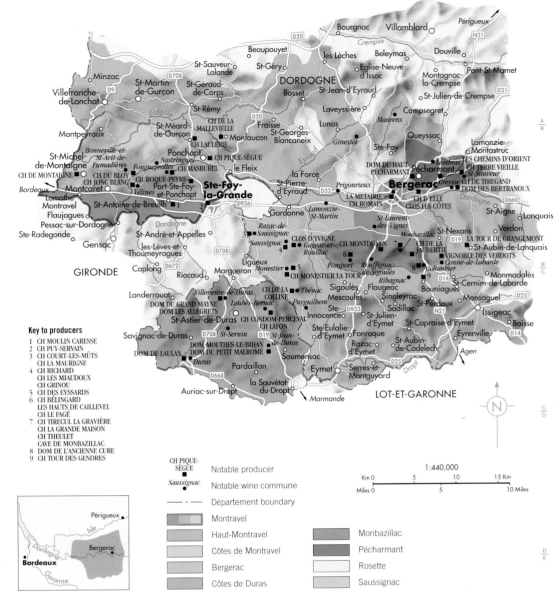

Key to producers
1 CH MOULIN CARESSE
2 CH PUY-SERVAIN
3 CH COURT-LES-MÛTS
   CH LA MAURIGNE
4 CH RICHARD
   CH LES MIAUDOUX
   CH GRINOU
5 CH DES EYSSARDS
6 CH BÉLINGARD
   LES HAUTS DE CAILLEVEL
   CH LE FAGÉ
7 CH TIRECUL LA GRAVIÈRE
   CH LA GRANDE MAISON
   CH THEULET
   CAVE DE MONBAZILLAC
8 DOM DE L'ANCIENNE CURE
9 CH TOUR DES GENDRES

CH PIQUE-SÈGUE — Notable producer
Saussignac — Notable wine commune
- - - - Département boundary
Montravel
Haut-Montravel
Côtes de Montravel
Bergerac
Côtes de Duras
Monbazillac
Pécharmant
Rosette
Saussignac

1:440,000

The leading lights of Dordogne wine have been Bruno and Claudie Balancini at Château Tirecul La Gravière, and Luc de Conti at Château Tour des Gendres. The Balancinis' Cuvée Madame is made only in the best years.

The Loire Valley

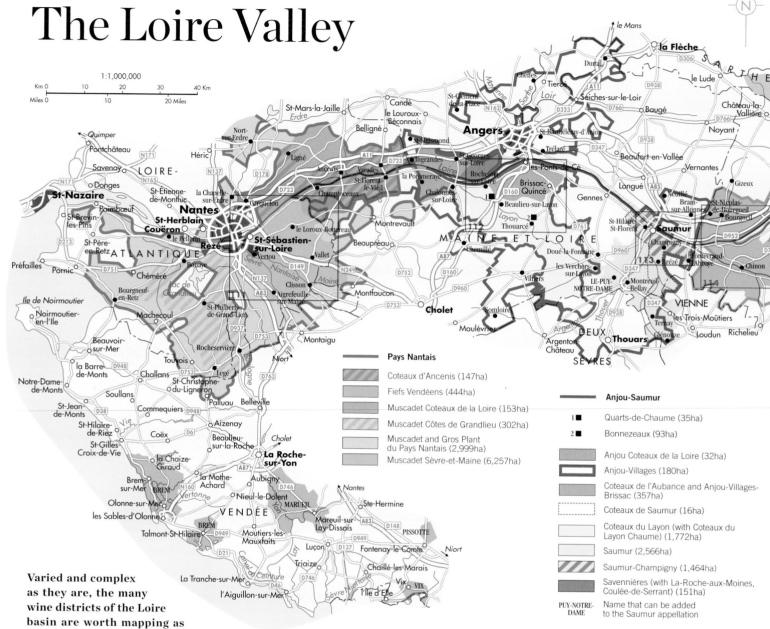

1:1,000,000

Pays Nantais

	Coteaux d'Ancenis (147ha)
	Fiefs Vendéens (444ha)
	Muscadet Coteaux de la Loire (153ha)
	Muscadet Côtes de Grandlieu (302ha)
	Muscadet and Gros Plant du Pays Nantais (2,999ha)
	Muscadet Sèvre-et-Maine (6,257ha)

Anjou-Saumur

1 ■	Quarts-de-Chaume (35ha)
2 ■	Bonnezeaux (93ha)
	Anjou Coteaux de la Loire (32ha)
	Anjou-Villages (180ha)
	Coteaux de l'Aubance and Anjou-Villages-Brissac (357ha)
	Coteaux de Saumur (16ha)
	Coteaux du Layon (with Coteaux du Layon Chaume) (1,772ha)
	Saumur (2,566ha)
	Saumur-Champigny (1,464ha)
	Savennières (with La-Roche-aux-Moines, Coulée-de-Serrant) (151ha)
PUY-NOTRE-DAME	Name that can be added to the Saumur appellation

Varied and complex as they are, the many wine districts of the Loire basin are worth mapping as a whole, for although they are so far-flung (see the map of France on p.47 for the outlying ones), with wide variations of climate, soil, and tradition, and four or five important grape varieties, the wines do have a family likeness. They are light and invigorating, with palpable acidity – and, generally, moderate prices. Well over half of all Loire wines are white. They divide clearly between the dry wines to the east (Sancerre and Pouilly) and west (Muscadet), with the often-sweeter wines of Touraine and Anjou in the middle, made from the Loire's own grape, Chenin Blanc. The best reds of Touraine and Anjou, however, have all of the fragrance and charm of Cabernet Franc.

Brittany's wine country – one might almost say "Neptune's vineyard" – is the Pays Nantais, the home of **Muscadet**, the first modern success story for the Loire. Beside a plate of shrimps, oysters or mussels this very dry, slightly salty, but firm rather than acidic white is one of gastronomy's most convincing clichés. Muscadet is the name of the wine, not of a place or a grape (which in Muscadet's case is a sibling of Chardonnay, Melon de Bourgogne). The **Sèvre-et-Maine** region, which is mapped in detail opposite, has 69% of Muscadet's vineyards, densely planted on low hills of varied origin, most notably of gneiss and granite. The heart of the district lies around Vertou, Vallet, St-Fiacre, and La Chapelle-Heulin – the area where the wines are ripest, liveliest, and most scented. **Muscadet Coteaux de la Loire**, made well inland on steep slopes of schist or granite, tends to be a little leaner, while **Muscadet Côtes de Grandlieu**, made on sandy, stony soils, is more supple and riper than most.

Muscadet has traditionally been bottled *sur lie* – straight from the fermentation vat, unracked – the lees deepening both flavour and texture. The best producers are, happily, determined to throw off Muscadet's reputation for simplicity, working for healthier, riper grapes, experimenting with long lees-ageing, distinguishing between different

soils, and treating some of their best wines to oak ageing in almost Burgundian idiom. Their ambitions are leading to interesting new, if still embryonic, label designations.

Outside the areas mapped in detail, **Jasnières** produces some fine, challengingly dry Chenin Blanc on what is effectively a single slope. And the **Coteaux du Loir** is worth watching for fresh, light red or rosé Pineau d'Aunis. **Cheverny**, meanwhile, flourishes in myriad forms, of which some quite piercing Sauvignon Blanc is probably best; sharp dry whites made from Romorantin grapes are labelled **Cour-Cheverny**.

Irregular quality dogs growers this far north. Although climate change is having a marked effect, ripeness in many vineyards varies so widely from year to year that they hardly seem to produce the same wine. A fine autumn ripens grapes almost to raisins, but a wet one can deliver a very acidic product. Hence the importance of the sparkling wine industry.

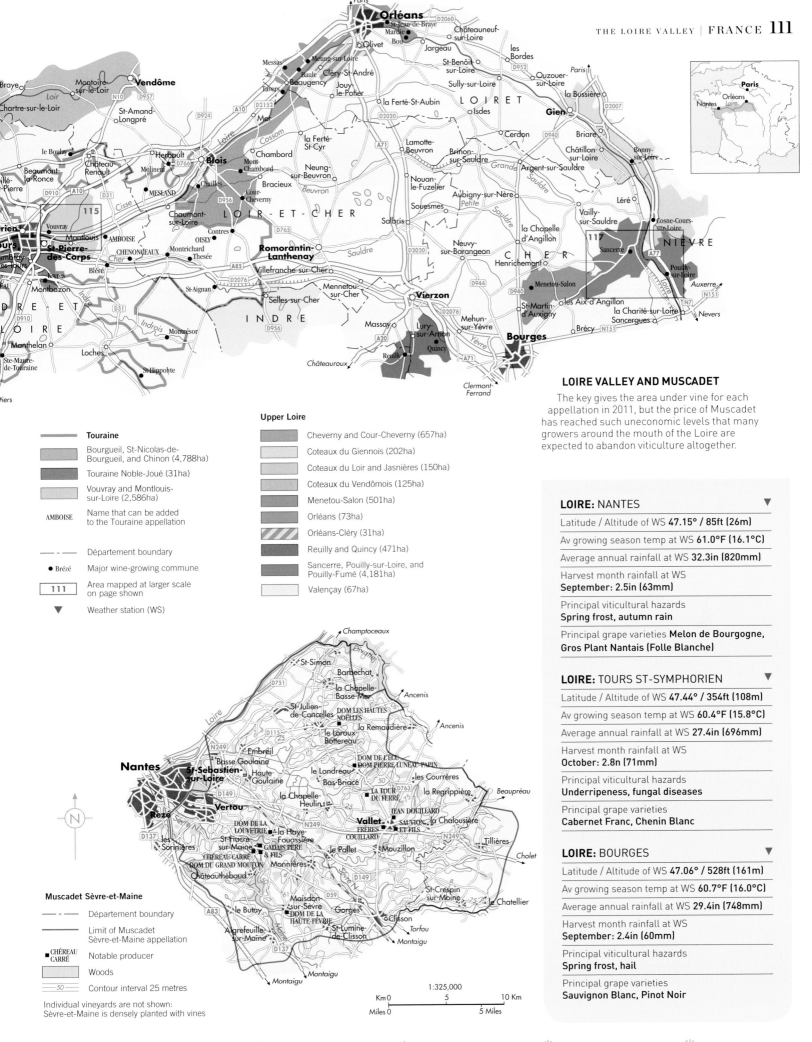

LOIRE VALLEY AND MUSCADET

The key gives the area under vine for each appellation in 2011, but the price of Muscadet has reached such uneconomic levels that many growers around the mouth of the Loire are expected to abandon viticulture altogether.

Touraine

- Bourgueil, St-Nicolas-de-Bourgueil, and Chinon (4,788ha)
- Touraine Noble-Joué (31ha)
- Vouvray and Montlouis-sur-Loire (2,586ha)

AMBOISE Name that can be added to the Touraine appellation

— - — Département boundary

● Brézé Major wine-growing commune

111 Area mapped at larger scale on page shown

▼ Weather station (WS)

Upper Loire

- Cheverny and Cour-Cheverny (657ha)
- Coteaux du Giennois (202ha)
- Coteaux du Loir and Jasnières (150ha)
- Coteaux du Vendômois (125ha)
- Menetou-Salon (501ha)
- Orléans (73ha)
- Orléans-Cléry (31ha)
- Reuilly and Quincy (471ha)
- Sancerre, Pouilly-sur-Loire, and Pouilly-Fumé (4,181ha)
- Valençay (67ha)

Muscadet Sèvre-et-Maine

— - — Département boundary

——— Limit of Muscadet Sèvre-et-Maine appellation

■ CHÉREAU CARRÉ Notable producer

Woods

—50— Contour interval 25 metres

Individual vineyards are not shown: Sèvre-et-Maine is densely planted with vines

1:325,000

Km 0 — 5 — 10 Km
Miles 0 — 5 Miles

LOIRE: NANTES ▼

Latitude / Altitude of WS	**47.15° / 85ft (26m)**
Av growing season temp at WS	**61.0°F (16.1°C)**
Average annual rainfall at WS	**32.3in (820mm)**
Harvest month rainfall at WS	**September: 2.5in (63mm)**
Principal viticultural hazards	**Spring frost, autumn rain**
Principal grape varieties	**Melon de Bourgogne, Gros Plant Nantais (Folle Blanche)**

LOIRE: TOURS ST-SYMPHORIEN ▼

Latitude / Altitude of WS	**47.44° / 354ft (108m)**
Av growing season temp at WS	**60.4°F (15.8°C)**
Average annual rainfall at WS	**27.4in (696mm)**
Harvest month rainfall at WS	**October: 2.8n (71mm)**
Principal viticultural hazards	**Underripeness, fungal diseases**
Principal grape varieties	**Cabernet Franc, Chenin Blanc**

LOIRE: BOURGES ▼

Latitude / Altitude of WS	**47.06° / 528ft (161m)**
Av growing season temp at WS	**60.7°F (16.0°C)**
Average annual rainfall at WS	**29.4in (748mm)**
Harvest month rainfall at WS	**September: 2.4in (60mm)**
Principal viticultural hazards	**Spring frost, hail**
Principal grape varieties	**Sauvignon Blanc, Pinot Noir**

Anjou

The ideal and goal of Anjou was traditionally sweet white wine, the product of autumn sunshine and noble rot. In the past, years without their benison produced little of value. But truly fine dry (*sec*) white is now produced every year, thanks to picking by hand (rather than the ubiquitous machine harvester), the strictest selection at harvest, and the sensitive use of oak.

The grape that gives us all this is the Chenin Blanc, called locally Pineau de la Loire. It can reach thrilling ripeness and sweetness with near perfect acid balance in the southeast of the area mapped here: **Coteaux du Layon**. Here the Parisian Basin bumps up against the Massif Amoricain, creating buttes fully exposed south-southwest to the sun and to drying winds straight off the Atlantic, which help to concentrate the grape sugars. The particularly well-protected **Quarts de Chaume,** with only 86 acres (35ha), is the Loire's first official Grand Cru. **Bonnezeaux** (with about 2.5 times the vineyard area) is also outstanding enough to have its own appellation.

The elusive River Aubance, parallel with the Layon to the south, also sees great sweet white wines, when Nature co-operates. **Coteaux de l'Aubance** has been invaded by what can seem like an army of talented wine producers.

Savennières lies north of the Loire, on one of its rare steep south-facing banks. Again it is Chenin Blanc, but here the wine is dry, as dense and rich in substance as it is rigid in structure. This combination of concentration and acidity deserves years in bottle. Within Savennières two vineyards have their own appellation: **La Roche aux Moines**, with just under 50 acres (19ha), and **La Coulée de Serrant**, with a mere 15 fiercely biodynamic acres (6ha).

These are historically the most distinguished wines of Anjou, but the region's basic Anjou appellation has also been in a state of benevolent transformation. **Anjou Blanc** can nowadays be firm and characterful. Even the sickly **Rosé d'Anjou** is being overtaken by the delicately scented, off-dry rosé **Cabernet d'Anjou**.

Although soils here seem generally better suited to whites, Cabernet Franc has its place, too. Anjou's growers are mastering their vines and new oak barrels to become accomplished producers of aromatic reds. The best of these, occasionally stiffened by Cabernet Sauvignon, earn the appellations **Anjou-Villages** and its heartland **Anjou-Villages-Brissac**. In the best vintages they can provide the subtle thrill of a great Touraine red at a fraction of the price.

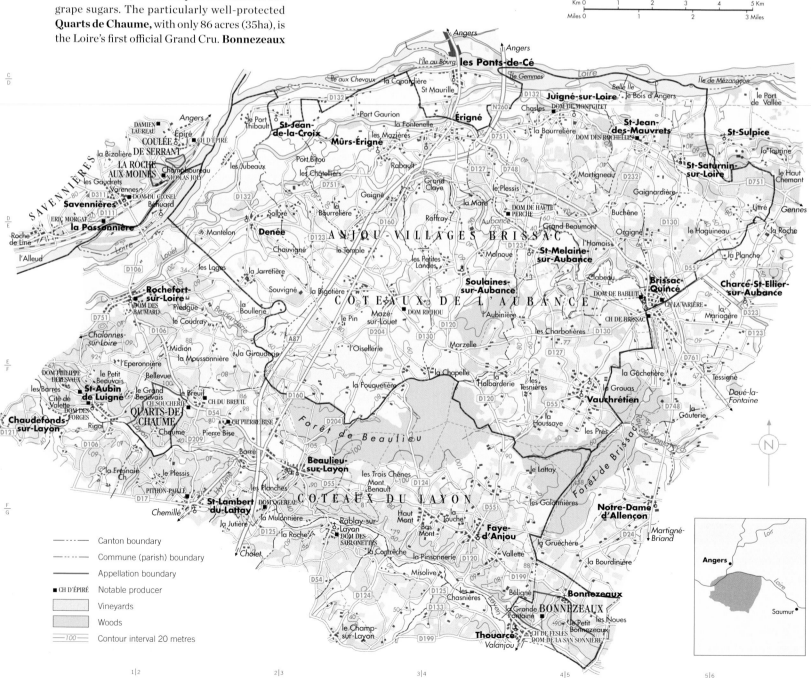

Km 0   1   2   3   4   5 Km
1:112,500
Miles 0   1   2   3 Miles

Canton boundary
Commune (parish) boundary
Appellation boundary
CH D'ÉPIRÉ Notable producer
Vineyards
Woods
100 Contour interval 20 metres

Saumur

Saumur in the past would have been nowhere without bubbles. As in Champagne, carbon dioxide makes a virtue of acidity. Sparkling Saumur (appellation Saumur Mousseux) mops up the Chenin Blanc (and up to 10% Chardonnay) grown all over Saumur, and even parts of Anjou, that is too tart to enjoy as a still wine.

The town of Saumur, lying 30 miles (48km) upstream of Angers, is the Loire's Reims and Epernay rolled into one, with kilometres of cellars carved in the soft local tuffeau. It is in the nature of Chenin Blanc to make more flirtatious, less flavoursome, fizz than champagne, but the best sparkling Saumurs – brut and made by the traditional method – are not without ambition. Parts of the blend may be fermented in oak or given extra ageing. On a higher level, though, comes the appellation **Crémant de Loire**: less geographically specific but stricter in the ground rules of its production, its wines generally considerably finer than Saumur Mousseux.

Still Saumur, without bubbles, comes in all three colours. It is much riper overall than it was a decade or two ago, but it is the **Saumur-Champigny** reds, from a small enclave on the left bank of the river, that deserve most attention. This is one of Cabernet Franc's most refreshing expressions, from tuffeau-dominated land that is effectively an extension of the best red wine country of Touraine just over the département boundary. Vines are densely planted along the white cliffs by the river, while inland, around the important wine centre of St-Cyr-en-Bourg with its reliable co-op, the local tuffeau becomes yellower and sandier and tends to produce slightly lighter wines.

Saumur Puy-Notre-Dame (about 12 miles/30km southwest of Saumur, see p.110) is a relatively new sub-appellation for fragrant, mainly Cabernet Franc reds made around the village of that name. As elsewhere in the Loire, reds are getting more potent and darker, thanks to much-improved vine-growing and climate change.

The Château de Saumur is just one of scores of grand châteaux that unfailingly draw visitors to the Loire Valley and help to introduce them to its glorious wines – which still struggle to make sufficient impact outside France. Too light? Too crisp to appeal to uneducated palates?

Map legend:
- Département boundary
- Canton boundary
- Commune (parish) boundary
- Appellation boundary
- DOM DE NERLEUX Notable producer
- Vineyards
- Woods
- —100— Contour interval 20 metres

This collection represents the wines of both Anjou – Chenins sweet and dry – and Saumur, which is better known for its Cabernet Franc-based reds, although L'Insolite is a nervy white based on particularly ancient Chenin Blanc vines.

Chinon and Bourgueil

Chinon, Bourgueil, and St-Nicolas-de-Bourgueil, are Touraine's – and the Loire's – best-known red wines. At this Atlantic-influenced western end of the Touraine, Cabernet Franc makes vigorous wine with raspberry fruitiness and the rasping savour of a sharpened pencil. In an average year the purple new wine is excellent drunk cool within a few months of the vintage. In outstandingly ripe years such as 2003, 2005, and 2009, the wine has the substance and structure, like a good red bordeaux, to mature for a decade. For its quality it is absurdly undervalued.

Chinon is grown on a patchwork of varied soils, whose produce is increasingly vinified separately. Vineyards on riverside sand and gravel make lighter, earlier-drinking styles of Chinon. Tuffeau, particularly the south-facing slopes of Cravant-les-Coteaux east of Chinon and the plateau above Beaumont to the west, tends to produce wines with the structure of a good **Bourgueil**, where steeper slopes and more limestone in the soil make wine which can improve for up to 10 years in bottle. **St-Nicolas-de-Bourgueil** has rather sandier soils than Bourgueil. Chinon's white wine ("taffeta" to

Rabelais) can be excellent, too. Chenin is Chinon's white grape and the appellation boundary is set to be extended south and west to incorporate communes devoted to Chenin, making more interesting wines than the Sauvignon that has become obligatory for white Touraine.

The greater Touraine region produces a host of other, usually less serious, reds, rosés, and whites, all called **Touraine** but sometimes with the geographical suffixes **Amboise**, **Azay-le-Rideau**, or **Mesland**. **Touraine Noble Joué** is an unusually dry, characterful rosé, or *vin gris*, made on the southern outskirts of Tours from Pinots Meunier, Noir, and Gris. For Touraine without a suffix, Gamay-based blends are *de rigueur* for reds, and Sauvignon Blanc – the best extremely good value – for zesty whites.

Three examples of Cabernet Franc, sometimes known here as Breton, at its very best – although this far north, vintages vary enormously, and underripe Cabernet Franc is not pretty. Furthermore, herbaceousness is seen as a fatal flaw by many.

– - – - – -	Canton boundary
– – – – –	Commune (parish) boundary
———	Appellation boundary
■ COULY-DUTHEIL	Notable producer
la Grille	Vineyard name/Lieu-dit
▨	Vineyards
▨	Woods
——100——	Contour interval 20 metres

1:127,500

Km 0   1   2   3   4   5 Km
Miles 0   1   2   3 Miles

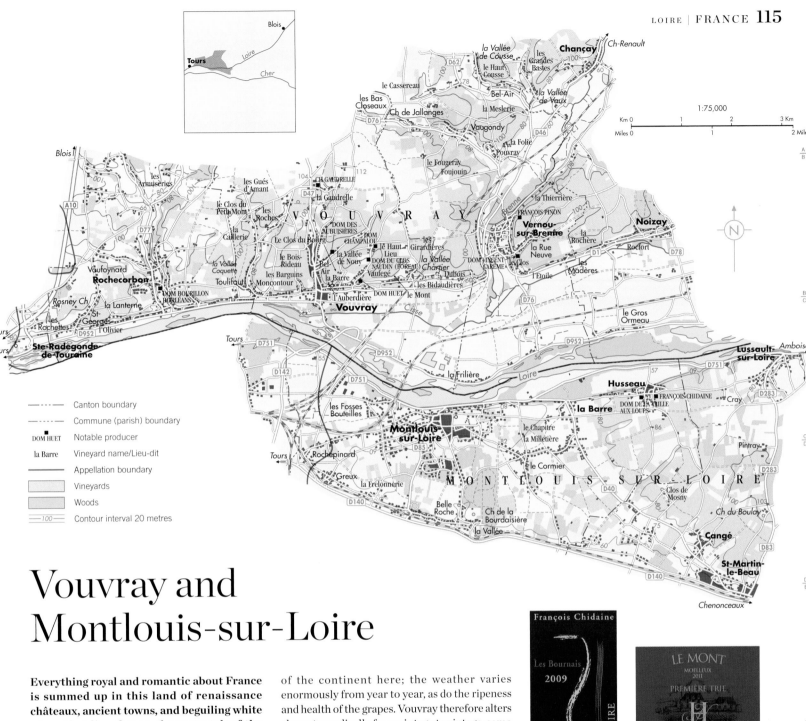

Vouvray and Montlouis-sur-Loire

Everything royal and romantic about France is summed up in this land of renaissance châteaux, ancient towns, and beguiling white wines that lies along a short stretch of the immense but lazy Loire. Low hills of soft tuffeau flank the river along the reach from Noizay to Rochecorbon. For centuries they have provided both cellars and cave-dwellings for the wine-growers of the district. The Chenin Blanc here, although often tarter than in Anjou, at its best is sweet, with the distinct taste of honey. What distinguishes it more than anything, however, is its long life. For a comparatively light wine its longevity is astonishing. You may expect port to live for half a century, but in a pale, firm, rather delicate wine, the ability to improve and go on improving for so long in bottle is matched only occasionally in Germany. The key is acidity.

The first distinction in **Vouvray** is whether any given bottle is dry (*sec*), off-dry (*sec-tendre*, an unofficial but increasingly popular style), medium-dry (*demi-sec*), sweet (*moelleux*), or for that matter sparkling. The influence of the Atlantic meets that

of the continent here; the weather varies enormously from year to year, as do the ripeness and health of the grapes. Vouvray therefore alters character radically from vintage to vintage: some years dry and austere, requiring many years' softening in the bottle (although fewer now that sulphur is used more sparingly); every now and then a gloriously rich expression of noble rot, requiring several different pickings through each vineyard. Less successful vintages may be converted into very good sparkling wines, which have a honeyed character and an ageing potential that sets them apart from sparkling Saumur.

Normally, only the richer vintages carry the name of one of the handful of famous vineyards on the best slopes, where clay and gravel overlie the riverside tuffeau. The best-known producer, Huet, owns three: Le Haut Lieu above the cellars, Le Mont, whose wines are the most concentrated, and the Clos du Bourg, the favourite of the famous former winemaker Noël Pinguet and the first of his conversions to biodynamic viticulture in the late 1980s.

The leading Vouvray producer, Huet, has been co-owned by American investor Anthony Hwang since 2005. He seems keener on producing dry Chenins like Chidaine's Montlouis than this super-sweet botrytised Moelleux from Le Mont.

Montlouis-sur-Loire has very similar conditions to Vouvray (even locals can find the wines difficult to differentiate), without the perfect sheltered, south-facing situation of the first rank of Vouvray's vineyards along the Loire. Soils tend to be sandier, and so Montlouis is stereotypically a little lighter and less intense, and more of it is destined to be made sparkling.

Sancerre and Pouilly

The aromatic white wines of Sancerre and Pouilly are perhaps the easiest to recognize in France. On these limestone and clay hills bisected by the upper reaches of the River Loire, in a near-continental climate, Sauvignon Blanc can make better, certainly finer and more complex, wine than anywhere else in the world. But it does so too rarely. The popularity of **Sancerre**, and **Pouilly-Fumé** made across the river, has allowed some less-than-thrilling examples on to our shelves and wine lists.

Pouilly-sur-Loire is the town; its wine is only called Pouilly-Fumé when it is made from the Sauvignon Blanc. Its other grape, Chasselas, once grown for Parisian tables, makes wine so mild that its survival here is a mystery.

It would be a brave taster who maintained he or she could always tell a Pouilly-Fumé from a Sancerre. The best of each are on the same level: the Sancerre perhaps slightly fuller and more obvious, the Pouilly-Fumé more perfumed. Many Pouilly vineyards are lower than those of Sancerre, which lie at altitudes of 650–1,150ft (200–350m) flanking the hilltop town, but most of the best are to the north of Pouilly itself. The soils here have a high proportion of clay-flint (silex), which confers the potential for age-worthy, almost acrid wines described as having a gunflint (*pierre à fusil*) character. Silex occurs in bands from northwest to southeast throughout both appellations, while vineyards in the west of the Sancerre appellation tend to be on *terres blanches*: white limestone soils with a high proportion of clay resulting in rather sturdier wines. In between these two zones, the limestone is often mixed with pebbles and the wines are more linear and refined.

Sancerre's extent

A total of 14 villages and three hamlets have the right to produce Sancerre. The two best Sancerre vineyards are generally acknowledged to be the pebbly, calcareous Chêne Marchand in the village of Bué, which makes particularly mineral, finely etched Sancerre, and the Monts Damnés in Chavignol, where kimmeridgean marl (clay-limestone) produces broader wines. The silex of Ménétréol gives steelier wine – provided the winemaker is committed to quality.

The total area of Sancerre vineyard more than trebled in the last quarter of the 20th century and by 2011 had reached 7,150 acres (2,900ha), more than two times the extent of Pouilly-Fumé.

The hilltop town of Sancerre seen at sunset in late spring from clay-flint (silex) vineyards. This is the French home of the much-travelled Sauvignon Blanc and the best wines have that fashionable quality called "minerality".

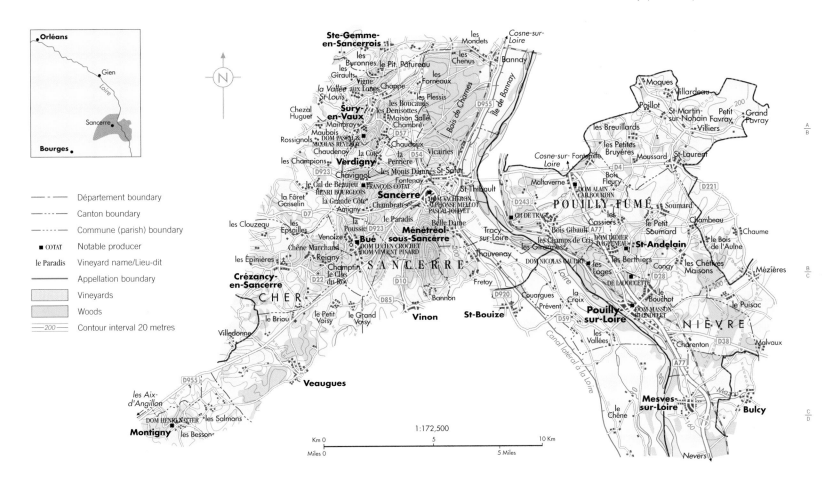

Legend:
- —·—·— Département boundary
- ——— Canton boundary
- ········· Commune (parish) boundary
- ■ COTAT Notable producer
- *le Paradis* Vineyard name/Lieu-dit
- ——— Appellation boundary
- Vineyards
- Woods
- —200— Contour interval 20 metres

1:172,500

Km 0 — 5 — 10 Km
Miles 0 — 5 Miles

In Pouilly, de Ladoucette's Disneyland-original Château du Nozet may be the biggest and best-known estate, but the late Didier Dagueneau pioneered seriously low yields and experimentation with oak (echoed by Vincent Pinard, Henri Bourgeois, Alphonse Mellot, and other leading producers in Sancerre).

Such ambitious growers are understandably interested in proving that their wines are worth ageing, but – in clear contrast to the great white wines of Vouvray, for example – the great majority of Sancerre and Pouilly-Fumé reaches its appetizing, flirtatious peak within a year or two of bottling. The search for quality tends to favour vines from old pre-1950s clones rather than recent higher-yielding ones. And not only in these vineyards. Sancerre's other passion is its Pinot Noir, popular in the region though rarely seen outside it. Its rare rosé form can be a beauty, but red versions tend to seem disconcertingly light to those expecting a lesser red burgundy. It may represent only about a seventh of total production (and none at all within the Pouilly-Fumé appellation), but some of the more ambitious producers are determined to prove that in good years it can provide just as much pleasure as many a wine at a similar price from the Côte de Beaune.

Well inside the great bend of the river are the other so-called Vignobles du Centre (see the map of the Loire Valley on p.111). The historic vineyards of Quincy and Reuilly, and a rapidly expanding fragment at Menetou-Salon, also make fruity Sauvignon Blancs and pale Pinot Noir to compete with Sancerre, at keener prices.

Quincy, on largely sandy soils, is the most rustic of these three appellations and applies only to white wine. **Reuilly** makes an increasing amount of all three colours on well-exposed, steep limestone marl (clay-limestone) and gravel and sand terraces. Pinot Gris makes fine *vin gris* here. **Menetou-Salon**, thanks to a high proportion of limestone in the soil, has its own charm: a light touch ideal for lunch in the sunshine. The best can be better value than the lazier exponents of its neighbour to the east, Sancerre.

SANCERRE AND POUILLY-FUME

The most important Sancerre and Pouilly vineyards are shown here (for the full extent of the appellations, see the map on p.111). The best producers of Pouilly-Fumé are all in the north, whereas Sancerre's most hardworking exponents are spread more widely throughout the appellation.

The most obvious omission here are the Pouilly-Fumés of Didier Dagueneau, whose packaging is typically wild, unconventional, and difficult to reproduce. Henri Bourgeois has another Sauvignon Blanc operation in Marlborough, New Zealand. If you can't beat them...

Alsace

The wine of Alsace reflects the ambivalent situation of a border province. There are two possible physical boundaries between France and Germany: the Rhine and the crest of the Vosges, which run 15 miles (25km) west and parallel of the river. The Rhine has been the political frontier throughout most of history, but the mountains have always been the line that makes the great climatic, stylistic, even linguistic difference. Alsace has never been German, except in periods of military occupation. Its language and its market may be, but its soul is entirely French. Alsace makes Germanic wine in the French way. The tone is set by the climate, the soil, and the choice of grape varieties: all comparable to German wine regions, the nearest of which is Baden just across the Rhine.

One of the attractions of Alsace for winemakers and more involved connoisseurs is the mosaic of soil types within the region and the increasingly pressing challenge of matching grapes to them. But what distinguishes Alsace from other French wine regions is the fact that it lies in the rain shadow of the Vosges. A comparison of the rainfall statistics overleaf with those on other pages shows that only Perpignan, on the Spanish border, is drier than Colmar, and even Toulon in Provence is wetter than Strasbourg. Drought may sometimes plague vineyards here but ripeness is usually guaranteed.

Traditionally, Alsace winemakers sought bone-dry, firm, strong wines, fermenting every ounce of the sugar produced by the long, dry summers of Alsace and, often, adding even more (chaptalizing) to make the wine stronger. This used to contrast with the traditional German model of feather-light wines with natural grape sugar lingering delicately therein. But of late these two stereotypes have been converging. The average residual sugar level of Alsace wine has been increasing while German wines are becoming drier and stronger. The best producers on both sides of the Rhine are proud that all of this is a result of lowering yields and concentrating on what each grape has to offer. But consumers complain that Alsace wine has become more difficult to match with food, and that labels fail to tell them how sweet the wine is likely to taste.

Hoar frost in winter accentuates the upright vertical training system used on vines encouraged to grow well off the ground. This is characteristic of Alsace (and many German) vineyards.

The grapes of Alsace

The major clues on typical Alsace labels, most unusually for France, are varietal. The grapes that give their names and special qualities to the wines of Alsace are the Riesling of the Rhine – responsible here and in Germany for the best wine of all: Sylvaner, Muscat, the uniquely perfumed Gewurztraminer, and Pinots Blanc, Gris, and Noir. Gewurztraminer is the best introduction to the aromatic wines of Alsace: heady with scent yet often totally clean and dry. The German *Gewürz* means "spiced". A more precise description would mention roses, grapefruit – sometimes lychees.

Riesling is king. It offers something much more elusive: a balance of hard and gentle, flowery and strong, which leads you on and never surfeits. Its consort is Pinot Gris, the fullest-bodied but least perfumed wine of the region; at table it offers a realistic alternative to a white burgundy. Alsace Muscat is usually a blend of Muscat Ottonel with Muscat Blanc grapes. At its best it keeps all of Muscat's characteristic grapey scent, but makes a dry wine as clean as a whistle: a playful apéritif. Klevener de Heiligenstein is a grape speciality of the area around the village of Heiligenstein just north of Barr, in a limestone-dominated area that extends as far north as Ottrott. The lightly spicy, sometimes slightly buttery wine is relatively light in alcohol, and in good vintages it can age well.

Much more important is Pinot Blanc – a name used both for Pinot Blanc itself, the everyday grape of Alsace which usually manages to transmit some of the characteristic smokiness of the region's whites, and for the softer Auxerrois (the two are frequently blended). To keep matters complicated, the Auxerrois is sometimes labelled "Klevner", or even "Clevner". It is also the most common base wine for sparkling Crémant d'Alsace, made in large quantities by the traditional method, which at its best can rival the Crémants of Burgundy, Jura, and the Loire.

In a class above the commonest wines of the region comes Sylvaner. Alsace Sylvaner is light, a touch leafy, and sometimes attractively tart. Without the tartness it can be a little dull and coarse in flavour. It is often the first wine to be served at a dinner in Alsace, to build up to the main wine, the Riesling.

Grand Cru sites

The term *Edelzwicker* ("noble mixture") is usually applied to a mixture of grape varieties, generally Pinot Blanc and Chasselas. Only Riesling, Pinot Gris, Gewurztraminer, and Muscat – the Alsace grape nobility – are generally allowed the controversial Alsace Grand Cru appellation discussed overleaf, although the quality of old Sylvaner vines in Zotzenberg, north of Mittelbergheim, has earned Grand Cru status. Those sites so far approved as Grands Crus that are not within the areas mapped in more detail overleaf are numbered on the map opposite, many of them clustered on a patch of particularly well-favoured clay-limestone due west of Strasbourg in some of the lowest-lying vineyards of the

André Ostertag and Marc Kreydenweiss stand out from the crowd in the less glamorous, lower vineyards of the Bas-Rhin by having gone their own way – especially in their winemaking – and both were early adopters of biodynamic practices in the vineyards. Ostertag, most unusually for Alsace, ages some of his wines in small oak barriques.

Bas-Rhin département. Steinklotz is known for Pinot Gris and Pinot Noir, Altenberg de Bergbieten for Riesling.

In the bottom left-hand corner of the map, 12 miles (20km) south of the main concentration of Haut-Rhin Grands Crus is the historic Rangen vineyard, which rises steeply above the village of Thann. Schoffit and Zind-Humbrecht make superbly expressive wines, especially Riesling and Pinot Gris, from these warm volcanic soils. In general, the vineyards of the Bas-Rhin are less sheltered by the Vosges and produce rather lighter wines, although the biodynamic wines of Domaine Ostertag at Epfig are thrilling exceptions. In 2012, 11 communes negotiated the right to append their name to the basic Alsace appellation for specific grape varieties. Specific vineyard names, or *lieux-dits*, may also now be cited on labels.

Colours and styles

Like its counterparts from the Loire and from Germany, Alsace wine is essentially about fruit rather than oak. If oak is used at all it is generally in the form of old oval casks incapable of imparting their flavour, although there are a few exceptions. Similarly, most Alsace winemakers have deliberately suppressed the second malolactic fermentation for their whites, but it is generally necessary to soften the 10% or so of Alsace wine that is red and made from Pinot Noir. Colours and styles vary enormously, from the traditional tart, dark rosé to some deep-crimson, oaky wines made from barrel-aged, low-yield fruit. As summer temperatures have risen, so has their quality.

Another challenge for the region's winemakers is to make the most of its finest autumns, when seriously ripe grapes can be picked to make either very sweet Vendange Tardive wines or, even sweeter, rarer, and generally botrytised, Sélection de Grains Nobles made from several pickings, with Sauternes as its model. A late-picked Gewurztraminer has perhaps the most exotic smell of any wine in the world, and can at the same time keep a remarkable cleanness and finesse of flavour.

HAUT-RHIN AND BAS-RHIN

Crucial to the quality of all Alsace wines, partly by sheltering the vineyards from rainfall, is the range of Vosges Mountains that rises immediately west of the vineyards mapped here. The map overleaf with its contour lines shows this clearly.

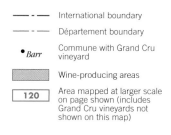

	International boundary
	Département boundary
• *Barr*	Commune with Grand Cru vineyard
	Wine-producing areas
120	Area mapped at larger scale on page shown (includes Grand Cru vineyards not shown on this map)

Grand Cru vineyards outside area of detailed map

1	STEINKLOTZ
2	ENGELBERG
3	ALTENBERG DE BERGBIETEN
4	ALTENBERG DE WOLXHEIM
5	BRUDERTHAL
6	KIRCHBERG DE BARR
7	ZOTZENBERG
8	KASTELBERG
9	WIEBELSBERG
10	MOENCHBERG
11	MUENCHBERG
12	WINZENBERG
13	FRANKSTEIN
14	PRAELATENBERG
15	OLLWILLER
16	RANGEN

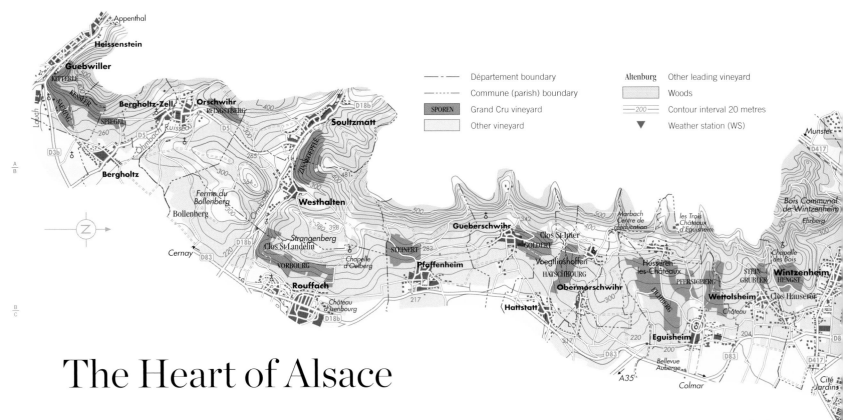

The Heart of Alsace

In the heart of the Alsace vineyard, as in Burgundy, a range of east-facing hills provides an ideal environment for the vine. Spurs and re-entrants offer extra shelter and a privileged sunwards tilt in places where the vines face east, southeast, or south. A dense pine forest nearby can lower the average temperature of a vineyard by a full degree centigrade compared with one next to a young oak wood. Every nuance of the unfolding landscape is echoed in the alignment of the vine rows to catch each minute of sunlight.

And Alsace is sunny. The high Vosges to the west are the secret of these vineyards, which lie along the mountain flank at an altitude of 600–1,200ft (180–360m) in a green ribbon that is rarely more than a mile wide. The lorry drivers grinding their way up through Kaysersberg towards St-Dié invariably encounter a thick bank of cloud as they reach the crest of the Vosges, with clouds banking up to the west. The higher the mountains, the drier the land they shelter from moist west winds. The map shows the central stretch of the Haut-Rhin vineyards, clustered under the wooded slopes to the north and south of the city of Colmar – where the mountains can keep the sky clear of clouds for weeks on end. In this protected climate, classic Riesling, fragrant but muscular, thrives.

Ironically, the wine-growing conditions are so propitious that Alsace was seen during long periods of its troubled history as a source of basic blending material – rather as France once regarded Algeria. Hence the lack of a long-established hierarchy of the better and the best vineyards in the manner of the Côte d'Or.

Instead, the modern wine industry developed through the enterprise of farmers (many of them working land that has been in the family since the 17th century) turning merchant and branding their own and their neighbours' wines, distinguishing them only by their grapes. Such well-known names as Becker, Dopff, Hugel, Humbrecht, Kuehn, Muré, and Trimbach are the result. Alsace also had France's first co-operative cellar, in 1895, and such co-ops as Beblenheim, Eguisheim, Kientzheim, Turckheim, and Westhalten rank high among some of the better producers today.

Grands Crus and the Clos

The Grand Cru appellation, an attempt to designate the best vineyards that was launched in 1983, has everyone arguing over exactly which land deserves exalted status. But the Grands Crus, marked on the map in violet, are slowly changing the way Alsace wines are perceived. Their restricted yields and increased levels of ripeness offer at least theoretically a higher quality level. They should promote the wines from being a mere varietal (an expression of a grape) to enjoying appellation status in the fullest sense: the specific linkage of terroir and grape variety based on soil, situation, and – up to a point – tradition. And an increasing number of wines are, like those of Marcel Deiss, an expression of the traditionally mixed plantings,

The well-worn *Route des Vins* takes a meandering course though the whole length of the Alsace wine country, enabling tourists to visit some of the prettiest wine towns in the world. Kaysersberg, to the northwest of the capital city of Colmar, is one of the most beautiful.

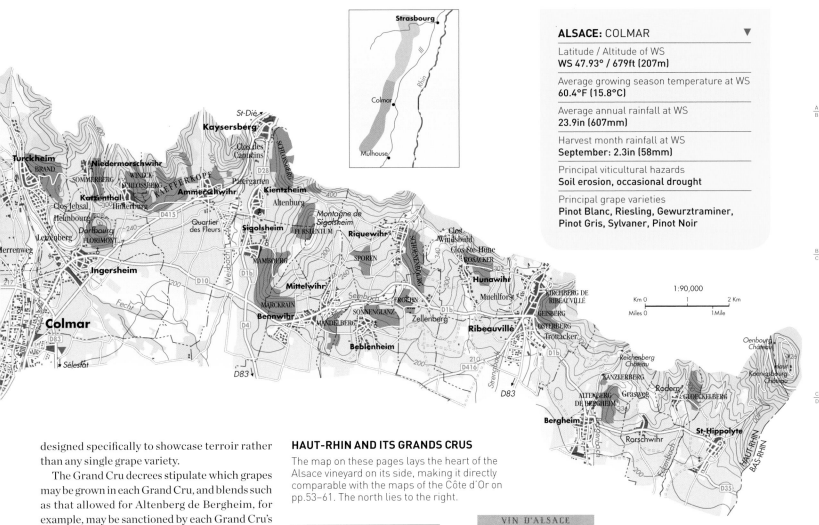

ALSACE: COLMAR ▼

Latitude / Altitude of WS
WS 47.93° / 679ft (207m)

Average growing season temperature at WS
60.4°F (15.8°C)

Average annual rainfall at WS
23.9in (607mm)

Harvest month rainfall at WS
September: 2.3in (58mm)

Principal viticultural hazards
Soil erosion, occasional drought

Principal grape varieties
**Pinot Blanc, Riesling, Gewurztraminer,
Pinot Gris, Sylvaner, Pinot Noir**

HAUT-RHIN AND ITS GRANDS CRUS

The map on these pages lays the heart of the Alsace vineyard on its side, making it directly comparable with the maps of the Côte d'Or on pp.53–61. The north lies to the right.

The Clos Ste Hune label gives no direct clue as to its location or status (technically Alsace Grand Cru), while Marcel Deiss's Altenberg label is uncommunicative about the grape varieties in this wine. Alsace labels are notoriously inexplicit – especially about sweetness.

designed specifically to showcase terroir rather than any single grape variety.

The Grand Cru decrees stipulate which grapes may be grown in each Grand Cru, and blends such as that allowed for Altenberg de Bergheim, for example, may be sanctioned by each Grand Cru's management committee. Many site/variety associations are already well in place, usually on the basis of growing and tasting experience, which often turns out to have some geological link. At Guebwiller, at the southern end of this stretch of vineyards, the sandstone of Kitterlé is famous for its luscious wines made from a range of grape varieties, particularly those grown by Schlumberger. Just north of here at Westhalten, the more limestone slope of Zinnkoepflé faces due south and concentrates Gewurztraminer and Riesling to new heights, whereas the marls and sandstone of the southeast-facing Vorbourg at Rouffach have a particular affinity for Muscat.

Hatschbourg at Voegtlingshofen is a splendid vineyard of marl and limestone, ripening dense-textured Gewurztraminer and Pinot Gris, like Goldert next door. Eichberg at Eguisheim grows fine Gewurztraminer and Riesling on marl and sandstone. Hengst at Wintzenheim is famous for the same varieties. The granite of the Vosges produces Rieslings with extra richness at Turckheim in the Brand Grand Cru, and at Kientzheim in Schlossberg. At Riquewihr the clay marls of Schoenenbourg also produce glorious Riesling, although the clay of the Sporen south of the village is more suitable for Gewurztraminer.

Nonetheless, some producers, proud of their own reputations, eschew the Grand Cru system. The finest Riesling in Alsace – some would say the

world – is grown in Trimbach's Clos Ste-Hune within the Rosacker Grand Cru above Hunawihr. The name "Rosacker" is never mentioned on the label because the Trimbachs do not believe that the rest of this mainly limestone vineyard matches Clos Ste-Hune in quality. Indeed, the word *clos*, signifying a self-contained vineyard often within another, can be shorthand for quality, as in Domaine Weinbach's Clos des Capucins, at the foot of the Schlossberg slopes in Kientzheim; Muré's Clos St-Landelin within the

Vorbourg vineyard; and Zind-Humbrecht's Clos Hauserer, near the Hengst Grand Cru, Clos Jebsal near Turckheim, Clos St-Urbain in Thann's Grand Cru Rangen (on the map on p.119), and Clos Windsbuhl near Hunawihr.

While the concepts of the Grand Cru and Clos appeal to many winemakers, others produce equally fine selections simply as cuvées of their best grapes, often labelled with what are in effect brand names. Alsace, it seems, will always be in dispute.

Northern Rhône

The vineyards of the Rhône Valley fall naturally into two parts: the north with less than a tenth of total production, almost all fine wine, and the much more extensive south, where the landscape, and wines, are quite different. A comparison of the rainfall in the two regions (see the key facts panels on pp. 123 and 129) is enough to explain why the northern Rhône is so much greener and less Mediterranean than the south. The break comes at about Montélimar, where for a short stretch the vine is absent from the valley, slowly funnelling out towards its delta. In the north the vine perches on terraced cliffs of crumbling granite wherever the best exposure to the sun can be found. The grape of the northern Rhône is Syrah, alias Shiraz. But the northern Rhône can also boast three highly distinctive and now-fashionable white wine grapes – Marsanne, Roussanne, and Viognier – even if they make relatively little wine in total.

On the following pages the best areas of the northern and southern Rhône are mapped in detail. Côte-Rôtie, Condrieu, and Hermitage, the most majestic Rhône wines, are all in the northern sector. Around them lie several others of strong local character, long traditions, and evolving reputations.

Cornas, for example, is the stubborn country cousin to the noble Hermitage, made of the same Syrah grapes grown on granite and with just as much authority and power, if rather less finesse.

Recently a number of producers have begun to make fruitier wines for earlier drinking, while at traditional estates, wines generally remain closed for their first-half dozen years. Jean-Luc Colombo (who has experimented with heavy oaking), the talented Thierry Allemand, and the venerable Auguste Clape are the most famous Cornas producers, but are no longer the only ones with an international reputation.

The appellation today shows encouraging signs of rejuvenation. The Courbis brothers, Eric and Joël Durand, Vincent Paris and Stéphane Robert of Domaine du Tunnel are newer producers to note. Over recent years, total plantings have grown to 308 acres (125ha). An east-facing amphitheatre of terraces is Cornas's heart.

The temptation to stretch a good name to breaking point long ago overtook **St-Joseph**, the west-bank appellation to the north of Cornas, which now stretches almost 40 miles (60km) from the St-Péray appellation to well north of Condrieu. It was once a group of just six communes, led by Mauves and Tournon, which have similar granitic soils to the hill of Hermitage across the river. But since 1969 St-Joseph was allowed to expand into a total of 26 communes, and to grow from 240 to 2,900 acres (1,180ha), resulting in some pretty light, bland wines.

Fortunately, since the 1990s an increasing proportion has been grown on the steep granite riverbanks rather than at the bottom of these slopes or on the much cooler, more clay-laden plateau. Wines from the latter are difficult to distinguish from a northern **Côtes du Rhône**, the catch-all appellation of the Rhône Valley, which applies to 47 communes north of Montélimar (and 124 in the south). The names of the original six St-Joseph communes – Glun, Mauves, Tournon, St-Jean-de-Muzols, Lemps, and Vion –

together with Chavanay in Condrieu country to the north, remain pointers to the best wines. Fine, sometimes vineyard-designated, wines are made here by Chapoutier, Jean-Louis Chave, Gonon, and Guigal, while good and consistent quality comes from domaines such as Courbis, Coursodon, Delas, Pierre Gaillard, Gripa, and Stéphane Montez. St-Joseph also produces one of the Rhône's least-known but most persuasive and food-friendly whites, often better and more intricate than its red, from the Hermitage grapes Marsanne and Roussanne.

From the same grapes, and often the same producers, increasingly fine, still white and a little traditional, golden sparkling are also made in **St-Péray**, south of Cornas. On the River Drôme, off the map to the east, totally different grapes (Clairette and Muscat, respectively) make substantial **Crémant de Die** and feather-light, grapey **Clairette de Die Tradition**.

The narrowness of the northern Rhône Valley has limited any expansion of the most venerable appellations here, but some growers are experimenting with areas not blessed with AOC status. Some of the more energetic producers of Côte-Rôtie and Condrieu (see overleaf) have recently sought out specially favoured schist slopes on the opposite left bank of the river, such as at Seyssuel between Vienne and Lyon, and planted Syrah and Viognier. The produce of these vineyards outside the approved areas must be sold as IGPs, in this case often des Collines Rhodaniennes (see the map on p.47). It gives them a little more glamour.

Côte-Rôtie's vineyards high above the little wine town of Ampuis, which could be renamed "Guigalville". Well over 40% of all grapes grown here are vinified in the expanding Guigal cellars.

NORTHERN RHÔNE'S WINE REGIONS

There is little room for expansion in the northern appellations of Condrieu and Côte-Rôtie, so restless younger vignerons are planting around Seyssuel on the opposite bank. St-Joseph has proved to be the most elastic appellation, although the superior crus being renovated by the top producers may eventually be officially distinguished from the less suitable vineyard land.

- — · — · — Département boundary
- Côte-Rôtie
- Château-Grillet
- Condrieu
- Condrieu/St-Joseph
- St-Joseph
- Hermitage
- Crozes-Hermitage
- Cornas
- St-Péray
- Côtes du Rhône
- Grignan-les-Adhémar
- 125 | Area mapped at larger scale on page shown
- ▼ | Weather station (WS)

1:450,000

Km 0   5   10   15 Km
Miles 0   5   10 Miles

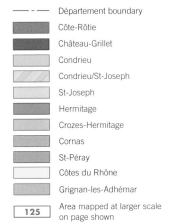

RHONE: VALENCE ▼

Latitude / Altitude of WS
44.91° / 525ft (160m)

Average growing season temperature at WS
64.1°F (17.9°C)

Average annual rainfall at WS
36.4in (923mm)

Harvest month rainfall at WS
September: 4.6in (118mm)

Principal viticultural hazards
Poor weather at flowering, fungal diseases

Principal grape varieties
Syrah, Viognier, Marsanne, Roussanne

These three St-Josephs are grown on the steep combes that produced fine wines long before the appellation was so generously extended. Vincent Paris is one of several new interpreters of the tiny Cornas appellation to the immediate south.

Côte-Rôtie and Condrieu

Côte-Rôtie's ribbon of vineyards, hugging the granite western walls of the valley at Ampuis in perilous terraces, has only recently known worldwide fame. Until the spotlight of fashion picked out the single-minded Marcel Guigal and his exceptional wines in the 1980s, Côte-Rôtie was an insider's wine, astonishing all who discovered it with its magical soft, fruity finesse, southern in warmth but closer to a great red burgundy in the way firm tannins supported delicate flavours – in marked contrast to the burliness of Hermitage, the northern Rhône's most famous emissary.

Like Hermitage, Côte-Rôtie is certainly Roman or earlier in origin. Up to the 19th century, its wine was sold by 76 litres (20 gallons): the measure of a double amphora. It long maintained its almost secret niche as one of France's greatest wines. When this Atlas was first published in 1971, the total area of vineyards was only 173 acres (70ha) and dwindling. Its price barely justified the hard work involved in cultivating the back-breakingly steep terraces. The world has since "discovered" Côte-Rôtie, prices have risen steeply, and in 40 years the vineyard area has almost quadrupled to 652 acres (264ha), definitively overtaking Hermitage in terms of the amount of wine produced.

As the name implies, this southeast-facing slope (so steep that gradients can reach 60% in places, and pulleys, even monorails, have to be used to transport anything as heavy as a box of grapes) is indeed "roasted" (*rôtie*) in summer. Many parts of this strip of vineyards, sometimes barely 1,640ft (500m) wide, are exposed to the sun all day. The hard rock (schist in the north) from which these riverside plots are hewn retains every degree of heat, which is why newer plantings on the plateau above rarely ripen anything like as fully and have arguably diluted Côte-Rôtie's reputation.

It may seem obvious where the boundaries should be: the northwestern one at the top of the famously roasted slope and the southeastern boundary now formed by the N86, the road that winds down the right bank of the Rhône south of Lyons, but just how far northeast and southwest true Côte-Rôtie terroir extends has been disputed for centuries. All are agreed, however, that the original vineyards are centred on the two most obvious slopes above the little town of Ampuis: the Côte Blonde on a south-facing spur just south of town and the southwest-facing bank that is the Côte Brune to the north. The Côte Blonde, being part of the greater Massif Central, has more granite, sometimes visible at the surface, with notably soft topsoils, comprising many different plots of sandy/slate soil with a pale limestone element. These yields softer, more charming, earlier-developing wines than those produced on the almost equally extensive and even more varied Côte Brune, whose schist and heavier clay are darkened by iron and whose wines are traditionally deeper and tougher.

The local map of individual vineyards lists even more than those mapped opposite, which include those most likely to be found on labels. Being equal in quality but not in style, the wines of the Côte Blonde and Côte Brune were in the past blended by merchants to produce a unified Côte-Rôtie. But today there is a fashion for vineyard-designated bottlings, a trend accelerated by the dominant producer, Guigal. By bottling separately wines labelled La Mouline (Côte Blonde), La Landonne, and La Turque (Côte Brune), after ageing them in new oak for a daring and dramatic 42 months, Guigal has come as close as any grower to creating a new Romanée-Conti. These are wines for millionaires, impressed by power and pungency, but not always for lovers of the classic, gentle Côte-Rôtie, matured in barrels that are themselves mature. Traditionalists might be more satisfied by wines from such as Barge, Gangloff, Jamet, and Jasmin, and Rostaing's Côte Blonde bottling.

The picture is further complicated by the divergence among the names on Guigal labels, the most famous names of Côte-Rôtie, and those on local maps. The toughest, longest-lived of all Guigal's wines comes from La Landonne vineyard, which is also bottled by Jean-Michel Gérin and René Rostaing. But this is the only one of Guigal's internationally traded so-called "La La" wines that is an officially recognized plot. La Mouline, a Guigal brand name since 1966, is a sumptuous, velvety monster produced from 60-year-old holdings in the Côte Blonde as marked on the map. La Turque, another Guigal brand created in 1985, is made from vines also marked on the map high above the centre of Ampuis, while the more traditional Côte-Rôtie bottling under Guigal's more recently acquired Château d'Ampuis label is a blend from seven quite different vineyards from both Côtes Brune and Blonde. It seemed inevitable that Marcel Guigal would acquire and glamorously renovate the down-at-heel Château d'Ampuis right on the river's edge, which is where his parents worked in their youth.

But Côte-Rôtie is far from being a one-man appellation. Gilles Barge, the Bonnefonds, Bernard Burgaud, Clusel-Roch, Duclaux, Jean-Michel Gérin, Jamet, Michel and Stéphane Ogier, and Jean-Michel Stéphan and many other producers based in Condrieu or St-Joseph can all make wines of great interest. Merchants with particularly significant Côte-Rôties include Chapoutier, Delas, Jaboulet, Vidal-Fleury (owned by Guigal), and, of course, Guigal itself.

It is not just geography that distinguishes Côte-Rôtie from Hermitage. In theory Côte-Rôtie growers have long been allowed to add up to 20% of Viognier to perfume and stabilize the Syrah on which the wine depends. Guigal's La Mouline is often enlivened by more than 10% Viognier, but 2–5% is the most common proportion.

Condrieu – the sumptuous white

The extraordinarily heady, recognizably perfumed Viognier grape, with its aromas of apricots and may blossom, is the speciality of the even smaller appellation of Condrieu into which the Côte-Rôtie vineyards merge to the south, where schist and mica give way to often crumbled, sanded granite. Many of the local growers make both of these sought-after white and red wines, to the chagrin of bigger merchants who would like to acquire their wines or, preferably, their vineyards. At one time, Condrieu was more

An increasing proportion of all Condrieu and Côte-Rôtie is labelled with the name of the vineyard or small parcel of vines where it was grown. All of these top bottlings cite their original site, even if Jamet's special cuvée carries nothing more specific than the major slope above the town.

Département boundary
Commune (parish) boundary
LE CLOS   Vineyard name
Appellation boundary
Condrieu, Château-Grillet, and Côte-Rôtie
St-Joseph
Woods
200   Contour interval 20 metres

CONDRIEU, COTE-ROTIE, AND CHATEAU-GRILLET

Note the tiny enclave of Château-Grillet overlooking the Rhône and its industrial flanks just south of Condrieu. The vineyards and cellars are being overhauled, the former possibly extended. Expect to hear more of François Pinault's new purchase.

commonly encountered as a sweet but decidedly obscure wine. The difficulty of growing such an unreliable, disease-prone, low-yielding vine as Viognier on the often relatively inaccessible slopes above the village of Condrieu compared unfavourably with other much easier, more

lucrative crops for which the area was well known. By the 1960s, the total planted area of the Condrieu appellation, created in 1940, had shrunk to barely 30 acres (12ha). Fortunately, the charms of Viognier in general and Condrieu in particular were so obvious that an increasingly international fan club developed. The variety is now much more widely planted in the Languedoc, California, and Australia than in Condrieu. But the enthusiasm has been sufficient to identify new clones of Viognier (not all of them predicated on wine quality) and encourage a new blast of creative energy in Condrieu itself.

Among the top producers of classical, fragrant, almost exclusively dry Condrieu are Georges Vernay, with Coteau du Vernon a speciality; Pierre Dumazet, André Perret, and Guigal, who now produces a de luxe bottling, La Doriane, blended from grapes grown in the Côte Châtillon and Colombier vineyards. Younger, equally ambitious producers who have also been experimenting with late-picked, botrytised, and oaked versions include Yves Cuilleron, Yves Gangloff, Pierre Gaillard, and François Villard.

All this creativity demands vineyards, and Condrieu has been growing, to 405 acres (164ha)

by 2011. The Condrieu appellation ambles north from the village of Chavanay, where growers may also produce St-Joseph and the higher granite content in the soil is said to imbue some minerality in the wines, as far north as the hills north of Condrieu itself, which can yield particularly rich Viognier.

New sites are not always in the awkward, inaccessible spots where the finicky Viognier vine flourishes – not least because, in order to produce an economic crop level, it should be sheltered from the cool north wind at flowering time. The most favoured vineyards in Condrieu tend to have a powdery, mica-rich topsoil locally called arzelle. They include Chéry, Chanson, Côte Bonnette, and Les Eyguets. Condrieu combines alcoholic power with a haunting but surprisingly fragile aroma. It is one of the very few luxury-priced whites that should be drunk young.

The most unusual Viognier of all is **Château-Grillet**: 9.4 acres (3.8ha) in a privileged amphitheatre of vines that has carved out its own appellation, an enclave within Condrieu's territory. The wine's price has recently reflected more its rarity than its obvious quality, but marked changes are afoot now that it belongs to François Pinault, who also owns Château Latour in Pauillac. It has long responded better to bottle-age than most Condrieu.

Hermitage

The Côte-Rôtie hunches its back against the north to ripen its northernmost Syrah. Thirty miles (50km) further south, the imposing hill of Hermitage does the same – on the other side of the river. It seems hard to square its world fame with its tiny area: with 336 acres (136ha) of vines, the entire Hermitage appellation is not that much more extensive than, say, Château Lafite in Pauillac. And, unlike appellations across the river such as St-Joseph, expansion is limited by long-standing decree.

But Hermitage has traditionally been celebrated as one of France's most glorious wines. The records of Bordeaux producers shipping in Hermitage to beef up their own wines date back to the mid-18th century. André Jullien's celebrated survey of the world's finest vineyards, *Topographie de Tous les Vignobles Connus*, first published in 1816 (see p.12), lists the individual *climats*, or small plots, of Hermitage alongside Château Lafite and Romanée-Conti as among the best red wines of the world. He also puts their white wines in the same class. The town of Tain l'Hermitage, squeezed on to the narrow riverbank at the foot of the hill of Hermitage, was known as Tegna in Roman times, and its wines were celebrated by both the scientist Pliny and the poet Martial.

The left bank

The Rhône is France's main north–south artery, directing its accompanying roads and railway, which snake under the narrow terraces of vines and make the hill's magnificent stance above Tain familiar to millions.

The slopes of Hermitage, uniquely in the northern Rhône, are on the river's left, or east, bank. Facing from west to due south, they are well protected from the prevailing north winds. This granite outcrop was once an extension of the Massif Central until the river burrowed a course around its western rather than eastern flank. The resulting escarpment, 1,150ft (350m) high, though not as precipitous as Côte-Rôtie, is steep enough in parts to demand terracing. Certainly, it is steep enough for mechanization to have been outlawed and make repairing the ravages of erosion a back-breaking annual task. The topsoil that slides down the hill after heavy storms is made up largely of decomposed flint and limestone with glacial deposits that are alpine in origin at the eastern end.

Although for the red wines of Hermitage nothing but Syrah is planted, each *climat* is subtly different in terms of soil type, exposition, and altitude with some benefiting from the shelter provided by a natural amphitheatre. Jullien in 1816 felt confident in listing Hermitage's *climats* in order of merit: Méal, Gréfieux, Beaume, Raucoule, Muret, Guoignière, Bessas, Burges, and Lauds. Spellings have changed, but the *climats* remain and, although Hermitage is typically, and

possibly ideally, a blend from several different *climats*, their names have been seen on an increasing proportion of wine labels as the urge to get to grips with individual vineyard characteristics has taken hold of both producers and consumers.

In general the lightest, most aromatic red wines come from the higher *climats* Beaume and L'Hermite, beside the little chapel on top of the hill that gave its name to Jaboulet's famous flagship, La Chapelle. Relatively fleshy wines come from Péléat. Les Gréffieux, in which Chapoutier has the largest holding, makes elegant, aromatic wines, while Le Méal can produce extremely dense, powerful wines. The particularly granitic *climat* of Bessards, turned south-southwest at its western end, tends to produce the most tannic and longest-lived wines.

Horses are no trendy new accessory in the vineyards of Hermitage, high above the town of Tain on the banks of the Rhône. They were reintroduced to work the steep granite hill as long ago as the 1980s. This horse and ploughman are toiling on behalf of Paul Jaboulet Aîné.

The adjective "manly" has stuck to Hermitage ever since it was first applied to it by the English scholar and oenophile Professor George Saintsbury in the 1920s. Indeed, it was as well known for boosting anaemic Bordeaux as for its unique style. It can be almost like port without the added brandy. Like vintage port, Hermitage throws a heavy sediment in, often on to, the bottle, so it needs decanting. Top vintages improve for many years until their scent and flavour are heady, inspiring – almost overwhelming.

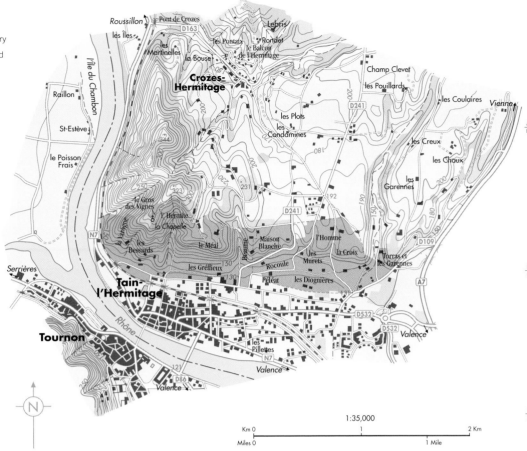

Young Hermitage of a good vintage is as closed and tannic as any young great red, but nothing can restrain its abounding perfume and the fistfuls of fruit that seem to have been crammed into the glass. As it ages, the immediacy of its impact does not diminish, but its youthful assault gives way to the sheer splendour of its mature presence. You could not drink it and fail to be impressed.

Unlike the appellations of Condrieu and Côte-Rôtie lying to the north, Hermitage has been in fashion for so long that virtually all of the available land has been planted; there is no more room for vines – or for new producers.

The appellation is dominated by four producers: Domaine Jean-Louis Chave, based across the river in Mauves, just south of Tain's twin town, Tournon, and the large merchant houses of Chapoutier, Jaboulet, and the smaller Delas, whose names, advertising to all that traffic motoring along below, adorn the walls that prop up their terraces.

Crozes-Hermitage

Like most great wines, Hermitage has its shadow. Crozes-Hermitage is to the Grand Cru what a village Gevrey-Chambertin is to Le Chambertin. Crozes, the village round the back of the hill, gives its name to an appellation that extends almost 10 miles (16km) both north and south of Tain and Hermitage itself, including more than 3,700 acres (1,500ha) of vineyard.

Crozes-Hermitage is the opportunity for enthusiastic newcomers to this area, joined by an increasing number of local producers who want to bottle the fruit of their own labours rather than sell it to the co-operative, the Cave de Tain l'Hermitage, however competently it handles the fruit of 20% of the vineyards.

Until the 1990s only one Crozes wine, Paul Jaboulet's Domaine de Thalabert, made in one of Crozes' most successful areas just north of Beaumont-Monteux, was regularly comparable with a Hermitage. Most of the rest was pallid stuff. Today, however, we can choose from two basic styles – one full of youthful blackcurrant fruit for early drinking, and the other, more serious

bottlings, even able to mimic the grandeur of Hermitage, that can be kept for up to 10 years. The better merchants and growers, such as Alain Graillot, Belle, Domaine Pochon, Domaine Marc Sorrel, and Domaine du Colombier, led the way, but new merchants such as Tardieu Laurent and the Tain co-op are also responsible for some admirable bottlings. Domaines Yann Chave, Combier, des Entrefaux, des Remizières, and Gilles Robin are also producing Crozes-Hermitage – and some of them Hermitage itself – that is increasingly to be reckoned with.

The Hermitage hill was historically almost as famous for its white wine, made from Roussanne and, mainly, Marsanne grapes. For Jullien it ranked with Montrachet as one of France's greatest. Even today it accounts for about a quarter of the Hermitage vines. Jullien named "Raucoule" as the best vineyard for white Hermitage; its wine is still known for its aroma.

White Hermitage can continue to evolve gloriously for decades. It starts life dense, stony, slightly honeyed but relatively dumb: a brooding presence (though much fresher today than in the past) that slowly gives way to glorious nuttiness.

HERMITAGE AND CROZES-HERMITAGE

The hillside vineyards of Hermitage may be renowned the world over, but they really are as limited as this map suggests. Only a fraction of the Crozes-Hermitage vineyards are mapped here (see p.123 for their full extent).

Chapoutier's and Jean-Louis Chave's are particularly fine. There is a general tendency (as with the reds) to produce *microcuvées*, often from individual *climats*, such as L'Ermite and Le Méal from Chapoutier, Ex-Voto from Guigal, Le Reverdy from Ferraton, and Jaboulet's white La Chapelle.

And there is still a trickle of the legendary, extraordinarily long-lived sweet *vin de paille*, made in tiny quantities in very ripe years from grapes that are traditionally shrivelled on straw (*paille*) mats. Gérard Chave resurrected this ancient, possibly Roman, speciality in the 1970s. Bottles from the 19th century still exist as the appellation's oldest souvenirs and are said to be still hauntingly rich. The Cave de Tain now makes an excellent version at a more affordable price.

Three different labels of one of France's greatest wines, with a much longer history than that of the famous wines of Bordeaux. White Hermitage can be just as thrilling as the red on which the Bordelais used to depend for strengthening their wines.

Southern Rhône

The funnel end of the Rhône Valley, where it releases its traffic to the Mediterranean, has a place in every traveller's affections. History and natural history combine to make it one of the richest regions of France for interests of every kind. Who cannot picture the vast engineering of the Romans, lizards alert on its slumbering stones, plots of early vegetables screened from the mistral, the pines and almonds yielding to olive groves in the far south – and always, on hillside or plain, sand or clay, the cross stitch of vines?

The basic appellation here is **Côtes du Rhône**, a general one for the red, white, or rosé of the Rhône Valley, encompassing almost 140,000 acres (56,400ha), making it France's second-biggest wine region after Bordeaux.

Within this there is, of course, wide variation of quality and style. Sandy soils are mixed up with ex-alpine limestone or mediterranean alluvial, suntraps with cooler zones. Some Côtes du Rhône is extremely ordinary, but even this portmanteau appellation has its treasures, often but not always the junior wines of producers in senior appellations such as Château de Fonsalette, from the same stable as the famous Château Rayas.

Grenache must now account for at least 40% of all red Côtes du Rhône; its most usual, but by no means only, blending partners being Syrah and Mourvèdre. White and rosé wines account for 4% and 7% of production, respectively. The 19,300 acre (7,800ha) **Côtes du Rhône-Villages** appellation is a very distinct step up, and one that can offer some of France's best value. Of the 95 communes eligible for the -Villages suffix, all of them in the south, the 17 best have the right to append their names to the already cumbersome moniker Côtes du Rhône-Villages. These favoured villages are marked in magenta on this map and overleaf. Those on this map that have established a reputation include Valréas, Visan,

and, on the right bank of the Rhône, Chusclan, which with nearby Laudun, makes fine rosés as well as reds. **Vinsobres**, whose cooler climate and elevation suit Syrah particularly well, won its very own appellation in 2006.

Between Vinsobres and the Rhône lies **Grignan-les-Adhémar**, an awkward elision of two village names in response to the collapse in sales of Coteaux du Tricastin after accidents at an eponymous nuclear centre. The parched mistral-swept landscape here is better known for its truffles than its wine. Mourvèdre will not ripen so far from the Mediterranean, so it is Cinsault that bolsters the fruity Grenache, along with stiffening Syrah (which does well in the higher vineyards).

Gigondas, overlooked and sheltered by the serrated Dentelles de Montmirail, is one of France's most charming wine villages. Local winemakers pride themselves on looking down on the vineyards of Châteauneuf-du-Pape. See overleaf for more details of the wines.

The organic pioneer Domaine Gramenon was one producer who proved that wines made carefully here can be aged for longer than the usual two or three years.

Mont Ventoux lies to the east. The scattered appellation (with 15,000 acres/6,100ha) reflects higher altitudes and cooler conditions than most Côtes du Rhône. The tradition here was for reds and rosés that were light in every way and lively when very young, but producers such as Fondrèche and Pesquié are now making increasingly serious wine, backed by good merchant blends such as La Vieille Ferme from the Perrins of Château de Beaucastel. Further south, just north of the River Durance, is the fashionable holiday region of the Luberon. The landscape can sometimes seem to have more personality than the produce of its almost 8,000 acres (3,200ha) of vineyards.

Lying on the right bank of the Rhône, the **Côtes du Vivarais**, dominated by the Cave de

Just some of the exciting wines being made in the southern Rhône outside the most famous heartland mapped in detail overleaf. Grenache vines dominate, but Syrah can do especially well in the cooler reaches, too.

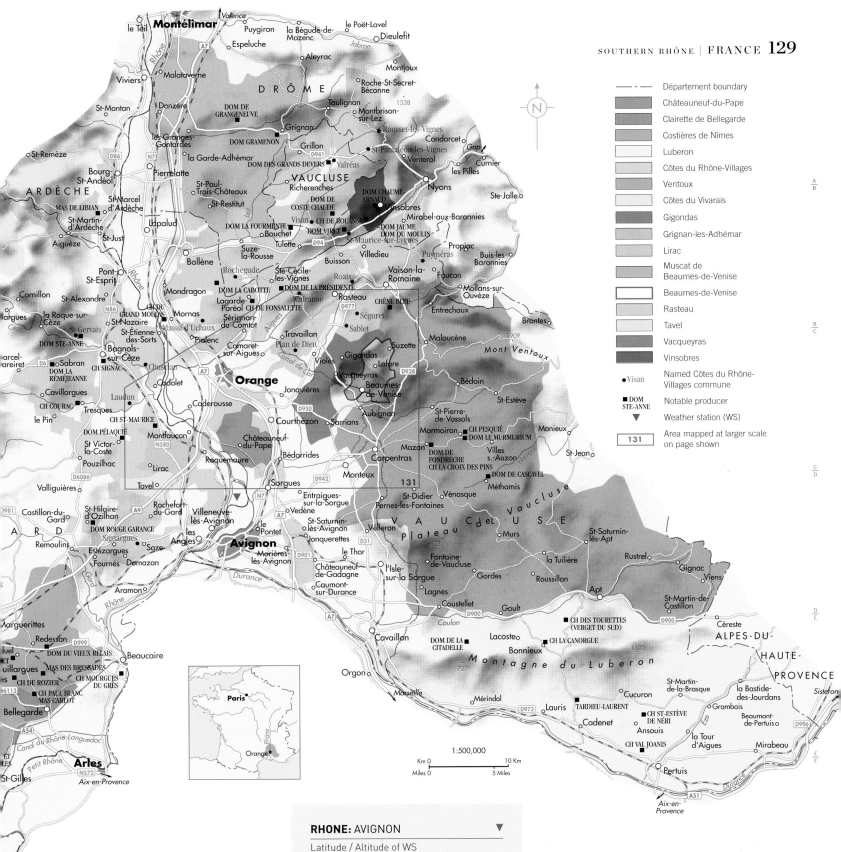

Map Legend

- – – – Département boundary
- Châteauneuf-du-Pape
- Clairette de Bellegarde
- Costières de Nîmes
- Luberon
- Côtes du Rhône-Villages
- Ventoux
- Côtes du Vivarais
- Gigondas
- Grignan-les-Adhémar
- Lirac
- Muscat de Beaumes-de-Venise
- Beaumes-de-Venise
- Rasteau
- Tavel
- Vacqueyras
- Vinsobres

- • Visan — Named Côtes du Rhône-Villages commune
- ■ DOM STE-ANNE — Notable producer
- ▼ — Weather station (WS)
- 131 — Area mapped at larger scale on page shown

1:500,000
Km 0 ... 10 Km
Miles 0 ... 5 Miles

RHONE: AVIGNON ▼

Latitude / Altitude of WS
43.91° / 112ft (34m)

Average growing season temperature at WS
67.4°F (19.7°C)

Average annual rainfall at WS
26.6in (677mm)

Harvest month rainfall at WS
September: 4.6in (117mm)

Principal viticultural hazards
Drought

Principal grape varieties
Grenache Noir, Syrah, Carignan, Cinsault, Mourvèdre

Ruoms, is almost invariably like featherweight Côtes du Rhône, thanks to conditions that are exceptionally cool for this torrid part of France.

Much hotter and more Mediterranean-influenced are the vineyards of the 8,600-acre (3,500ha) **Costières de Nîmes** north of the Camargue, now rightly considered a westward extension of the vineyards mapped overleaf rather than part of the Languedoc. These are robust, sun-swept wines of interest, particularly the juicy expressions of Grenache Noir.

SOUTHERN RHONE'S WINE REGIONS

This is not just wine country. It is holiday country *par excellence*, the gateway to Provence. The hills of the Luberon are dotted with luxurious second homes and glamorous, artfully rustic small hotels. In the southwest, the Costières de Nîmes gives way to the eastern Languedoc, but its reliance on Grenache Noir allies it to the southern Rhône.

The Heart of the Southern Rhône

Around Châteauneuf-du-Pape (mapped in detail overleaf) lies a cluster of villages with their own sweet, spicy story to tell, related by a swelling band of ambitious producers. Just as in Châteauneuf, the vines are baked in summer by the Provençal sun, serenaded by drowsy cicadas, and scented by the herby *garrigue* that punctuates the vineyards.

The dominant grape for red wines is the versatile Grenache, supplemented by Syrah in cooler, higher terrains and Mourvèdre in some of the warmer ones. Small but increasing amounts of characterful, full-bodied white wine is made from grapes such as Grenache Blanc, Clairette, Bourboulenc, Roussanne, Marsanne, and Viognier.

There is a clear path for promotion for the wine villages of the southern Rhône, with Côtes du Rhône being the region's most basic appellation. A distinct step up are the named Côtes du Rhône-Villages communes, marked in magenta, mainly in the north of the map. Once their wines have established a reputation, they can apply to have the name of their village appended to Côtes du Rhône-Villages on the label. Thereafter, they may progress to having their own appellation, which the locals term cru.

Gigondas was the first to win its own appellation back in 1971, and its tight-knit reds can rival those of Châteauneuf-du-Pape itself. The late-ripening vineyards extend from the plain east of the River Ouvèze up to, and in some cases embedded in, the spectacular jagged limestone landmark of the Dentelles de Montmirail (see p.128) which dominates the pretty hillside village of Gigondas. Thanks to altitude, and more calcareous soils, Gigondas tends to

be more aromatic and slightly gentler than Châteauneuf. But winemaking techniques are just as varied as throughout the southern Rhône. Ambitious producers such as Domaine Santa Duc and Château de St-Cosme have successfully experimented with new oak, while traditionalists such as Domaine Raspail-Ay and St-Gayan make sumptuous wines of great depth and prolonged flavour, capable of living over 20 years in the best vintages. The current trend to vinify each plot separately according to its requirements is relatively advanced in Gigondas. A flirtation with Syrah is on the wane and all-Grenache wines have been allowed since 2009. A small amount of Gigondas is made deliberately as a rosé, and Clairette is the pale grape of choice locally.

Vacqueyras earned its own appellation in 1990 and, with its earlier-ripening sandy and stony terrain, can be headier, more immediate, and a little more rustic than Gigondas. New oak is a rarity here; the fruit, mainly Grenache with some Syrah, speaks for itself. Vacqueyras can offer the spice and herbs of the southern Rhône at a very fair price and is the only appellation on the left bank of the Rhône that may be applied to wines of all three colours, including some fine, smoky, full-bodied dry white based on Grenache Blanc. **Beaumes-de-Venise**, with its potent reds from

some Jurassic clay, gained AOC status for its reds in 2004, having been entitled since 1945 to its own appellation for its strong, sweet, aromatic golden Muscat Vin Doux Naturel, a local speciality that recalls the Muscats of the Languedoc. In similar fashion, **Rasteau** already had AOC status for its rather rustic strong, sweet Vins Doux Naturels when in 2009 it, along with neighbouring **Vinsobres**, in the north of the mapped area, won its own appellation for its dry wines. **Cairanne** is one of the most exciting wine villages of the southern Rhône, its reds and whites in the hands of vignerons as accomplished as the Alary family, the Brusset family and Marcel Richaud. The wines of Rasteau can be rather less sophisticated

Some of the finest examples of Châteauneuf's satellites. This is one of the last of Gourt de Mautens' Rasteaus. Owner Jérôme Bressy has been expelled from the appellation for insisting on blending such traditional varieties as Picardan and Counoise with Grenache.

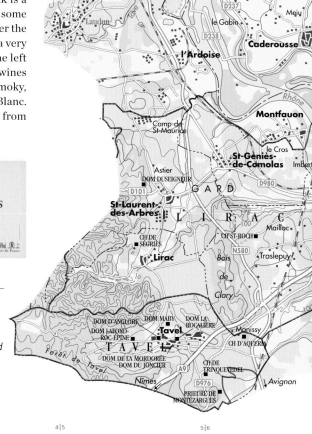

Grenache is king in the southern Rhône, but it may not ripen properly until sugar levels are so high that extremely potent wines result.

than the best Cairannes, but the likes of Gourt de Mautens have won a loyal following.

Rosé is the historic speciality of Tavel and Lirac across the Rhône from Châteauneuf. For long **Tavel** was France's most powerful dark-pink wine, a fiery partner for the strong flavours of many Mediterranean dishes. But this century there has been a certain dalliance with a more Provençal style and some lighter, fresher wine has been emerging from many domaines. **Lirac**, formerly also best known for rosé, can be better value. With lower permitted yields, it inclines more today to softly fruity reds less dominated by Grenache than Tavel. Several well-known Châteauneuf-du-Pape estates have bought vineyards in Lirac, which has encouraged quality in recent years. Its food-friendly whites are enlivened by a minimum of one-third Clairette grapes.

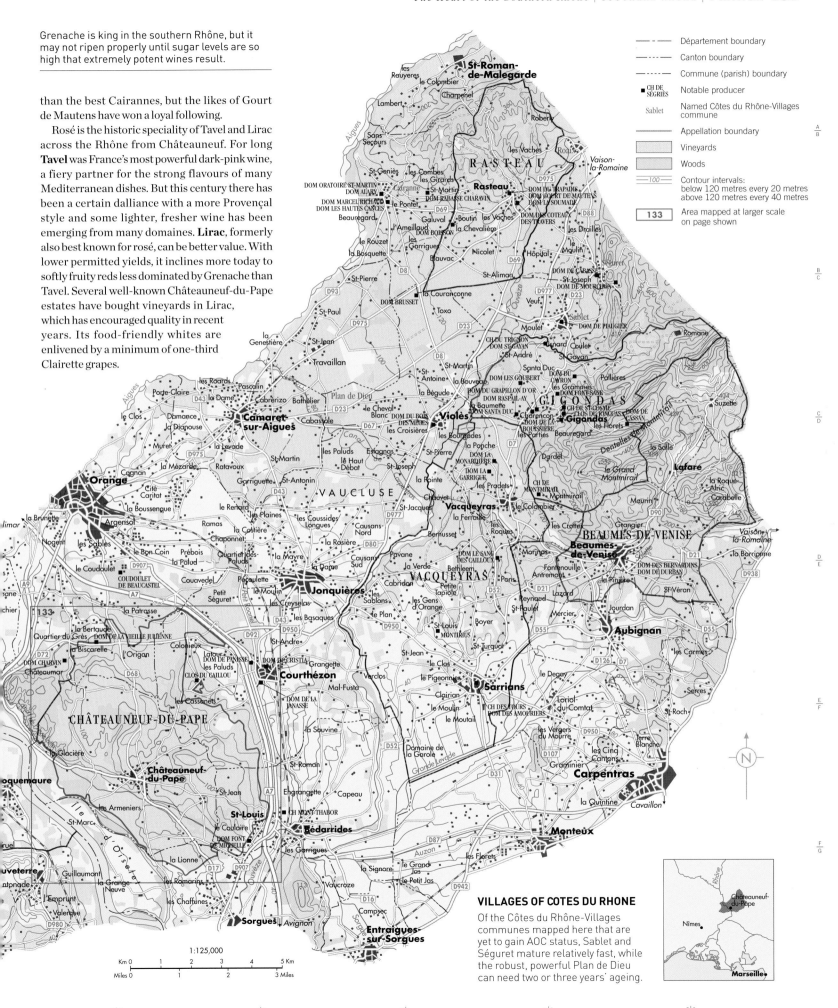

–·–·–	Département boundary
–··–··–	Canton boundary
–––––	Commune (parish) boundary
■ CH DE SÉGRIÈS	Notable producer
Sablet	Named Côtes du Rhône-Villages commune
∙∙∙∙∙∙	Appellation boundary
	Vineyards
	Woods
══100══	Contour intervals: below 120 metres every 20 metres above 120 metres every 40 metres
133	Area mapped at larger scale on page shown

1:125,000

Km 0 1 2 3 4 5 Km
Miles 0 1 2 3 Miles

VILLAGES OF COTES DU RHONE

Of the Côtes du Rhône-Villages communes mapped here that are yet to gain AOC status, Sablet and Séguret mature relatively fast, while the robust, powerful Plan de Dieu can need two or three years' ageing.

Châteauneuf-du-Pape

Châteauneuf-du-Pape the place is no more than a stoney village in arid, scented Provençal countryside, dominated by a ruined papal summer palace. The wine that bears its imposing name, though, is the magnificent standard-bearer for the dynamic southern Rhône, making France's most potent, and some of its most individualistic, wines – both red and white.

Châteauneuf-du-Pape has always had the distinction of having the highest minimum strength of any French wine: 12.5% alcohol. But in this era of global warming, its wines are rarely less than 14.5% and occasionally reach 16%, presenting a challenge to growers, winemakers – and wine drinkers. The region is also the birthplace of France's famous Appellations d'Origine Contrôlées (AOC). In 1923 its most famous grower, Baron Le Roy of Château Fortia, delimited the land arid enough to support both lavender and thyme, thereby laying the foundation stones for the entire AOC system.

Well over 90% of Châteauneuf-du-Pape is red but is hugely variable in style. Most is easy to like, being spicy, rich, and strong. Big companies and co-operatives may blend a lightish, sweetish version for relatively early drinking, but Châteauneuf today is much more likely to be the produce of an ambitious, family-owned estate making highly individual, age-worthy wines that express their particular combination of terroirs and grape varieties. Châteauneuf-du-Pape is unusual in its cocktail of as many as 18 permitted varieties (once 13, but different colours of the same grape are now listed as separate varieties).

Grenache is the backbone of the AOC, often blended with Mourvèdre and Syrah together with some Cinsault, Counoise (a local speciality), and small amounts of Vaccarèse, Muscardin, Picpoul, and Terret Noir, and the light-skinned Clairette, Bourboulenc, Roussanne (which is much easier to grow in the southern than the northern Rhône), and the neutral Picardan. Château de Beaucastel and Clos des Papes, unusually, persist with all 13. (The other five listed in the AOC regulations are Clairette Rosé and both white and pink forms of Grenache and Picpoul.)

A flirtation with Syrah, which can lack freshness this far south, has been widely replaced by an increasing affection for the late-ripening Mourvèdre now that summers are generally so warm. Its inclusion in a blend can help rein in the alcoholic excesses of Grenache in hot years. The red wines, often tough in youth thanks to the dry summers, can age to sumptuous, sometimes gamey, depths of flavour. The much rarer whites, succulent in the first few years, can develop even more exotic scents when fully mature, after an often-sulky middle age. Many producers use heavy, burgundy-shaped bottles embossed according to which of several rival producers' associations they belong to.

Sand, clay, and stones

The Châteauneuf-du-Pape cliché is the *galet*, the rounded, heat-absorbing stone found almost exclusively in some of its vineyards, but in reality soils within this relatively small area are extremely varied. The famous vineyards of arch-traditionalist Château Rayas, for instance, situated on the plateau behind Château de Vaudieu, have hardly any *galets* but instead a high proportion of chipped clay stones, alluvial deposits, clay, and sand. The map opposite shows with unparalleled precision exactly which soil type predominates where in Châteauneuf.

Many producers own parcels of vines in several different soil types, typically blending them into one cuvée, but more and more of them are also bottling one or even several premium-priced special cuvées which may showcase one particular terroir, or may be made from the producer's oldest vines, or a single grape variety. Other variables include the amount of new wood (no great friend of Grenache) used, size and material of cask, and the precise proportions of the different grape varieties in the blend.

The soils of Châteauneuf-du-Pape

Thin soils on bedrock

Hard Cretaceous limestone

Thin soils on slightly weathered rock

Cretaceous limestone modified by ploughing

Miocene sandstone and molasse

Immature soils on valley alluvium

Coarsely fragmented sandy clay

Finely fragmented sandy clay

Sandy clay with many pebbles

Slopes covered by immature soils

Unrefined scree rich in Cretaceous limestone fragments

Colluvium (fine scree) rich in sand on Miocene molasse

Colluvium rich in sand and clay from the valley floor

Brown soils (moderately weathered) rich in limestone

Clay soil on Cretaceous marl

Sandy soil on Miocene molasse

Soils rich in limestone

on ancient gravelly alluvium

on ancient alluvium and modified molassic sand

Red, iron-rich soils from the plateau

Red soil on ancient gravelly alluvium

Red and limestone soils on Cretaceous limestone

Deep-red soil on ancient alluvium and quartzite pebbles (*galets*)

Clay-rich soils from the valley floor

Thin, fine-textured soil (clay and fine sand)

Thick, fine- and medium-textured soil (clay, sand, small pebbles)

Appellation boundary

Commune (parish) boundary

Lieu-dit boundary

■ VILLENEUVE Notable producer

The most established estates, such as progressive Château de Beaucastel, modernist La Nerthe, and determinedly mono-cuvée Clos des Papes, are being challenged by the likes of the Férauds at Domaine du Pegau with their limited-edition bottlings such as Da Capo.

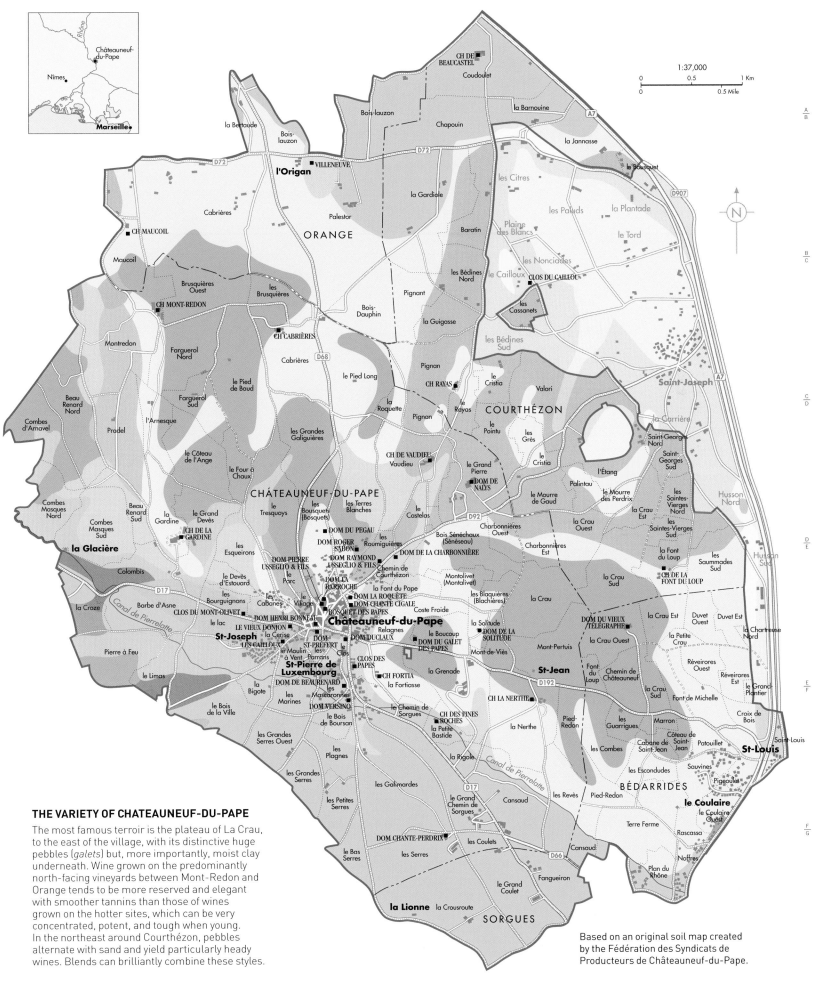

Marseille

Nîmes

Châteauneuf-du-Pape

1:37,000

0   0.5   1 Km
0   0.5 Mile

N

CH DE BEAUCASTEL
Coudoulet
la Barnouine
Bois-lauzon
Chapouin
la Jannasse
la Bertaude
Bois-lauzon
le Bousquet
l'Origan
VILLENEUVE
la Gardiole
les Citres
les Paluds
la Plantade
Cabrières
Palestor
le Tord
ORANGE
Baratin
Plaine des Blancs
les Nonciades
CH MAUCOIL
Maucoil
les Bédines Nord
le Caillou
CLOS DU CAILLOU
Brusquières Ouest
les Brusquières
Bois-Dauphin
Pignant
les Cassanets
CH MONT-REDON
la Guigasse
les Bédines Sud
Montredon
Farguerol Nord
CH CABRIÈRES
Cabrières
le Pied Long
Pignan
Saint-Joseph
Beau Renard Nord
le Pied de Baud
CH RAYAS
le Cristia
Valori
la Carrière
Combes d'Arnavel
Farguerol Sud
la Roquette
le Rayas
COURTHÉZON
Saint-Georges Nord
Pradel
l'Arnesque
Pignan
le Pointu
le Cristia
Saint-Georges Sud
les Grandes Galiguières
les Grès
l'Étang
le Côteau de l'Ange
CH DE VAUDIEU
Vaudieu
le Grand Pierre
Palintau
les Saintes-Vierges Nord
Combes Masques Nord
le Four à Chaux
DOM DE NALYS
la Crau Est
les Saintes-Vierges Sud
Combes Masques Sud
Beau Renard Sud
la Gardine
le Grand Devès
CHÂTEAUNEUF-DU-PAPE
les Tresquoys
les Bousquets (Bosquets)
les Terres Blanches
le Castelas
le Mourre de Gaud
le Mourre des Perdrix
Husson Nord
Combolis
CH DE LA GARDINE
les Esqueirons
DOM DU PEGAU
les Roumiguières
Charbonnières Ouest
la Crau Ouest
la Font du Loup
les Saummades Sud
la Glacière
DOM ROGER SABON
Bois Sénéchaux (Sénéseau)
Charbonnières Est
CH DE LA FONT DU LOUP
Husson Sud
les Devès d'Estouard
DOM PIERRE USSEGLIO & FILS
le Parc
DOM RAYMOND USSEGLIO & FILS
Chemin de Courthézon
DOM DE LA CHARBONNIÈRE
Montolivet (Montalivet)
la Crau Sud
les Bourguignons
DOM LA BARROCHE
la Font du Pape
les Blaquières (Blachières)
la Crau
Canal de Pierrelatte
les Cabanes
le Village
DOM LA ROQUETTE
DOM CHANTE CIGALE
Coste Froide
DOM DU VIEUX TÉLÉGRAPHE
la Crau Est
Duvet Ouest
Duvet Est
la Croze
CLOS DU MONT-OLIVET
DOM HENRI BONNEAU
BOSQUET DES PAPES
la Solitude
la Petite Crau
CH de Chartreuse Nord
Barbe d'Asne
le lac
LE VIEUX DONJON
Châteauneuf-du-Pape
Relagnes
DOM DE LA SOLITUDE
la Crau Ouest
St-Joseph
la Cerise
DOM ST-PREFERT
DOM DUCLAUX
le Boucoup
Mont-Pertuis
Réveirores Ouest
Réveirores Est
le Grand Plantier
LES CAILLOUX
le Moulin à Vent
Parrans
les Clos
DOM DU GALET DES PAPES
Mont-de-Viès
Font du Loup
Chemin de Châteauneuf
la Crau Sud
St-Pierre de Luxembourg
CLOS DES PAPES
St-Jean
Font de Michelle
le Limas
la Bigote
CH FORTIA
la Grenade
Croix de Bois
DOM DE BEAURENARD
les Mascaronnes
la Fortiasse
le Chemin de Sorgues
CH LA NERTHE
Pied-Redon
les Guarrigues
Marron
Saint-Louis
les Marines
DOM VERSINO
CH DES FINES ROCHES
la Nerthe
Côteau de Saint-Jean
Patouillet
St-Louis
le Bois de la Ville
le Bois de Boursan
la Petite Bastide
Cabane de Saint-Jean
les Combes
Sauvines
les Grandes Serres Ouest
les Plagnes
la Rigole
Pied-Redon
BÉDARRIDES
Pigeoulet
les Grandes Serres
la Petite Serres
les Galimardes
Canal de Pierrelatte
les Escondudes
le Coulaire
le Coulaire Ouest
le Grand Chemin de Sorgues
Cansaud
les Revès
Terre Ferme
Rascassa
DOM CHANTE-PERDRIX
les Coulets
Cansaud
Noffres
la Lionne
la Crousroute
le Bas Serres
les Serres
le Grand Coulet
Fangueiron
Plan du Rhône
SORGUES

THE VARIETY OF CHATEAUNEUF-DU-PAPE

The most famous terroir is the plateau of La Crau, to the east of the village, with its distinctive huge pebbles (*galets*) but, more importantly, moist clay underneath. Wine grown on the predominantly north-facing vineyards between Mont-Redon and Orange tends to be more reserved and elegant with smoother tannins than those of wines grown on the hotter sites, which can be very concentrated, potent, and tough when young. In the northeast around Courthézon, pebbles alternate with sand and yield particularly heady wines. Blends can brilliantly combine these styles.

Based on an original soil map created by the Fédération des Syndicats de Producteurs de Châteauneuf-du-Pape.

Western Languedoc

The Languedoc, described in more detail overleaf, is France's new world, a scene of new ideas coming good and growing expectations. Money and talent are immigrating here to replace old bad habits; it deserves close study. While most of the region is firmly Mediterranean, its far west is influenced by the Atlantic. All its highest, wildest vineyards are mapped on these pages. The character of their wines ranges from Bordelais in structure, if not in flavour, in the westernmost vineyards to Rhône-like (or at least Rhône-influenced) in the east.

Of the two most important appellations of the western Languedoc, **Minervois** is slightly more civilized, more polished. The terrain is not quite so rugged as that of Corbières, although at its northern limit where vineyards push up into the foothills of the dominating Montagne Noire, their hold on the rocky, garrigue-covered foothills of the Cévennes looks every bit as precarious as that of the gnarled Corbières vines on what are effectively the foothills of the Pyrenees. Clinging above the village of Minerve are some of the appellation's highest, latest-ripening vineyards. Those around La Livinière produce so many wines that seem to combine the rugged scents of the high vineyards with the suppleness of lower-altitude wines that they have earned their own appellation.

Southwest of here Atlantic influence impinges, in the form of higher acid levels and a slightly lighter build. The hotter, drier land sloping down towards the River Aude and that closest to the Mediterranean provide much of the dreary blended Minervois found at come-hither prices in every French supermarket.

The producers' names on the map are those of more ambitious individuals and co-operatives making particularly toothsome wine. They include respected names from Burgundy. About 85% of all Minervois is red, and 12% is now rosé, typically based on various combinations of Grenache, Syrah, and Mourvèdre with no more than 40% Carignan.

The ancient white grape Bourboulenc, commonly called Malvoisie, comes into its own on a strange western outpost of the Languedoc called La Clape, an eccentric detached limestone massif south of Narbonne which in Roman times was an island. These whites can be memorably marine-, not to say iodine-, scented. An increasing array of sweet wines is also made in Minervois, not least the aromatic Vin Doux Naturel (see p.138) **Muscat de St-Jean de Minervois**.

The **Corbières** landscape is even more dramatic: a geological chaos of mountain and valley reaching from the sea 40 miles (60km) back into the Aude département. Limestone alternates with schist, clays, marls, and sandstone; the influence of the Mediterranean with intermittent

influence from the Atlantic blowing down the Aude Valley and over its western hills.

Made from the same southern cocktail of grape varieties, red Corbières, other than at its most mundane, tastes less tamed and more concentrated, often rather tougher, than Minervois, whose vineyards enjoy less extreme summers. Drought and summer fires are constant threats in many parts of the varied Corbières appellation. The low, barren hills around **Boutenac** have earned their own cru in the northern Corbières.

Fitou, granted the Languedoc's first appellation in 1948 and a long-standing producer of Rivesaltes Vins Doux Naturels (see p.138), consists of two distinct enclaves within Corbières: Fitou Maritime, a clay-limestone band around the saltwater lagoons on the coast, and Fitou Haut, a patch of mountainous schist 15 or so miles (24km) inland, separated by a great wedge of Corbières. For much of the 1980s and 1990s, Fitou lagged behind its northern neighbours, but today several producers such as Domaine Maria Fita and Bertrand-Bergé are giving the two prominent co-operatives, Mont Tauch and Cascastel, a run for their money. The proportion of Grenache is increasing at the expense of Carignan in Fitou Haut, while Syrah and Mourvèdre are gaining ground in Fitou Maritime.

Atlantic influence

The extent of the cooling Atlantic influence here is most graphically seen in the western hills south of Carcassonne, where **Limoux** long ago established at least a national reputation for its fine traditional-method fizz, whether Blanquette, based on the original Mauzac grape, or the more delicate Crémant de Limoux made from Chardonnay, Chenin Blanc, and Pinot Noir. Still white Limoux is oak-fermented (the only AOC white for which oak is mandatory), obviously raised in a much cooler environment than expected this far south, and based on Chardonnay. The relatively recent red Limoux appellation is for oaked blends, of which Merlot must constitute half; the rest may be drawn from the other Bordeaux grapes and Grenache and Syrah, although surely Pinot Noir should be added for this is clearly the Languedoc's most promising spot for Pinot, currently sold as IGP.

All of these wines have much finer acidity than those made in the warmer eastern Languedoc, as do those of **Malepère** to the immediate north. Malepère wines, never blockbusters, are dominated by Merlot and Malbec (or Côt). Just north of Carcassonne, **Cabardès** is the only appellation in which Mediterranean and Atlantic (Bordeaux) grapes are mandatorily combined. The increasingly well-made wines reflect this.

St-Chinian is mapped on this page but is described overleaf with its neighbour Faugères.

WESTERN LANGUEDOC'S WINE REGIONS

This map, on which only the land deemed promising enough to grow AOC wine is highlighted, reveals vividly the plain around Béziers, which used to be effectively a cheap wine factory but is now much more sparsely planted with vines, thanks to financial encouragement from the EU authorities. See the France map p.47 for the location of the various Languedoc and Roussillon IGPs/Vins de Pays.

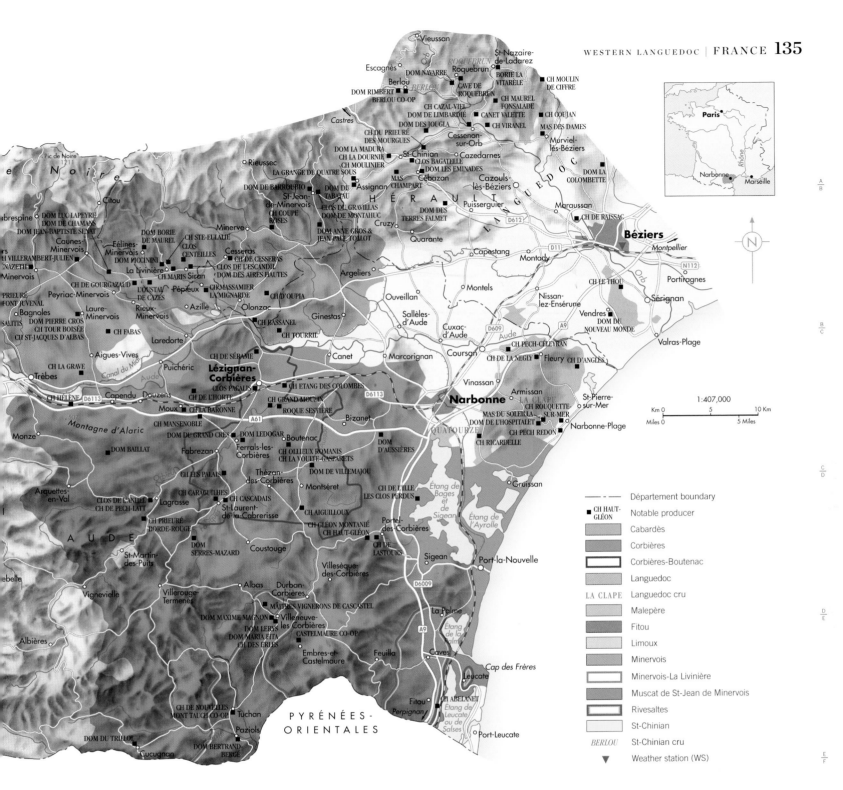

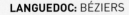

Hecht & Bannier, Les Clos Perdus, and Rives-Blanques are examples of admirable wine producers set up relatively recently by incomers, thanks to the relatively low cost of vineyard land currently available in the Languedoc. Castelmaure in the Corbières hills is one of the finest of the Languedoc's many co-ops.

LANGUEDOC: BÉZIERS ▼

Latitude / Altitude of WS
43.32° / 49ft (15m)

Average growing season temperature at WS
66.7°F (19.3°C)

Average annual rainfall at WS
22.8in (579mm)

Harvest month rainfall at WS
September: 2.8in (70mm)

Principal viticultural hazards
Drought

Principal grape varieties
Carignan, Grenache Noir, Cinsault, Syrah, Merlot, Cabernet Sauvignon

Eastern Languedoc

The sweep of vines around France's central Mediterranean coastline has shrunk considerably and beneficially in recent years, the Languedoc having been the single most responsive region to EU inducements to pull out vines in less suitable terrains. The total vineyard area of the Languedoc-Roussillon fell from 721,500 acres (292,000ha) in 2005 to 584,400 acres (236,500ha) just four years later. Most of the uprooted vineyards have been from the least interesting flatlands of the coastal hinterland, leaving the Languedoc increasingly dominated by more propitious zones, generally on higher ground and poorer soils, producing wines with real local character, a strong French accent, and remarkably attractive prices. While most of the maps in this book show the extent of all the vineyards in a particular region, the vine has been planted so extensively in the area mapped here that only those areas producing Appellation d'Origine Contrôlée wines are highlighted.

In the bad old days this part of the world was dominated by (often badly run) co-operatives, and relatively few of the region's tens of thousands of vine-growers made wine. But in recent years there has been a new wave of energetic individuals, many of them from outside the region, as keen to make wine as to grow grapes. Although more than 300 of them are still in operation, co-ops have been amalgamating in an attempt to pool resources and gain muscle in the competitive modern wine market. They vary enormously in their abilities to make and sell exportable wine. Wine enthusiasts would be well advised to concentrate on the wines that emerge from the coloured zones of the eastern Languedoc appellations. The most exciting wines tend to be made by passionate individuals, often first-generation wine producers. They typically operate where the Romans grew vines (some of the first in Gaul) on hillsides such as the Terrasses du Larzac, an increasingly important area, with such poor, shallow soils that nothing else would flourish.

In 2006 the Coteaux du Languedoc appellation was recast simply as the overarching regional appellation **Languedoc**, but that now will not

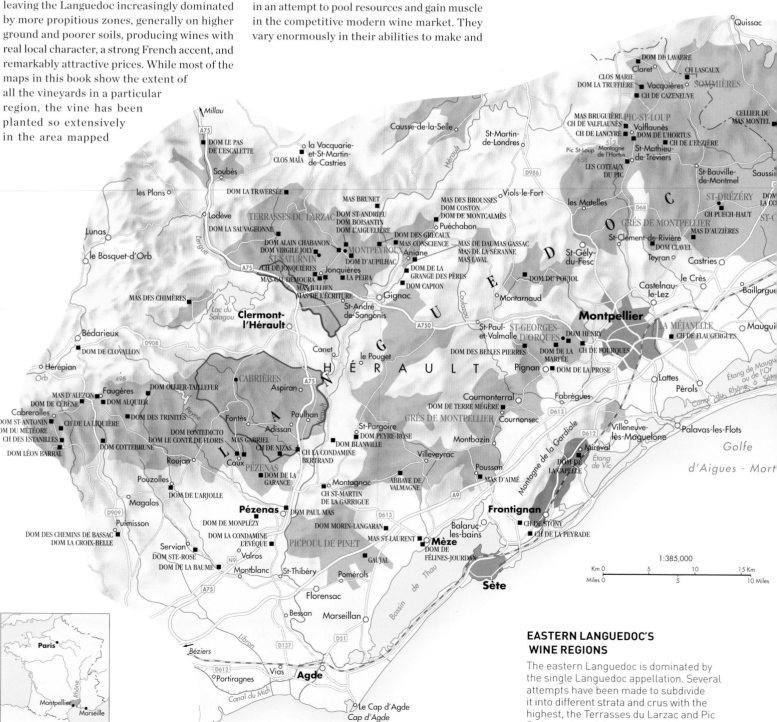

EASTERN LANGUEDOC'S WINE REGIONS

The eastern Languedoc is dominated by the single Languedoc appellation. Several attempts have been made to subdivide it into different strata and crus with the highest, the Terrasses du Larzac and Pic St-Loup, two of the most promising.

come into final effect, if at all, until 2017. Its crus (see the names in magenta) encompass most, but not all, of the likely spots for top-quality viticulture in the eastern Languedoc – as the distribution of notable producers clearly shows.

Distinctive terroir

One of the most obviously distinctive terroirs within the Languedoc is Pic St-Loup, in the far north of the area mapped here, on the foothills of the dramatic Cévennes. The wines produced

on the flanks of the rocky finger that is the Pic St-Loup itself, and on the Montagne de l'Hortus, by such estates as Clos Marie, Mas Bruguière, Domaine de l'Hortus, and châteaux de Cazeneuve, de Lancyre, and Lascaux, are obviously the products of southern sunshine. They reflect the herbs of the region but also the definition conferred by altitude and relatively cool nights. This is one of the northernmost parts of the Languedoc; Syrah does well here.

Producers such as domaines l'Aiguelière, d'Aupilhac (with Cinsault and old-vine Carignan), Alain Chabanon, La Pèira, and La Sauvageonne, now part of the important Gérard Bertrand empire run from just outside Narbonne, have confirmed the high potential of the relatively cool, windy hills north of Clermont. Back in the 1970s ambitious Hérault wine production was pioneered at Mas de Daumas Gassac, on the distinctive gritty soils of Aniane (but with an emphasis on Cabernet Sauvignon rather than Syrah or more traditional Midi varieties).

The extensive cru of Grés de Montpellier incorporates a wide swathe of vineyards with varied soils southwest and north of this ancient university city. They all benefit from the moderating influence of sea breezes throughout the heat of high summer. The medieval town of Pézenas lends its name to a cru extending north of the town as far as Cabrières, rich in the schist that characterizes both Faugères to the immediate west and its neighbour St-Chinian mapped on p.135.

St-Chinian has one of the most distinctive reputations for Languedoc wines of all three colours, perhaps most characterfully from the rugged schists of the north and west of the zone, at altitudes often well above 1,970ft (600m) in spectacularly mountainous country. There are fine whites, Carignan-marked reds from St-Chinian-Berlou, and St-Chinian-Roquebrun reds more heavily influenced by Rhône varieties, particularly sharply etched Syrah grown on schist. Vines grown at lower altitudes on the bizarre purple clay and limestone soils around the village of St-Chinian itself tend to be softer and more supple. **Faugères** (red, rosé, and now white)

is made up almost entirely of schist and demands hard work on meagre soils and vineyards up to 2,300ft (700m) overlooking Béziers and the plain, no longer a sea of vines, that stretches towards the coast (see p.135).

Of the vast production of the Languedoc, almost 80% is red, and mainly blends of Mediterranean varieties such as Carignan (often vinified by carbonic maceration in an effort to soften it) with increasing proportions of Grenache, Syrah, Mourvèdre, or Cinsault. White winemaking has become increasingly sophisticated, however, and there are now many intriguing blends of such grapes as Grenache Blanc, Clairette, Bourboulenc, Picpoul, Roussanne, Marsanne, Vermentino (also known as Rolle), and Viognier.

Clairette du Languedoc and **Picpoul de Pinet** are specifically white wines embraced by the AOC system. The first is made to a limited extent, just north of Pézenas, in a modern, fresh style to flatter what can be a very refreshing grape variety. It can also be late-harvest and sweet. The second, most unusually for France, is a varietal appellation, in this case dependent on the quirky, lemon-scented Picpoul grape grown between Pézenas and the lagoon behind the port of Sète, much of it vinified by two dynamic co-ops. The result is a sort of Midi Muscadet. These represent Languedoc tradition as much as the sweet golden Vins Doux Naturels (see p.138) based on Muscat, of which Muscat de Frontignan was once world-famous. Muscats de Mireval and de Lunel south of Nîmes rarely show the zest of a Frontignan wine, but there is now some experimentation with unfortified late-harvest wines.

Country wines

Those are the principal appellations of the eastern Languedoc but many producers, whether in an AOC zone or in the flatlands in between, make a range of IGP wines (mapped on p.47). And many, particularly but not exclusively those outside the official appellation zones, make nothing but these local "country wines" – whether carrying the name of some small local IGP zone or the more internationally recognizable name "Pays d'Oc", often with a grape name.

The reliably hot summers can ripen a usefully wide range of grape varieties, and here at least French prejudice against *vins de cépage* – those that Anglo-Saxons call varietal wines – is much less marked. And more and more wine made here is sold simply as Vin de France: the flexible category available for those who wish to stray outside the confines of AOC and IGP regulations and/or are unwilling to deal with the paperwork involved. The Languedoc has proved that it can be a fine source of serious, terroir-driven, often hand-crafted essences of southern France, but an area as extensive and varied as this can be as difficult to understand as it is to sell. As much as in Burgundy, the name of the producer holds the key to wine quality. Remarkably few wines made here could ever be described as overpriced, however.

Map legend:

- — · — Département boundary
- **DOM CLAVEL** ■ Notable producer
- Languedoc
- **PÉZENAS** Languedoc cru
- Clairette du Languedoc
- Faugères
- Muscat de Frontignan
- Muscat de Lunel
- Muscat de Mireval

There may not be much visual variety in these labels but the wines have been made from a wide range of grape varieties and terroirs. Servières, for example, is one of the world's finest varietal Cinsaults, while Clos Marie's Manon is a firm white made from Vermentino, Grenache Blanc, and Roussanne. Bergerie de Hortus is a more usual blend of Grenache, Syrah, and Mourvèdre.

Roussillon

Once a mere suffix to the Languedoc, Roussillon is exerting its individuality: physical, cultural, and viticultural. Its inhabitants consider themselves Catalans who happen to find themselves in France, but only since 1659. Their yellow-and-red-striped banners are everywhere, their local dialect with its double Ls more closely resembles Spanish than French.

The landscape here may be more dramatic – at the eastern end of the Pyrenees the peaks of the Canigou, snow-covered most of the year, swoop more than 7,500ft (2,500m) down to the Mediterranean – but the region is softer, less wild than the rocky lower contours of the Corbières hills to the north. Sunshine (an average of 325 days a year) helps, and explains the fields and groves (and vineyards) of fruit and vegetables to which the Perpignan plain and Agly, Têt, and Tech valley floors are devoted. The effects of that sunshine are concentrated by the east-facing amphitheatre created by the Corbières, Canigou, and Albères mountains which separate modern France from Spain.

Vins Doux Naturels

France's first fruits of the season regularly come from Roussillon, and the vineyards on the plain are some of the driest and hottest in France, their low bushes yielding only small crops of fully ripe Grenache grapes of all hues as early as mid-August. They were traditionally used for the most basic of Roussillon's famous Vins Doux Naturels (VDN). These once-popular apéritifs are not in fact naturally sweet wines, as the name implies, but part-fermented grape juice stopped from becoming wine by adding alcohol, according to the sweetness and strength sought but usually later than for port.

Roussillon makes 90% of all of France's Vins Doux Naturels, and **Rivesaltes**, made in a vast area of Roussillon mainly from Grenache Noir, Blanc, and Gris, is France's most popular VDN by far. **Muscat de Rivesaltes**, a more recent creation, comes from the same generous zone, incorporating all but the highest vineyard land of the Pyrénées-Orientales département, together with the two enclaves of Fitou in the Aude mapped on p.135.

But it is the curious inland region of the upper Agly Valley, with its distinctive black schist around Maury that has become the focus of the most exciting recent wine activity in Roussillon. The sheer individuality of its deep-flavoured dry red wines and firm, long-living, mineral-scented dry whites has drawn winemakers from all over the world.

These dry wines are certainly easier for outsiders to understand than VDN, even if they are evolving in style and composition every year, with a notable preponderance of followers of the "natural wine" cult (see p.29). Record sunshine

and low-yielding bush-vines combine to make tough tannins a potential problem. Fermenting whole bunches and retiring the destemmer is increasingly the solution. **Côtes du Roussillon** is the base level, still made largely from old-vine Carignan, with Grenache, Cinsault, Syrah, and Mourvèdre all on the increase.

Many reds and whites, including Agly's best, are sold as IGP Côtes Catalanes however, the haunting dry whites benefiting from an exotic palette of pale-skinned grape varieties (see key facts panel).

Côtes du Roussillon-Villages are bolder, more positive wines (reds only), thanks to even lower yields and higher strength. **Côtes du Roussillon Les Aspres** was devised expressly for superior wines from those villages not included in Côtes du Roussillon-Villages. Many of these wines offer good value for age-worthy reds and whites whose aromas come from the soil rather than from following international fashion. At the time of writing the dramatic landscape of the Agly Valley does not even have its own appellation, but **Maury** has one for its VDN, which can be as splendid, and certainly as long-lived, as a good Banyuls.

Banyuls is France's finest VDN, grown at yields that sometimes average less than 20hl/ha on France's southernmost vineyards, steep windswept terraces of brown schist sloping to the

Looking down on the steep Banyuls terraces of mixed Grenache plantings at harvest time. The proportion of Roussillon grapes made into strong sweet Vins Doux Naturels has shrivelled in recent years.

sea just north of a rather sleepy Spanish frontier post. Grapes come predominantly from ancient Grenache Noir bushes, often shrivelling to raisins on the vine. For Banyuls Grand Cru, made only in particularly good years, 30 months of barrel-ageing and 75% of Grenache Noir is mandatory. Ageing techniques, and therefore hues and wine styles, vary just as widely as for port (see p.209), and sometimes for similar reasons. Pale wines heady with *rancio* flavour may result from long ageing in old wooden barrels in relatively warm conditions, while wines labelled Rimage are aged, like vintage port, at a much more stately pace in bottle.

Dry wines made from the Banyuls vineyards are called after the pretty fishing port of **Collioure**, traditionally home to artists and anchovy-packers. Deep crimson essences, almost more Spanish than French, also testify to the robust alcohol levels achieved by the vines, mainly Grenache but increasingly supplemented by Syrah and Mourvèdre. Powerful white Collioure is also made, usually from Grenache Blanc and Gris.

AUDE

Opoul-
Périllos

Narbonne

DOM DES CHÊNES

DOM DU CLOS
DES FÉES

Vingrau

Salses-
le-Château

Étang de
Leucate
ou de
Salses

Caudiès-
de-Fenouillèdes

Prugnanes

DOM LE SOULA
St-Paul-de-
Fenouillet

DOM DE MAJAS

DOM GRAIN
D'ORIENT

DOM LAGUERRE

DOM POUDEROUX
CH ST-ROCH
CALVET THUNEVIN
DOM PERTUISANE
DOM DES ENFANTS
DOM MAS AMIEL
CAVE JEAN-LOUIS LAFAGE
Maury
CLOT DE L'ORIGINE
LA PETITE BAIGNEUSE
CLOS DES VINS D'AMOUR

MAS KAROLINA
MAS MUDIGLIZIA

Lesquerde

CLOS DU ROUGE GORGE
PRECEPTOIRE
DE CENTARNACH
DOM DU POSSIBLE
DOM DU BOUT DU MONDE
Lansac
DOM DE L'AUSSEIL
DOM J-L TRIBOULEY
DOM RIVATON
Caramany

Tautavel

DOM DES SOULANES
DOM GARDIÉS

DOM
DANJOU-BANESSY
CH DE JAU

DOM DEPEYRE
DOM DES
SCHISTES
DOM DE
L'HORIZON
Estagel
DOM VINCI
DOM DE RANCY
ROC DES ANGES
Montner
DOM MATASSA
DOM PADIÉ
DOM GAUBY

Espira-
de-l'Agly DOM DU MAS CRÉMAT
CH LES PINS
DOM BOUDAU
DOM PIQUEMAL

Rivesaltes

DOM CAZES

Port-
Barcarès

DOM SINGLA

St-Laurent-
de-la-Salanque

A
B

Sournia

DOM FONTANEL

Latour-
de-France

Calce
DOM PITHON

Baixas

Agly

DOM RIBERACH

Cassagnes

CH DE CALADROY
DOM DU CLOT DE L'OUM
Belesta

PYRÉNÉES-

St-Estève

Bompas

Perpignan

Canet-en-
Roussillon

D617

Canet-Plage

B
C

1314

Millas

DOM FORÇA RÉAL

Têt

Touleuges

DOM LAPORTE
DOM SARDA-MALET

MAS BAUX

Cabestany

Étang de
Canet et de
St-Nazaire

Ille-sur-Têt

N116

ORIENTALES

Canohès

D900

A9

Molitg-les-Bains

Vinça

Thuir

CH MOSSÉ
DOM FERRER-RIBIÈRE
Terrats

Trouillas

DOM DE CAZENOVE
Bages

St-Cyprien

C
D

Prades

Cantarrane

D612

Elne

DOM SOL-PAYRÉ

Fourques

DOM PUIG-PARAHY
DOM VAQUER

Passa

CH PLANÈRE

Banyuls-
dels-Aspres
GOUME DEL MAS
DOM MADELOC
DOM ST-SEBASTIEN

Massif du Canigou

2784
Pic du Canigou

Valmanya

Tech

St-Genis-
des-Fontaines

D618

DOM LÉONINE

Argelès-sur-Mer

DOM LA TOUR VIEILLE
Collioure

DOM DE L'ÉTOILE
DOM BRUNO DUCHÈNE

Port-Vendres
Cap Béar

le Boulou

DOM DU
MAS ROUS

Sorède

DOM
LE SCARABÉE

LE CLOS DE PAULILLES

DOM DU MAS BLANC
CELLIER DES TEMPLIERS
CASOT DES
MAILLOLÈS

Banyuls-sur-Mer
DOM DE LA
RECTORIE

Andorra

D115

Céret

Amélie-les-
Bains-Palalda

D900

Albères

Pic Neulos
1256

Barcelona

le Perthus

Chaîne des

Cerbère
Cap Cerbère

Barcelona

Arles-
sur-Tech

Montferrer

ESPAÑA

D
E

N

1:250,000

Km 0 1 2 3 4 5 Km
Miles 0   1   2   3 Miles

International boundary

Département boundary

DOM CAZES Notable producer

Lesquerde Villages that may append
their name to Côtes du
Roussillon-Villages AOP/AOC

Banyuls and Collioure

Côtes du Roussillon Les Aspres

Côtes du Roussillon

Côtes du Roussillon-Villages

Maury

Rivesaltes and Muscat de Rivesaltes

Weather station (WS)

ROUSSILLON'S WINE REGIONS

The distribution of interesting producers on the map above suggests that the Agly Valley may be due for its own detailed map in our next edition. See p.135 for the northern part of the Rivesaltes and Muscat de Rivesaltes zone.

ROUSSILLON: PERPIGNAN ▼

Latitude / Altitude of WS
42.74° / 138ft (42m)

Average growing season temperature at WS
67.6°F (19.8°C)

Average annual rainfall at WS
22.0in (558mm)

Harvest month rainfall at WS
September: 1.5in (38mm)

Principal viticultural hazards
Drought

Principal grape varieties
Carignan, Grenache Noir, Maccabeu, Syrah, Grenache Blanc, Muscat, Grenache Gris, Mourvèdre, Lladoner Pelut, Cinsault, Rolle, Marsanne, Roussanne, Malvoisie du Roussillon

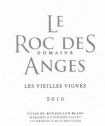

Just one Vin Doux Naturel here, Mas Amiel's riposte to port. Among dry Roussillon wines, whites (typically IGP rather than AOC) often trump reds, though Bertrand-Bergé's Fitou, made just north of the area mapped, is masterful.

Provence

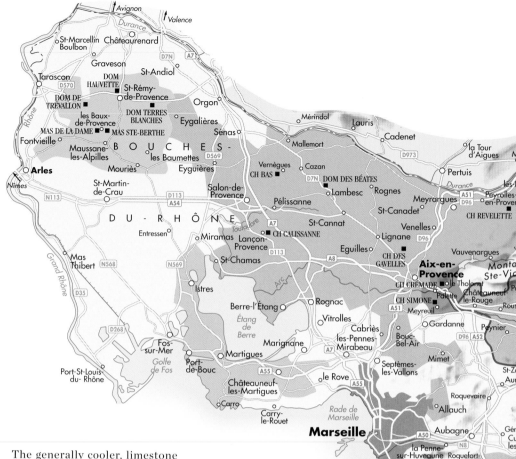

The Romans, overflowing from Italy, invented Provence without greatly changing the Italian model. Their cities and monuments are still its grandest features. Its wine, until very recently, was nothing much: largely overstrong and underflavoured rosé. But now a spell has come over it – as it has over Chianti. Ambitious, stylish, often very rich incomers, drawn to Provence's legendary countryside and climate, have reinvented its wine. An increasing proportion of its rosé is gently made, intriguingly perfumed, and dry enough to be the perfect foil for the garlic and olive oil that characterize the region's cuisine. Seriously interesting reds are also being made all over Provence.

A glance at the map explains why these reds may vary considerably in character. The classic appellation **Côtes de Provence,** France's most extensive, encompasses the northern outskirts of Marseille, the southern flanks of the Montagne Ste-Victoire, Mediterranean islands, the warm coastal hinterland of resorts such as Le Lavandou and St-Tropez, cooler, subalpine retreats north of Draguignan, and even a pocket of vines around Villars well north of Nice.

The generally cooler, limestone enclave of **Coteaux Varois,** a much more recent recruit to AOC status, is sheltered from softening maritime influence by the Massifs de la Ste-Baume and Besillon. Some vineyards in the wooded hills north of Brignoles may not be picked until early November, while vintage time on the coast is early September. Louis Latour from Burgundy has had remarkable success with Pinot Noir grown even further north, near Aups, hinting at just how cool it is here.

In the west, the landscape of **Coteaux d'Aix-en-Provence** (of which the university town itself is in fact on the southeastern border) is less dramatic, as the wines tend to be – although Counoise grapes add interest to some rosés.

Between Coteaux d'Aix-en-Provence and the River Rhône itself is the splinter appellation created in 1995 and named after the extraordinary hilltop tourist trap **Les Baux-de-Provence.** Warmed by the sea and buffeted by Provence's famous mistral, this area is even better suited to organic viticulture than most of the rest of Provence. The AOC regulations now permit white Les-Baux-de-Provence, made mainly from Clairette, Grenache Blanc, and the more and more popular Vermentino – often known in Provence as Rolle.

Having been ruled by successive waves of invaders from the east, north, west, and south

Provence, which spreads south and east from the Luberon, has a languorous magic: warm stone, sun-baked orange tiles, cicadas, blossom, wild yellow daisies, lavender, thyme, and of course wine, traditionally rosé, are all part of it.

(Sardinians for much of the 19th century), Provence boasts a varied legacy of grape varieties. Tibouren (also known over the Italian border in Liguria as Rossese di Dolceacqua) is one useful example. Although old Carignan vines are well regarded, the INAO's current preoccupation seems to be to reduce and eventually eliminate the Carignan that was planted here, as in the Languedoc, to supply cheap reds for northern France, while encouraging the Grenache and Cinsault (so useful for rosés), and the sturdier Mourvèdre and Syrah, which is making some excellent wines in the cool Coteaux Varois. Cabernet Sauvignon is officially viewed as a somewhat sinister intruder. Certainly its ripening here can be uncertain. As a result some fine Provençal reds (and whites) are sold as IGPs, including all of those from Les Baux's Domaine de Trévallon, arguably the region's finest red wine producer of all.

As might be expected of a region with a history of wine-growing that dates back to Roman times, Provence harbours some well-established individual wine zones. Perhaps the most historic is **Palette** on the north-facing, limestone-influenced bank of the River Arc just east of Aix, where the Rougier family of Château

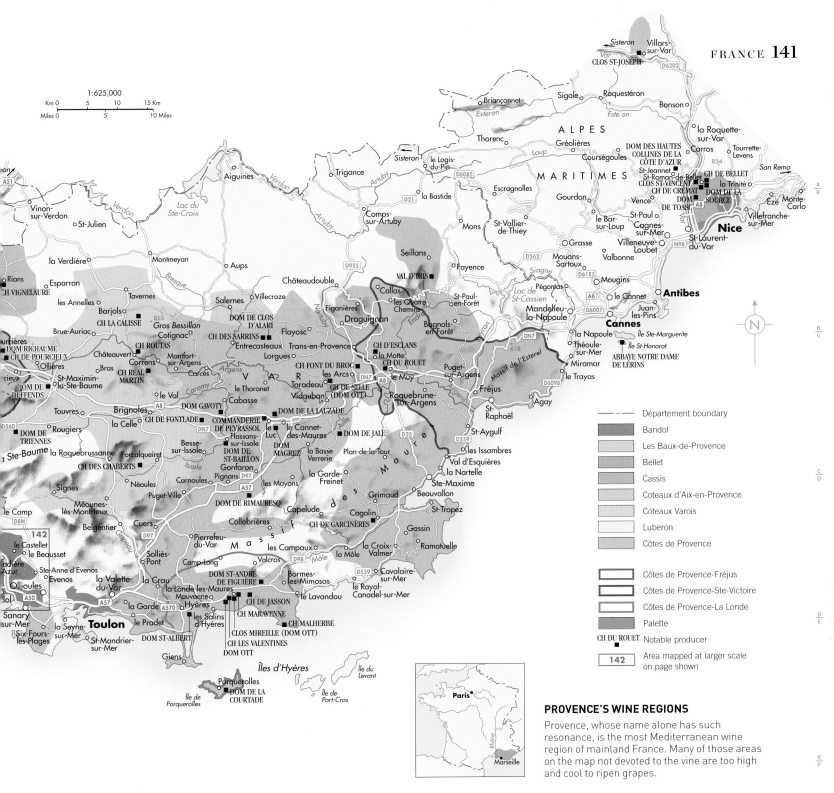

Provence's wine regions

— · — · —	Département boundary
▮	Bandol
▮	Les Baux-de-Provence
▮	Bellet
▮	Cassis
▮	Coteaux d'Aix-en-Provence
▮	Coteaux Varois
▮	Luberon
▮	Côtes de Provence
▭	Côtes de Provence-Fréjus
▭	Côtes de Provence-Ste-Victoire
▭	Côtes de Provence-La Londe
▮	Palette
CH DU ROUET	Notable producer
142	Area mapped at larger scale on page shown

PROVENCE'S WINE REGIONS

Provence, whose name alone has such resonance, is the most Mediterranean wine region of mainland France. Many of those areas on the map not devoted to the vine are too high and cool to ripen grapes.

Simone has been making extraordinarily dense wine of all three colours for more than 200 years from a palette (hence the name?) of local grape varieties, more numerous even than are allowed in Châteauneuf-du-Pape.

Cassis, centred on the small port to the east of Marseille, also makes a serious effort with its characteristically herbal white: de rigueur with bouillabaisse. In the far east of Provence, a handful of vignerons continue to resist the encroachment of Nice on the vineyards of **Bellet**, (they have a documented history going back 200 years), cooled by winds from the sea and the Alps, and enriched by such Italianate grapes as Braquet (Brachetto), Folle Noire (Fuella), and Rolle (Vermentino). Wines made close to tourist centres are rarely underpriced.

Garrus is the top cuvée of Sacha Lichine's Château d'Esclans, which has pushed Provençal rosé into the luxury price bracket. Château Vignelaure, when acquired by Georges Brunet of Bordeaux, pioneered Provençal blends of Syrah and Cabernet Sauvignon.

Bandol

On south-tilted terraces among the pines, well inland of the touristy port but open to Mediterranean breezes, the appellation Bandol feels both its isolation and its unique status keenly. In size it may be dwarfed by the oceans of Côtes de Provence that make up the bulk of wine produced in this sunny corner of southeast France. But in stature it is arguably Provence's most recognized appellation.

The wine is mainly red, made substantially from the fashionable Mourvèdre grape (the only such French appellation) often blended with some Grenache and Cinsault, and with its full-blooded, almost feral herbiness it is extremely easy to appreciate. Thanks to a climate benign enough to ripen a vine variety with one of the longest growing cycles of all, most red Bandol is voluptuously ripe and can easily be enjoyed at only six or seven years. Grenache is a common choice for any north-facing vineyard; its potential alcohol level needs taming. A

substantial, often Cinsault-dominated dry rosé is much drunk in the region and small quantities of full-bodied white Bandol are also made, mainly from Clairette, Bourboulenc, and Ugni Blanc.

Terroirs in this relatively small appellation vary enormously. On the red clay soils that predominate south of La Cadière d'Azur (central on the map) the wines can be extremely opulent, sometimes even a bit heavy. On the chalky plain northeast of St-Cyr in a sweep eastwards to Le Brûlat the soils at are their most neutral, and the wines supple and obliging. Bandol is at its nerviest when grown on the stony, more limestone-dominated soils northeast of the zone, while from the oldest soils of the zone south of Le Beausset come a mixed bunch of wines. At higher altitudes (such as vineyards at 1,000ft (300m) around Château de Pibarnon) soils tend to be less fertile than most, and here the vintage may extend to mid-October.

Yields are some of the lowest in France, and fortunately any rain tends to be followed by a sharp mistral that blows away the risk of rot. The low-acid Mourvèdre may not be the easiest grape to vinify, with a tendency to develop the unappetizing farmyard smells associated with reduction, but winemaking techniques in Bandol are becoming increasingly sophisticated. Mourvèdre has never been a great friend of barriques and most wine is matured in large oak *foudres*. Bandol's signature grape variety must constitute at least half the blend, but in warmer years some estates make cuvées that are almost 100% Mourvèdre.

Bandol was once shipped from the port after which it is named. Today most of the wine is made well inland, on terraces called restanques that are sheltered from cool north winds and soak up so much sunshine that Mourvèdre always ripens here.

Département boundary
Canton boundary
Commune (parish) boundary
CH PRADEAUX Notable producer
Appellation boundary
Vineyards
Woods
100 Contour interval 50 metres

1:100,000
Km 0   1   2   3 Km
Miles 0   1   2 Miles

Corsica

The island of Corsica is sunnier and drier than anywhere in mainland France, but its mountainous terrain means its patchwork of terroirs has only a fiercely dry, flavour-concentrating July and August in common. Corsica is closer to Italy than France in many respects, including the simple one of distance, but France has been the major influence on its modern wine history. When France lost Algeria in the 1960s, an army of skilled growers, the *pieds noirs*, migrated to the then-malarial east coast. By 1976 Corsica's vineyard had quadrupled, almost entirely with bulk-producing vines.

Corsica's contribution to the European wine lake has since been stemmed and, thanks to vast subsidies from Brussels and Paris, the island's cellars are now well-equipped, its winemakers often trained at one of the mainland's wine colleges, and its vineyards much reduced and planted with superior vine varieties. Even so, most of the more interesting wine produced on the island has also been sold there, at prices boosted by tourist demand. The wine most commonly exported is basic IGP blessed only by Corsica's seductive *nom de verre*, L'Ile de Beauté, under which almost half of all wine made on the island now travels.

Heritage vines

More and more Corsican wine, however, is serious stuff that has rediscovered its birthright in the hardy traditional grape varieties and the rocky hills where they grow best. Research continues into Corsica's grapevine heritage. Nielluccio, Tuscany's Sangiovese, which may have been imported by the Genoese who ruled the island until the late 18th century, accounts for almost one-third of the island's vines and dominates the northern appellation of **Patrimonio**, inland from the port of Bastia. The only area on the majestically craggy island to have limestone soil, Patrimonio produces some of the island's best and longest-lived wines: firm Rhônish reds, well-balanced whites, and rich Muscat Vins Doux Naturels (see p.138) of high quality.

The much softer Sciaccarello grape (Tuscany's Mammolo), grown in about 15% of the island's vineyards, is associated principally with Corsica's oldest wine region on the granitic west coast around the capital Ajaccio, at Calvi, and in the Sartène region around Propriano (schist is found in the south of the island). It makes highly drinkable, soft yet spicy red and a rosé that can be lively despite its high alcohol content.

Sweet wines, of Muscat or the local Vermentino (known as "Malvoisie de Corse" in the north of the island), are also the speciality of Cap Corse, the long northward point of the island and can be excellent. Rappu is a strong sweet red made here, around Rogliano, from Aleatico grapes. Wines made on this northern tip of Corsica are labelled **Coteaux du Cap Corse**. Vermentino, the principal white grape in all of Corsica's AOCs, also produces crisp, dry wines, varying from intensely aromatic to steely citrus, and deeply savoury with age.

The appellation of **Calvi** in the northwest uses Sciaccarello, Nielluccio, and Vermentino, as well as some of the more international grapes, to produce full-bodied table wines; **Figari** and **Porto-Vecchio** do the same in the south. It is thirsty country, with wines that could scarcely be called thirst-quenching, although Figari and Sartène seem to have come furthest in making wines, particularly whites, with a degree of modern, fruity crispness.

In comparison with these concentrated wines of traditional character, the regular Vins de Corse with no further geographical suffix (typically made around Aléria and Ghisonaccia on the eastern coastal plain) are of no special interest. Blending local with international varieties has proved to be commercially successful for the island's better co-ops.

A new generation of growers is eager to make the most of their terroir, and a local, some would say captive, market eager to find in their wines the elusive scents of the island.

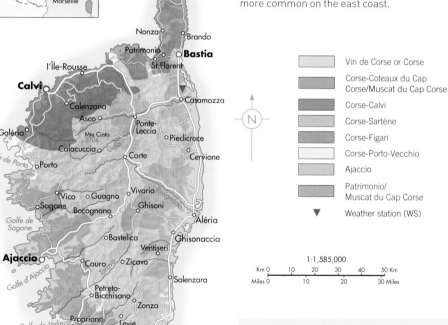

CORSICA'S WINE REGIONS

Most of the vineyards are within sight of the coast, for the mountainous interior is too rugged for viticulture. The west coast has granite, the south and the Cap Corse Peninsula have some schist, while alluvial soils and some marl and sand are more common on the east coast.

- Vin de Corse or Corse
- Corse-Coteaux du Cap Corse/Muscat du Cap Corse
- Corse-Calvi
- Corse-Sartène
- Corse-Figari
- Corse-Porto-Vecchio
- Ajaccio
- Patrimonio/Muscat du Cap Corse
- ▼ Weather station (WS)

1:1,585,000
Km 0 10 20 30 40 50 Km
Miles 0 10 20 30 Miles

Summer rainfall is so low here that all flavours in the island's fruits and vegetables are unusually concentrated, including those of the Muscats of Cap Corse, the island's intriguing Vin Doux Naturel.

CORSICA: BASTIA ▼

Latitude / Altitude of WS
42.33° / 33ft (10m)

Average growing season temperature at WS
67.6°F (19.8°C)

Average annual rainfall at WS
31.5in (799mm)

Harvest month rainfall at WS
September: 3.2in (81mm)

Principal viticultural hazards
Drought

Principal grape varieties
Nielluccio, Merlot, Vermentino, Grenache Noir, Sciaccarello

Jura

The Jura *vignoble*, a little enclave of vines scattered among woodland and meadow in what seem like France's remotest hills, may have shrivelled considerably since the twin scourges of mildew and phylloxera at the end of the 19th century, but its varied wines are hugely original, and increasingly fashionable – not least because of their organic and "natural" credentials. Its appellations Arbois, Château-Chalon, l'Etoile, and the all-encompassing Côtes du Jura hold special fascination for students of the art of food and wine pairing.

This is a verdant land of trenchermen, heavily influenced by the gastronomic traditions, and indeed, soils and weather, of Burgundy to the immediate west, except that in the Jura's much more jumbled terrain winters can be even more severe. As in the Côte d'Or, the best vineyards slope, sometimes steeply, south and southeast to catch the sun. Jurassic limestone is, not surprisingly, characteristic of Jura as well as of Burgundy (the l'Etoile AOC takes its name from tiny, star-shaped fossils in the soil). Blue and grey marls are especially prized for Savagnin grapes.

Jura grows the Burgundy grapes – some Pinot Noir and a great deal of Chardonnay, made increasingly in the imported Burgundian, non-oxidative style some locals call floral. The most intriguing Jura wines, however, are made from local vine varieties, particularly the late-ripening Savagnin, and are often deliberately exposed to oxygen during ageing. Savagnin, traditionally blended with Chardonnay, can taste like its close relative Traminer when young and simple, but ageing in wood brings rigour and a hazelnut note to white table wines – a pleasure not found elsewhere.

Vin Jaune

This noble grape is also wholly responsible for Jura's famous strong yellow wine, Vin Jaune. Savagnin grapes are picked as ripe as possible, fermented and then left in old Burgundy barrels for at least six years. The wine evaporates and on its surface grows a film of yeast, usually thinner than the famous flor of the Jerez region (see p.198). The traditional bottle for these firm, intensely nutty wines is the *clavelin* containing 62cl, supposedly the volume left of an original litre put into cask. Not for neophytes, this is a wine that can last for decades and is often best opened well in advance of serving, preferably with mature Comté cheese or a local *poulet de Bresse*. The **Château-Chalon** appellation is limited to this odd but potentially excellent style of wine, but Vin Jaune, of distinctly varying quality, is made throughout the region.

The most common red wine grape is the perfumed Poulsard, often called Ploussard, especially around Pupillin (a subappellation of Arbois), where it is most popular and makes light, rose-scented wine. A silky Poulsard rosé and even some medium-sweet Pétillant Naturel are also made. Trousseau is a deeper-coloured but rarer Jura grape whose peppery, violet-scented wine is grown mainly around Arbois – although its latest address is northern California. Pinot Noir tends to do best around Arlay, due west of Château-Chalon and south of Lons-le-Saunier. This southern part of the **Côtes du Jura** produces mainly white wines, including Vin Jaune, while the appellation l'Etoile is restricted specifically to whites.

Jura has always produced good sparkling wine. Traditional-method **Crémant du Jura** represents almost a quarter of Jura's wine production and can be excellent value. Jura's unctuous *vin de paille* is also made throughout the region, from Chardonnay, Savagnin, and/or Poulsard grapes, generally picked early and dried in carefully ventilated conditions until January when these raisins are fermented (to more than 14.5% alcohol by volume) and then aged in old barrels for two or three years. Like Vin Jaune, these rarities are for very long keeping.

One final speciality is Macvin du Jura, a fragrant and often characterful mixture of grape juice and grape spirit drunk as an apéritif in the region.

JURA'S HEARTLAND

As indicated by the boundary of the Côtes du Jura and Arbois appellations, the area mapped here is only part, arguably the most important part, of Jura wine country, with its rolling green hills and pretty villages.

DOM MACLE ■ Notable producer
— Arbois
— Château-Chalon
— l'Étoile
— Côtes du Jura
Vineyards
Woods
—400— Contour interval 50 metres

Key to producers
1 DOM A & M TISSOT
  DOM TISSOT
  FRÉDÉRIC LORNET
  JACQUES PUFFENEY
  MICHEL GAHIER
2 DOM DE LA TOURNELLE
  DOM DE L'OCTAVIN
  DOM ROLET
  JACQUES TISSOT
3 DOM BERTHET-BONDET
  DOM MACLE
4 DOM BAUD PÈRE ET FILS

1:310,000
Km 0 — 5 — 10 Km
Miles 0 — 5 — 10 Miles

For such a small region, Jura produces a remarkably wide range of wine styles. Table wines are divided into those that are deliberately oxidized such as Vin Jaune, and those that are not, such as this Chardonnay grown under a cherry tree.

Savoie

Savoie is France's alpine country, complete with all the demands of tourism: winters cold enough to attract hordes of skiers and lakes that warm the nearby vineyards in summer. A small but growing area of Savoie is now devoted to the vine, but the wine areas, and even individual vineyards, are widely dispersed. Mountains so often get in the way, and most of the original *vignoble* was abandoned after phylloxera, mildew, and the First World War. The wines are so varied, from such a rich mix of local vine specialities, that it seems extraordinary to the outsider that almost all of them go under the same basic appellation, **Savoie**, or **Vin de Savoie**.

A Savoie AOC is more than twice as likely to be white as red or rosé. It is also about 10 times more likely to be light, clean, and fresh – at one with Savoyard mountain air, lakes, and streams – than it is to be deep and heady, although some producers have been experimenting with extracting more from the region's most valuable dark-skinned grape, the peppery Mondeuse. Some make their Mondeuse like Beaujolais; others carefully restrict yields and may put it in a barrique to stiffen it; the best keep a juicy note of plums and a streak of tannin which are highly appetizing. The great majority of wine sold as straight Savoie is made from the Jacquère grape and the result is light, white, dry, and usually with a discernibly alpine quality.

But within the greater Savoie region, 16 individual crus are allowed to append their name to Savoie on the label, provided certain conditions, different for each cru but stricter than for basic Savoie appellation wine, are met. On the southern shores of Lac Léman (Lake Geneva), for example, only the Chasselas grape, so beloved by neighbouring Switzerland, is allowed for wines labelled with the crus Ripaille (which can be quite a rich, golden wine), Marin, Marignan, and Crépy. South of here in the Arve Valley is the cru of Ayze, which produces still and especially sparkling whites from the rare Gringet grape.

Southeast of Bellegarde is Frangy, an isolated cru specializing in this case in the local, characterful, and age-worthy Altesse. The superiority of this grape is recognized by a special appellation, Roussette de Savoie, for any Savoie wine made from it, within certain conditions. (The four crus authorized only for the production of Roussette de Savoie are marked in magenta on the map above.)

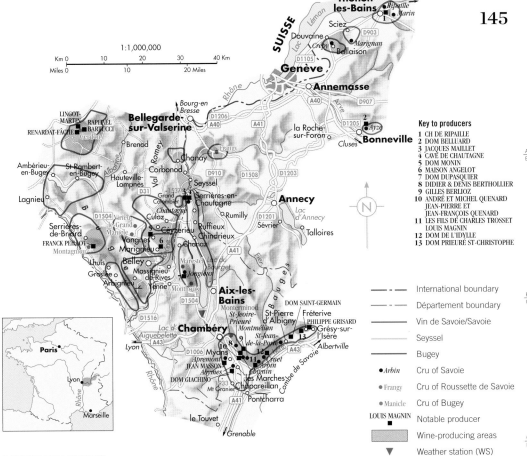

SAVOIE AND BUGEY

By no means all of Bugey's vineyards are shown here; they continue west and north of the area mapped, as can be seen on the map of France on p.47. Just a glance at the concentration of wineries and vineyards suggests how narrow some of these subalpine valleys are.

South of Frangy, **Seyssel** has its own appellation, once quite well-known for its sparkling wines made from Altesse with some local Molette grapes. Still wines made mainly from Altesse predominate today. And south of Seyssel are the extensive vineyards of Chautagne, a cru best known for its reds, particularly its grainy Gamay. To the west of the Lac du Bourget is Jongieux. A wine labelled simply "Jongieux" is made exclusively from Jacquère but some Altesse is grown here, too, especially on the Marestel vineyard slope, which has its own Roussette de Savoie cru.

Lying to the south of the town of Chambéry is Savoie's largest vineyard area, facing south and southeast on the lower slopes of Mont Granier and including the popular crus of Apremont and Abymes. Following the Isère River up the Combe de Savoie is a cluster of crus where all of Savoie's varieties are grown, but especially Jacquère and some Altesse. Of these, Chignin is responsible for one of the best-known ambassadors of fine Savoie wine. As well as growing Jacquère under its own name, its speciality, Chignin-Bergeron, made exclusively from the Roussanne grape of the Rhône grown on the steepest slopes, is one of Savoie's more powerful and powerfully scented whites. The Combe de Savoie, especially the village of Arbin southeast of Chambéry, is best suited to ripening Mondeuse to the full.

Bugey won its own appellation in 2009. Its pround native Brillat-Savarin would have been delighted. Sparkling wines predominate with light, frothy, medium-sweet, pink Cerdon – based on Gamay grown on very steep, south-facing slopes up to 1,600ft (500m) – its most distinctive and popular ambassador. Chardonnay provides backbone for the traditional-method fizz and still whites, with Pinot Noir is responsible for most of the small amount of varietally labelled still red.

Key to producers
1 CH DE RIPAILLE
2 DOM BELLUARD
3 JACQUES MAILLET
4 CAVE DE CHAUTAGNE
5 DOM MONIN
6 MAISON ANGELOT
7 DOM DUPASQUIER
8 DIDIER & DENIS BERTHOLLIER
9 GILLES BERLIOZ
10 ANDRÉ ET MICHEL QUENARD
  JEAN-PIERRE ET
  JEAN-FRANÇOIS QUENARD
11 LES FILS DE CHARLES TROSSET
  LOUIS MAGNIN
12 DOM DE L'IDYLLE
13 DOM PRIEURÉ ST-CHRISTOPHE

Symbol	Meaning
— · —	International boundary
— – —	Département boundary
—	Vin de Savoie/Savoie
—	Seyssel
—	Bugey
● Arbin	Cru of Savoie
● Frangy	Cru of Roussette de Savoie
● Manicle	Cru of Bugey
LOUIS MAGNIN ■	Notable producer
▨	Wine-producing areas
▼	Weather station (WS)

SAVOIE: CHAMBÉRY ▼

Latitude / Altitude of WS
45.64° / 771ft (235m)

Average growing season temperature at WS
61.5°F (16.4°C)

Average annual rainfall at WS
48.1in (1,221mm)

Harvest month rainfall at WS
September: 4.4in (112mm)

Principal viticultural hazards
Hail and humidity in the growing season

Principal grape varieties
Jacquère, Gamay, Mondeuse, Altesse, Roussanne, Chasselas

ALTESSE
WHITE TABLE WINE
ROUSSETTE DU BUGEY - MONTAGNIEU
Appellation d'Origine Contrôlée
MIS EN BOUTEILLE À LA PROPRIÉTÉ
FAMILLE PEILLOT, VIGNERONS
MONTAGNIEU · Bugey · France
ALC. 12.5% BY VOL.   PRODUCT OF FRANCE   750 ML

The label of Les Filles, Gilles Berlioz's all-Roussanne Chignin-Bergeron is one of the most striking in this book. The village of Chignin is just south of Arbin and Cruet in the Combe de Savoie, its vineyards facing southeast towards the River Isère.

ITALY

Vernazza in the white wine DOC of Cinque Terra, Liguria

Italy

Is there a country so stylishly creative as Italy? Or less easily governed? Italy has the world's richest variety of individual wine styles, distinctive terroirs, and indigenous grape varieties. At the top end her wines have a vivacity, originality, savour, and flair all their own. At the bottom end, like other countries, she still has too many dull, overproductive vines, but their wines are avoidable. The middle ground is what is most important, and these wines have already improved.

Some would say there is no excuse. Colonizing Greeks called Italy Oenotria – "the land of wine" (or, strictly, staked vines – a sure sign of viticultural ambition). The map reminds us that there is little of Italy that is not, at least marginally, wine country. Only France – sometimes – makes more wine than Italy.

In terms of geography, Italy cannot fail to produce good wine in great variety, if slopes, sunshine, and a temperate climate are the essentials. Her peculiar physique, that of a long spine of mountains reaching south from the sheltering Alps almost to North Africa, means that there can hardly be a desirable combination of altitude with latitude and exposure that is absent (a possible saviour as climate changes). Many of her soils are volcanic; much is limestone; there is plenty of gravelly clay. But with such variety generalization seems futile. If there is anything lacking, it is order. Italian wine labels remain a labyrinth. If Italy is viticultural heaven and offers us so much, it is easy to forget just how recent all this is. Just two generations ago, only a tiny proportion of Italian wine was even bottled by the producer. The great majority was shipped to the cities for local use, and such wine as was exported was mostly blended by the big shippers.

Italy's wine law

It is hardly surprising then that wine labels are distinctly unevolved, their chief problem being a sometimes impenetrable confusion of names, with an obscure town often the only geographical reference. Italy still needs a labelling system (which is not necessarily the same thing as a new wine law) that sets out clearly who made the wine, where, when, and how. From the 1960s on, the Italian government undertook the monumental task of devising an answer to France's Appellation d'Origine Contrôlée system: the DOC (Denominazione di Origine Controllata), complete with boundaries (often

too generous), maximum yields (ditto), and specified grape varieties and production methods. A superior form of DOC, DOCG (for which the origin was not just controlled, but guaranteed – a nice distinction) was created and has been increasingly bestowed since the 1980s.

In 1992, a law was passed to restructure the whole system of classification with tighter restrictions, including maximum permitted yields, decreasing steadily from the pinnacle of DOCG to DOC and then down to the IGT (Indicazione Geografica Tipica), category. Like France's Vins de Pays, IGTs can use the geographical and varietal name and, crucially, vintage, which was outlawed for the most basic category, Vino da Tavola, to persuade producers

to use IGT rather than calling their top wines Vino da Tavola – a way, one often felt, of mocking the whole system.

Of the 60-plus IGTs, by far the most common are those carrying the name of one of Italy's 19 regions. IGTs have appeared on an increasing proportion of labels – not least because many of the names (Umbria, Toscana, for example) have more market resonance than those of individual DOCs.

In theory an IGT does not have the status of a DOC, but the market has said otherwise about many of them – particularly those made from the non-traditional grape varieties that are now planted, often encouraged by official regulations, all over Italy. Cabernet Sauvignon (which was

ITALY'S WINE-PRODUCING AREAS

This map is intended as a reminder of the whereabouts of the regions and as a key to the subsequent, more detailed maps. The most important current DOCs and DOCGs appear on the four pages that carve up the country into northwest, northeast, centre, and south, except those in the most complex centres of quality wine-growing, which are given large-scale maps of their own.

1:6,000,000
Km 0   100   200 Km
Miles 0   50   100 Miles

- –·–·– International boundary
- –·–·– Regione boundary
- Wine-producing area
- Land above 600 metres
- 151 Regional map page number

first introduced in the early 19th century) and Chardonnay spearheaded this invasion, but Merlot, Syrah, and others have become almost commonplace. This is gradually becoming a disadvantage in a global market saturated with international varieties, and has led to a long-overdue reappraisal of Italy's own often glorious grapes. Grapes such as Fiano, Greco, Erbaluce, Malvasia, and Nosiola for white wines and Aglianico, Cesanese, Gaglioppo, Marzemino, Negroamaro, Nerello Mascalese, Perricone, and Uva di Troia for reds have already established a reputation outside their region of origin. Others will follow.

Good whites, too

There was a time when all Italy's best wines were red, but no longer. Italy learned to make "modern" (that is, fresh and crisp) white wine in the 1960s. In the 1980s, she began to add back the character that was lost in the process, and by the late 1990s had succeeded. Soave, Verdicchio, and Friuli's range of white varietals are by no means the only whites that can now be found in deliciously fruity, sometimes complex form. And a retro trend in Italian winemaking has seen skins increasingly left in the fermentation vat for varieties such as Ribolla Gialla, Pinot Grigio, and Albana.

Italy's red wines continue to get better and better, too, again not least because of the rediscovery of local grape varieties and techniques. They range from the silky and fragile to the purple and potent, in every

Tuscany as seen looking north from Montepulciano. Is it any wonder that so many outsiders have been tempted to acquire a stake in a landscape like this – and what more bucolic activity than wine-growing?

style and aroma, from redoubtable natives to Bordeaux blends to rival first growths. This extraordinarily rapid revolution in wine quality has been achieved partly with Euro-money, and once to a certain extent depended on advice from a band – some would say too small a band – of well-travelled consultant oenologists. But their often-predictable influence is now declining as individuality, expression of truly local terroir, and ancient vine varieties and techniques are seen as fashionable virtues. Another sort of consultant is more valued today: agronomists with a grasp of organics and biodynamic viticulture, the likes (sometimes French) of Michel Barbaud, and Claude and Lydia Bourguignon. This has led in some vineyards to a re-evaluation of such traditional vine-training techniques as the overhead tendone and pergola systems, which can protect vines from sunburn in Italy's hottest summers. Alberello bush-vines are similarly being reappraised.

Yet to be true to the spirit of Italy, the qualities of all her wine must be seen in the context of the incredibly varied, sensuous Italian table. The true genius of Italy lies in spreading a feast. In the great Italian feast, wine plays a role as vital as food.

THE LANGUAGE OF THE LABEL

QUALITY DESIGNATIONS

Denominazione di Origine Controllata e Garantita (DOCG) wines either recognized as Italy's best, or supported by the most skilful politicians

Denominazione di Origine Controllata (DOC) Italy's original answer to France's AOP/AOC (see p.46) and equivalent to the EU's Denominazione di Origine Protetta (DOP), which also includes DOCG

Indicazione Geografica Protetta (IGP) the EU denomination gradually replacing Indicazione Geografica Tipica (IGT)

Vino or **Vino d'Italia** the basic EU denomination replacing Vino da Tavola

OTHER COMMON EXPRESSIONS

Abboccato lightly sweet

Amabile semi-sweet

Annata vintage year

Azienda agricola wine estate which does not buy in grapes or wine, unlike an azienda vinicola

Bianco white

Cantina cellar or winery

Cantina sociale, cantina cooperativa co-operative winery

Casa vinicola wine firm

Chiaretto very pale red

Classico original, rather than expanded, wine zone

Consorzio growers' association

Dolce sweet

Fattoria literally, farm

Frizzante semi-sparkling

Gradi (alcool) alcoholic strength as a percentage by volume

Imbottigliato (all'origine) bottled (at source)

Liquoroso strong, usually fortified

Metodo classico, metodo tradizionale bottle-fermented sparkling wine

Passito strong, usually sweet wine made from dried grapes

Podere very small agricultural property, smaller than a fattoria

Recioto wine made from half-dried grapes, a Veneto speciality

Riserva special, long-aged selection

Rosato rosé (relatively rare in Italy)

Rosso red

Secco dry

Spumante sparkling

Superiore wine that has undergone more ageing than normal DOC and contains 0.5–1% more alcohol

Tenuta small holding or estate

Vendemmia vintage

Vendemmia tardiva late harvest

Vigna, vigneto vineyard

Vignaiolo, viticoltore vine-grower

Vino wine

Northwest Italy

Northwest Italy means Piemonte (Piedmont in English) to any foreign wine-lover, but the hills around Alba and Asti (the Langhe and Monferrato mapped in detail overleaf) are not the only great vineyards of this subalpine corner. Their noblest grape, Nebbiolo, gives excellent, if different, results in several parts of the region – most notably in the hills above Novara and Vercelli (famous for rice), where under the name of Spanna it rejoices in no fewer than seven different DOCs, each for a different sort of soil.

The DOCG **Gattinara** (above all from Le Colline Monsecco) is considered the noblest form of Spanna, with Antoniolo and Travaglini providing other convincing proof, **Ghemme** (also DOCG) and **Lessona** are almost as good and **Bramaterra** is not far behind. All benefit from a subalpine climate, a southern exposure and fast-draining glacial soil that is notably more acid than the soils of the Langhe. In practice all depends on the grower and the amount of Bonarda or Vespolina grapes added. The weight and intensity of Barolo may be lacking, but not the perfume. Producers such as Proprietà Sperino in Lessona and Le Piane in Boca are doing their best to restore the region's wines to the fame they enjoyed 150 years ago, when they were more highly regarded than the then-emergent Barolo.

Nebbiolo also grows in the far northeast corner of the map opposite, where Lombardy meets Switzerland. In Valtellina, on south-facing suntraps on the north bank of the River Adda, the grape, known here as Chiavennasca, makes muscular reds. The heartland, **Valtellina Superiore** DOCG, which includes the Grumello, Inferno, Sassella, and Valgella subzones, makes infinitely better wine than that sold simply as **Valtellina** Rosso. Some dry Sfursat (Sforzato) is made from semi-dried grapes – a local and potentially excellent amarone-style wine. Notable producers include Arpepe, Fay, Nino Negri, and Rainoldi.

North of Turin on the road up to the Valle d'Aosta and the Mont Blanc tunnel to France there are two more Nebbiolos, of high reputation but low output, Carema and Donnaz. In tiny

Carema, still in Piemonte but with its own name for Nebbiolo – Picutener – both Ferrando and the local co-op are excellent. **Donnaz** is made in Donnas over the provincial boundary in the Valle d'Aosta, Italy's smallest wine region. Alpine conditions may make these Nebbiolos paler and less potent than those from lower latitudes but they have their own finesse. Aosta's own red grape is Petit Rouge, which tastes not unlike the Mondeuse of Savoie: dark, fresh, berryish, and bracing. It forms the basis of Enfer d'Arvier and Torrette, among other wines subsumed into the **Valle d'Aosta** DOC. The Fumin grape makes longer-lived reds. The busy valley also makes some recherché whites from imported grapes: the very light Blancs de la Salle and de Morgex, some winter-weight Malvoisie and Petite Arvine from Switzerland, and some lively Chardonnay.

Where the hilly turbulence of Piemonte merges with the Lombard plain to the east, conditions become less alpine and extreme. The fulcrum of Lombardic viticulture is Oltrepò Pavese, the part

Wine has been grown in the Valtellina Superiore subzone of Grumello since Roman times. The dramatically spotlit Castello di Grumello dates back to the 13th century and today houses a restaurant popular with both tourists and locals.

of the province of Pavia that lies beyond the River Po. Many of Italy's best Pinot Nero and some Pinot Bianco for the making of sparkling wines come from here, without necessarily mentioning the fact.

The DOC **Oltrepò Pavese** Rosso calls for two-thirds Barbera mollified with a variety of local grapes, of which Bonarda (the local alias for the Croatina grape) is the most prevalent and characterful, although Uva Rara can add spice to a blend. The zone's leading estate is Frecciarossa, "red arrow", from Castéggio. See p.158 for details of Lombardy's flourishing sparkling wine industry around Brescia.

The **Colli Piacentini** south of Piacenza is bidding for recognition with international varietal bottlings and an often frizzante red made from Barbera and Bonarda.

South from Piemonte over the final curling tail of the Alps, known as the Ligurian Apennines, we are on the Mediterranean, with scarcely enough room between the mountains and the sea to grow grapes. Liguria's production is tiny, but highly individual and worth investigating. Of its grapes only Vermentino (also known as Pigato here) and Malvasia are widely grown elsewhere. **Cinque Terre** is the white wine served with fish on the

Three wines from different points along the base of the Italian Alps. The Valle d'Aosta is the coolest, while Valtellina's steep, south-facing vineyards, responsible for dried-grape Sfursat, can be really quite warm in summer.

MAJOR DOCGS AND DOCS

Italy has so many wine appellations – hundreds of them – that we have had to restrict this and the other regional maps to the most significant. Note how they cluster on hillsides. The flat plain of the Po is not fine wine country.

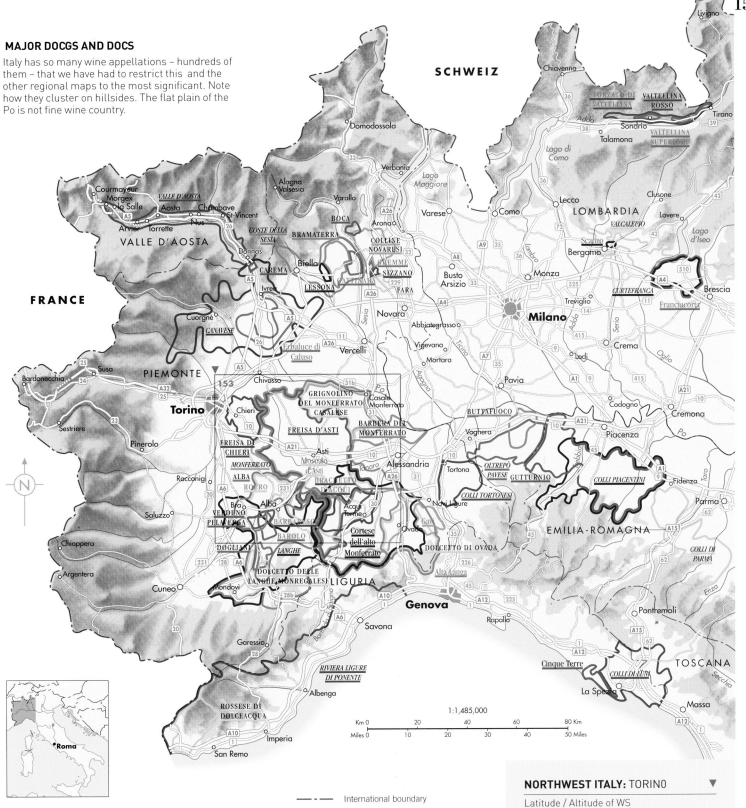

steep coast near La Spezia. Its liquorous version is called Sciacchetrà, made from dried grapes grown in vertiginous seaside vineyards – a real labour of love.

Potentially the most memorable Ligurian wine, however, is the red **Rossese**, whether **di Dolceacqua** near the French border or **di Albenga**, nearer Genoa. Unlike anything made in Provence, Rossese can be truly fresh, fruity, and inviting. And, while attractive in youth, it also has the benefit of getting better with age.

—————	International boundary
—— · ——	Regione boundary
CAREMA	Red wine
LANGHE	Red and white wine
Cinque Terre	White wine

DOCG/DOC boundaries are distinguished by coloured lines

Land above 600 metres

153   Area mapped at larger scale on page shown

▼   Weather station (WS)

NORTHWEST ITALY: TORINO ▼

Latitude / Altitude of WS
45.2° / 991ft (302m)

Average growing season temperature at WS
63.8°F (17.7°C)

Average annual rainfall at WS
29.2in (741mm)

Harvest month rainfall at WS
October: 3.0in (75mm)

Principal viticultural hazards
Downy mildew, hail, underripeness

Principal grape varieties **Barbera, Dolcetto, Moscato Bianco, Nebbiolo**

Piemonte

Piemontese food and wine are as inseparable as those of Burgundy. They are strong, rich, individual, mature, somehow autumnal, with white truffles playing an important part. Piemonte means "at the foot of the mountains" – in this case the Alps. The Alps almost encircle this hilly region, so that from its heart, the rolling Monferrato hills around Asti, they form a continuous dark – or in winter and spring, sparkling white – horizon. Less than 5% of Piemontese vineyards are officially classed as flat. Every slope of vines, it can seem, faces in a slightly different direction and is governed by a slightly different aspect and altitude, determining which vines are planted where. If each vineyard is characterized by its very own mesoclimate, the Piemonte region has a macroclimate of its own, with what can be a very hot growing season followed by a misty autumn and a cold, often foggy, winter.

At vintage time in Barolo the hills are half-hidden. Ramps of copper and gold vines – dotted with peach trees and such hazel bushes (for Nutella) as survived a cull to make way for Chardonnay plantings – lead down to the valley of the Tanaro, often lost in the fog. It is a magical experience to visit the region and see the dark grapes coming in through the mist.

The two best red wines of Piemonte, Barolo, and Barbaresco, take their names from villages mapped in detail on the next pages. Most of the rest of Piemonte's most famous wines are named after the grapes from which they are made: Barbera, Brachetto, Dolcetto, Grignolino, Freisa, Moscato, Nebbiolo. If to the grape they add a district name (for example, Barbera d'Asti), it means they come from a limited and theoretically superior area. The notable exceptions to this format are the relatively recent Langhe, Roero, Monferrato, and catch-all Piemonte denominations devised to avoid what the Piemontese see as the ignominy of IGT wines.

The haunting Nebbiolo has no rival as the finest red grape of northern Italy. It does not have to be grown in Barolo or Barbaresco to make mellow, fragrant wine – indeed, some seriously worthwhile Nebbiolo d'Alba, Langhe Nebbiolo, and red **Roero** are made nowadays. This last, made DOCG in 2004, is grown in the Roero hills northwest of Alba on the sandy soils of the Tanaro's left bank. The fragrant, pear-scented old local white grape Arneis also thrives here, too.

The DOC **Langhe,** on the other hand, extends south of Alba on the opposite bank of the river. It has been designed for the varietal likes of Nebbiolo, Dolcetto, Freisa, Arneis, Favorita, and Chardonnay grown on the heavier clay marl soils of the Tanaro's right bank. The many geographically specific wines produced in these Langhe hills, including Barolo and Barbaresco, may be declassified to DOC Langhe, either a varietal version or merely Rosso or Bianco.

Monferrato has its own DOC, its boundaries very similar to that of Barbera d'Asti, while the Piemonte DOC is designed specifically for Barbera, Brachetto, Chardonnay, Cortese, Grignolino, Moscato, Uva Rara, and the three Pinots: not exactly an exclusive club.

Once despised as too common to inspire respect, Barbera is now Piemonte's second most glamorous red grape. Nebbiolo makes pale, tannic wines that demand time and attention. Barbera, treated to ageing in new French oak barriques, conforms more closely to the modern red wine stereotype: big, bold, and deep purple. Barbera grapes were traditionally picked earlier than Nebbiolo, but they need relatively warm sites and later picking to bring the acidity down to palatable levels, as growers in Asti and Alba have shown. **Barbera d'Asti,** in general the most quintessential Barbera, has three official subzones: Nizza, Tinella, and Astiano or Colli Astiani. **Barbera d'Alba** is typically solid and age-worthy whereas most **Barbera del Monferrato,** produced in virtually the same area as Barbera d'Asti, is the opposite. But styles evolve with fashion.

It seems impossible to eat badly in Piemonte. Chocolate and hazelnuts are as much a speciality of the Langhe hills as Nebbiolo.

Piemonte's third red grape is Dolcetto, which will still ripen in the coolest, highest sites: soft, where Barbera often bites, but capable of a marvellous balance between fleshy, dusty-dense, and dry with a touch of bitter that goes perfectly with rich local dishes. The best Dolcetto comes from Alba, Diano d'Alba, Dogliani, and Ovada (for its most potent style).

Grignolino is consistently a lightweight cherry red but can be a fine and piquant one; at its best (from Asti or Monferrato Casalese) extremely clean and stimulating. All these are wines to drink relatively young.

Moscato is Piemonte's signature white grape, responsible for sparkling Asti and, distinctly superior, fizzy **Moscato d'Asti,** the epitome of sweet Muscat grapes in its most celebratory form. It also has the considerable merit of containing less alcohol – only about 5% – than virtually any other wine. It can amaze and delight guests after a heavy dinner.

White Cortese grapes are grown south of Alessandria (see p.151) to produce still-fashionable dry **Gavi.** Arneis may have colonized Roero but these sandy soils are also particularly suitable for zesty Favorita, the local variant of Vermentino.

Other specialities of this prolific region include another frothy sweet red wine, Brachetto d'Acqui; light red Verduno from Pelaverga grapes; sweet pink or red Malvasia di Casorzo d'Asti; the interesting yellow wine with the Erbaluce di Caluso DOCG (the sweet form, Caluso Passito, is made from semi-dried grapes; the sparkling one benefits from prolonged lees ageing); and Freisa, often from Asti, a fizzy and frequently sweet red wine not unlike a tarter, less fruity form of Lambrusco that is either loved or loathed. Alta Langa DOC was created in 2002 for traditional method fizz, while some surprisingly good sparkling Riesling, sold as simple Langhe Bianco, is also produced. No one has ever accused Piemonte of a paucity of grapes, flavours, or names.

In the 1980s, Giacomo Bologna's Bricco dell'Uccellone changed the fortunes of Piemonte's most planted grape variety, Barbera, by introducing it to new French oak and making it much more concentrated.

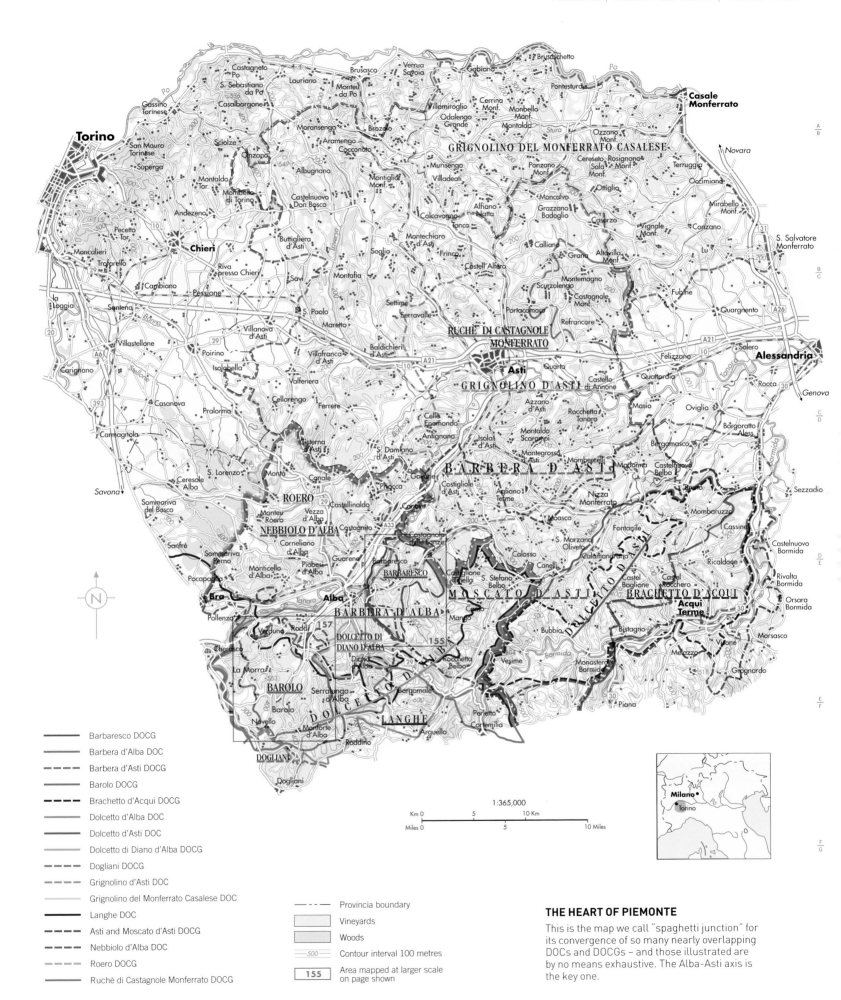

Torino

Casale Monferrato

GRIGNOLINO DEL MONFERRATO CASALESE

Chieri

RUCHÈ DI CASTAGNOLE MONFERRATO

Asti

"GRIGNOLINO D'ASTI"

Alessandria

BARBERA D'ASTI

ROERO

NEBBIOLO D'ALBA

Acqui Terme

BARBERA D'ALBA

MOSCATO D'ASTI

BRACHETTO D'ACQUI

Bra

Alba

DOLCETTO DI DIANO D'ALBA

LANGHE

BAROLO

DOLCETTO D'ALBA

DOGLIANI

Barbaresco DOCG

Barbera d'Alba DOC

Barbera d'Asti DOCG

Barolo DOCG

Brachetto d'Acqui DOCG

Dolcetto d'Alba DOC

Dolcetto d'Asti DOC

Dolcetto di Diano d'Alba DOCG

Dogliani DOCG

Grignolino d'Asti DOC

Grignolino del Monferrato Casalese DOC

Langhe DOC

Asti and Moscato d'Asti DOCG

Nebbiolo d'Alba DOC

Roero DOCG

Ruchè di Castagnole Monferrato DOCG

Provincia boundary

Vineyards

Woods

―500― Contour interval 100 metres

155 Area mapped at larger scale on page shown

1:365,000

Km 0   5   10 Km

Miles 0   5   10 Miles

THE HEART OF PIEMONTE

This is the map we call "spaghetti junction" for its convergence of so many nearly overlapping DOCs and DOCGs – and those illustrated are by no means exhaustive. The Alba-Asti axis is the key one.

Barbaresco

Nebbiolo finds its most dazzling expression in the Langhe hills, on the calcareous clay soils of the right bank of the River Tanaro, to the northeast of Alba in the Barbaresco zone, and to the southwest of the city around the village of Barolo (mapped and discussed overleaf). The Nebbiolo grape is a particularly late ripener so the finest wine tends to come from slopes with a southern tilt that are not too high: between about 490 and 1,150ft (150 and 350m) altitude.

Today, the grower and his or her vineyard (the terms *sorì* and *bricco* recur continually for distinguished sites) hold the key to Barolo and Barbaresco. Tastings reveal consistent differences of quality, of aroma, of potency, and of finesse that in the Côte d'Or would justify the term and yet the emergence of these great wines from the limbo of legend into the critical limelight has been accomplished only since the 1980s.

Late picking, long extraction, and endless ageing in huge old casks was the rule until the 1970s and 1980s. Around this time a newly critical public, putting "fruit" firmly on the agenda, began to turn away from wines that were vastly tannic, and often simply dried out by having waited too long for a maturity that never came.

Modern vinification had no problem finding the "solutions": choosing the right moment to pick (sometimes pushing phenolic ripeness to the limit); fermentation in stainless steel at controlled temperatures; shorter macerations; shorter ageing periods in large old oak or, much more controversially, ageing in small, new or newish French barriques. Two schools and their fans slugged it out for years; now the best producers combine the virtues of both. However it is made, Barbaresco is always a tannic wine that needs to age, one in which the tannin merely frames a stunning array of haunting flavours. Great Barolos and Barbarescos can overlay smoky woodland notes on deep sweetness, the flavour of raspberries on leather and spice, leafy lightness on jam-like concentration. Older wines advance to animal or tarry flavours, sometimes suggesting wax or incense, sometimes mushrooms or truffles and dried cherry. What unites them is the racy cut of their tannins and acidity, freshening rather than overwhelming the palate.

Although there has been considerable new planting, Barbaresco, with 1,680 acres (680ha), has less than half as much vineyard as Barolo. The village of just 600 people lies on a ridge that wobbles west towards Alba, flanked all the way by vineyards of renown. Asili, Martinenga, and Sorì Tildin are bywords for the finest reds. A little lower and to the east lies Neive, in whose castle the French oenologist Louis Oudart, imported by local landowner Count Cavour, experimented with Nebbiolo, and in whose vineyards Barbera, Dolcetto, and, especially, Moscato, are still more important than Nebbiolo. So thrilling were the wines produced from some of Neive's best sites in the 1990s that grower labels from here are increasingly seen. South on higher slopes, some of which are too cool to ripen Nebbiolo and are therefore more suitable for Dolcetto, lies the commune of Treiso, whose Nebbiolo tends to be particularly elegant and perfumed. Pajorè was the most important cru historically. Roncagliette produces wines with the sort of balance so characteristic of those made around the village of Barbaresco to the north. The authorities have divided the entire Barbaresco zone into contiguous subzones, some of very much better quality than others. Only the best Barbaresco vineyards are marked on the map opposite, and named as they are most likely to be found on a label (although spellings vary – especially since Piemonte has its own dialect).

Leading producers

Barbaresco once played understudy to the much more famous Barolo, until Angelo Gaja, in a dazzling Missoni sweater, strode onto the world stage as Italy's wine prophet and unstoppable promoter. Gaja has no inhibitions; his wines, whether classic Nebbiolo, experimental Cabernet, Chardonnay, or Sauvignon Blanc, or Barbera are treated like first-growth claret, state their case, and cost a fortune.

Bruno Giacosa had shown in the 1960s that Barbaresco could have the intensity (if not always the sheer physical weight) of Barolo, but it was Gaja who modernized the message, importing new barriques and new ideas without apparently a second thought in this most traditional of regions. In 2000 Gaja announced that he was renouncing the name he had made so famous and labelling his fabulously expensive single-vineyard bottlings – Sorì San Lorenzo, Sorì Tildin, and Costa Russi, previously sold as Barbaresco – DOC Langhe Nebbiolo, the catch-all appellation for declassified Barolo and Barbaresco and for wines containing up to 15% of "foreign" varieties such as Cabernet, Merlot, and Syrah.

Other outstanding producers in Barbaresco today include not only Giacosa, Marchesi di Gresy, and the excellent Produttori del Barbaresco co-op, but also Ca' du Rabajà, Ceretto for its Bricco Asili, Cigliuti, Moccagatta, Fiorenzo Nada, Rizzi, Albino Rocca, Bruno Rocca, and Sottimano. But historically a much higher proportion of the grapes were sold to the region's large merchant bottlers and co-operatives than in Barolo.

The grape harvest in the commune of Neive. Flat vineyards do not exist in the Langhe hills, but precise position and altitude are key to whether the slope is devoted to Barbera, Dolcetto, or the late-ripening Nebbiolo.

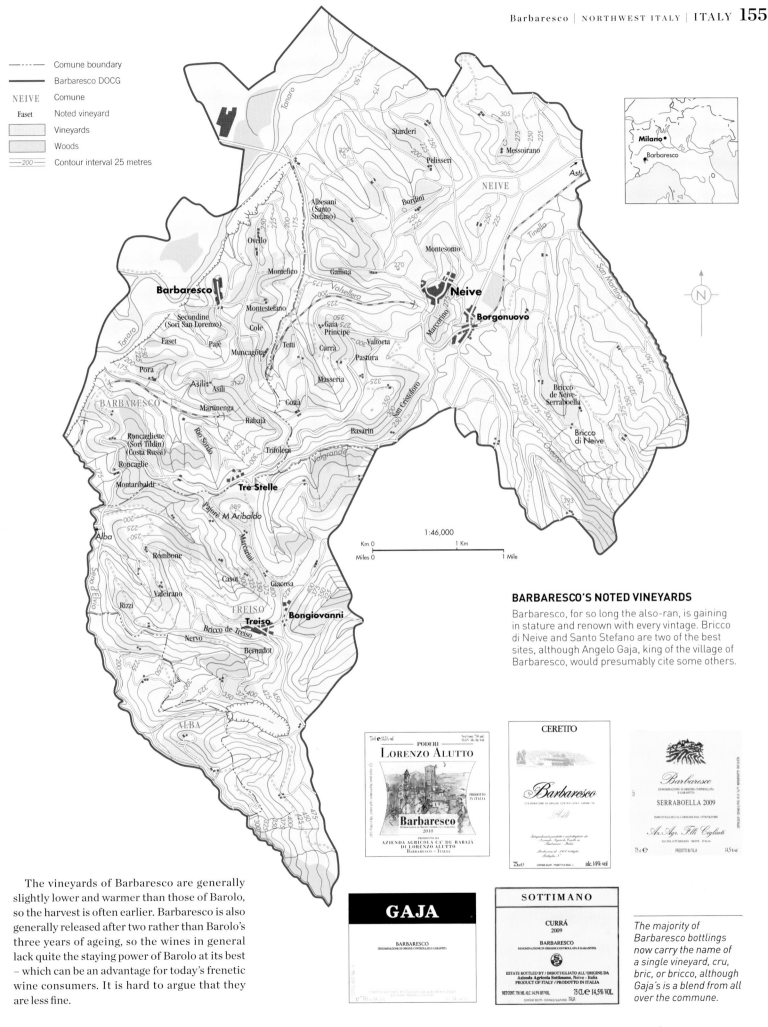

Key

- - - - Comune boundary
───── Barbaresco DOCG
NEIVE Comune
Faset Noted vineyard
Vineyards
Woods
──200── Contour interval 25 metres

Milano
Barbaresco

BARBARESCO'S NOTED VINEYARDS

Barbaresco, for so long the also-ran, is gaining in stature and renown with every vintage. Bricco di Neive and Santo Stefano are two of the best sites, although Angelo Gaja, king of the village of Barbaresco, would presumably cite some others.

The vineyards of Barbaresco are generally slightly lower and warmer than those of Barolo, so the harvest is often earlier. Barbaresco is also generally released after two rather than Barolo's three years of ageing, so the wines in general lack quite the staying power of Barolo at its best – which can be an advantage for today's frenetic wine consumers. It is hard to argue that they are less fine.

PODERI
LORENZO ALUTTO
Barbaresco
2010
PRODOTTO DA
AZIENDA AGRICOLA CA' DU RABAJA
DI LORENZO ALUTTO
BARBARESCO – ITALIA

CERETTO
Barbaresco
Asij
alc. 14% vol.

Barbaresco
DENOMINAZIONE DI ORIGINE CONTROLLATA
E GARANTITA
SERRABOELLA 2009
IMBOTTIGLIATO ALL'ORIGINE DAL VITICOLTORE
Az. Agr. F.lli Cigliuti
DI CIGLIUTI RENATO – NEIVE – ITALIA
75 cl e   14,5 % vol

GAJA
BARBARESCO
DENOMINAZIONE DI ORIGINE CONTROLLATA E GARANTITA

SOTTIMANO
CURRÁ
2009
BARBARESCO
DENOMINAZIONE DI ORIGINE CONTROLLATA E GARANTITA
ESTATE BOTTLED BY / IMBOTTIGLIATO ALL'ORIGINE DA
Azienda Agricola Sottimano, Neive - Italia
PRODUCT OF ITALY / PRODOTTO IN ITALIA
NET CONT. 750 ML ALC. 14.5% BY VOL.   75 cl 14,5% VOL

The majority of Barbaresco bottlings now carry the name of a single vineyard, cru, bric, or bricco, although Gaja's is a blend from all over the commune.

Barolo

Barbaresco is a great example of Nebbiolo, but Barolo is the greatest. The Barolo zone starts just two miles southwest of Barbaresco, with the Dolcetto vineyards of Diano d'Alba lying between, and is subject to many of the same influences and characteristics already described on p.154. Two little tributaries of the Tanaro, the Tallòria dell'Annunziata and Tallòria di Castiglione, split Barolo into the three main though highly convoluted ranges of hills mapped opposite, rising nearly 165ft (50m) higher than the Barbaresco zone.

Thanks to an increase in vineyard area of more than 40% since the late 1990s, there are now 4,460 acres (1,886ha) of Barolo vineyards, although some of the new ones may prove to be too cool to ripen Nebbiolo reliably, despite climate change. All Barolo vineyards are concentrated in this zone, just big enough for 11 communes in the relatively populous Langhe hills. So many different positions, altitudes, and mesoclimates – and two main soil types – have provided endless fodder for the discussion of possible subzones. And the discussion only intensified after some (but by no means all) communes chose dramatically to extend (devalue?) their best crus in the 2011 official listing of them, notably Monforte d'Alba's 8-mile (13km) stretch of Bussia.

The east–west divide
To the west of the Alba road around La Morra, soils are very similar to those in Barbaresco, calcareous marls from the epoch geologists know as Tortonian. These western hills of the zone in the communes of Barolo and La Morra tend to offer slightly less tense, more openly fragrant wines. The great vineyards here include Brunate, Cerequio, Le Rocche, and La Serra in La Morra, and the Barolo commune's most famous site, Cannubi, on slightly lower ground.

To the east, however, in the vineyards of Castiglione Falletto, Serralunga d'Alba, and those to the north of Monforte d'Alba, soils are Helvetian, much less fertile, with more sandstone. They tend to produce even more concentrated wines, Barolo's beefiest, which demand extremely long ageing. Some vineyards in Castiglione Falletto produce wines that are notably softer than those of Serralunga, while the spur of land that divides the valleys of Serralunga and Barolo again produces distinctive wines, combining

Rooftops in the village of Barolo. The landscape is almost Mediterranean, but not full-on olives and pines. There is a distinctly subalpine feel about the whole region – as well there might be in view of its name.

the power of Serralunga and the perfume of the Barolo made in Castiglione Faletto and northern Monforte. Prime examples include Bussia and Ginestra in Monforte and, in Castiglione Falletto, Vietti's Villero, Mascarello's Monprivato and the wine that Scavino calls in Piemontese dialect Bric dël Fiasc (Bricco Fiasco in Italian). The only exception to the sternness of Castiglione Falletto's Barolos might be Bricco Rocche, which, with its relatively sandy soils, can produce particularly perfumed wines.

Serralunga d'Alba is home to the famous Francia cru and to the former royal estate of Fontanafredda, an association that helped develop Barolo's status as "the wine of kings, the king of wines". The commune has some of Barolo's highest vineyards, but enough warmth builds up in the narrow valley that separates Serralunga from Monforte d'Alba to the west to compensate for the altitude, so that Nebbiolo can be ripened on suitable sites most years. It was in Serralunga that Angelo Gaja expanded from Barbaresco into the Barolo zone in the late 1980s, both wines having been awarded DOCG status as early as 1980.

The aristocracy of northwest Italy is represented here – for wine drinkers who can afford to pay and wait. Barolo is quintessentially for the patient, and for those with a keen grasp of local geography.

Map labels

Montvigliero

Verduno

VERDUNO

San Giacomo
Neirane
Olmo
Plaustra

Alba

GRINZANE CAVOUR

Gallo d'Alba

Grinzane Cavour

Talloria

Moltarone

Bricco San Biagio
Perretto
Bricco Manescotto

LA MORRA
Roggeri
Monfalletto
Rocchettevino
Arborina
Gattera
Le Turnote
Bricco Manzoni
Gancha

Talloria dell'Annunziata
La Rosa

Rocchette
Annunziata
Marcenasco
Conca
Bricco Luciani
La Morra
Rocche dell'Annunziata
Giachini
Conca dell'Abbazia

Montanello
CASTIGLIONE FALLETTO
Codana
Bricco Boschis

SERRALUNGA D'ALBA
Cerretta
Baudana
Prapò

Berri

Torriglione
Bricco Fiasco
Monprivato

La Serra
Brunate
Fossati
Cerequio
Bergeisa
Pugnane
Bricco Roche
Colombera
La Delizia
Case Nere
Sarmassa
Castiglione Falletto
Villero
Fontanile
Disa
Gabutti-Parafada
Lazzarito
Brea

Cannubi Boschis
Albarella
Cannubi
Castellero
Bussia Sottana
Perno
Serralunga d'Alba
Cucco

Le Liste
Rue
San Lorenzo
Cannubi Valletta
Margheria
Marenca Rivette

Bricco delle Viole
BAROLO
La Villa
Cannubi Muscatel
Preda
Barolo
Vigna Rionda
Collaretto
Serra

Vergne
Paiagallo
Bussia Soprana
Fossano
Le Coste
Rivassi
Bussia
Santo Stefano
Castelletto Monforte
La Villa
Briccolina
Ornato

Terlo
Ravera
Dardi
Gramolere
Falletto

Pianplume

NOVELLO
Visette
Arnulfo
Pianpolvere
MONFORTE D'ALBA

Gavarini
Francia

Sottocastello di Novello
Ginestra

Novello
Moscoei
Arione

Monforte d'Alba
Manzoni Soprana
Le Coste

Mondovì

BAROLO'S NOTED VINEYARDS

It may seem strange to have quite so many named vineyards in only a few square kilometres, but the contour lines alone help to explain why. And one name can be so much more valuable than another – boundary disputes are common.

Legend

- - - Comune boundary
—— Barolo DOCG
LA MORRA Comune
Briccolina Noted vineyard
Vineyards
Woods
—400— Contour interval 25 metres

1:54,000
Km 0 1 2 Km
Miles 0 1 Mile

Milano
Barolo

Body text

Even before this, however, Barolo could boast dozens of dedicated grower-bottlers ("domaines" seems a better word than "estates" for this most Burgundian of Italy's wine regions). Traditions here are, as in Burgundy, that the same family who tends the vines makes the wine – even if there has been considerable evolution in the way that vivacious, expressive, almost burgundian wine is made over the last two or three decades. Good Barolo is arguably the world's most uncompromising wine,

depending on decades of bottle-age to show its true allure, its ethereal bouquet. A few traditionalists have such a faithful, knowledgeable following that they can afford to continue to make such a wine. Others have adapted Barolo to modern times to a greater or lesser degree by reducing fermentation and barrel-ageing times so that wines can be broached earlier. No one is right, and only those who decided to ignore the unique qualities of this grape and this place would be wrong.

Northeast Italy

The cosmopolitan area mapped opposite is now Italy's most prolific producer of wine – most of it white, much of it Pinot Grigio. In the far west, **Franciacorta** has built itself the reputation of Italy's best *metodo classico* wine. Its sparkling success story began in the 1970s with the Berlucchi family's direct imitation of champagne, subsequently taken up by farm after farm in the region south of Lake Iseo. Chardonnay and Pinot Nero are perfectly suited to a climate without extremes. The finest wines, both sparkling and still, come from the charismatic Maurizio Zanella of Ca' del Bosco, whose Cuvée Annamaria Clementi exhibits a finesse seen only in Champagne's very best wines. But others such as Bellavista, Ferghettina, Gatti, Majolini, Monte Rossa, and Uberti are all pressing hard on Zanella's heels. Their red Bordeaux blends and Burgundian whites are sold as Curtefranca DOC.

The intensive Veneto wine belt is described in detail on pp.162-63. Its western extreme produces an appealing dry white from the south end of Lake Garda based on its own local relative of the Verdicchio grape, known simply as Lugana. Ca' dei Frati and Ca' Lojera have shown that it can even be aged and that this territory has potential for fully ripened reds, as well as the light red **Bardolino** and pink Chiaretto traditional on this resort-lined lake. Both of these, made from the same grapes as Valpolicella, are made to be drunk young, preferably on a vine-shaded terrace, though the **Bardolino Superiore** DOCG is designed for more substantial, even more Bordeaux-like, blends. The **Garda** name has been given to the catch-all DOC that allows blending among the standard-issue Veneto zones of Soave, Valpolicella, and **Bianco di Custoza**. Bianco di Custoza, made to the south, can be a surer bet than basic Soave, while in **Gambellara** to the east Angiolino Maule and Giovanni Menti make some of the purest expressions of Garganega.

Prosecco and Lambrusco

The most popular wine of the far eastern Veneto is the Venetian tourist's lubricant, sparkling **Prosecco**. So great is world demand for this easy-drinking fizz that the production area was expediently enlarged in 2008 to encompass nine entire provinces (see the massive area enclosed by a pink boundary on the map). And to protect their precious Prosecco from imitation, the producers changed the name of the grape responsible to "Glera" and registered its original name "Prosecco" as a geographical name so as to keep it for themselves. Prosecco from the hill of Cartizze in Valdobbiadene was traditionally the most sought-after, but there is increasing interest in bone-dry *col fondo* (or *sur lie*) versions sold "with sediment" still in the bottle. Verduzzo and the grape now known as Friulano in Friuli and Tai Bianco in the Veneto are the white grapes of the Venetian hinterland, while light Cabernet (Franc mainly) and Merlot, supplemented by the uncompromising but improving local Raboso, dominate the plains of Piave and Lison-Pramaggiore.

As can be seen clearly from the map, the valley of the River Po as it descends from the plain south of Milan to the Adriatic is wide and flat – not the most prepossessing wine country. Only one Po Valley wine name is famous for some, infamous: the sparkling red **Lambrusco** from around Modena, above all from Sorbara. There is something decidedly appetizing about this vivid wine bursting with red-berry flavours and its unusual bright-pink foaming head. It cuts the fatty richness of Bolognese food admirably. Producers such as Francesco Bellei are pushing the boundaries of Lambrusco di Sorbara, producing classic wines in various ways, including *frizzante* (lightly sparkling) and the *metodo ancestrale* (bottle-fermented wines sold with sediment) that was traditional until the more industrial, expedient tank method largely took over in the 1970s.

The grapes that used to be known as Prosecco – until the producers realized that the name would be more valuable as a geographical one.

The wine becomes much more varied in the Veneto and eastwards. On green volcanic islands in the plain near Vicenza and Padova are the increasingly successful **Colli Berici** and Euganei, the latter home to the sweet sparkling Moscato Giallo now called **Colli Euganei Fior d'Arancio** DOCG. The red grapes are the Cabernets and Merlot of Bordeaux and Grenache, known locally as Tai Rosso, which is the classic Berici red. White grapes are a mix of international and traditional: Garganega of Soave; Glera; light and sharp Verdiso; and the more solid Friulano, formerly Tocai Friulano, now called Tai Bianco in its own Lison DOCG (see p.164). The interplay of local and Euro-political interests here is enough to make your head spin. The DOCs of the region are a series of defined areas that give their names to whole groups of red and white wines, generally varietally labelled.

Breganze, north of Vicenza, is a case of a DOC brought to prominence (like Franciacorta) by one fanatical winemaker. Fausto Maculan resurrected the old Venetian taste for sweet wines from dried local Vespaiola grapes with his golden Torcolato. For details of wines made east of here in the eastern Veneto, see p.164.

The reputation of Emilia Romagna as a wine producer is steadily growing. The hills around Bologna, the **Colli Bolognesi**, now produce some very respectable Cabernet, Merlot, and Chardonnay, as well as the local white Pignoletto. The country south of Bologna and Ravenna still produces oceans of varietal Romagna wine, with Trebbiano di Romagna the least remarkable. In 1986, **Albana di Romagna** was the first white wine in Italy to be elevated to DOCG status (on what grounds it was hard to see). Like so many Italian whites, it comes in all levels of sweetness. Some of the best, including the dried-grape Scacco Matto *passito* version, are made by Zerbina. This extensive zone's red, **Sangiovese di Romagna**, is even more variable. It can be thin and overcropped, but it can also be gutsy and sophisticated enough to show why some of the Sangiovese clones most popular with discerning Tuscan producers come from Romagna.

In the northeast of Italy, Alto Adige/Südtirol is challenging Friuli's crown as leading white wine producer. Climate change is improving reds, too. For more details see p.161.

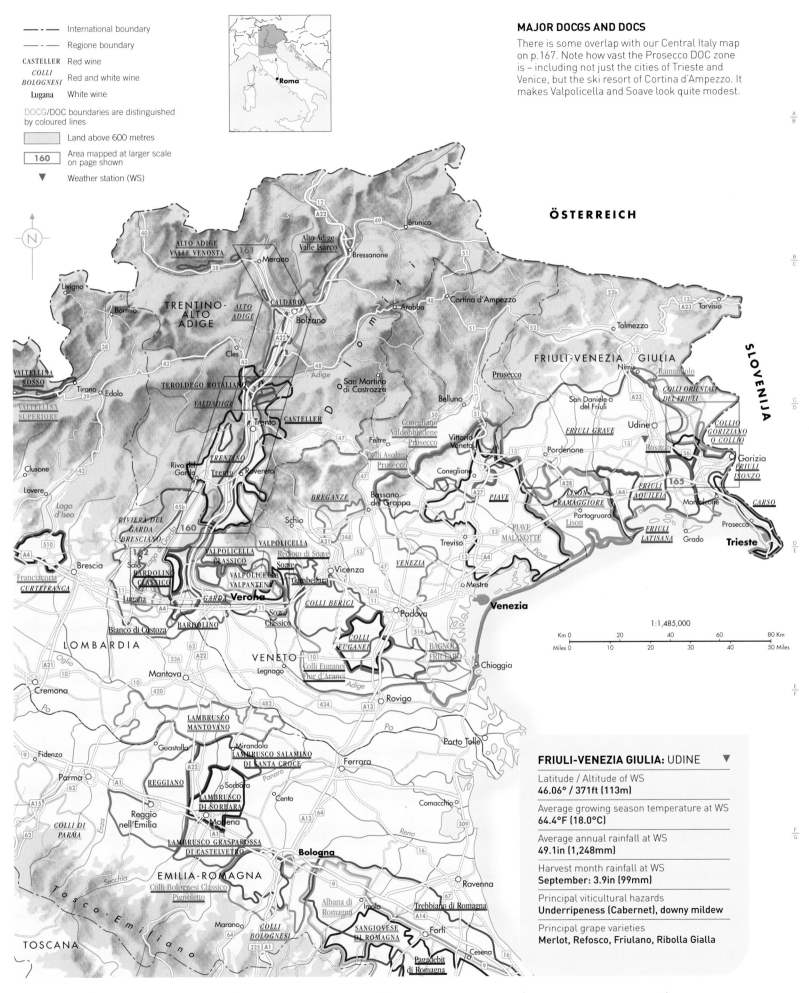

International boundary
Regione boundary
CASTELLER Red wine
COLLI BOLOGNESI Red and white wine
Lugana White wine

DOCG/DOC boundaries are distinguished by coloured lines

Land above 600 metres

160 Area mapped at larger scale on page shown

▼ Weather station (WS)

MAJOR DOCGS AND DOCS

There is some overlap with our Central Italy map on p.167. Note how vast the Prosecco DOC zone is – including not just the cities of Trieste and Venice, but the ski resort of Cortina d'Ampezzo. It makes Valpolicella and Soave look quite modest.

FRIULI-VENEZIA GIULIA: UDINE ▼

Latitude / Altitude of WS
46.06° / 371ft (113m)

Average growing season temperature at WS
64.4°F (18.0°C)

Average annual rainfall at WS
49.1in (1,248mm)

Harvest month rainfall at WS
September: 3.9in (99mm)

Principal viticultural hazards
Underripeness (Cabernet), downy mildew

Principal grape varieties
Merlot, Refosco, Friulano, Ribolla Gialla

Trentino

The Adige Valley forms the dramatic corridor into the Alps that links Italy with Austria over the Brenner Pass. It is a rock-walled trench, widening in places to give views of distant peaks but also, like the Rhône Valley, an inevitably crowded north–south link with all the valley floor excesses of traffic and industry that go with it.

There is a tendency to cling to the valley floor, but its best vineyards form a lovely contrast to the thundering traffic below. They pile up every available slope from river to rock-walls in a pattern of pergolas that look from above like deeply leafy steps.

The catch-all DOC for the whole valley is **Trentino**. But each part of the valley has its own specialities – indeed, its own indigenous grapes. They are inevitably threatened by a flood of Pinot Grigio (by popular demand) and Chardonnay for *metodo classico* fizz (Trento DOC), but are now fighting back and finding new friends. On the way north to Trento, the snaking gorge known as the Vallagarina is home to Marzemino, a perfumed, light-bodied, historic red.

From the northern end of Trentino comes purple Teroldego, grown on the cliff-hemmed, pergola-carpeted, gravelly plain known as the Campo Rotaliano between Mezzolombardo and Mezzocorona. **Teroldego Rotaliano** is one of Italy's great characters, with hallmark bracing acidity and the hint of bitterness that marks it as a native. The queen of fine, fully ripe Teroldego Rotaliano is Elisabetta Foradori. Her improved clones, and experiments with fermenting in amphoras, impress her clients more than they do the authorities, so she sells them as IGT Vigneti delle Dolomiti. Schiava or Vernatsch, from the Tyrol (also known in Germany as Trollinger), was once widely grown, but has fortunately lost ground. Schiava is perhaps best appreciated as a rosato produced in the village of Faedo at the northern end of this map.

The eastern Adige slopes round San Michele are particularly successful for white grapes and, in recent years, for the international red varieties, too. Some of the world's very few interesting Müller-Thurgaus are produced here.

The western arm of the valley near Trento, linking it with three small lakes, grows the same wide range of grapes (all these zones grow good base wine for spumante) but specializes in sweet Vino Santo of high quality from yet another revived indigenous variety, Nosiola. Its best wines come from the villages of Pressano and Lavis in the Valle dei Laghi.

Co-ops necessarily predominate in such parcellated terrain, but Trentino's current voyage of rediscovery is being undertaken by some of the region's most energetic small producers.

EITHER SIDE OF THE AUTOSTRADA

With Franciacorta to the southwest, Trentino has long been Italy's focus for dry sparkling wine production, and for still wines made on a commercial scale, but wines of real interest are also made here, such as the exceptional San Leonard claret in the far south, and Foradori's Teroldego in the north.

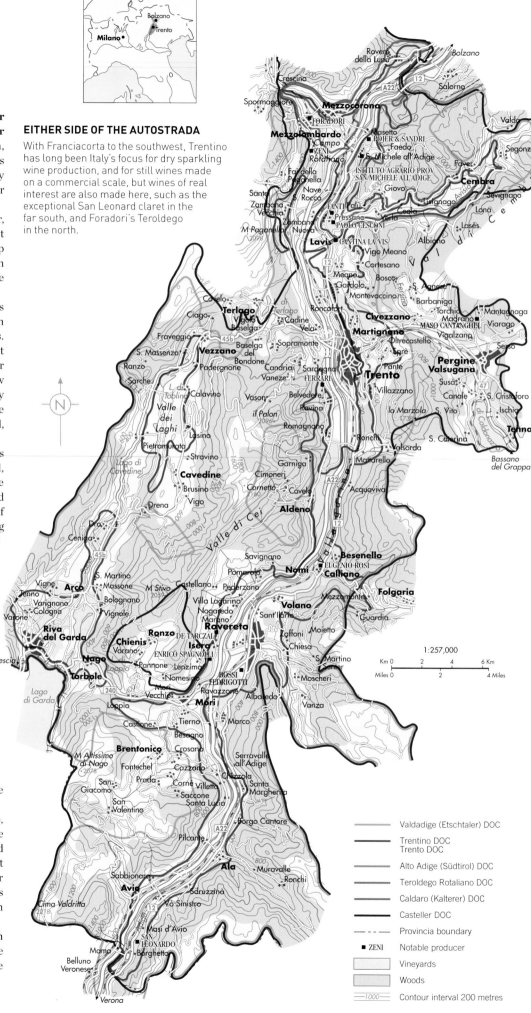

1:257,000

Km 0   2   4   6 Km
Miles 0   2   4 Miles

———	Valdadige (Etschtaler) DOC
▬▬▬	Trentino DOC / Trento DOC
———	Alto Adige (Südtirol) DOC
———	Teroldego Rotaliano DOC
———	Caldaro (Kalterer) DOC
▬▬▬	Casteller DOC
– – –	Provincia boundary
■ ZENI	Notable producer
▢	Vineyards
▨	Woods
=1000=	Contour interval 200 metres

Alto Adige

The Alto Adige, the southern tip of Austria's Tyrol, is Italy's most northerly wine region and one of its most vigorous, its serious aspirations to quality increasingly fulfilled. Its Alpine peaks proclaim both a cultural and a viticultural melting pot. German is a more common language than Italian, yet French grape varieties have been more widespread than Teutonic ones (even if the latter are catching up). Its vineyards produce both the racy, fruity, varietal whites on which its modern reputation is based and varieties that will produce serious red wines in warmer areas. Most wines are sold under the blanket DOC **Alto Adige** (Südtirol) plus the name of the grape.

Production is centred on the benchland and lower slopes of the Adige Valley. Vineyard altitudes vary from 650 to almost 3,300ft (200–1,000m) but 1,148–1,804ft (350–550m) is best for avoiding frost and optimizing ripeness.

Higher vineyards, often steep and terraced as in the **Valle Venosta** (Vinschgau) to the northwest and **Valle Isarco** (Eisacktal), which stretches for 15 or 20 miles (24 or 32km) northeast of Bolzano (see p.159 for both), are especially good for Riesling, Sylvaner, Kerner, and various Veltliners.

On slightly lower slopes Chardonnay, Pinot Bianco, and Pinot Grigio are fruity and lively, while the village of Terlano, on the way north to Merano, is highly rated for Sauvignon Blanc. Here, instead of the usual white outcrops of calcareous soils moved by ancient glaciers, is hard granitic porphyry, specifically trumpeted on labels such as that shown on p.158. For obvious reasons, the Traminer grape is associated with the village of Tramin (Termeno in Italian) south of Bolzano. Hofstätter's is particularly notable.

The workhorse red grape is the Schiava (alias Vernatsch), whose wines are pale, soft, and simple. The local Lagrein, originally grown around Bolzano, produces much more serious stuff, including the deeply fruity rosé Lagrein-Kretzer and darker Lagrein-Dunkel, both of which have ageing potential and a growing number of followers around the world. An intricate system of locally valued crus hover on steep slopes over Bolzano.

Red varieties imported in the 19th century – Pinot Noir, Merlot, and Cabernet – can also be very good. Indeed, Alois Lageder at Magrè makes a Pinot Noir that is among Italy's most subtle and stylish. All of these, together with Lagrein, are replacing Schiava in the region's warmest sites east of Lake Caldaro and on the slopes above Bolzano, benefiting from afternoon breezes off Lake Garda and the cool nights. Irrigation is generally essential.

Local co-ops, or cantine, are a valuable and important force in Alto Adige and the best can compete with some of the better-known independent producers indicated on this map.

VINEYARDS OF THE DOLOMITES

This is the historical heartland of this bilingual wine region, with Trentino part of the vast area that can give its IGT wines the romantic name Vigneti delle Dolomiti ("Vineyards of the Dolomites"), although permitted crop levels are decidedly unromantic.

Alto Adige DOC subzones:

- Meranese (Meraner)
- Santa Maddalena (Sankt Magdalener)
- Caldaro (Kalterer)
- Terlano (Terlaner)
- Colli di Bolzano (Bozner Leiten)

- Teroldego Rotaliano DOC
- Trentino DOC
- Provincia boundary
- ▪ FRANZ HAAS — Notable producer
- Vineyards
- Woods
- ─1000─ Contour interval 200 metres
- ▼ Weather station (WS)

ALTO ADIGE: BOLZANO ▼

Latitude / Altitude of WS
46.46° / 790ft (241m)

Average growing season temperature at WS
64.1°F (17.8°C)

Average annual rainfall at WS
23.5in (596mm)

Harvest month rainfall at WS
October: 2.1in (54mm)

Principal viticultural hazards
Spring frosts

Principal grape varieties
Schiava, Pinot Grigio, Pinot Bianco, Chardonnay, Lagrein, Gewürztraminer, Pinot Noir

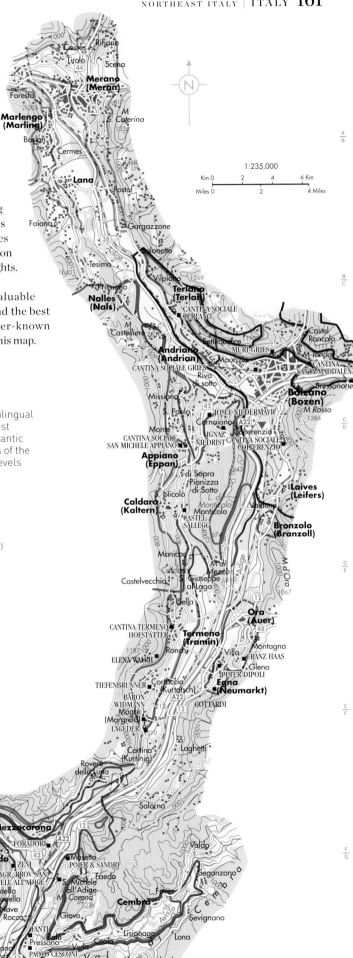

Verona

The hills of Verona, stretching from Soave westwards to Lake Garda, have such fertile volcanic soil that vegetation grows uncontrollably; the vine runs riot on every terrace and pergola, among villas and cypresses that are the image of Italian grace – not always, sadly, reflected in the wine they produce. For the Veneto has become Italy's most productive wine region. High yields, with an official limit of 105hl/ha, are the bane of quality, especially in **Soave** DOC, the Veneto's most important wine zone. Almost 80% of the vineyards are cultivated by growers who deliver their grapes straight to the local co-op with no personal reputation for quality to uphold.

Real Soave is incomparable, with its insistent combination of almonds and lemons. A bottle from Pieropan or Anselmi will leave you in no doubt. In an effort to distinguish the authentic from the mass of wine that usurps its name the authorities have devised two superior denominations. **Soave Classico** DOC, from the original historic production zone, and **Soave Superiore** DOCG, grown on the less fertile hillsides, have maximum yields of 98hl/ha and 70hl/ha, respectively – which is at least a start.

Such generous yields are far higher than those actually practised by the top producers. Pieropan and Anselmi have been joined by such conscientious companies as Cantina di Castello, La Cappuccina, Coffele, Filippi, Gini, Inama, Prà, modernist Suavia, and Tamellini. With the exception of Filippi in Soave Colli Scaligeri, the highest part of the DOC, they all operate in the original area of Soave Classico, centred on the eastern end of the Lessini Hills northeast of the village of Soave.

The important grapes are Garganega and Verdicchio (called Trebbiano di Soave), which make wines of an intensity and mouth-filling texture that bring the meaning of Soave (suave) into focus. Pinot Blanc and Chardonnay are also allowed, so long as Garganega makes up at least 70% of the wine.

The best producers typically make a range of single-vineyard or cru bottlings, expressing such characterful local sites as Vigneto La Rocca and Capitel Foscarino, and some, such as Prà, make fine Soave in oak. **Recioto di Soave** is a wonderfully lively, and historic, sweet DOCG version made from dried grapes.

Soave cohabits with **Valpolicella**, whose DOC zone has been extended far beyond the original Classico zone until it reaches the boundaries of Soave. The improving Valpantena is a permitted subzone, dominated so far by Bertani and the local co-op. Plain Valpolicella should have a lovely cherry colour and flavour, lively acidity, a gentle sweet smell, and just a trace of almond bitterness. The mass-produced article rarely does, but there are now as many producers here as in Soave who recognize the need to make truly distinctive as opposed to commercially viable wine – and the last decade of the 20th century saw a return to some of the more difficult-to-work but higher-quality hillside sites. Most superior Valpolicella is grown in the Classico zone on four fingers of higher-altitude vineyard sheltering Fumane, San Ambrogio, and Negrar, but there are exceptional operators such as Dal Forno and Trabucchi elsewhere.

Vines are being planted on white-pebbled terraces at much higher densities and vertically trained to extract more flavour from every grape, above all late-ripening Corvina, the best of the region. Neutral Rondinella and the relatively tart (and optional) Molinara can also play a part. There is also experimentation with rarer indigenous grapes such as Oseleta and Corvinone.

Recioto and Amarone

The most potent form of Valpolicella is a Recioto or Amarone, respectively the sweet (occasionally fizzy) and dry (also bitter) results of drying selected, healthy grapes off the vine to make more concentrated and potent wines. Such heady productions (they have been losing weight of late) are the direct descendants of the Greek wines shipped by the Venetians in the Middle Ages. The old practice of *ripasso* strengthens Valpolicella by refermenting it on the pressed grape skins, preferably of Corvina, after an Amarone has finished fermentation, in which case it may qualify as Valpolicella Superiore or Ripasso, constituting a sort of "Amarone Lite". Amarone is often the climax of a Veronese feast.

THE VERONA HILLS

The area mapped extends to the western shore of Lake Garda and Bardolino, as well as the complexities of the many subzones of the now-exciting Valpolicella and Soave zones. Garda is the catch-all DOC.

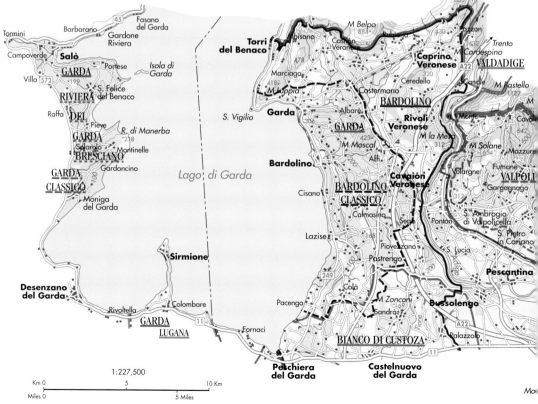

VERONA: VERONA ▼
Latitude / Altitude of WS
45.38° / 239ft (73m)
Average growing season temperature at WS
66.4°F (19.1°C)
Average annual rainfall at WS
30.8in (783mm)
Harvest month rainfall at WS
September: 3.2in (81mm)
Principal viticultural hazards
Hail, fungal diseases
Principal grape varieties
Garganega, Corvina, Pinot Grigio, Merlot

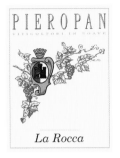

All of these wines prove that Verona is a fine-wine region as well as satisfying the demands of the mass market. The three white wines at the top are serious wines by any measure, and by no means overpriced compared with their peers in Burgundy.

Even in co-ops such as this one in Negrar, Corvina grapes are painstakingly hung out to dry to concentrate sugars, as part of making the Amarone that is so popular today.

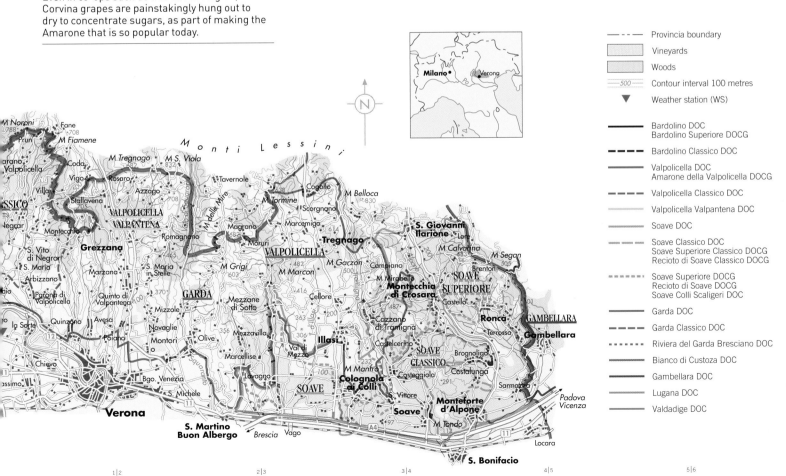

– – – –	Provincia boundary
	Vineyards
	Woods
—500—	Contour interval 100 metres
▼	Weather station (WS)
■■■	Bardolino DOC Bardolino Superiore DOCG
– – –	Bardolino Classico DOC
■■■	Valpolicella DOC Amarone della Valpolicella DOCG
– – –	Valpolicella Classico DOC
	Valpolicella Valpantena DOC
	Soave DOC
– – –	Soave Classico DOC Soave Superiore Classico DOCG Recioto di Soave Classico DOCG
·······	Soave Superiore DOCG Recioto di Soave DOCG Soave Colli Scaligeri DOC
	Garda DOC
– – –	Garda Classico DOC
·······	Riviera del Garda Bresciano DOC
	Bianco di Custoza DOC
	Gambellara DOC
	Lugana DOC
	Valdadige DOC

Friuli-Venezia Giulia

Italy's northeastern corner has long been her powerhouse of fine white wine production. White winemaking may have progressed enormously all over the country in the last decade or two, but Friuli, or to give the region its full name, Friuli-Venezia Giulia, has been famous for fresh, modern whites since the early 1970s. Now its best are some of the world's finest whites, typically varietal, perfumed, sharply etched, clean as a whistle, and these days very rarely overoaked.

The country's most revered DOCs for white wines are **Friuli Colli Orientali**, in the northern half of the map opposite, and **Collio Goriziano**, named after the province of Gorizia but more often than not called simply "Collio", in the southern half of the map. The vineyards of western Primorska have also been included because although they are politically part of Slovenia (and are therefore described in detail on p.265) they belong geographically to Friuli. Some producers even have vineyards on both sides of the border. As elsewhere in Italy, there are wine co-operatives in Friuli but, unlike Italy's other notable source of refreshing dry whites, Trentino-Alto Adige, Friuli is essentially dominated by family-owned wine producers.

The vineyards of Colli Orientali, although protected from harsh north winds by the Julian Alps in Slovenia to the northeast, are marginally cooler and certainly more continental than those of Collio, closer to the tempering influence of the Adriatic. These "eastern hills", or Colli Orientali, reaching altitudes of between 330 and 1,150ft (100–350m) above sea level, were once below it and the soils still bear the traces of marl and sandstone deposits, often layered in the characteristic soil type known as "flysch of Cormons", named after the town in the centre of the map.

Increasingly accomplished reds

The principal grape, known here as Friulano and in the Veneto as Tai Bianco, is identical to Sauvignonasse, or Sauvignon Vert. It can be rather crude elsewhere, but it seems to thrive in this corner of Italy. The ubiquitous Pinot Grigio, Pinot Bianco, Sauvignon Blanc, and the local speciality Verduzzo are also grown, but a good third of the vineyards of Colli Orientali are devoted to the production of increasingly accomplished red wine. "Cabernet" and, particularly, Merlot dominate, but the local Refosco, Schioppettino, and Pignolo can all be found in refreshing, clear-cut varietals and an increasing array of generally oaked blends.

Most of the Cabernet planted in Friuli was long thought to be Cabernet Franc (sometimes spelt Frank), but some is the old Bordeaux variety Carmenère (formerly misidentified in Chile as Merlot). Parts of the Colli Orientali feel more alpine than maritime, but the southwestern end between Búttrio and Manzano is warm enough to ripen even Cabernet Sauvignon. Global warming and better winemaking both contribute to the continuing upgrade in general wine quality here, although some of the less glorious producers grow a wider range of vines than suits their terrain, and at too high a yield.

In the far north of the Colli Orientali, around Nimis to the northwest of the area mapped here (see p.159), the slopes of the **Ramandolo** DOCG are particularly steep and cool, and can be damp. Sweet amber Verduzzo is the speciality here. A great deal of local pride is also invested in **Picolit**, a strong white varietal dessert wine which could be described as the Italian Jurançon: a wine more hay-like and flowery, while less pungently honeyed, than Sauternes.

The smaller **Collio** DOC to the south of Colli Orientali makes very similar wines, including the lion's share of Friuli's finest whites, but far fewer reds, and such reds as there are often taste

Vines follow the contour lines in Collio, but with enough space for machines between each pair of rows. This is border country, even if the Italy–Slovenia border is not one of the most actively policed.

light and underripe – particularly if autumn rains arrive too early to achieve full ripeness. Such is worldwide demand for Pinot Grigio that this variety long ago overtook Friulano and Sauvignon Blanc. Historic Ribolla Gialla, often fermented on the skins (Gravner was the pioneer) to produce deep-yellow wine, is Collio's increasingly fashionable and respected signature white, known as Rebula over the border in Slovenia. As in Colli Orientali, Chardonnay and Pinot Bianco are more likely to be lightly oaked than the other white wine varietals. Other local light-skinned grape specialities include Traminer Aromatico, Malvasia Istriana, and Riesling Italico (Welschriesling), all found in Slovenia, too.

Where red wine works

On the whole the "Cabernet" of Friuli-Venezia Giulia is heartiest to the west of this region, especially in **Lison-Pramaggiore** (see p.159). Going east, early-ripening Merlot seems better suited to the large crops and coolish climate of this part of Italy and dominates the **Grave** and **Isonzo** DOCs. The coastal areas with their flat vineyards make less concentrated wines from these grapes than those from hillside plantations in the Colli Orientali, although Isonzo, with better-drained vineyards north of the Isonzo river, has good concentrated examples, too. Indeed, for many years some producers in the Colli Orientali quietly sourced their red wines from better Isonzo growers. The wines made on the lower, flatter, more fertile land between the river and the sea more closely resemble those of the productive Grave del Friuli plain to the west. Competent white wines, notably Friulano and Pinot Grigio, are also made in Isonzo, with Vie di Romans the outstanding producer.

The speciality of **Carso**, along the coast around Trieste, is red Refosco, known here as Terrano, and widely grown by producers just over the border in Slovenia, too.

FRIULI AND WESTERN SLOVENIA

Brda, the most northwestern wine region in Slovenia, is included here because it is geographically virtually indistinguishable from Collio. Small hills and steep slopes shape the vineyards, sometimes the same vineyard, on each side of the border. See p.264 for how this fits into the greater Slovenian picture.

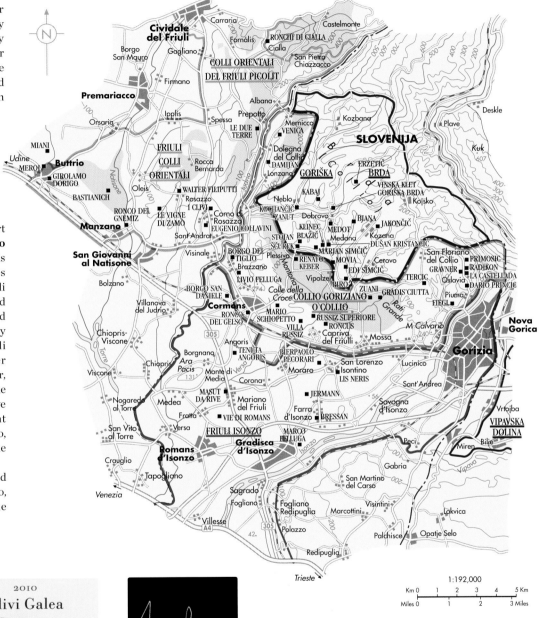

1:192,000

International boundary

Provincia boundary

Friuli Colli Orientali DOC
Colli Orientali del Friuli Picolit DOCG

Collio Goriziano o Collio DOC

Friuli Isonzo DOC

Primorska wine region, subregion named

RONCUS Notable producer

Woods

Contour interval 100 metres

PINOT GRIGIO

Slovenian influence is clear on the Pinot Grigio label above. And Gravner's influence can be seen, and tasted, throughout Friuli and Brda. Skin contact is in; amphorae abound; cloudiness is no sin – presumably a reaction to the squeaky-clean whites that once characterized this part of the world.

2010
clivi Galea

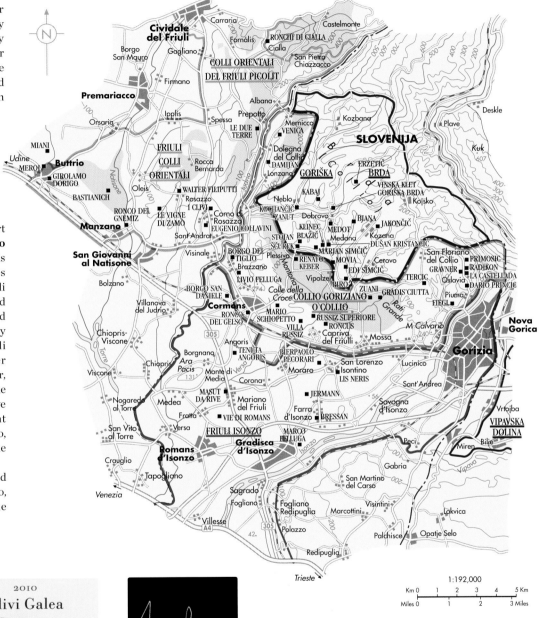

Livio Felluga

Sossò

2008
Flors di Uis

VIE DI ROMANS

Central Italy

The heart and perhaps the soul of Italy lie in this central, slightly skewed slice of the peninsula: the cities best-known to foreigners, Florence and Rome, the iconic countryside of Chianti, the tombs of the Etruscans... Does it sound predictable? It is anything but. Altitude, terrain, and above all ideas vary enormously. The seas on either side wash maritime wine regions of wildly differing characters. Ancient identities are thickly overlaid with creativity and, nowadays, underwritten by considerable inward investment. Nothing can be taken for granted. In this era of global warming, even the late-ripening Sangiovese can succeed on Italy's Apennine spine at altitudes as high as 1,970ft (600m). Lamole is an example.

Sangiovese country

With the exception of its coastal regions this is Sangiovese country, Italy's most planted vine, whose wines can vary from pale, thin, tart mouthwash to the most sumptuous expressions of Italian gastronomic brio in a glass. At higher altitudes on this map it needs a warm growing season to ripen fully, and the results are generally much more delicate than lower-altitude Sangioveses. This was particularly true of the clones selected in the 1970s for their huge yields, regardless of quality. The process of replacing them with better clones has revolutionized our expectations of (especially) Tuscan wine. Central Italian Sangiovese is now likely to be much deeper in both colour and flavour, but retaining the structural zest that makes such wines sit so definitively on the dinner table. Light-skinned grapes tend to be planted on higher or less-protected land, and much of the dominant

Trebbiano Toscano, the workhorse white grape that has been grown in Sangiovese country for more than a century, generally produces pretty dull wine, though blending with Malvasia Bianca can add interest to Tuscan dry whites.

Soils on these foothills of the Apennines vary, but the two most characteristic types are galestro, a local, particularly crumbly variant on clay-limestone, and the more solid, heavier albarese. Local lakes and rivers are welcome warming influences, as are, of course, the two seas.

East coast zones

In the Marche the **Verdicchio dei Castelli di Jesi** zone is vast, and the so-called Classico heart constitutes as much as 90% of the area, which seems like a fudge, but producers such as Colonnara and Umani Ronchi pull out all the stops for their top bottlings, which combine refreshment with substance. The smaller **Verdicchio di Matelica** zone tends to produce more characterful wine on its rather higher, hillier terrain. To the immediate south distinctive dry whites made by smaller producers from Passerina and/or Pecorino grapes in the Falerio DOC and Offida DOCG zones have been attracting attention.

The reds of the Marche have been slower to carve out their identity, but **Rosso Conero** DOC, based on juicy Montepulciano grapes, shows some character. **Rosso Piceno**, made from Sangiovese with Montepulciano, generally with lower yields and judicious oaking, can be good value.

Montepulciano is the red grape of this part of the Adriatic coast and **Montepulciano d'Abruzzo** is rarely overpriced, even if it is highly variable (Cerasuolo d'Abruzzo is the satisfyingly full-blooded, dry, pink version). The finest zone for Montepulciano, in the wild Abruzzi hills around the town of Teramo, has DOCG status for its **Montepulciano d'Abruzzo Colline Teramane**. Superior producers include Illuminati and Villa Medoro. Trebbiano d'Abruzzo (not the same as

Sangiovese is by far the most planted red wine grape in Central Italy, and indeed the most planted variety in all of Italy. But there is enormous variation among clones of this ancient variety and the quality of the wine they produce.

Trebbiano Toscano) is also extremely variable but it can hit great heights, not least because of some confusion as to exactly which grape variety is involved. The quixotic late Eduardo Valentini of Loreto Aprutino created an international reputation for his fastidiously selected, magnificently age-worthy, full-bodied version.

West coast zones

On the west coast, the Roman region Lazio is oddly inert in terms of wine. A handful of producers are trying hard with both imported international varieties and such local specialities as the light red Cesanese, but Rome is essentially a white wine city. **Marino** and **Frascati**, from the increasingly built up Castelli Romani, are downed in vast quantities but rarely with much attention.

Moving north, Cerveteri looks much more important on the map than it is on the ground. It is north of here on, and in the hinterland of, the Tuscan coast that there has been the most dramatic change to the winescape in recent years. For more details see overleaf.

Most significant wine zones on this map have been mentioned above, or in the case of Emilia-Romagna's wines on p.151, or are described on the pages that follow, but an increasingly important exception is the thoroughly modern **Cortona** DOC zone to the immediate east of Montepulciano. A host of international grape varieties are permitted but Syrah seems the most promising and complex, with those of Tenimenti Luigi d'Alessandro and Stefano Amerighi the most impressive producers.

Some of the finest Central Italian wines made, on both coasts, outside the regions mapped in detail on the pages that follow. Verdicchio in particular has been undergoing a dramatic upgrade, not least via the identification of superior terroirs. Geography is always the answer.

Genova

COLLINE LUCCHESI

Lucca
Pisa

MONTECARLO

Pistoia

CHIANTI
MONTALBANO

Prato

CARMIGNANO

Borgo San
Lorenzo

COLLI
BOLOGNESI

Bologna

EMILIA-ROMAGNA

Imola

Faenza

Lugo

Reno

Ravenna

Cervia

Firenze

CHIANTI COLLI
FIORENTINI

Albana
di Romagna

Forlì

SANGIOVESE DI
ROMAGNA

Trebbiano di
Romagna

Cesena

Cesenatico

Livorno

CHIANTI
COLLINE PISANE

Pontedera

CHIANTI
MONTESPERTOLI

Poggibonsi

G. Figline
Valdarno

POMINO

Pagadebit
di Romagna

Cesena

TERRATICO DI BIBBONA

Cecina

MONTESCUDAIO

Volterra

Vernaccia
di San
Gimignano

CHIANTI
CLASSICO

CHIANTI
COLLI ARETINI

Rimini

SAN MARINO

Cattolica

BOLGHERI

San
Gimignano

CHIANTI
COLLI SENESI

CHIANTI

Siena

Arezzo

Sansepolcro

Pesaro

COLLI PESARESI

Fano

VAL DI CORNIA

Piombino

Massa
Marittima

Val d'Arbia

CHIANTI
COLLI
SENESI

VALDICHIANA

Città di
Castello

Urbino

Bianchello
del Metauro

Isola
d'Elba

Portoferraio

MONTEREGIO DI
MASSA MARITTIMA

BRUNELLO DI
MONTALCINO

Montalcino

CORTONA

Cortona

Umbertide

Metauro

LACRIMA DI
MORRO D'ALBA

Senigallia

ELBA

ELBA ALEATICO
PASSITO

MONTECUCCO
SANGIOVESE

MONTECUCCO

Moscadello di
Montalcino

SANT'ANTIMO

Montepulciano

Lago
Trasimeno

Gubbio

Verdicchio dei
Castelli di Jesi

Jesi

Esino

Ancona

Grosseto

Scansano

VINO NOBILE
DI MONTEPULCIANO

VIN SANTO DI
MONTEPULCIANO

Perugia

TORGIANO ROSSO
RISERVA

Fabriano

ROSSO
CONERO

MORELLINO
DI SCANSANO

COLLI DEL
TRASIMENO

COLLI
PERUGINI

Assisi

TORGIANO

Verdicchio
di Matelica

ROSSO
CONERO

MAREMMA TOSCANA

Bianco di
Pitigliano

PARRINA

ORVIETO

ASSISI

Foligno

ROSSO PICENO

Isola del
Giglio

SOVANA

Orvieto
Classico

UMBRIA

Macerata

VERNACCIA DI
SERRAPETRONA

MARCHE

Argentario
Ansonica Costa
dell'Argentario

Porto
Ercole

Orbetello

Fiora

Orvieto

MONTEFALCO
SAGRANTINO

COLLI
MARTANI

COLLI MACERATESI

Falerio

Fermo

Est! Est!! Est!!!
di Montefiascone

Lago di
Bolsena

LAGO DI
CORBARA

Orvieto

Spoleto

Norcia

OFFIDA

Montefiascone

COLLI
AMERINI

Narni

Terni

Nera

**Ascoli
Piceno**

ROSSO PICENO
SUPERIORE

Tuscania

Viterbo

Rieti

MONTEPULCIANO
D'ABRUZZO COLLINE
TERAMANE

Civitavecchia

CERVETERI

Civita
Castellana

Teramo

CASTELLI
ROMANI

Bracciano

Lago di
Bracciano

LAZIO

MONTEPULCIANO
D'ABRUZZO

L'Aquila

Loreto
Aprutino

Roma

Cannellino
di Frascati

Tivoli

Trebbiano
d'Abruzzo

Pescara

Marino
Colli Albani

Frascati

Subiaco

Celano

Chieti

Colli Lanuvini

CESANESE
DI AFFILE

Avezzano

CERASUOLO
D'ABRUZZO

ABRUZZO

Lanciano

VELLETRI

CORI

Fiuggi

CESANESE
DEL PIGLIO

MONTEPULCIANO
D'ABRUZZO

Sulmona

Aprilia

Anzio

Latina

CESANESE DI
OLEVANO ROMANO

Frosinone

Trebbiano
d'Abruzzo

CERASUOLO
D'ABRUZZO

Sora

Vasto

Priverno

Trebbiano
d'Abruzzo

Sangro

Sisto

Terracina

Pontecorvo

Cassino

Isernia

BIFERNO

MOLISE

PENTRO DI ISERNIA

Gaeta

Formia

Napoli

Biferno

International boundary

Regione boundary

BIFERNO Red wine

TORGIANO Red and white wine

Zagarolo White wine

DOCG/DOC boundaries are distinguished
by coloured lines

Land above 600 metres

169 Area mapped at larger scale
on page shown

1:1,500,000

Km 0   20   40 Km
Miles 0   10   20   30 Miles

Roma

MAJOR DOCGS AND DOCS

Exceptionally, this map has been rotated so that
it does not point due north. The Apennines are
too high for viticulture, and divide those regions
influenced by the Mediterranean and Adriatic. The
greatest concentration of fine wine is in the west,
but the east coast is slowly catching up.

Maremma

The map opposite shows only the original, northernmost quarter of what might be called Tuscany's Gold Coast, the Maremma Toscana, a stretch of land from Bibbona as far south as the Argentario Peninsula that has attracted a fever of interest and outside investment.

This once-malarial coast has no long wine tradition; the flame was lit in the 1940s when the Marchese Incisa della Rocchetta chose a stony hectare of his wife's extensive San Guido estate in Bolgheri to plant Cabernet. He hankered after the Médoc. The nearest vineyards were miles away. His young vines were surrounded by neglected peach orchards and abandoned strawberry fields, but he was pleased enough with his house wine to plant more, under the guidance of his oenologist, Giacomo Tachis. When the Marchese's early wines eventually lost their tannin they revealed flavours not seen in Italy before.

His nephews, Piero and Lodovico Antinori, tasted the wines. Piero talked to Professor Peynaud in Bordeaux. Antinori started to bottle and market Sassicaia with the 1968 vintage. By the mid-1970s it was world-famous. Then, in the 1980s, Lodovico Antinori began planting the neighbouring property he then owned, Ornellaia, with Cabernet Sauvignon, Merlot, and, less successfully, Sauvignon Blanc.

In 1990 his brother Piero produced a Cabernet/Merlot blend called Guado al Tasso from his Belvedere estate on higher ground to the southwest. The soil turns sandier here; the wine lighter. This may well be the westernmost site for great reds, but the last two decades have seen a land-grab throughout the Maremma. Investment has poured in, not just from such substantial Florentines as Antinori, Frescobaldi, and Ruffino but a host of smaller producers in the Chianti hills inland seeking extra ripeness in the 15% of coastal grapes they are allowed to add to their inland produce. Soon the grape-rush brought northern Italian producers such as Bolla, Gaja, Loacker, and Zonin. Even some from California.

The **Bolgheri** DOC evolved, with pioneer Sassicaia having its own DOC within it – and a new winery almost on the Roman coast road, the Via Aurelia. Cabernet and Merlot have been the grapes of choice for most newcomers, even if some of the land grabbed, extensively in some cases, has proved too flat and fertile to produce wines of special quality. With much of the best vineyard land in Bolgheri accounted for, the focus has continued to shift south. Now the two **Val di Cornia** zones and Suvereto, on higher ground up in the hills, have attracted considerable numbers of hopeful investors.

The **Maremma Toscana** DOC was created to encompass all DOCs and DOCGs on this map as well as all those shown on the map on p.167 north of the Lazio border and west of Montalcino.

Within this labyrinth of DOCs and DOCGs, most of them very new, there are signs of life for Tuscany's signature grape, indeed the central and southern Maremma seem generally better suited to Sangiovese than to Bordeaux grapes, with the finest examples coming from higher, less fertile sites. **Montecucco Sangiovese** DOCG with at least 90% Sangiovese (as opposed to the Montecucco DOC with its minimum 70%) seems particularly promising, and its soft, rolling hills are much easier to plant than the higher, wilder reaches of **Monteregio di Massa Marittima**, which stretches out over the Colli Metallifere, the mineral-rich coastal ridge. Potential vineyard sites may need extensive restructuring, but on soils not unlike those of Montalcino at altitudes up to 1,970ft (600m) there can be some very elegant Sangiovese.

Just south of Grosseto is the **Morellino di Scansano** DOC, which was created as long ago as 1978; Morellino is the local name for Sangiovese and Scansano its hilltop capital. This is the Maremma's classic Sangiovese zone, even if arguably the most famous wine grown here is a Bordeaux blend with a little Alicante. It is made

---

The wine library at Ornellaia could easily be in California. Indeed, this particular winery was at one stage part-owned by Robert Mondavi of the Napa Valley. The wine country around Bolgheri has attracted more than its fair share of foreign investment.

Black seems to be in fashion with designers of Maremma labels. Owners of these include Angelo Gaja of Barbaresco, the Antinoris and Frescobaldis of Florence, and the noble family who started it all with Sassicaia, the Incisa della Rochettas.

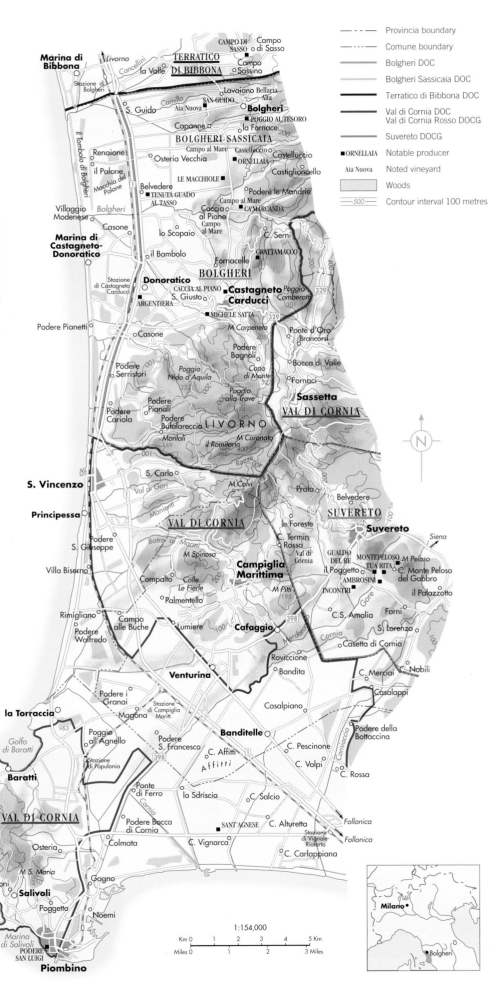

by the pioneering Le Pupille estate, Saffredi, and was originally produced with the help of Giacomo Tachis. Ripeness is not a problem in balmy conditions nearer sea level. As at the single-estate seaside DOC **Parrina**, the wines are much fleshier, more supple, and arguably more "international", than anything made in the hills of Chianti Classico inland.

But recent expansion has been to the north as well as south of the map on this page. Both Antinori brothers with their Biserno estate, and now Gaja with a few hectares of red and white wine vines, have also invested in higher, windier, warmer Terratico di Bibbona, which tends to produce more robust wines than Bolgheri. The whole Maremma region has been transformed from marshland to Italy's Napa Valley in a remarkably short time.

NORTH TUSCAN COAST

Seriously interesting wines are also made well to the south of the area mapped, such as in Morellino di Scansano, and in Parrina and Montecucco further inland. See map on p.167.

1:154,000

Km 0 1 2 3 4 5 Km
Miles 0 1 2 3 Miles

Legend:
- Provincia boundary
- Comune boundary
- Bolgheri DOC
- Bolgheri Sassicaia DOC
- Terratico di Bibbona DOC
- Val di Cornia DOC / Val di Cornia Rosso DOCG
- Suvereto DOCG
- ■ ORNELLAIA Notable producer
- Aia Nuova Noted vineyard
- Woods
- —500— Contour interval 100 metres

Chianti

The hills between Florence and Siena can come as near to the Roman poet's idea of gentlemanly country life as anywhere on earth. The blending of landscape, architecture, and agriculture is ancient and profound. The villas, cypresses, olives, vines, rocks, and woods compose pictures that could be Roman, Renaissance, Risorgimento – there is no way of telling (provided all the tourists park their cars discreetly).

In this timeless scene, once a promiscuous tangle of the crops deemed necessary to Tuscan peasant life, vineyards now march uphill and down dale, many of them owned and regimented by well-heeled outsiders.

The original Chianti zone, the first anywhere in the world to be delimited, in 1716, was limited to the land around the villages of Radda, Gaiole, and Castellina, with Greve added later. The red line on the map opposite shows the extended historic zone which today produces what is one of Italy's finest wines, **Chianti Classico**.

Of the six other Chianti subzones, **Chianti Rufina**, east of Florence and partly mapped here, is the most distinctive, making elegant wines that can age remarkably. (A pass through the Apennines north of here, which allows maritime breezes to cool the vineyards, is largely responsible for the finesse of Chianti Rufina, and for the fact that it can need time to show its

best. Some estate cellars have fine bottles 50 or 60 years old.) Some of the most distinguished estates are found around San Gimignano in the subzone of **Chianti Colli Senesi**, the hills above Siena. Chianti made in the hills above Florence, Pisa, and Arezzo (respectively the **Chianti Colli Fiorentini**, **Colline Pisane**, and **Colli Aretini** subzones) tends to be less fine, as are the wines of the **Chianti Montalbano** subzone northwest of Florence.

The map on p.167 shows just how large an area – almost 100 miles (160km) from north to south, more extensive than the Bordeaux wine region – is allowed to produce wine labelled simply "Chianti", at best a tangy, ultra-digestible mouthful of fruit ready for drinking in a year or two, but a very much less ambitious drink than Chianti Classico, which is made according to much stricter conditions.

As long ago as 1872 Barone Ricasoli (sometime Prime Minister of Italy) at his castle of Brolio distinguished between these two forms of Chianti: a simple one for drinking young and a more ambitious version aimed at the cellar. For the early-drinking Chianti he allowed some of the then prevalent white grape Malvasia into the blend with the red grapes then grown, Sangiovese and Canaiolo. Unfortunately the proportion of prolific white wine vines grew and the dreary Trebbiano Toscano crept in.

When the DOC laws defined Chianti in 1963 they insisted on 10% and allowed up to 30% – far too much – of white grapes into Chianti of any style. Pallid Chianti (too often beefed up with

red imported from the south of Italy) became the rule, and it became clear that either the rules must change, or the zone's producers must make their best wine in their own way and give the wine a new name.

The rise and fall of the Super Tuscan

In 1975, the ancient Antinori family launched their rebel flag Tignanello, made, like Carmignano to the west of Florence, from Sangiovese with a small proportion of Cabernet. To underline the point they rapidly added Solaia, with the proportions of Cabernet and Sangiovese reversed. Within a few years there seemed scarcely a *castello* or villa in Chianti that had not followed them with a "Super Tuscan" (sold initially as a defiant Vino da Tavola, but nowadays coralled into the IGT category) of their own construction, many of them excellent and some original.

But as the character of many of these rebel wines became increasingly distant from anything obviously Tuscan, and as new, much higher-quality clones of Sangiovese were identified, as well as the best sites and better ways of growing them, the concept of Chianti Classico – and its Riserva version – as a truly fine wine emerged. Today, Riserva represents about 20% of the total production of the region.

Chianti Classico is now an extremely serious wine made substantially (80–100% of the blend) from low-cropped, top-quality Sangiovese vines, aged in wood – large and/or small oak – with a life expectancy of 10 years or even more. The other varieties now allowed in Chianti Classico up to a total of 20% are the traditional Canaiolo, the deeply coloured Colorino, and "international varieties", notably Cabernet and Merlot. From 2006 onwards, white grapes were completely banned from Chianti Classico (though they are allowed in straight Chianti).

The vineyards of Chianti Classico are at fairly high altitudes of 820–1,640ft (250–500m), or higher, but the producers marked on our map, which shows the chaotic hilliness of the Chianti countryside and the scattering of vines (and olives) among the woods, manage to transform the light-coloured, high-acid Sangiovese into

As in Piemonte, single vineyards are increasingly finding their way on to wine labels in Chianti. Most of the labels illustrated are from Chianti Classico, the heartland of the Chianti zone. Selvapiana in Chianti Rufina is a noble exception.

TUSCANY: FIRENZE ▼

Latitude / Altitude of WS
43.80° / 144ft (44m)

Average growing season temperature at WS
68.3°F (20.1°C)

Average annual rainfall at WS
30.2in (767mm)

Harvest month rainfall at WS
October: 3.4in (85mm)

Principal viticultural hazards
Underripeness, downy mildew, esca

Principal grape varieties
Sangiovese, Trebbiano, Canaiolo Nero

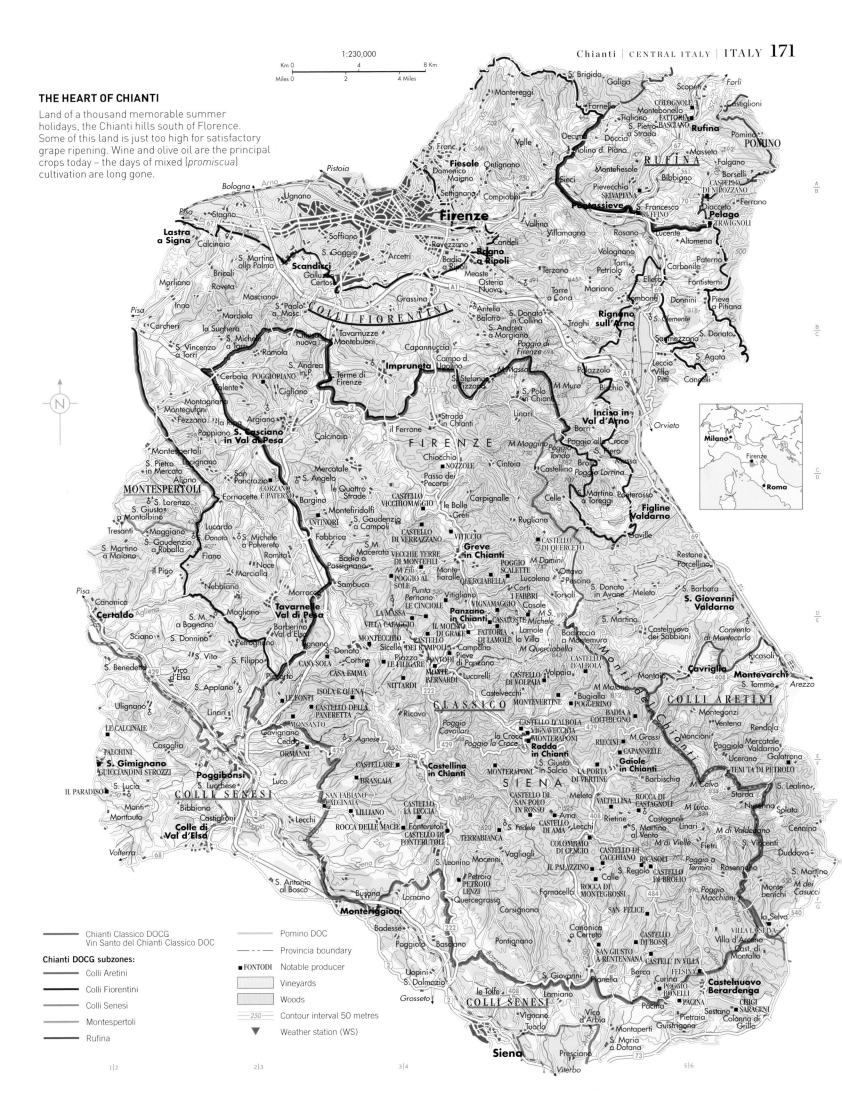

THE HEART OF CHIANTI

Land of a thousand memorable summer holidays, the Chianti hills south of Florence. Some of this land is just too high for satisfactory grape ripening. Wine and olive oil are the principal crops today – the days of mixed (*promiscua*) cultivation are long gone.

Chianti Classico DOCG
Vin Santo del Chianti Classico DOC

Chianti DOCG subzones:
Colli Aretini
Colli Fiorentini
Colli Senesi
Montespertoli
Rufina

Pomino DOC
Provincia boundary
FONTODI Notable producer
Vineyards
Woods
250 Contour interval 50 metres
Weather station (WS)

wines that are complex, satisfyingly tannic, and savoury rather than voluptuous.

The rest of their output often includes olive oil, a Riserva Chianti Classico to drink after extended bottle-ageing, sometimes a fairly inconsequential local dry white and increasingly a *rosato*, perhaps a Vin Santo (Central Italy's famous dried-grape, long-aged, sweet white, or rather tawny; see p.174), and perhaps a Super Tuscan IGT or two – though these seem to be on the wane as Chianti Classico waxes. It may now even be made from nothing but Sangiovese, the most Tuscan grape of all. These wines are typically fastidiously made, and there has been a return to the traditional large

oak vats known as *botte* after a dalliance with the French barriques, the fashion of the 1980s.

The best way for the highly individual wines of Chianti Classico to distinguish themselves from mere Chianti would probably be to develop an identity for the individual communes, rather as has been done in France's Côtes du Rhône. The wines of Gaiole, for example, are generally higher in acidity because of the Gaiole vineyards' altitude, while the wines from lower-lying Castellina in Chianti are generally fuller and a little richer. The wines from Castelnuovo Berardenga in the very south of the Chianti Classico zone are often characterized in youth

No one ever accused the Chianti hills of lacking drama. This decidedly apocalyptic scene is of dawn over the vineyards of Badia a Passignano in the west of the Chianti Classico zone.

by their compact, grainy tannins. And although Panzano is actually administratively part of the much more varied commune of Greve, the wines grown on its amphitheatre of vineyards are quite distinct. Bathed in the sun all day long, they tend to be fruit-driven wines with particularly fine tannins. To an outsider, making these geographical distinctions clear on the label seems to make perfect sense.

Montalcino

In the 1970s, Montalcino was the poorest hilltop town in southern Tuscany. Little was heard of this part of Italy. It was purely local knowledge that the climate here was more equable than farther north or south. Monte Amiata, rising to 5,600ft (1,700m) just to the south, collects the summer storms that come from that direction. Montalcino has the warm, dry climate of the Tuscan coast (see p.168) with, in the best vineyards, the rockier, less fertile soils of the cooler Chianti Classico zone.

At the same time as Ricasoli was devising an ideal formula for Chianti, Clemente Santi and his kin (now called Biondi-Santi) were establishing a model for what they labelled **Brunello** (a local selection of Sangiovese clones) **di Montalcino**. Odd bottles of such ancient vintages of this wine as were made were not just revered rarities, but also impressively muscular and worthy of emulation. Many did. In the 1970s, the mammoth US Banfi corporation, flushed with success with its Lambrusco in the USA, tried to repeat the trick with a sweetish white Moscadello di Montalcino, planting hundreds of Montalcino acres. It was a flop. The company rapidly converted the vineyards to Brunello and thus, from the 1980s, thanks to Banfi's clout and distribution network, Montalcino has been engulfed in American, then international, interest. It became Tuscany's answer to Barolo.

The old Brunello di Montalcino, wine for heroes, aged almost to destruction, has adapted considerably to modern tastes. The mandatory minimum of four years in oak was reduced to two and some producers started to deepen the Sangiovese, legally 100% of Brunello di Montalcino, with illegal "international" grape varieties. This came to a head in a flurry of accusations in 2008. Producers eventually voted not to allow foreign grapes into the blending vat; recent vintages have been more recognizably Tuscan, and the Sant'Antimo DOC – same boundaries as Brunello, different name – is designed for grapes other than Sangiovese. Montalcino was the first DOCG to be graced with a "junior DOC", **Rosso di Montalcino**, a (relatively) lighter Sangiovese that can be released at only one rather than four years old.

Encouraged by Brunello's high prices, the zone has been expanded enormously, from just over 150 acres (60ha) in 1960 to more than 5,000 acres (2,000ha) today. Altitudes vary from 490ft (150m) above sea level in the Val d'Orcia in the south, where the most potent wines tend to be made on heavy clay soils, to 1,640ft (500m) just south of Montalcino itself, where wines grown on galestro marls are more elegant, aromatic, and, to some tastes, "true". Some areas are definitely better than most, but individual site classification has so far been regarded as too politically sensitive.

---- ---- ----	Provincia boundary
	Chianti Colli Senesi DOCG
	Brunello di Montalcino DOCG Rosso di Montalcino DOC Moscadello di Montalcino DOC Sant'Antimo DOC
■ LISINI	Notable producer
	Vineyards
	Woods
—500—	Contour interval 100 metres

1:135,000

Black is back – though, alas, it will be some time before Gianfranco Soldera applies any labels to his irreproachable Case Basse Brunello. An intruder broke into his cellar late in 2012 and opened the taps on all six of his most recent vintages.

Montepulciano

Montalcino's neighbours to the east, across an intervening enclave of "mere" Chianti, have ancient pretensions of their own embodied in their aristocratic DOCG, Vino Nobile di Montepulciano. Montepulciano is a hill town of great charm surrounded by vineyards planted with a mixture of Sangiovese, called here Prugnolo Gentile, and some local and Bordeaux varieties. Vino Nobile must contain a minimum of 70% Sangiovese – some producers prefer 100%, others a blend – so its varietal make-up is more like Chianti Classico than Brunello di Montalcino.

As in Montalcino, minimum oak-ageing periods have been reduced (to just one year in wood for both normal and Riserva versions), though Vino Nobile di Montepulciano cannot be released until it is two years old, a Riserva three. But while a young Vino Nobile may taste not very different from a Chianti Classico or Brunello di Montalcino of the same age, the best repay five, even 10 years cellaring. If young Vino Nobile is often pretty chewy, the earlier-maturing junior version, **Rosso di Montepulciano**, can be almost surprisingly soft.

Vineyards are in two separate zones separated by the Val di Chiana plain and must be at altitudes of 820–1,970ft (250–600m). The average annual rainfall, around 29in (740mm), is slightly higher than in Montalcino, which, with soils rich in clay with some limestone, tends to make the wines more accessible, although the pervading warmth of south Tuscany leaves no shortage of ripeness.

Led by the house of Avignonesi, now in Belgian hands, a swelling band of accomplished wine producers here has dallied with various Super Tuscan formulae, and several of them have branched out to the immediate northeast into the Cortona DOC zone (see p.167).

Vin Santo, the forgotten luxury

Another of Montepulciano's triumphs is its Vin Santo, the forgotten luxury of many parts of Italy, Tuscany above all. It is orange-coloured, smoky scented, extraordinarily sweet, intense, and persistent, made typically from Malvasia Bianca, Grechetto Bianco, and Trebbiano Toscano – grapes that are carefully dried in well-ventilated premises at least until December before being fermented and aged for three years (sometimes under roof tiles) in tiny flattened barrels called *caratelli*. Grapes for **Vin Santo di Montepulciano** Riserva are dried and the wine aged even longer, while Avignonesi's sumptuous speciality, Vin Santo di Montepulciano Occio de Pernice "eye of the partridge", made of Prugnolo Gentile, is often aged in cask for eight years before bottling.

1:138,460

| | Km 0 | 1 | 2 | 3 | 4 | 5 Km |
| Miles 0 | | 1 | | 2 | | 3 Miles |

– ⋅ – ⋅ –	Regione boundary
– – – –	Provincia boundary
▬▬▬	Chianti Colli Senesi DOCG
▬▬▬	Vino Nobile di Montepulciano DOCG Rosso di Montepulciano DOC Vin Santo di Montepulciano DOC
▬▬▬	Valdichiana DOC
▪ FASSATI	Notable producer
▢	Vineyards
▢	Woods
═500═	Contour interval 100 metres

There is a certain sameness to these labels of Vino Nobile di Montepulciano, made from at least 70% of the local clone of Sangiovese, known here as Prugnolo Gentile. Avignonesi, the zone's most famous estate, is being steadily enlarged.

Umbria

Land-locked Umbria's climate varies enormously, from cooler-than-Chianti highlands in the north around Lake Trasimeno, to a Mediterranean climate at Montefalco, and Terni in the south. Its great gifts to the world of wine are its Grechetto grape, for full-bodied white wines capable of nutty intensity, and Sagrantino for reds. Sagrantino is thick-skinned, packed with flavour and potential longevity. It was long a local secret around the town of Montefalco, where it made sweet red passito. But, in the early 1990s, Marco Caprai brought it to international attention by creating dramatic dry wines of extraordinary fruit and vivid tannins. Today, **Montefalco Sagrantino** is a DOCG of more than 1,235 acres (500ha) already producing wine on well over 40 estates, with a further 740 acres (300ha) coming on stream.

Umbria has wine traditions as ancient as any. Orvieto was an important Etruscan city. The magnificent cellars cut in the volcanic rock of its dramatic hilltop 3,000 years ago are unique examples of prehistoric technology, specifically designed for long, cool fermentation, the object being sweet, amabile, white wine. Alas for **Orvieto**: the 1960s and 1970s fashion for dry white wines turned it into yet another Central Italian blend based on Trebbiano Toscano (called Procanico here). The Grechetto that gave it character fell out of use, and the fortunes of this supposed leader of Umbrian wine foundered.

Enter Dr Giorgio Lungarotti, who, on his estate at Torgiano near Perugia, was the first in modern times to prove, in the late 1970s, that Umbria could make Sangiovese-based reds as good as Tuscany's, and even to explore what might be called Super Umbrians. His daughters, Teresa and Chiara, continue to keep **Torgiano**, whose Riserva is now DOCG, on the map.

It was in the southwest, at Antinori's Castello della Sala estate, that Umbrian wine history moved on again via a revolutionary range of non-traditional whites. A barrel-fermented Chardonnay was perhaps only to be expected, but Cervaro della Sala had almost from the start a purity and singularity to establish it as one of Italy's greatest white wines. The botrytised Muffato, made from a range of international grapes plus Grechetto, showed other possibilities. Today, Umbria makes a truly Italian farrago of reds and whites, including some Orvieto of real interest.

UMBRIA AND NORTHERN LAZIO

Lazio is not one of Italy's most dynamic regions for wine production, but the northeast corner may be regarded as an honorary extension of the region that gives us, most notably, the wines of Orvieto and Montefalco.

— - —	Regione boundary
— - —	Provincia boundary
MONTEFALCO SAGRANTINO	DOCG
ORVIETO	DOC
■ LA FIORITA	Notable producer

DOCG/DOC boundaries are distinguished by coloured lines

▼   Weather station (WS)

1:695,000

Km 0   5   10   15   20   25 Km
Miles 0   5   10   15 Miles

UMBRIA: PERUGIA ▼

Latitude / Altitude of WS
43.10° / 682ft (208m)

Average growing season temperature at WS
64.6°F (18.1°C)

Average annual rainfall at WS
30.6in (778mm)

Harvest month rainfall at WS
September: 3.5in (89mm)

Principal viticultural hazards
Some esca in older vineyards

Principal grape varieties
Sangiovese, Ciliegiolo, Sagrantino, Trebbiano, Grechetto

Montiano, a particularly luscious Merlot, is the most celebrated wine from the Falesco winery in northeast Lazio. It was established by the Cotarello brothers, who made their names working for, inter alia, the Antinoris in Tuscany.

Southern Italy

In Roman times, it was the inland parts of Campania, particularly the province of Avellino east of Naples, which set the pace for the whole of Italy with the empire's most famous wines. Aglianico is one of Italy's greatest dark-skinned grapes, making wines with a powerful, obviously noble, brooding character. In the volcanic hills of the **Taurasi** DOCG zone, where it finds its finest expression, it can ripen as late as November and is naturally so high in acidity that the malolactic fermentation is no routine achievement.

The name of **Greco di Tufo**, a substantial white from inland Campania of remarkably original flavour, apple-peel fragrance, and mineral depths, shares the credit between its long-assumed Greek origins and the tuff rock on which it grows. In the same hilly province, Avellino, the classical Fiano grape makes a more delicate, subtle white, a wine that combines emphasis with firmness and a hauntingly floral scent. With age, it reveals powerful, smoky, stony notes. Both Greco di Tufo and **Fiano di Avellino** are now DOCG.

These are the established names of modern Campanian wine, but some encouragingly good wines are emerging from less expected areas. Naples' own DOC, **Campi Flegrei**, produces fine Falanghina, which is also the dominant grape in the white wines of **Capri** and the **Costa d'Amalfi** (both DOCs). In the Furore subzone of Amalfi, Marisa Cuomo makes some of Italy's most celebrated whites.

Centenarian vines of ancient varieties are common on this dramatic stretch of coast and its hinterland, the Tramonti Valley. **Lacryma Christi** whites and reds grown on the slopes of Mount Vesuvius are finally earning a reputation for more than just their name.

Notable producers around Taurasi

1 TERREDORA DI PAOLA
2 I FEUDI DI SAN GREGORIO
3 MOLETTIERI
4 BENITO FERRARA
5 PIETRACUPA
6 CAGGIANO
7 LUIGI TECCE
8 COLLI DI LAPIO
9 MASTROBERADINO

MAJOR DOCGS AND DOCS

How strange the contrast between the almost frenetic wine activity in Campania, Molise, and Puglia, and the isolation of the pockets of celebrated wines and vines in Basilicata and Calabria.

What is is about black? The first two labels are especially fine Taurasis based on Aglianico, while Fatalone's is one of Puglia's most consistently complex Primitivos, and Graticciaia is made of sun-dried Negroamaro grapes.

Map legend:

— · —	Regione boundary
BIFERNO	Red wine
SOLOPACA	Red and white wine
Greco di Tufo	White wine
■ MAFFINI	Notable producer

DOCG/DOC boundaries are distinguished by coloured lines

IGT Salento	
Land above 600 metres	
177	Area mapped at larger scale

1:2,348,000

Basilicata, the region to the south, has only one significant DOC: **Aglianico del Vulture**, grown (with unusual skill for this part of the world) on the relatively cool slopes of an extinct volcano up to 2,500ft (760m), using its own distinct Aglianico. Less famous than Taurasi, it can often offer better value, although winemaking standards vary wildly. In 2010, the Superiore version of the wine was promoted to DOCG status. Aglianico is also grown on the Adriatic coast in the little-known region of **Molise**, where Di Majo Norante does an outstanding job – as this organic producer continues to do with his Montepulciano and Falanghina grapes.

On the east coast, in the wilds of Calabria, there is just one strong red of reputation, Cirò, made from the delicate, hauntingly perfumed Gaglioppo grape. The best-known producer is the family-owned firm of Librandi, which has been working hard to rescue such other local grapes as the Magliocco Canino, from which it makes the velvety Magno Megonio. Calabria's most original wine, however, may be the strong, tangy, and sweetly perfumed **Greco di Bianco** made around a village itself called Bianco, near the very tip of the Italian "toe".

Puglia's transformation

The wines of Calabria and Basilicata may be works in progress, but Puglia's wine scene has been radically transformed. Generous EU grants for pulling up vines have had mixed results, too, often at the expense of the low bush-vines yielding concentrated, interesting wine. Puglia is much the flattest southern Italian wine region, which makes it easy to work compared with its neighbours, but provides little in the way of altitude to afford relief from the unremitting summer heat.

Three-quarters of the region's output is still blending wine for the north (including France) or fodder for the producers of grape concentrate, vermouth, or the stills that dispose of Europe's embarrassing wine surplus. However, the proportion of Puglian wine made expressly for discerning drinkers has certainly been increasing. The flatland around Foggia in the north churns out undistinguished Trebbiano, Montelpulciano, and Sangiovese, but some more ambitious bottlings have been emerging from producers based in **San Severo**.

Castel del Monte DOC, in the north of the "heel" of Italy mapped in detail above, boasts some modest hills and produces some notable dark reds based on its late-ripening Nero di Troia, especially Torrevento's age-worthy single-vineyard Vigna Pedale and Rivera's Cappellaccio. But most of Puglia's more interesting wines are made on the flat Salento Peninsula, where there may be no great variation in exposition and mesoclimate, but the vines benefit from the cooling winds that blow off both the Adriatic and Ionian seas. Today, thanks to much-improved

viticulture, the better grapes are rarely picked before the end of September.

At the turn of the century, it was the peninsula's ability to provide such anodyne shelf-fillers as IGT Chardonnay del Salento that drew international attention, but there has been a perceptible increase in interest in Salento's local grapes. Negroamaro, "black-bitter", is the cautionary name of the principal red grape of eastern Salento, yet it can make attractive rosé and fruity reds for early drinking if it is not macerated for long or left too long in bottle. Its darker face is almost port-like, roasted reds in such DOCs as **Squinzano** and **Copertino**. Malvasia Nera, with different strains identified respectively with Lecce and Brindisi, is Negroamaro's usual blending partner and can add a certain velvet to the texture.

But the most famous Puglian variety is Primitivo – identical to California's Zinfandel and with its roots now established as Croatian – traditionally a speciality of western Salento, particularly on the red soils over limestone of Manduria and also in higher Gioia del Colle. Fiendish alcohol levels are the risk here. It takes the right hands to strike the voluptuous note. Fiano, Greco, and the perfumed Minutolo are being planted for white wines.

Pergolas such as these in Campania, being associated with overcropping, have been viewed with suspicion. But as temperatures rise, their use as grape sunscreens is starting to be acknowledged.

PUGLIA

On Italy's "heel", the hills that characterize the rest of the country suddenly disappear, with Gioia del Colle being one of the few wine zones with any elevation. Usefully cooling winds off both coasts are generally uninterrupted.

1:1,575,000

Km 0   20   40   60 Km
Miles 0   20   40 Miles

— ∙ — ∙ —   Regione boundary

— ∙ ∙ — ∙ ∙ —   Provincia boundary

CASTEL DEL MONTE
NERO DI TROIA RISERVA   DOCG

SQUINZANO   DOC

■ FELLINE   Notable producer

DOCG/DOC boundaries are distinguished by coloured lines

▼   Weather station (WS)

Key to producers
1 TORMARESCA (ANTINORI)
2 DUE PALME
3 MASSERIA LI VELI
4 CANDIDO
5 CANTINA SAN DONACI
6 TAURINO
7 CASTELLO MONACI
8 AMATIVO
9 LEONE DE CASTRIS
10 CUPERTINUM
11 MONACI

SOUTHERN ITALY: BRINDISI ▼

Latitude / Altitude of WS
40.65° / 33ft (10m)

Average growing season temperature at WS
69.9°F (21.0°C)

Average annual rainfall at WS
22.5in (572mm)

Harvest month rainfall at WS
August: 0.8in (19mm)

Principal viticultural hazards
Rapid ripening, water stress, sunburn

Principal grape varieties
Negroamaro, Primitivo, Malvasia Nera, Nero di Troia

Sicily

After centuries of stagnation, the Mediterranean's biggest and most historically fascinating island is now Italy's most vital and improved wine region. Sicily retains the visible remnants of more civilizations more obviously than anywhere else in the world of wine – from the near-intact Greek temple of Agrigento to the Roman mosaics of Piazza Amerina, the Crusader castles and Moorish churches of Palermo to the Baroque splendour of Noto and Ragusa, and, most recently, the giant EU wine factories that appeared in the late 1980s and early 1990s. This is Sicily, as rich and varied culturally as it is viticulturally – with so many different terroirs and terrains that one might even suggest it should be regarded as a continent rather than a mere island.

The southeastern tip is further south than Tunis. Sicily can be very hot, its grapes, especially in the interior, regularly warmed to boiling point by winds from Africa. Irrigation is a necessity for

a good half of Sicilian vineyards, especially for the sea of trellised vines around Alcamo. Indeed, so dry is the climate that the vines need little spraying, making these areas close to ideal for organic viticulture. But the landscape can be greener inland, and the mountains in the northeast are usually snow-capped for several winter months (Etna retains its cap for much of the year).

Geography is a constant but the political complexion of the island's wine industry has recently been anything but. In the mid-1990s Sicily competed only with Puglia for the title of Italy's most productive wine region, but now even the Veneto churns out much more, and the island has definitively, and sensibly in view of 21st-century economics, opted for quality over quantity and focused on its own vine heritage rather than more anodyne imports.

The indigenous grape that made Sicily's vinous reputation abroad is Nero d'Avola (Avola is in the extreme southeast with its own cru and DOC **Eloro**), making rich, brightly fruited reds, notably around Agrigento near the south-central coast, and in the far west, too. This popular grape

has now been planted all over the island. Another native grape, Frappato, enlivens Nero d'Avola in the blend for **Cerasuolo di Vittoria**, the island's only DOCG, and is itself increasingly appreciated for its freshness, vigour, and delicately fruity appeal for early drinking.

Of potentially even more interest, however, is Nerello Mascalese, traditionally grown up to 3,300ft (1,000m) on the slopes of Mount Etna, where more and more ambitious vine-growers are braving the volcano's portentous rumblings and very real eruptions. Etna, with its rich mix of different altitudes and exposures and densely planted centenarian vines sprouting from soils that include congealed magma, has become a magnet for terroir-conscious wine producers in much the same way that Burgundy is. Vine holdings are similarly parcellated. Some see it as a new Côte d'Or. The local guru, Salvo Foti, who gained credit for re-igniting Etna's wine reputation while working with the long-established Benanti family, bottles (for I Vigneri) several separate wines from ancient vines on the eastern slopes of Etna. Committed new investors

MAJOR DOCGS AND DOCS

The oft-conquered island of Sicily is well used to conflict. Today, in the field of wine, the battle is between west and east: Nero d'Avola versus Cerasuolo and Nerello Mascalese. Recently, the east seems to have been winning, but we all dream of a revival of Marsala's fortunes.

Provincia boundary

ELORO   Red wine

ETNA   Red and white wine

Moscato di Pantelleria   White wine

■PLANETA   Notable producer

DOCG/DOC boundaries are distinguished by coloured lines

Land above 500 metres

179   Area mapped at larger scale on page shown

1:1,786,000

in Etna include Firriato and Tasca d'Almerita, whose Rosso del Conte was the first serious Sicilian red of the modern era, and US wine importer Marc De Grazia. Andrea Franchetti has come from Trinoro in southern Tuscany, and the ultra-naturalist (he uses no sulphur) winemaker Frank Cornelissen from Belgium.

A vine with rather softer results, Nerello Cappuccio, is also grown on Etna and blended with Nerello Mascalese. Yet another Sicilian red grape, Nocera, is blended with both in the ancient **Faro** DOC on the far northeastern tip of the island. Faro (meaning "lighthouse") was revived by an architect, Salvatore Geraci, on steep terraces at Palari, overlooking the Strait of Messina. Like the wines of Etna, the best Faro wines show precision and a level of acidity surprising so far south.

Sicily's white and fortified wines

If there is a white equivalent it is found in wines made of the crisp Carricante grape on Etna. The Benanti family showed (in their Pietramarina) that Carricante can mature impressively for up to 10 years. Catarratto is very different: the workhorse white grape of the west. The 1990s influx of flying winemakers occasionally managed to fashion interesting wines from it, but more often from its partner Inzolia (the Ansonica of Tuscany) or Grillo, a vital ingredient in **Marsala**, Sicily's classic fortified wine, grown in the far west of the island, around Trapani, in vineyards cooled by sea breezes and the influence of Mount Erice. Marsala is a very distant cousin of cream sherry, invented by British settlers to fortify Nelson's navy, which was based in Naples. In much of the late 20th century Marsala seemed to be in the deepest of doldrums, found only in the kitchen. The flame is still alive, though, in the delicate, largely Grillo, wines of De Bartoli and the Gruali of Rallo, which are unfortified and therefore non-DOC.

Sicily's celebrated Moscato is usually strong and sweet. The Planeta family that put Sicily on the map with its early, skilfully made, international varietals rescued **Moscato di Noto** from near oblivion. Nino Pupillo did the same for the distinctly different **Moscato di Siracuso** – both of them made from Moscato Bianco/Muscat Blanc grapes, but in very different environments. The Sicilian Moscatos best-known off the island, however, are made from Muscat of Alexandria, called Zibbibo here. The luscious **Moscato of Pantelleria**, a volcanic island closer to Tunisia than Sicily, has keen admirers. Less well-known are the sumptuous Malvasias of Lipari and the Aeolian Islands to the north, off Palermo. One of the finest of these orange-scented elixirs is made by Barone di Villagrande.

Although not immune, Sicily is less dominated by the itinerant consultant oenologists who guide so many of Italy's most famous cellars. Co-operatives are still extremely important, but the future lies with ambitious independent enterprises, most of them home-grown.

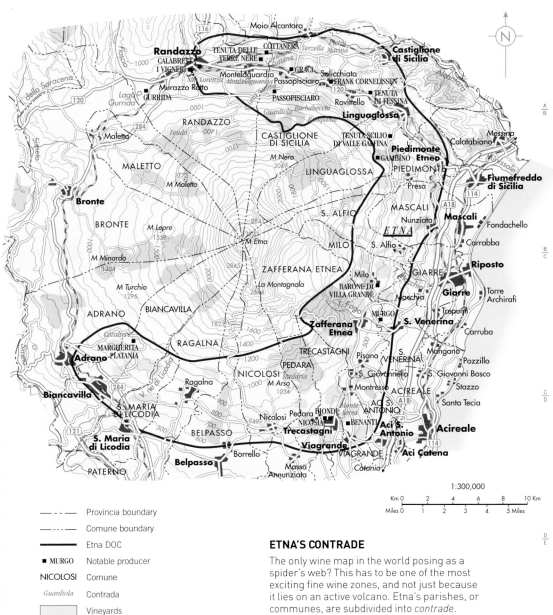

1:300,000

Km 0   2   4   6   8   10 Km
Miles 0   1   2   3   4   5 Miles

- – – –   Provincia boundary
- - - -   Comune boundary
———   Etna DOC
■ **MURGO**   Notable producer
NICOLOSI   Comune
Guardiola   Contrada
  Vineyards
  Woods
—500—   Contour interval 100 metres

ETNA'S CONTRADE

The only wine map in the world posing as a spider's web? This has to be one of the most exciting fine wine zones, and not just because it lies on an active volcano. Etna's parishes, or communes, are subdivided into *contrade*.

Pietramarina is acknowledged as Etna's finest white wine, and Etna Bianco Superiore may be made only in the commune of Milo. Vinupetra is made by I Vigneri, a small consortium of growers advised by Etna's celebrated oenologist Salvo Foti.

Sardinia

Wine has not played an important part in Sardinian culture since the island supplied ancient Rome, although there was a flurry of heavily subsidized planting in the mid-20th century to provide reds, so alcoholic they tasted almost sweet, for blending on the mainland (notably in Chianti). Even today many of Sardinia's greatest, if least-exported, wines are sweet – rare and rich Moscatos, Malvasias, and **Vernaccia di Oristano** (which can also be dry). During the 1980s, however, the subsidies to plant vines became bribes to pull them out and the island's total vineyard shrank by almost three-quarters, much of it concentrated on the flat Campidano plain in the south.

For four centuries (to 1708) Sardinia was ruled by Aragón, and many of its vines came from Spain. Bovale Sardo and Bovale Grande have been shown by DNA profiling to be the Spanish grapes Graciano and Mazuelo (Carignan), respectively. Widely planted Monica makes undistinguished reds, while Giròs, dry and sweet, can taste cherry-like. Nuragus is the white equivalent of Monica, and Nasco, another possibly ancient Sardinian grape, makes soft, often sweet whites.

Cannonau is the local hero, and accounts for 20% of production. It is the local form of Spanish Garnacha (Grenache), a chameleon of potentially high quality, sweet or dry. Crisp, lemony Vermentino is Sardinia's original gift to the wine world, now found on the Ligurian coast as Pigato, in Piemonte as Favorita, and all over southern France as Rolle. In the rocky, arid northeast of Sardinia, inland from the famous Costa Smeralda, Gallura's combination of heat and marine winds concentrate Vermentino to such an extent that **Vermentino di Gallura** was the island's first DOCG.

Sardinia's most successful red wine DOC is **Carignano del Sulcis**, made in the southwest of the island from the produce of seriously old Carignan bush-vines, although even here yields of 105hl/ha are considered quite acceptable. Along with Catalunya, this is probably the world's most promising territory for the Carignan vine. Such is the confidence of Giacomo Tachis, the renowned oenologist behind Barrua, the joint venture between the producers of Sassicaia on the Tuscan coast and Santadi of Sardinia, that he based it on old-vine Carignan. In the Sulcis Meridionale zone a daily average of seven hours of sunshine throughout the year and the hot scirocco from Africa irons out its usual creases. Santadi already made concentrated, velvety bottlings of Carignano del Sulcis as Terre Brune and Rocco Rubia.

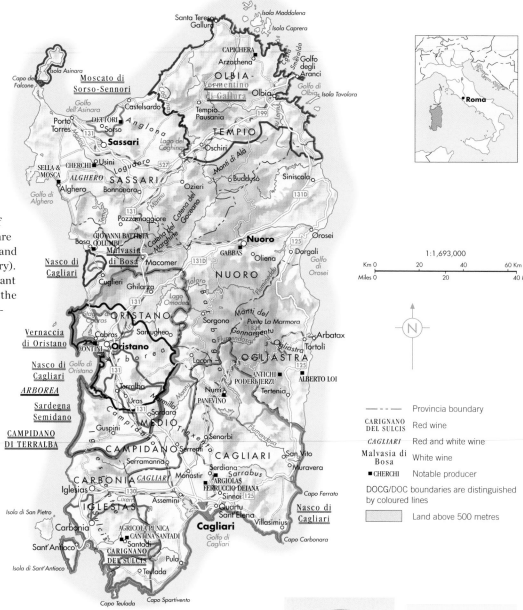

SARDINIA'S WINE ZONES

Cannonau's DOC production zone has generously been increased to encompass the whole of the island, as has that of Vermentino di Sardegna, which may be produced at yields as high as 130hl/ha and still qualify for DOC status.

Meanwhile, north of the capital, Cagliari, also on the flatter land in the south of the island, Argiolas had already made Sardinia's modern reputation with Turriga, a combustively concentrated barrique-aged blend of old-vine Cannonau and Carignano – another Tachis project.

In the northwest, near the town of Alghero, Sella & Mosca has bet on Cabernet Sauvignon for its long-lived Alghero, Marchese di Villamarina, and on the rare, local Torbato grape (known as Tourbat or Malvoisie in Roussillon) for its distinctive Terre Bianche white.

Sardinia undoubtedly has an unusually varied cache of raw ingredients. It has countless old bush-vines of the sort of fashionable and interesting grape varieties the modern world demands growing in a perfect climate. The potential is there.

Sardinian wine gives the wine-lover the impression of work in progress. So much potential, not all of it realized. Capichera's Vermentino di Gallura (a DOCG) is called Santigaini – "October" in the local dialect – which is when the grapes are picked.

Map legend

- – – – – Provincia boundary
- **CARIGNANO DEL SULCIS** Red wine
- *CAGLIARI* Red and white wine
- **Malvasia di Bosa** White wine
- ■ CHERCHI Notable producer
- DOCG/DOC boundaries are distinguished by coloured lines
- Land above 500 metres

1:1,693,000
Km 0   20   40   60 Km
Miles 0   20   40 Miles

SPAIN

Torres' vineyard terraces ripple along the slopes above Porrera, Priorat

Spain

Spain and Italy, the two great wine nations of the Mediterranean, have remarkably little in common. Italy is a peninsula where you are never far from mountains or sea, a conglomerate of many separate states, a land full of local industries and crafts. Spain is a great land mass whose history is one of central direction and overseas empire. Until recently her range of wines was limited. What has happened in the past 20 years is revolution; there are new stars fizzing and crackling everywhere.

Spain may be in the warmer latitudes, but a good 90% of all Spanish vineyards lie at altitudes higher than any major French wine region – most of Castilla y León and Castilla-La Mancha for a start – which helps to maintain enough acidity to keep their wines relatively fresh. The cold winters and very hot summers, with sunshine often so relentless that the vines shut down and the grapes stop ripening, can leave the early autumn a scramble to accumulate sugar and aroma before temperatures drop. The big problem in the south, east, and some of the north of the country is summer drought. Dry soils cannot support many vines, so in most regions they are planted unusually far apart, traditionally trained (if that is the word) in bushes only just above ground level. Spain, as a result, has long had more land under vine than any other country – which has not discouraged her ambitious vintners from planting with gay abandon – until, from 2008, the money ran out. There were enormous vineyards, but very small crops.

The situation began to change in 1995, when the law officially allowed Spanish growers to irrigate, although only the rich can afford to bore for water and install the systems to distribute it. Despite some dangerously dry years, irrigation has increased yields dramatically. In regions such as La Mancha that lend themselves to machine harvesting, installing wires to train the vines has made a difference, too.

Spain's *denominaciónes* keep multiplying. At the time of writing there were 67 DOs; two DOCas, Rioja and Priorat; 14 single-estate appellations (Vinos de Pago); plus six Vinos de Calidad. But many of the most exciting developments are in vineyards outside the official system, which is why the accuracy and topicality of the map on this page presents this Atlas's single greatest challenge. The DO system is less complicated than France's AOC hierarchy – or indeed Italy's DOCs. Most DOs are so large that they include all sorts of different terrains and conditions. There is more than a streak of Latin anarchy (see Italy) in Spaniards' attitudes to these regulations, too:

SPAIN'S WINE REGIONS

There seems no end to new discoveries of ancient Spanish vines that can be persuaded to yield wines of great quality. The Gredos Mountains west of Madrid, Ribeira Sacra, the Canaries, and the island of Mallorca are just a few examples.

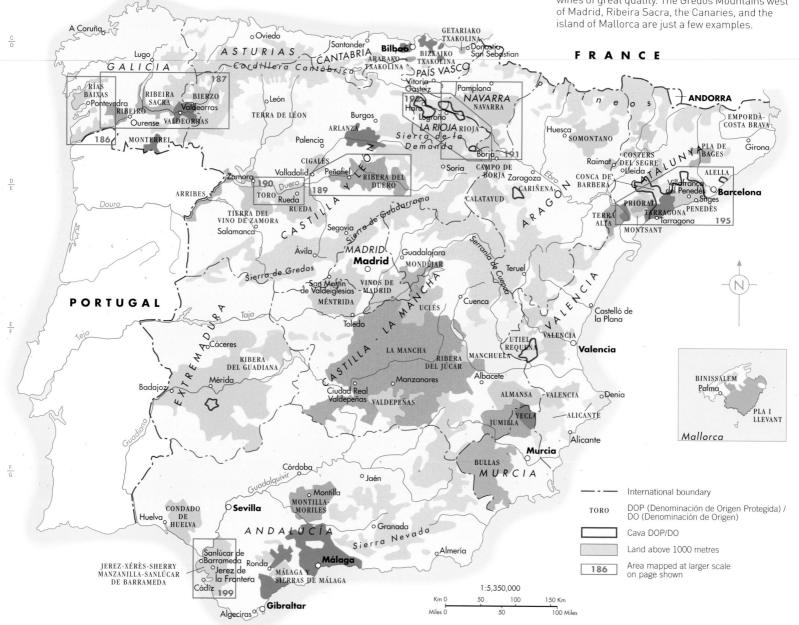

particularly in the matter of grape varieties, where there can be some disparity between what is permitted and what is planted. In most cases this is all to the good, as so many wine producers are anxious only to make better wine. A defining characteristic, however, is that buying in grapes, and often wine, is still far more common in Spain than the practice of estate bottling.

Spanish bodegas were traditionally places where wine was aged, convenient for the market – often for much longer than is customary or, in some cases, advisable. Nevertheless, the Spanish habit of releasing wine when it is ready to drink rather than ready to sell is appealing, to say the least. But things have been changing in the bodegas. For centuries American oak was the wood of choice for barrels, thanks to the country's transatlantic seafaring. From the 1980s, however, Spanish new wave winemakers were some of the most avid buyers of French oak, even if most of the barrels are actually coopered in Spain, notably at Logroño in Rioja.

Not only the source of oak, but also time in barrel has become more French. The Reserva and Gran Reserva categories were devised implicitly to honour extended oak ageing, but an increasing number of producers now value intensity over antiquity and are abandoning or devaluing their Gran Reservas and bottling even their top wines much younger.

The North

The majority of Castilla y León's vineyards lie in the high, landlocked Duero Valley. Toro, Rueda, and Ribera del Duero are mapped in detail on pages 188–90, but **Cigales**, just north of the Duero, is also making some serious reds (as well as inexpensive traditional reds and *rosados*) from ancient Tempranillo vines in particularly rocky soils. The climate is dry and harsh. At 2,100–2,600ft (650–800m) altitude, and with relatively low rainfall, fungicide sprays have rarely been needed. Drought and frost are the chief enemies here, not disease. Cigales is higher and cooler than Toro to the southwest, so its wines tend to be more structured.

Way up in the Bay of Biscay, around the cities of Bilbao and San Sebastián, are the piercing, appley Basque whites of, respectively, **Bizkaiko Txakolina/Chacolí de Vizcaya** and **Getariako Txakolina/Chacolí de Guetaria** (Spanish political courtesy embraces four languages: Gallego, Basque, Catalan, and mainstream Castilian). **Arabako Txakolina/Chacolí de Alava** is made in small quantities in the province of Araba/Alava. They are served locally by pouring from a great height into tumblers.

The River Ebro flows southeast from the Cantabrian Cordillera on the north coast to the Mediterranean in Catalunya. The Upper Ebro embraces Rioja and Navarra (see pages 191–93), where Tempranillo and Garnacha meet, but also **Campo de Borja**, whose high-altitude plantings of old bush-vine Garnacha yield some extremely juicy reds at low cost, as well as much more ambitiously oaked, concentrated wines tuned to the current American taste. The continental climate and the local *cierzo*, a cold, dry northwest wind, help. The climate is similar in **Cariñena**, to the south, but Garnacha is challenged here by Tempranillo and Cabernet as producers from e.g.Rioja move in. Neighbouring **Calatayud** is home to some of Spain's most successful co-operative exporters, notably San Gregorio. A Master of Wine called Norrel Robertson has fashioned first-class wines from the local Garnacha bush-vines, still one of Spain's undervalued resources. (In EU eyes old vines in little-known regions should be pulled up; little do they know their potential in these deep slate soils.)

Somontano, meaning "at the foot of the mountains", is an adolescent DO brought into being, for once, by the local government. In the late 1980s it encouraged Viñas del Vero to plant Tempranillo and international varieties to add cosmopolitan glamour to the local Moristel and Parraleta vines. The total area planted, however, has more than doubled since the late 1990s, to nearly 12,000 acres (4,750ha) in 2011. Aragón has a proud history, but in wine terms it lags far behind its neighbours Catalunya and Navarra. Much of it to the west is too open to Atlantic blasts for vines to flourish; to the south there is desert. But Somontano offered a mild climate and more rain than most of the central Spanish plateau, even if the average of about 20in (500mm) a year is only just adequate.

Today, Somontano wines may not equal the best of Ribera del Duero, Rioja, and Priorat, but they are among the most consistent and best value in Spain. Three in four bottles is filled by either Viñas del Vero, the privately owned Enate, or the former co-op Pirineos, now joined by several other good bodegas such as Blecua, Dalcamp, Irius, Laus, and Olvena.

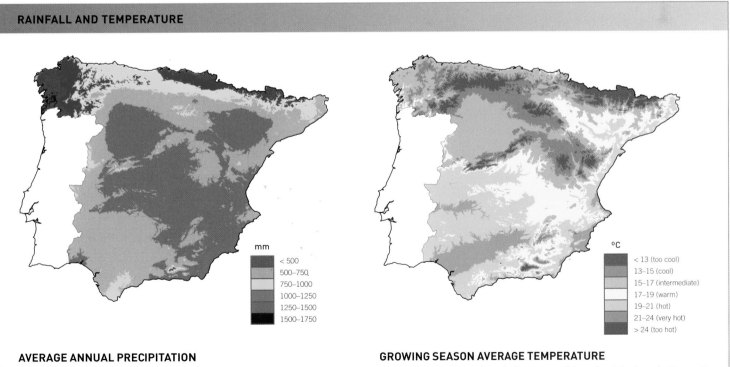

RAINFALL AND TEMPERATURE

mm
< 500
500–750
750–1000
1000–1250
1250–1500
1500–1750

°C
< 13 (too cool)
13–15 (cool)
15–17 (intermediate)
17–19 (warm)
19–21 (hot)
21–24 (very hot)
> 24 (too hot)

AVERAGE ANNUAL PRECIPITATION
A country of extremes: from the dry south and interior of the country (less than 500mm/20in per year in many places) to the moderately wet Galicia in the northwest (some places have over 1,000mm/40in per year).

GROWING SEASON AVERAGE TEMPERATURE
Range from moderately cool climate conditions for viticulture in the north and northwest to hot and very hot growing seasons in the south. (Data source for both maps: WorldClim, 1950–2000.)

The Sun sets over the village of San Vicente de la Sonsierra in Rioja Alta (mapped in detail on p.193), but note in the foreground just how large an area of vineyard is needed to supply enough water for each vine. Typically Spanish.

International-style wines in general, and from Somontano in particular, have sold less well than was hoped; individuality and personality are more prized nowadays than they were in the 1980s. Taking advantage of lean times, the sherry giants swooped in to control a large part of production; González Byass acquired Viñas del Vero and Barbadillo took over Pirineos. The wines are attractively plump though never too massive, thanks to predominantly sandy soils. Crisp acidity comes naturally, not least because soils here are low in potassium, which keeps pH levels low, too. There are mouth-filling Bordeaux-variety reds, some savoury Tempranillo, much more convincing Chardonnay than most of Spain can manage, and some of Spain's rare dry Gewürztraminer.

Bodega Pirineos works hardest at maintaining the local grapes, squeezing every ounce of flavour out of the light, loganberry-scented Moristel by encouraging malolactic fermentation. Pirineos also perseveres with low-yielding, tight, mineral-scented Parraleta. Both are well worth preserving.

No one could accuse Spanish wine producers, or their label designers, of a lack of creativity. Compare and contrast with labels from, for example, Bordeaux and Burgundy. Some, such as Enrique Mendoza's Estrecho Monastrell from Alicante and An Negra from Mallorca, are positively gnomic.

The East

In many ways the vineyards inland from Spain's central Mediterranean coast have been making even more rapid progress than those in the north. For long, Manchuela, Valencia, Utiel-Requena, Almansa, Yecla, Jumilla, Alicante, and Bullas were regarded as fit only to provide strong bulk wine for a dwindling export market. But some of these DOs are putting new money and ideas to good use to make fruity and even stylish reds. Wine is still made that is deliberately strong and sweet, but the best can compete with "premium" super-ripe reds from California and Australia. Local varieties are typically blended with international imports, but such growers as Casa Castillo in **Jumilla** have shown how to tame varietal Monastrell (Mourvèdre). In **Alicante** Enrique Mendoza led the way, with wines varying in sweetness, if not in strength. Others have followed. The DO **Manchuela**, on a high plateau with limestone deposits, was justified by Finca Sandoval's blend of Syrah with Monastrell. The beefy Bobal, Spain's second most-planted red grape after Tempranillo, is characteristic of this region and neighbouring **Utiel-Requena**, which is also more than 1,970ft (600m) above sea level.

South of Madrid

Most central of all to Spanish life is the *meseta*, the high plateau south of Madrid, whose endless flat vineyards weary the eye. The extent of **La Mancha**, its chief DO, is clear from the map. Its DO-classified vineyards alone, less than half of the total, cover more ground than all of Australia's vineyards put together. The town of **Valdepeñas** gave its name to a large part of this production: strong but pale red made from Airén (Spain's most-planted white grape, on which Brandy de Jerez depends) tinted with some red. From the late 1990s La Mancha has been changing just as dramatically as the rest of Spain's winescape, with a steady conversion from white to red varieties. By 2005 more than two-thirds of all the wine made in this vast region was red, much of it inexpensive and made from Cencibel, the local strain of Tempranillo. Some Garnacha has also long been grown, but international varieties have also invaded in strength. Cabernet, Merlot,

Syrah, and even Chardonnay and Sauvignon Blanc can be found here – although it can be difficult to imbue them with much character in a region where picking has to begin by mid-August.

Between here and Madrid are the DOs of **Méntrida**, **Vinos de Madrid**, and **Mondéjar**, all ripe for transformation. The most innovative vineyards here have been the Marqués de Griñon's near Toledo. With a novel palette of imported grape varieties (including Syrah and Petit Verdot) and new ways of growing and watering vines, the Marqués engineered the first DO Pago (see panel) in Spain, **Dominio de Valdepusa**. Some good wines from old Garnacha and local Albillo vines are also being made in the granitic and occasionally slate foothills of the Sierra de Gredos to the northwest by such bodegas as Bernabeleva, Jiménez-Landi, and Marañones. Due west of La Mancha, in Extremadura near the Portuguese frontier, is the extensive and relatively recent DO **Ribera del Guadiana**. Here, too, there is considerable potential for robust, ripe wines, similar to those of Alentejo over the Portuguese border. Castillo de Naos makes a good example from Tempranillo.

The islands

The **Canary Islands**, once the source of Spain's most famous sweet wines, lie far to the southwest in the Atlantic, but they have joined in the DO game with zest. The islands of Gran Canaria, La Palma, El Hierro, the volcanic Lanzarote, and La Gomera each have one DO, while the proud island of Tenerife has no fewer than five (see map below) and, at least officially, 15,000 acres (6,500ha) of vines of a dozen local varieties. Red wine is in a minority. For the moment the best wines are the zesty, citrus-peel whites made from such local grape varieties as Marmajuelo (Bermejuela) and Gual (Madeira's Boal).

The past 20 years have seen the ancient vineyards of Mallorca recover from near extinction with both local grapes and imports. Manto Negro gives light reds, the rare Callet something more seriously red, especially in the exceptional Anima Negra. The two DOs are **Plà i Llevant** to the east and **Binissalem** in the centre of the island.

ABONA DOP/DO
DOP/DO boundaries are distinguished by coloured lines

Islas Canarias

THE CANARY ISLANDS

These volcanic islands off the coast of Morocco have a unique viticultural heritage – vines which have never known phylloxera – and a long history of making distinctive sweet whites from low, windswept bush-vines. The regional government is helping put them back on the map with a plethora of denominations.

Rías Baixas

Galicia's best-known wines are as far from the Spanish stereotype as it is possible to imagine: delicate, lively, aromatic whites that go perfectly with the shellfish that is the standard Galician diet. With the one exception of Martín Códax, a producer now part-owned by E & J Gallo of California, everything about Rías Baixas (pronounced "ree-ass by-shuss") wine is small scale. Some of the best bodegas make only a few hundred cases of wine a year; most growers have only a few hectares of vines. This damp, green corner of Spain (compare the annual rainfall of Vigo with that of any other Spanish weather station) was until recently extremely poor and virtually ignored by the rest of the country. Any Gallego with any gumption emigrated, but tended to cling fiercely to ownership of minuscule parcels of inherited land. This, and Galicia's physical isolation, meant that it was not until the 1980s that these singular wines found a ready and rapturous market outside Galicia.

Like the wines, the landscape is exceptional for Spain: irregular Atlantic inlets called rías, which are effectively shallow fjords, lined with hills that are densely forested with local pine and rapacious eucalyptus imported in the 1950s. Even the vines look quite different.

As in Portugal's very similar Vinho Verde country across the River Miño, vines have traditionally been trained on pergolas, horizontal trellises well above light-dappled shoulder height. The widely spaced, spindly trunks are often trained up posts of granite, the common building material of this part of the world. For the thousands of small farmers who grow vines simply to make wine for themselves, this high canopy allows them to use every square foot of precious earth; their cabbages grow beneath. But it can also help ventilate the grapes, an important consideration where sea mists regularly invade the vineyards, even in summer.

The thick-skinned Albariño grape dominates here. Of all grapes it can best resist the mildew that persistently threatens, and young Albariño has a faithful following. There is increasing experimentation, however, with blends, oak, and deliberately aged wines.

RIAS BAIXAS SUBZONES

Val do Salnés is the most important subzone, and the coolest and dampest. In O Rosal to the south, the best vineyards are carved out of terraced clearings on the south-facing hillsides and produce wines notably lower in acidity. Condado do Tea is the warmest subzone, being furthest from the coast, and its wines tend to be more powerful and less refined.

—·— International boundary
—·— Provincial boundary
═══ Rías Baixas DOP/DO

Rías Baixas subzones:
Condado do Tea
O Rosal
Ribeira do Ulla
Soutomaior
Val do Salnés
FILLABOA Notable producer
—400— Contour interval 200 metres
▼ Weather station (WS)

RÍAS BAIXAS: VIGO ▼	
Latitude / Altitude of WS	**42.24° / 856ft (261m)**
Average growing season temperature at WS	**62.2°F (16.8°C)**
Average annual rainfall at WS	**70in (1,786mm)**
Harvest month rainfall at WS	**September: 4.0in (102mm)**
Principal viticultural hazards	**Fungal diseases, high winds**
Principal grape varieties	**Albariño, Treixadura, Loureira Blanca**

Two of the most established labels and admired wines, both Albariño. But red wines, from Caiño Tinto, Loureiro Tinto, Espadeiro, and even Pinot Noir, are becoming more common, thanks to the efforts of winemaker Rodrigo Méndez, abetted by Raúl Pérez of Bierzo.

Inland Northwest Spain

In recent years the climate has grown steadily warmer in eastern and southern Spain. At the same time the pendulum of fashion has swung back in favour of wines that refresh rather than merely impress – a cue for cool, damp northwest Spain and its wines. They are attracting more and more attention from wine enthusiasts – and not just the crisp dry whites of Rías Baixas described opposite. Almost all Spanish whites need added acidity to give them zip, but not in Galicia.

Traditions here are Celtic (as the Gallic name suggests). The Atlantic, the hills, the wind, and a good deal of rain (see the map on p.183) are the chief physical factors. Wines are mainly light, dry, and refreshing. The Palomino and red-fleshed Alicante Bouschet vines that were pressed into service here after phylloxera having been largely replaced by the much more characterful local grape varieties.

The white wine region **Ribeiro**, just up the Miño river from Rías Baixas, shipped wine to England in the middle ages, long before the Douro Valley to the south. The trade disappeared and vineyards were abandoned – all over this corner of Spain. Today producers are more bullish and consumers more receptive. The grape varieties that are typically blended to produce dry white Ribeiro: Albariño, Treixadura, Loureira, Torrontés, and, increasingly, the Godello of Valdeorras have a positive future. A little red is made here, too, mainly from the highly coloured Alicante grape.

Ribeira Sacra, further inland, makes Galicia's potentially most interesting red wine (and some fine white Godello), in archaic conditions on almost impossibly steep slate terraces above the rivers Sil and Miño. The fruitily scented Mencía is the best red grape, also grown in the small but revitalized **Monterrei** region (which is warm enough to ripen Tempranillo). Quinta da Muradella is a leading exponent.

Valdeorras has already established a name for its firm white Godello, which can yield extremely fine varietal wines worth ageing, but its reds are also carving out a reputation. Mencía is important here, too, but less widely planted Galician red wine grapes are gaining ground in all these zones, both in blends and even varietal wines. Merenzao/Bastardo (Trousseau), Mouratón (Juan García), Carabuñeira (Touriga Nacional), Sousón (Vinho Verde's Vinhão), Brancellao (northern Portugal's Alvarelhão), Ferrón (Manseng Noir), and Caíño Tinto (Vinho Verde's Borraçal) are no longer rarities.

Mencía is also the basis of fashionable **Bierzo**, one Spain's fruitiest, most aromatic, distinctively refreshing reds, grown just over the border into Castilla y León but in conditions very like those of Galicia. Alvaro Palacios of Priorat and his nephew Ricardo put Bierzo, and indeed Mencía, on the international map. It was the slate terraces of Bierzo, rather than the predominating clay, that persuaded them. They produced wines with a grace and finesse not found in a generation of concentrated, oak-heavy products. Now there are 50 bodegas in Bierzo, not all expressing the same refinement. Raúl Pérez is the consulting winemaking wizard in this green corner of Spain.

The Palacios family introduced the racy reds of Bierzo to the outside world but Bierzo-born Raúl Pérez, who made the Ultreia, became the leading light of wine production in all four regions mapped below.

---------- Provincial boundary

━━━━━ Bierzo DOP/DO

━━━━━ Ribeira Sacra DOP/DO

━━━━━ Ribeiro DOP/DO

━━━━━ Valdeorras DOP/DO

● Villafranca del Bierzo — Wine centre

VALDESIL ■ — Notable producer

〜1200 — Contour interval 300 metres

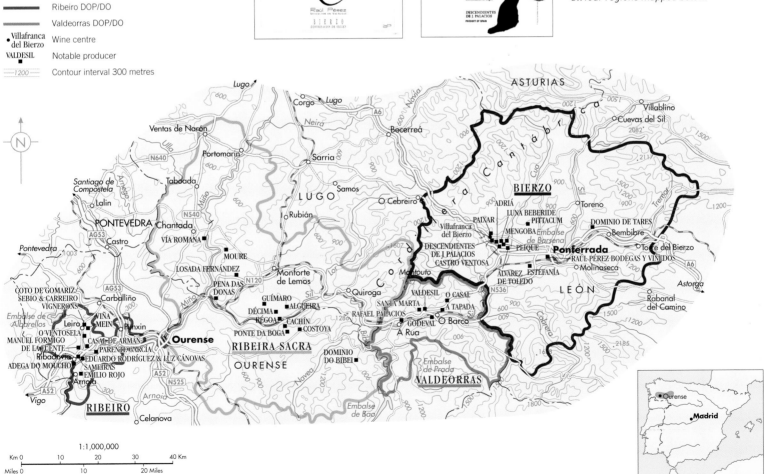

1:1,000,000

Ribera del Duero

Ribera del Duero is the modern red wine miracle of northern Spain. Barely known in the early 1980s, it now rivals Rioja as Spain's foremost red wine region. The plain of Old Castile, stretching in tawny leagues north from Segovia and Avila to the old kingdom of León, is traversed by the adolescent Duero, the river that in Portugal becomes the Douro and the home of port (see pp.206–09). At 3,000ft (850m) the nights here are remarkably cool: in late August it can be 95°F (35°C) at noon and 54°F (12°C) at night. Spring frosts are all too common. Grapes are routinely picked in late October. The light and air have a high-altitude dryness and brightness about them, as do the wines, which have particularly lively acidity thanks to those cool nights. These are concentrated reds of remarkably intense colour, fruit, and savour – quite different in style from the typical produce of Rioja less than 60 miles (100 km) to the northeast.

Vega Sicilia provided the initial proof that very fine red wine could be made here. The estate was initially planted in the 1860s, at the same time as Rioja was being invaded by Bordeaux merchants and influence. Vega Sicilia's Unico, made only in good vintages, aged longer in oak than virtually any other table wine, and sold at 10 years (after some years in bottle nowadays), is a wine of astonishing, penetrating personality. But here Bordeaux grapes, unusually, add a little cosmopolitan glamour to the native Tempranillo (a locally adapted version known here as Tinto Fino or Tinta del País).

Rapid expansion

Ribera became hugely fashionable in the 1990s. There were just 24 bodegas in the region when the DO was created in 1982. In 2012 there were more than 200, down from a peak of 230, thanks to Spain's economic crisis. (Many of these bodegas, it should be said, are unencumbered by vineyards). This wide, high plateau has seen a quite remarkable transformation of land previously devoted to cereals and sugar beet. Today it has more than 49,400 acres (20,000ha) of vines. Many of the new plantings depend not on Ribera's own strain of Tempranillo but on cuttings imported from other regions, hence of more doubtful value. Viticulturists can easily be foxed by Ribera's extremely varied soils, even within a single vineyard, where grapes may ripen at infuriatingly different paces. Limestone

Baskets really are still used for the harvest in parts of Ribera del Duero, such as here in García Figuero's vineyard in La Horra, where some of the region's finest grapes are grown.

outcrops, more common north of the Duero, help to retain rainfall that is far from generous.

The tradition of buying in grapes is just as strong here as in Rioja (even Vega Sicilia, with 600 acres/250ha, has contracts with other growers), and many of these new bodegas vie with each other for fruit. Some of the best comes from round La Horra, but top winemakers such as Peter Sisseck, the Dane who made Dominio de Pingus Spain's rarest and most expensive wine, are cagey about their sources – invariably the oldest and truest of gnarled, crouching Tinto Fino bushes.

Two of the most successful producers in the region are not even within the DO boundaries. Abadía Retuerta, a vast property founded in 1996 by the Swiss pharmaceutical company Novartis, is at Sardón de Duero, just west of the official boundary. (In 1982 when the DO regulations were being drawn up there were no vines here, but there had been vines almost continuously from the 17th century. The abbey was one of Valladolid's chief suppliers of wine until the early 1970s.) Even further west, in Tudela, is Mauro, founded in 1980 and now established in a handsome old stone building by Mariano García, once Vega Sicilia's

winemaker. García is also involved in making Aalto, just one of many relatively new names in Ribera del Duero, where, it seems, reputations can be made in a single vintage.

More recent investors have included Félix Solis (Pagos del Rey), Alonso del Yerro, Marqués de Vargas (Conde de San Cristóbal), Torres (Celeste), Faustino – many of them already well established in other wine regions, especially neighbouring Rioja. Others, including a prominent Madrid publisher, Alfonso de Salas, the Marqués de Montecastro, could be said to be diversifying (in his case with a notably soft red radically untypical of the region).

THE WINE CENTRES OF THE DUERO

The broad, high valley of the Duero and its tributaries have made wine for centuries, presumably more because of local thirst – Valladolid, as the capital of 17th-century Spain, formulated strict wine laws – than because the fierce continental climate favoured the vine.

Key to producers

1 DOMINIO DE PINGUS
2 ARZUAGA NAVARRO
3 VEGA SICILIA
4 DEHESA DE LOS CANÓNIGOS
5 HACIENDA MONASTERIO
6 MATARROMERA
7 EMILIO MORO
8 CONDE DE SAN CRISTÓBAL
9 LEGARIS
10 MONTECASTRO
11 PAGO DE LOS CAPELLANES
12 RODERO
13 ALONSO DEL YERRO
14 REAL SITIO DE VENTOSILLA
15 GOYO GARCÍA VIADERO (BODEGAS VALDUERO)
16 CILLAR DE SILOS

1:671,000

Km 0   10   20 Km
Miles 0   5   10   15 Miles

— — — Provincial boundary
——— Ribera del Duero DOP/DO
● La Horra   Wine centre
PESQUERA   Notable producer
—1000—   Contour interval 100 metres
▼   Weather station (WS)

Of these much-admired reds only one, the leading estate Vega Sicilia, has a history of winemaking longer than two decades. They are all based on Tempranillo, called Tinta del País here and grown on more than 80% of vineyard land.

RIBERA DEL DUERO: VALLADOLID ▼

Latitude / Altitude of WS
41.70° / 2,7775ft (846m)

Average growing season temperature at WS
60.3°F (15.7°C)

Average annual rainfall at WS
17in (435mm)

Harvest month rainfall at WS
October: 2.1in (52mm)

Principal viticultural hazards
Spring frost, autumn rain

Principal grape varieties
Tinto Fino / Tinta del País (Tempranillo)

Toro and Rueda

In 1998, the medieval town of Toro, in the far west of Castilla y León, had eight bodegas and its wine was widely and justly regarded as rustic, if full-throttle. But the sheer exuberance of its local strain of Tempranillo, Tinta de Toro, became too obvious to ignore – especially in the era when wine drinkers were looking for drama rather than subtlety – and by 2006 there were 40 bodegas, by 2012, 50. High-profile Spanish investors included the owners of glamorous Ribera del Duero bodegas Vega Sicilia, Pesquera, and Mauro as well as the roving winemaker Telmo Rodríguez. Even the French moved in. François Lurton from Bordeaux and famous oenologists Michel and Dany Rolland of Pomerol were so impressed by Tinta de Toro's ripeness levels, they embarked on a joint venture, Campo Eliseo. And LVMH acquired the highly regarded Numanthia bodega from its Riojano owners at the top of the market in 2008.

The key to Toro's quality is, as so often in Spain, its altitude. At 1,970–2,460ft (600–750m) above sea level the region's growers can depend on cool nights to "fix" colour and flavour in the grapes ripened during the torrid summer days on the region's various red clays and sandy soils.

The average age of Toro's vines is relatively high. Most of them are still grown as individual bush-vines, spaced as far as 10ft (3m) apart: a record low vine density imposed by Toro's near-desert conditions – under 16in (400mm) of rain a year. Some of the Tinta de Toro that constitutes 85% of all plantings in the region is vinified quickly by carbonic maceration and sold young and juicy, but the great majority of the wine is aged in oak, in the case of Reservas for at least 12 months.

Rueda

Neighbouring Rueda is historically a producer of white wine from its local Verdejo vine, rescued from a long decline when Rioja's powerful Marqués de Riscal decided to move its white wine production here in the 1970s. Verdejo can yield wines every bit as refreshing as the Sauvignon Blanc that was planted here more recently. It holds its acidity well and, to develop its full mineral potential can be picked much later than the rather simpler Sauvignon Blanc.

Most red wine made here, generally from Tempranillo and sometimes Cabernet Sauvignon, is sold as Vino de la Tierra Castilla y León rather than red Rueda.

The tentacles of Bordeaux have long stretched into northern Spain. Dominio del Bendito is an acclaimed Toro estate run by young Bordelais Antony Terryn, while the original co-founder of Belondrade was a member of the sprawling Lurton clan of Bordeaux.

TORO AND NORTHWESTERN RUEDA

The map includes all of Toro but only the vinously most important, far northwestern portion of the Rueda zone, which extends outside the province of Valladolid into Segovia, and Avila (see map on p.182). Several producers make both wines.

– – – –	Provincial boundary
———	Toro DOP/DO
———	Rueda DOP/DO
• Venialbo	Wine centre
PINTIA ■	Notable producer
	Woods
—500—	Contour interval 100 metres

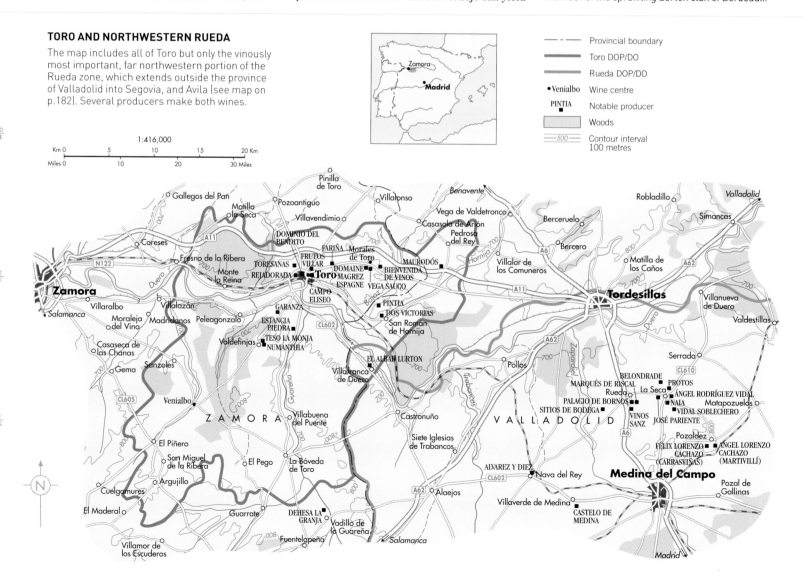

1:416,000

Km 0 — 5 — 10 — 15 — 20 Km
Miles 0 — 10 — 20 — 30 Miles

Navarra

Camped round the northeastern boundary of Rioja, the wine region of Navarra was long in competition with it (and indeed part of France), until the Bordeaux merchants chose to place their post-phylloxera trade not with this green land of asparagus and nurseries but with Rioja and its ready rail link from Haro (see p.192). For most of the 20th century Navarra's scattered vineyards were dedicated chiefly to Garnacha and the useful *rosados* and strong, deep, blending reds that it produced. But then came a revolution in the form of Cabernet, Merlot, Tempranillo, and Chardonnay. Tempranillo overtook Garnacha in total area. and Cabernet Sauvignon became the region's third most-planted grape, yet curiously few Navarra wines from these newer varieties have enjoyed real commercial success.

It is blends that make the running, while wines such as Chivite's Gran Feudo Viñas Viejas Reserva show just how good old-vine Navarra Garnacha can be. While the all-important co-operatives continue to soak up much of the region's run-of-the-mill Garnacha, the best producers turn to older vineyards planted with Navarra's traditional varieties – Garnacha and Moscatel de Grano Menudo – to make either single-variety examples or to increase the percentage of them in ambitious blends. Domaines Lupier and Emilio Valerio are among the newer prospectors to have followed this line with notable success.

International appeal

The most exported wines of Navarra taste like a cross between Rioja and Somontano: obviously oaked but using a full palette of both Spanish and international varieties. French oak is used more commonly than in Rioja, perhaps because oak ageing came so much later to Navarra, but also because more of the vineyard is devoted to French grape varieties.

Navarra is no more homogeneous than Rioja, however. There is a world of difference between the hot, dry, flat **Ribera Baja** and **Ribera Alta** subzones in the south, which lie on the banks of the River Ebro and have to be irrigated (with a system of canals initiated by the Romans) and the less-planted cooler climate, and more varied soils, of the north.

Ribera Alta is measurably warmer and more exposed to the influence of the Mediterranean than Ribera Baja, protected by the Sierra del Moncayo to the south. The best Garnachas in Ribera Baja come from Fitero because its poor, Châteauneuf-like soils are open to Mediterranean warmth. Just to the north of Fitero, Corella has earned a reputation for excellent botrytised Moscatel de Grano Menudo (Muscat Blanc à Petits Grains) – again the work of the dominant Navarra producer, Bodegas Chivite. Camilo Castilla, meanwhile, is

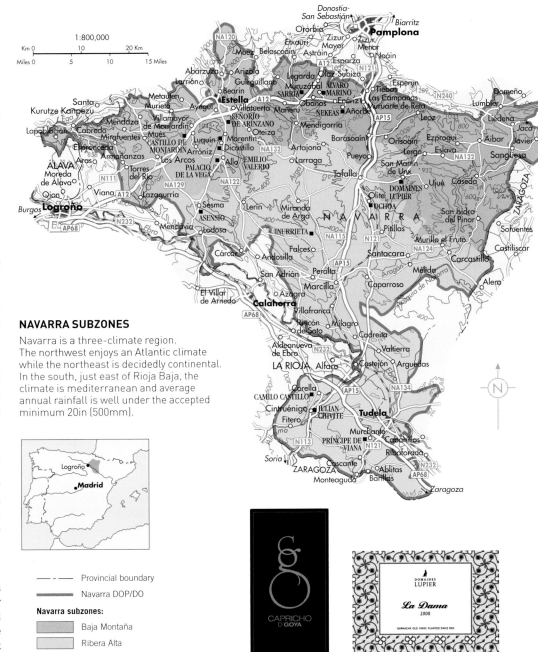

NAVARRA SUBZONES

Navarra is a three-climate region. The northwest enjoys an Atlantic climate while the northeast is decidedly continental. In the south, just east of Rioja Baja, the climate is mediterranean and average annual rainfall is well under the accepted minimum 20in (500mm).

- – · – Provincial boundary
- ——— Navarra DOP/DO

Navarra subzones:

- Baja Montaña
- Ribera Alta
- Ribera Baja
- Tierra Estella
- Valdizarbe
- OCHOA ■ Notable producer
- —400— Contour interval 200 metres

Two of the relatively rare fine wines: late harvest Muscat (left) and old vine Garnacha, made in Navarra where far too much wine is relatively ordinary stuff – typically pink Garnacha or rather thin red churned out by co-operatives.

the bodega that nurtured the variety and remains Spain's master of traditional *rancio* Muscats, aged for many years in old oak.

A day that is positively torrid in the south of Navarra can be quite cool in the mountainous north, closer to the Atlantic, where the persistence of the westerlies has spawned virtual forests of wind-powered generators on mesas above the vineyards. As in Rioja, northern Navarra's altitude means that the Bordeaux grape varieties are picked considerably later than in Bordeaux itself – sometimes as late as December in the highest vineyards. **Baja Montaña** (clay with some limestone) produces mainly *rosados*. In

the northern subzones of **Tierra Estella** and **Valdizarbe**, aspects and elevations are so varied that their pioneering growers have to select sites with extreme care. Spring frosts and cold autumns lie in wait for them. Nonetheless, it was in Tierra Estella, perhaps with climate change in mind, that Chivite chose to invest heavily in an historic estate, Arínzano. Arínzano's blend of Tempranillo with Cabernet and Merlot is outstanding enough to earn it Pago status, Spain's highest: a single-estate denomination of its own. Pago status is earned only by estates with genuinely distinctive natural characteristics and a commercial history of at least five years.

Rioja

Rioja established itself 150 years ago as Spain's nearest shot at French-style wine. That may be an irrelevance today; Spain has many styles, but Rioja is still its most familiar name abroad. Its recent challengers in international esteem, Ribera del Duero and Priorat, have wobbled in contrary market winds. Rioja's roots are too deep for that.

Without the massive wall of the rocky Sierra de Cantabria, Rioja would be too buffeted by Atlantic winds for vines to survive. In the far northwest of the region some of the highest vineyards above Labastida can struggle to ripen at all. In the east, on the other hand, vines ripen fully as high as 2,600ft (800m), thanks to the warming influence of the Mediterranean, felt as far west as Elciego. Growers in Alfaro in the east may harvest four to six weeks before those around Haro, where the last grapes may not be picked until the end of October.

The region is divided into three zones, two Spanish and one Basque. **Rioja Alta** is the western, higher part south of the winding, poplar-lined River Ebro. It includes land around San Vicente de la Sonsierra north of the river but still in the Spanish province of La Rioja. **Rioja Alavesa**, that part of Rioja in Alava province, is Basque and – quite literally nowadays – another country, with its own language, its own police force, and some tax breaks that have perhaps encouraged the rash of new bodegas on this north bank of the river. **Rioja Baja**, the extensive hotter eastern section, again Spanish, has its own anomalous enclave carved out of it just east of the industrial capital of the region, Logroño. The historic Marqués de Murrieta Castillo Ygay bodega could not be allowed to belong to Rioja Baja, which was for long considered inferior.

In Rioja Alta and Alavesa vines are virtually the only crop; the landscape is a spotted patchwork of small plots of low bush-vines on soils variously soft clay-red and limestone-white, tinted with yellow alluvial deposits. These terraces, eroded to different levels by the river (the higher the better), are more likely to be dominated by clay in Rioja Alta and limestone in Rioja Alavesa. The red soils around Fuenmayor are some of Rioja's most productive, and clay is so important there that it has spawned a huge ceramics factory. The soils of Rioja Baja are even more varied than those of Rioja Alta and its vines much more sparsely cultivated.

Tempranillo is by far the most important variety of Rioja, accounting for 61% of vineyards. It blends well with the plumper Garnacha (Grenache, 18%), best in Rioja Alta upstream of Nájera and in Rioja Baja in the high vineyards of Tudelilla. Graciano (known as Morrastel in the Languedoc, in Portugal as Tinta Miúda) is a fine but finicky Rioja speciality that now seems at least safe from extinction. Mazuelo (Carignan) is allowed, and experimentation with Cabernet Sauvignon uneasily tolerated.

Rioja's true character

Oddly enough, Spain's most famous, most important wine began the 21st century with a search for its true character. The reputation of the region was made in the late 19th century, when Bordeaux négocians came here to fill the embarrassing voids in their blending tanks left by phylloxera north of the Pyrenees. They had their proof of Rioja's potential in the wines of the two marquéses, de Riscal and Murrieta, who had established their own estates, in 1860 in Elciego and in 1872 just east of Logroño, respectively.

With its rail links to the Atlantic coast Haro was the ideal centre for blending wine brought in by cart from as far away as Rioja Baja. The Bordeaux merchants showed how to age it in small barrels, and thus were born many of Haro's most important bodegas, all founded around 1890 and clustered about the railway station – some even with their own platforms.

Until the 1970s most Rioja was juicy stuff made by small-scale farmers (in villages such as San Vicente you can still see stone *lagares*, or troughs, behind half-open doors hung with the handwritten claim *Se Vende Rioja*). Blending and *élevage*, not even winemaking, let alone geography, were the key. Rioja was fermented fast and then aged for many years in old American oak. The result was pale wines, sweet with vanilla, that could be beguiling provided the grapes were of impeccable quality. With the bottlers' control on growers so dangerously loose, however, the temptation to cut corners and increase yields has at times been overpowering.

The end of the 20th century saw a revision in winemaking techniques in many bodegas (most of which now make their own wine, if not grow their own grapes). The thin-skinned, gentle Tempranillo was macerated much longer and bottled much earlier, after ageing in oak that was often French rather than American. The result was wine that was deeper and fruitier – in short, more modern. But today a return to more traditional styles is perceptible, not just from the old practitioners but from such new practitioners as Bodega Valenciso at Ollauri.

New French oak had been introduced to the region in 1970 by the Marqués de Cáceres bodega at Cenicero, the midpoint of Rioja without extremes of climate. Grapes grown west of here tend to have more acid and tannin, those to the east, less. Another, less controversial, development is the rise of single-estate wines such as Allende, Contino, Remelluri, and Valpiedra, and a new breed of younger, terroir-driven producers such as Abel Mendoza, Olivier Rivière, David Sampedro, and Tom Puyaubert (Exopto) whose model is more Burgundian than Bordelais.

About a seventh of all the vines grown in Rioja produce white grapes, almost invariably the tart Viura (Macabeo) supplemented by limited amounts of Malvasía Riojana and Garnacha Blanca. Easy-drinking neutrality with a good fresh cut is the most the majority aim for – a pity, because oak-aged white Rioja, enriched and refined for a decade or two in barrel and bottle, can challenge the greatest whites of Bordeaux. López de Heredia is the name to conjure with. Its Viña Tondonia (white and red) is one of the great originals.

The two top left were founded in the late 19th century. Owned by CVNE, another survivor from this period, Contino is an example of the new, single-estate Riojas. The other three producers are much younger, but showcase the greatness of older vines.

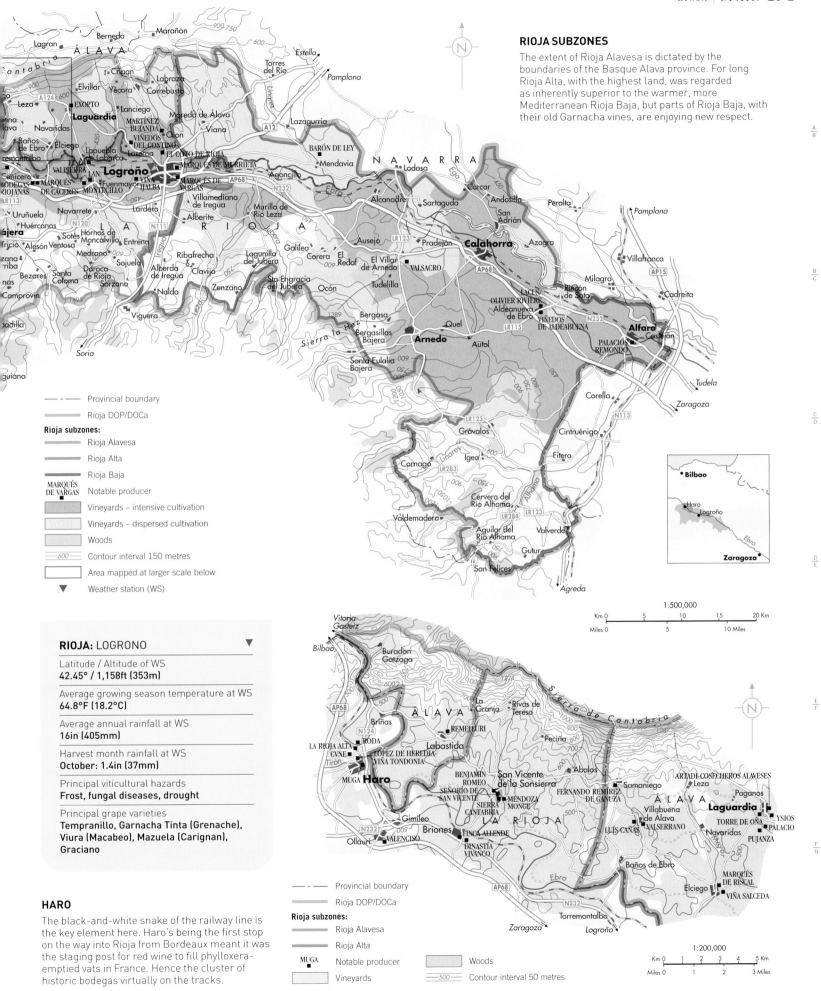

RIOJA SUBZONES

The extent of Rioja Alavesa is dictated by the boundaries of the Basque Alava province. For long Rioja Alta, with the highest land, was regarded as inherently superior to the warmer, more Mediterranean Rioja Baja, but parts of Rioja Baja, with their old Garnacha vines, are enjoying new respect.

Provincial boundary
Rioja DOP/DOCa
Rioja subzones:
Rioja Alavesa
Rioja Alta
Rioja Baja
MARQUÉS DE VARGAS Notable producer
Vineyards – intensive cultivation
Vineyards – dispersed cultivation
Woods
600 Contour interval 150 metres
Area mapped at larger scale below
▼ Weather station (WS)

1:500,000

RIOJA: LOGRONO ▼

Latitude / Altitude of WS
42.45° / 1,158ft (353m)

Average growing season temperature at WS
64.8°F (18.2°C)

Average annual rainfall at WS
16in (405mm)

Harvest month rainfall at WS
October: 1.4in (37mm)

Principal viticultural hazards
Frost, fungal diseases, drought

Principal grape varieties
Tempranillo, Garnacha Tinta (Grenache), Viura (Macabeo), Mazuela (Carignan), Graciano

HARO

The black-and-white snake of the railway line is the key element here. Haro's being the first stop on the way into Rioja from Bordeaux meant it was the staging post for red wine to fill phylloxera-emptied vats in France. Hence the cluster of historic bodegas virtually on the tracks.

Provincial boundary
Rioja DOP/DOCa
Rioja subzones:
Rioja Alavesa
Rioja Alta
MUGA Notable producer
Vineyards
Woods
500 Contour interval 50 metres

1:200,000

Catalunya

Catalunya (Catalonia in English) has convinced the world – or least most certainly itself – that it is a country apart from Spain. A visitor to Barcelona and its coast feels it in the air. From its culture to its gastronomy, Barcelona is one of Europe's dynamic cities, as close to France as to Castile. Catalans are not given to siestas; they are busy, and on the wine front, exceptionally creative. Between the Mediterranean conditions of their coast to a much cooler subalpine climate in their northern hills they have the chance of a vast range of wines. And they don't waste it.

Most obviously, on shelves and wine lists throughout Spain, there is **Cava**, Spain's answer to champagne, of which 95% is produced in Catalunya, mainly from the vineyards on the fertile plateau, 600ft (200m) up in and around the wine capital of Sant Sadurní d'Anoia in Penedès. The industry, for that is what it is, is dominated by arch-competitors Codorníu and Freixenet. The winemaking method may be that of Champagne; the grapes are very different. Macabeo dominates most Cava blends, its late budding promising good insurance against spring frost. Distinctive local flavour, occasionally too much flavour, comes from the local Xarel-lo, best planted at lower altitudes. The relatively neutral Parellada yields appley wine of real crispness, at least in the northern Penedès, if not allowed to overproduce. Chardonnay constitutes about 5% of all plantings while Pinot Noir is permitted for the increasingly popular pink

Cava. Lower yields and longer bottle ageing are steadily improving the quality of the best Cava.

For still wines, which tend to have particularly frank, direct flavours, **Penedès** is the leading DO. International vine varieties are more widespread in Penedès than anywhere else in Spain; it was here they began, in the 1960s, with such pioneers as Jean León and Miguel Torres, the Catalan giant of still wine producers. Having made the point with Cabernet and Milmanda Chardonnay (Milmanda is in the quite distinct inland **Conca de Barberá** region, on limestone hills north of Tarragona), the Torres bodega now showcases local Catalan grapes for its extraordinary and original red (also grown in Conca de Barberá), Grans Muralles. The increasingly common **Catalunya** DO, which encompasses all Catalan regions and sanctions blending between them, was introduced in 1999, largely because the expanding Torres operation found the Penedès appellation too constricting.

The hottest, lowest vineyards of the Baix-Penedès by the coast pour forth Monastrell, Garnacha, and Cariñena for blended dry(ish) reds. At medium altitudes Cava is the main thing, but more ambitious growers, often with vineyards carved out of the Mediterranean scrub and pines on higher land, up to 2,600ft (800m), are doing their best to squeeze serious local character out of relatively low-yielding vines, both indigenous and imported varieties.

The **Tarragona** DO, immediately west of Penedès around the city of that name, also supplies raw material for Cava in its hills, but the eastern coastal plain still produces its traditional sweet, heavy red wine, sometimes long aged in barrel to take on a *rancio* character.

Higher, western vineyards have their own DO of **Montsant**, encircling the Priorat DOCa described overleaf. The greatest concentration of notable bodegas is around Falset, a high-altitude one-horse town that is the gateway to Priorat but lies just outside it. Seriously concentrated dry reds can be produced here from a wide range of grape varieties, although they lack the benefit of Priorat's distinguishing soil. Celler de Capçanes and Joan d'Anguera set the pace here, while world-class Garnacha is grown in the Espectacle vineyard of Cannan-Barbier.

To the south and west in the high country of the hot, sunny **Terra Alta** DO, imported red varieties have been replacing the region's Garnacha Blanca, which can make full-bodied whites of some character. Vinos Piñol and the natural wine pioneer Laureano Serres make refined red Garnacha and Cariñena.

The **Costers del Segre** DO is only hinted at on this map, consisting of seven widely scattered subzones (see the map of Spain on p.182). Les Garrigues is just over the Montsant range from fashionable Priorat in similar, though slightly less wild, terrain. Old Garnacha and Macabeo bush-vines at altitudes of up to 2,460ft (750m) have considerable potential, but now it is Tempranillo and international varieties that are being trellised among the almonds and olives. Breezes from the Mediterranean minimize the risk of frost.

Lightish but spicy international varietal wines are made on lower ground to the northeast in the Valls del Riu Corb zone, while Artesa de Segre, way to the north, has more in common with Somontano to the west in Aragón. And then there is the vast Raimat estate, quite literally an oasis in the semi-desert northwest of Lleida, thanks to

Many of the labels here are in Catalan rather than Castilian Spanish. The bottom two labels are of some of the finest Cava, both 100% Catalan wines, the Gramona proudly based on the Catalan grape Xarel-lo, which is enjoying a revival.

COASTAL CATALUNYA

This is a complicated map, and it doesn't include the outlying wine zones of Catalunya (see map on p.182), many of which are increasingly worthy of serious interest.

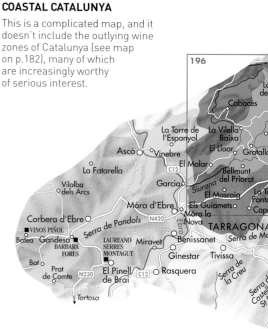

Through his pupils and disciples, modernist Catalan architect Gaudí influenced the design of many a bodega, particularly the co-operatives that proliferated in the early 20th century. This wine cathedral is the Gandesa co-op in Terra Alta, designed in 1919 by César Martinell (after which one of its wine is named).

an irrigation system developed by the Raventós family of Codorníu. The wines produced here are more New World than Catalan.

On the coast immediately north of Barcelona the vine-growers of **Alella** do battle with its real-estate developers and have also leapt aboard the international varietal bandwagon.

Off this detailed map, but on the introductory map of Spain, is the **Pla de Bages** DO, centred on the town of Manresa, due north of Barcelona. Although it has some interesting old Picapoll (called Clairette in Languedoc), it too is being planted with Cabernet and Chardonnay. The northernmost of Catalunya's DOs, **Empordà** on the Costa Brava, used to be known only for its tourist rosé made from Cariñena. Today it offers a burgeoning range of well-made blends, both red and white, and many in the image of the best of Roussillon over the Pyrenees. All in all, Catalunya could be said to be in full ferment.

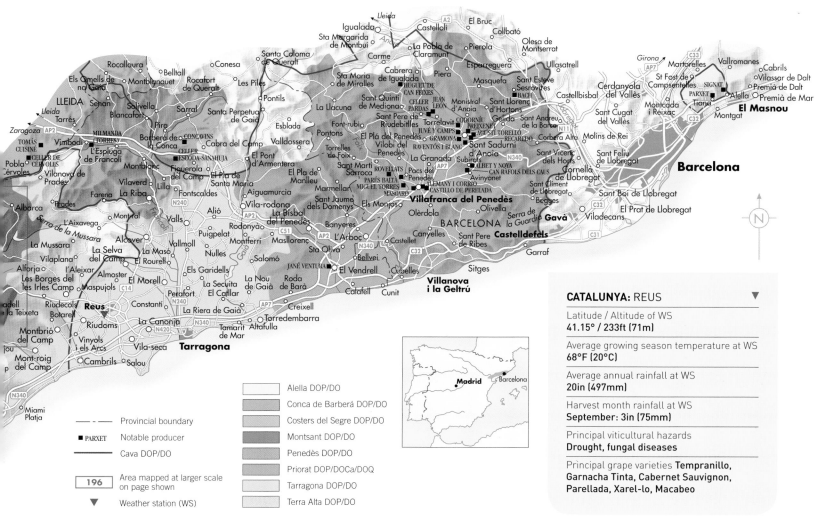

| Provincial boundary |
| **■ PARXET** Notable producer |
| Cava DOP/DO |
| 196 Area mapped at larger scale on page shown |
| ▼ Weather station (WS) |

	Alella DOP/DO
	Conca de Barberá DOP/DO
	Costers del Segre DOP/DO
	Montsant DOP/DO
	Penedès DOP/DO
	Priorat DOP/DOCa/DOQ
	Tarragona DOP/DO
	Terra Alta DOP/DO

CATALUNYA: REUS ▼

Latitude / Altitude of WS
41.15° / 233ft (71m)

Average growing season temperature at WS
68°F (20°C)

Average annual rainfall at WS
20in (497mm)

Harvest month rainfall at WS
September: 3in (75mm)

Principal viticultural hazards
Drought, fungal diseases

Principal grape varieties **Tempranillo, Garnacha Tinta, Cabernet Sauvignon, Parellada, Xarel-lo, Macabeo**

Priorat

Priorat is not a name you will find in old reference books. In the first, 1971, edition of this one it appeared only as "Priorato [the Castilian name], a strong dry red wine". Yet before the arrival of phylloxera there were 12,350 acres (5,000ha) of vineyards in this dizzying landscape of crinkle-folded hills (this is not country for the nervous driver). By 1979, when René Barbier of Clos Mogador first saw the potential of this historic region, there were only 1,500 acres (600ha) of mainly Cariñena (Carignan) vines left. In 1989 he persuaded five friends to share winemaking premises and grapes in the village of Gratallops. Their wines were quite distinct from the rustic, raisiny ferments that were then standard for Priorat – concentrated, mineral-laden wines that were very different from the oaky Spanish norm.

Inspired, the pioneers soon set up bodegas of their own. Such was the international acclaim for these wines (their scarcity helped, too) that the region has since been invaded and quite literally reshaped by incomers – some from Penedès, some from as far away as South Africa. By the turn of this century there were 2,500 acres (1,000ha) either under vine or being bulldozed into tractor-friendly terraces ready for planting, with another 2,500 acres earmarked by planting rights. Now bodegas number 90, and all this activity has been superimposed on a region where shepherds and donkey carts were until very recently commonplace.

So why are the wines so special? Priorat is admittedly protected from the northwest by the Sierra de Montsant, a long ridge of craggy outcrops. But it is its particularly unusual soil, llicorella, a dark-brown slate whose jagged rock faces sparkle in the sun with their sprinkling of quartzite, that makes the best Priorat the almost chewable essence that it is. Annual rainfall is often less than 16in (400mm) a year, which in most wine regions would make irrigation a necessity. Priorat's soils are unusually cool and damp, however, so that the vine roots tunnel Douro-style through faults in the llicorella to find water. The result in the best sites is almost ridiculously low yields of arrestingly concentrated wine.

Cariñena is still the most widely planted vine by far and, especially in the north of the region around Torroja and Poboleda, the vines are old enough to yield top-quality grapes, vinified by (among others) Terroir al Lìmit, Trio Infernal, Mas Doix, and Cims de Porrera. Ancient Garnacha planted in cooler, slower-ripening sites such as L'Ermita vineyard is also highly valued, but of the more recently planted imports, only Syrah seems successful. Garnacha and Cariñena are favoured by the rules of Vi de Vila, or village, wines that were introduced in 2009.

Alvaro Palacios's L'Ermita was the wine that put Priorat on the map and is one of Spain's most expensive wines. His counterpart in South Africa, Eben Sadie, was originally involved in Terroir al Límit.

1:146,000

| Km 0 | 1 | 2 | 3 | 4 | 5 Km |
| Miles 0 | | 1 | | 2 | 3 Miles |

- - - - - - Municipal boundary
———— Priorat DOP/DOCa/DOQ
———— Montsant DOP/DO
EL LLOAR Vi de Vila/Vin de Vila
MAS MARTINET Notable producer
Gran Clos Named vineyard
Vineyards
Woods
—500— Contour interval 100 metres

PRIORAT'S VILLAGE WINES

The 12 village zones of the Vi de Vila, or village wine, scheme are mapped above. Montsant is on Priorat's southern doorstep but lacks the special llicorella soil that can be tasted in so many of the wines produced in the topographical cocktail that is Priorat.

Andalucía – Sherry Country

For perhaps 20 centuries, perhaps more, wine in Andalucía meant *vinos generosos*, **a self-translating term: in modern terms sherry above all, but also the similar-but-different wines of Montilla-Moriles and Málaga.** Sherry is arguably, indeed, still Spain's greatest wine – but modern history here has been moving in other directions. Breakneck development on the Costa del Sol has been matched by the rapid spread of vineyards destined for unfortified wines, both dry and, more surprisingly, sweet.

The key to producing wines with freshness as well as southern ripeness is, yet again, altitude. The mountains rise straight up from the villas, golf courses, and building sites along the coast. A vineyard planted just a few miles from the Mediterranean could well be more than 2,600ft (800m) above the sparkling blue sea, its nights as cool as the days are hot.

Málaga

The **Málaga** DO once applied exclusively to seriously diminishing quantities of wine made sweet and strong either by adding grape spirit during fermentation or by drying the grapes, but in 2001 it was transformed into Málaga and Sierras de Málaga (see the map on p.182). Málaga is used for both fortified wines between 15 and 22% alcohol and naturally sweet wines over 13% which depend entirely on the Andalucían sunshine for their sugar and alcohol. **Sierras de Málaga** is the DO for the dry wines under 15% that have proliferated from the rash of newer plantings.

The most dynamic subzone is around the hilltop tourist magnet of Ronda, where there have been considerable plantings of international varieties, including Petit Verdot and unexpectedly successful Pinot Noir, as well as Tempranillo. For white wines, the Montilla-Moriles grape Pedro Ximénez, Moscatels, and Macabeo are allowed, as well as Sauvignon Blanc and Chardonnay, which the F Schatz bodega, to name one, has made into something quite surprising, considering the latitude.

There are other subzones: those on the coast well west of here towards Cádiz, where Moscatel reigns and both Atlantic and Mediterranean influences are felt; the large plateau well north of the town of Málaga towards Montilla-Moriles, where limestone under russet soils ripens Pedro Ximénez and the local Doradilla of surprising finesse; the rugged Axarquia Mountains to the east, best known for Moscatel and the local grape

Romé grown on slate; and historic but almost extinct vineyards in the hills around Málaga itself.

While the Sierras de Málaga wines are remarkable for their existence this far south, it is Málaga itself, in its two forms, light or treacley, that is most distinctive. Bodegas Málaga Virgen and Gomara continue to make a dazzling array of traditional *vinos generosos*. At the same time Telmo Rodríguez, orginally from Rioja but a force for good in several parts of Spain, revived Málaga Moscatel as a fresh, fragrant but delicate wine with his tangy, tangerine-flavoured Molino Real. It was left to a creative US-based importer of Spanish wines, Jorge Ordóñez, himself a native of Málaga, to trump this with a nectar made from ancient Moscatel vines grown high in the hills. Almijara's Jarel is another notable example.

As fast as DOs are created they are overtaken by creative winemakers. The hinterland of the Costa del Sol, the most mountainous part of Spain, has even been described as the new La Mancha

in terms of expansion. Some of the Vinos de la Tierra made around Granada, at altitudes of up to 4,485ft (1,386m) for Barranco Oscuro's vineyard, continental Europe's highest, suggest that this may eventually be one of Spain's most exciting regions for unfortified wines. Barranco Oscuro and H Calvente are the names to look out for.

Chalk and grapes

But what of Jerez-Xérès-Sherry and Montilla-Moriles, the heart of Andalucía's wine industry for 2,000 years? Upwardly mobile they are not, with both a surplus of grapes and, shockingly for those of us who treasure unique qualities in wine, a deficit of customers. Despite this widespread and misplaced apathy towards sherry outside Andalucía, **Jerez** has seen the recent emergence of some exceptional new bodegas to add to its roster of great names: Fernando de Castilla, Bodegas Tradición, and Equipo Navazos, a particularly fastidious small-scale négociant.

Jerez's chalk-white *albariza* soil retains moisture that is invaluable for the relatively neutral-tasting Palomino Fino grapes during a growing season when not a drop of rain may fall. Emilio Lustau's Montegilillo vineyards are near Carrascal just north of Jerez.

And Valdespino winemaker Eduardo Ojeda and criminal law professor Jesús Barquín have unexpectedly breathed new life into fine sherry by unearthing and bottling great individual casks or butts (*bota*) in the bodegas of Jerez, Sanlúcar, and Montilla.

Sherry's great distinction is finesse. It is a question of chalk, of the breed of the Palomino Fino grape, of huge investment and long-inherited skill. Not every bottle of sherry, by a very long way, has this quality – in fact the sherry aristocracy could be said to have been ruined by the high proportion of poor wine shipped from Jerez in the 1970s and 1980s. But a real fino or manzanilla, the finely judged produce of the bare white chalk dunes of Macharnudo or Sanlúcar de Barrameda, is an expression of wine and wood as vivid and beautiful as any in the world.

The sherry country, between the romantic-sounding cities of Cádiz and Seville, is almost a caricature of grandee Spain. Here are the patios, the guitars, the flamenco dancers, the night-turned-into-day. Jerez de la Frontera, the town that gives its name to sherry, lives and breathes sherry as Beaune does burgundy and Epernay champagne – even if consolidation, closure, and takeover have meant that there are far, far fewer sherry exporters than there were even 10 years ago.

The comparison of sherry with champagne can be carried a long way. Both are white wines with a distinction given them by chalk soil, both needing long traditional treatment to achieve their special characters. Both are revivifying apéritifs, of which you can drink an astonishing amount in their home countries and only feel more alive than you have ever felt before. They are the far-northern and the far-southern European interpretation of the same equation: the white grape from the white ground.

Not all the ground is white. The chalk areas (*albarizas*) are best; the *pagos* (districts) of Carrascal, Macharnudo, Añina, and Balbaína the most famous. Some vineyards are on *barros* (dark lands) and sand and produce second-rank wines for blending – although sandy coastal vineyards can suit Moscatel grapes well.

The shippers' headquarters and bodegas are in the sherry towns of Sanlúcar, El Puerto de Santa María, and, especially, Jerez. There are little bars in each of these towns where the tapas, the morsels of food without which no Andalucían puts glass to mouth, constitute a banquet. Your *copita*, a glass no more imposing than an opening tulip, fills and empties with a paler wine, a cooler wine, a more druggingly delicious wine than you have ever tasted – although even this is a tradition on the wane. Such a fine wine, say modern connoisseurs, needs as big a glass as burgundy.

The most celebrated sights of Jerez are the historic bodegas. Their towering whitewashed aisles, crisscrossed with sunbeams, are irresistibly cathedral-like. In them, in ranks of butts typically three tiers high, the new wine is put to mature. Most will not leave until they have gone through the elaborate blending process of the solera system, although wines of notable distinction may be sold unblended, either as a single vintage wine, a fairly recent revival designed to kick-start the connoisseur market for sherry, or one straight from an *almacenista*, or stockholder.

When fermentation of the new wine is complete, it is sorted into categories: better or worse, lighter or more full-bodied. Then each wine begins its journey within the solera system, which is simply a progressive topping-up of older barrels from younger of the same style. The new wine is put into the youngest level of a specific *criadera* or nursery (the Spanish term reflecting the idea of raising children) according to its category. Each year a proportion of wine from the solera, the oldest and final stage of the *criadera*, is bottled so that the younger wines move up into the next nursery class to continue their education. The more stages, the finer the wine.

Styles of sherry

All young sherry is originally classified as either a wine light and delicate enough to be a fino, or a fuller wine that is classified as an oloroso. A fino, light in alcohol, will mature under a protective, bread-like layer of a strange Jerez yeast called flor. Olorosos are matured in contact with air and deliberately fortified to more than 15.5% alcohol, normally 17.5%, to prevent the growth of flor.

Sherries bottled as finos are the finest and palest: distinctive, bone-dry wines which need a minimum of blending. Even lighter and drier are the manzanillas of Sanlúcar de Barrameda, made just like a fino and blessed with a faintly salty tang which is believed to come from the sea. An aged manzanilla (the term is *pasada*) is sublime with seafood. You need look no further than the most popular (and mostly rapidly drunk) brands – Tio Pepe for fino, La Gitana for manzanilla – for a good example.

Amontillado, a darker, more complicated wine, is the next category. The best amontillados are old finos, finos which lacked the perfect zing for drinking young and put on weight with age – although the name has more often been used for export blends that are medium in every sense

Working with the flames that toast the interior of oak barrels must be particularly punishing in the heat of Andalucía, but sherry would not be sherry without the barrels, or butts. New barrels are eschewed for sherry and have to be broken in for many years – 20 or more – with table wines.

JEREZ: JEREZ DE LA FRONTERA ▼

Latitude / Altitude of WS
36.75° / 89ft (27m)

Average growing season temperature at WS
71.4°F (21.9°C)

Average annual rainfall at WS
23in (582mm)

Harvest month rainfall at WS
August: 0.2in (5mm)

Principal viticultural hazards
Drought

Principal grape varieties
Palomino Fino, Pedro Ximénez

of the word. True classical oloroso, dry, dark, and biting, is less common, but a great favourite with Jerezanos themselves. Such wines can age superbly but are too heavy for a fino solera. Commercial brands labelled oloroso or cream are younger, coarser examples blended with sweetening wines; pale cream is similar but robbed of colour. Palo cortado, on the other hand, is a true, classical, rich-yet-dry rarity, something between amontillado and oloroso.

In a further attempt to attract fine wine drinkers to their neglected wines, sherry producers have devised a way of signalling and certifying notable age and quality: VOS and VORS sherries are more than 20 and 30 years old respectively. And 12- and 15 year-old designations of age have also been implemented.

But no blend – medium-sweet or sweet as most blends are – can compare with the best natural sherries. They are as much collectors' pieces as the great domaine-bottled burgundies. They are also the least expensive fine wines in the world.

Montilla

Like the sherry region, sandier **Montilla-Moriles** just south of Córdoba (its name incorporates two of its towns), is also shrinking. By 2010, it was down to 15,320 acres (6,200ha). Until 50 years ago its produce was blended in Jerez as though the two regions were one.

But Montilla is different. The Montilla grape is not Palomino but Pedro Ximénez, which is still regularly shipped to Jerez for making sweet wine there. Montilla's much higher altitude and more extreme climate naturally results in even stronger musts, which has always allowed it to be shipped without fortification, in contrast to sherry. Unlike sherry, Montilla loses alcohol as it ages and very old examples may be little more than 10% from cask. Once the two-year minimum ageing period is up the wine is ready, heavier but softer than sherry, slipping down like table wine. The blackest, stickiest, most tooth-rottingly syrupy renditions have recently enjoyed the spotlight of fashion, in Spain at least, and are far from overpriced. Alvear, Toro Albalá, and Pérez Barquero are the bodegas that set the standard.

THE SOILS OF JEREZ

When sales were booming in the early 1980s, all sorts of soils were used for sherry production. But the total sherry vineyard has shrunk by more than half since then and the great majority of the remaining vines are on the best, *albariza* soils (see p.197).

Provincial boundary
Jerez DOP/DO
Tehigo   Vineyard area
Chalk soil
Clay and sandy soil
200   Contour interval 100 metres
▼   Weather station (WS)

There are signs of life in sherry production. Each of the three left-most and the Solear Manzanilla labels are for what might be called connoisseur bottlings of barely filtered sherries. The other two labels on the top row are fine Montillas, while the remaining two labels are very fine Málaga Moscatels.

PORTUGAL

Harvest time in this top-rated vineyard above Pinhão in the Cima Corgo subregion of the Douro Valley

Portugal

Portugal's isolation, cut off behind Spain on the Atlantic fringe of Europe, has given the country a unique selling point a more eager marketer might never have thought of. While other countries were all busy planting French vines, Portugal stuck to her indigenous varieties and her unreconstructed tastes. And these grapes include a number with qualities capable of beguiling a much wider world.

Touriga Nacional, for example, has emerged as Portugal's flagship red variety. While its heartland is the Dão and Douro (where this once minor player is now major in both port and table wines), it has taken hold throughout the country, typically as the lead variety in blends. Touriga Franca is another port grape clearly capable of making the transition from fortified to less potent wine, while Trincadeira (the Tinta Amarela of port) has great richness, and Jaen (Mencía in Spain's Galicia)

can make distinguished, juicy young wine. And these are not the only ones. The grape known as Tempranillo in Spain is also extremely successful in Portugal, called Tinta Roriz in the north and Aragonês in the south. In Bairrada, Baga makes Portugal's most age-worthy and distinguished single-variety reds, while the balance of Alfrocheiro is increasingly valued, even outside Dão.

But in this century Portugal has emerged as a serious white wine producer, too. The quality of Vinho Verde has improved enormously (see p.204). Arinto, the dominant variety of the Bucelas region, is increasingly prized for the acidity it brings to blends, especially in Alentejo. Bairrada's Bical can also age well, and Encruzado, native to the Dão region, has great potential for full-bodied, rather burgundian whites. Perhaps most surprising of all is the torrid Douro's ability to produce such exciting, full-bodied white blends of grapes such as Viosinho, Rabigato, Côdega de Larinho, and Gouveio (Spain's Godello). And this is without taking into account the great white grapes of Portugal's wine island, Madeira (see p.214).

Portugal has retained her individuality, but she has at long last joined the greater world of wine, as the following pages demonstrate. This contrasts strongly with all the years when Portugal was known to the world's wine drinkers only for her great sweet fortified wine, port (examined in detail on p.209), and the country's other wine style conceived specifically for export in the

mid-20th century – wines neither red nor white, sweet nor dry, still nor sparkling – of which Mateus and Lancers were the leading ambassadors.

The country is not vast, but different regions are subject to the very different influences of Atlantic, Mediterranean, and even continental climates. Soils, too, vary enormously: granite, slate, and schist in the north and inland; limestone, clay, and sand by the coast; and the schist that, once again, finds favour among quality-focused producers in the south.

A new generation

Portugal's table wines have caught up fast with the evolution in modern winemaking, thanks to a new generation of well-educated Portuguese winemakers who have played their part in capturing the fruit of Portugal's distinctive grape varieties in the bottle, and in producing wines that do not require ageing for a decade before they are drinkable. Not that Portuguese wine has been without laws and regulations. The Douro lays claim to be the world's first demarcated and regulated wine region (in 1756), and long before Portugal's entry into the EU in 1986 many other districts had been demarcated and every aspect of their wines controlled. This was not always to the benefit of their quality, or to the liking of merchants and their local clients, who routinely ignored what the law prescribed to blend the kinds of wines they preferred, typically labelled Garrafeira.

In most of the Alentejo, the scale is big, wide and open, as in this vineyard near Reguengos de Monsaraz, the most important wine town in a region that accounts for almost a third of Portugal's land mass.

THE LANGUAGE OF THE LABEL

QUALITY DESIGNATIONS

Denominação de Origem Controlada (DOC) Portugal's answer to France's AOC/AOP (see p.46) and equivalent to the EU's Denominações de Origem Protegidas (DOP)

Indicações Geográficas Protegidas (IGP) the EU denomination that is gradually replacing Vinho Regional (VR)

Vinho or **Vinho de Portugal** the basic EU denomination replacing the old Vinho de Mesa

OTHER COMMON EXPRESSIONS

Adega winery

Amarzém or **Cave** cellar

Branco white

Colheita vintage

Doce sweet

Engarrafado (na origem) bottled (estate bottled)

Garrafeira merchant's special reserve

Maduro old or mature

Quinta farm or estate

Rosado rosé, pink

Séco dry

Tinto red

Verde young

Vinha vineyard

Portugal's wine map, like that of Spain, has sprouted a rash of demarcated regions. The regulations of Portugal's DOCs (DOPs), emulating those of France's Appellations d'Origine Contrôlées (AOCs/AOPs), prescribe the permitted local grape varieties. Increasingly important, however, is the Vinho Regional (VR/IGP) category of wines from much larger regions and with more flexible regulations. The map shows the approved wine names; the key reveals their status. **Duriense** is a Vinho Regional generally used for declassified Douro wines, for example, typically made from international, or at least non-local, grape varieties such as Syrah, Sauvignon Blanc, Alvarinho, and Sémillon.

The productive **Tejo** region is named after the River Tagus (Tejo), which flows southwest from the Spanish border to Lisbon. The fertile river banks used to produce vast quantities of decidedly light wine, but towards the end of the last century EU subsidies persuaded hundreds of growers here to uproot their vines. Total production has shrunk and the focus of Tejo wine production has now moved away from the riverbank towards the clays of the north and sandier scrub in the south. There has also been a move towards the nobler indigenous grapes, notably Touriga Nacional and Alicante Bouschet (which enjoys honorary Portuguese status), as well as imports such as Cabernet Sauvignon, Merlot, and more recently Syrah (which seems to have a promising future in Portugal). Fruity, if relatively simple, Castelão is the most important local red wine grape although some Trincadeira is also grown. Whites are typically based on the arrestingly perfumed Fernão Pires, although Chardonnay, Sauvignon Blanc, Arinto, and latterly Alvarinho and Viognier have made promising inroads.

In the south of Portugal the Vinho Regional category is much more important than DOC, so that most Algarve wine, for instance, is sold as Vinho Regional **Algarve** rather than under the name of one of its four DOCs. Algarve wine quality has risen as the hold of the co-ops, and quantity produced, has shrunk. The Azores in the middle of the Atlantic grow some of the same grapes as Madeira but without such dramatic results.

The grapevine is not the only plant in Portugal of interest to wine drinkers. The southern half of the country has the world's greatest concentration of cork oaks, so that Portugal is the principal supplier of wine corks. It is a brave Portuguese wine producer who pursues a screw-capped path.

PORTUGAL'S WINE REGIONS

Portugal has been working on rationalizing its wine nomenclature. Names in red apply to the most precise, often historic, wines while those in black refer to an IGP or Vinho Regional with looser regulations.

— · — · — International boundary

BAIRRADA DOP/DOC

MINHO IGP/Vinho Regional

▢ Land 500-1000 metres

▢ Land above 1000 metres

▢ 212 Area mapped at larger scale on page shown

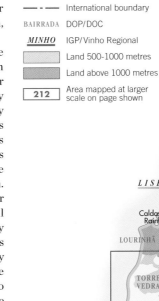

1:2,500,000

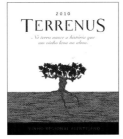

Malhadinha and Terrenus are made in the south and north of Alentejo, respectively, while Porta Velha is a well-priced blend from Trás-os-Montes, and Lagoalva de Cima Alfrocheiro is grown in Tejo.

Vinho Verde

Of Portugal's many wildly differing styles of wine, the most singular remains Vinho Verde, the youthful "green" (*verde*, as opposed to *maduro*, or aged) wine of the northernmost province, the **Minho**. The Minho is the river that defines the northern frontier between Portugal and Spanish Galicia. Its province accounts for an eighth of Portugal's wine harvest. Green is an apt word for this Atlantic-washed region's verdant landscape, and for many years it was also appropriate for the tart wines it produced made from grapes that were less than fully ripe.

This has changed dramatically, however, as the domestic market for the most basic, thinnest Vinho Verde has shrivelled and a new generation of vine-growers and winemakers is favouring quality over quantity. The Minho is Portugal's wettest region, and well-watered vines, unless disciplined, tend to sprout leaves rather than ripen fruit. But these days vines are trained on trellises designed to maximize ripeness rather than being allowed to climb unfettered up granite posts – the dominant stone here – and even trees. More ambitious farmers are planting their most fertile and prolific sites by streams with other crops, while winemakers do what they can to preserve and enhance every nuance of fruit and aroma. In the past Vinho Verde was often 9–10% alcohol. The more commercial examples had to have their searing acidity disguised by added sweetness and fizz. Today's wines are in the main perfectly well balanced and can occasionally reach natural alcohol levels as high as 14% – quite a transformation in a very short time.

As Vinho Verde producers have become more focused on export markets, white wines have become much more important than the tart, deep-purple Vinho Verde once drunk in great quantity locally, sometimes in white china bowls. The local Vinhão grape dominates the production of red Vinho Verde, the best of which can be bracingly fruity. Most white Vinho Verde on the other hand is made from a blend of grapes, typically including Azal, Loureiro (Loureira in northwest Spain), Trajadura (Treixadura), Avesso, and Arinto, (here known as Paderná). The exception to this is the growing amount of very fine Vinho Verde made exclusively from the regional celebrity grape, Alvarinho, which grows as well in the northernmost subregion, **Monção and Melgaço**, as it does in Rías Baixas just across the River Minho in Spain as Albariño.

The Loureiro-only wines made in the **Lima** subregion immediately south of Monção and Melgaço are also extremely convincing, often the ripest and most complex white Vinho Verdes, some of them even robust enough to take oak maturation, and deeper-flavoured than their Spanish counterparts.

Altitude and proximity to the Atlantic are the major influences on wine grape choices and their results in the subregions of this large area. The average rainfall in Monção and Melgaço is around 47in (1200mm) compared to 55–63in (1400–1600mm) in Lima. Hills shelter Monção and Melgaço from the ocean and its influence, making this subregion relatively dry and warm, although it is high enough for nights to be usefully cool. Similarly, the areas most likely to produce high-quality red Vinho Verde are well inland, in the interior of Lima, in Basto, Amarante, and Paiva in the extreme south.

MONCAO AND MELGACO

The locator map below left and the country map on p.203 show just how small a proportion of the Vinho Verde zone is mapped below. But this is because the Monção and Melgaço subregion produces such a high proportion of the finest wines in this rapidly improving region.

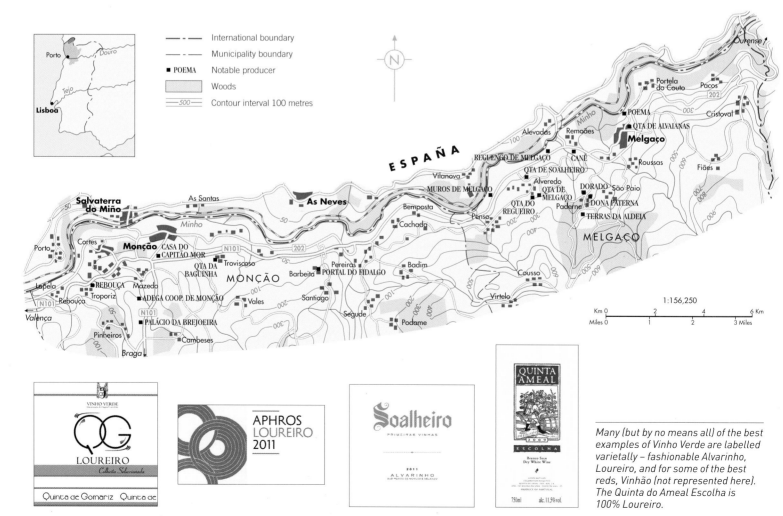

Many (but by no means all) of the best examples of Vinho Verde are labelled varietally – fashionable Alvarinho, Loureiro, and for some of the best reds, Vinhão (not represented here). The Quinta do Ameal Escolha is 100% Loureiro.

Douro – Port Country

The Douro Valley, the home of port, has embraced a new vocation. After centuries of being known only for fortified wine labelled port, it has now established an international reputation for its distinctive unfortified wines labelled Douro DOC (or the more flexible Duriense VR). With the determined exception of the Fladgate Partnership, port producers invariably make table wines, too, which makes financial sense now that vineyards and wineries that were predicated on unlimited supplies of cheap labour have been redesigned. More than 6,280 acres (2,500ha) of vineyards were replanted as part of a major World Bank investment programme, typically with a handful of approved varieties rather than the traditional jumble. Just as significant, the quality of life and wages have improved notably in the region, dramatically increasing production costs and making the sort of cheap port once sold in such quantity (especially to France) almost uneconomic to produce. The economic climate of the Douro, where individual farmers, many of them smallholders, are granted the right to produce a set amount of port each year, is more fragile than ever. It is hoped that tourists will be part of the answer.

Of all the places where men have planted vineyards, the Upper Douro is the most improbable. To begin with there was hardly any soil: only 60-degree slopes of schist, flaking and unstable, baked in a 100°F (38°C) summer sun and plagued by malaria. It was a land of utter desolation and the locals were careful to settle only well above the reach of riverside mosquitoes, as can be seen by the location of most of the villages on the map overleaf.

A feat of engineering

The vine, however, is one of the few plants not quite deterred by these conditions. The harsh climate, ranging from Atlantic-influenced in the west and increasingly continental away from the coast, suits it. What was needed was simply the engineering feat of building walls along the mountainsides, thousands of them, like contour lines, to hold up the patches of ground (one could hardly call it soil) where vines could be planted. Once the ground was stabilized and rainwater no longer ran straight off – an enterprise undertaken as early as the 17th century – olives, oranges, oaks, chestnut trees, and vines flourished.

Long after phylloxera had laid waste the region's vineyards, in the efficient 1970s, some of the old stone-walled terraces were replaced by bulldozed, wider terraces (*patamares*) supported by banks of schist rather than walls. Their great advantage is that they are wide enough for tractors and mechanization. Their disadvantage is the reduction in vine density, and for this reason, but mostly because of erosion of that scarcest of commodities, soil, narrow single-row terraces are back in fashion. Wherever the angle of elevation allows, growers are now increasingly planting vine rows up, rather than across, the slope, which encourages denser planting, more even ripening, and also allows mechanization – provided the slope is less than 30%. Many of the original terraces dating from the 17th century survive in the mountains above Régua, in the original port wine zone, first delimited in 1756, which then extended only as far as the Tua tributary. Today, this area of the Cima Corgo remains the heartland of port production, but the search for quality has led further and further upstream.

The Douro reaches Portugal from Spain in a wilderness that has been accessible by road only since the late 1980s, when funds started to flood into Portugal. The river has carved a titanic canyon through the layered rock uplands: the so-called Upper Douro, or Douro Superior, the driest, flattest, least developed part of the Douro (see the

---

It is hardly surprising that the Douro Valley is a UNESCO World Heritage Site. It is truly extraordinary. In the foreground are the terraced vineyards of Quinta do Ventozelo, in the distance the town of Pinhão, one of the few on the river itself.

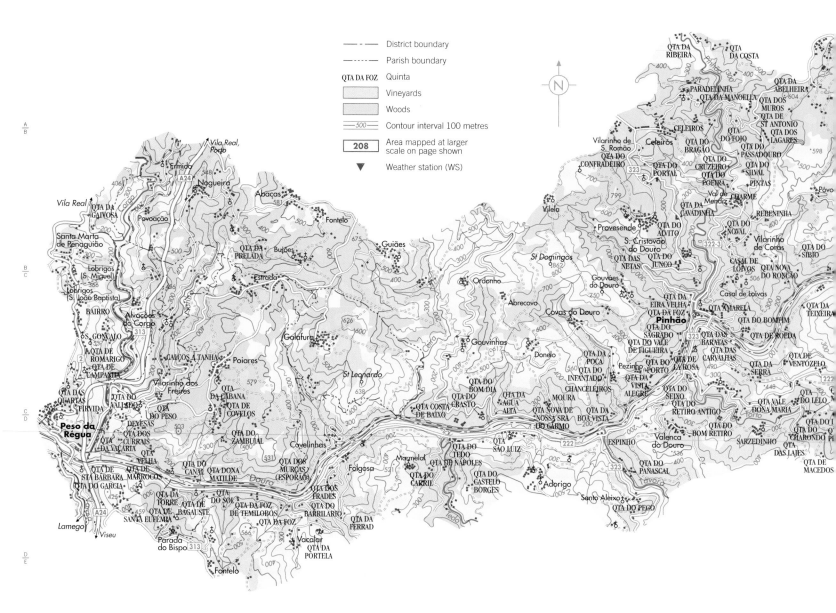

District boundary
Parish boundary
QTA DA FOZ — Quinta
Vineyards
Woods
—500— Contour interval 100 metres
208 — Area mapped at larger scale on page shown
▼ — Weather station (WS)

regional map, above right) which can, despite its extremely continental climate, produce some very fine grapes, as witness the ports of Quinta do Vesuvio and the iconic Douro DOC pioneer, Barca Velha. This easternmost part of the valley has seen a frenzy of planting in the last decade,

especially in the cooler, elevated reaches of the Douro river's left bank between the River Côa and the Spanish border (see the detailed map overleaf). With ready access to irrigation water from the river and afternoon shade, the benefits are obvious. Its steep, schist-strewn slopes are

reminiscent of the Cima Corgo but harder to work than the rest of the Upper Douro's relatively rolling landscape.

To the west, the 4,640ft (1,415m) Serra do Marão and Serra do Montemurro stop the Atlantic rain clouds of summer from refreshing the schists of the heart of port country, Cima Corgo, mapped in detail above. Average annual rainfall varies from 20in (500mm) in Douro Superior to 26in (650mm) in Cima Corgo and 35in (900mm) in the heavily planted Baixo Corgo, with the wettest, coolest climate downstream of the Corgo tributary and off the main map to the west where the basic, low-price ports are (or were) made by co-ops.

The Baixo Corgo is reckoned to be too damp for top quality. To make great port the vines have to be forced to insinuate their roots as far down into the schist as possible in their search for water, up to 26ft (8m) deep as at Quinta do Vesuvio in the east of the section mapped. Yields in this dry climate are some of the world's lowest.

The vineyards that are conventionally recognized as the best of all for port are those around and above the railway town of Pinhão,

Some of the great Douro table wines that have emerged from the valley in the last decade or so. Wine & Soul Guru and the Quinta de la Rosa are high-quality white wines. Poeira is one of the most elegant reds, while Duas Quintas is grown in the Douro Superior.

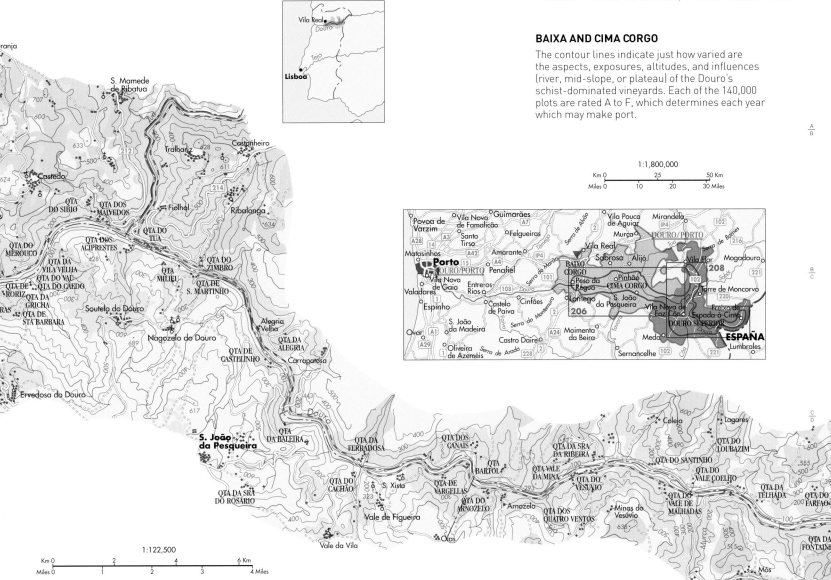

BAIXA AND CIMA CORGO

The contour lines indicate just how varied are the aspects, exposures, altitudes, and influences (river, mid-slope, or plateau) of the Douro's schist-dominated vineyards. Each of the 140,000 plots are rated A to F, which determines each year which may make port.

including the valleys of the Tedo, Távora, Torto, Pinhão, and Tua tributaries.

Because orientations and altitudes vary so dramatically, the character of wine produced even in neighbouring vineyards can be quite different. In the Tedo Valley, for instance, wine tends to be tannic, while that made just across the river around Quinta do Crasto, famous for its Douro table wine, is relatively light and fruity. The mild climate of the Torto tributary makes it good table wine country since maturation is slower and sugar levels tend to be lower than in the main Douro Valley. Higher vineyards, wherever they are, tend to ripen later and produce lighter wines, while those that face south and/or west attract the most sunlight and produce the strongest musts.

Vineyard classification

Each port vineyard is classified, from A down to F, according to its natural advantages – altitude, location, yield, soil, inclination, orientation – and the age, density, training, and varieties of vine grown on it. The higher the classification, the more money will be paid for the grapes in the highly regulated market that governs relations

between the grape growers and port producers. Until pioneering work in the 1970s by José Ramos Pinto Rosas and João Nicolau de Almeida, little was known about the vines that grew in the Douro, typically a tangled jumble of different bush-vines. They identified Touriga Nacional, Touriga Franca, Tinta Roriz (various clones of Spain's Tempranillo), Tinto Cão, and Tinta Barroca as those varieties that most regularly made the best port. These constitute the majority of the Douro's now much more disciplined vineyards, but Sousão is increasingly valued, as is Tinta Amarela in the Cima Corgo and Douro Superior.

To make white port – a local favourite – Viosinho, Gouveio, Malvasia, and Rabigato are some of the best light-skinned grapes that yearly do battle with the Douro's baking-hot summers and freezing-cold winters. More and more of these varieties, as well as Côdega de Larinho, are also being used for increasingly convincing white table wines, such as Dirk Niepoort's pioneering Redoma.

Vintage time anywhere is the climax of the year, but picking these grapes in the Douro, perhaps because of the hardship of life there, can be almost

DOURO: VILA REAL ▼

Latitude / Altitude of WS
41.32° / 1,578ft (481m)

Average growing season temperature at WS
63.4°F (17.4°C)

Average annual rainfall at WS
40.3in (1,023mm)

Harvest month rainfall at WS
September: 1.0in (27mm)

Principal viticultural hazards
Rain during fruit set, drought, erosion

Principal grape varieties
Touriga Franca, Tinta Roriz (Tempranillo), Touriga Nacional, Tinta Barroca, Tinta Amarela

Dionysiac, even if the nocturnal ritual of treading grapes to music is being systematically replaced by prosaic, computerized alternatives.

The famous shipping firms have their own quintas, or wine farms, up in the hills where they go to supervise the vintage. They are rambling

DOURO SUPERIOR

For a long time the Douro Superior was regarded as the back of beyond, but Portugal's road network has improved immeasurably recently. Now producers here are able to take advantage of this, even if the climate up here by the Spanish border is even more extreme.

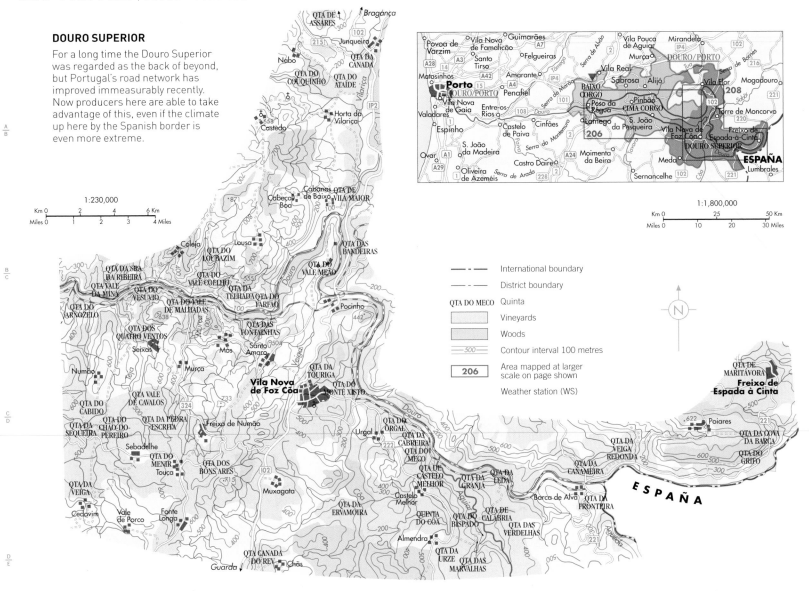

International boundary

District boundary

QTA DO MECO — Quinta

Vineyards

Woods

Contour interval 100 metres

Area mapped at larger scale on page shown

Weather station (WS)

---

white houses, vine-arboured, tile-floored, and cool in a world of dust and glare. Most of the famous port quintas are shown on the map on these pages, names that have become much more familiar since the late 1980s with the rise in single-quinta ports. Quinta do Noval, above Pinhão (renovated by AXA), has been world-famous for years, but there are now scores more "single-quinta ports", the products of a single estate in a single year, often in vintages not quite fine enough to be generally declared. Taylor, for instance, sells the wine produced on its Quinta de Vargellas in lesser vintages. But many other single-quinta ports are now produced, year in and year out, more like a Bordeaux château. The main source of grapes and wine for port, however, is still a multitude of small farmers, even if more and more of them are being tempted to sell what they make under the name of their own quintas.

This is particularly true for the table wines – all labelled Douro – that have been emerging from this spectacular valley since international investment arrived. Winemaking niceties such as temperature control have revolutionized the lives of the increasing number of Portuguese-trained oenologists. Douro table wines used to be an afterthought, made from grapes left over from making port, but light wines have become so important that some producers have been planting, or selecting, vineyards specifically for table wines. High-altitude and north-facing sites are especially suitable. These wines vary enormously in style according to the provenance of the grapes and the intentions of the winemakers – from the almost burgundian Charme of Niepoort through the sophisticated intensity of Pintas to the schistous solidity of Quinta da Gaivosa, but there is a real air of excitement in the Douro that this extraordinary terrain can now express itself in two such different types of wine.

The many styles of port. Taylor's 2007 represents classic vintage port. Vesuvio represents the single-quinta alternative. Tawny, Colheita, and Garrafeira (see p.209) ports are aged much longer in wood. White ports, such as Santa Eufêmia's 30-year-old, are on the up.

The Port Lodges

The grapes for port may be grown in the wilderness of the Douro Valley, but about two-thirds of the wine is still aged in the huddles of shippers' lodges in Vila Nova de Gaia across the river from the recently revitalized city of Oporto. Before it can be shipped downstream, however – in the old days by Viking-style boat and nowadays by rumbling tanker – those grapes must be transformed into the uniquely strong sweet wine that is port. No other wine can use the name.

Port is made by running off partially fermented red wine, while it still contains at least half its grape sugar, into a tank or barrel a quarter full of (often chilled) spirits – fair-quality brandy these days, not always in the past. The brandy stops the fermentation so that the resulting mixture is both strong and sweet. But the wine also needs the pigmentation of the grape skins to colour it, and their tannin to preserve it. In normal wines these are extracted during fermentation, but since with port the fermentation is unnaturally short, pigments and tannin have to be extracted thoroughly and at speed. This used to mean late-night treading in stone troughs or *lagars*. In a few perfectionist houses (Taylor's is one) it still does. In most, computer-controlled "robotic *lagars*" or their equivalents have lightened the burden. Douro living is not as hard as it was.

Port is traditionally shipped in the spring to Vila Nova de Gaia, before the sweltering summer can imbue the young wine with a character known as "Douro bake". But this is changing, too. As Gaia's narrow streets become increasingly clogged by traffic, and electricity for air conditioning has become much more reliable up the Douro, more and more port is being kept and matured where it is made.

The city of Oporto and Vila Nova de Gaia across the river were once rich in English influence, with the port trade dominated by English and Anglo-Portuguese families. Oporto's handsome Georgian Factory House was the weekly meeting place for British port shippers for 200 years.

Styles of port

Across the river, the port lodges, with their dusty stacks of ancient, blackened barrels have much in common with the sherry bodegas. Superior tawny port is traditionally matured in barrels called pipes containing 550–600 litres (a pipe as a notional unit of commercial measurement is 534 litres) for anything from two to 50 years. The influence of the nearby Atlantic is particularly treasured for this style of port. Perhaps three years out of 10 conditions are near perfect for port-making. The best wine of these years needs no blending; nothing can improve it except time. It is bottled at two years like red Bordeaux, and is named simply with its shipper's name and the year. This is vintage port, and it is made in tiny but much-heralded quantities. Eventually, perhaps after 20 years, it will have a fatness and fragrance, richness and delicacy that are incomparable – although so dramatically has the standard of vine-growing and winemaking in the Douro risen in recent decades that it is now possible to enjoy even vintage port within four or five years.

Most other port, from near-vintage standard to merely moderate, goes through a blending process to emerge as a branded wine of a given character. This wine, aged in wood, matures in a different way, more rapidly, to something much mellower. A very old wood port is comparatively pale ("tawny" is the term) but particularly smooth. The best aged tawnies, usually labelled 10 or 20 years (although other permitted age claims are 30 and over 40 years), can cost as much as vintage ports; many people prefer their gentleness to the full, fat fieriness which vintage port can retain for decades. Chilled tawny is the standard drink of port shippers.

Ports labelled Colheita (Portuguese for "harvest") are wood-aged ports from a single year, expressive tawnies which may be drunk at any point after the bottling date, which should appear on the label. The iconoclastic Dirk Niepoort persists with the extremely rare Garrafeira style of port, whereby wines start off like Colheitas but are taken out of wood at between three and six years old and kept for many a year in large glass demijohns, resulting in particularly elegant ports.

Run-of-the-mill "wood" ports labelled simply ruby are not kept for nearly so long, nor would such age reveal any great qualities in them. Low-price wines labelled tawny with no indication of age are usually a blend of emaciated young ruby ports. White port is made in exactly the same way but from white grapes (and some of the best is now sold with a specific age). Rosé – or "pink"–port emerged at the end of the last century but currently occupies only a small niche. A noticeable notch above these basic ports are those designated Reserve, young rubies with some real guts to them and respectable tawnies bottled at under 10 years old.

As vintage port is bottled very young and unfiltered, the sediment forms a "crust" on the side of the bottle. A port sold as a crusted or crusting port is a blend of different years bottled early enough to be sure of throwing a sediment in bottle. Like vintage port, it demands a decanter.

The more common compromise between vintage and wood port is the extremely varied late bottled vintage (LBV) category – port kept in barrel for four to six years, and bottled once it has rid itself of its crust. Accelerated and cleaned in this way, it is the modern man's vintage port. Most commercial LBVs have nothing like the character of vintage port, but both Warre and Smith Woodhouse produce a serious LBV, made just like vintage port but bottled unfiltered after four rather than two years. They, too, demand decanting.

Oporto, Porto in Portuguese, which gave its name to port, is now a popular tourist destination. The old boats that used to ship port down to Vila Nova de Gaia in barrel are now harnessed to add to the city's visual appeal.

Bairrada and Dão

Bairrada and Dão are two long-established names that had lost their way in the 20th century. Now they are in the throes of (entirely beneficial) transition. Bairrada is a thoroughly rural district lying astride the highway that links Lisbon and Oporto, extending over most of the area between the granite hills of Dão and the Atlantic coast. Its nearness to the Atlantic makes its wines naturally fresh, and its vineyards relatively damp, although its low hills encompass some extremely varied and expressive terroirs. The best wines tend to come from the clay-limestone that gives body and typical Portuguese bite to its overwhelmingly (85%) red wine. The defining ingredient, though, is Bairrada's indigenous Baga grape. Luís Pato has been one of Bairrada's most passionate exponents and likens Baga to the Nebbiolo of Piemonte in its uncompromisingly heavy charge of acids and tannins. Baga produces wines of formidable character which, until the recent introduction of some softening methods in the winery, demanded patience (some traditional bottlings need 20 years' cellaring) and sympathy – not qualities that mark out the typical modern wine drinker.

The perhaps inevitable consequence is that many old Baga vines have been pulled out – not least because, since 2003, Bairrada may be made from non-local varieties. Campolargo, one of the region's great modernizers, had led the charge. Its eclectic and far from atypical range features Touriga Nacional, Tinta Roriz, Cabernet Sauvignon, Merlot, Syrah, and even Pinot Noir. But is it Bairrada? Not that the purists are defeated. Pato and other leading Baga exponents, including his daughter Filipa, have founded Baga Friends to defend and promote a grape whose time has been a long while coming.

The white companion of Baga is Bical, another local grape notable for its acidity but capable of quality and a degree of complexity. Both varieties find their way into some very fine traditional-method sparkling wines, a revived regional strength since 1890. Maria Gomes (Fernão Pires) is another traditional, if much less distinguished, white grape variety.

Dão

The Dão DOC is at least thoroughly Portuguese in terms of permitted grape varieties. Until the 1990s, the name was associated with aggressively tannic, dull reds, almost all vinified by heavy-handed co-operatives. But in the last 20 years, the number of independent quintas has increased fivefold and the result has been far juicier, friendlier wines. These range from well-priced collections from the substantial likes of Sogrape (Quinta dos Carvalhais) and Dão Sul (Quinta de Cabriz) to some of Portugal's finest wines with a keen sense of terroir from winemakers as talented as Alvaro Castro.

Named after the river that runs through it, Dão is effectively a granite plateau, where bare rocks show through the well-drained soil – although there is some schist in the flatter south and west, which is less obvious wine country. Vineyards are only a subplot in the landscape, cropping up here and there in clearings in the sweet-scented pines and eucalypts, ideally at altitudes of 1,300–1,640ft (400–500m), but some can be found as high as 2,620ft (800m). The higher the vineyard, the more marked the difference between day- and night-time temperatures. Dão's capital, Viseu, is one of Portugal's prettiest towns. The Serra do Caramulo shields the region from the Atlantic and the Serra da Estrela mountains protect it in the southeast. This means that in winter Dão is cold and wet (its annual rainfall averages as much as 43in/1,100mm); in summer warm and dry – much drier than Bairrada, although the wines of both regions are characterized by real structure and freshness.

As is usual in Portugal, a dizzying range of grapes is grown in the Dão region to produce increasingly fruity reds – though still with a certain granitic substance – as well as firm,

Grape-picking does not look like young people's work at Casa do Santar, the largest estate in Dão, which is now part of the ambitious Dão Sul group that has holdings all over Portugal.

--- · — District boundary
■ LUÍS PATO · Notable producer
BAIRRADA · DOP/DOC

Appellation boundaries are
distinguished by coloured lines

1:588,000
Km 0 · 10 · 20 Km
Miles 0 · 5 · 10 Miles

ATLANTIC INFLUENCE

Bairrada wines are heavily influenced by the
Atlantic, while Dão wines, made inland and
protected by two mountain ranges, are more likely
to express the varying altitudes of the vineyards.

fragrant whites suitable for ageing. This affinity
for the cellar, in whites as well as reds, was already
obvious from the traditional Dãos that were
sold by merchants, who would buy, blend, and
age wines from the co-operatives as their own
Reservas or Garrafeiras.

The finest individual estates, such as Luis
Lourenço's Quinta dos Roques/Quinta das Maias
and Alvaro Castro's Quinta da Pellada/Quinta
de Saes, have been producing single varietals as
well as blends as they experiment with individual
grapes, but traditional blends are the mainstay
of Dão's output, not least because a good 60% of
its older, generally better vineyards are planted
with a jumble of different varieties. Touriga
Nacional, possibly at its best in Dão, has shown
great promise for long ageing; Jaen (Galicia's
Mencía) for fruity early drinking; and Tinta Roriz
can provide body. The deep-coloured Alfrocheiro
is also promising in various judicious blends.
Responding well to burgundian winemaking
techniques, full-bodied Encruzado has already
proved itself to be one of Portugal's finest single-
varietal white wine grapes.

The potential of this part of the world for
truly remarkable table wines was always clear,
thanks to one eccentric, mysterious, and highly
idiosyncratic example. Right on Barraida's

eastern boundary, the Bussaco Palace Hotel,
originally designed as a "cathedral of wine" to
showcase the region, has selected and matured
its own red and white Buçaco wines in a wholly
original way for generations. The reds are a blend,
typically of Baga from Bairrada and Touriga
Nacional grown in the Dão. For whites, Dão's
Encruzado has been blended with Bical and Maria

Gomes from Bairrada. These famous blends are
aged for years in barrel in the Palace cellars and
sold exclusively from the hotel's wine list, which
still goes back for decades. The "current" vintages
are 2008 for white and 2007 for red, although the
vintages on the hotel wine list stretch back to the
1940s. They look and taste like relics of another
age, in the most fascinating sense.

*Luís Pato, bottom left, demonstrates
his attitude to local wine regulation
while Doda, bottom right, is a
whacky 50:50 blend of Dão and
Douro. Pato's daughter Filipa makes
Nossa, newcomer Julia Kemper
the fine white Dão, and Quinta das
Bageiras the 2008 red Bairrada.*

Lisboa and Península de Setúbal

Vinho Regional Lisboa, once called Estremadura or simply Oeste ("the west"), is one of Portugal's most productive wine regions. Its potential was not obvious while co-operatives made its wine, but its long, Atlantic-coastal growing season, its choice of soils, and new interest in better grapes (notably Syrah and Touriga Nacional) are giving ambitious new estates their chance. Most prefer to use the Vinho Regional label rather than the DOCs Torres Vedras, Arruda, and Alenquer, the part of the Oeste sheltered from Atlantic influence by the Montejunto range producing some of the region's best reds. See the map on p.203 for the full extent of both Lisboa and Península de Setúbal VRs.

The hinterland of Lisbon has been known for centuries for three historic wines, now all threatened with extinction. **Colares** on the west coast is, or was, a tannic red; **Carcavelos** now refers to the surfing beach of Cascais. **Bucelas** soldiers on, a fresh-enough white (the main grape is the lemony Arinto) for modern tastes – even for real quality. Its Quinta da Romeira is successful enough to attract other investors to the DOC.

But much more important today are the vineyards across the Tagus on the Setúbal Peninsula. Between the Tagus (Tejo) and Sado estuaries, southeast of Lisbon, there are clay-limestone hills round Azeitão, whose slopes are cooled by Atlantic winds, and the much hotter, more fertile inland sandy plain of the River Sado, east of **Palmela**.

Setúbal's most important producers, José Maria da Fonseca and especially Bacalhôa Vinhos, were pioneers of Portugal's new wave of easy-drinking varietals. The local red grape Castelão, well suited to the sandy soils just east of Palmela, has given way to Syrah, Aragonês (Tempranillo), and Douro red grape varieties.

The region's traditional wine is **Moscatel de Setúbal**, a rich, pale-orange Muscat (tinged pink if made from the rarer Moscatel Roxo), which is lightly fortified and highly perfumed by long maceration with the headily aromatic Muscat of Alexandria skins. Aged it can bedazzle; young it is just the job with Portugal's custard tarts.

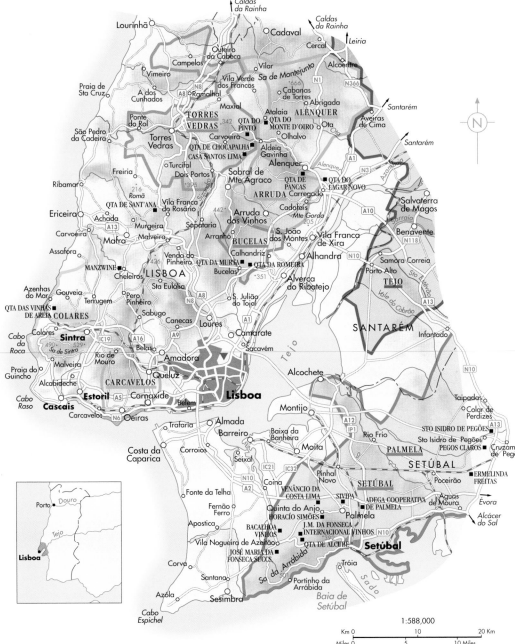

- – – District boundary
- ■ PEGOS CLAROS Notable producer
- ARRUDA DOP/DOC

Appellation boundaries are distinguished by coloured lines

▼ Weather station (WS)

A wide variety of different wine styles is made in the unruly area mapped above. The Moscatel Roxo is an aged blend of Horácio Simões's best wines of the 1990s, while Monte Cascas makes one of the best Colares from 80-year-old Ramisco vines.

ESTREMADURA: LISBON ▼

Latitude / Altitude of WS
38.72° / 253ft (77m)

Average growing season temperature at WS
68.7°F (20.4°C)

Average annual rainfall at WS
30.5in (774mm)

Harvest month rainfall at WS
September: 0.2in (6mm)

Principal viticultural hazards
Rain during fruit set, autumn rain

Principal grape varieties
Castelão, Camarate, Trincadeira, Fernão Pires, Arinto

Alentejo

In comparison with the tapestry of vines that seems to smother northern Portugal, in the vast and diverse Alentejo region vineyards are concentrated in four main DOC enclaves: Borba, Redondo, Reguengos, and Vidigueira. However, some exciting new pockets of excellence have sprung up in recent years (see below). The Alentejo's wide, sun-browned spaces are dotted with silver olive trees and dark cork oaks, browsed bare by sheep, but only occasionally green with vines. Smallholdings are rare here. Ranch-like estates, unknown in the densely populated north, are the norm.

Even in midwinter, this is a land of sun and open vistas. The visitor is aware that Spain is just over the border; winemakers do their shopping there. Rainfall is low and temperatures so routinely high that picking starts in the third week of August. Rich, loamy soils are interspersed with the granite and, especially, schist to which vines are more suited.

Six of the the Alentejo's eight DOC subregions are based on an important co-op, none more important than that of **Reguengos**, which, in Monsaraz, produces a best-seller within Portugal. A large proportion of the region's wine, whether qualifying for DOC or not, is sold as Vinho Regional Alentejano, often varietally labelled.

When José Roquette, owner of one of Lisbon's rival football teams, blessed his Reguengos estate Herdade do Esporão with an Australian winemaker and almost Napa-like dream winery in the late 1980s, he started a trend. By 2010, the region could boast 260 producers (there were 45 in 1995).

The part of the Alentejo mapped here is on the move. But so is the cooler, wetter enclave of **Portalegre** to the north, where the land rises to 3,280ft (1,000m) of granite and schist. And Beja on the southwestern edge of our map combines wine, fashion, and tourism in developments such as the winemaking spa hotels Malhadinha Nova and L'AND. Many a Portuguese oenologist has followed in the footsteps of João Portugal Ramos to make his name in the well-equipped cellars of the Alentejo.

The thirst-quenching whites that tourists want in this arid region may variously be made from the tropical-fruited Antão Vaz, the floral white Roupeiro, Arinto for freshness, and, increasingly, some Verdelho and Alvarinho. But this is now red wine country. Aragonês (Tempranillo) and the local speciality, Trincadeira, have risen to the fore. So has the red-fleshed Alicante Bouschet, which seems to take on a certain unaccustomed nobility in Alentejo. Quinta do Mouchaõ is its finest exponent. Touriga Nacional, Cabernet Sauvignon, and Syrah have inevitably been imported. This is an evolving region to watch.

CENTRAL ALENTEJO

Only the central part of Alentejo is mapped here (see p.203). To the north the granite hills around Portalegre are wetter, estates tend to be smaller, and in general, vines older and less international.

--- | International boundary
--- | District boundary
—— | Alentejo DOP/DOC
ALENTEJANO | IGP/Vinho Regional
BORBA | Alentejo subregion
■ CORTES DE CIMA | Notable producer
400 | Contour interval 200 metres
▼ | Weather station (WS)

Quinta do Mouro in Borba belongs to a dentist, while Pedra e Alma is the reserve, old-vine bottling of wine writer Richard Mayson's Quinta do Centro in Reguengos. Local grape varieties dominate both.

ALENTEJO: EVORA ▼

Latitude / Altitude of WS	38.57° / 1,014ft (309m)
Average growing season temperature at WS	68.1°F (20.1°C)
Average annual rainfall at WS	23.0in (585mm)
Harvest month rainfall at WS	August: 0.3in (8mm)
Principal viticultural hazards	Drought, isolated spring frosts
Principal grape varieties	Aragonês (Tempranillo), Trincadeira, Alicante Bouschet, Arinto, Roupeiro, Antão Vaz

Madeira

The ancients knew these old off-shore volcanoes as the Enchanted Isles. They cluster 400 miles (640km) off the coast of Morocco, right in the path of sailing ships crossing the Atlantic, their modern names Madeira, Porto Santo, Selvagens, and the Desertas. Madeira (the only one mapped here) is the largest of the little archipelago and one of the prettiest islands in the world, as steep as an iceberg and as green as a glade. The story goes that when the Portuguese landed on the island (in 1419, at Machico in the east) they set fire to the dense woods that gave the island its name. The fire burned for years, leaving the already fertile soil enriched with the ashes of an entire forest.

Certainly it is fertile today. From the water's edge to over halfway up the 6,000ft (1,800m) peak it is steadily terraced to make room for patches of vine, sugarcane, corn, beans, potatoes, bananas, and little flower gardens. As in northern Portugal the vines are grown in arbours, making room for yet more cultivation beneath. The mystery to the visitor is where the vineyards are. There are no big ones. Hundreds of miles of *levadas*, little irrigation canals, distribute water to the crops, from the northern slopes to the southern.

Wine has been the principal product of the Madeira Islands for 400 years. Porto Santo, low, sandy, and with a North African climate, looked much more promising than tall, green, rainy Madeira. The settlers planted the island with the Malvasia grape (which is assumed to be named after the southern Greek port of Monemvasia), concentrated its sugar in the sun, and found a ready market for the sweet wine that resulted – even at the court of François I of France.

The planting of Madeira itself – with both vines and sugarcane – came later. Settlement of the American colonies meant increased traffic and trade and the bigger island, with its port of Funchal, became the victualling place for westbound ships. Conditions here are very different from those on Porto Santo; rain is rarely far off, especially on the north coast, which is unprotected from the winds off the Atlantic; Malvasia, Verdelho, and the other vines introduced often struggled to ripen. The marriage of sugar with these acid and astringent wines was an obvious expedient.

Warming the wine

The sweet-and-sour result was more than adequate as ballast on sailing ships, and an effective anti-scurvy protection into the bargain. And it was this travelling as ballast that made madeira. A bucket or two of brandy (or cane spirit) fortified it for its long sea voyages. One crossing of the equator would finish off any normal wine, but it was found to mellow madeira wonderfully – and a double equator crossing even more so.

Instead of long, hot sea voyages, madeira today is subjected to (gentle) ordeal by fire. An effect similar to the tropical heat is produced by warming the wine to almost 122°F (50°C) in hot stores (*estufas*) for at least three months. When it comes out it has the wonderfully revitalized combination of heat, acidity, and refreshing tang by which all madeiras can be recognized.

Modern-day Madeira shippers blend their most commercial wine into consistent brands, most of them using the *estufagem* process. But some finer wines gain their complexity by gentle barrel-ageing alone, a process called *canteiro* after the racks on which barrels were stacked. Madeira was originally blended by a solera system like that used for sherry, a practice once again allowed by the EU. Some older bottled solera wines are very fine, if you can find them, but the very highest quality of madeira, as of port, has traditionally been the reserve wine of a single vintage. Today, to be labelled Frasqueira (vintage), a madeira must be from a single year, of a single grape variety, and aged in cask for at least 20 years. In practice the very finest wines may spend a century undergoing the slowest of oxidations in the barrel, and/or decanted into glass demijohns, before being bottled.

Increasingly popular commercially are Colheita madeiras, made from the produce of a single year and bottled after spending five years in wood. If there is no grape variety on the label it will have been made substantially from Tinta

MADEIRA'S VINES

The green lines enclose those parts of this densely planted island where viticulture is most common, but vines are almost always interspersed with other crops. The colour-shaded areas refer strictly to the past. Inland areas tend to be too high to cultivate.

Every available square inch of this terraced vineyard close to Ribeira da Janela, near Porto Moniz in the northwest, is planted. Madeira is truly an Atlantic wine.

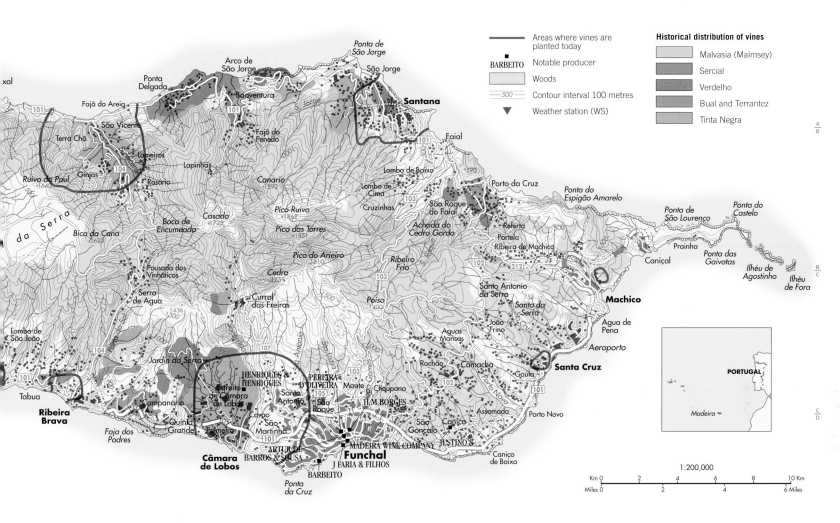

Negra, the grape variety that invaded the island after the double disaster of oidium in the 1850s and phylloxera in the 1870s. Damp-resistant American hybrids invaded the island's vineyards and the most planted vinifera vine became Tinta Negra, which still accounts for about 86% of all grapes grown on the island.

Styles of madeira

The practice until Portugal joined the EU in 1986 was to cite the classic vine varieties of madeira on labels whether the wine was really made from them or (more likely) not. Today, unless made from one of the traditional varieties, they must be labelled simply according to the average age of the blend (3, 5, 10, 15, 20, 30, and more than 40 years) and style (dry, medium, and rich, for example), generally determined, as in port production, by when the fermentation is halted by the addition of grape spirit (96% alcohol as opposed to 77% for port).

The traditional grape varieties are associated with a particular level of sweetness. The sweetest of the four, and the earliest maturing, is Malmsey or Malvasia: dark-brown wine, very fragrant and rich, soft textured and almost fatty, but with the sharp tang that all madeiras have. Bual madeira is lighter and slightly less sweet than Malmsey – but still definitely a dessert wine. A smoky note steals in to modify its richness. Verdelho (now the most planted white wine grape on the island) is made less sweet and softer than Bual. The faint honey and distinct smoke of its flavour make it good before or after meals. The tiny plantings of the Sercial (Esgana Cão on the mainland) vine, which makes the driest, most revitalizing wine of Madeira, are in the island's highest vineyards and are harvested late. Sercial wine, the slowest-developing of them all, is light, fragrant, distinctly sharp – unpleasantly astringent young, in fact – but marvellously appetizing old. It is more substantial than a fino sherry, but still a perfect

apéritif. A small but noticeable revival of the historic Terrantez vine variety is also underway.

In bottle madeira develops at a snail's pace. The older it is, the better it is – and an opened bottle of virtually any good madeira can retain its freshness for months, even years.

Barbeito is the single most conscientious madeira producer today and this is a highly individual bottling from a single cask. The dominant company Blandy's has followed along the dated varietal Colheita route, while in the middle is an unfortified table wine from the variety most suited to that style.

MADEIRA: FUNCHAL ▼

Latitude / Altitude of WS
32.63°C / 190ft (58m)

Average growing season temperature at WS
69.8°F (21.0°C)

Average annual rainfall at WS
24.7in (627mm)

Harvest month rainfall at WS
September: 0.1in (2mm)

Principal viticultural hazards
Fungal diseases

Principal grape varieties
Tinta Negra, Verdelho, Bual, Sercial, Malvasia

GERMANY

The village of Achkarren in the Kaiserstuhl region, Baden-Württemburg

Germany

After a late-20th-century wobble German wine has steadily been working its way back into international favour as new wine drinkers discover its unique qualities, its freshness, vibrancy, and perfume. Sheer mass in wine eventually loses its appeal; German wines offer positive refreshment. And a new generation of growers has taken up the reins. Their interpretation of their country's great traditions is turning the tide in Germany's favour again.

Many of Germany's best vineyards lie almost as far north as grapes can be persuaded to ripen. Some of the best are on land unfit for normal agriculture; if there were no vines there would be forest and bare mountain. All in all their chances of giving the world's best white wine look slim. And yet they can, and stamp it with a racy elegance that no one, anywhere, can imitate.

Their secret is the balance of two ingredients that don't sound, on the face of it, specially appealing: sugar and acidity. Sugar without acid would be flat; acid without sugar would be sharp. But in good years the two are so finely counterpoised that they have the inevitability of great art. They provide the stage for a stirring fusion of essences from the grape and the ground that is more apparent in German wines than any others, perhaps because they are generally unadorned by such winemaking layers as malolactic fermentation, lees stirring, and ageing in new oak and are therefore more brilliantly transparent. Thanks to all that acidity, the best also age magnificently – far better than most other white wines.

The classic gems in Germany's crown are sweet wines that are best enjoyed, unlike most wines, alone in all their glory rather than with food. They are delicate ferments, often stopping at a mere 8% alcohol, retaining much of the natural grape sugar in the wine. But sweetness is unfashionable and this has been seen as a commercial handicap. The result? Far drier German wines, growers making many, sometimes all, of their wines completely or almost completely dry and offering them as wines for the table like any others. In 2010, for example – a vintage which, if anything favoured fruitier wines – 64% of all German wine was classified *trocken* (dry) or *halbtrocken* (medium dry), the same proportion as in the very different 2011 vintage.

Since the vogue for *trocken* wines began in the early 1980s the genre has advanced from thin productions (early examples of fully dry Mosel Kabinett were painfully tart) to wines of firm and convincing elegance; principally dry Spätlesen and, top of the tree, wines from some of the finest vineyards labelled Grosses Gewächs. These command enormous respect and high prices within Germany and are rapidly winning friends abroad.

GERMANY'S WINE REGIONS

The locator map together with the main one show how the vine is limited to the southern two-thirds of the country. Rivers define most of the wine regions. The eastern regions of Saale-Unstrut and Sachsen (in English, Saxony) have a much more continental climate than the other wine regions.

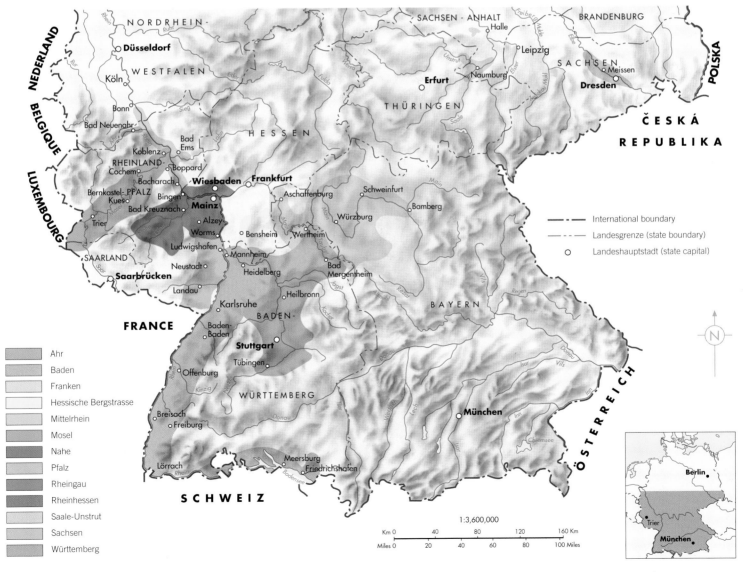

Ahr
Baden
Franken
Hessische Bergstrasse
Mittelrhein
Mosel
Nahe
Pfalz
Rheingau
Rheinhessen
Saale-Unstrut
Sachsen
Württemberg

International boundary
Landesgrenze (state boundary)
Landeshauptstadt (state capital)

1:3,600,000

Km 0   40   80   120   160 Km
Miles 0   20   40   60   80   100 Miles

Germany's determined new generation of growers, inspired by the potential of historically glorious vineyard sites, and often influenced by peers in very distant countries, has also been helped by the effects of climate change. Grapes are now easier to ripen fully, and the threat of rot and other vine diseases is no longer routine. German dry wines with 12% or even 14% alcohol are now common. The result in the right hands is dry wines with much more character and flavour, even if not all winemakers are aware that too much alcohol can make German wines unbalanced, tasting dangerously hot or oily.

While German wine's image abroad was seriously damaged in the late 20th century by the vast quantities of sugar water exported from Germany under such names as Liebfraumilch and Niersteiner Gutes Domtal, this sort of bulk wine is now firmly in retreat. And not a minute too soon.

The German wine label, one of the most explicit yet confusing on earth, has been both cause and instrument of some of the industry's problems.

The most regrettable deception was the legal creation (in 1971) of Grosslagen, commercially useful, large geographical units whose names are indistinguishable to most wine drinkers from those of Einzellagen, individual vineyards. But these are playing a dwindling role in the dynamic German wine scene. Progressive producers are finding more internationally acceptable (and indeed accurate) ways of labelling their wines.

Significant grapes

Riesling is the great grape of Germany. A very significant proportion of Germany's best wines are made from it, and it is planted to the exclusion of almost everything else in the best sites of the Mosel, Rheingau, Nahe, and Pfalz. In a lesser site in a lesser year it stands no chance of really ripening.

To deliver quantity (if not quality) reliably, Germany turned during the mid-20th century to Müller-Thurgau, a much earlier-ripening, more productive crossing, bred in 1882. Although there has been a certain limited renaissance of the

The south-facing Bockstein vineyard is tilted towards the all-important sun above the village of Ockfen in a side valley off the River Saar, a tributary of the upper Mosel (see p.223). The Romans planted vines where snow melted first.

variety in Franken and around the Bodensee in the far south, Müller-Thurgau generally produces rather soft, coarse wines that lack Riesling's lovely backbone of fruity acidity. In 1996, lovers of fine German wine had the satisfaction of seeing Riesling regain its rightful place as the country's most planted vine, and by 2010 Müller-Thurgau's share of the total vineyard area had fallen to 13%. Nevertheless, standard cheap German wines with no mention of any grape on the label can still be assumed to be made (at least mainly) from Müller-Thurgau.

Silvaner is now the third most-planted vine for white wine, far behind these two varieties, but historically important, especially in Franken, where it makes better wine than Riesling. Silvaner brings a hint of earth and vegetation that can be green, but on its favourite soil type of clay limestone it seems to seize the minerals to become almost like Chablis. In Franken it represents 22% of vines planted, in Rheinhessen 10%.

On many sites in Baden and some sites in the Pfalz, Grauburgunder (Pinot Gris) and Weissburgunder (Pinot Blanc) are valued above any other variety and have become hugely popular with German drinkers. Between 1995 and 2010 both varieties saw their total plantings throughout Germany more than double. Hotter summers have yielded wines full-bodied enough to withstand ageing in small oak barrels – a novelty that has been welcomed within Germany.

But the most notable development in Germany's varietal make-up in the last two decades has been the rise in popularity of red wine. Plantings of Spätburgunder (Pinot Noir) have tripled in a generation, so that in terms of total plantings it does not lag far behind Müller-Thurgau. Germany's fourth most-planted variety is the 1956 crossing Dornfelder, which can make particularly appetizing red wine in the Pfalz. German Syrah is not unknown; Merlot and Cabernets are quite common. About 36% of all Germany's vineyards are now planted with red wine grapes: a revolution.

These new plantings of red grape vines have been very largely at the expense of crossings such as Huxelrebe, Optima, and Ortega, created to boost ripeness levels in the sweet white wines that briefly enjoyed a great vogue in the early 1980s, particularly in Rheinhessen and the Pfalz. Kerner, Bacchus, and Scheurebe are the most popular, and refined, of the established light-skinned crossings. But Germany has also been planting newly created red wine vines, such as the rot-resistant Regent, by 2005 already planted on more than 5,000 acres (2,000ha).

Sachsen, Saale-Unstrut, and Mittelrhein

In the far east of the map on p.217 are two small wine regions, Sachsen and Saale-Unstrut. They lie roughly on the same latitude as London, but their much more continental climate frequently blesses them with magnificent summers, even if the risk of serious spring frosts is high. Substantial replanting in the 1990s after reunification had increased the total vineyard area by 2010 to almost 1,700 acres (700ha) in Saale-Unstrut and over 1,100 acres (450ha) in Sachsen.

Steady progress has been made by estates such as Pawis in Freyburg and Gussek in Naumburg (both Saale-Unstrut), as well as Schloss Proschwitz near Meissen and Zimmerling at Dresden-Pillnitz (Sachsen), which all manage to produce dry wines with remarkable substance and character for their northerly location. Saale-Unstrut, of which a good 25,000 acres (10,000ha) were under vine in the Middle Ages, produces nothing but dry wines while Sachsen makes a small proportion of sweet ones.

Although the workhorse grape of both regions is the ubiquitous Müller-Thurgau, Weissburgunder, Grauburgunder, Riesling, and Traminer grapes dominate the many steep, south-facing sites with which each region is blessed. These wines are often compared with those of Franken (see pp.240–41), although they are lighter, more aromatic, and less earthy.

Another wine region not considered in detail in the pages that follow is the increasingly successful Rhineland tourist magnet the Mittelrhein, in the west of the country (see map, p.217). Its most important vineyards are southeast of Koblenz, between Boppard and Bacharach. Weingart and Matthias Müller are growers of outstanding calibre who manage to produce some filigree Spätlesen and Auslesen from the Engelstein, Mandelstein, and Feuerlay sites at Bopparder Hamm.

Vineyard classification

For many years German wine law made no attempt to limit yields (which are some of the highest in the world) or to classify vineyards as the French do, but this has changed, at least within the influential VDP (Verband Deutscher Prädikatsweingüter), the association of 200 top growers. The VDP sets its members strict limits on permitted yields, and in 2000 undertook the politically extremely sensitive task of classifying Germany's Erste Lagen (top sites) for various grape varieties specified for each region. These, of course, are limited to its members' holdings and, like any such classification, the VDP's list of top site and variety combinations has attracted a certain amount of criticism.

In this book we continue to highlight our own selection of that small proportion of vineyards we consider consistently superior by shading them in lilac and (best of all) purple. This bold vineyard classification was made in collaboration with Germany's top-quality growers, local wine organizations, and experts, and to a certain extent the VDP, but is not identical to the classification the VDP made in 2000.

MATTHIAS MÜLLER

2011
Riesling Spätlese
feinherb
Mandelstein

Weingart
mittelrhein

2011 Bopparder Hamm Ohlenberg

Riesling Kabinett
trocken
Gutsabfüllung

Mittelrhein vineyards totalling just 1,200 acres (500ha) are strung out along the spectacular Rhine Gorge and as far upriver as Bonn. They grow a higher proportion of white wine grapes, mainly Riesling, than any region other than the Mosel. Most of the crisp wine is consumed locally.

Ahr

The Ahr is a little river that makes its way from the Eifel Mountains to the Rhine through a beautiful narrow valley, a gorge in places. Its vineyards, despite being so far north, have long been devoted to Spätburgunder. It is only since the 1990s, however, that its wines have been able to bewitch Pinot Noir enthusiasts. Before that, the Ahr Valley attracted coachloads of up to two million thirsty visitors a year, happy with its cheap, pale, often sweet red.

This did not make economic sense; many of the vineyards are planted on steep and stony slopes, requiring long hours of intensive manual labour. As German palates became more refined, and in the 1980s turned gradually to drier wines, a handful of pioneers risked the change from mass production to planting Burgundian clones, reducing yields, and ageing Spätburgunder in barriques. The estates of Meyer-Näkel, Deutzerhof and Jean Stodden took only took a few years of fine-tuning before they made the breakthrough into the German red wine elite with, respectively, their Dernauer Pfarrwingert, Altenahrer Eck and Recher Herrenberg. Their success has since encouraged many others, with Adeneuer, Kreuzberg, and Nelles among the first.

The well-preserved remains of a large Roman villa at the foot of the Ahrweiler Silberberg suggest that it was the Romans who brought the vine to the valley, but the earliest recorded reference to vineyards "*ad Aram*" is dated 770. In many parts of the valley the slopes are so vertiginous that they have to be terraced. In the first half of the 19th century, rising wine taxes and a collapse in the price of grapes drove many Ahr growers to emigrate to America. In 1868, 18 of those who remained founded Germany's first wine co-operative, the Mayschosser Winzerverein, with such success that by 1892 the number of members had risen to 180. Ever since then growers' co-operatives have played an important part in the Ahr. They still receive the majority of the harvest to this day.

In 2011, red wine grapes accounted for 85% of the 1,360 acres (550ha) under vine. Spätburgunder (62%), the early-ripening Pinot Noir mutation Frühburgunder (6.5%), and Portugieser (6%) dominate, with Riesling (7%) the only white wine variety of any relevance. Geologically, the 15-mile (25km) stretch of vineyards may be divided into the Mittelahr (Middle Ahr), between Altenahr and Walporzheim, and the Unterahr (Lower Ahr), from Ahrweiler to Heimersheim. The rocky slopes of the narrow Middle Ahr Valley, largely weathered slate and greywacke, store summer heat; temperatures are unexpectedly high for so far north. The combination of an almost Mediterranean mesoclimate and the stony ground results in wines with a strongly mineral signature and firm structure. The soils of the wider Lower Ahr are higher in loess and loam, resulting in slightly richer, juicier, softer wines.

Pinot Noir, known here as Spätburgunder, is what Ahr wine is all about. Nowadays the grapes ripen fully and can produce respectably deep red wines.

THE MIDDLE AND LOWER AHR

The Ahr Valley extends many miles further west and a little further east, but the most admired vineyards, those coloured darkest purple, are in the stretch mapped here. They are all on the left bank of the river facing due south.

ROSENTHAL	Einzellage
- - - - -	Kreis (rural district) boundary
- - - - -	Gemeinde (parish) boundary
	Exceptional vineyard
	Excellent vineyard
	Other vineyard
	Woods
—200—	Contour interval 20 metres

1:77,000
Km 0 — 1 — 2 Km
Miles 0 — 1/2 — 1 Mile

Meyer-Näkel is probably the Ahr producer best known outside Germany (not least for having won awards), but the structured Pinots of Kreuzberg, Jean Stodden, and Nelles are also widely admired in Germany. Many taste of the slate on which they are (unusually) ripened.

Mosel

The sinuous River Mosel is lined by vines all the way from its source in the Vosges Mountains to its union with the Rhine at Koblenz. In France and then Luxembourg, it is known as the Moselle. All the great Mosels are made from Riesling, but this far north Riesling will only ripen on near-ideal sites. With every twist and turn of the river comes a dramatic change in vineyard potential. In general all the best sites face south and slope steeply down towards the reflective river. But the gradient that makes them the source of some of the finest wine in the world also makes them nearly impossible to work. Many are seriously threatened by a shortage of vineyard labour as younger Germans are unwilling to spend their working days in the open, fighting gravity, hunched over truculent vines. In recent years, often overqualified vineyard workers have been imported from Eastern Europe, but this may not provide a long-term solution to this perennial problem. The Mosel's total area of vines has shrunk by about a third since the mid-1990s, although this is largely because the inferior Müller-Thurgau vine has been uprooted and vineyards on flat sites have been put to other uses.

The Mosel's two great vinous side valleys are the Saar (see overleaf) and the Ruwer, both famous for their Riesling grown on grey slate. The Ruwer is a mere stream. Its vineyards add up to about half those of one Côte d'Or commune. Before the advent of global warming, there were years when most of its wine was just too faint and sharp. And even today many of the lesser vineyards are being abandoned because their names are not famous enough to justify the work involved. Yet like the Saar, when conditions are right it performs a miracle: its wines are Germany's most delicate: gentle yet infinitely fine and full of subtlety.

Waldrach, the valley's first wine village of real note, makes good light wine but rarely more. Kasel is already one step up the ladder; its Nieschen vineyard can produce outstanding wines in hot years. The extensive von Kesselstatt estate, the Bischöfliches Weingut of Trier, and Karlsmühle of Mertesdorf all have holdings here.

Mertesdorf and Eitelsbach are not themselves famous names, but each has one supreme vineyard, solely owned by one of the country's best growers. In Eitelsbach, the Karthäuserhofberg vineyard extends proudly above an old monastic manor of the same name making superlative wines: lime or lemon playing against honey. Across the stream in Mertesdorf, Maximin Grünhaus echoes that situation, set obliquely to the left bank of the river with the manor house, also former monastic property, at its foot. A subterranean aqueduct, still passable by foot, connects the Grünhaus property with

Trier, the Roman (and actual) capital of the Mosel 5 miles (8km) upstream.

Upstream of Trier the rolling farmland is regularly under threat from spring frosts and is almost completely devoted to the hardy, historic, if rustic, Elbling vine. Elbling makes light, tart wine, sometimes lightly sparkling, both in the limestone Obermosel and in Luxembourg across the river. Luxembourg's growers, routine

chaptalizers, rely largely on Rivaner (Müller-Thurgau) and on such low-acid grapes as Auxerrois. Their strong suit is sparkling wine.

Most of the Mosel's great wine is made between Serrig and Zell on those sections mapped in detail on the pages that follow, but see p.226 for details of the increasingly exciting wine-scape between Zell and Cochem. Downstream of Cochem Riesling comes into its own again.

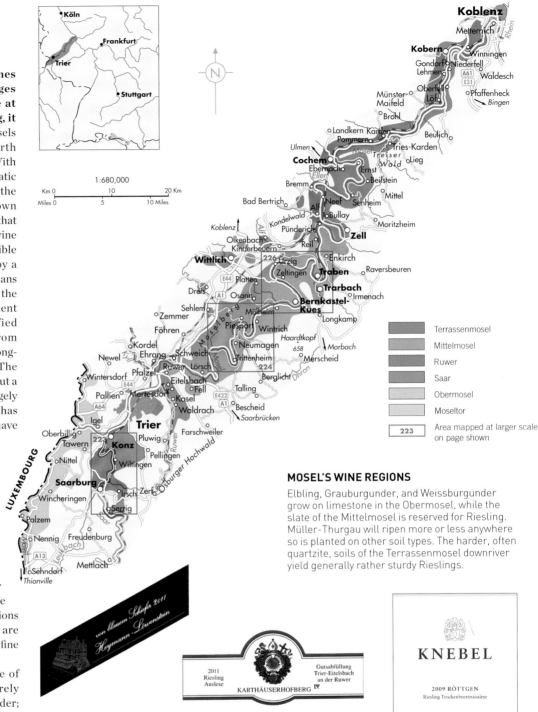

MOSEL'S WINE REGIONS

Elbling, Grauburgunder, and Weissburgunder grow on limestone in the Obermosel, while the slate of the Mittelmosel is reserved for Riesling. Müller-Thurgau will ripen more or less anywhere so is planted on other soil types. The harder, often quartzite, soils of the Terrassenmosel downriver yield generally rather sturdy Rieslings.

	Terrassenmosel
	Mittelmosel
	Ruwer
	Saar
	Obermosel
	Moseltor
223	Area mapped at larger scale on page shown

Fine wines, all Rieslings of course, made outside the areas mapped in detail on the following pages – all of them downriver of the Mittelmosel except for the Karthäuserhofberg Auslese representing the Ruwer tributary, also home to von Schubert.

Saar

German wine, its problems and its triumphs, is epitomized nowhere better than in the valley of the Saar, the Mosel tributary. The battle for sugar in the grapes has raged most fiercely in this cold corner of the country where, until the climate began to grow warmer, it was won only perhaps three or four years in 10. Recent years, however, have delivered a succession of glorious successes: some of the least potent but most thrillingly nuanced wines in the world. They are all Rieslings of inimitable delicacy, most of them vibrating with fruit and extract.

A mere 1,775 acres (720ha) of vines share the valley with orchard and pasture. This is calm, open agricultural country. The map opposite shows more clearly than any other the way the south-facing slopes – here nearly all on steep hillsides at right angles to the river – offer wine-growers the greatest chance of enough sunshine to reach full ripeness. Unlike the Mittelmosel, the Saar Valley is in many parts open to cold easterly winds. You can taste the resulting frisson in the wines.

As in the best parts of the Mosel, the soil is primarily slate. The qualities of Mosel wine – apple-like freshness and bite, a marvellous mingling of honey in the scent and steel in the finish – can find their apogee in Saar wine. It is drier here than on the Ruwer, resulting in lower yields and more restrained aromas. If anything, the emphasis here is more on the steel than the honey.

In unsuccessful vintages (there are a few) even the best growers may have to sell their produce to the makers of sparkling Sekt, who need high acidity in their raw material. But when the sun shines and the Riesling ripens and goes on ripening far into October, even November, the great waft of flowers and honey which it generates would be almost too lush, were it not for the rapier-like acidity. Then the Saar comes into its own. It makes sweet wine that you can keep for years and never tire of; the balance and depth make you sniff and sip and sniff again.

Superlative sites are few. Most are in the hands of rich and ancient estates that can afford to wait for grapes to ripen and make the most of them. The most famous estate of the Saar is that of Egon Müller, whose house appears on the map as Scharzhof at the foot of the Scharzhofberg in Wiltingen. Müller's sweetest Trockenbeerenauslesen are among the world's most expensive white wines. Egon Müller also manages the Le Gallais estate, with the famous Braune Kupp vineyard, at the other end of Wiltingen.

Geltz Zilliken singlehandedly demonstrated the greatness of the Rausch vineyard across the river from Saarburg, while rising stars include the

These cellars, underneath the Vereinigte Hospitien in Trier, would have looked quite remarkably similar 1,600 years ago when they were built by the Romans. A little less electric light, perhaps, and the wines in barrel would probably have tasted rather different.

über-traditionalist Roman Niewodniczanski of Van Volxem (Müller's neighbour in Wiltingen; he makes only what he calls "harmonic" dry wines), Claudia Loch of Weinhof Herrenberg in Schoden, and von Othegraven in Kanzem (now owned by TV star Günther Jauch). Von Kesselstatt owns part of the Scharzhofberg vineyard, while St Urbans-Hof downstream in Leiwen (see p.225), Peter Lauer of Ayl (a Feinherb specialist), von Hövel at Oberemmel, and Schloss Saarstein near Serrig make marvellous Saar Rieslings too.

Almost 320 acres (130ha) of the Mosel's vineyards, many of them in the Saar and Ruwer, belong to a group of religious and charitable bodies incorporating the estates of Hohe Domkirche (the cathedral), Bischöfliches Konvikt (a Catholic boarding school), Friedrich-Wilhelm-Gymnasium (Karl Marx's old school), and Bischöfliches Priesterseminar (a college for priests). Another spiritual organization with sizable vineyard holdings is the Vereinigte Hospitien (an almshouse) at Trier. In its deep, damp Roman cellars under the city one has the feeling that wine is itself an act of charity rather than mere vulgar trade.

All of these classics are quite sweet – in the case of the Eiswein very sweet – yet feather-light in terms of alcohol – only about 7 or 8% – except for Van Volxem's Gottesfuss, in which vines planted in 1880 produce a hugely dense wine that is just off-dry.

HERRENBERG
SONNENBERG
FALKENSTEINER HOFBERG
219
200
326
Niedermennig
Könzer Bach
Obermennig
EUCHARIUSBERG
ALTENBERG
↑ *Trier*
Konz
ALTENBERG
200
260
220
URBELT
PULCHEN
287
KUPP
SAND-BERG
AUF DE WILTINGERKUPP
BRAUNE KUPP
Kommlingen
322
300
Golgen Berg
272
Krettnach
KARLSBERG
ALTEN-BERG
KIRCH-BERG
Filzen
STEIN-BERGER
HERREN-BERG
HÖLLE
GOTTES-FUSS
Rauhof
300
312
Der Oberste Weiher
FELS
Weingut von Othegraven
ALTEN-BERG
HÖRECKER
Forsthaus
240
ALTENBERG
Weingut Priesterseminar
UNTER-BERG
Kanzem
240
AGRITIUSBERG
LIEBFRAUEN-BERG
ALTENBERG
SCHLOSS-BERG
KLOSTERBERG
Kloster Berg
230
ROSENBERG
200
Oberemmel
HÜTTE
Hamm
Hammerfahre
Jagdhütte
ROSENBERG
RAUL
ALTENBERG
263
SCHLOSSBERG
Wiltingen
Oberemmeler Bach
200
312
HERRENBERGER
GOLDBERG
RITTERPFAD
JESUITEN-BERG
200
BRAUNFELS
Scharz Berg
ROSENBERG
ROSENBERG
300
SCHARZHOFBERG
Scharzhof
Links der Saar
Wawern
Weyerbach
SONNENBERG
Winzergenossenschaft
Scharzhof
RITTERPFAD
JESUITTEN-BERG
323
Staatsforst Wawerner Hochwald
SCHLANGENGRABEN
SAARFEILSER MARIENBERG
280
Saarburg-West
BRAUNFELS
HERRENBERG
Jungenwald
51
Aylerwald
240
HERRENBERG
N
Biebelhausen
Schoden
Ayler Kupp
Graubusch
KUPP
Irminer-Wald
KUPP
HERREN-BERGER
Ayl
SCHEIDTER-BERG
Mohlems Kopf
321
KUPP
BOCKSTEIN
440
300
KUPP
Hohe Köpchen
KUPP
630
Ockfen
KLOSTER-BERG
Ockfener Bach
KREUZ Berg
342
FUCHS
STIRN
SONNENBERG
300
Niederleuken
KUPP
KLOSTER-BERG
251
BERG-SCHLÖSSCHEN
337
SCHLOSS-BERG
Kaselbach
SONNENBERG
200
ANTONIUS-BRUNNEN
RAUSCH
51
081
Saarburg
182
Irsch
SONNENBERG
Beurig
407
Perl
Staatsforst
285
407
SONNENBERG
Saarburg Ost
269
300
Hasenheide
SCHLOSS SAARSTEINER
VOGELSANG
Serriger Bach
280
Merzig
ANTONIUSBERG
SCHLOSS SAARFELSER SCHLOSSBERG
KUPP
Schloss Saarfels
Serrig

Koblenz
Rhein
Mosel
Trier
Nahe
Saarburg

1:50,000
Km 0 .... 1 .... 2 Km
Miles 0 .... 1 Mile

_ _ KUPP   Einzellage

_ · _ · _   Kreis (rural district) boundary

_ _ _ _   Gemeinde (parish) boundary

Exceptional vineyard

Excellent vineyard

Other vineyard

Woods

——200——   Contour interval 20 metres

STAR OF THE SAAR

The most famous vineyard here by far is the 69 acre (28ha) Scharzhofberg, a south-facing site some way from the river but one that manages, especially in the hands of an Egon Müller (IV is currently in charge), to produce wines that are truly ethereal.

Middle Mosel: Piesport

The spectacular river walls of slate mapped here, rising over 700ft (200m) in places, were first planted with vines by the Romans in the 4th century. They provide perfect conditions for Riesling, introduced here in the 15th century and firmly rooted in the best sites during the 18th.

The wines of the river vary along its banks even more than, say, the wines of Burgundy vary along the Côte d'Or. But all the best sites face south, held up to the sun like toast to a fire. So hot are these vineyards in midsummer that working in them after noon is unthinkable. The vineyards also benefit both from the hill north of Minheim, which effectively closes this stretch of the valley to cold eastern winds, and the wooded slopes above the vineyards, which exude cold air at night, encouraging dramatic

differences between day and night temperatures and retaining acid and aroma in the wines.

The Mittelmosel (Middle Mosel) is generally accepted as virtually identical to the legally delimited Bereich Bernkastel, from Trier in the southwest to Pünderich in the northeast. Here and overleaf we map beyond the central and most famous villages to include several whose wine is often underrated.

One obvious candidate is Thörnich, whose Ritsch vineyard has been brought to glorious life by Carl Loewen. Another in this category is Klüsserath just downstream, where Kirsten and Clüsserath-Eifel have been making exceptional wines from the Bruderschaft vineyard, a typical Mosel steep bank curving from south to southwest. There is an important difference

between delicacy and faintness; these wines are delicate. The long tongue of land that ends in Trittenheim is almost a cliff where the village of Leiwen jumps the river to claim the vineyard of Laurentiuslay. Fine examples abound, thanks to a concentration of ambitious young vintners in this area.

The best-exposed site of Trittenheim is the Apotheke vineyard, which lies over the bridge next to Leiterchen, a monopoly of Weingut Milz. Like many sites here the vineyards are so steep that a monorail is necessary to work them. The town of Neumagen-Dhron, a Roman fort and landing place, keeps in its little leafy square a remarkable Roman carving of a Mosel wine ship, laden with barrels and weary galley slaves. Reinhold Haart, St Urbans-Hof, von Kesselstatt, and Hain are outstanding producers here, all with fine holdings in the south-facing bowl of vines that is Piesporter Goldtröpfchen. Its dramatic amphitheatre gives Piesport a standing far above its neighbours. Its honeyed wines have magical fragrance and breeding, which can, thanks to the particularly deep, clay-like slate here, exude almost baroque aromas. According to our classification, half of the slopes can be regarded as exceptional, the other half as excellent.

Michelsberg is the Grosslage (amalgam of vineyards) name for this part of the river, from Trittenheim to Minheim. "Piesporter Michelsberg", therefore, has not normally been Piesporter at all – typical of how Grosslagen names, fortunately now in retreat, have misled the consumer.

Wintrich and Kesten can all make fine wines, with Ohligsberg probably the best. But there are no perfectly aligned slopes in this stretch until the beginning of the great ramp of vines that rises opposite the village of Brauneberg. In Kesten it is called Paulinshofberg. In Brauneberg it is the Juffer and Juffer Sonnenuhr (the part of Juffer with the sundial). Fritz Haag-Dusemonder Hof and Max Ferd. Richter have made glorious golden examples in both parts of the Juffer.

This view of the famous Goldtröpfchen vineyard across the Mosel from Piesport shows vividly how much light may be reflected from the river on to the vines. The foreground suggests just how painful it can be to work these steep vineyards.

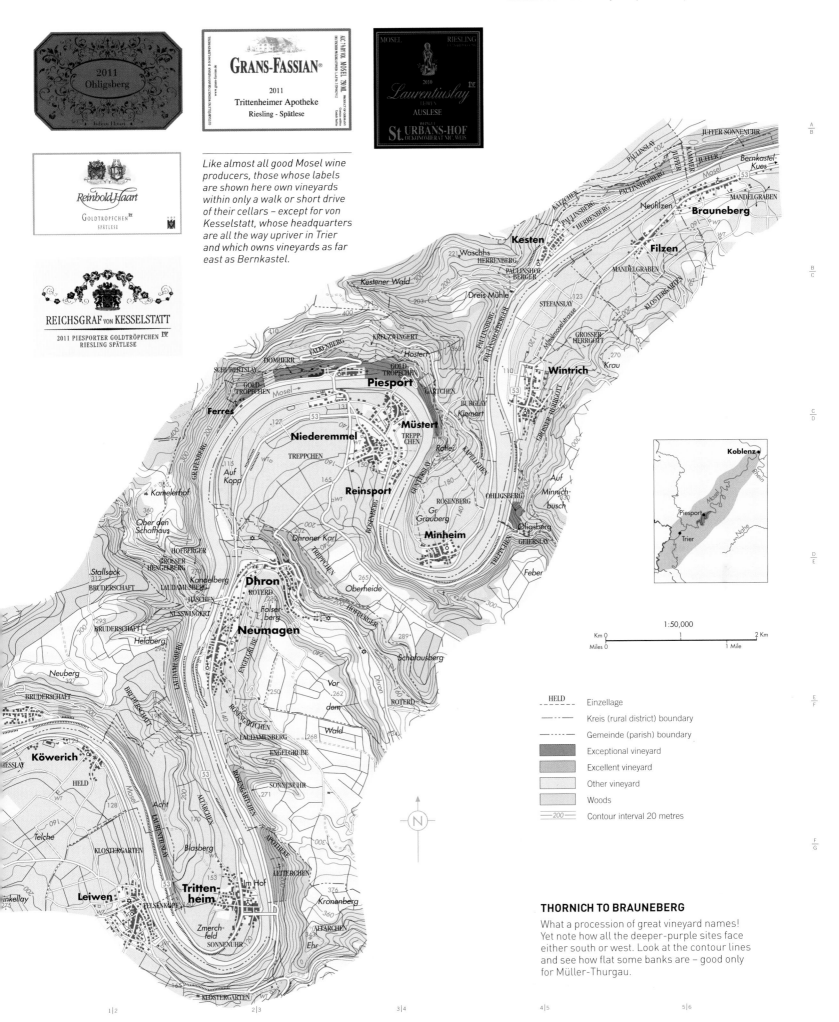

Like almost all good Mosel wine producers, those whose labels are shown here own vineyards within only a walk or short drive of their cellars – except for von Kesselstatt, whose headquarters are all the way upriver in Trier and which owns vineyards as far east as Bernkastel.

1:50,000

HELD	Einzellage
	Kreis (rural district) boundary
	Gemeinde (parish) boundary
	Exceptional vineyard
	Excellent vineyard
	Other vineyard
	Woods
200	Contour interval 20 metres

THORNICH TO BRAUNEBERG

What a procession of great vineyard names! Yet note how all the deeper-purple sites face either south or west. Look at the contour lines and see how flat some banks are – good only for Müller-Thurgau.

Middle Mosel: Bernkastel

The view from the ruined castle above Bernkastel is of a green wall of vines 700ft (200m) high and 5 miles (8km) long. Only the Douro, in Portugal, in the whole gazetteer of rivers to which the vine is wedded, has anything approaching a comparable sight. From Brauneberg to the Bernkastel suburb of Kues many of the hills are relatively modest – the wines, too. One of the more notable products of this stretch is the Eiswein regularly gathered by Max Ferd. Richter from the Helenenkloster vineyard above Mülheim. The top sites are exceptionally steep, however, in Lieser, a village perhaps best known for the grim mansion owned by Thomas Haag's excellent Schloss Lieser estate at the foot of the Rosenlay. In the Niederberg-Helden, Schloss Lieser has a perfect south-facing slope.

The Mosel's most famous vineyard starts abruptly, rising almost sheer above the gables of the tourist mecca that is Bernkastel: dark slate frowning at slate. The butt of the hill, its one straight south elevation, is the Doctor vineyard. From its flank the proudest names of the Mosel follow one another in unbroken succession. Comparison of the first growths of Bernkastel with those of Graach and Wehlen, often with wines from the same growers in each place, is a fascinating game. The trademark of Bernkastel is a touch of flint. Wehleners, grown on shallow stony slate, are rich and filigreed while those grown on the deeper, heavier slate of Graach are somehow earthier.

The least of these wines should be something with a very obvious personality. The greatest of them, long-lived, pale gold, piquant, frivolous yet profound, are wines that beg to be compared with music and poetry.

Many world-famous producers cluster here, although a hike through the vineyards (too steep for a stroll) quickly demonstrates that not all the growers are equally conscientious. JJ Prüm has long been the leading grower of Wehlen. Markus Molitor (also of Wehlen) has won his reputation more recently, not just with fine Riesling but with some unusually excellent Spätburgunder, too. Erni (Dr) Loosen of Bernkastel, Selbach-Oster, and Willi Schaefer also command worldwide respect, while von Kesselstatt continues its excellent work this far downstream. Controversy rages meanwhile over a huge bridge: Europe's highest, planned to cross the river at Urzig, bringing a highway through the sensitive drainage area of these superlative Riesling sites.

Zeltingen brings the Great Wall to an end. It is the Mosel's biggest wine commune, and among its best. At Urzig, across the river, red slate, in rocky pockets instead of a smooth bank,

The period charm, and myriad Weinstuben, of Bernkastel-Kues act like a magnet for the crowds of tourists who flock to the Mosel Valley from spring to summer. The vineyards surrounding the town are too steep to attract any but the fittest visitors.

gives the Würzgarten (spice garden) wines a different flavour: more penetrating and racy than Zeltingers. Erden's finest vineyard, the Prälat, is probably the warmest in the entire Mosel Valley, sandwiched between massive and precipitous red slate cliffs and the river. Dr Loosen makes some of his best wines here. Wines from the Treppchen vineyard are usually more austere.

It used to be thought that the drama of Mosel wine ended at Kinheim, but a new generation of producers such as Swiss-born Daniel Vollenweider of Wolf, Martin Müllen of Traben-Trarbach, Weiser-Künstler with the Enkircher Ellergrub, Thorsten Melsheimer in Reil, and biodynamic Clemens Busch in Pünderich (the latter two off the map to the north) are proving otherwise in a delicious and indeed dramatic way.

Just downstream from here at Zell, the landscape changes dramatically, with most of the vineyards planted on narrow terraces, inspiring this lower section of the Mosel Valley's name, Terrassenmosel. Of the many excellent sites here the most important today are Europe's steepest vineyard, Calmont in Bremm, Gäns in Gondorf, and the Uhlen (an exceptional site) and Röttgen of Winningen. Such exciting producers as Heymann-Löwenstein and Knebel in Winningen, Franzen in Bremm, and Lubentiushof in Niederfell provide the proof in bottles of Riesling both sweet and dry.

Joh.Jos.Prüm
2007
Wehlener Sonnenuhr
Kabinett

Willi Schaefer
2009
Graacher Domprobst
Riesling Beerenauslese
Mosel

SELBACH-OSTER
2011
ZELTINGER SCHLOSSBERG
RIESLING AUSLESE

rdener Prälat
Riesling
Alte Reben

MARKUS MOLITOR
2007
Graacher
Himmelreich***

Pinot Noir
Mosel

Among all the overachieving craftspeople represented here, the one whose wines last longest, is Joh. Jos. Prüm, currently run by Dr Manfred and his daughter, Dr Katharina Prüm.

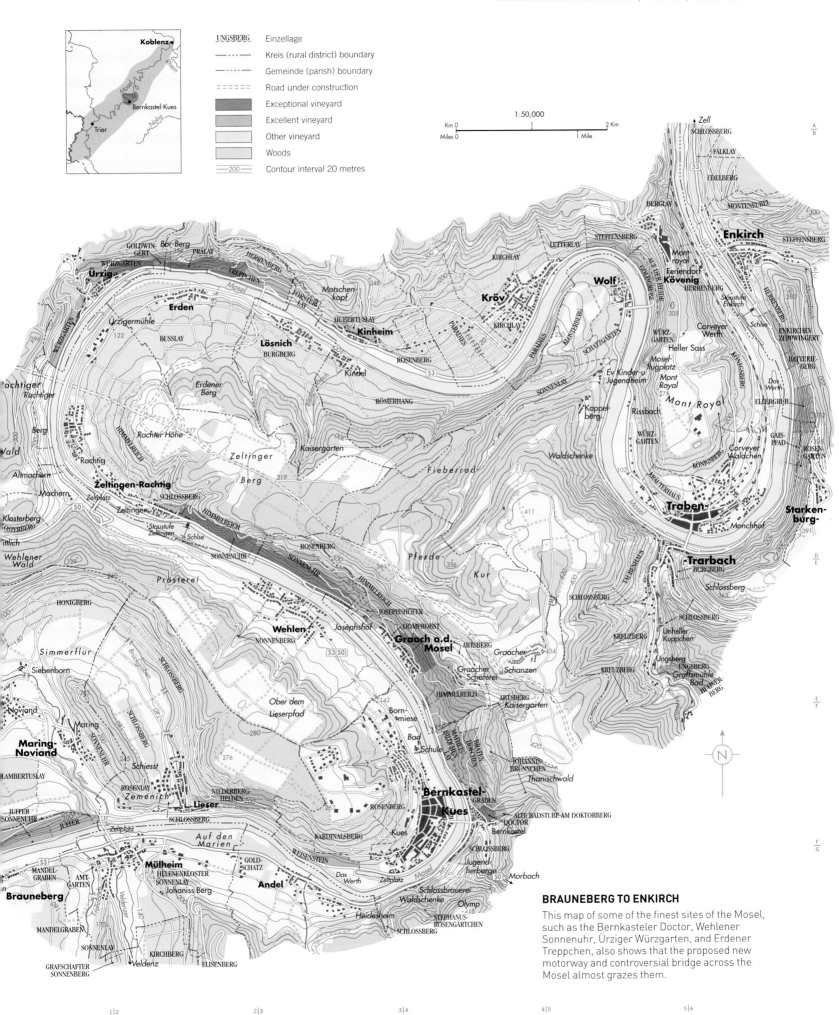

UNGSBERG — Einzellage
— · — · — Kreis (rural district) boundary
— ·· — ·· — Gemeinde (parish) boundary
= = = = = = Road under construction
Exceptional vineyard
Excellent vineyard
Other vineyard
Woods
—200— Contour interval 20 metres

1:50,000
Km 0   2 Km
Miles 0   1 Mile

BRAUNEBERG TO ENKIRCH

This map of some of the finest sites of the Mosel, such as the Bernkasteler Doctor, Wehlener Sonnenuhr, Ürziger Würzgarten, and Erdener Treppchen, also shows that the proposed new motorway and controversial bridge across the Mosel almost grazes them.

Nahe

What would you expect of a region neatly inserted between the Mosel, Rheinhessen, and the Rheingau? Precisely. At their best, Nahe wines capture the precise vineyard expression of those from the Mosel, and live as long, but also reveal the body and grapey intensity of Rhine wines. Then there is that extra ingredient: a hint of alchemical gold.

The River Nahe flows northeast parallel to the Mosel, out of the Hunsrück hills, to join the Rhine at Bingen. Whereas the Mosel is the very spine of its vineyards, the Nahe is flanked by scattered outbreaks of wine-growing where either its own banks or its tributaries' face south. Most of its best wines today are made by quite recently established winemakers. The best vineyards are no easier to work than the Mosel's, however, and the number of growers has been declining.

If the majority (just) of white Nahe wine is still made in the fruity, sweeter style, wine-growers such as Helmut Dönnhoff and his son Cornelius, Werner Schönleber and his son Frank, and Tim Fröhlich of the Schäfer-Fröhlich estate have shown that brilliant dry wines can be made from the region's best vineyards.

The westernmost of these are above Monzingen, whose two first-class sites are the stoney, slatey Halenberg, and the more sprawling, variable and damp Frühlingsplätzchen, with redder, softer soil. Emrich-Schönleber and Schäfer-Fröhlich are the outstanding exponents in this broad, open valley, which contrasts with the narrow drama of the Nahe's most concentrated stretch of great vineyards. Mapped in detail on the opposite page, they lie on the left, south-facing bank of the river as it winds around Schlossböckelheim, Oberhausen, Niederhausen, and Norheim. They were classified by the Royal Prussian Surveyor in 1901 (on a map revived in the 1990s by the VDP as a blueprint for vineyard quality). Niederhäuser Hermannshöhle was rated first, encouraging the Prussian government to establish a new Staatsweingut (State Wine Domain) here the following year. Scrub-covered arid hillsides and old copper mines (Kupfergrube) were cleared using convict labour to create several new vineyard sites. Its wines then challenged those of the long-established Felsenberg downstream of Schlossböckelheim, today rendered so eloquently by Schäfer-Fröhlich, whose other great vineyard is, confusingly, the steep Felseneck of Bockenau well north of the river.

From the 1920s, the Nahe Staatsweingut and several large estates based in Bad Kreuznach but with vineyards upstream produced wines of a brilliance and pungent minerality as spectacular as the rocky landscape. At last, in 1930, the Nahe was recognized as an independent wine-growing region, but the fame of the top growers was always greater than that of the region itself. From the late 1980s, the Staatsweingut failed to play the leading role for which it was established and is now, as Gut Hermannsberg, rebuilding both its cellars and reputation in private hands. The major beneficiary of this turmoil has been the exceptional Helmut Dönnhoff, based in Oberhausen, who put this stretch of vineyards

THE WINE CENTRES OF NAHE

The vineyards of the Nahe are particularly widely dispersed, as this map of all significant wine towns and villages shows. Vineyards cluster not just on the banks of the River Nahe but also on those of the Alsenz, Ellerbach, Gräfenbach, and Guldenbach.

MONZINGEN

The sprawl of Frühlingsplätzchen is clear when compared with the much more restricted Halenberg – although it also looks very odd that Halenberg has a bite taken out of it. This is the section from which Emrich-Schönleber makes its A de L (*Auf der Lay*, or "on the slate") Riesling.

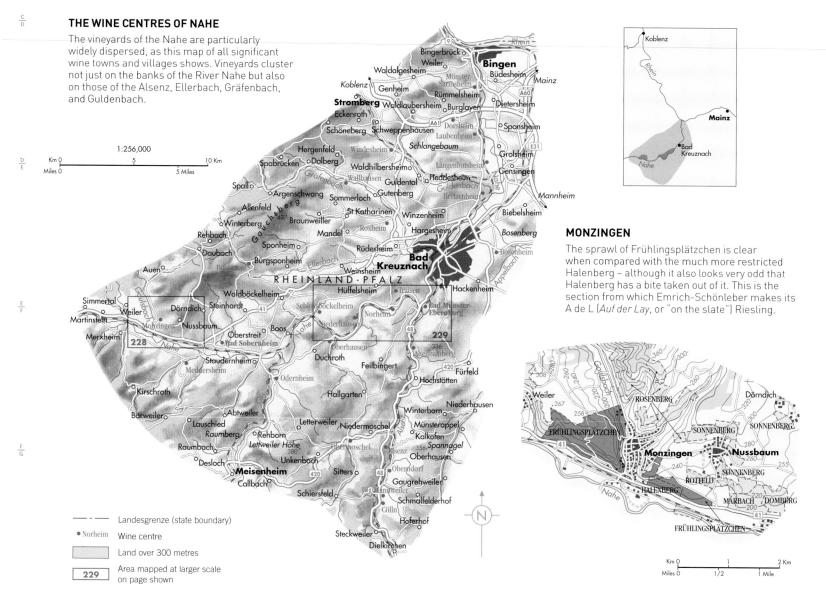

Landesgrenze (state boundary)

Norheim · Wine centre

Land over 300 metres

229 · Area mapped at larger scale on page shown

The Traiser Bastei vines are squeezed between the Nahe, the railway, and the road on one side and on the other the craggy Rotenfels precipice, which stores and radiates warmth between Traisen and Bad Münster. The vineyard has been shrunk by the extent of falling rocks.

– in some cases recuperating them from almost unworkably steep scrub – on the map. He has been able to add some of the old Staatsweingut's most valuable holdings in the Hermannshöhle to his estate, and has more recently been recuperating the Höllenpfad vineyard above Roxheim, northwest of Bad Kreuznach. Many other vineyards have been sold off by the once-great estates of Bad Kreuznach. But south of the town, just upstream of the Bad Münster bend, the red precipice of the Rotenfels, said to be the highest cliff in Europe north of the Alps, can still yield fine wine from the strip of fallen rubble at its foot. Dr Crusius is the principal custodian of the short ramp of a red-earth suntrap that is the potentially great Traiser Bastei.

Downstream of here, and north of the area mapped in detail below, is an increasingly vibrant wine scene. In Langenlonsheim, Martin Tesch captures the essence of enviably mature vineyards in dramatically labelled bottles of ultra-modern, single-vineyard dry wine. Wine writer Armin Diel and his daughter Caroline of Schlossgut Diel have put Dorsheim on the map with a range of sometimes dazzling wines, while Kruger-Rumpf makes exciting wine from holdings in Münster-Sarmsheim, almost on the outskirts of Bingen, where the Nahe meets the Rheingau.

Of these five great Nahe producers, only one, Dönnhoff, has vines in the stretch of top-quality vineyards below, demonstrating just how scattered the Nahe's vinelands are. The Brücke ("bridge") vineyard is a monopole that regularly produces luscious sweet wines.

STEINBERG — Einzellage
---·---·— Kreis (rural district) boundary
— – — – — Gemeinde (parish) boundary
       Exceptional vineyard
       Excellent vineyard
       Other vineyard
       Woods
— 200 — Contour interval 20 metres

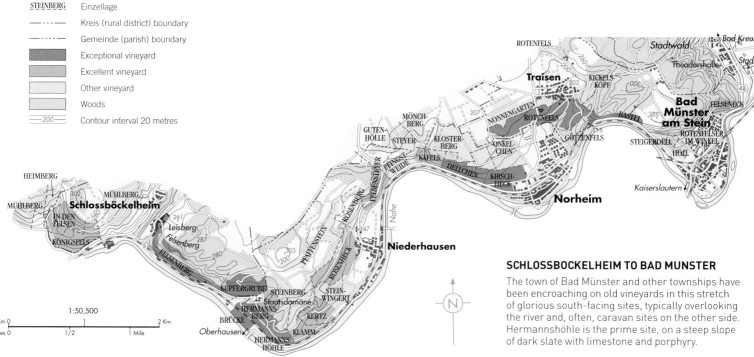

SCHLOSSBÖCKELHEIM TO BAD MUNSTER

The town of Bad Münster and other townships have been encroaching on old vineyards in this stretch of glorious south-facing sites, typically overlooking the river and, often, caravan sites on the other side. Hermannshöhle is the prime site, on a steep slope of dark slate with limestone and porphyry.

1:50,500
Km 0   1   2 Km
Miles 0   1/2   1 Mile

Western Rheingau

The Rheingau is the spiritual heart of German wine, the birthplace of Riesling and the site of its most historic vineyard, planted by Burgundian Cistercians as a rival to the Clos de Vougeot. At its best its wines can unite depth, subtlety, and austerity to make the noblest wine of the great wine river. Did these attributes make it complacent? It has certainly been overtaken in the past decades by the less aristocratic Rheinhessen and Rheinpfalz. Its potential, though, still glitters in its finest bottlings. The names of Rüdesheim, Johannisberg, Erbach, Rauenthal, and Hochheim still spell Riesling at its most compelling.

The broad stretch of south-facing hillside mapped here is sheltered to the north by the Taunus range and warmed to the south by reflection from the Rhine, here running from east to west. It has obvious advantages for vine-growing. The river, more than half a mile wide and a throbbing highway for slow strings of enormous barges, also promotes the mists that encourage botrytis as the grapes ripen. Decidedly mixed

soils, crumbling from the hills, include various forms of slate and quartzite as well as marls.

At the western end of the Rheingau the south-facing Rüdesheimer Berg Schlossberg, by far the Rheingau's steepest slope, drops almost sheer to the river. The Rüdesheimer Berg is distinguished from the rest of the parish by having the word Berg before each separate vineyard name. At their best (which is not always in the hottest years, since the drainage is too good at times), these are superlative wines, full of fruit and strength and yet delicate in nuance. In hotter years, the vineyards behind the town of Rüdesheim come into their own. Georg Breuer and Leitz are the outstanding names here.

The Rheingau's white wine output is even more dominated by Riesling than the Mosel's,

but today 12% of Rheingau vineyards are planted with Spätburgunder (Pinot Noir) and Assmannshausen, around the river bend to the northwest, is no longer the sole red wine outpost.

Ambitious, cosmopolitan growers such as August Kesseler of Assmannshausen revolutionized the colour and structure of such wines, from pale and suspiciously smoky to deep, sturdy, and barrique-aged. Dry Assmannshäuser Spätburgunder has for long been Germany's most famous red wine. Krone, Robert König, the Hessische Staatsweingüter Assmannshausen (State Wine Domain), and newcomer Chat Sauvage maintain a high standard. Assmannshausen's extraordinary pink Trockenbeerenauslese is a revered rarity.

The Rheingau wines of all hues that fetch the highest prices are the super-sweet Beerenauslesen

THE RHEINGAU

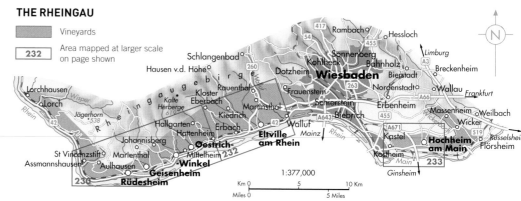

- Vineyards
- 232 — Area mapped at larger scale on page shown

1:377,000

ASSMANNSHAUSEN TO HALLGARTEN

The map above shows how we have sliced up this venerable stretch of the vineyards sloping down to the broad, busy Rhine in order to map as much of the important terrain as possible. Alas, there is no room on the map below for vineyards around Lorch, whose reputation has been steadily growing.

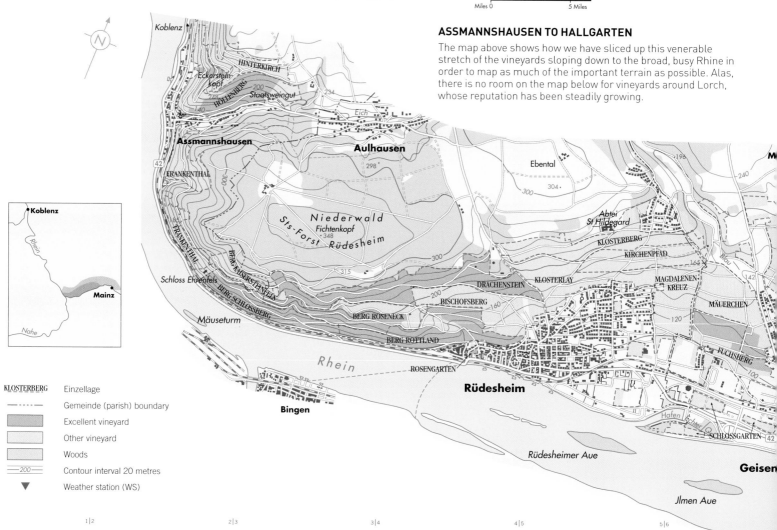

- KLOSTERBERG — Einzellage
- - - - - — Gemeinde (parish) boundary
- Excellent vineyard
- Other vineyard
- Woods
- —200— — Contour interval 20 metres
- ▼ — Weather station (WS)

and Trockenbeerenauslesen: wines with another purpose than accompanying food. Its less rare wines had drifted into being sweet, too, before its current leaders, like so many of their peers to the south, deliberately moved away from this tradition. By 2005, 84% of all Rheingau wine was dry – as it had been 100 years before. The Charta organization of top growers led the way in the 1980s, encouraging low yields and dry wines of Spätlese quality. Since 1999, this torch has been carried by the VDP top growers' association.

Geisenheim, just upstream from Rüdesheim, is home to the world-renowned teaching and research centre for oenology and, especially, viticulture. Just upriver and uphill from here is Schloss Johannisberg, standing above a great apron of vines, dominating the landscape between Geisenheim and Winkel. It is credited with the introduction in the 18th century of late harvesting

to make nobly rotten, sweet rarities and, after a lull, it once again deserves its landmark status.

Schloss Vollrads, above Winkel, is another magnificent and historic estate whose reputation has recently been restored. Even Winkel's second-best site, Hasensprung ("hare's leap"), is capable of richly nuanced, aromatic wine.

Mittelheim, squeezed between Winkel and Oestrich, has less distinction, but the best wines of Oestrich, from the Doosberg and Lenchen

vineyards, have real character and lusciousness, whether sweet or dry. Peter Jakob Kühn, Spreitzer, and Querbach make both with distinction.

In Hallgarten, the Rheingau vineyards reach their highest point. Heavier marl soil predominates here. The Hendelberg and Schönhell sites yield strong, long-lived wines, although many regard Jungfer as the finest site. Fürst Löwenstein and Fred Prinz are the Jungfer's most notable producers.

RHEINGAU: GEISENHEIM ▼

Latitude / Altitude of WS
49.59° / 377ft (115m)

Average growing season temperature at WS
59.4°F (15°C)

Average annual rainfall at WS
21in (537mm)

Harvest month rainfall at WS
October: 1.9in (48mm)

Principal viticultural hazards
Fungal diseases

Principal grape varieties
Riesling, Spätburgunder

Schloss Johannisberg is the granddaddy of them all, boasting nine centuries of vine-growing, while the others are more contemporary stars. Kesseler is a red wine specialist, and the great majority of Rheingau wines of either colour are now dry.

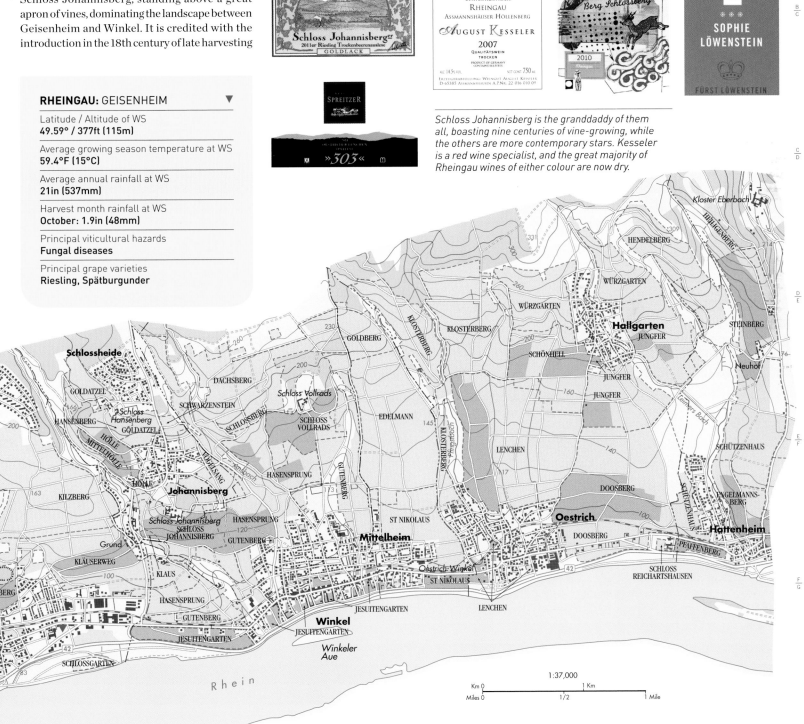

Eastern Rheingau

The boundaries of Hattenheim (in the west of the area mapped below) stretch back into the hills to include the high ridge of the Steinberg. This 80-acre (32.4 ha) vineyard was planted and walled in the 12th century by the Cistercians. Below, in a wooded hollow, stands their monastery, Kloster Eberbach. If German wine had a headquarters this great complex of medieval buildings in its woodland valley would be it. Today, it houses music festivals, a hotel, restaurant, and an extraordinary collection of ancient wine that tells the story the Rheingau. In 2008, its owners, the Hessische Staatsweingüter Kloster Eberbach (State Wine Domain), intent on restoring the Steinberg to its full glory, built a thoroughly modern winery on the outskirts of Eltville (see photo, opposite) for its vast vineyard holdings, the biggest in Germany and some of the best.

Like Hallgarten, Hattenheim has marl in the soil. Mannberg on its eastern boundary is 90% owned by Langwerth von Simmern. Nussbrunnen and Wisselbrunnen are capable of producing wines just as good. Straddling the border with Erbach is Marcobrunn, unusually close to the river in a situation that looks as though the drainage would be far from perfect. Wine from either side of the parish boundary is very full-flavoured and often rich, fruity, and spicy: the characteristics of these marl-based vineyards. The owners of Marcobrunn include Schloss Schönborn, Schloss Reinhartshausen, and the Staatsweingut. Erbacher Siegelsberg, which lies parallel with Marcobrunn, is next in quality.

The beautiful and musical Gothic church of Kiedrich is the next landmark, set back from the river and 400ft (120m) higher. Kiedrich makes exceptionally well-balanced and delicately spicy wine. Robert Weil (part Japanese-owned) is the biggest estate of the parish and today makes many of the Rheingau's most impressive sweet wines. Gräfenberg is reckoned the best part of the vineyard, although Wasseros is also highly regarded. Weil concentrates on its substantial holdings in Gräfenberg and the smaller but equally outstanding Turmberg, and makes fine Trockenbeerenauslesen in enviable quantity in both. (Turmberg was incorporated into the Wasseros in 1971, but in 2005 was restored, under its original name and size of 9.4 acres/3.8ha, as a monopoly of the Weil estate.)

Rauenthal, the last of the hill villages and the furthest from the river, can make a different kind

HATTENHEIM TO WALLUF

Note that for entirely practical reasons, the orientation of this map, like that of the Western Rheingau, is not due north. The vines occupy the great majority of the slope between the woods and the water. Vines are also grown on the narrow island between Hattenheim and Erbach.

KLOSTERBERG	Einzellage
- - - - -	Gemeinde (parish) boundary
	Excellent vineyard
	Other vineyard
	Woods
—200—	Contour interval 20 metres

For location map, see p.230

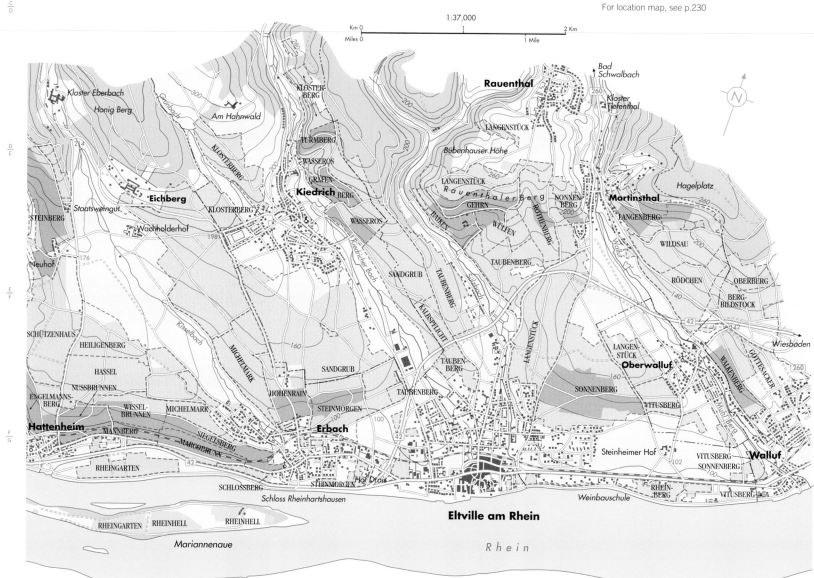

1:37,000

of superlative wine. The complex Rauenthalers of the estate of Georg Breuer continue to be some of the most sought-after in Germany. Auslesen from two lordly growers, Baron Langwerth von Simmern and Count Schönborn, as well as those of several smaller growers on the Rauenthaler Berg, are prized for the combination of power and delicacy in their flowery scent and in their spicy aftertaste.

Eltville makes larger quantities of wine but without as much cachet, although J Koegler is a grower to watch. Not far from the town are the headquarters of the Staatsweingüter Kloster Eberbach, whose wines (especially Steinbergers) have in the past been among the Rheingau's best.

Without the fame of their neighbours, Walluf and Martinsthal share much of their quality. At Walluf the stars are JB Becker and Toni Jost, one of the most celebrated producers of the Mittelrhein across the river.

Hochheim

In the far east of the Rheingau, separated from the main stretch of vineyards mapped opposite by the southern suburbs of sprawling Wiesbaden, the Rheingau has an unexpected outpost: Hochheim (which gave us the word "hock"). Hochheim vineyards lie on gently sloping land just north of the warming River Main, isolated in country that has no other vines. Good Hochheimers, with their own thrilling full-bodied earthiness, thanks to deep soils and an unusually warm mesoclimate, match the quality of the best Rheingauers and the style of those of Nackenheim-Nierstein in Rheinhessen.

During the 1980s and 1990s, Domdechant Werner injected new life into the region, with Domdechaney its flagship site. Today, Franz Künstler is the undisputed leader for the consistency and the brilliance of his wines, particularly those from the Kirchenstück and Hölle vineyards. Kirchenstück grows the most elegant wines, while Hölle and Domdechaney produce wines so rich enough to be atypical of the Rheingau's elegant signature.

Hochheim was previously most readily associated with Queen Victoria, whose visit to the source of wines then so popular with her subjects is commemorated by the Königin Victoriaberg vineyard and label. The sole owner of Königin Victoriaberg is now Reiner Flick, who not only makes excellent dry and sweet wines from the vineyards of Hochheim, but is also putting the historic vineyards of Wicker, especially Nonnberg, to the northeast of Hochheim, back on the map – though not, alas, this one.

Flick and Künstler are the bright sparks of Hochheim today. The Czech Künstler family made wine for three centuries in Moravia before being expelled from the country in the mid-20th century.

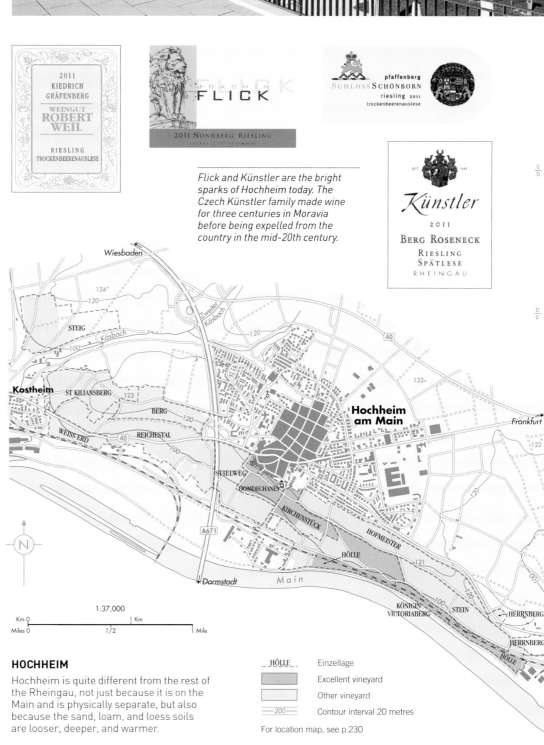

HOCHHEIM

Hochheim is quite different from the rest of the Rheingau, not just because it is on the Main and is physically separate, but also because the sand, loam, and loess soils are looser, deeper, and warmer.

HÖLLE	Einzellage
	Excellent vineyard
	Other vineyard
—200—	Contour interval 20 metres

For location map, see p.230

1|2   2|3   3|4   4|5   5|6

Rheinhessen

Today, Rheinhessen rivals Pfalz as the most exciting wine region in Germany. For years this area between the Rheingau and Pfalz, bounded to the east and north by a long, slow bend in the Rhine, seemed to be asleep. A handful of strong traditionalists around the Nierstein "Rheinfront" made fine wines; most of the area just churned out the Liebfraumilch and Gutes Domtal that did Germany's reputation so much harm.

But by the turn of the century it was apparent that much was set to change in and around the 150-odd Rheinhessen villages, spaced out over an area 20 by 30 miles (30 by 50km), virtually all named Something-heim, where wine is just one crop among many. A group of highly trained and motivated, enviably well-travelled young winemakers have demonstrated that not just the steep terraces right on the Rhine, but the dull, undulating, fertile mixed-farming country in the

hinterland can produce wines of thrilling integrity and quality. They are concentrated in the south in the area mapped opposite, for the first time in this Atlas, known as Wonnegau. Many of these younger winemakers belong to organizations such as Message in a Bottle, Rheinhessen Five, and Vinovation, inspired in particular by a remarkable pair of overperforming neighbours, Philipp Wittmann and Klaus Peter Keller, in the area around Flörsheim-Dalsheim in the south.

The revolution has been taking place in villages no one had heard of. Dittelsheim owes its arrival to Stefan Winter; Siefersheim, far to the west, to Wagner-Stempel; Hohen-Sülzen to Battenfeld-Spanier; Bechtheim to Dreissigacker; and Weinheim to Gysler. In many cases they are not so much trailblazing as recovering historic sites, for the vine has been cultivated in Rheinhessen since Roman times. Charlemagne's uncle presented

vineyards in Nierstein to the diocese of Würzburg in 742. Typically these new-wave winemakers are returning to traditional winemaking methods, including most obviously low yields and ambient, rather than added cultured yeasts. The result is wines that are more intense but reveal their aromas rather more slowly than the German norm. Nor do they limit themselves to Riesling. Serious dry Silvaner is made here and the quality of the Spätburgunder produced is soaring.

A mixed bag of vines

No German wine region grows a more varied mix of vines. Even the once ubiquitous Müller-Thurgau today accounts for barely 16% of all Rheinhessen's vineyard. Riesling is now Rheinhessen's second most-planted variety, having overtaken the Dornfelder that is popular for fruity reds. Silvaner, Portugieser, Kerner, Spätburgunder (Pinot Noir), Scheurebe, and Grauburgunder can all lay claim to between 4 and 9% of the region's vineyard.

Silvaner has a particularly long and noble history in Rheinhessen and can be found today in two distinct styles. The majority is light, fresh, reasonably fruity wine for early drinking (notably with the early-summer white asparagus the locals love). At the other end of the scale are powerful, dry Silvaners with high extract and longevity. Their foremost protagonist is Michael Teschke of Gau-Algesheim, whose estate is almost solely dedicated to the variety, although Keller and Wagner-Stempel are both practitioners of this style.

One traditional characteristic persists. The proportion of Rheinhessen wine that is sweeter than *halbtrocken* is still almost half. Only the Mosel and Nahe produce a lower proportion of dry wine than Rheinhessen – although many of the region's finest new-wave wines are bone-dry.

For centuries, Worms was one of the great Rhineland cities, seat of the famous "Diet" of 1521 that excommunicated Martin Luther, translator of the Bible into German. Its Liebfrauenstift-Kirchenstück vineyard around the local church, the Liebfrauenkirche, has the doubtful distinction of having christened Liebfraumilch, the rock on which quality German wine so nearly foundered. But two growers, Gutzler and Liebfrauenstift (formerly Valckenberg), are now making serious wine from this vineyard.

At the other, northern extreme of Rheinhessen, the town of Bingen, facing Rüdesheim (see p.230) across the Rhine, has excellent Riesling vineyards on the steep slopes of its first-growth Scharlachberg.

In the distant past, the town of Nierstein was famous for its wonderfully luscious, fragrant

1:331,000

Km 0 .... 5 .... 10 Km
Miles 0 .... 5 Miles

Landesgrenze (state boundary)

• Nierstein — Wine centre

Land over 200 metres

235 — Area mapped at larger scale on page shown

THE WINE CENTRES OF RHEINHESSEN

Germany's most productive region has more than 400 named single-vineyard sites but, although things have been changing for the better, most wine is still sold either as Liebfraumilch or as bland, geographically confusing Niersteiner Gutes Domtal.

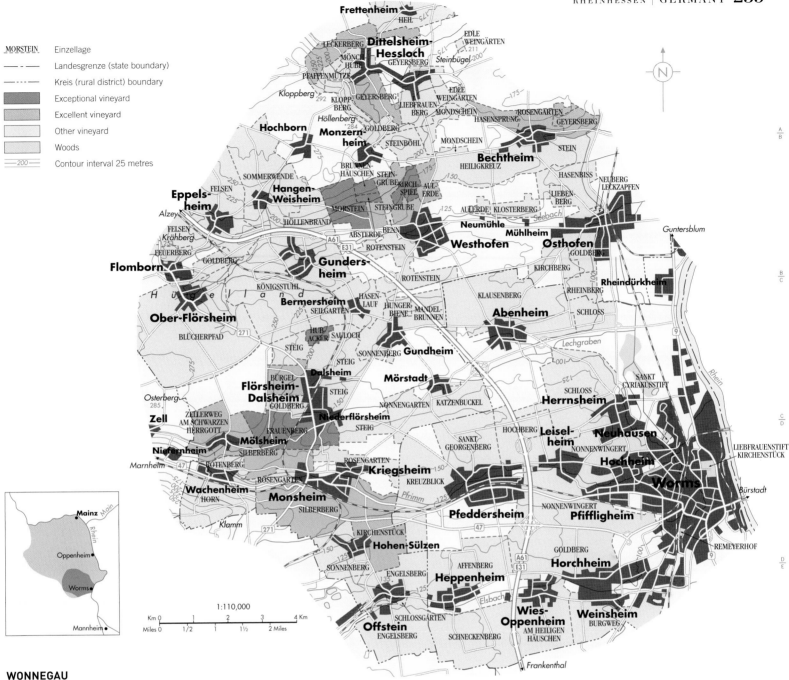

Legend:

MORSTEIN — Einzellage

— — — Landesgrenze (state boundary)

—·—·— Kreis (rural district) boundary

Exceptional vineyard

Excellent vineyard

Other vineyard

Woods

—200— Contour interval 25 metres

Map labels (towns and vineyards):

Frettenheim, HEIL, Dittelsheim-Hessloch, EDLE WEINGÄRTEN, LECKERBERG, MÖNCH HUBE, GEYERSBERG, Steinbügel, PFAFFENMÜTZE, Kloppberg, KLOPPBERG, LIEBFRAUENBERG, MONDSCHEIN, ROSENGARTEN, GEYERSBERG, Höllenberg, GOLDBERG, HASENSPRUNG, Hochborn, Monzernheim, STEINBÖHL, MONDSCHEIN, STEIN, Bechtheim, HEILIGKREUZ, HASENBISS, NEUBERG LECKZAPFEN, SOMMERWENDE, BRUNNEN-HÄUSCHEN, STEIN-GRUBE, KIRCH-SPIEL, AUL-ERDE, LIEBEN-BERG, Eppelsheim, FELSEN, Hangen-Weisheim, MORSTEIN, STEINGRUBE, AULERDE, KLOSTERBERG, Seebach, Alzey, HÖLLENBRAND, ABSTERDE, BENN, Neumühle, Mühlheim, Östhofen, Guntersblum, FELSEN Krähberg, FEUERBERG, ROTENSTEIN, Westhofen, GOLDBERG, Flomborn, GOLDBERG, Gundersheim, ROTENSTEIN, KIRCHBERG, Rheindürkheim, KÖNIGSSTUHL, RHEINBERG, Hügelland, HASEN-LAUF, HUNGER-BIENE, MANDEL-BRUNNEN, KLAUSENBERG, Abenheim, SCHLOSS, Bermersheim, SEILGARTEN, Ober-Flörsheim, HUB-ACKER, SAULOCH, SONNENBERG, Gundheim, Lechgraben, SANKT CYRIAKUSSTIFT, BLÜCHERPFAD, STEIG, STEIG, Mörstadt, SCHLOSS, Herrnsheim, Dalsheim, BÜRGEL, STEIG, NONNENGARTEN, KATZENBUCKEL, Osterberg, Flörsheim-Dalsheim, GOLDBERG, Zell, ZELLERWEG AM SCHWARZEN HERRGOTT, FRAUENBERG, Niederflörsheim, STEIG, HOCHBERG, Leiselheim, Neuhausen, Niefernheim, Mölsheim, SILBERGER, ROTENBERG, SANKT GEORGENBERG, NONNENWINGERT, Hochheim, Marnheim, ROSENGARTEN, Wachenheim, HORN, RÖSENGARTEN, Kriegsheim, KREUZBLICK, Monsheim, SILBERGER, Pfrimm, NONNENWINGERT, Pfiffligheim, Worms, Bürstadt, Klamm, Pfeddersheim, LIEBFRAUENSTIFT KIRCHENSTÜCK, REMEYERHOF, KIRCHENSTÜCK, Hohen-Sülzen, AFFENBERG, GOLDBERG, Horchheim, SONNENBERG, ENGELSBERG, Heppenheim, Wies-Oppenheim, Weinsheim, BURGWEG, Offstein, SCHLOSSGÄRTEN, ENGELSBERG, SCHNECKENBERG, AM HEILIGEN HÄUSCHEN, Frankenthal

Scale: 1:110,000 — Km 0, 1, 2, 3, 4 Km — Miles 0, 1/2, 1, 1½, 2 Miles

Inset map: Mainz, Main, Rhein, Oppenheim, Worms, Mannheim

Grid letters (right margin): A/B, B/C, C/D, D/E, E/F, F/G

Grid numbers (bottom margin): 1|2, 2|3, 3|4, 4|5, 5|6

WONNEGAU

This new map shows where the greatest concentration of the new stars of the region is to be found, in gentle farming country rather than in a dramatic landscape like the "Rheinfront" between Nackenheim and Nierstein.

wines from such illustrious vineyards as Hipping, Brudersberg, and Pettenthal, but in the 1970s the name was sullied by its association with the bloated Grosslage Niersteiner Gutes Domtal, a wine from anywhere except Nierstein. Today, it is no longer the leading light in Rheinhessen, although Kühling Gillot and Keller are doing their best to bring back the glory days.

Just to the north of the town lies the village of Nackenheim. The most famous stretch of vineyard here is the sand-red near-cliff called Roter Hang, where the Gunderloch estate consistently excels with uniquely spicy, unctuous Riesling from the Rothenberg site.

KELLER 2011 Kirchspiel Riesling

Wittmann AULERDE Riesling GG 2011

GUNDERLOCH 2011 ROTHENBERG Riesling Auslese

RHEINHESSEN SYLVANER TROCKEN VOM MÜHLWEG DEUTSCHER QUALITÄTSWEIN 0,75 L. 2011 13,0% VOL

BATTENFELD SPANIER KIRCHENSTÜCK 2011 RIESLING GG

DREISSIGACKER 2011 GEYERSBERG

The four left-most labels are for wines produced on the land mapped in detail above, while Gunderloch is perhaps the most famous "Rheinfront" producer. Michael Teschke is based in the far northwest of the region.

Pfalz

The Pfalz (in English, Palatinate) is Germany's biggest, and these days perhaps most exciting, wine region; a 50-mile (80km) stretch of vineyards north of Alsace, under the lee of the German continuation of the Vosges – the Haardt Mountains. Like Alsace, it is the sunniest and driest part of its country and has the never-failing charm of half-timbered, flower-bedecked villages among orchards. A labyrinthine road, the Deutsche Weinstrasse, like the Route du Vin of Alsace, starts at the gates of Germany and winds northwards through vines and villages, culminating in the Mittelhaardt, the area mapped in detail opposite. A great part of the wine of the area has been made by efficient co-operatives, but the Pfalz is now known for its ambitious individual wine producers, many of them members of such informal organizations as Fünf Freunde, Pfalzhoch, and Südpfalz Connexion.

Riesling is the most-planted vine, but the red wine craze has swept through the Pfalz, too. In 2010, almost 40% of all its wine was red, and Dornfelder was the second most-planted variety; Müller-Thurgau has fallen to almost exactly the same area as the even less distinguished red Portugieser. A rich mix of other varieties makes up 45% of the region's vines. The Pfalz is Germany's workshop for a range of whites and reds of every complexion, including the whole Pinot family, with the emphasis on dry, often barrique-aged wines for the table. The three Pinots (Weissburgunder, Grauburgunder, and Spätburgunder), with and without oak, are firmly established and even Cabernet Sauvignon can be ripened. Two bottles in every three of Pfalz wine are dry: *trocken* or *halbtrocken*.

Exciting wines throbbing with fruit are now made not just in the Mittelhaardt, the home of some of Germany's biggest and most famous estates, but throughout the region. There are Pfalz wines of serious interest, made from Viognier and Sangiovese as well as the more traditional varieties, from as far north as Laumersheim, as far south as Schweigen, and as far east as Ellerstadt.

In the Mittelhaardt, however, Riesling is still king. Mittelhaardt Riesling's special quality is succulent honeyed richness and body, balanced with thrilling acidity – even when it is finished dry. Historically, three famous producers (known as the "three Bs") dominated this, the kernel of the Pfalz: biodynamic purist Bürklin-Wolf, von Bassermann-Jordan, and von Buhl. But any monopoly of quality they had has disappeared in a surge of ambitious and original winemaking on all sides.

The Einzellagen on the hilly west side of the villages are the ones that most often attain the summits of succulence. In the south, Ruppertsberg is one of the first villages of the Mittelhaardt; its

This harvest scene of terraces near Bad Dürkheim looks almost as though it belongs on a medieval tapestry.

THE WINE CENTRES OF THE PFALZ
The Mittelhaardt, mapped opposite, is but a very small proportion of the sprawling Pfalz, where summers of late have been warmer than ever.

International boundary
Landesgrenze (state boundary)
Forst   Wine centre
Land over 300 metres
237   Area mapped at larger scale on page shown

best sites (Gaisböhl, Linsenbusch, Reiterpfad, Spiess) are all on moderate slopes, well-exposed, and mostly Riesling.

Forst has a reputation for the Pfalz's most elegant wine. Locals draw parallels with the tall, graceful spire of the village church. The top vineyards of Forst lie on water-retentive clay, while black basalt above the village provides dark, warm soil, rich in potassium, sometimes quarried and spread on other vineyards, notably in Deidesheim. The Jesuitengarten, Forst's most famous vineyard, and the equally fine Kirchenstück, lie just behind the church. Freundstück (largely von Buhl's) and Pechstein are in the same class. Georg Mosbacher is an outstanding Forst grower.

Although Forst was the most highly rated Pfalz village in the classification of 1828, Deidesheim to the south has at least caught up, besides being one of the prettiest villages in Germany. Its best wines have a very special sort of succulence. Von Bassermann-Jordan and von Buhl have their cellars here. Hohenmorgen, Langenmorgen, Leinhöhle, Kalkofen, Kieselberg, and Grainhübel are the top vineyards.

The village of Wachenheim, where Bürklin-Wolf is based, marks the end of the historic kernel of the Mittelhaardt with a cluster of famous small vineyards. Böhlig, Rechbächel, and Gerümpel are the first growths. Richness is not a marked characteristic of Wachenheim; its great qualities are finely poised sweetness and purity of flavour.

Bad Dürkheim is the biggest wine commune in Germany, with 2,000 vineyard acres (800ha). Riesling is in the minority except in the best sites of the terraced Michelsberg and Spielberg. For long Bad Dürkheim was an under-performer but now Thomas Hensel and Karl Schaefer and others challenge them. One of Germany's most reliable co-ops, the Vier Jahreszeiten, has been a reliable producer of bargains here for decades.

From here north we are in the Unterhaardt, whose most renowned parishes are Kallstadt (star performer: Koehler-Ruprecht) and Ungstein. Their best sites are Saumagen, in what was a Roman chalk pit, and Herrenberg, famous for rich Scheurebe from the Pfeffingen estate. Knipser and Philipp Kuhn of Laumersheim make a wide range of thrilling wines, from barrique-aged whites and reds to substantial Grosses Gewächs dry Rieslings.

THE MITTELHAARDT

Bad Dürkheim is famous for its riotous sausage and wine fair every autumn. But most of the great Pfalz vineyards are little further south, between Wachenheim and Deidesheim.

The warm, dry summers of the Pfalz make the region well suited to producing dry wines full of fruit and flavour, although there is also one of the Pfalz's Trockenbeerenauslese in this collection of labels. Alcohol is just 6.5% but the sugar level will be extraordinary.

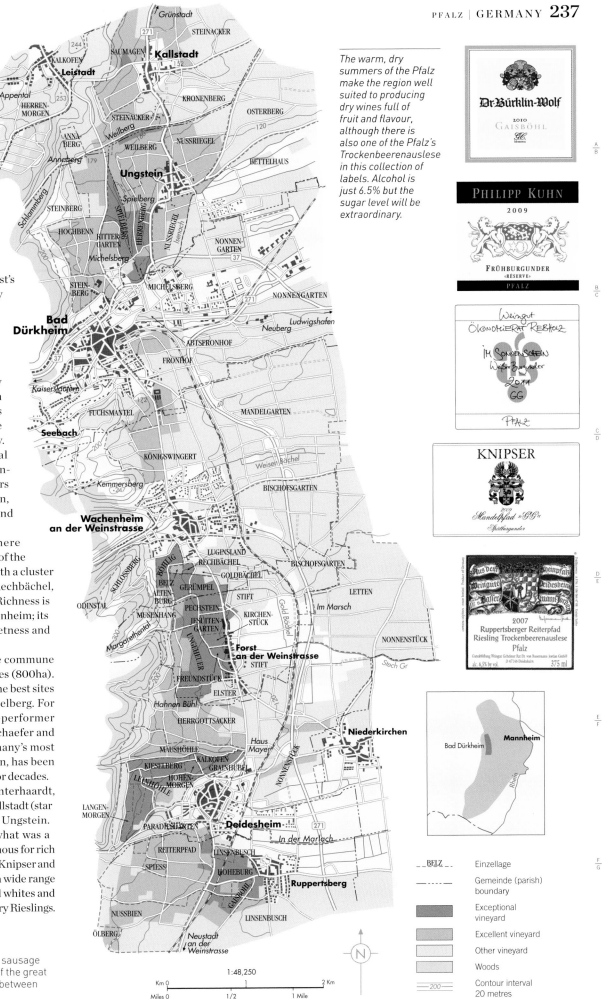

BELZ	Einzellage
	Gemeinde (parish) boundary
	Exceptional vineyard
	Excellent vineyard
	Other vineyard
	Woods
200	Contour interval 20 metres

1:48,250

Km 0 ... 1 ... 2 Km
Miles 0 ... 1/2 ... 1 Mile

Baden

Germany is profiting more from climate change than any wine country. In the far south, its growers are setting off in quite new directions. Their wines are invariably dry, very full-bodied, and often oaked. These are incontrovertibly wines to be drunk with food; the best are keenly sought at Germany's well-kept tables, even if they are too rarely exported. France may have provided the original models for the Spätburgunder, Grauburgunder, and Weissburgunder that are, respectively, the first, third, and fourth most-planted vine varieties in Baden, but a new generation of winemakers is confident enough to carve out its own local styles of wine.

Among German wine regions only the Ahr has a higher proportion of red wine than Baden and Württemberg, where 44% and 71% respectively, of total vineyard area are planted with dark-skinned varieties. The second half of the last century saw massive restructuring of the Baden winescape, both physical in the form of re-landscaping of difficult-to-work steep slopes, and social in the form of the domination of Baden's super-efficient co-ops, which at one stage handled 90% of each crop. Today, that proportion has fallen to 72%, although the mammoth Badischer Winzerkeller at Breisach, the frontier town on the Rhine between Freiburg and Alsace, is still Baden's principal marketer.

The co-ops are making better and better wine, but it is what is happening at the other end of the scale that makes Germany look at Baden with new eyes. Smaller producers such as Dr Heger in Kaiserstuhl, Bernhard Huber in Breisgau, Andreas Laible in Durbach, and Salwey of Oberrotweil are the ones who pioneered Burgundian techniques and clones. Other top Kaiserstuhl growers include Bercher, R & C Schneider, Karl Heinz Johner, and Fritz (son of Franz) Keller, whose wine-importing and gastronomic background is heavily influenced by France.

Baden is the warmest German region, only slightly damper and cloudier than Alsace, just across the Rhine. Two-thirds of its vineyards skirt the legendary Black Forest, with the bulk of them in a narrow 80-mile (130km) strip between the forest and the river. The best of them lie either on privileged southern slopes in the forest massif or on the Kaiserstuhl, the remains of an extinct volcano which forms a distinct island of high ground in the Rhine Valley.

The Kaiserstuhl (mapped opposite) and Tuniberg furnish one-third of all Baden's wine. While the dominant soil type is loess, most of the finest red Spätburgunders and full-bodied white Grauburgunders grow on volcanic soils and are positively stiff with flavour. Immediately east of here is the Breisgau, where Bernhard Huber of Malterdingen is making some of Germany's finest Spätburgunder. To the north, in Lahr, the Wöhrle family has breathed new life into the Weingut Stadt Lahr, which is now making particularly pure, pristine whites – Chardonnay as well as Pinot Blanc.

BADEN, WURTTEMBERG, AND HESSISCHE BERGSTRASSE

Just north of Mannheim, and not an exporter of its dry Rieslings, is Germany's smallest wine region, Hessische Bergstrasse (see p.217 for its full extent). Baden and Württemberg beween them have 60 times as much vineyard.

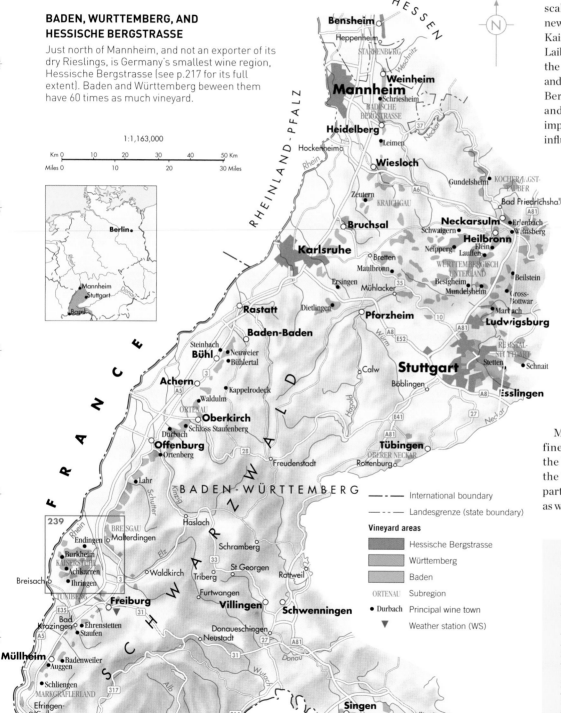

1:1,163,000

Km 0	10	20	30	40	50 Km
Miles 0		10	20	30 Miles

International boundary
Landesgrenze (state boundary)

Vineyard areas
- Hessische Bergstrasse
- Württemberg
- Baden
- ORTENAU — Subregion
- • Durbach — Principal wine town
- ▼ — Weather station (WS)

SCHWEIZ

BADEN: FREIBURG ▼

Latitude / Altitude of WS
48° / 918ft (280m)

Average growing season temperature at WS
61.2°F (16°C)

Average annual rainfall at WS
37in (929mm)

Harvest month rainfall at WS
September: 3.4in (87mm)

Principal viticultural hazards
Spring frost

Principal grape varieties
Spätburgunder, Müller-Thurgau, Grauburgunder, Riesling, Gutedel

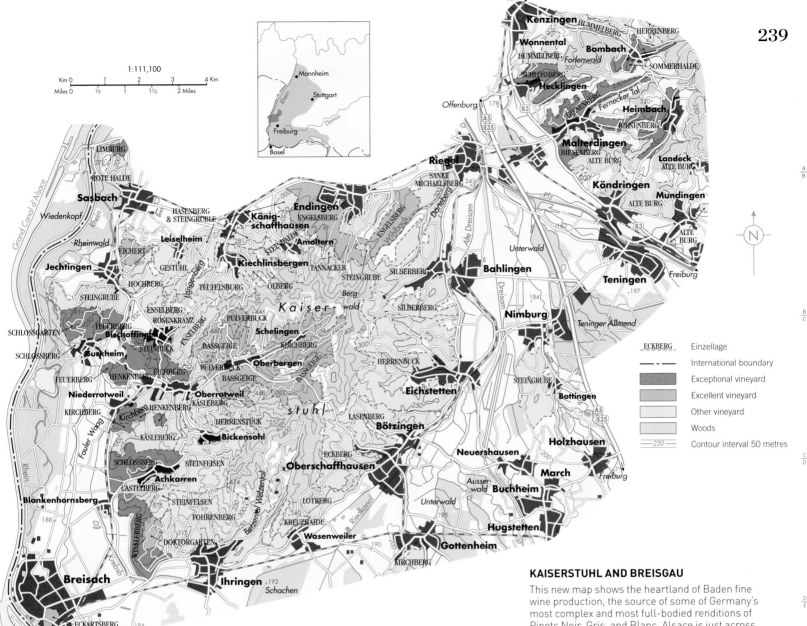

KAISERSTUHL AND BREISGAU

This new map shows the heartland of Baden fine wine production, the source of some of Germany's most complex and most full-bodied renditions of Pinots Noir, Gris, and Blanc. Alsace is just across the Rhine from here.

Map legend:

- ECKBERG — Einzellage
- — — International boundary
- Exceptional vineyard
- Excellent vineyard
- Other vineyard
- Woods
- 250 — Contour interval 50 metres

North again, just south of the luxurious Black Forest spa of Baden-Baden, the Ortenau is Baden's second most important pocket of vineyards with a long-established emphasis on red wine. Andreas Laible, Schloss Neuweier, and newcomers Enderle & Moll are the over-achievers here.

Still further north, the diversity of soils of the Kraichgau encourages a wider range of varieties, but Riesling is popular and Auxerrois something of a local speciality. Around the historic university town of Heidelberg the Badische Bergstrasse is best known for the Seeger estate's various Pinots.

Far to the south, in the Markgräflerland, the corner of Germany between Freiburg and Basel, the favourite grape has been Gutedel, the local name for the Chasselas planted across the border in Switzerland. It makes refreshing, if reticent, wine. Chardonnay is also very much at home here and rival winemaking brothers Martin and Fritz Wassmer of Bad Krozingen-Schlatt, together with Ziereisen of Efringen-Kirchen, have put the local Spätburgunder on the map.

Wine from the southernmost area of all, around Meersburg on the Bodensee, is known as Seewein ("lake wine") and off-dry, pink-tinted Weissherbst of Spätburgunder is a cheerful local speciality. Aufricht of Meersburg-Stetten and Staatsweingut Meersburg are making some remarkable Müller-Thurgau (the principal grape) here as well as some elegant white Pinots.

Württemberg

Württemberg, extensive though its vineyards are (it is Germany's fourth-largest wine region), is very much better known in Germany than abroad. Producers such as Aldinger and Rainer Schnaitmann in Fellbach on the outskirts of Stuttgart suggest that Württemberg is poised for the sort of revolution recently witnessed in

Rheinhessen. The region, which, like Baden, extends far beyond the limits of this map (see p.217), is still dominated by the dark Trollinger grape, but Lemberger, the fourth most-planted variety after Riesling and Schwarzriesling (Pinot Meunier), produces some thoroughly convincing and distinctive Württemberg red. There have also been some convincing experiments with Frühburgunder and even some red Bordeaux varieties. The climate is more continental so sites are chosen with care, lining the River Neckar and its tributaries, with three-quarters of the region's vineyards to the north of the state capital, Stuttgart.

Salwey and Dr Heger are two of Baden's most admired producers and, like their peers, take Grauburgunder extremely seriously, (Endingen has hosted an annual Grauburgunder event). About half of all the region's grapes are Pinots of some hue.

Franken

Franken (in English, Franconia) is out of the mainstream of German wine both geographically and by dint of its quite separate traditions. Politically it lies in the otherwise beer-centric former kingdom of Bavaria, which gives its State cellars a grandeur found nowhere else in Germany. Franken is unusual in that it makes greater wines from Silvaner than Riesling, and has long specialized in dry wines. The name Steinwein ("stone wine") was once loosely used for all Franken wine. Stein is, in fact, the name of one of the two famous vineyards of the city of Würzburg, Franken's wine capital on the Main. The other is Innere Leiste. Both distinguished themselves in the past by making wines that were incredibly long-lived. A Stein wine of the great vintage of 1540 was still (just) drinkable in the 1960s. Such wines were Beerenauslesen at least, thus immensely sweet. Franken makes few such rarities today; indeed, less than 10% of production is anything other than *trocken* or *halbtrocken*.

Franken's climate is decidedly continental, but climate change has largely solved the region's problem of too short a growing season. Indeed, 1996 was the last vintage that saw any underripe Riesling – and Silvaner is frequently as concentrated and alcoholic these days as some of the more substantial wines from the Austrian Wachau.

But even in Franken, unfortunately, Müller-Thurgau seems to offer a better return, at least on less-than-ideal sites. It is the most-planted variety, on about a third of all vineyard land, but Silvaner (grown on more than a fifth) is king, magically producing wines of crackling intensity here, even if it demands the most propitious vineyard sites. Franken wines may also be made from the super-aromatic grape varieties Kerner, and, especially, Bacchus. Scheurebe and Rieslaner, an even later-ripening Silvaner x Riesling crossing, can make very good dessert wines and substantial dry wines here, provided they reach full ripeness.

The heart of Franken

The heart of wine-growing Franken is in Maindreieck, following the fuddled three-cornered meandering of the Main from Escherndorf and Nordheim upstream of Würzburg, south to Frickenhausen, then north again through the capital to include all the next leg of the river and the outlying district around Hammelburg. Escherndorf stands out from these many villages for its celebrated Lump vineyard,

Vineyards near the magnificent city of Würzburg in autumn, before the relatively early arrival of Franken's particularly cold winter – which historically limited the planting of Riesling in Franken and encouraged the planting of dreary Müller-Thurgau.

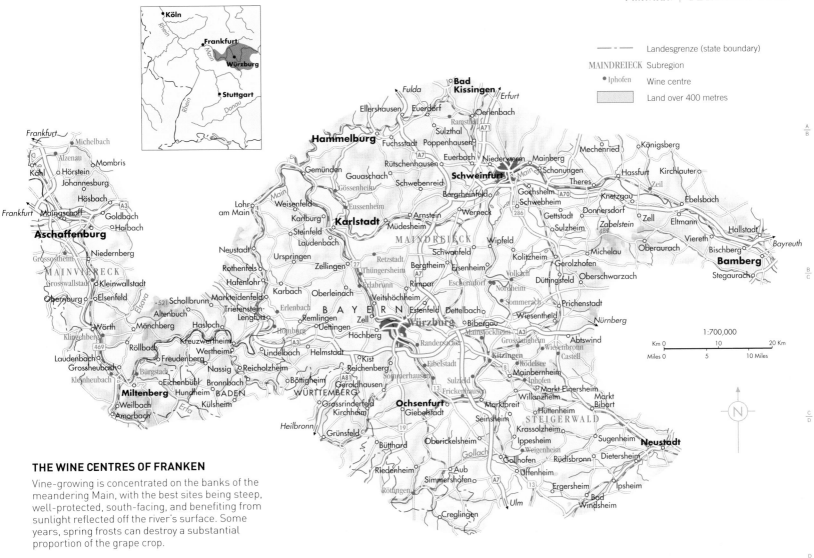

THE WINE CENTRES OF FRANKEN
Vine-growing is concentrated on the banks of the meandering Main, with the best sites being steep, well-protected, south-facing, and benefiting from sunlight reflected off the river's surface. Some years, spring frosts can destroy a substantial proportion of the grape crop.

and such talented producers as Horst Sauer and neighbour Rainer Sauer. What distinguishes all these scattered south-facing hillsides is the peculiar limestone known as Muschelkalk (whose origins are not so different from the Kimmeridgian clay of Chablis, or indeed of some of Sancerre's soils). This gives the wines an elegant raciness, particularly so in the case of the famous Würzburger Stein and noticeably so even in the more honeyed wines of Escherndorfer Lump.

Würzburg is the essential visit: one of the great cities of the vine, with three magnificent estate cellars in its heart belonging respectively to the Bavarian State (Staatliche Hofkeller), a church charity (the recently revived Juliusspital), and a civic charity (the Bürgerspital). The city is also home to the Knolls' exceptional 66-acre (27ha) Weingut am Stein estate. The Staatliche Hofkeller lies under the gorgeous Residenz of the former prince-bishops, whose ceiling paintings by Tiepolo are reason enough to visit the city. There is also the noble Marienburg Castle on its hill of vines, the great baroque river bridge, and the bustling Weinstuben (wine bars) belonging to these ancient foundations, where all their wines can be enjoyed with suitably savoury food.

Mainviereck, further downstream to the west, has lighter loam based on sandstone. It

has much less land under vine, but ancient steep vineyards such as Homburger Kallmuth (off the map to the south) can produce extraordinary, age-worthy wines. This is also Franken's red wine area, where exceptionally arid terraces of red sandstone can produce Spätburgunders and Frühburgunders (an early-ripening strain of Pinot Noir) of real interest. Stars such as red wine magician Rudolf Fürst and Fürst Löwenstein are based here.

In the Steigerwald in the east, the vine looks almost a stranger in the setting of arable fields with forests of magnificent oaks crowning its sudden hills. The seriously steep slopes are of gypsum and marl, which makes its mark in particularly strongly flavoured wines. Some of the finest wines come from the parishes of Iphofen (home of Hans Wirsching and Johann Ruck) and Rödelsee, as well as the doll's-house princedom and wine estate of Castell.

All of these labels, from some of Franken's most admired producers, are designed for the wide, flat Bocksbeutel that has been the characteristic bottle shape for Franken wines for centuries – which is why so many wine labels are oval.

THE REST OF EUROPE

The village of Riex nestled among the UNESCO-listed vine terraces of Lavaux, Switzerland

England and Wales

Climate change has played straight into the hands of those growing vines in the British Isles. England's wine-growers now have such confidence that nearly 4,000 acres (1,600ha) of vineyard are scattered widely over the southern half of the country, with the greatest concentration in the southeast – the counties of Kent, East and West Sussex, and Surrey. A large number of smaller vineyards (there are more than 500 in total) are also found across the south to the West Country, along the Thames and Severn valleys, and in East Anglia, the driest part of England, as well as in southern Wales and Ireland. The largest grower is sparkling pioneer Nyetimber, with 410 acres (166ha) of vines in West Sussex and Hampshire – very much an exception in an industry where the average is 6.5 acres (2.65ha), and many of even the larger ones depend heavily on tourism for sales. Well over 100 wineries now process the crop, which fluctuates dramatically but averages over 2.5 million bottles per year.

About 80% of English wine is white, with most of the rest rosé. The Champagne varieties Chardonnay, Pinot Noir, and Meunier already account for 45% of the total area, a proportion expected to rise to 75% as new vineyards are planted and older ones pulled out. Bacchus, Seyval Blanc, Reichensteiner, Müller-Thurgau, Madeleine x Angevine 7672 (a variety unique to the UK, bred by Georg Scheu in Germany in the 1930s), the red-fleshed hybrid Rondo, Schönburger, Ortega, and Pinot Blanc (in that order) are the next most widely grown varieties. A few light red wines and an increasing number of good rosés (especially sparkling) are being made from Pinot Noir and Meunier, with other reds and pinks being made from Rondo, Dornfelder, and Regent.

English sparkle

Bottle-fermented sparkling wines – most of the best based on the Champagne grapes – are England's strongest suit; the best match champagne selling at the same price. There is little difference in the chalk soil between Champagne and England's Downs, and climate change has been decidedly in England's favour. Heavy chaptalization was once routine but this century natural sugar levels have risen, and in the ripest years many wines have no added sugar at all. Generally warmer spring and summers, better viticultural and winemaking skills, more experience, and better equipment mean that many wineries can make very respectable whites and pinks almost every year. Imports can (easily) be cheaper, but the wines being made in England and Wales today, especially those that sparkle, have their own uniquely crisp, bright-fruited, lively style. They can – and often should – improve with time spent in bottle.

ENGLAND: EAST MALLING ▼

Latitude / Altitude of WS
51.29° / 105ft (32m)

Average growing season temperature at WS
57.3°F (14.1°C)

Average annual rainfall at WS
26in (648mm)

Harvest month rainfall at WS
October: 2.9in (74mm)

Principal viticultural hazards
Poor fruit set, high acids in cooler years, low yields

Principal grape varieties
Chardonnay, Pinot Noir, Bacchus, Seyval Blanc, Reichensteiner

Ridgeview of Sussex and Camel Valley of Cornwall, both run by dedicated and charismatic individuals, have a consistent and admirable record of winning awards for their well-made sparkling wines – not just in the UK, but in blind tastings abroad, too.

■ SHARPHAM Notable vineyard
▼ Weather station (WS)

1:3,225,000

Switzerland

Even now, in a more open and curious wine world than ever before, Swiss wine remains little-known beyond its national borders. Less than 1% is exported, and tourists tend to stick to a few staples that are far from being the best. Hardly anyone knows that over 200 different wine grapes are grown in this small country. And this despite the fact that, after decades of vinous isolation, Switzerland has stripped away her protective layers. The wine market was opened up in 2001, and from 2006 the once-routine stretching of Swiss with imported wine was banned.

The Swiss are enthusiastic wine drinkers and import about 60% of their needs – including a great deal of Burgundy's best. Making any sort of wine in a country with Switzerland's prices is inevitably expensive. The land of milk and money will never be able to produce bargains for the mass market. Producers know this, and concentrate more and more on making wines with a story. This should not be too difficult since every vineyard – almost every grape – is tended as and by an individual. The country's total of 36,922 acres (14,942ha) of vineyards (such precision is very Swiss) are divided between thousands of full- and part-time growers, whose impeccable and often spectacular plots are attentively gardened, rather than commercially farmed.

By scrupulous care of their vines, making use of irrigation, especially in the drier parts of the Valais, the Swiss have regularly achieved yields as high as Germany's. By producing such big quantities, adding sugar when necessary, they make growing grapes pay in spite of the steep slopes and the equally steep costs. In the winery, malolactic fermentation (unlike in Germany or Austria) has often compensated for any natural excess tartness.

Switzerland has some of the highest vineyards in Europe and is home to the first vineyards on two of the world's great wine rivers, the Rhine and the Rhône, which both rise, remarkably close to one another, in the Gotthard Massif.

Every Swiss canton grows some grapes for winemaking. In recent years more than four-fifths of Swiss wine has come from the western cantons of French-speaking Switzerland: la Suisse romande. **Valais** is the most productive canton, followed by **Vaud** and then, some way behind, **Geneva**. The Italian-speaking **Ticino** is fourth and produces virtually nothing but red wine.

The Swiss drink twice as much red wine as white, and the late 1990s saw widespread conversion of what were largely white wine vineyards to red, notably Pinot Noir. Today these constitute 58% of all plantings.

The most-planted white grape by far is the pale Chasselas, a neutral grape – in fact, usually an eating grape elsewhere – which manages to achieve real personality in Switzerland's most favoured sites (see overleaf). In the German-speaking east of the country, Müller-Thurgau, originally bred from Riesling and Madeleine Royale by the Swiss Dr Müller in the canton of Thurgau, is the most important white wine grape, though it is losing ground today to red varieties.

For Switzerland's fashionable and rapidly improving red wines, the vine known here variously as Pinot Noir, Blauburgunder, or Clevener is grown all over the country, with the exception of Ticino, which concentrates on Merlot, introduced in 1906 from Bordeaux after phylloxera all but destroyed the region's vines. In this Italian-speaking canton quality has risen strikingly in recent years. The best Merlots, nurtured on the sunniest slopes, can occasionally achieve Pomerol-like richness.

A taste of history

But the country's most interesting and original wines come from her long list of historic vine specialities: in the Valais, Arvine (or Petite Arvine), Amigne, Humagne Blanc, Païen (or Heida), and Rèze for whites, and Cornalin (or Rouge du Pays) and Humagne Rouge for reds; in east Switzerland, Completer and the old German vines Räuschling and Elbling; and in Ticino, red Bondola. Of these, Arvine, Completer, and the red Cornalin and Humagne Rouge can make some very fine wine indeed. Any chance to taste them

Through very deliberate planning, the Swiss have been extraordinarily effective at retaining their stunning landscape and viticultural heritage. Syrah is one of the most successful varieties in these Valais vineyards above Sion.

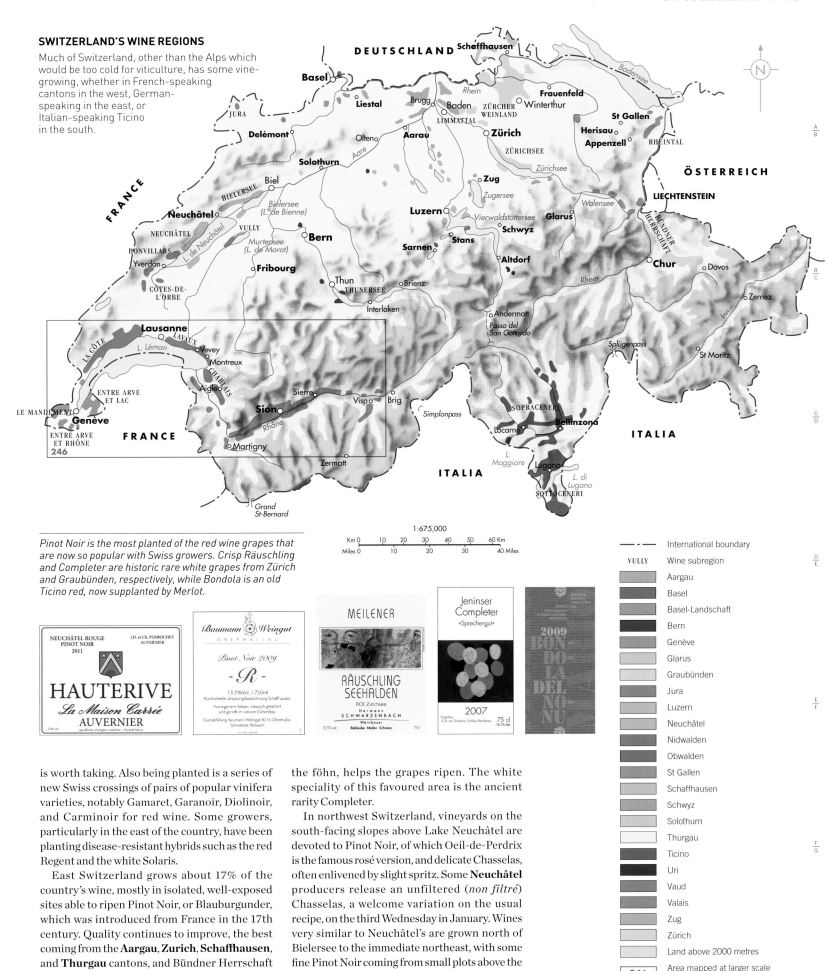

SWITZERLAND'S WINE REGIONS

Much of Switzerland, other than the Alps which would be too cold for viticulture, has some vine-growing, whether in French-speaking cantons in the west, German-speaking in the east, or Italian-speaking Ticino in the south.

Pinot Noir is the most planted of the red wine grapes that are now so popular with Swiss growers. Crisp Räuschling and Completer are historic rare white grapes from Zürich and Graubünden, respectively, while Bondola is an old Ticino red, now supplanted by Merlot.

1:675,000

| Km | 0 | 10 | 20 | 30 | 40 | 50 | 60 Km |
| Miles | 0 | | 10 | 20 | 30 | | 40 Miles |

Legend:

- – ⋅ – ⋅ – International boundary
- VULLY Wine subregion
- Aargau
- Basel
- Basel-Landschaft
- Bern
- Genève
- Glarus
- Graubünden
- Jura
- Luzern
- Neuchâtel
- Nidwalden
- Obwalden
- St Gallen
- Schaffhausen
- Schwyz
- Solothurn
- Thurgau
- Ticino
- Uri
- Vaud
- Valais
- Zug
- Zürich
- Land above 2000 metres
- 246 Area mapped at larger scale on page shown

is worth taking. Also being planted is a series of new Swiss crossings of pairs of popular vinifera varieties, notably Gamaret, Garanoir, Diolinoir, and Carminoir for red wine. Some growers, particularly in the east of the country, have been planting disease-resistant hybrids such as the red Regent and the white Solaris.

East Switzerland grows about 17% of the country's wine, mostly in isolated, well-exposed sites able to ripen Pinot Noir, or Blauburgunder, which was introduced from France in the 17th century. Quality continues to improve, the best coming from the **Aargau**, **Zurich**, **Schaffhausen**, and **Thurgau** cantons, and Bündner Herrschaft in **Graubünden**, where the warm autumn wind,

the föhn, helps the grapes ripen. The white speciality of this favoured area is the ancient rarity Completer.

In northwest Switzerland, vineyards on the south-facing slopes above Lake Neuchâtel are devoted to Pinot Noir, of which Oeil-de-Perdrix is the famous rosé version, and delicate Chasselas, often enlivened by slight spritz. Some **Neuchâtel** producers release an unfiltered (*non filtré*) Chasselas, a welcome variation on the usual recipe, on the third Wednesday in January. Wines very similar to Neuchâtel's are grown north of Bielersee to the immediate northeast, with some fine Pinot Noir coming from small plots above the villages of Schafis, Ligerz, and Twann.

Valais, Vaud, and Geneva

The steep sides of the Valais, the valley which the young River Rhône carved through the Alps, are followed by gentler slopes in Vaud, where the waters broaden into Lac Léman (Lake Geneva). An almost continuous south-facing band of vines hugs the north bank of the river, then the lake. The Valais is a hotbed (literally) of vinous experimentation. Vaud is the traditional heart of Swiss wine, where Cistercian monks introduced viticulture from Burgundy more than 900 years ago. Geneva, at the end of the lake, is hard at work upgrading its wines.

In the high **Valais**, peculiarly alpine conditions – brilliant sun and summer drought – can make concentrated, super-ripe wines. The average rainfall in Sion, a major wine centre, is less than two-thirds that of Bordeaux; Valais growers have built *bisses*, steep channels of mountain water, to irrigate their vines since the Middle Ages.

Along the Rhône

The Rhône's first vines grow near Brig: historic varieties such as Lafnetscha, Himbertscha, Gwäss (Gouais Blanc), and Heida (Savagnin Blanc, also called Païen in French-speaking Valais), throwbacks to the age before the Simplon Tunnel and its railway transformed the Valaisian economy. Just southwest of here are some of Europe's highest vines at Visperterminen, at 3,600ft (1,100m) lying almost in the shadow of the Matterhorn. Heida in particular achieves splendid density and richness.

Large-scale wine production begins just before Sierre (one of the driest places in Switzerland) and continues as far downstream as Martigny.

The Valais' 12,530 acres (5,070ha) of vineyards are tended by as many as 20,000 growers, only about 500 of whom make wine. About a fifth of Valais grapes are processed by the dominant co-operative, Provins. Fendant (as Chasselas is known here) is the dominant white, usually soft but deceptively strong, while its red counterpart is Dôle, a medium-weight blend dominated by Pinot Noir, then Gamay. Traditional varieties such as the cherry-scented Cornalin (or Rouge du Pays) and rustic Humagne Rouge are now challenged not just by Pinot Noir and Gamay but by spicy Syrah, which has travelled remarkably well upstream from its home in the French Rhône Valley.

Of the 27 white grapes grown in the Valais, Arvine (or Petite Arvine) is the most widely successful of the natives. Its combination of nervy acidity and considerable extract works best in the arid climate around Sion and Martigny. Valais whites are in general extremely potent, whether Johannisberg (Silvaner), Ermitage (Marsanne), Malvoisie (Pinot Gris; sometimes flétri: strong, sweet wines traditionally from raisined grapes), Chardonnay, Amigne (a speciality of the village of Vétroz), Humagne

Blanc (not related to Humagne Rouge), or Heida. Rèze is grown in Sierre, and aged high in the Alps in the Val d'Anniviers, to produce the rare Vin du Glacier, a little like Jura's Vin Jaune.

Around the lake

The vineyards in **Vaud** are quite different, not concentrated by alpine sunshine but gently ripened by the mild climate round the lake. Although red wine is gaining ground, 61% of vineyards are devoted to a single white grape, Chasselas – never specified on Vaud labels, which favour geographical names. Yields are generally relatively high, but the best lakeside vineyards manage to produce the world's most characteristic expressions of this mild grape.

Chablais is the easternmost of Vaud's wine regions and Chasselas can reach record ripeness levels around Aigle, Ollon, and Yvorne. The vine-terraces initially built by the Cistercians

in the 11th century on the north shore of the lake in Lavaux (encompassing the area between Montreux in the east and Lausanne) are so beautiful they were recognized as a World Heritage Site in 2007. Vines luxuriate in direct sunshine, glare reflected from the lake, and heat radiated by the stony terraces, with two specially designated Grands Crus, Calamin and Dézaley, enjoying the greatest esteem. Calamin, all 40 clayey acres (16ha) of it, lies within the village of Epesses, while next door the 136 acres (54ha) of Dézaley, in the commune of Puidoux, have more limestone. Calamin is typically flinty, Dézaley smoky – but these are fine distinctions. Both are nectar with a fried perch at a table beside the lake.

The best Chasselas wines of the less spectacular vineyards of La Côte, which stretches in an arc from west of Lausanne to the city of Geneva, come from such villages as Féchy, Mont-sur-Rolle, and Morges. The traditional red of La Côte

LAKE GENEVA AND THE RHONE VALLEY

The map of France on p.47 shows how the River Rhône flows through Valais and Lake Geneva (Lac Léman) before turning towards the Mediterranean, with vineyards planted on its banks practically all the way. Note how essential a south-facing slope is in Switzerland, although Visp, as usual, provides exceptions.

1:450,000

Km 0 ⋯ 10 Km
Miles 0 ⋯⋯ 3 ⋯⋯ 6 Miles

SWITZERLAND: SION ▼	
Latitude / Altitude of WS	
46.22° / 1,581ft (482m)	
Average growing season temperature at WS	
58.7°F (14.9°C)	
Average annual rainfall at WS	
24in (599mm)	
Harvest month rainfall at WS	
September: 1.5in (38mm)	
Principal viticultural hazards	
Spring frost	
Principal grape varieties	
Gamay, Chasselas	

*Climate data from 1971 to 2000

Some of the Vaud vineyards on the north bank of Lake Geneva are so steep that a monorail is needed for transporting grapes and vineyard equipment. This is in Lavaux, east of Lausanne.

is Salvagnin, a blend of Gamay and Servagnin (a local clone of Pinot) that is the Vaud's answer to the Valais' Dôle, though some fine Merlot and Gamaret are emerging.

Geneva's vineyards have changed more than any in Switzerland in recent years. Gamay is now the principal grape, having overtaken Chasselas, and is followed by Pinot Noir, Gamaret, and Chardonnay. There are three main vineyard areas, the largest being Mandement (Satigny is Switzerland's biggest wine commune), which has the ripest and tastiest Chasselas. The vineyards between the Arve and the Rhône make rather mild wine, while the produce of those between the Arve and the lake is pretty dry and pallid. The co-operative Cave de Genève has recently switched from making mainly everyday wines to becoming the main ambassador of Geneva's winemaking renaissance.

As in the Valais, the pace is being set by a small group of ambitious individuals who have shown that innovation (planting Merlot and Sauvignon Blanc, for example) can be more rewarding than following local custom. The picture-book village of Dardagny, for instance, has adventurously planted Scheurebe, Kerner, and Findling as well as its unusually invigorating Pinot Gris.

The Mitis and Zufferey (centre) are made from Valais's traditional grapes – Amigne and Cornalin respectively – but Dôle, as from Domaine des Muses, is the Swiss classic blend of Pinot Noir with Gamay. Curzilles is a classic Vaud blend based on Chasselas.

	International boundary
	Canton boundary
CHABLAIS	Wine subregion
AIGLE	Grand Cru
SATIGNY	Other notable wine commune
	Vineyards
	Woods
1000	Contour interval 200 metres
▼	Weather station (WS)

Austria

Austria's array of intensely pure wines have their own distinct, finely etched personality. There is something of the freshness of the Rhine in them, more perhaps of the fieriness and high flavour of the Danube (*Donau* in German), but almost nothing in common with Austria's wines of 30 years ago, before the country underwent vinous revolution – all of it benign.

So-called Weinland Osterreich in the far east of the country around Vienna, where the Alps descend to the great Pannonian Plain that reaches across Hungary, is where most Austrian wine is made, in hugely varied conditions. There is slate, sand, clay, gneiss, loam, and fertile loess, parched fields and perpetually green ones, craggy precipices above the Danube, and the tranquil shallow mere of the Neusiedler See.

Austria's fiercely continental climate and relatively modest average yields generally result in more potent wines than Germany's. The most commonly encountered fruit flavours are those of Austria's own white grape, Grüner Veltliner, grown on more than a third of the country's vineyard. "Grüner" or "GrüVe" can be thirst-quenchingly fresh and fruity, with plenty of acidity and a flavour that reverberates on a wavelength somewhere between grapefruit and dill (typically in the vast Weinviertel). In the right hands and places (especially upriver of Vienna), it can also be a full-bodied, intriguingly spicy, perhaps peppery white well worth ageing.

The rolling, wooded countryside of the prolific **Weinviertel** north of Vienna, with its baroque churches and pretty villages, is the very essence of Middle Europe. The hills of Slovakia form a barrier between it and the warming influence of the Pannonian Plain to the southeast, so that its wines are Austria's freshest and lightest. Some of the best reds come from Mailberg, with a warming combination of loess and sand in a well-sheltered valley. Blauer Portugieser is the workhorse red grape, but Austria's own Zweigelt is better.

Austria has been busy developing its counterpart to France's Appellations d'Origine Contrôlées, with eight DAC (Districtus Austriae Controllatus) regions in 2013, as shown on the map. The general appellation **Burgenland** is widely used for all wines produced in that region which do not qualify for one of its four DACs – Eisenberg, Mittelburgenland, Leithaberg, and Neusiedlersee – including all those grown in vineyards in the celebrated village of Rust, whose growers decided to opt out of the DAC scheme.

White wine country

Austrian wine is still almost 65% white. Grüner Veltliner was (and still is) dominant; Welschriesling and Riesling are also important, but today the market demands red. Austria's own juicily intense Zweigelt, refreshing Blaufränkisch and, especially, velvety Sankt Laurent are catching up on the bland, workhorse Blauer Portugieser. Although mixed farming predominates in **Traisental** and **Wagram**, these regions produce seriously fine Grüner Veltliner and the unrelated, red-skinned Roter Veltliner. Markus Huber von Reichersdorf of Traisental, Bernhard Ott of Feuersbrunn, and Karl Fritsch of Oberstockstall in Wagram are three of the country's most admired wine-growers. On the outskirts of Vienna, but still technically in Wagram, are the monastic cellars and influential national wine school of Klosterneuburg.

Easy-drinking reds are the speciality of **Carnuntum**, south of the Danube, and the Marchfeld plains of the southern Weinviertel. Göttlesbrunn and Höflein are Carnuntum's best-sited villages, with Prellenkirchen and Spitzerberg hotspots for new, improved Blaufränkisch – although Zweigelt and Zweigelt-based blends still dominate production.

Leutschach, right on the border with Slovenia, is an important wine-producing commune. Styria has a character all of its own and produces crisp, racy, dry wines, mainly whites, and – most dazzlingly – Sauvignon Blancs.

Elsewhere it can be fatally cold for vines in winter or dangerously dry in summer. Muhr-van der Niepoort is challenging Gerhard Markowitsch as Carnuntum's star performer, with Johannes Trapl in hot pursuit further west.

No capital city is so intimate with wine as Vienna (or **Wien**), where more than 1,536 acres (622ha) of vineyards still hold their ground right up to the tramlines within the heart of the residential districts, and surge up the side of the surrounding hills into the Vienna woods. For many years Viennese growers focused mainly on supplying relatively simple young wines for *Heurigen*, local inns run by wine producers. However, since the turn of the century there has been widespread determination to produce more serious wine, notably Gemischter Satz, made from at least three different varieties grown and vinified together with no perceptible oak. Top sites include Nussberg on the south bank of the Donau/Danube, Bisamberg on the north shore, and Mauer and Maurer Berg on the boundary with the **Thermenregion** (famous for its hot springs), the most southerly and hottest wine region of Niederösterreich. The Thermenregion is sheltered to the north by mountains and the Vienna woods, but is wide open to Pannonian influence, not unlike Burgenland to the south. It also has the *Heurigen* tradition, without nearly so many tourists. In red wine country in the south growers are concentrating on Pinot Noir and St Laurent, while in the north there is new determination to research and upgrade the characteristic white wine grapes of Gumpoldskirchen: the lively Zierfandler and the heavier Rotgipfler and Neuburger.

Evidence of Austrian wine's versatility. The first three of these wines prove that great wine can come from the Weinviertel. Gerhard Markowitsch is the leading light of Carnuntum, while Franz Wieninger makes some of the best Viennese wine from old vines (Alte Reben).

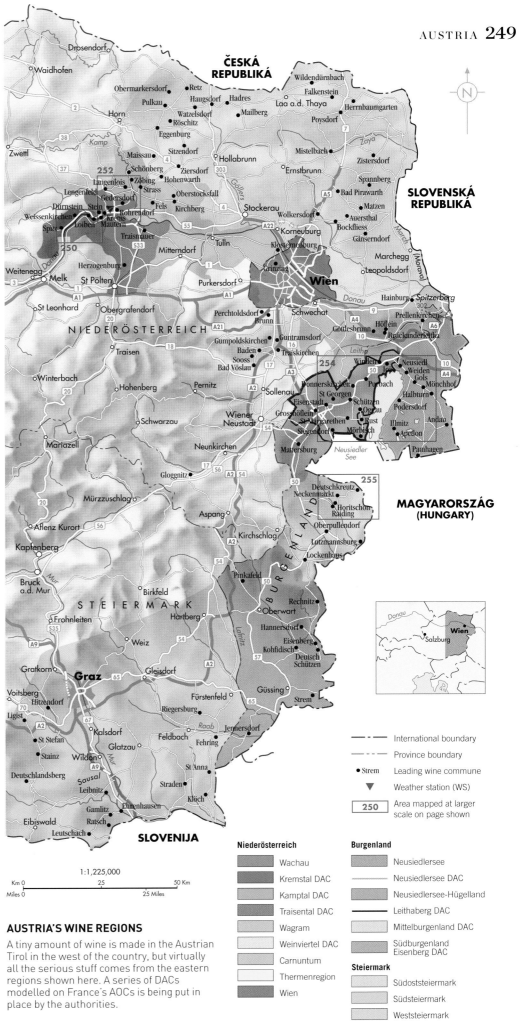

Steiermark (Styria), away to the south, has little in common with Austria's northerly regions. For decades it has produced exclusively dry wines, not unlike those over the border in eastern Slovenia where some Austrian producers now operate. It may have only 7% of the country's vineyards, and those widely dispersed, but its reputation for intense, piercing Sauvignon Blanc (sometimes oaked), Chardonnay, and Welschriesling is unmatched within Austria. Chardonnay, some of it travelling most unusually under a local alias, Morillon, is well entrenched here.

Südsteiermark has the greatest concentration of revered producers; names such as Gross, Lackner-Tinnacher, Polz, Sattlerhof, Tement, as well as energetic newcomers such as Hannes Sabathi. And then there are Wohlmuth and Harkamp on the high schists of Sausal, which yield some of Südsteiermark's most elegant wines. Traminer is a speciality of the volcanic soils of Klöch in Südoststeiermark, while pink Schilcher made from the rare Blauer Wildbacher grape is that of Weststeiermark.

*Climate data from 1971 to 2000

AUSTRIA: KREMS ▼

Latitude / Altitude of WS
48.42° / 679ft (207m)

Average growing season temperature at WS
58.5°F (14.7°C)

Average annual rainfall at WS
20in (516mm)

Harvest month rainfall at WS
September: 1.8in (46mm)

Principal viticultural hazards
Spring frost

Principal grape varieties
Grüner Veltliner, Zweigelt, Blauer Portugieser, Welschriesling, Riesling, Blaufränkisch

1:1,225,000

Km 0 — 25 — 50 Km
Miles 0 — 25 Miles

AUSTRIA'S WINE REGIONS

A tiny amount of wine is made in the Austrian Tirol in the west of the country, but virtually all the serious stuff comes from the eastern regions shown here. A series of DACs modelled on France's AOCs is being put in place by the authorities.

—·—·— International boundary
—·—·— Province boundary
● Strem   Leading wine commune
▼   Weather station (WS)
250   Area mapped at larger scale on page shown

Niederösterreich
- Wachau
- Kremstal DAC
- Kamptal DAC
- Traisental DAC
- Wagram
- Weinviertel DAC
- Carnuntum
- Thermenregion
- Wien

Burgenland
- Neusiedlersee
- Neusiedlersee DAC
- Neusiedlersee-Hügelland
- Leithaberg DAC
- Mittelburgenland DAC
- Südburgenland Eisenberg DAC

Steiermark
- Südoststeiermark
- Südsteiermark
- Weststeiermark

Wachau

If ever a region needed an atlas to tell its story, it is the Wachau, a complex meeting point of northern and southern climates and a rich mosaic of different soils and rocks. Forty miles (65km) before it reaches Vienna, the broad grey Danube broaches a range of 1,600ft (490m) high hills. For a short stretch the craggy north bank of the river, as steep as the Mosel or Côte-Rôtie, is patchworked with vines on ledges and outcrops along narrow paths leading up from the river to the crowning woods. There are plots of deep soil and others where a mere scratching finds rock, patches with day-long sunlight and others that always seem to be in shade. This is the Wachau, Austria's most famous wine region, even if, with only 3,335 acres (1,350ha), it constitutes just 3% of the country's vineyard.

What gives the (almost invariably dry, or dryish, white) wines of the Wachau their distinction is the geography. Hot Pannonian summers reach their furthest west here, heating the Danube Valley as far as the eastern end of the Wachau. Grapes in these low-yielding vineyards can reach potential alcohol levels of 15% or more. Yet the wines are far from flabby monsters; the vineyards are cooled at night by refreshing northern air from the woods above. These steeply terraced vineyards may need irrigation in high summer (rainfall often falls below the practical natural minimum of 20in/500mm a year) but the cool nights help, and the Danube acts as a natural heat regulator.

Grüner Veltliner was the traditional Wachau grape and makes its most vivid wines here – at their best green-tinged, high-spirited, almost peppery performances. The best have been shown to age as long as, and with results as interesting as, fine white burgundies. Grüner Veltliner can thrive on the lower banks in loess and sand, so growers have been dedicating their highest and steepest sites, on less fertile gneiss and granite at the top of the hill, to Riesling, and their clientele is enraptured.

Top Wachau Rieslings can have the steely cut of the Saar in a mouth-filling structure that is every bit as full as an Alsace Grand Cru. Growers who have long made superlative examples of such wines include Hirtzberger at Spitz, Prager at Weissenkirchen, FX Pichler at Oberloiben, Emmerich Knoll, the Tegernseerhof family and Leo Alzinger at Unterloiben, Johann Schmelz at Joching, and Rudi Pichler at Wösendorf, as well as the admirable Domäne Wachau co-op at Dürnstein. New oak does not feature here, although there have been experiments with botrytised grapes.

Cool northern influence is at its strongest west of Spitz in the Spitzer Graben side valley, where growers such as Peter Veyder-Malberg and Johann Donabaum are taking full advantage of the mica schists and lower temperatures to make seriously elegant wines. The Loibens (Unter-

and Ober-) enjoy a noticeably softer climate than even Weissenkirchen. Dürnstein, in whose castle Richard the Lionheart was imprisoned, is the natural capital of the Wachau and the scenic climax of the valley. The baroque steeple, the ruined castle, and the village's tilting vineyards are irresistibly romantic.

Most of the Wachau's finest wines are grown on the north bank of the river, but at least one grower, Nikolaihof, makes some firm biodynamic wines around Mautern on the south bank – fungicides are rarely called for in this dry climate: good for organic viticulture.

It is no surprise to learn that this 12-mile (20km) mosaic of vineyards has accumulated no fewer than 900 different named sites, or *Rieden*. Their boundaries are still too debatable to map precisely here, but if one must be singled out, it is **Achleiten**, to the northeast of Weissenkirchen. Slate and gneiss combine to give its wines a mineral signature that is a boon to those at blind wine tastings.

Code of honour

Members of the Vinea Wachau growers' association have to sign up to the Codex Wachau, whereby they agree not to buy in grapes and to make the purest, most expressive wines possible. They also have their own system of designating wines; local taste codified, in fact. Steinfeder is a light wine up to 11.5% alcohol for early drinking. Federspiel is made from slightly riper grapes, 11.5–12.5% alcohol, good in its first five years. Wines labelled Smaragd (after a local green lizard) can be seriously full-bodied, with alcohol levels above – often far above – 12.5%; they repay six or more years' ageing. Some producers, however – particularly some of younger generation such as Pichler-Krutzler and Peter Veyder-Malberg, who are already making waves – prefer to operate independently, making one wine that they feel

CENTRAL AND EASTERN WACHAU
Most of the Wachau's great wines come from steep terraces facing the sun on the left bank of the Danube, but especially refined wines are grown in the cool side valley west of Spitz. The distinctive Nikolaihof of Mautern is arguably the best-known producer on the right bank.

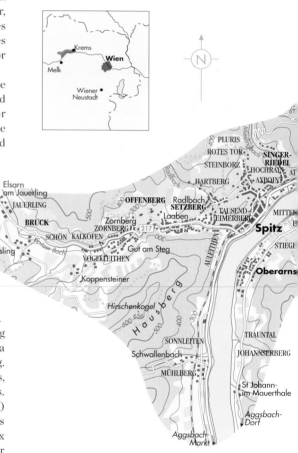

perfectly expresses each combination of grape, vineyard, and vintage without necessarily worshipping ripeness for its own sake.

Riesling and Grüner Veltliner are what the Wachau does best, and these labels represent some of the most reliable practitioners, from the baroque splendour of the Knoll label to the more discreet offerings of Prager and relative newcomer Pichler-Krutzler.

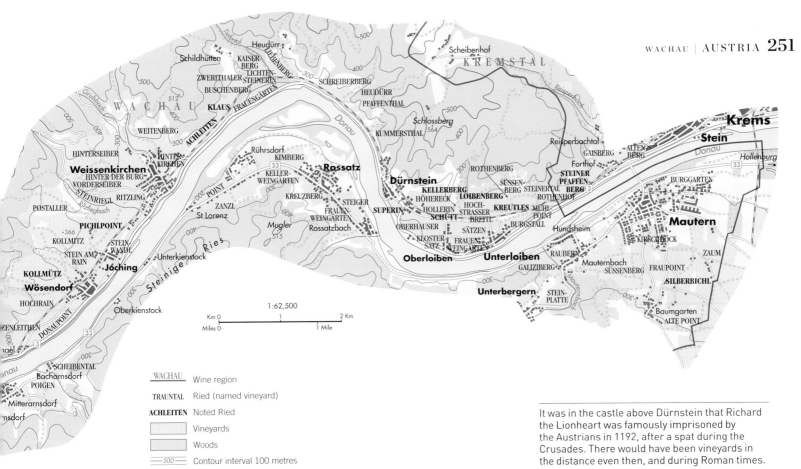

Krems

Stein

Weissenkirchen

Rossatz

Dürnstein

Mautern

Oberloiben

Unterloiben

Unterbergern

SILBERBICHL

Jöching

Wösendorf

1:62,500

Km 0   1   2 Km

Miles 0   1 Mile

WACHAU   Wine region

TRAUNTAL   Ried (named vineyard)

ACHLEITEN   Noted Ried

   Vineyards

   Woods

—500—   Contour interval 100 metres

It was in the castle above Dürnstein that Richard the Lionheart was famously imprisoned by the Austrians in 1192, after a spat during the Crusades. There would have been vineyards in the distance even then, and during Roman times.

Kremstal and Kamptal

If the Wachau made the running in Austria's initial assault on the world's lovers of dry white wines, it did not take long for them to notice that the neighbouring Kremstal and Kamptal made wines of similar quality and style – and in many cases charged less for them.

The pretty twin towns of Stein and Krems mark the eastern end of the Wachau and the start of the very similar but slightly less dramatic **Kremstal**. The clay and limestone vineyards around here, including the famous Steiner Hund, can give particular density to both Riesling and Grüner Veltliner. The south-facing Pfaffenberg, almost in the Wachau, produces particularly subtle wine, thanks to granite and gneiss.

The Kremstal region extends both north and south of the Danube, much of it on strangely soft loess – half soil, half rock – source of some famous Grüner Veltliners but also of full-bodied reds. Kremstal is an intermediate zone between the sharp focus of the Wachau and the greater variety of Kamptal. Parts of the region are high and steep enough to need terracing, as in the Wachau.

Among the talented producers, Malat and Nigl make racy whites with every bit as much concentration as many Wachau wines. Salomon-Undhof, which has a related wine operation in South Australia, is another notable producer with some good-value bottlings. Sepp Moser is an outspoken fan of biodynamism, and Ilse Maier at Gayerhof follows the same philosophy to produce fine whites on the south bank of the Danube. The Stadt Krems winery and vineyards (owned by the town) are in the hands of Fritz Miesbauer, who also makes the wines of the massive baroque abbey of Gottweig. The municipality's ancient holdings include the 12th-century Wachtberg vineyard.

Kamptal, the productive buffer zone between Kremstal and Weinviertel, is the source of such outstanding wine that it has been called the K2 of Austria (Wachau being Mount Everest). Its south-facing vineyards, with largely loess soil, are protected by mountains from northern chill and benefit from much the same climate and aspect as Kremstal and Wachau to the west. Kamptal is about 1.8°F (1°C) warmer than the Wachau, being lower, and produces similarly dense Riesling and Grüner Veltliner, as well as a slightly greater range of other varieties. The main river influence is not the broad, east-flowing Danube but its south-flowing tributary, the Kamp, which can bring cooler temperatures at night and trigger often livelier wines.

The most important wine centres are Langenlois, which has been a wine town for centuries; Zöbing, famous for its Heiligenstein vineyard; and Gobelsburg, where the grand Schloss Gobelsburg has been splendidly

1:73,500

Km 0   1   2 Km
Miles 0   1 Mile

KREMSTAL	Wine region
GOLDBERG	Ried (named vineyard)
LAMM	Noted Ried
	Vineyards
	Woods
—500—	Contour interval 100 metres

NORTHERN KREMSTAL AND SOUTHERN KAMPTAL

The map on p.249 shows that we highlight only the most exciting sections of the valleys of Krems and Kamp here. Terracing and many of the soils are very similar to those of the Wachau (pp.250–51), but most vineyards are much further from the Danube. Many of the finest vineyards cluster round Langenlois.

restored by Michael Moosbrugger. His partner at the Schloss is Willi Bründlmayer, the star producer of Langenlois – although Jurtschitsch, in the determinedly organic hands of Alwin Jurtschitsch since 2009, is making better wines than ever, while Hirsch has been leading the way towards lighter, more precise wines.

Another key player is Fred Loimer, not least because of his dramatic "black box" of a winery. Returning to traditional methods in his underground cellars, he has experimented with large oak casks for fermentation. Loimer has provided inspiration for a whole new generation of dedicated younger producers.

Of serious note to wine tourists in Kamptal is the exceptional Loisium Hotel in Langenlois, devoted to wine via its wine museum, "wine spa", and a restaurant with a wine list that has admirably preserved Grüner Veltliners going back to the 1930s.

The small-berried Grüner Veltliner is Austria's signature grape, but has been losing ground to even more fashionable red wine grapes in its homeland. Meanwhile, growers as far afield as Oregon and New Zealand have been planting the Austrian white wine grape.

Most of the best wines of Kremstal and Kamptal carry the name of a named vineyard, or Ried. After a flirtation with relatively rich wines at the end of the 20th century, most growers now produce full-bodied but dry Rieslings and Grüner Veltliners, and wines are generally becoming increasingly refined.

Burgenland

The flat and often sandy shores of Lake Neusiedl, an extraordinary giant marshy pool more than 20 miles (32km) long and only 3ft (1m) deep, are today the slightly improbable source of Austria's greatest red and sweet white wines. For a long time, Burgenland seemed as though it was from an earlier era of Middle Europe, the days of the Hapsburgs and the Esterhazys, when Austria and Hungary were the same empire. After the Second World War, fewer than 250 acres (100ha) of vines were grown between the marshy ponds of the Seewinkel on the east shore of the lake, around villages such as Illmitz and Apetlon, which then knew only dirt roads and had no electricity. But of all the Austrian provinces, Burgenland benefitted most from the improvement grants available when the country joined the EU in 1995. Now it grows about 34,600 acres (14,000ha) of carefully tended vines – 4,940 acres (2,000ha) of them in Seewinkel – and is home to hundreds of well-equipped, immaculate cellars.

The country is so flat in **Neusiedlersee**, and the lake so surrounded by waist-high reeds, that views of the water are few and far between. One small 80ft (25m) rise is revered as a hill. This may sound an unlikely description of great wine country. The secret is that elusive shallow lake, enveloped by mist through its long, warm autumns, encouraging so much botrytis, or noble rot, that bunch after bunch of grapes look as though they have been dipped in ash.

The late Alois Kracher almost single-handedly put Illmitz on the world wine map with an extraordinary range of intensely sweet, rich, even dramatic white wines (often carefully designed blends, notably Chardonnay and Welschriesling). His son Gerhard carries the torch with aplomb. Angerhof-Tschida is another Illmitz superstar.

Burgenland grows a wider range of different grapes than any other Austrian region, with Weissburgunder (Pinot Blanc), Neuburger, Muskateller (small-berried Muscat), Muscat Ottonel, and Sämling 88 (Scheurebe) all of interest to white winemakers.

The red revolution

But the most recent revolution has been in Burgenland's red wines. This is Austria's hottest wine region, with Mittelburgenland in particular wide open to Pannonian warmth, so red grapes (grown in a landscape not too dissimilar to the Médoc's) ripen reliably each year, yet morning mists help keep their acidity in balance. Led by producers such as the Pannobile group in Gols (headed by Hans and Anita Nittnaus), Roland Velich of Moric in Mittelburgenland, and Uwe Schiefer, Hermann Krutzler, and Wachter-Wiesler in the south, red wines have become much more subtle, less alcoholic and less obviously oaked. Burgenland's total area devoted to red grapes overtook that for white varieties in 2009. The racy, juicy Blaufränkisch is the most popular variety, but Zweigelt, Sankt Laurent, Pinot Noir, and even Merlot and Cabernet Sauvignon are all much more widely planted than they were 10 years ago.

The best Neusiedlersee red wines tend to come from (slightly) higher ground further away from the lake, around the villages of Mönchhof, Gols, and Weiden in the northeast and, across the lake in the west, from the limestone and schist soils of the considerably higher Leithaberg. The **Leithaberg** DAC is arguably Austria's strictest and most terroir-driven, and its mineral-laden reds are some of the country's most distinctive, exemplified by the wines of Birgit Braunstein, Prieler, and Kloster am Spitz. Producers such as Paul Achs, Gernot Heinrich, Hans and Anita Nittnaus, Juris, Umathum, and Pöckl have been standard-bearers for other Neusiedlersee reds.

The most historically famous wine of Burgenland comes from the photogenic village of Rust in **Neusiedlersee-Hügelland**, where Feiler-Artinger, Ernst Triebaumer, and Heidi Schröck

NEUSIEDLERSEE AND LEITHABERG

Most of the best wine made around the shallow Neusiedler See comes from the northern end: full-bodied reds from the northeast and the Leithaberg DAC, and exceptional sweet whites from the eastern shore and Rust, the Leithaberg refusenik.

— · —	International boundary
— —	Province boundary
— — —	Parish boundary
<u>NEUSIEDLERSEE</u>	Wine region
LEITHABERG	DAC
UNTERE LÜSS	Ried (named vineyard)
TIGLAT	Noted Ried
	Vineyards
	Woods
	Marsh
250	Contour interval 50 metres

2009
NECKEN MARKT
ALTE REBEN
BLAUFRÄNKISCH BURGENLAND ÖSTERREICH
QUALITÄTSWEIN TROCKEN MIT STAATLICHER PRÜFNUMMER L-9 5134/11
PRODUZIERT UND ABGEFÜLLT VON ROLAND VELICH, A-7051 GROSSHÖFLEIN
ENTHÄLT SULFITE/CONTAINS SULFITES
WWW.MORIC.AT
13,5%VOL 750 ML
MORIC

Roland Velich of Moric (pronounced "Moritz") is credited with re-energizing the reputation of Blaufränkisch in Austria thanks to his exceptional, hand-crafted, terroir-driven, refreshing dry reds made around Lutzmannsburg and Neckenmarkt, Mittelburgenland's heartland of the grape.

are the leading producers. Ruster Ausbruch was traditionally compared with Tokaji (see p.258), despite having less acidity and more alcohol, and ranks in sweetness between Beerenauslese and Trockenbeerenauslese. But the village, which has bowed out of the Burgenland DAC, also produces fine reds and dry whites.

Vineyards slope east down to the villages of Purbach, Donnerskirchen, Rust, and Mörbisch and, being higher and further from the water than those on the east of the lake, are slightly less prone to botrytis. Serious amounts of red wine are made here and in the vineyards that stretch west almost as far as Wiener Neustadt and south past Mattersburg. Andi Kollwentz of the Römerhof estate in Grosshöflein is considered Austria's best all-round cellarmaster.

In **Mittelburgenland**, to the immediate south of the Neusiedlersee, one vine in every two is Blaufränkisch, which really comes into its own here. The result has been increasingly sophisticated versions of this invigorating red grape, not just from Moric but also Albert Gesellmann, the Hans Igler winery, Paul Kerschbaum, and Franz Weninger.

Blaufränkisch also reigns in **Südburgenland**, a much more diffuse wine region well south of the lake and which encompasses the **Eisenberg** DAC. The wines are lighter than in Mittelburgenland, with distinct minerality and spice: a reflection of the high iron content in the soil. The best producers are the Krutzler family, whose best-known bottling is Perwolff, while Uwe Schiefer's single-vineyard Reihburg Blaufränkisch is also notable. Wachter-Wiesler has joined them on the red wine podium. A younger generation promises even greater things.

NORTHEAST MITTELBURGENLAND

Right on the Hungarian border is a nucleus of particularly propitious red wine vineyards, where Blaufränkisch flourishes, resulting in new respect for this remarkably successful Austrian (and Hungarian) grape variety. Its relatively high acidity is a useful counterbalance to Pannonian warmth.

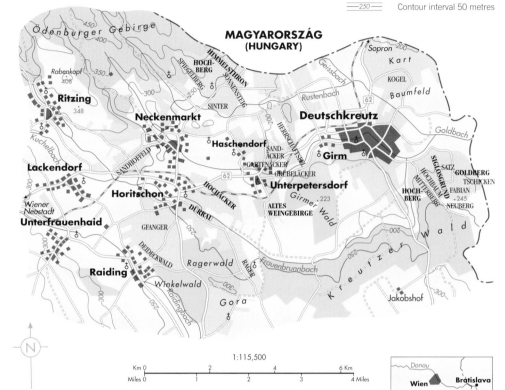

Barrels of Blaufränkisch in the immaculately kept cellars of Hans Igler in Deutschkreutz. Just over the border is Sopron, one of Hungary's finest regions for the same variety, known there as Kékfrankos (see map on p.257).

Hungary

For centuries, Hungary has had the most distinctive food and wine culture, the most varied native grapes, and the most refined wine laws and customs of any country east of Germany – and these are once again being cherished. The country's extraordinary palette of indigenous white grape varieties, with Furmint currently to the fore, is at last recognized as an asset rather than a liability. Today, Hungarian wine producers confidently offer definitively well-made, post-communist wines in a wide range of recognizably Magyar/Hungarian styles.

The characteristic traditional Hungarian wine is white – or rather warmly gold – and spicy. It tastes, if it is a good one, distinctly rich – not necessarily sweet but full of fire and even a shade fierce. It is wine for meals cooked with more spice and pepper and fat than a light wine could stand. These are dishes for Hungary's savage winters. The grapes are ripened in warmer autumns than in many parts of continental Europe, although the climate is relatively cool and the growing season shorter than in most Mediterranean regions. Average annual mean temperatures are

warmest in the south, reaching 52.5°F (11.4°C) around the town of Pécs, and coolest in the north, reaching a low of around 49°F (9.5°C) at Sopron. (See over for Tokaj.) Almost all of the country's historic wine regions have evolved in the shelter of high ground; varied terrain results in a range of mesoclimates, reflected in the diversity of each region's wines.

Hungary's great grape varieties begin with the firmly structured, racy Furmint and the softer, more perfumed Hárslevelű – the grapes of Tokaj, but not only of Tokaj. Quite different – lighter – are the aromatic, lively Leányka and the even grapier Királyleányka. Other varieties grown mainly for crisp, lighter, unoaked whites are Sauvignon Blanc and the popular crossing Irsai Olivér, while Furmint, Hárslevelű, Olaszrizling (Welschriesling), Chardonnay, and Szürkebarát (Pinot Gris) are more likely to be fuller-bodied and oaked.

Specifically Hungarian varieties, in many cases rare today, include Kéknyelű ("blue-stalk") of Lake Balaton; the fresh, even tart, Ezerjó of Mór; and the austerely stylish Juhfark of Somló that

needs aeration and age to shed its harshness. Hungarian red varieties are still in the minority, and grown mainly in Eger, Sopron, Szekszárd and Villány. Kékfrankos (called Blaufränkisch in Austria) is the most-planted red wine grape and has real potential, its innate crispness being an asset in the Pannonian warmth. It is grown in almost every region but does particularly well in Szekszárd, Sopron, and Eger, as well as in Mátra. The traditional clones of the workmanlike Kadarka (called Gamza in Bulgaria) produce spicy, red-fruited, relatively simple wines, notably in Szekszárd in the south, and as a seasoning in Bikáver blends.

Half of Hungary's vineyard area lies on the easily mechanized Great Plain, between the Duna (Danube) and the Tisza in the southern centre of the country, in the regions now known as **Kunság**, **Csongrád**, and **Hajós-Baja**. The sandy soil is of little use for anything but vines. Great Plain wine, mainly white Olaszrizling and Ezerjó, with some red Kékfrankos and Kadarka, is the everyday wine in Hungarian cities, although producers such as Frittmann Testvérek show that better wines are possible.

Hungary's better-quality vineyards are scattered among the hills that traverse the country from southwest to northeast, culminating in the Tokaj region described overleaf.

In the warm south, the districts of Szekszárd, Villány, Pécs, and Tolna grow both red and white wines. Kadarka is the historic grape, with Kékfrankos well-entrenched. **Villány** is southernmost, warmest, and makes the running with full-bodied reds of increasing interest and complexity; with Eger in the north, this is the region that shows up on foreigners' radar and top wine lists in Budapest. Such growers as Attila Gere, Ede Tiffán, József Bock, Sauska, and Vylyan have substantial followings for their Cabernet Sauvignon, Cabernet Franc (especially), and Merlot, sometimes blended with Kékfrankos or Zweigelt, or even Portugieser for a Magyar twist. On the slopes of Szekszárd, the deep loess

"Cuvée" in this part of the world (Austria as well as Hungary) signifies a blend of different grape varieties. The Heimann family has been growing grapes on the slopes of Szekszárd, red wine country, since 1758.

produces structured Kékfrankos, Kadarka, Merlot, and the Cabernets. The names to look for here are Heimann, Takler, Vesztergombi, and Vida. **Szekszárd** also produces a Bikavér blend of (usually) Kékfrankos with Cabernet and Merlot. The Bikavér tradition is otherwise limited to Eger.

Egri Bikavér was once Hungary's famous wine in the West, a rugged red sold as Bull's Blood. **Eger**, at the eastern end of the Mátra Hills in the northeast of the country, is one of Hungary's most important wine centres, a baroque city with huge cellars, magnificent caverns cut in the hills' soft, dark tuff. Hundreds of time-blackened oak casks, 10ft (3m) across and bound with bright-red iron hoops, line 8 miles (13km) of tunnels. Their age and less-than-pristine condition played a part, along with the substitution of Kékfrankos for Kadarka, in an apparent thinning of the blood in this historic wine, but the 21st century has seen a renaissance in red wine-making here. St. Andrea, Gróf Buttler, Thummerer and the late Tibor Gál's GIA (continued by his family), are the modern face of Eger, with Bikavér only part of much larger red and white portfolios, including some very promising Pinot Noir.

West of Eger along the south-facing slopes of the Mátra range is Hungary's second-biggest vineyard region, **Mátra**, with the town of Gyöngyös at its heart. White wines make up 80% of its output but some reasonably successful, artisanal reds are now joining the Olaszrizling, Tramini, and Chardonnay. In the far west, almost on the Austrian border, is **Sopron**, a red wine outpost growing mainly Kékfrankos, which has

been revitalized by producers such as Franz Weninger from across the Austrian border in Burgenland. He has been followed in his redevelopment of the best sites by locals Luka, Pfneiszl, and Ráspi.

To the east of Sopron, **Neszmély** was best-known for dry whites from traditional grapes but today produces a range of thoroughly international varietals from ultra-modern wineries designed with exports in mind. Hilltop is the best known. **Etyek-Buda**, just west of Budapest, is another flourishing source of largely internationally styled whites, including sparkling wine, vast quantities of which are made in the cellars of Budafok, just south of the capital. Chateau Vincent is probably the best. József Szentesi makes more artisanal traditional-method fizz in co-operation with other small producers across the country. Hollóvár, Kreinbacher, and Meinklang of Austria are the top producers on the strangely isolated volcanic hill of **Somló** north of Lake Balaton. Here, Furmint, Hárslevelű, Olaszrizling, and the rare Juhfark, are especially firm and mineral. The clay-limestone of **Mór** to the northeast results in Ezerjó that is especially tart, high-flavoured, and sometimes nobly sweet. Both are among Hungary's "historical wine regions".

Lake Balaton, besides being the biggest lake in Europe, has a special significance for Hungarians. In a country with no coast, it is the "sea" and chief beauty spot. Balaton's shores are thick with summer villas and holiday resorts, fragrant with admirable cooking. It has good weather and a busy social life. The north shore of Lake Balaton

HUNGARY'S WINE REGIONS

Hungarian wine authorities have been changing the names of the recognized wine regions with a regularity apparently designed to infuriate compilers of reference works. But Eger, source of Egri Bikavér (Bull's Blood), has remained constant.

has all the advantages of good southern exposure and shelter from cold winds, as well as the air-conditioning effect of a big body of water. It is inevitably a vineyard.

Its special qualities come from the climate, and from the combination of a sandy soil and extinct volcano stumps (Mount Badacsony is the most famous) that sprout from otherwise flat land. The steep basalt slopes drain well and absorb and hold the heat. Except in exceptional years when botrytised sweet wines – above all Szürkebarát or Pinot Gris – are made, most wines made here are dry, and with their strong mineral element can benefit from aeration. Olaszrizling is the common white grape. Rhine Riesling can be excellent.

The Lake Balaton region has been divided into four appellations. On the north shore are the classic **Badacsony**, where Huba Szeremley, József Laposa, and Endre Szászi are the most renowned producers, and **Balatonfüred-Csopak**, where Mihály Figula and István Jásdi are notable. On the south shore, **Balatonboglár** is best-known on export markets for Chapel Hill. The best growers are János Konyári and Ottó Légli, with Garamvári for sparkling wine. Various outlying vineyards to the west, where the finest producer is Lászlo Bussay, are grouped as **Zala**.

Tokaj

The word "legend" is more often used about Tokaji than any other wine. (Tokay is the old English spelling; the town that inspired the name, at the bottom of the map below, Tokaj). And with good reason. Although it suffered a temporary total eclipse of standards during the communist era, Tokaji has been legendary for 400 years. Only champagne has spawned as many anecdotes. History relates how the sumptuous Tokaji Aszú, made from botrytised grapes, was first produced – methodically, rather than by chance – by the chaplain of the Rákóczi family in their vineyard called Oremus (his name was Szepsy Lackó Máté; the year 1630). How in 1703 the patriot Prince Rákóczi of Transylvania used Tokaji to woo Louis XIV and drum up support against his Habsburg overlords. How Peter and Catherine (both Great) kept Cossacks in Tokaj to escort their supplies to St Petersburg – and how its restorative properties led potentates to keep Tokaji by their bedsides.

Tokaji was the first wine knowingly to be made from botrytised or "nobly rotten" grapes: over a century before Rhine wine, and perhaps two before Sauternes. The conditions that cause the rot, the shrivelling of the grapes, and the intense concentration of their sugar, acid, and flavour are endemic to the Tokaj region.

The Zemplén Mountain range is volcanic, rising in typically sudden cones from the north edge of the Great Plain. Two rivers, the Bodrog and the Tisza, converge at the southern tip of the range, where Mount Kopasz, also known as Tokaj Hill, rises above the villages of Tokaj and Tarcal. From the plain come warm summer winds, from the mountains shelter, and from the rivers the rising autumn mists that promote botrytis. October is usually sunny.

Of the three grape varieties in Tokaj today, some 70% of the vines are the late-ripening, sharp-tasting, thin-skinned Furmint, highly susceptible to botrytis infection. Another 20–25% is Hárslevelű ("linden-leaf"), less susceptible but rich in sugar and aromas. Since most of the vineyards were mixed plantings, traditionally Furmint and Hárslevelű were often harvested, pressed, and fermented together. Between 5-10% is Muscat Blanc à Petits Grains, known locally as Sárgamuskotály – either used as a seasoning grape, as Muscadelle is in Sauternes, or as a sumptuous speciality on its own.

The vineyards of Tokaj (locally known as Tokaj-Hegyalja) were first classified in the early 1700s and divided into first, second, third, and unclassified growths. In 1737, by royal decree, this became the world's first delimited wine region. The map shows the principal villages of the region (there are 27 in all; Makkoshotyka is to the north of the area mapped), whose slopes form a wide V, thus facing southeast, south, or southwest. The northernmost make delicate and fine Aszús from sandy soil. It was here that the original Oremus vineyard of the Rákóczis made the first of all Aszú wines. The new Oremus cellar, owned by Vega Sicilia of Spain, has been moved south to Tolcsva.

In Sárospatak, with a splendid Rákóczi castle on the river, Megyer and Pajzos were two of the first vineyards to be privatized. Kincsem is the great vineyard of Tolcsva, named after Hungary's greatest racehorse. The old Imperial Cellars in Tolcsva are still owned by the state and operate under the old name Tokaj Kereskedőház; the new headquarters are in Sátoraljaújhely. To this day it buys so many grapes from the region's smallholders that it is still the largest wine producer of all.

Olaszliszka (*Olasz* means "Italian") is a 13th-century Italian settlement; legend has it that the Italians introduced winemaking. Here the soil is clay with stones, producing more potent wines. Erdőbénye lies up by the oak forests, the source of barrels. Szegilong has a number of classed growths, and is seeing a revival. Bodrogkeresztúr and Tokaj itself, by the river, have the most regular botrytis.

From Tokaj, around the south side of Mount Kopasz into Tarcal, the steep and sheltered vineyards are the Côte d'Or of the region; a succession of once-famous site names (the greatest is Szarvas) which continues through Tarcal onto the road to Mád with Terézia and the great growth Mézes Mály. In Mezőzombor, Disznókő was one of the first vineyards to be privatized in the early 1990s and spectacularly restored by AXA of France. Mád, the former centre of the wine trade, has the famous first growths Nyulászó, Szt Tamás, Király, and Betsek, as well as the steep, abandoned Kővágó. All forces now point towards lower yields and single-vineyard wines able to express these very distinct terroirs. The names of the first growths are once again becoming familiar. In recognition of its return to precise, wine-producing glory, the Tokaj region was made a UNESCO World Heritage Site in 2002.

If the current renaissance of Tokaji has a figurehead, it is István Szepsy, an inspirationally fastidious grower. If it has an international market leader, it is Royal Tokaji, also in Mád, founded in 1989 by Hugh Johnson (founder and co-author of this book) and others, and the first independent company of the new regime.

Styles of Tokaji

Tokaji Aszú, a wine notable for its combination of sweetness, acidity, and uncannily apricot-like fruit, is made by a unique two-stage process. Vintage starts in late October. Shrivelled Aszú grapes and unaffected grapes full of juice are picked at the same time but kept apart. The latter are then pressed and fermented to make various styles of dry or semi-dry wine, including a powerful base wine. The Aszú grapes meanwhile are stored in an almost-dry heap, gently leaking the fabulous Eszencia – juice with up to 850g/l of sugar – to be reverently kept as the region's greatest treasure (see below).

As the harvest ends, the vintner soaks the Aszú berries, crushed or not, for one to five days in fresh must or in partly or fully fermented base wine, in the proportion of one kilo to one litre, prior to pressing. Fermentation starts, controlled by a combination of the sugar content and the cellar temperature (the higher the former and the lower the latter, the slower the fermentation). The richest and finest wines maintain the highest degree of natural sugar; hence the lowest of alcohol (10.5% is typical), while humbler styles tend to have slightly more alcohol (12–13%) and lower natural sugar levels.

The measure of sweetness is still expressed as the number of 20-kilo *puttonyos*, or vineyard hods, of Aszú added to 136 litres (one *gönci* barrel) of base wine, although today sweetness is, more conventionally, measured in grams of residual sugar per litre and wines are fermented in barrels of various sizes, sometimes even in stainless steel. Wine sold as a 6-*puttonyos* Aszú must have more than 150g/l sugar; Aszúeszencia is effectively 7 *puttonyos*. Three *puttonyos* make it the rough equivalent of a German Auslese (at least 60g/l), four or five put it into the Beerenauslese class of sweetness and concentration. The minimum age for these Aszú wines is three years, two in

There's a sameness about Tokaji labels, even if the style of the wines themselves varies more than it has done for decades. We can now choose from dry, varietal, late harvest, and single vineyard wines as well as the traditional Aszú and super-rich Eszencia.

barrel and one in bottle. Traditionally they were aged longer but earlier bottling is increasingly common, resulting in wines with more freshness in youth but still awesome potential for ageing. If no Aszú has been added, the wine is Szamorodni (literally "as it comes" in Polish) suggesting the fruit was picked and crushed with the botrytised berries. The *száraz* (dry) version develops rather like a light sherry while the *édes* (fairly sweet) is a different style. The (now regulated) use of the term Late Harvest (*Késői szüretelésű*) on labels has added to an already complicated picture. These naturally sweet wines may be made simply of overripe grapes, but more often they are also made with botrytised grapes and, in contrast to Aszú wines, are matured only briefly.

Eszencia, the most luxurious Tokaji, is so sweet it will hardly ferment at all. And of all the essences of the grape it is the most velvety, oily, peach-like, and penetrating. Its fragrance lingers in the mouth like incense. Eszencia has the lowest alcohol level of any wine – if you can call it wine

A vineyard near Mád is lined with piles of the volcanic pumice rocks that litter the ground all over the Tokaji region. They have to be picked out and put on one side so as not to damage vineyard machinery.

at all. No age is too great for it (or, indeed, for any great Aszú wine).

As an increasingly important second string to its bow, Tokaji is rediscovering the qualities of dry wines, notably but not exclusively dry Furmint, that are generally intriguing and distinctive: intense, slow to unfurl, and with very obvious middle European nobility. Inspired by the dramatic improvements in making Aszú wines (and the not-inconsiderable difficulty of selling them), most producers now offer dry wines in the image of those that played a significant role in Tokaji three or four centuries ago. And the increasing emergence of exciting single-vineyard wines serves only to underline the wisdom of the 18th-century vineyard classification.

TOKAJ'S BEST VINEYARDS

Vineyard names have become increasingly important over the last two decades, since Tokaj production fell once more into the hands of individuals keen to express the region's distinctive topography in liquid form.

OREMUS	Notable producer
Hatalos	Noted vineyard
Mád	Wine town/village
	Classed vineyard
	Other vineyard
	Woods
500	Contour interval 100 metres
▼	Weather station (WS)

1:183,000

Km 0   2   4   6 Km
Miles 0   1   2   3 Miles

TOKAJ: TOKAJ ▼

Latitude / Altitude of WS
48.10° / 436ft (133m)

Average growing season temperature at WS
60.4°F (15.8°C)

Average annual rainfall at WS
24in (620mm)

Harvest month rainfall at WS
October: 1.6in (41mm)

Principal viticultural hazards
Autumn rain, grey rot

Principal grape varieties
Furmint, Hárslevelű, Sárgamuskotály

Czech Republic and Slovakia

A wine prospector in these cultured but battered countries 20 years ago would have found very little. But the Czechs and Slovaks are becoming wine drinkers again. Quality has risen with quantity. Little is exported yet, but the potential is there. **Bohemia**, the hinterland of Prague, across Germany's eastern border from Sachsen (Saxony), has about 1,800 acres (720ha) of vines, mainly along the right bank of the Elbe. The region makes light wines, supplying Prague's cafés, most notably of Pinot Noir at Mělník, Svatovavřinecké (Austria's Sankt Laurent) at Roudnice, and Ryzlink Rýnský (Riesling) at Velké Žernoseky. Kosher wines are produced at Most.

Moravia, with 44,000 acres (18,000ha) of vineyard, makes by far the majority of Czech wine from vineyards just over the border from Austria's Weinviertel, concentrated south of the capital Brno. The warm limestone slopes of the Pálava hills here are locally famous for their flora. The most successful wines of the Znojmo subregion are zesty Sauvignon Blancs from well-equipped cellars at Nový Šaldorf and Nové Bránice, and also Veltlínské Zelené (Grüner Veltliner) and Riesling from Šatov. Ryzlink Vlašský (Welschriesling), Chardonnay, and the two white Pinots are the flagship wines of the Mikulov subregion. The northern part of Slovácko grows Riesling, while the southern part is better at reds such as Frankovka (Austria's Blaufränkisch). The aromatic white Moravian crossings of Traminer Rot and Müller-Thurgau (from Lechovice, Rakvice, and Šatov) and Muškát Moravský (Moravian Muscat) also have a certain following. Moravian reds are not usually so interesting, although Svatovavřinecké and Zweigeltrebe (Zweigelt) from the Velké Pavlovice subregion and Frankovka from Kobylí, Bořetice, and Dolní Kounice are better than most.

Slovakia

Wine was traditionally more important in Slovakia than the Czech Republic, land of Pilsner, but the total area of Slovak vineyard halved to 37,000 acres (15,000ha) between 1980 and 2010. Progress – bringing, for example, malolactic fermentation, oak ageing and lees contact – is changing the picture. Sweet Icewine and straw wine, made from dried grapes, have been revived. White wines predominate, with international grapes (Riesling, Chardonnay, Sauvignon Blanc, as well as Cabernet Sauvignon and various Pinots) in the forefront. But winemakers and their customers have recently become interested in new Slovak crossings, bred to ripen early with high sugar levels and full flavours. According to the latest (2009) wine law, combining German and French principles, wines are divided into three quality levels defined mainly by ripeness and yield. The finest wines are denoted DSC (Districtus Slovakia Controllatus).

In general, the warmer climate and deeper, fertile soils of southern Slovakia are more suitable for reds, particularly Cabernet Sauvignon, Frankovka, and the new crossings. The less fertile, stonier soils of the Malé Karpaty hills, which lie in a sweep eastwards from the capital Bratislava, are more suitable for such white wine grapes as Silvaner, Veltliner, Welschriesling, Riesling, Chardonnay, and various Muscats.

A handful of big Slovakian producers tend to make distinctly ordinary wines, while hundreds of small winemakers grow their own grapes in tiny vineyards, mainly for their own consumption. Most of the best wines emerge from medium-sized wineries such as Mrva & Stanko, Karpatská Perla, and Elesko. One of relatively few exported Slovak wines is the crisp, dry Château Belá Riesling made by Egon Müller of Germany near Štúrovo.

Very little Czech and Slovak wine is exported, but these labels show a keen appreciation of drama and typography on a wine label. The wines are light, dry, and white.

BOHEMIA, MORAVIA, AND SLOVAKIA

Three very different wine regions can be associated with what lies just over their respective borders with Sachsen in Germany, Weinviertel in Austria, and northern Hungary (including Tokaj). Moravia is now the most productive, since Slovakian viticulture shrivelled.

1:3,650,000

	International boundary
ČECHY	Wine region
ZNOJMO	Wine subregion
• Mělník	Wine town/village
	Land above 1000 metres

Western Balkans

If few wines of more than local interest come from the regions on this map today it is for political reasons rather than geographical ones. On the latitude of Italy and similarly diverse and mountainous, the western Balkans have equally propitious conditions for vines. They have ancient histories of winemaking and the many native grape varieties that inevitably result. Albania apart, they formed the short-lived Yugoslavia. As they emerge from years of political strife they are offering glimpses of rich wine-making potential.

Mountainous **Bosnia and Herzegovina** was once an important vineyard of Austro-Hungary. Some memorable full-flavoured, dry, apricot-scented white wine is still made of the now-rare Žilavka around Mostar. But the dominant grape today is the much more ordinary dark-skinned Blatina. The civil war of the early 1990s left less than 9,900 acres (4,000ha) of vineyards, mainly in Herzegovina to the south of Mostar.

Wine production in **Serbia** (Srbija) has a chequered history. The Turks did their best to rout the vine; the Hapsburgs positively encouraged it. Today Serbia claims to have even more vineyards than Croatia, – around 148,000 acres (60,000ha) – but certainly not all in production. If Serbia succeeds in joining the EU, however, there will have to be a vineyard census and updated wine laws. Production is still dominated by five large industrial wineries, but some of the output of the now 40-plus smaller producers is genuinely encouraging.

The northern autonomous province of Vojvodina shares the climatic extremes of the Pannonian Plain with Hungary to the north. Welschriesling is common here, but Pinots of all three colours currently offer most promise. The vineyards with the best potential (and a long history) are on the Fruška Gora, the hills that relieve the flatness of Vojvodina along the Danube north of Belgrade. The countryside here is very similar to that of inland Croatia, to the west, while the sandy Subotica-Horgoš and Čoka wine regions in the far north are both geographically and culturally much more Hungarian than Serbian, and the wines distinctly Magyar in character. The town of Smederevo south of Belgrade gives its name to the white Smederevka grape, producing scarcely memorable off-dry whites, but a few producers are making more interesting wines from Riesling, Chardonnay, and Cabernet Sauvignon.

In southern Serbia, the most invigorating reds are made from the local Prokupac grape, while the Oplenac subregion, situated in the hilly Šumadija region along the Velika Morava River, is increasingly good at Riesling, Sauvignon, Chardonnay, Frankovka, and Pinot Noir.

Until the disintegration of Yugoslavia, **Kosovo**'s wine industry was maintained largely by exports of Amselfelder, a sweet red blend for the German market. A Serbian blockade put paid to wine exports for many years. Rahovec (Orahovac) is the main wine area, claiming 54,300 acres (22,000ha) of vines. The largest winery here, StoneCastle, privatized in 2006 and advised by international consultants, clearly has exports on its agenda.

Albania's ancient wine industry managed to survive Ottoman rule, then the communist fixation with volume at all costs, but its vineyards today total a mere 9,900 acres (4,000ha). Wines are clean and fresh, but the country's unique combination of Mediterranean climate and indigenous grapes such as Shesh i Bardhë, Pules, and Debinë for whites and Shesh i Zi, Kallmet, Vlosh, and Serina for reds are ripe for development. The requisite expertise has tended to come from Italy.

Montenegro became an EU candidate in 2010. Its wine industry is small, with 10,600 acres (4,300ha) of vines dominated by one winery: 13 Jul-Plantaže. With 5,708 acres (2,310ha), it is claimed to be the largest single vineyard in Europe. A good 70% is planted to Vranac, a deep-coloured, tannic red variety that has real character and ageing potential. The other important local grape is Krstač for whites. The wine industry, including the first private producer, Sjekloća, is based around Lake Skadar.

Even further south, on the border with Greece, the hot winelands of the **Republic of Macedonia** (not to be confused with the Greek region) are making much better wine now that the industry is in private hands. There are around 80 wineries and three wine regions, of which Povardarje, or Vardar Valley, is by far the most important. Vranac grapes dominate; white wines are often distilled into brandy. The biggest (and improving) producer Tikveš crushes around 25% of the country's harvest.

Much of the wine produced in the terrain mapped here travels without a label, either straight from vineyard to table, or in bulk from one of a handful of large industrial producers. Both these wines are grown in the south, but there is no reason why interesting wine should not be made in the north too.

Croatia

Istria and Dalmatia have always been the frontispiece of Croatia (Hrvatska), the sublime coast of golden Venetian ports and hundreds of islands. Emperors, crusaders, and doges passed up and down without, perhaps, doing much wine tasting. Today's yacht-owners know better. Croatia's wines are original, well-made, and fetching good prices.

Croatia is split into two very different regions by the Dinaric Alps mountain range that follows the coast. Coastal Croatia consists of Croatian Istria (**Hrvatska Istra**), the Croatian Coast (**Hvratsko Primorje**), Northern Dalmatia (**Sjeverna Dalmacija**), Central and Southern Dalmatia and associated islands (**Srednja i Južna Dalmacija**), and the Dalmatian Highlands (**Dalmatinska Zagora**). It is a white wine coast in the main.

Continental Croatia, which lies inland north and east to the Hungarian border (see map, p.261), is also white wine country. Graševina, Croatia's Welschriesling, is not a grape of legend. It covers a quarter of Croatia's vineyards, but needs all the artistry that is now being applied around Kutjevo in **Slavonia** (Slavonija) and Baranya and Ilok, bordering the Danube to make it thrilling enough to compete with the more recent plantings of Chardonnay, Traminac, and true Riesling; also the reds that are emerging here. It is cooler to the north and west of Zagreb, especially in Plešivica and even Zagorje. Aromatic whites such as Riesling and Sauvignon Blanc show real promise here, as do some of the best sweet wines.

North to south

Istria, the most northerly of the coastal regions, is blessed with a better grape: its very own Malvasia, Malvazija Istarska. It reliably makes firm whites redolent of honey and apple skins, especially when its makers follow the Slovenian fashion of macerating the grape skins in their juice. Acacia rather than oak is often the barrel-wood of choice in Istria – despite the fact that Slavonia, not far to the east, is famous for the quality of its oak. The result is often lively, full-bodied, complex wines – some even fit for ageing. The distinctive Istrian red is Refosco or Teran, distinct from Friuli's Refosco dal Peduncolo Rosso and tough enough to tempt producers to add some of their Merlot.

There is more excitement, though, going south down the coast, where the Malvasia may not have the same qualities, but is varied by local grapes of characters only now being exploited. Red Plavac

Vineyards on the island of Brač, south of Split. Presumably in the middle of winter they look less paradisiacal, but to the increasing number of summer tourists who visit this beautiful corner of the world, most wine – however ordinary – must seem relatively ambrosial.

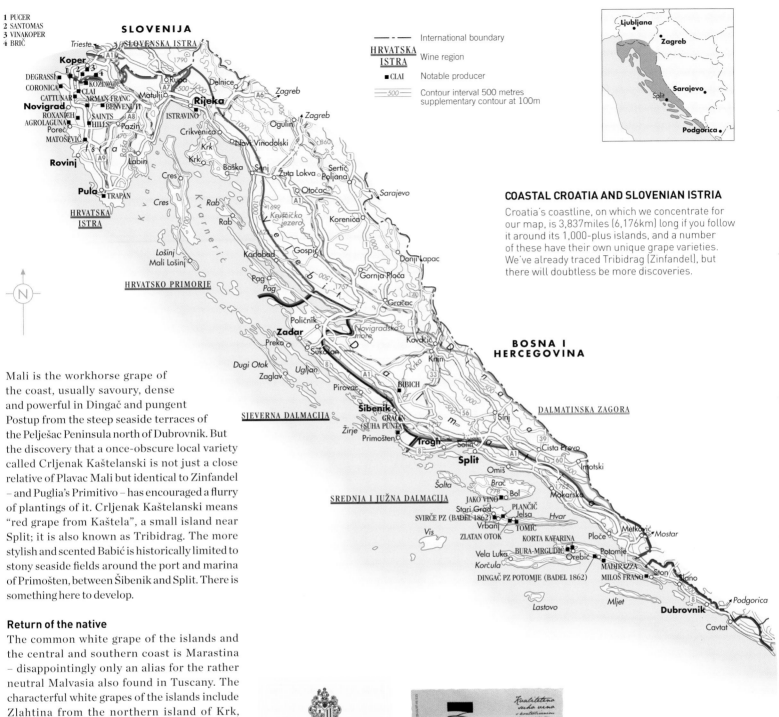

1 PUCER
2 SANTOMAS
3 VINAKOPER
4 BRIČ

International boundary

HRVATSKA
ISTRA   Wine region

■ CLAI   Notable producer

500   Contour interval 500 metres
supplementary contour at 100m

COASTAL CROATIA AND SLOVENIAN ISTRIA

Croatia's coastline, on which we concentrate for our map, is 3,837miles (6,176km) long if you follow it around its 1,000-plus islands, and a number of these have their own unique grape varieties. We've already traced Tribidrag (Zinfandel), but there will doubtless be more discoveries.

Mali is the workhorse grape of the coast, usually savoury, dense and powerful in Dingač and pungent Postup from the steep seaside terraces of the Pelješac Peninsula north of Dubrovnik. But the discovery that a once-obscure local variety called Crljenak Kaštelanski is not just a close relative of Plavac Mali but identical to Zinfandel – and Puglia's Primitivo – has encouraged a flurry of plantings of it. Crljenak Kaštelanski means "red grape from Kaštela", a small island near Split; it is also known as Tribidrag. The more stylish and scented Babić is historically limited to stony seaside fields around the port and marina of Primošten, between Šibenik and Split. There is something here to develop.

Return of the native

The common white grape of the islands and the central and southern coast is Marastina – disappointingly only an alias for the rather neutral Malvasia also found in Tuscany. The characterful white grapes of the islands include Zlahtina from the northern island of Krk, aromatic Vugava on the tiny Vis, refreshing Bogdanuša on Hvar, otherwise almost entirely covered in lavender, and both promising Pošip and the celebrated intense Grk on Korčula. New energy and ambition came to the island wine-growers when the native Mike Grgich returned in 1996 from his dazzling career as a founder of Grgich Hills in the Napa Valley. Grgich helped to introduce Americans to Croatian wine, and played a part in what became known as Zinquest, the search for Zinfandel's Croatian roots. As visitors now know, with Dalmatian food – tiny oysters, raw ham, grilled fish, smoky and oniony grilled meats, and mounds of sweet grapes and figs – the fire and flavour of the local wines of the coast can seem ambrosial.

1:2,175,000

Km 0   25   50   75 Km
Miles 0   25   50 Miles

The best Croatian wines are designated Vrhunsko Vino, superior wines are Kvalitetno Vino, while table wines are Stolno Vino. These are fine examples of Malvazija (both of the top labels), Graševina (Welschriesling), Pošip (from Korčula), and Plavac (Tribidrag's progeny).

Slovenia

Even in the Iron Curtain era it was hard to tell where Italy stopped and Slovenia began. It was the first of the old Yugoslav nations to declare independence (in 1991), and the only one whose wine has always been acknowledged and drunk in Western Europe. In the 1970s, Lutomer "Riesling" from eastern Slovenia was almost the only wine shipped from Eastern Europe.

Slovenia stretches eastwards from the Adriatic to the Pannonian Plain with its continental climate. The green rolling hills provide some excellent grape-ripening sites, now grouped into three distinct wine regions: Primorska (on the coast), Posavje (along the Sava River and not mapped in detail), and Podravje (along the Drava River), including the historic wine centres of Maribor, Radgona, and Lutomer-Ormož.

It was at Maribor that in 1823 the Austrian Archduke Johann ordered "all noble vine varieties that exist" to be planted on his property. Thus Chardonnay, Sauvignon Blanc, Pinot Gris, Pinot Blanc, Traminer, Muscat, Riesling, Pinot Noir, and many other grapes were introduced to inland Slovenia.

In this century the country's total area of vines has been declining, as the number of Slovenians interested in being part-time vignerons shrinks, but 40,412 acres (16,354ha) of vineyards are officially registered, and there are many that are not. Average holdings are tiny and although the Slovenian wine industry is gradually becoming more professional and less fragmented, there are still more than 27,000 wine-growers in the country.

SLOVENIA'S WINE REGIONS

ÖSTERREICH

PODRAVJE

SLOVENIJA
Ljubljana

PRIMORSKA

POSAVJE

HRVATSKA
(CROATIA)

CENTRAL PRIMORSKA

Slovenia's wine country is mapped in three different sections. Part of Goriška Brda in the far northwest is mapped in detail p.165. Posavje is shown on the locator, left, while the most important section of the Primorska region to its immediate southeast is mapped below.

International boundary

KRAS Wine region

■ OTAR Notable producer

Contour interval 100 metres

1:362,500

Km 0 — 10 — 20 Km
Miles 0 — 10 Miles

Was the heart shape of this vineyard in the Spicnik-Stajerska area of Podravje, north of Maribor, deliberate? It is not difficult to see how well suited much of Slovenia is to the vine.

Primorska

Primorska, the westernmost Slovenian wine region, with 16,040 vineyard acres (6,490ha), never lost historic links with Friuli across the border in Italy and is still the most dynamic. Summers here are hot, but autumn rains arrive early. Most of the Primorska vineyards are influenced both by the Adriatic and the Alps and tend to produce aromatic, powerful wines. Predictably, given its proximity, Primorska favours the Friulian style of aromatic, dry, varietally named whites and firm reds which, unusually for Slovenia, represent as much as half of production. Indeed in some cases, Brda in the north of the region is simply a continuation of Collio across the border in Friuli (and is mapped with Friuli on p.165).

Rebula (Ribolla Gialla) is the dominant white wine grape here, though red Bordeaux blends and Pinot Noir can be good. Rebula can be made in every imaginable style, from razor-sharp and raised in stainless steel to the product of dramatically extended skin contact and long maturation in amphorae. It is often used to give freshness to local sparkling wines and premium blends. Some of the blends are defiantly "natural", including whites that are the distinctly orange product of months of skin contact.

In Primorska, as in Friuli, a wide variety of local and international varieties are grown, including aromatic, vegetal Sauvignonasse (known as Friulano in Friuli). But Primorska Pinot Grigio typically has much more structure and character than its Veneto counterpart.

The **Vipava Valley** district, especially its upper reaches, is noticeably cooler, resulting in wines with more lift, elegance, and less alcohol than in Brda. The indigenous grapes Zelen and Pinela (known as Pinella in northeast Italy) have been in the spotlight recently.

Kras, the harsh karst limestone plateau above Trieste, with its red, iron-rich soils, is the eastern extension of Italy's Carso. It is famous for its dark, tart Teran made from grapes also known as Refosco Terrano (and often confused with Refosco dal Peduncolo Rosso), which are also grown around Koper on the Istrian coast. Teran matches a rustic kebab to perfection. Malvasia is the white wine grape par excellence over the border in Croatian Istria and is becoming increasingly important in Slovenian Istria, too (see map p.263).

Podravje

Podravje, with 16,750 acres (6,780ha) of vines, is Slovenia's most widespread and most continental region. It is divided into the sprawling **Štajerska Slovenija** district and the relatively minute **Prekmurje**. After two decades of being in the shadow of Primorska, Podravje is now firmly back in the game.

The dominant variety has long been Laški Rizling (Welschriesling), but increasing attention, both in Slovenia and abroad, is being paid to Sipon (Furmint). Renski Rizling (Rhine Riesling) can produce some fine wines, and Sauvignon Blanc is also seen as having great potential. Chardonnay and Pinots of all three hues are grown around Ljutomer, Ormož, Maribor, and Radgona, where Ranina (Austria's Bouvier) and Dišeči Traminec (Gewürztraminer) make full-bodied wines with historic resonance. Radgona has been Slovenia's sparkling wine capital since 1852.

Podravje wines today are almost exclusively white and made reductively with cold fermentation, and stainless-steel maturation, bottled early, sealed with screwcaps, and sold in their first year. The aim is pungent aromas, low alcohol, and crisp acidity – although there are promising experiments with large oak barrels and Burgundian winemaking techniques. Traditionally, many wines retained unfermented sugar, but nowadays most are dry, except for some exceptional sweet botrytised wines and Icewines in favourable years.

Reds account for less than 10% of all Podravje wine production but Modri Pinot (Pinot Noir), Modra Frankinja (Blaufränkisch), and Zweigelt are slowly increasing in both quality and quantity. According to Guinness World Records, the famous ancient vine in Maribor is the oldest on the planet at more than 400 years old, and it still yields 77–121b (35–55kg) of Žametovka grapes every year. The warm Prekmurje district produces fuller, softer wines than the norm with some promising reds.

Posavje

Posavje is relatively unimportant in terms of the total amount of wine produced, from vineyards widely dispersed southwest of Podravje. The region has only 6,680 acres (2,703ha) of vines, growing much the same grapes as Podravje but often blending them to make such locally (rather than varietally) named specialities Cviček, Metliška črnina, and Bizeljčan. Posavje wines tend to be even lighter, tarter, and less polished than in Podravje. The rare, crisp white Rumeni

CENTRAL PODRAVJE

Slovenia's wine region furthest from the coast is just south of Styria in Austria, and produces similarly finely etched, mainly white, aromatic wines. Ljutomer in the far east was the name of a Welschriesling brand exported in vast quantity in the 1960s and 1970s.

	International boundary
	Boundary of Okoliš (appellation)
■ VINAG	Notable producer
	Vineyards
600	Contour interval 150 metres

Ales Kristančič of Movia in Brda has been Slovenia's best-known wine producer outside the country and has also been influential in persuading his peers, such as Marjan Simčič to adopt extremely "natural" winemaking techniques. Verus and Dveri Pax make great-value varietals in Podravje.

Plavec can enliven the local fizz of Bizeljsko Sremič. The standard issue in Dolenjska district is pink, light, tart Cviček, a popular local answer to the Austrian Schilcher. Bela Krajina district is

famous for Yellow Muscat, and sweet wines that can often outshine those from Podravje. Spicy Modra Frankinja (Blaufränkisch) is a regional speciality that benefits from time in barrel.

Bulgaria

In the 1970s, Bulgarian Cabernet Sauvignon was a byword for value. By the mid-1990s, it all had all gone horribly wrong, thanks largely to the maladroit way in which land was privatized. Now, however, there is reassuring evidence once more that Bulgaria can make fine wines from both international and indigenous grapes.

Massive plantings of international varieties on fertile land in the 1950s were intended to pump out a river of everyday wine for the Soviet Union. They did better than that. For a while the river was seen as cheap and palatable in the West. Advice, it was surprisingly said, came from (among other places) California. But Gorbachev's 1980s anti-alcohol purge had a profound effect. As the economy foundered and the market for its produce shrank, the country's vineyards were simply neglected or abandoned, often because no one quite knew who owned them.

During the late 1990s, the wineries and bottling plants that were once state-owned were privatized, some of the better wineries attracting investors from Western Europe and EU investment funds. The years in the run-up to EU accession at the start of 2007 saw huge EU subsidies for wineries and vineyards. In the last few years a number of smaller, private estates have emerged. By 2009, the country's total area of wine grapevines had shrunk to 138,700 acres (56,130ha), with as much as 15% of this destined for private use or the local rakia spirit. But at least vineyards are now much better looked after. Wineries increasingly own their own vines, even if they are often rather young ones at present, which can result in some rather simple wines.

To satisfy EU wine laws, Bulgaria has designated two zones for regional wine: the **Thracian Lowlands** in the south and **Danubian**

BULGARIA'S WINE REGIONS

With an eye on EU wine bureaucracy and ease of blending between districts, Bulgarian wine country has been divided into just two vast principal regions: the plain to the immediate south of the River Danube and the "Thracian Lowlands" – anywhere producing wine in the south of Bulgaria.

—·—·—	International boundary
DANUBIAN PLAIN	Principal wine region
•*Varna*	Wine town/village
■ TERRA TANGRA	Notable producer
(shaded)	Quality wine regions
(shaded)	Land above 1000 metres
▼	Weather station (WS)

BULGARIA: PLOVDIV ▼

Latitude / Altitude of WS
42.13° / 587ft (179m)

Average growing season temperature at WS
64.9°F (18.3°C)

Average annual rainfall at WS
21in (541mm)

Harvest month rainfall at WS
September: 1.3in (33mm)

Principal viticultural hazards
Fungal diseases, winter freeze, hail

Principal grape varieties
Merlot, Cabernet Sauvignon, Pamid, Red Misket, Muscat Ottonel, Rkatsiteli, Chardonnay, Dimyat, Melnik

Plain in the north. Just as in Italy, a distinction is made between the 21 regions that make wine with guaranteed origin and the further 23 for wines of controlled and guaranteed origin.

While cheap bottled wine exports to Russia and Poland are still significant – a good half of all Bulgarian wine is exported – many of the new producers have serious quality (and price) ambitions. They include an Italian textile magnate, Edoardo Miroglio, whose new plantings of Pinot Noir on a boutique estate at Elenovo in the mountains show real promise. The French distribution company Belvedere has been a major force, especially at the Katarzyna estate. Bessa Valley has benefited from investment by the owner of Château Canon-la-Gaffelière in St-Emilion, and Château de Val is owned by a Bulgarian who has returned from a successful career in the US.

The arrival of temperature control, modern equipment, and better winemaking has been transformative. Most winemakers are locally trained, but French consultant Marc Dworkin has been influential first at Damianitza and then Bessa Valley, while Michel Rolland of Pomerol consults at Telish's Castra Rubra winery.

International and local grapes

Bulgaria's most-planted red wine grape is now Merlot, with 26,125 acres (10,570ha); Cabernet Sauvignon comes second with 20,850 acres (8,440ha), but there is a conscious effort now to match variety and terrain and to stray beyond the Bordeaux staples. Impressive examples of Shiraz, Pinot Noir (especially in the cool northwest), Cabernet Franc, and Malbec have appeared among reds, and good Chardonnay, Traminer, and occasionally Sauvignon Blanc and Viognier among whites.

Of the local grape varieties, Mavrud has received most attention. This indigenous late-ripening variety can produce strapping, spicy reds suitable for a long life, though it is arguably at its best imbuing top blends (Santa Sarah

Privat and Rumelia's Erelia are two examples) with some local personality. Since it needs a long growing season it is increasingly appreciated, and mainly planted, in the south around Plovdiv and Assenovgrad. Shiroka Melnishka Losa ("broadleaved vine of Melnik") is another southern speciality, grown exclusively in the hot Struma Valley right on the Greek border over the Rhodope and Pirin mountains (Zapadni Rodopi and Pirin Planina). It makes scented, robust wines, some of them strangely sweet, but they can be impressive survivors of long ageing in old oak.

The Valley of the Roses is around Karlovo in the far north of the central section of the Thracian Lowlands, at the highest limit of viticulture there. The Stara Planina rise in the distance.

Much more common than either of these, though, is Pamid, which gives pale, innocuous wine. Rubin is a promising Bulgarian crossing of Nebbiolo and Syrah whose best examples can display more than a whiff of Nebbiolo's perfume.

The great majority of Bulgaria's Cabernet and Merlot grapes are grown in the south of the country where wines are typically riper and more structured, while the reds produced on the best sites in the north, especially in the northwest, have more finesse and longevity.

Red wines predominate (just) in all regions apart from those on the Black Sea. Most of Bulgaria's best white wines come from around Shumen and Veliki Preslav in the coolest, northeast part of the country, although Belvedere has shown that its new vineyards in the Sakar Mountains can yield truly aromatic Sauvignon Blanc. The most-planted white wine variety is Red Misket, a pink-skinned local crossing of the Balkan speciality Dimyat and Riesling.

The Valley of the Roses between the Balkan (Stara) and Sredna Gora mountains, famous for its damask roses, which are grown for their attar, or essential oils, produces perfumed wines, too: both Red Misket and Muscat Ottonel as well as some Cabernet Sauvignon.

Enira is Bessa Valley's top bottling; Dux is the same from Valley Vintners in the far northwest, where reds tend to be rather more complex and subtle than those grown in the higher temperatures of the Thracian Lowlands.

Romania

Romania is a Latin country in a Slav sandwich, whose affinities are closer to France than to its neighbours. In both latitude and attitude there are parallels. Its wine literature even shares the sort of hard-headed lyricism of much of French gastronomic writing. True, the Black Sea is no Atlantic in its influence, but together with the Carpathian Mountains, which curl like a giant conch in the middle of the country, it moderates the hot, dry summers of a continental climate.

The mountains rise from the surrounding plain to 8,000ft (2,400m) at their peaks, and enclose the high Transylvanian plateau. Across Wallachia, the south of the country, the Danube (Dunărea) flows through a sandy plain, turning north towards its delta and isolating the Black Sea province of Dobrogea.

In Romania, as in the old Soviet Union, a great planting programme in the 1960s turned huge tracts of arable land into vineyard, but by 2009 this had shrunk considerably, to 448,100 acres (181,340ha). Romania is still the seventh-biggest producer of wine in Europe, and by far the most important in the old Soviet Bloc. By no means all is serious or exportable; it includes a considerable proportion of hybrids, and home-made wines sold illegally by the roadside. Indeed, Romania is still a net importer of wine.

The favourites are the local Fetească Regală and slightly meatier Fetească Albă (Hungary's Leányka), with aromatic Tămâioasă Românească (a small-berried Muscat) much favoured for the future. Welschriesling and Aligoté are also common, as is Merlot. Cabernet Sauvignon, Sauvignon Blanc, Pinot Gris, and Muscat Ottonel are other international varieties with a track record in Romania and there is also a little Chardonnay and Pinot Noir. Of Romania's own red wine grapes, Băbească Neagră makes light, fruity wines, and Fetească Neagră more serious stuff.

Like Hungary, Romania has one wine whose name was once famous all over Europe. But while Tokaji struggled on through communism to re-emerge in splendour, Cotnari is now virtually unknown outside Romania. It was historically a botrytised dessert wine made in the northeast. Most contemporary examples are rather ordinary medium-dry to medium-sweet whites.

Seven regions

The country today is divided into seven wine regions, of which Romanian **Moldova**, to the east of the Carpathians, is by far the biggest, with

The Prince Ştirbey estate was restored in the early years of this century by Baroness Ileana Kripp-Costinescu, a descendant of the original owner, who is concentrating on local grape varieties and has done much to put the Drăgăşani region on the map.

over a third of the country's vineyards. Northern Moldova is white wine country. The great concentration of production, though, is further south in the central Moldavian Hills: the county of Vrancea, with Focşani as its capital, has 50,000 acres (20,000ha) under vine. Coteşti, Nicoreşti, Panciu (known for sparkling wine), and Odobeşti (a brandy centre) are the lilting names of its wine towns. The terrain varies but much of it is sand, as it is over the western border in the Great Plain of Hungary.

Following the curve of the Carpathians, Moldova gives way to hilly **Muntenia** and **Oltenia**, the former better known by the name of its most famous vineyards at Dealu Mare. These hills, well-watered, south-sloping, and with the highest average temperatures in Romania, are largely dedicated to Cabernet, Merlot, Pinot Noir, full-bodied Fetească Neagră, and also now some promising Shiraz. Dealu Mare is Romania's most exciting region for ambitious red wines, notably those of Davino, SERVE, Lacerta, Rotenberg, and Vinarte. The unctuous and aromatic dessert Tămâioasă from Pietroasa (northeast of Dealu Mare) is one white wine speciality.

West of Dealu Mare the small but dynamic zone of Drăgăşani was recently revived by its old princely family of Ştirbey, making fresh and lively wines of such local red grapes as Crâmpoşie Selecţionată, Novac, and Negru de Drăgăşani as well as aromatic fresh whites from Fetească Regală, Muscat, and Sauvignon Blanc. There are small estate growers as well, Avincis and Via Sandu among them.

The outcrops of Carpathian foothills scattered through Muntenia and Oltenia each have their own specialities. Stefăneşti is known for aromatic white wines, while Cabernet Sauvignon is Sâmbureti's forte. Vânju Mare to the west also has an established name for Cabernet, and a growing one for Pinot Noir. Crama Oprisor even further southwest is owned by Carl Reh of Germany. Domeniul Coroanei Segarcea, south of Craiova, is the revived and replanted former royal estate.

On Romania's short Black Sea coast **Dobrogea**, across the Danube to the east, has the country's sunniest climate and lowest rainfall. The Murfatlar subregion has a reputation for soft red wines and luscious white ones, including sweet Chardonnays, from exceptionally ripe grapes grown on limestone soils, tempered by onshore breezes. The dominant producer, with 7660 acres (3,100ha) of vines, is also called Murfatlar and recruited a Romanian-born consultant winemaker from South Africa in 2011.

Hungarian influence is evident in the northwestern corner of Romania. Many of the red wines of **Banat** have been made from Pinot Noir, Merlot, and Cabernet Sauvignon but the introduction of Fetească Neagră and Shiraz promises well. Recaş is the leading producer. Fetească Regală, Welschriesling, and Sauvignon Blanc dominate white wine production.

Transylvania, meanwhile, remains like an island in the centre of the country: a plateau

ROMANIA'S WINE REGIONS

The Carpathians dominate Romanian geography and most Romanian wine is made east and south of them. West of them, Transylvania has a name that would resonate on export markets, but relatively little Romanian wine, made anywhere, escapes the country.

1:3,750,000

| Km 0 | 50 | 100 | 150 Km |
| Miles 0 | | 50 | 100 Miles |

- – - – Internationalboundary
BANAT Wine region
COTNARI Wine subregion
• *Sadova* Wine town/village
■ RECAŞ Notable producer
Wine-producing area
Land above 1000 metres
▼ Weather station (WS)

UKRAINA

MAGYARORSZÁG (HUNGARY)

MOLDOVA

UKRAINA

REPUBLIKA SRBIJA

BÂLGARIJA

MAREA NEAGRĂ (BLACK SEA)

Baia-Mare · Cernăuţi · Suceava · COTNARI · Cotnari · BUCIUM IAŞI · IAŞI · VINIA · Iaşi · MOLDOVA · COLINELE TUTOVEI · Huşi · HUŞI · ZELETIN · Bacău · MARAMUREŞ · SILVANIA · DIOSIG · Oradea · LECHINŢA · Cluj-Napoca · Târgu-Mureş · TRANSILVANIA · AIUD · Aiud · Târnăveni · JIDVEI · Blaj · ALBA · Alba Iulia · TÂRNAVE · SEBEŞ APOLD · Deva · CRIŞANA · MINIŞ MĂDERAT · Siria · Ghioroc · Arad · WINE PRINCESS · RECAŞ · PETRO VASELO · Timişoara · VERITAS PANCIU · NICOREŞTI · Nicoreşti · DEALUL BUJORULUI · PANCIU · Panciu · Odobeşti · IVEŞTI · ODOBEŞTI · Focşani · COVURLUI · CRAMA GIRBOIU · SENATOR · COTEŞTI · VINCON · Galaţi · DEALURILE VRANCEA · BUZĂULUI · VINARTE · DAVINO · DOMENIILE TOHANI · CRAMA CEPTURA · Buzău · ROTENBERG · DOMENIILE SĂHĂTENI · SERVE · LACERTA · CRAMA BUDUREASCA · HALEWOOD · BASILESCU · DEALU MARE · VINTERRA · PIETROASA VECHE · Braşov · Argeş · Ştefăneşti · VINARTE · Piteşti · ŞTEFĂNEŞTI · PRINCE ŞTIRBEY · Dobroteasa · SÂMBUREŞTI · Ploieşti · VIA SANDU · Drăgăşani · AVINCIS · MUNTENIA · Bucureşti · VINARTE · Rogova · OLTENIA · DRĂGĂŞANI · VINTERRA · VINARTE · PLAIURILE DRÂNCEI · DEALURILE CRAIOVEI · PODGORIA DACILOR · CRAMA OPRIŞOR · Craiova · VIE VIN · VÂNJU MARE · Segarcea · SADOVA-CORABIA · CALAFAT · DOMENIUL COROANEI SEGARCEA · Sadova · PODGORIA SEVERINULUI · BANAT · Beograd · DOMENIILE OSTROV · ALIRA · MURFATLAR · Medgidia · MURFATLAR · Ostrov · OSTROV · Lipniţa · Varna · SARICA NICULIŢEL · Niculiţel · DOBROGEA · ISTRIA BABADAG · Constanţa

•Bucureşti

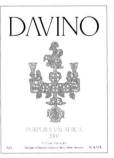

The two Feteascăs, represented by the unusually refined examples made by Davino and Crama Basilescu, are Romania's most widely planted grape varieties and are Moldovan in origin.

ROMANIA: BACAU ▼

Latitude / Altitude of WS
46.53° / 604ft (184m)

Average growing season temperature at WS
60.7°F (16°C)

Average annual rainfall at WS
23in (587mm)

Harvest month rainfall at WS
August: 2in (52mm)

Principal viticultural hazards
Spring frost, drought, September rain, winter freeze

Principal grape varieties
Fetească Regală, Fetească Albă, Merlot, Welschriesling, Aligoté, Sauvignon Blanc, Cabernet Sauvignon, Muscat Ottonel Băbească Neagră

1,500ft-plus (460m) above sea level, cool and relatively rainy, favouring much fresher and crisper whites than are produced in the rest of Romania, together with some promising Pinot Noir. For the moment potential is greater than reality, but recent winery investments may change this. EU membership has encouraged a sizeable flow of subsidy and investment into Romania's wine industry. Imports seem to be providing a competitive spur to the best local enterprises, if not (yet) to the five large oufits that control almost 70% of the Romanian market.

1|2   2|3   3|4   4|5   5|6

The Black Sea Region

In the 1970s, the Soviet Union was the world's third-biggest wine producer. By the end of the 20th century, the same area was reduced to producing a mere 3% of the global total. President Gorbachev's campaign to cut alcohol consumption included domestic wine producers (and neighbouring suppliers), with devastating effect. When the Soviet Union broke up in the early 1990s, many vineyards had already been pulled up and others abandoned for lack of a market. In 2006 Russian president Vladimir Putin banned wine imports from Moldova and Georgia altogether, an underhanded blow for two countries so dependant on wine (see overleaf for more on Georgia).

Moldova

Lying on the eastern border of Romania, Moldova is the ex-Soviet republic with the most vines, and claims to have the highest density of vines in the world. Almost 4% of the country is vineyard and one-quarter of the working population is involved with wine in some way. As with all the winelands mapped here, the total vineyard area has shrunk considerably since Gorbachev's putsch against alcohol. Moldova's vineyard area reached a peak of 593,00 acres (240,000ha) during the Soviet era. But in 2010, the country still had 368,00 acres (149,000ha) of vineyards, with 262,000 acres (106,000ha) of them in production for wine.

Historically, the Kremlin cellars of the tsars looked to what was then Moldavia (and anciently **Bessarabia**) for their finest table wines. Moldova's history has been a tug-of-war between Russia and Romania. Happily for its (largely Romanian) people, neither side prevailed and Moldova won the prize of independence in 1991 (see p.268 for details of wine production in Romanian Moldova).

As a wine producer, Moldova has much going for it: the same latitude as Burgundy, varied and vine-friendly topography, and a climate tempered by the Black Sea. Winters are occasionally cold enough to kill unprotected vines, but long-established vineyards in the best sites enjoy almost ideal conditions. The great majority of vines are planted in southern and central Moldova around the capital Chișinău. Its most prestigious red, then and now, is Negru de Purkar, a striking blend of Cabernet Sauvignon, Saperavi, and Negra Rara from Purcari in the **Stefan Voda** district in the southeast. There is real potential here.

Having established its three official wine regions along EU lines, the Moldovan wine industry has attracted millions of euros from the European Investment Bank, as well as considerable investment from Russia, and a smattering of foreign wine consultants.

Thanks to Moldova's historic links with France, over 80% of her vines are respectable vinifera varieties. Most planted currently is Aligoté (23% of all vines planted), followed by the Georgian white wine grape Rkatsiteli (15%), Sauvignon Blanc (9%), then Merlot (9%). But Cabernet and Merlot do not always ripen fully and it may well be that there is more potential for Pinot Noir, Pinot Gris, Sauvignon Blanc, and sparkling wine.

The industry is still struggling to recover from the (partially rescinded) Russian ban. Moldovan wine has traditionally been casually made medium-dry whites designed for export

MOLDOVA TO AZERBAIJAN

The map shows clearly how valuable maritime influence is to viticulture on the shores of the Black and Caspian seas. It is hardly surprising that vines in Russia's inland Don region have to be banked up each year to protect them from freezing in winter.

*Climate data from 1971 to 2000

UKRAINE: SIMFEROPOL ▼
Latitude / Altitude of WS **44.95° / 672ft (205m)**
Average growing season temperature at WS **61.7°F (16.5°C)**
Average annual rainfall at WS **20in (501mm)**
Harvest month rainfall at WS **September: 1.4in (36mm)**
Principal viticultural hazards **Winter freeze**
Principal grape varieties **Rkatsiteli, Aligoté, Cabernet Sauvignon**

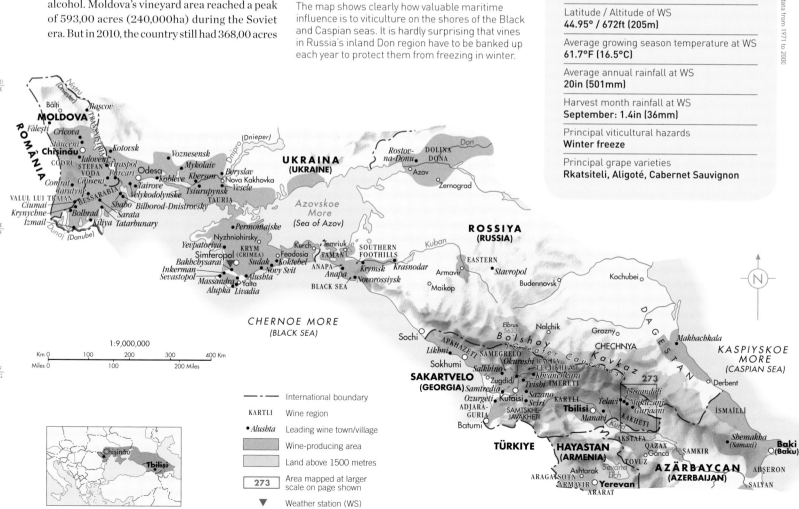

1:9,000,000

International boundary

KARTLI Wine region

• *Alushta* Leading wine town/village

Wine-producing area

Land above 1500 metres

273 Area mapped at larger scale on page shown

▼ Weather station (WS)

to the old Soviet bloc, but things are gradually changing. Wines are becoming drier and better made. And at last some small-scale producers of real interest such as Pelican Negru, Et Cetera, and Equinox have managed to fight their way through the bureaucracy. The most significant exporter to western Europe is Acorex, making competent international varietals, notably Pinot Gris and Sauvignon Blanc.

Ukraine

The second most important vine-grower among the ex-Soviet republics is Moldova's eastern neighbour, Ukraine. Most of Ukraine (and Russia) is too cold to ripen grapes, but even the Phoenicians and ancient Greeks recognized that the warming effect of the Black and Azov seas was sufficient to allow vine-growing on their shores. While there are significant vineyards around the Black Sea ports of Odessa and Kherson, the wine region with the most interesting history is the **Crimea** (Krym).

The Crimea became part of the Russian Empire under Catherine the Great at the end of the 18th century. The Mediterranean climate of its south coast soon made it the natural resort area for the more adventurous aristocracy. It was developed by the famously rich and cultured anglophile Count Mikhail Vorontsov in the 1820s. Vorontsov built a winery, and later his palace, at Alupka, southwest of Yalta, and founded a wine institute (wine being his passion) at Magarach nearby. It continues to be the most important wine research centre in the ex-Soviet republics, and specializes in breeding cold-hardy grape varieties.

In a precise parallel with what was going on in Australia at the same time (and California a generation later), Vorontsov began by imitating as closely as possible the great wines of France. His success was as limited as someone trying to make burgundy in Barossa. The south coast was too hot. Only 6 miles (10km) inland, on the other hand, it was too cold. A generation after Vorontsov, Prince Leo Golitsyn was more scientific. After the Crimean War of 1853–56, the tsar built a summer palace, Livadia, between Alupka and Yalta. Golitsyn had remarkable success making Russia's second-favourite drink, sparkling "shampanskoye", 30 miles (50km) east along the south coast at his Novy Svit ("New World") estate – a tradition that continues.

But the destiny of the Crimea clearly lay in dessert wines. In 1894 the tsar built "the world's finest winery" at Massandra, near Livadia, with Golitsyn in charge, to develop the potential of the south coast, a narrow 80-mile (130km) belt between mountains and sea. It produced strong sweet wines of all sorts, which established a fabulous reputation in pre-revolutionary Russia. They were called "Port", "Madeira", "Sherry", "Tokay", "Kagor" (a wine named after the French Cahors with historic status within the Russian Orthodox church), or even "Yquem", as well as Muscats, White, Pink, and Black. The most planted varieties in Ukraine's recently revitalized wine industry, however, are the thoroughly modern Chardonnay, Riesling, Aligoté, Pinot Noir, Merlot, Cabernet Sauvignon, and Rkatsiteli.

Russia

Most of Russia's vines are planted somewhere on this map, not too far from the tempering influence of the Black and Caspian seas on the country's harshly continental climate. More than half of them are planted in Krasnodar Krai in the west, where maritime influence is such that they survive most winters without protection. But vines have to be buried to survive in the **Don** region and in Stavropol and Dagestan, where most grapes are used for brandy.

While the old industrial wineries of the Soviet regime were rapidly becoming too obsolete even for reliable bottling, let alone winemaking, there have been considerable signs of increasing interest in modern wine production with revamped old enterprises such as Myskhako and Fanagoria, and several new, foreign-influenced ones such as Château Le Grand Vostock and Château Tamagne. A number of these more modern enterprises are already exporting wine – mainly competent if unexciting international varietals – to the West.

The majority of new vines planted are imported from France, but some growers are exploring the potential of such indigenous varieties as Tsimlansky Black (Cherny), and Krasnostop (meaning the same as Piedirosso – "red foot" – in Italian) as well as Ukraine's Golubok. Georgia's Saperavi also grows well in the Russian south. The principal white wine varieties are Chardonnay, Sauvignon Blanc, Aligoté, and Rkatsiteli.

As was long the Soviet tradition, semi-industrial plants near the major cities process wines and grape concentrate imported in bulk, notably through the port of Novorossiysk, from all over the world. Russia's lack of an effective wine and grape law hardly inspires confidence in what is written on the country's wine labels. Much of what is imported in bulk caters particularly to Russians' historic love of sparkling wines. Nevertheless, traditional-method all-Russian examples of fizz can still be found at the Abrau Durso winery (also founded by Golitsyn) in Krasnodar, which has become an extremely important tourist centre. The Tsimlansky plant in Rostov-on-Don is working on its rather less sophisticated sparkling wines.

In the past, a heavy dose of sweetening, in reds just as much as whites, covered a multitude of winemaking sins, but as more and more Russians are exposed to western influences and tastes, not least via the vibrant restaurant scene in Moscow and St Petersburg, Russian taste in wine may well increasingly favour drier styles.

Armenia and Azerbaijan

The former Soviet republic of **Armenia** is sandwiched between Georgia, Turkey, Iran, and Azerbaijan. Its population is just 3 million people, though an estimated 8 million people worldwide claim Armenian descent, ensuring a certain international demand for wine labelled Armenian. Most of the country's limited grape supplies are distilled into the national drink, grape brandy. Wine is very much a minority interest in Armenia, but the Italian-Armenian Zorah estate, near Areni village in the Yeghegnadzor region southeast of the capital Yerevan, has shown that Armenia can make fine wine – in this case from the promising indigenous Areni grape fermented, Georgian-style, in clay jars. Some vineyards here are as high as 5,250ft (1,600m). Armenia has a strong claim to be the birthplace of wine culture with the recent discovery of the oldest known winery dating back around 6,000 years. Excavations of the Areni-1 cave between 2007 and 2010 found grape seeds, vine twigs, remains of pressed grapes, a rudimentary wine press, and a large clay vat apparently used for fermentation.

Azerbaijan also produces wine, much of it sweet red, notably from its Matrassa grape.

The three labels on the left come from Russia's Black Sea region, just across the strait from the Crimea, which the tsars chose as their centre of wine production. Et Cetera is a Moldovan label, while the only one in the local language is from Ukraine.

Georgia

Two hundred years of generally unfriendly attention from Russia would be enough to put most countries in conformist mood. Not Georgia. Her position south of the high barrier of the Caucasus, a bridge from the Black Sea to the Caspian and Persia, between Europe and Asia, was never going to give the Kartli people (their proper name) a quiet life. It has forged an extraordinary national identity, ready repeatedly to challenge the big bear across the mountains. And a powerful part of this identity is its claim to have invented wine.

Certainly the earliest archaeological evidence of winemaking is here (or in Armenia; it depends on the most recent discovery, and on where Georgia then began and ended). The date is around 6,000 BC. How do we know there were vineyards then? The pips of cultivated grapes are different from those of wild ones, and they have been found in quantities that could not be accidental. Noah's vineyard on Mount Ararat, of course, was not far away. Harder evidence is that the pips were in clay jars, ancestors of the *qvevri* the Georgians still use for fermentation today.

The *qvevri* is a jar like a huge pot-bellied amphora buried in the ground. At vintage time everything goes into its mouth: trodden grapes,

skins, stalks and all. Traditionally it stays there until a celebration calls for supplies. The result, whether fermented dry or not, is seriously tannic, a taste to acquire, but at best is remarkably good wine. This is not the way industrial wine is made; its demise has often been expected, but the flavours of Georgia's best grapes blossom in the *qvevri*: pale-skinned Mtsvane Kakhuri, the sterling, deeply coloured Saperavi, and characterful, reliably crisp Rkatsiteli. These and the sweet, fizzy shampanskoye (which can't be made in *qvevris*) lubricate a lively social life.

Georgians are notorious for their relish and capacity for wine, seeing a natural connection between their famously long lives and the potency and nutritional value of Saperavi. Georgian wine has commanded a premium in Russia since the time of Pushkin. Sadly the temptation to fake it seems to have been too strong. That at least is the reason the Kremlin gave in 2006 for banning its import, despite the fact that Muscovites rate Georgian Saperavi as their old empire's most reliable red. This blow fell at the same time the Kremlin banned Moldova's potentially excellent wines. In 2013, it looks as though Russia's thirst will overcome its politics; Georgian wine will get its reprieve.

Georgia has three historic wine regions. Kakheti, where more than two-thirds of all Georgian grapes are grown, is the driest, spanning the easternmost foothills of the Caucasus. Kartli, where *qvevri* are rare, lies on flatter land round the capital, Tbilisi; Imereti, to the west towards the Back Sea, has more humid conditions. North of here in Racha-Lechkumi the climate is much wetter and local Aleksandrouli and Mujuretuli grapes mainly produce semi-sweet wines. Local varieties and naturally sweet wines also predominate in the humid, subtropical zone around the Black Sea coast.

Modern winemaking came to Georgia with Russian settlers early in the 19th century. Pushkin preferred the results to burgundy, and such estates as Tsinandali became famous. Under the Soviets, decline was inevitable, but after independence progress was slow until, ironically, Russia turned vicious.

International appeal

The Russian embargo unintentionally forced Georgia to improve its wines. It inspired greater focus both on little-known native grapes, such as the white Kisi and red Shavkapito, and the *qvevri* technique. Winemakers started needing to enter the new, more sophisticated markets of Europe, China, Hong Kong, Japan, and the US, which demand high quality, but also wines with a Georgian passport that had thorough-going Georgian character. This challenging exercise has raised awareness both at home and abroad of what makes Georgian wine special. It had another unforeseen effect, in America particularly: wine made in a way as different as possible from modern industrial methods, from thoroughly alternative grapes, has a counter-cultural appeal. It offers a way for wine merchants to show they don't buy the Cabernet–Chardonnay conventions. Far from being a relic of the past, the *qvevri* may be a pointer to the future – and a number of visionary winemakers in other countries from Austria to Sicily are seeing it that way.

To enter the international market forced Georgia to delineate regions and subregions, EU-style, and 18 appellations of origin are EU registered. Much the most important of the eight main wine regions are Kartli and Kakheti, both in the eastern half of the country, the region that was historically known as Iberia. **Kakheti** produces roughly 80% of the wine produced today, making full-flavoured wines largely from Saperavi, sharp Rkatsiteli, and the softer white Mtsvane Kakhuri. Its subregions, shown on the map, include most of the names familiar from history, whether as estates or districts. **Tsinandali**, for example, is a 19th-century château celebrated for white wine, now a brand name for its district. **Kvanchkara** (in

The Alaverdi monastery north of Telavi is the spiritual home of viticulture in Georgia, or at least in Kakheti. In cellars dating from around the 8th century AD, a monk takes a sample of wine from a traditional *qvevri*.

KHAKETI'S WINE REGIONS

Four-fifths of all Georgian wine is made here in Kakheti, whose appellation system is surprisingly intricate and developed. All of these appellations are registered with the EU, presumably with an eye to increasing exports.

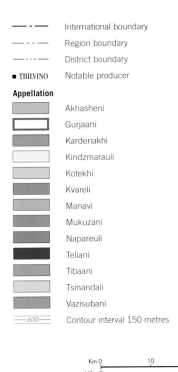

International boundary
Region boundary
District boundary
■ TBILVINO Notable producer

Appellation

Akhasheni
Gurjaani
Kardenakhi
Kindzmarauli
Kotekhi
Kvareli
Manavi
Mukuzani
Napareuli
Teliani
Tibaani
Tsinandali
Vazisubani

Contour interval 150 metres

1:763,000

Km 0   10   20   30   40 Km
Miles 0   10   20 Miles

western Georgia) and **Kindzmarauli** are historic rival producers of sweet Saperavi reds.

Alaverdi is an 8/10th-century AD monastery rehabilitated in 2005, where the monks make typical *qvevri* wines. Telavi is the capital of Kakheti, still in its ancient walls, and the home of a major cellar. Schuchmann is a German company that varies the offering with Chardonnay as well as *qvevri* Saperavi. Pheasant's Tears was started by an American painter determined to breathe new life into ancient traditions.

Central **Kartli** is cooler and windier, creating lighter wines then in Kakheti, sometimes with some natural spritz . Western Georgia feels the influence of the Black Sea with a less extreme climate and higher rainfall. The two provinces of what was once the kingdom of Colchis, Imereti in the lowlands and the highland region of Racha, have grape varieties of their own: Tsitska and Tsolikouri are most common (and are often blended with each other). Imeretian wines tend to have lively acidity and a playful character, usually with less skin contact than in Kakheti. In the higher Racha-Lechkhumi, where the growing season is long and grapes are often picked late, resulting in naturally off-dry and semi-sweet wines, the local varieties are Mujuretuli and Aleksandrouli. The coastal areas of Samegrelo, Adjara, and Guria were historically famous for their wines, but have less importance today.

With such a rich heritage of indigenous grapes, Georgia has no need for imported international vine varieties. Saperavi, like Rkatsiteli, has such a strong personality (and deep colour) that it has been appropriated by growers in Russia, and even further afield.

The red Saperavi can make great wines – many of them sweet, but with lively tannins and acidity that keeps them fresh in the mouth. Georgian winemakers are very self-aware, and despite shortages of equipment (and even of bottles), compete to exhibit better and better wines, in both the old style and the new. For the moment politics stand in the way of real progress, but no one doubts that Georgia's grapes, its climate, and its temperament have extraordinary potential.

Greece

Greece started the modern era of wine (which in all of Europe's Mediterranean countries coincided with the European Union and its largesse) with several disadvantages. The first was language – Greek script is illegible to most wine drinkers. The second was unfamiliarity; the only Greek wine name in circulation was Retsina – Greek grapes and terroirs alike were unknown. The third, and most important, was her geography: as complex and mountainous as Italy's, with drought and stormy weather as constant threats.

These have been largely overcome. Greece has triumphantly introduced original tastes to the world at high levels of quality. (Not to have a substantial bulk-wine industry has saved her from banal associations.) Her main problems today are economic: an incapable government in a country with Levantine traditions of probity.

Indeed, far from being too hot and dry to produce good-quality wine, most of Greece is mountainous and infertile, with only a small percentage of low flatland with rich soils, land that is routinely reserved for more lucrative crops. The wine regions' combination of high altitudes, steep slopes, complex topography, and unpredictable rainfall is responsible for some fascinating, if sometimes demanding, terroirs. In Náoussa in Macedonia in the north of Greece, some vintages are critically plagued by rain and rot, while some of the many north-facing vineyards can have trouble ripening the fruit at all. Some wines made in cooler vintages on the Mantinía plateau in the Peloponnese interior (see overleaf) have to be deacidified, and occasionally the juice is bolstered by chaptalization.

The new era for Greek wine began in the mid-1980s with the return of a handful of agronomists and oenologists from formal training in France. An influx of funds from both the EU and ambitious individuals allowed them to upgrade technology in some of the larger négociants (notably Boutari and Kourtakis) and to establish a host of new, much smaller wineries in cooler areas where land was relatively cheap. Their successors, in thoroughly modern wineries, are just as likely to have learned their skills in Bordeaux or California as in Athens, and are making wines that are aeons away from the oxidized ferments once typical of Greek wine.

The revitalized Greek wine industry initially focused on the then-buoyant domestic market, for which imported grape varieties had a certain glamour. But in 2009, faced with a shrivelling home market, the Greek Wine Federation determined that the future lay in a much less introspective wine industry, oriented towards exports, to markets much more interested in novel Greek grapes.

Mainland Greece

Northern Greece is the area with the most unrealized potential – and where the Greek wine revolution was heralded prophetically in the 1960s at Chateau Carras. Physically **Macedonia** relates more to the Balkan land mass than to the Aegean limbs of Greece. This is red wine country, dominated by one variety, Xinomavro, whose name ("acid black") denotes sourness, but whose slow-maturing wines are some of the most impressive in the country. **Náoussa** is the most important appellation and the country's first (1971). With age the best-made Náoussa wines can acquire a bouquet as haunting as all but the finest Barolo – even if some wineries here in the north are still poorly equipped. There is snow on the slopes of Mount Vermio in winter but summers are so dry that irrigation is essential. The land is sufficiently varied and extensive for individual crus to deserve identification.

Gouménissa, lower on the slopes of Mount Piako, produces a rather plumper version of Náoussa. **Amindeo** on the northwest-facing side of Mount Vermio is so cool that it can produce aromatic whites, a denominated Xinomavro rosé, and good sparkling wine. In the windy, lake-influenced region not far from the border with the Republic of Macedonia, Alpha Estate produces a fine, dense, consistent, cool-climate Xinomavro blended successfully with Syrah.

An increasing number of international varieties have been grown around Kavála. Biblia Chora makes super-zesty, mainly white blends, and in Dráma in the far northeast of the country Lazaridi, Pavlidis, and Wine Art are examples of modern Greek confidence in wine, seen in isolated developments all over northern Greece. Gerovassiliou of Epanomí, just south of Thessaloníki, has experimented with Viognier as well as the indigenous white Malagousia and black Mavrotragano and Limnio.

Zítsa is the only appellation in **Epirus** in the northwest, with Debina the most-planted white grape for still and fizzy dry wines. Epirus has Greece's highest vines at Métsovo, at nearly 4,000ft (1,200m), and the oldest Cabernet Sauvignon, planted at Katogi Averoff in 1963.

Thessaly's potential is huge but as yet unrealized. The recently rescued dark-skinned Limniona is just one of the rare but intriguing indigenous grapes grown here. Rapsáni is the area's flagship red.

Central Greece is dominated by négociants and co-ops. The traditional Athenian wine, from the capital's backyard, **Attica** (Attiki), is retsina, the curious resinated ferment that for so long dogged Greece's vinous reputation. In fact fresh, well-made retsina can be as intriguing and idiosyncratic as a good fino sherry, and goes particularly well with the vivid flavours and textures of Greek cooking. Attica is the country's single biggest wine region, with 27,000 acres (11,000ha) under vine, mostly on the arid, infertile plain of Mesogia. An increasing number of fine unresinated wines are now made in Attica, although Savatiano, the base for retsina and the country's most widely planted vine variety, accounts for 95% of plantings. Old Savatiano vines can make surprisingly good whites that can age for at least five years, but the produce of younger plants is less inspiring.

The islands

Of the Greek islands the southernmost, **Crete** (Kríti), is much the biggest wine producer, and the island's once-moribund wine industry has recently attracted much-needed funds and enthusiasm. The best vineyards are relatively high and many growers have started investing in almost extinct varieties, the firm of Lyrarakis in particular making fine varietal Vidiano, Plyto, and Dafni. Way to the northwest, **Cephalonia** (Kefalloniá) and its Ionian neighbour **Zante** (Zákinthos), with its own lively red Avgoustiatis grape, come next in importance, especially for fresh white Robola and Tsaoussi, as well as for imported grapes. Corfu is not an island for wine connoisseurs.

In the Aegean, several islands make sweet wines of Muscat. **Sámos** is the best and most famous, and the prime exporter, with utterly

---

The Greek alphabet can be a bar to export markets, but these wines, from Dráma, Rapsáni, and the islands of Cephalonia and Santorini, have clearly been dressed to impress non-Greeks. Greek whites can be stunning; only the Rapsáni is red.

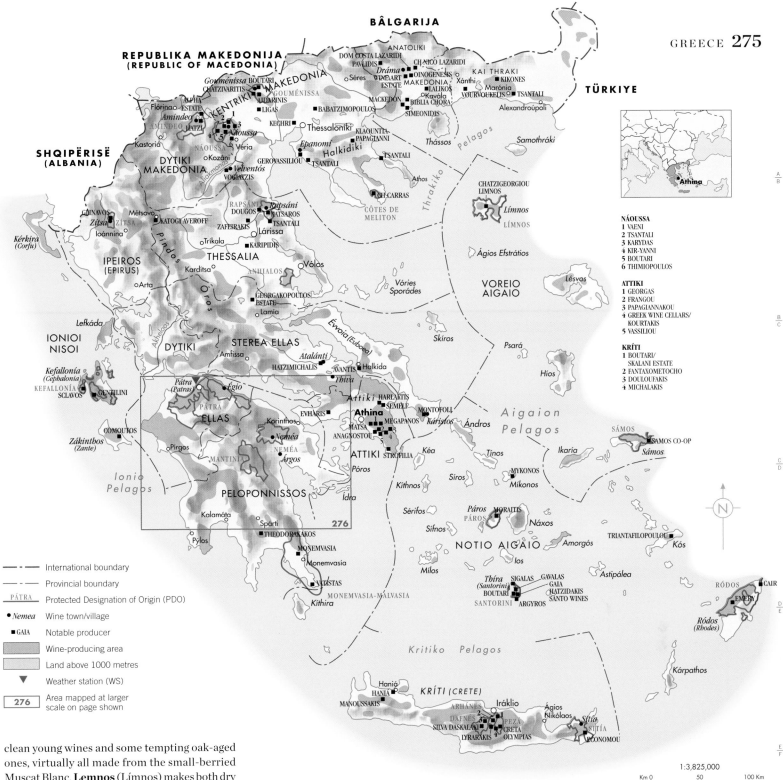

clean young wines and some tempting oak-aged ones, virtually all made from the small-berried Muscat Blanc. **Lemnos** (Límnos) makes both dry and sweet Muscats. **Páros** grows Monemvassia. Mandilaria is another tough island red grape found on Páros, Crete, and Rhodes. Its wines can lack concentration. On **Rhodes** (Ródos) white wine is more important than red. Curiously its sparkling white has built something of a name. The full-bodied white Athiri has recently made some remarkably elegant whites, both still and sparkling, grown at high altitudes.

Of all the islands, however, **Santorini,** in the southern Aegean, is the most original and compelling. Its potent, intense, and very dry wines, white, scented with lemon and minerals, are made mainly from ancient Assyrtiko vines, trained in little nests crouching on the windswept heights of this dormant volcano. Sigalas, Hatzidakis, and Gaia's Thalassitis are all fine examples that can

age for at least a decade. The island also produces a particularly rich white Vînsanto, made mainly from Assyrtiko, that deserves international recognition. The problem on Santorini is not shortage of winemaking enthusiasm and ingenuity but that the thriving tourist business has pushed up land prices, calling into question the very survival of these extraordinary vineyards.

GREECE'S WINE REGIONS

Notable wine producers cluster on Crete, where there has been a quiet wine revolution recently; around Athens, for obvious reasons; and in Náoussa, where the terroir proved many years ago so very propitious for top-quality reds worth ageing.

GREECE: PATRAS	▼

Latitude / Altitude of WS
38.25° / 3ft (1m)

Average growing season temperature at WS
70.1°F (21.1°C)

Average annual rainfall at WS
26in (658mm)

Harvest month rainfall at WS
August: 0.2in (5mm)

Principal viticultural hazards
Drought, sudden storms

Principal grape varieties
Savatiano, Roditis, Agiorgitiko

*Climate data from 1971 to 2000

Peloponnese

The northern half of the Peloponnese, mapped here, has seen even more energy and activity on the part of the new generation of Greek wine producers than anywhere else in recent years. It is accessible, beautiful, full of ancient sites... No wonder.

Neméa, in the east, is the most important appellation, making luscious red wines exclusively from Agiorgitiko (St George) grapes grown in such varied terrains that areas such as Koútsi, Asprókambos, Gimnó, ancient Neméa, and Psari are already starting to earn their own reputations. Neméa has milder winters and cooler summers than one might expect, thanks to the influence of the sea (and rains that can threaten the harvest.). It can be roughly divided into three zones. The fertile red clays of the Neméa valley floor produce perhaps the least age-worthy wines. The mid-altitude zone seems best-suited for the most modern, richest, most

dramatic styles, although even here there is wide variation in character. And some vineyards in the highest zone, some as high as 2,950ft (900m), which were once thought fit only for rosé production, are now producing some fine, elegant, almost "cool-climate" reds. For the moment, a single, all-encompassing appellation seems far too capacious and imprecise.

Pátra, in the far north, is predominantly a white wine region and source of the finest Roditis, the principal grape grown there. The rediscovered mineral-scented white Lagorthi grape has also been making waves, initially because of Antonopoulos's Adoli Ghis (meaning "guileless earth") bottling, and Parparoussis is one of the few to make a fine, steely white from the endangered local Sideritis. The restrained, precise styles created by these producers contrasts with the region's traditional sticky Muscat and Mavrodaphne – which admittedly

have the potential to be every bit as fine as the famous Muscat of Sámos, if made with more care.

Other ambitious new ventures are busy experimenting with such new varieties as the tasty Mavro (black) Kalavritino.

The cool **Mantinía** plateau in the south of the area mapped is already known as the home of the delicate Moschofilero grape and its (at best) ethereally floral wine. Producers such as Tselepos and Spiropoulos make both oaked and sparkling versions. Like so many ambitious Greeks, they grow a range of international grape varieties, too.

Much is expected of the new **Monemvasia-Malvasia** appellation in the south of the Peleponnese (see previous page), spearheaded by the Vatistas family and the Monemvasia Winery. The aim is to remind the world of wine of past, sweet glories shipped from this medieval port, thought to have inspired the grape name "Malvasia" (Malmsey is a derivation). The main grapes are varying proportions of Kydonitsa, meaning "quince-like", Monemvassia, and Assyrtiko and initial results are stunning.

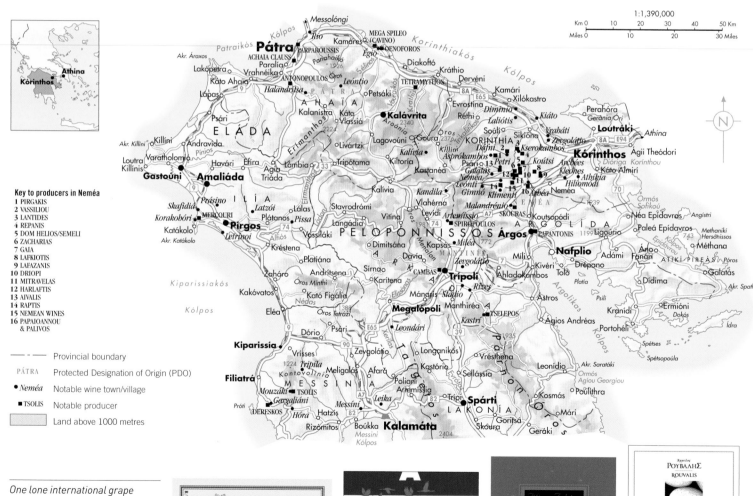

Key to producers in Neméa
1 PIRGAKIS
2 VASSILIOU
3 LANTIDES
4 REPANIS
5 DOM HELIOS/SEMELI
6 ZACHARIAS
7 GAIA
8 LAFKIOTIS
9 LAFAZANIS
10 DRIOPI
11 MITRAVELAS
12 HARLAFTIS
13 AIVALIS
14 RAPTIS
15 NEMEAN WINES
16 PAPAIOANNOU & PALIVOS

Provincial boundary
PÁTRA — Protected Designation of Origin (PDO)
•Neméa — Notable wine town/village
■TSOLIS — Notable producer
Land above 1000 metres

One lone international grape variety here: Merlot grown for Tselepos near Tripoli at 2,400ft (750m) above the Aegean. The Agiorgitiko of Neméa, grapey white Moscofilero, and widely planted white Roditis are more likely to be of interest on export markets.

Turkey

Despite onerous taxation and its powerful Muslim influences, Turkey has been fermenting a wine culture at a furious pace in recent years. The country has always had one of the world's most extensive areas of vineyard, but the proportion of grapes made into wine was still only 2–3% in 2010. The rest are eaten, fresh or dried, or find their way into *raki*, the country's aniseed-flavoured spirit. The wine industry may have been held back by the lack of a domestic market, but tourism, the abolition of a ban on foreign imports, and the early 21st-century privatization of the state monopoly Tekel, whose wines were rebranded Kayra and hugely improved from 2005, is changing that. Kemal Atatürk, founder of the secular republic, built state wineries in the 1920s in the hope of persuading his people of the virtues of wine, thereby ensuring the survival of indigenous Anatolian grape varieties, which may yet yield clues to the origins of viticulture itself. Younger and more cosmopolitan Turks are beginning to take an interest in wine, but progress is hampered by the lack of any serious wine law.

Turkey's climate varies enormously. Thrace's **Marmara** in the hinterland of Istanbul has the greatest concentration of wineries, though it grows less than 16% of the grapes turned into wine. This is the most European part of the country in every way, including its varied, wine-friendly soils and warm coastal mediterranean climate, which are similar to those of Bulgaria's Black Sea coast to the north and the northeastern corner of Greece. The Turkish wine revolution began here in the late 20th century with the emergence of small, foreign-inspired estate wineries Gülor, and Sarafin, now part of the big Doluca group. International grapes are grown here, but there is increasing interest in the local Papaskarasi and tougher Karalahna red wine grapes. The islands just south of here, virtually within sight of the ancient city of Troy, also have their own vine varieties which are being developed by ambitious producers such as Corvus.

More than half of all Turkish wine is grown in the **Aegean** region in the hinterland of Izmir that is so rich in classical relics and remains, such as the brilliant white temple of Ephesus. White wines have tended to be made from Misket (small-berried Muscat) and Sultaniye (Sultana), grown mainly for eating and drying but also vinified into clean, fresh, if rather neutral wines. More recently, promising vineyards have been developed further inland by Turkey's biggest producer, Kavaklidere, and Sevilen. Of the country's 140 official wine producers, more than 100 are based in either Marmara or the Aegean region. Likya has pioneered winemaking in the tourist country of Antalya on the south coast's **Mediterranean** region.

Diren is the only producer of note in the northeast around Tokat in the **Black Sea** region where the pale grape Narince is a speciality.

The rest of Turkey's wine is grown in the higher-altitude vineyards of Central Anatolia (about 14% of total production), and Eastern and Southeastern Anatolia, which together grow more around 12% of all Turkish wine, typically on smallholdings with just a few rows of vines. Kavaklidere has long had its headquarters in the capital Ankara in **Central Anatolia**, where there are now several other wineries. Its new vineyard area, called Côtes d'Avanos, is in the bizarre, bleak, volcanic landscape of Cappadocia, where wine has been made since the time of the Hittites. The firm, fresh Emir is the local white wine grape. The town of Kalecik in north Central Anatolia gives its name to the cherry-like, fruity Kalecik Karasi grape, one of Turkey's popular favourites.

Eastern and **Southeastern Anatolia** suffer such harsh winters that vines have to be banked up to protect them from fatal subzero temperatures, and the growing season tends to be shorter than

TURKEY'S UNOFFICIAL WINE REGIONS

One country, but vast variation in climate and culture. The Thracian hinterland of Istanbul is Mediterranean in both respects, while Eastern Anatolia (possibly the birthplace of viticulture) is viciously continental, and strictly Muslim – not an obvious combination for wine production.

in milder Marmara and the Aegean wine regions. Kayra's large red wine facility in Elazığ, Eastern Anatolia, produces wines such as Buzbağ – for many years the country's best-distributed brand. In the depths of Southeastern Anatolia, the Shiluh winery, founded in 2003, makes natural wines according to 1,000-year-old local traditions. But most of the characterful grapes of Eastern and Southeastern Anatolia are shipped west for vinification – which can pose problems in the heat of a Turkish summer. The most popular fine red wine grapes, both probably from Elazığ in Eastern Anatolia, are Oküzgözü and the rather more tannic Boğazkere, traditionally blended together. Turkey's wine future is bright.

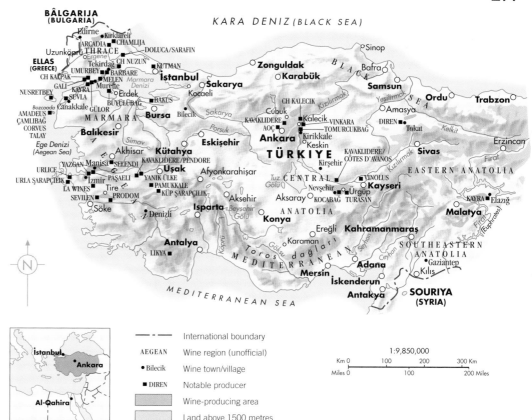

Map key:

- –·– International boundary
- AEGEAN — Wine region (unofficial)
- • Bilecik — Wine town/village
- ■ DIREN — Notable producer
- Wine-producing area
- Land above 1500 metres

1:9,850,000
Km 0 – 100 – 200 – 300 Km
Miles 0 – 100 – 200 Miles

Kavaklidere's extensive new Pendore estate (advised by Stéphane Derenoncourt of Bordeaux) lies at altitudes of up to 1,475ft (450m), while Sevilen's aromatic dry Sauvignon Blanc is made from vines growing up to 2,950ft (900m). Corpus from the island of Bozcaada is Corvus's blend of international grapes.

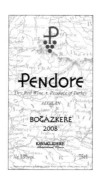

The Eastern Mediterranean

No matter where wine was first made, there is no doubt that the Middle East is the birthplace of the culture of drinking wine.

Cyprus

Recent archaeological evidence proves that Cyprus was producing wine from at least 3500 BC. In the Middle Ages it was acknowledged as producing the best of all sweet wines – the ancestor of Commandaria. The Ottoman Empire ended a great tradition, but EU membership in 2004 has given Cyprus a new chance. In place of the subsidies that used to be paid for exporting vast quantities of nondescript wine in bulk to manufacturers of cheap drinks, more than 6 million euros in EU subsidies have gone on grubbing up the worst vineyards, planting new ones, and establishing winemaking centres in the mountainous interior. The total area of vineyard has shrunk to just over 22,200 acres (9,000ha), mainly on the southern slopes of the Troodos Mountains, where a combination of altitude and valuable precipitation make viticulture possible. The best vineyards lie where the rains fall, in valleys at heights of 1,980–4,950ft (600–1,500m).

The old clear distinction among the four big wineries and about 50 boutique wineries has now become blurred, with the only really large enterprise being the grower-owned SODAP co-operative, whose wines are now reliable and cheap. The other producers have changed focus from quantity towards quality, too, and today the best producers (such as Vlassides, Zambartas, Vasa, Kyperounda, Hadjiantonas, Tsiakkas, and Fikardos) are making genuinely exciting wines from their own vineyards.

Cyprus has never been invaded by phylloxera, and its ungrafted vines are still protected by strict quarantine, which has slowed the introduction of international varieties. Even now, almost half of the island's wine-grape vineyards are planted with the indigenous and rather unexciting grape Mavro, so common that its name simply means "black". The local Xynisteri, planted on a further quarter of the total, can make reasonably delicate whites, and some ambitious ones from the highest vineyards. Shiraz has overtaken Cabernet Sauvignon, Cabernet Franc, and Carignan as the most significant incomer for red wine, having proved especially well-suited to the island's hot, dry terrain. The indigenous Maratheftiko is making quite impressive reds from better-managed vineyards, while tannic Lefkada can add a touch of local spice to blends.

Still the most individual of Cyprus wines is the liquorous Commandaria, made of raisined Mavro and Xynisteri grapes, grown in 14 designated villages on the lower slopes of the Troodos Mountains. Commandaria, which must be aged in oak for at least two years, can be simply sticky, or almost alarmingly concentrated, with four times as much sugar as port. The best have a haunting, fresh grapiness that explains their ancient reputation.

Lebanon

For now, however, the modern Lebanese wine industry is much better known abroad than that of Cyprus. If pressed to name an Eastern Mediterranean wine, many drinkers would cite Chateau Musar of Lebanon which, war notwithstanding, somehow continued to produce dry-farmed Cabernet Sauvignon, Cinsault, and Carignan blended into an extraordinarily aromatic red – like exotic Bordeaux, long-aged before sale and capable of ageing for decades after. Musar, however, is an anomaly. The majority of Lebanese wines are powerful (perhaps too much so for some tastes), concentrated, and just what you would expect from a hot, dry country whose vines are virtually disease-free and which has around 300 days of sunshine a year.

In 1990, there were three wine producers in Lebanon, but by 2012 there were more than 40, most making no more than 50,000 bottles a year. Châteaux Kefraya and Ksara are by far the biggest producers.

In the absence of indigenous red wine grapes, Lebanese producers have embraced foreign varieties, especially those from Bordeaux and the Rhône, but also from the warmer Mediterranean areas. Cabernet Sauvignon, Merlot, and Syrah may have been fashionable, but there is a gradual realization that drier-climate grapes such as Cinsault, Carignan, Grenache, and Mourvèdre (and to a lesser extent Tempranillo) might provide a more authentic expression of Lebanon's formidable and varied terroirs.

The Bekaa Valley is still the epicentre of the modern industry, with the majority of the vineyards in the western Bekaa towns of Qab Elias, Aana, Amiq, Kefraya, Mansoura, Deir El Ahmar, and Khirbit Qanafar. There are also vineyards in the hills above Zahlé, where altitudes of around 3,280ft (1,000m) help to produce fresh wines not spoiled by sun-baked flavours, as well as in the more arid regions of Baalbek (home to the famous Temple of Bacchus) and Hermel. Massaya (set up by an impressive triumvirate from Bordeaux and the Rhône), Domaine Wardy, and Château St Thomas are all serious, second-generation enterprises. They have been joined by a resurgent Domaines des Tourelles (it was founded in 1868 but fell into decline during the war), as well as the newer Chateau Khoury, Domaine de Baal, and Château Marsyas.

Israel

Across the much-disputed border, Israel is the other seat of wine revolution in this part of the world. Plantings have been so enthusiastic that Israel now has 13,600 acres (5,500ha) of wine grapes, to Lebanon's 7,400 acres (3,000ha) and

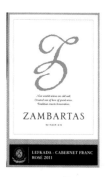

Evidence of Cyprus' progress as a wine producer. Zambartas' rather fine rosé is a blend of Lefkada and Cabernet Franc, while Kyperounda's Petritis, the label on the right, is the island's best Xynisteri.

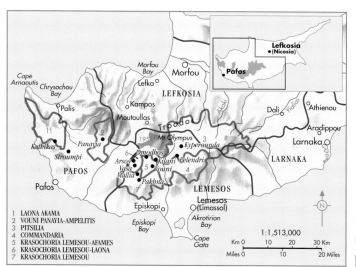

CYPRUS

To satisfy EU requirements, a controlled appellation scheme has been developed, although it has so far been little used. Wines carrying the name of one of the four PGI regions – Pafos, Lemesos, Larnaca, and Lefkosia – account for nearly half of production.

• *Arsos*   Wine village

PAFOS   PGI/regional wine

[3]   PDO/Wine of Controlled Appellation of Origin

   Land above 1000 metres

1 LAONA AKAMA
2 VOUNI PANAYIA-AMPELITIS
3 PITSILIA
4 COMMANDARIA
5 KRASOCHORIA LEMESOU-AFAMES
6 KRASOCHORIA LEMESOU-LAONA
7 KRASOCHORIA LEMESOU

1:1,513,000
Km 0   10   20   30 Km
Miles 0   10   20 Miles

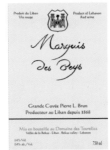

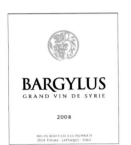

The finest wine produced in the Eastern Mediterranean is arguably the most surprising: Bargylus, a blend of Cabernet, Merlot, and Syrah grown near the ancient Roman city of Antioch in Syria by the Saade brothers, who also make wine in their native Lebanon. On the left above are two of Israel's best; the rest are Lebanese.

exports far more, largely to satisfy world demand for kosher wine. Sweet red kiddush wines were for years the standard output of the original co-operative wineries of Carmel at Rishon LeZiyyon and Zikhron Ya'aqov in the coastal regions of Samson and Shomron, a gift to Israel from Baron Edmond de Rothschild. They have recently reduced production considerably in their search for quality, and have been planting better-designed vineyards, especially in the Upper Galilee.

It was the late-1970s planting on the volcanic soils of the Golan Heights, from 1,300ft (400m) above the Sea of Galilee up to 4,000ft (1,200m) towards Mount Hermon, that signalled a new direction. There are now considerable vine plantings at these altitudes, not just in the Golan Heights but in the scenic foothills of Mount Meron, on the Lebanese border (just south of the Bekaa Valley) in Upper Galilee and on the shallow calcareous soils of the Judean Hills west of Jerusalem.

A wine culture is now well and truly established in Israel – a culture that celebrates Israeli wine rather than solely kosher wine – complete with wine magazines, international wine lists in restaurants, recognized wine regions, and scores of small but ambitious new wineries. Castel, Clos de Gat, and Flam are in the cool Mediterranean climate of the Judean Hills near Jerusalem, Margalit is in the Sharon Plain, and Yatir has to fend off grape-scoffing camels in the northern Negev.

The three leading wineries are supporting the wine-quality revolution by diligent vineyard site selection and by investment in technology. Israeli farming prowess and determination is good at coaxing wine from challenging environments that will stand international comparison. Cabernet Sauvignon, Merlot, Chardonnay, and Sauvignon Blanc are clearly at home but, as in Cyprus, Shiraz is challenging Cabernet as the most popular red wine grape. Cabernet Franc shows promise, but for many the old Carignan and Petite Sirah bush-vines are most characteristically Israeli.

ISRAEL AND LEBANON

Lebanese viticulture is no longer restricted to the crowded Bekaa Valley (see Batroun), and at least five very distinct wine regions have emerged in modern Israel where the improvement in wine quality has been nothing short of miraculous. Many of the better producers choose not to make kosher wine.

1:2,380,000

Km 0 — 50 — 100 Km
Miles 0 — 50 Miles

Batroun
Bekaa Valley
Galilee
Shomron
Samson
Judean Hills
Negev
— ·· — International boundary
■ CH MUSAR Notable producer
Land above 1000 metres

NORTH AMERICA

O'Shaughnessy Estate's barrel cave in the Howell Mountain region of California's Napa Valley, USA

North America

The USA is the world's most important consumer of wine, and only France, Spain, and Italy make more of it. Canada has become a serious producer in recent years, and even Mexico is starting to show signs of catching up. Not just the long-established West Coast but scattered spots all over the continent hold at least local interest for wine drinkers. America is entering a new era as the second wine continent.

When the early colonists first landed in North America, they were impressed by the rampant grapevines whose fruit festooned the forests. The grapes were sweet, if strange, to taste. It was natural to assume that wine would be one of the good things of the New World. Yet more than 300 years of American history were a saga of the shattered hopes of would-be wine-growers. European vinifera vines planted in the new colonies withered and died. The colonists did not give up. Having no notion what was killing their vines, they assumed it was their fault and tried different varieties and methods.

As late as the Revolution, Washington tried, and Jefferson, a great amateur of wine and one of France's early wine tourists, made a determined attempt. Nothing came of it. The American soil was riddled with the European vine's deadliest enemy, phylloxera. The hot, humid summers of the south and east encouraged diseases unknown in Europe. In the north, European vines died in the harsh winters. Native American vines had developed resistance to all of these hazards.

We now know of well over a dozen vine species indigenous to North America, many of them (and particularly *Vitis labrusca*) producing wine so feral that it has long been described as "foxy" – a flavour familiar today in grape juice and jelly but disgusting to drinkers accustomed to Europe's only vine species, *Vitis vinifera*.

Accidental hybrids

Once American and European vines coexisted on this continent new to wine, their genes commingled in random and spontaneous combinations from which various varieties with less obvious foxiness emerged. The Alexander grape, discovered in Pennsylvania, was the earliest of these accidental American–European hybrids; Catawba, Delaware, and Isabella followed. Norton is an all-American grape still producing powerfully distinctive and not-at-all foxy reds.

Settlers tried vine-growing and winemaking wherever they were, especially in New York (where winters were bitterly cold), Virginia (where summers were sultry), and New Jersey (somewhere in between). But it was at Cincinnati, Ohio, that the first commercially successful American wine was born: Nicholas Longworth's famous Sparkling Catawba. By the mid-1850s the wine was celebrated on both sides of the Atlantic. Success was short-lived. Black rot, the Civil War, and finally Longworth's death in 1863 ended Cincinnati's challenge to Reims. But the point was

made. By the time of the Civil War, vine-breeding had become a deliberate activity, resulting in scores of new varieties adapted for American conditions, including the almost rudely hardy but extremely foxy Concord, introduced in 1854 and today the mainstay of the great grape belt along the southern shore of Lake Erie through northern Ohio, Pennsylvania, and New York, which supplies America's grape juice and jelly.

In the South, the Carolinas and Georgia had their own indigenous Muscadine vines, particularly Scuppernong, whose viscous juice made wine even further from the European model than these American hybrids, although they are at least resistant to Pierce's Disease (see p.15).

The vine in the West

Winemaking reached the West Coast by quite a different route. The earliest Spanish settlers in Mexico had imported vinifera there in the 16th century with tolerable success. Their primitive vine, known as the Mission and identical to Argentina's Criolla Chica, flourished in Baja California. But not for 200 years did the Franciscan fathers move north up the coast of California. In 1769 the Franciscan Junípero Serra, founding a mission in San Diego, is credited with having planted California's first vineyard.

Pierce's Disease apart, there were none of the problems of the East Coast here. *Vitis vinifera* had found its Promised Land. The well-named Jean-Louis Vignes brought better vine varieties than the Mission from Europe to Los Angeles. The Gold Rush brought massive immigration. By the 1850s, northern California had been well and truly conquered by the vine.

Thus by the mid-19th century, America had two wine industries, poles apart. California, where vinifera was well established by the late 19th century, enjoyed an early golden age in the 1880s and 1890s, only to see its burgeoning wine industry besieged by the scourges of mildew and phylloxera – just like Europe.

Prohibition and repeal

But then came a blow greater than any of these: the prohibition of alcohol throughout North America between 1919 and 1933. Both western and eastern vine-growers limped through, making supposedly sacramental wine and shipping huge quantities of grapes, juice, and concentrate to a nation that suddenly discovered home winemaking, with the warning "Caution – do not add yeast or the contents will ferment".

The lasting legacy of the culture that spawned this outright ban on all things alcoholic, long after the repeal of Prohibition in 1933, has been a wine industry long thwarted by unnecessarily complex organization and obstructive legislation. Despite this, wine is currently basking in the glow of fashion and enthusiasm bordering on obsession among a growing proportion of Americans. This has translated into a flurry of activity and experiment on the part of would-be wine producers all over the continent. Ever

Some of America's best wines are featured here, although, sadly, far too few Americans will be aware of them. They tend to sell strictly locally. Vignoles and Norton are two of the finest white and red wine grapes grown in the US that are not members of the European vinifera vine species commonly used for wine.

Country boundary

State/provincial boundary

Phoenix State/provincial capital

▼1,200 Acres of vineyard area per state/province (over 1,000 acres), 2011

▲10 Number of wineries per state/province, 2012

since the development of the railroads, grapes and wine have been shipped from viticulturally well-endowed states, particularly California, for blending and bottling in less fortunately situated wineries, some of which grow relatively few vines. All 50 states, including Alaska, now produce wine, although a few rely on fruit other than grapes for their fermentations, and some buy in wine, grapes, and/or grape juice to supplement what they grow themselves.

United states of the vine

The mushrooming wine industries of Canada, Mexico, Texas, New York, Virginia, and all of the USA west of the Rockies are considered in detail on the following pages, but there are hundreds of wineries and thousands of acres of vines elsewhere. They may produce juice or jelly or heavily flavoured drinks based on the produce of American vines or, increasingly, more subtle and sophisticated ferments from either vinifera or the so-called French hybrids. This generation of varieties such as white Vidal, Seyval Blanc, and Vignoles,

and red Baco Noir and Chambourcin, was bred in post-phylloxera Europe from American and vinifera vines and introduced to North America (where they have enjoyed far more success than in Europe) by Philip Wagner of Boordy Vineyards, Maryland, in the mid-20th century.

French hybrids dominate vine-growing in the Midwest, although the all-American Norton variety also thrives here, and a new generation of such cold-hardy hybrids as Brianna, La Crescent, and Traminette for white wines and Frontenac, Marquette, and St. Croix for reds is increasingly planted in the Midwest and occasionally Northeast. **Missouri** is the only state with a long history of vine-growing on any scale and was Ohio's only serious 19th-century rival east of the Rockies. Augusta in Missouri made this point, when in 1980 it became America's first AVA, or American Viticultural Area. These 224 vine-growing areas (often delineated with more regard for political than natural boundaries, and producer rather than consumer sensitivities) represent the first steps towards a controlled appellation system for US wine.

Michigan, surrounded by the Great Lakes, almost rivals Oregon's position as the fourth most important vine-grower of all the states after California, Washington, and New York, but it falls to seventh in the table when vinifera-only

USA AND CANADA

The three different sizes for the vineyard area and number of wineries symbols are misleading in the case of California – its vineyard area is 13 times that of Washington, the next largest grower.

vines are counted. Vinifera vineyards – especially Riesling, Pinot Blanc, and a shrinking minority of French hybrids on the lake-girt Old Mission and Leelanau peninsulas – are promising.

Pennsylvania has almost as much vineyard as Michigan, and **Ohio** is also important. **New Jersey**'s wine industry has almost as long a history as Virginia's, but is much smaller; that of **Maryland** is smaller still. Both hedge bets between vinifera and French hybrids.

The rest of the South, those states bordering on the Gulf of Mexico as far as Texas, has a small but growing wine industry of its own, expanding from the usefully loose-berried Muscadine vines native to its hot, damp woods to French hybrids, vinifera, and newer Muscadine hybrids which can produce quite mainstream flavours. Cooler, higher parts of the South can have conditions very similar to Virginia's.

All over this great and thrilling continent, an exciting trend is discernible: to produce wines that will be appreciated outside their region while truly expressing their origins.

Canada

Canada may, on the face of it, seem a decidedly chilly place to grow vines, and only in the past 20 years or so has any wine made in Canada merited export, but good wine is now made with increasing élan in four different provinces. The modern industry dates only from the signing of the Free Trade Agreement with the USA in the late 1980s, which encouraged the revolutionary replacement of American and hybrid grape varieties with European *Vitis vinifera* vines. The state liquor boards that control the distribution of wine have an uneven track record, some of their labelling being decidedly imaginative. "Canadian" in particular is a term open to wide interpretation, as indeed is "wine". Buyers should read the small print.

Ontario was long the dominant wine province, but British Columbia is catching up fast. Wines made in the brilliant blue light and almost desert conditions of the **Okanagan Valley** are distinguished by the same sort of brightness of fruit as is found in Washington State to the south. British Columbia now has nearly 10,000 acres (almost 4,000ha) of mostly vinifera vines, more than 200 wineries, and 900 mostly small vineyards.

The Okanagan Valley lies in a rain shadow 200 miles (320km) east of Vancouver, where a series of lakes, the largest being the long, narrow, deep Lake Okanagan, ward off winter freeze. Irrigation is essential in the southern Okanagan. Summer days may be torrid but nights are almost always cool. Autumn arrives early so early-ripening grapes are generally favoured and this may be one of Pinot Blanc's perfect spots. Riesling and Chardonnay tend to shine although there are some fine reds, including Bordeaux blends, and not just in the far south of Okanagan, where Lake Osoyoos repeats the long format of Lake Okanagan. Land prices have been inflated by the winemaking ambitions of local entrepreneurs.

Similkameen Valley to the southwest of the Okanagan is British Columbia's second most important wine region and favours red wines. **Fraser Valley** just outside Vancouver is usefully frost-free. In the far west, on **Vancouver Island** and the **Gulf Islands**, the climate may be much cooler and wetter than Okanagan's but winemaking enthusiasm is by no means dampened. New viticultural areas are also being explored to the north of the Okanagan, though plantings remain small and experimental for the time being.

Eastern Canada

On Canada's east coast, Nova Scotia has 16 wineries and more than 70 growers with almost 500 acres (200ha) of vines, mainly winter-hardy hybrids planted in sheltered valleys and areas overlooking the Bay of Fundy and the Atlantic seaboard. Some wineries in Nova Scotia, like those in England, are pinning their hopes on sparkling wines made from both vinifera and hybrid grape varieties. Some of the finest have come from Benjamin Bridge and L'Acadie Vineyards.

Québec also has a small wine industry, with about 500 acres (200ha) of vineyard but more than 100 small wineries. The French-speaking province is also dependent on winter-hardy hybrids, many of them bred at the University of Minnesota, for clean if light wines. Some adventurous wineries, such as Les Brome, Vignoble Carone, and biodynamic Les Pervenches, have nevertheless managed to produce some successful Pinot Noir and Chardonnay.

The Okanagan Valley has Canada's most spectacular wine country, although its continental climate means the growing season is relatively short.

Meyer Family Vineyards
Tribute Series - Sonia Gaudet
Chardonnay
2010
13.5 % alc./vol.   Old Main Road Vineyard - Naramata   750 mL.

PENTÂGE
W I N E R Y
2010 ROUSSANNE
MARSANNE ~ VIOGNIER
DIRTY DOZEN VINEYARDS
ESTATE BOTTLED   750 mL
WHITE WINE-VIN BLANC   13.5% alc./vol.
PRODUCT OF CANADA / PRODUIT DU CANADA

British Columbia grows a particularly wide range of grapes successfully, with whites generally even more impressive, or at least distinctive, than reds. The wines are effortlessly ripe and bright.

1:1,000,000
Km 0   10   20 Km
Miles 0   10 Miles

OKANAGAN VALLEY   ■ HERDER   Notable producer

The semi-desert conditions in inland British Columbian wine country are not very dissimilar from those across the border in southeastern Washington described on pp.290-92.

Ontario

The province of Ontario, its climate moderated by the Great Lakes, produces more than three out of every four bottles of Canadian wine, from more than 200 wineries in four Designated Viticultural Areas (DVAs). It was the discovery of the potential for Icewine, pressed from grapes frozen solid, their sugar concentrated to formidable intensity, that kick-started the industry in the 1970s. Most of Ontario's wine is sold in the province, although the prodigious quantities of Icewine produced each year are a lucrative export commodity, especially to Japan.

The **Niagara Peninsula** is Canada's most important wine region, with 13,500 acres (5,450ha) of Ontario's total 16,000 acres (6,500ha) of vineyard. A combination of geographical quirks has long made viticulture possible in the semi-continental climate here. This narrow mosaic of glacial deposits is protected by the Great Lakes both north and south and the deep Niagara River to the east. These vast bodies of water delay budbreak in spring thanks to the accumulated cold of winter, and prolong ripening in autumn by storing summer sunshine in relatively warm water. Lake Ontario in particular moderates the effect of Arctic air masses in winter, while the temperature difference between this cooler lake and the warmer Lake Erie to the south encourages cooling breezes in summer. The lake's offshore breezes are kept circulating by the Niagara Escarpment (responsible for the Niagara Falls), which helps minimize frost damage and fungal disease. The land here tilts slightly north so that vineyards benefit even more from the influence of Lake Ontario.

Summers in Niagara have been increasingly warm and long in recent years, which has boosted the quality of its dry table wines considerably. But Ontario still manages to make an average of 750,000 litres of tinglingly sweet Icewine every year, either from Riesling or, more commonly,

from the luscious, curranty French hybrid Vidal, whose wines tend to mature early. Pale-red Icewine made from frozen Cabernet Franc grapes is also an increasingly popular speciality.

Riesling is arguably Niagara's strength for bone-dry wines, too, although individual producers have shown occasional brilliance with Chardonnay, Pinot Noir, Gamay, and even Syrah. The relatively short growing season is no disadvantage for traditional-method sparkling wine, whose production has doubled recently. Most Niagara vines are grown on the Lake Iroquois Plain but the well-protected benches, with their calcareous soils, are particularly suitable for delicate Riesling and Pinot Noir. An ambitious series of 12 Niagara Peninsula regional appellations and sub-appellations is already in place (see map below).

Ontario's other small appellations lie to the east and southwest of the Niagara Peninsula. **Lake Erie North Shore** depends solely on Lake Erie to temper its climate and is warm enough to ripen Merlot and both Cabernets. **Pelee Island** is Canada's southernmost point; it is completely surrounded by the lake and, like Lake Erie North Shore, enjoys a longer growing season than the Niagara Peninsula. The most recent DVA, **Prince Edward County** on Lake Ontario's north shore, is much cooler, but its shallow limestone soils are already showing potential for fine Chardonnay and Pinot Noir. However, these less-hardy vinifera vines have to be buried under mounds of earth to protect them in winter, when temperatures here can fall as low as -22°F (-30°C).

Wines made from 100% Canadian-grown grapes are designated VQA (Vintners Quality Alliance) and regulated provincially in both Ontario and British Columbia. Several of the larger Canadian companies have a long tradition of bottling blends of imported "grape products" and Canada's cheapest wine.

It is not surprising that our selection here is of wines that don't need much heat, but the quality of red wines in Ontario has also been improving, thanks to climate change.

NIAGARA PENINSULA

The Niagara Escarpment is part of the greater Niagara region and is shared with New York State across the border. The peninsula, which includes Niagara-on-the-Lake as another regional appellation, has been subdivided into no fewer than 10 sub-appellations.

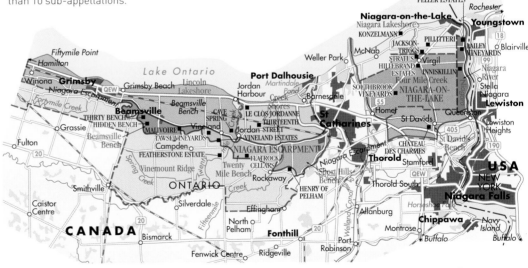

*Climate data from 1971 to 2000

NIAGARA PENINSULA: ▼
ST CATHARINES

Latitude / Altitude of WS
43.18° / 259ft (79m)

Average growing season temperature at WS
60.1°F (15.6°C)

Average annual rainfall at WS
29in (746mm)

Harvest month rainfall at WS
October: 2.7in (69mm)

Principal viticultural hazards
Winter freeze, underripeness

Principal grape varieties
Chardonnay, Riesling, Cabernet Franc, Merlot

NIAGARA-ON-THE-LAKE		International boundary
Niagara River		Regional appellation
		Sub-appellation
■ CAVE SPRING		Notable producer
		Woods
▼		Weather station (WS)

Pacific Northwest

Oregon and Washington, the two major players in the Pacific Northwest, could hardly be more different. Damp, green Oregon has always been the home of the craftsman winemaker, vinifying grapes grown in small, personally managed, mainly estate vineyards, many of which are organic. The Coast Range lines up as a sheltering sea wall, as it does in northern California, but here the ocean's warm North Pacific current brings rain instead of fog, modifying what might otherwise be more severe temperatures and resulting in some of America's most nearly Burgundian wines. Arid, continental eastern Washington, on the other hand, originally operated on a quasi-industrial scale, with heavily irrigated grapes picked mechanically and shipped back to the wineries that clustered round Seattle.

Contrasting landscapes

The roots of this difference lie in the terrain. The great concentration of Oregon's wine-growing is in the settled valleys west and south of Portland, which have raised cattle, fruit, nuts, and a wide range of crops for more than a century. Vineyards have been slipped piecemeal into this busy, well-worked landscape. But when the grapevine came to Washington, it moved straight out east onto the farmland –mostly desert – beyond the Cascade mountain range. Here a variety of row and orchard crops, vitally sustained by water from the Columbia, Yakima, and Snake rivers, were the primary form of agriculture.

Washington (described in more detail on pp.290–93) has been changing fast, however, and artisan operations are now common, with as much emphasis on growing, or at least finding, great grapes as on making wine. It is still relatively rare for Washington vintners to grow all their own grapes (in contrast to the Oregon model), but the vine is colonizing new areas of Washington all the time. The tourist destination **Lake Chelan**, for example, has proved capable of ripening a much wider range of grape varieties than the vineyards once hopefully planted around Seattle's rain-sodden **Puget Sound**.

Today, Washington is the second most important wine-growing state in the US, with 40,000 acres (16,200ha) of vines producing some of America's most admired Cabernet, Merlot, Riesling, and, especially, Syrah.

Oregon, meanwhile, has become a little less homespun in its organization, with a modest injection of capital and marketing skills from the big wide world outside. The total area devoted to the vine grew by 50% to 20,500 acres (8,300ha) in the six years to 2011.

If the Willamette Valley, the heartland of Oregon wine production described overleaf, suffers the same sort of capricious weather as Burgundy, **Southern Oregon** is notably warmer and drier, and proves there is more to the state than Pinots Noir and Gris. In fact, Oregon's first Pinot Noir was planted, at HillCrest Vineyard in 1961, in the **Umpqua Valley**. This AVA is coolest and wettest in the north, but as far south as Roseburg it benefits from much warmer summers and drier autumns. The dynamic Abacela winery has shown that Spanish varieties such as Albariño and Tempranillo can flourish here. **Red Hill Douglas County** is a single-vineyard AVA in the northeast of the Umpqua Valley. **Elkton Oregon** is the most recent AVA, established in February 2013.

South again, near the California border, the slightly more densely planted **Rogue Valley** is even warmer, and the annual rainfall (about 12in,

Fir trees, here overlooking Erath's Prince Hill Vineyards in Dundee Hills, are everywhere in Oregon wine country. The state supplies around a third of the US's Christmas trees.

or 300mm) in the east of the region is almost as low as that of far eastern Washington. Red Bordeaux grapes and Syrah will usually ripen here (in contrast to the Willamette Valley). **Applegate Valley** is a sub-AVA in the middle of the Rogue Valley.

Crossing borders

The vine is no respecter of state lines. The dramatic **Columbia Gorge** wine country straddles the river and includes vineyards in both Washington and Oregon. Washington's improbably vast **Columbia Valley** AVA also includes parts of Oregon, while one of the more surprising wine regions in the US is in the **Snake River Valley**, which is mainly in Idaho but also encompasses a bit of eastern Oregon. As in eastern Washington, the climate is continental, all the more extreme for being further south, and also considerably higher, at nearly 3,000ft (900m). Summer days can be very hot, the nights usefully cool, but winter arrives early. Some 48 wineries now flourish in Idaho, and there is considerable cross-border traffic in grapes and wine with eastern Washington, although Idaho's own vineyard area is over 1,600 acres (650ha).

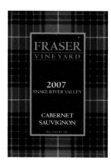

The first three wines are fine examples of Oregon wines made outside the most famous area, the Willamette Valley. Tsillan Cellars is one of the leading lights of Washington's new Lake Chelan AVA, while Fraser Vineyard is in Idaho's Snake River Valley.

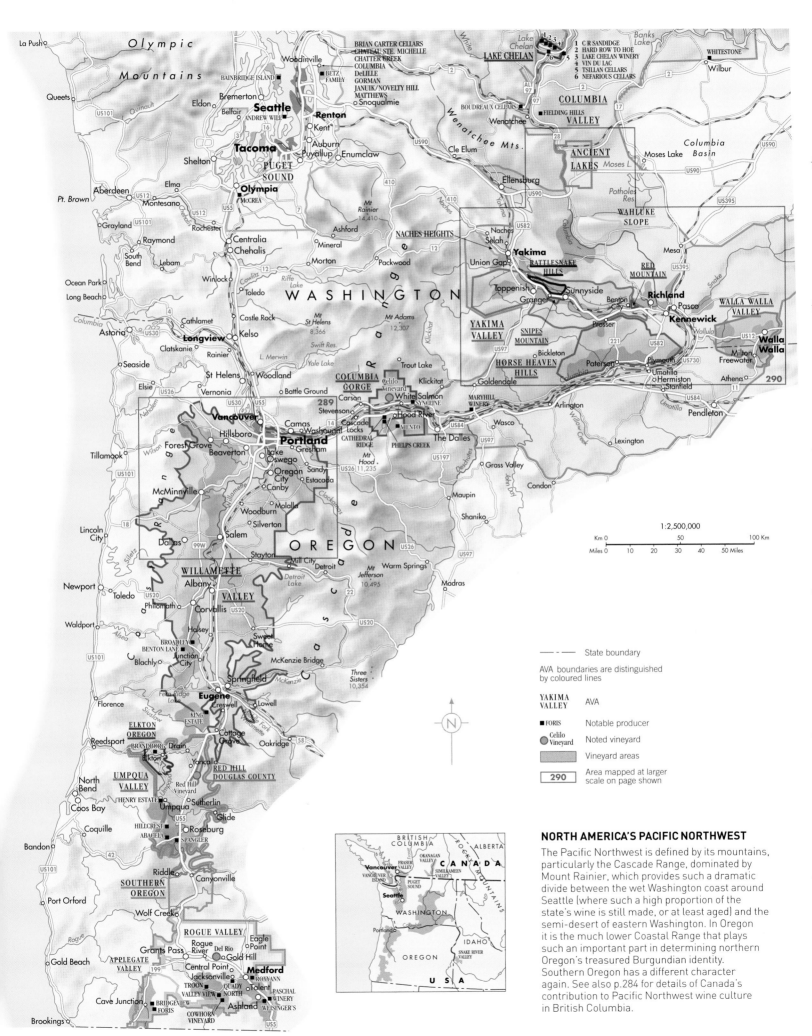

La Push

Olympic
Queets

Mountains

Woodinville

BRIAN CARTER CELLARS
CHATEAU STE. MICHELLE
CHATTER CREEK
COLUMBIA
DeLILLE
GORMAN
JANUIK/NOVELTY HILL
MATTHEWS
Snoqualmie

LAKE CHELAN

1 2 3 4
%
5

1 C R SANDIDGE
2 HARD ROW TO HOE
3 LAKE CHELAN WINERY
4 VIN DU LAC
5 TSILLAN CELLARS
6 NEFARIOUS CELLARS

WHITESTONE

Wilbur

BAINBRIDGE ISLAND

BETZ FAMILY

BOUDREAUX CELLARS

COLUMBIA
VALLEY

Bremerton
Eldon
Belfair

Seattle

Wenatchee

FIELDING HILLS

Banks
Lake

Moses Lake

Columbia
Basin

Shelton

ANDREW WILL
Renton
Kent

Tacoma

Puyallup
Auburn
Enumclaw

PUGET
SOUND

McCREA
Olympia

Aberdeen

Montesano

Elma

Grayland

Raymond

South Bend

Pt. Brown

Ocean Park

Long Beach

Astoria

Longview

ANCIENT
LAKES

Ellensburg

Moses L.

Potholes
Res.

Cle Elum

Mt
Rainier
14,410

Ashford

Mineral

Centralia

Chehalis

Winlock

Toledo

Morton

Packwood

WASHINGTON

Naches
Selah

Yakima

Union Gap

WAHLUKE
SLOPE

Mesa

NACHES HEIGHTS

RATTLESNAKE
HILLS

RED
MOUNTAIN

Toppenish

Sunnyside

Benton
City

Richland

WALLA WALLA
VALLEY

Rochester

Castle Rock

Mt
St Helens
8,366

Mt Adams
12,307

YAKIMA
VALLEY

SNIPES
MOUNTAIN

Granger

Prosser

Pasco

Kennewick

Cathlamet

Kelso

HORSE HEAVEN
HILLS

Bickleton

Paterson

Plymouth

Milton
Freewater

WALLA
WALLA

Longview

Rainier

Clatskanie

St Helens

Woodland

COLUMBIA
GORGE

Goldendale

Umatilla
Hermiston
Stanfield

Athena

290

Seaside

Elsie

Battle Ground

Trout Lake

Klickitat

White Salmon
SYNCLINE

Hood River

MARYHILL
WINERY

Arlington

Pendleton

Vernonia

Vancouver

Camas
Washougal

Carson
Stevenson

289

Celilo
Vineyard

MIENTO

PHELPS CREEK

Wasco

Lexington

Hillsboro

Portland

Forest Grove

Beaver ton

Gresham

Cascade
Locks

CATHEDRAL
RIDGE

The Dalles

Grass Valley

Condon

Tillamook

Lake
Oswego

Sandy

Mt
Hood
11,235

Oregon
City

Estacada

Canby

Maupin

Lincoln
City

McMinnville

Woodburn

Molalla

Shaniko

Madras

Dallas

Salem

Silverton

OREGON

Stayton

Mill City

Detroit

Warm Springs

Newport

Toledo

WILLAMETTE

Albany

Philomath

VALLEY

Corvallis

Detroit
Lake

Mt
Jefferson
10,495

Waldport

Halsey

Sweet
Home

Three
Sisters
10,354

1:2,500,000

Km 0   50   100 Km
Miles 0 10 20 30 40 50 Miles

BROADLEY

BENTON LANE

Blachly

Junction
City

McKenzie Bridge

Florence

Springfield

N

Eugene

Creswell

Lowell

— — —   State boundary

AVA boundaries are distinguished
by coloured lines

ELKTON
OREGON

KING
ESTATE

Cottage
Grove

Oakridge

YAKIMA
VALLEY

AVA

Reedsport

BRANDBORG

Drain

FORIS

Notable producer

Elkton

Yoncalla

Celilo
Vineyard

Noted vineyard

North
Bend

UMPQUA
VALLEY

RED HILL
DOUGLAS COUNTY

Vineyard areas

Coos Bay

HENRY ESTATE

Red Hill
Vineyard

Sutherlin

290

Area mapped at larger
scale on page shown

Coquille

HILLCREST

Umpqua

Glide

ABACELA

Roseburg

Bandon

SPANGLER

Riddle

Canyonville

SOUTHERN
OREGON

Port Orford

Wolf Creek

NORTH AMERICA'S PACIFIC NORTHWEST

The Pacific Northwest is defined by its mountains,
particularly the Cascade Range, dominated by
Mount Rainier, which provides such a dramatic
divide between the wet Washington coast around
Seattle (where such a high proportion of the
state's wine is still made, or at least aged) and the
semi-desert of eastern Washington. In Oregon
it is the much lower Coastal Range that plays
such an important part in determining northern
Oregon's treasured Burgundian identity.
Southern Oregon has a different character
again. See also p.284 for details of Canada's
contribution to Pacific Northwest wine culture
in British Columbia.

ROGUE VALLEY

Grants Pass

Rogue
River

Del Rio

Gold Hill

Eagle
Point

Gold Beach

APPLEGATE
VALLEY

Central Point

Jacksonville

Medford

ROXYANN

Cave Junction

TROON

QUADY
NORTH

VALLEY VIEW

Talent

PASCHAL
WINERY

Ashland

WEISINGER'S

BRIDGEVIEW

FORIS

COWHORN
VINEYARD

Brookings

BRITISH
COLUMBIA

FRASER
VALLEY

OKANAGAN
VALLEY

ALBERTA

ROCKY MOUNTAINS

Vancouver

SIMILKAMEEN
VALLEY

CANADA

Vancouver Island

PUGET
SOUND

Seattle

WASHINGTON

Portland

OREGON

IDAHO

SNAKE RIVER
VALLEY

USA

Willamette Valley

Climate is Oregon's great point of difference: difference from both California to the south and Washington State to the north. While Willamette Valley summers are cooler and cloudier than those of sunny California (see the key facts panels), its winters are considerably milder than those of Washington's deeply continental wine country in the east of the state. Pacific Ocean clouds and humidity wash across Oregon's wineland, especially the northern reaches of the Willamette Valley, through breaks in the Coastal Range, so that cool summers and damp autumns rather than harsh winter freeze are the perennial threats.

The discovery (or rather the invention) of the **Willamette Valley** as a modern wine region was made in the late 1960s at Dundee in Yamhill County by David Lett, when he established his Eyrie Vineyards. Had Lett planted Chardonnay and Cabernet, fame would have been slow to follow (especially since the latter would hardly ever have ripened properly). But he hit on Pinot Noir. Since the mid-1970s Oregon and Pinot Noir have been inextricably linked. This lush, pastoral country can do what California had long found next to impossible: conjure up the illusion of drinking fine red burgundy, even if Oregon Pinots are, in general, softer, more obviously fruity, and earlier-maturing than their European counterparts.

Almost as though this were the way Pinot Noir liked to be grown, the Willamette Valley has largely remained small-scale. The area attracted a different type of would-be winemaker from the high-rollers who headed for Napa or Sonoma. Modest means and big ideas produced a range of unpredictable wines, from the mesmerizing to the seriously flawed. Most of the early wines were fragrant but ethereal. But by the mid-1980s it was obvious that some of the Pinots had exciting staying power.

Whether or not this was what convinced them, high-profile foreigners moved in: from California, a succession of wine producers looking for a moodiness in Pinot that sunny skies could not give them; from Australia, Brian Croser of Petaluma, who set about making Argyle sparkling and still wines in an old hazelnut-drying plant next to Dundee's fire station; and, most importantly for Oregonian pride, from Burgundy itself, Robert Drouhin and his daughter Véronique at Domaine Drouhin. Pinots made today vary from the suave, gently understated Drouhin style (which has well withstood comparison with Drouhin's wines back home) to the richly oaky style initially adopted at Beaux Frères, the winery part-owned by Oregon's other internationally famous outside investor, wine guru Robert Parker.

Broadly, the Willamette summer is coolest in the vineyards of Washington County (as opposed to State). These are the most open to Pacific incursion, making them particularly suitable for aromatic varieties. Pinot Noir tends to be fine rather than fat here. The Ponzi family and others have shown that such wines can have staying power, however.

The valley's sub-appellations

After considerable debate and degustation, several sub-appellations are now officially recognized within the 150-mile (240km)-long Willamette Valley. **Dundee Hills** has established itself as the epicentre for top-quality wine, thanks to its famous heavy, red-tinged Jory loam soils. The Red Hills of Dundee enjoy the combination of good drainage and propitious exposure to rainfall and light that is so crucial to optimum ripeness in cloudy Oregon. **Yamhill-Carlton District** has very slightly more warmth but more frost problems, so vines are planted well above the frost-prone valley floor, ideally on east-facing slopes on the west side of the valley at between

200 and 700ft (60 and 210m). **McMinnville** is named after the university town that is a focus for the Oregon wine industry, while both **Eola-Amity Hills** (northwest of Salem) and **Chehalem Mountains**, the gateway to the heart of Oregon wine country, gained AVA status in 2006. **Ribbon Ridge**, a privileged sub-AVA of the Chehalem Mountains, lies just above the Dundee Hills.

Successful grape-growing in the Willamette Valley is about ripening grapes fully and making picking decisions that successfully navigate the inevitable autumn rains. Just where and when they occur, and for how long, determine how damaging the rains are, and this varies enormously each year. Many grape varieties such as Cabernet Sauvignon and Sauvignon Blanc are too late-ripening to be viable here. But even for early-ripeners, Willamette Valley's vintage pattern is as wilful as any in France and perhaps more wildly varied than in any other American wine region. Wine drinkers outside Oregon tend to fall in and out of love with the state's Pinot Noirs according to the success, or at least the obvious fruitiness, of the vintage on offer.

But there is another, superficially surprising, problem: summer drought. The rains can arrive in September or October, but generally only after what is often a very dry summer. This means that many older vines can start to turn a nastily inconvenient yellow long before the photosynthesis needed for ripening is completed. Newer vineyards, therefore, tend to be designed with irrigation systems in place so that the vines are stressed only if and when the grower deems it useful.

Rootstocks and clones

The early pioneers, often operating on extremely limited budgets, tended to establish vineyards as cheaply as possible, thus with wide-spaced vines, but higher-density planting is now commonplace. Another relatively recent change to Oregon vineyard design is the use of rootstocks. Ever since phylloxera was first spotted here in 1990, sensible growers have planted vines grafted on to rootstocks that will both resist the fatal root-muncher and limit the amount of vegetation that distracts from the grape-ripening process.

Yields in these vineyards therefore tend to be more consistent and vines tend to ripen earlier, but the most important influence on the continually improving quality of Oregon Pinot Noir and Chardonnay has been the introduction of Burgundian clones of each variety. For at least the first two decades, most Oregon Pinot Noir was made from the Wädenswil clone, originally from Switzerland, and/or the clone, so popular in California, known as Pommard. They tended to yield wines that had fruit and charm (in a good year) but not necessarily structure and subtlety. The introduction of smaller-clustered clones such as (for fans of detail) 113, 114, 115, 667, 777, and 882, called Dijon clones in Oregon, has added new dimensions to Oregon Pinot, even if in most instances they are used as elements in a blend.

Just some of the many exciting, often rather Burgundian, wines made in the Willamette Valley. The quality of Chardonnays has been slowly catching up with that of the dominant Pinot Noir grape. Bergström's are exemplary.

NORTHERN WILLAMETTE VALLEY

Six sub-appellations were carved out of the northern Willamette Valley AVA in the early 21st century. Boundaries are either straight or almost impossibly wiggly lines, it would seem. The number of noted vineyards is surely likely to increase. This is a state of individualists.

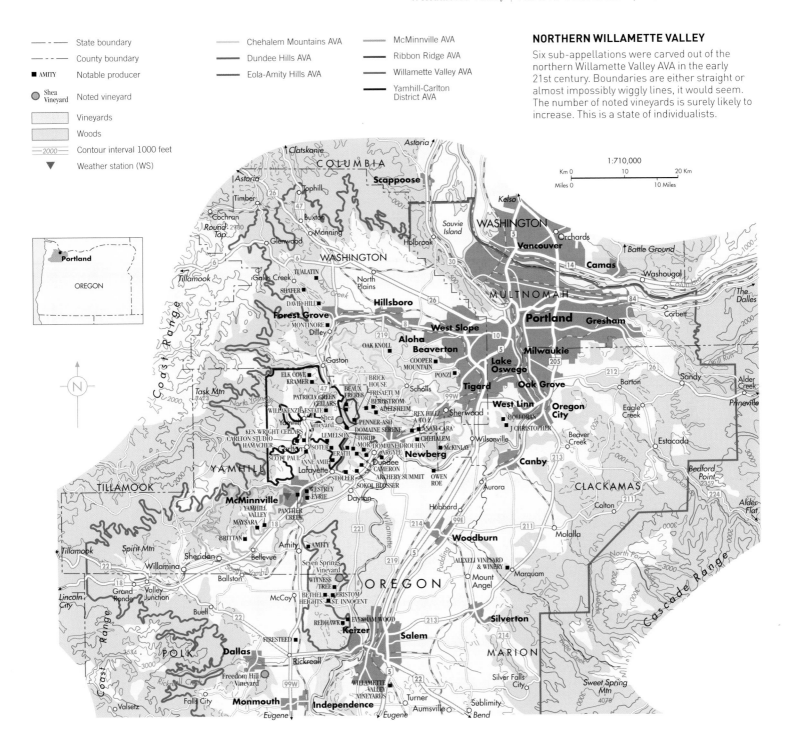

Legend:
- ‒ ‒‒ ‒ State boundary
- ‒ ‒ ‒ ‒ County boundary
- ■ AMITY Notable producer
- ⬤ Shea Vineyard Noted vineyard
- Vineyards
- Woods
- 2000 Contour interval 1000 feet
- ▼ Weather station (WS)

- Chehalem Mountains AVA
- Dundee Hills AVA
- Eola-Amity Hills AVA
- McMinnville AVA
- Ribbon Ridge AVA
- Willamette Valley AVA
- Yamhill-Carlton District AVA

1:710,000

For similar reasons, Oregon Chardonnays were relatively disappointing. The principal clone planted initially was Davis 108, whose main attribute in California was the length of its growing season before ripening. Most years in Oregon this was a distinct disadvantage, and many Chardonnays seemed rather thin and tart. The more suitable, and subtle, Dijon clones 76, 95, and 96 are now planted and the best Oregon Chardonnays made today have a distinctive verve and minerality that can seem almost Burgundian. For long, Oregon vintners' white wine hopes were pinned instead on Pinot Gris, which in Oregon is generally more like an aromatic Chardonnay than a rich Alsace Pinot Gris. Less common but well worth seeking

out are racy aromatic Rieslings from such notable producers as Trisaetum.

To its credit, and despite a notably humid climate, Oregon viticulture is today distinguished by notably widespread commitment to sustainable, often organic and sometimes biodynamic, practices.

One quirky institution that has done much to put the Willamette Valley on the international wine map and emphasize Oregon's distinction, however, is the International Pinot Noir Celebration held every July. This three-day Pinotfest sees fans and producers from all over the world congregate in the town of McMinnville to worship at the altar of Pinot and mutter about the iniquities of Cabernet.

WILLAMETTE VALLEY:
MCMINNVILLE ▼

Latitude / Altitude of WS
45.13° / 154ft (47m)

Average growing season temperature at WS
60.6°F (15.9°C)

Average annual rainfall at WS
41.7in (1,060mm)

Harvest month rainfall at WS
October: 3.1in (80mm)

Principal viticultural hazards
Fungal diseases, underripeness

Principal grape varieties
Pinot Noir, Pinot Gris, Chardonnay

Washington

COLUMBIA VALLEY

Washington's wine country, like Oregon, is a repository for deposits from as far away as Montana, thanks to the Missoula floods of the last ice age. The Columbia Valley has been sprouting new AVAs in the north. See Ancient Lakes opposite and Lake Chelan mapped on p.287. Red Mountain, mapped in detail bottom left, is virtually in Richland.

Not much of eastern Washington, where all but 80 acres (30ha) of the state's vines are grown, looks like wine country. Most visitors reach it from the city of Seattle, around which so many of the state's wineries still cluster. They drive through damp Douglas fir and ponderosa pine forests, over the mighty Cascades and descend suddenly into semi-desert, where in summer the sun shines reliably for up to 17 hours each day and where in winter Arctic blasts sometimes prove fatal for vines.

During eastern Washington's relatively short growing season, the fertile farmland of the Yakima Valley and the rolling wheatfields around Walla Walla are now punctuated by oases of green vines alongside the apples, cherries, and hops. This is low-cost farmland (far cheaper than California, for example). Many of the vines may be Concord for juice and jelly, but the total area of vinifera

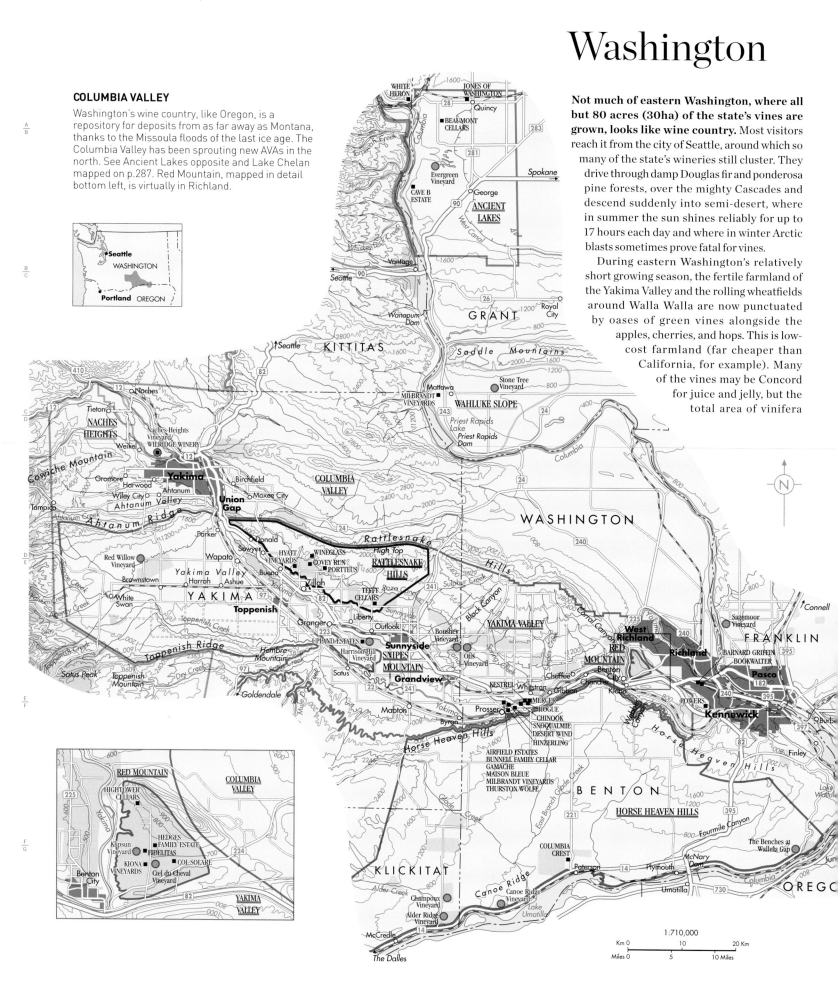

1:710,000

Km 0   10   20 Km

Miles 0   5   10 Miles

vines has been expanding fast, surpassing 40,000 acres (16,200ha) in 2010. Washington is the USA's second-biggest vine-grower and producer of vinifera wine, albeit making less than 10% of California's output.

The continental climate here has proved excellent for ripening fine wine grapes, on a latitude between those of Bordeaux and Burgundy, with the very important proviso that there is access to irrigation water – from rivers, reservoirs, or from much more expensive wells. Rainless summers and autumns minimize disease problems while the hot days and cold nights of the desert induce good colour and singularly well-defined flavours. Winters may be cold and dry but at least they help keep phylloxera at bay (virtually all vines are planted on their own roots), as do the fast-draining, relatively uniform sandy soils.

The trend is to blend

Vine-growing here was initially even more distinct from winemaking than in most American states, but this has been changing. For example, the dominant wine company, which owns Chateau Ste. Michelle, Columbia Crest, Snoqualmie, and many other labels, now grows and/or controls almost two-thirds of the grapes it needs. The great majority of Washington's hundreds of small wineries buy in grapes, however, often trucking them west over the Cascades, although the number of wineries – and estate vineyards – in eastern Washington has been steadily increasing. They also tend to buy from a wide range of growers and blend heavily, so winery location is rarely much clue to wine provenance. Partly so as to keep all blending options open, the giant **Columbia Valley** AVA (encompassing eastern Washington's more specific AVAs mapped here) and the ultra-flexible term Washington State are widely used in preference to more specific appellations.

The **Yakima Valley** is Washington's oldest designated wine region, carved by the Yakima River on its way east to join the Columbia, its fertile farmland and cattle ranches overlooked by snowy Mount Adams. Red Willow Vineyard in the northwest of the valley was one of the first to show that Syrah has considerable potential as a savoury but fruity addition to Washington's more traditional roster of grapes, and it is now being planted furiously throughout the state. **Rattlesnake Hills** is a fairly new AVA along the southern slopes of the Rattlesnake ridge within the Yakima Valley and makes the state's most Bordeaux-like reds. **Snipes Mountain**, a hill to the south, has some of the state's oldest vines, and is another relatively recent, and tiny, AVA. In the far southeast of the Yakima Valley, the town of Prosser, site of the new Walter Clore Wine and Culinary Center, is rapidly establishing itself as the prime focus of the valley's wine industry.

Between the Yakima Valley and the Columbia River, the **Horse Heaven Hills** boast some of the state's largest and most important vineyards. The extensive vineyards on the bluffs above the river, and those clustered around Champoux, are especially noteworthy. The lower south-facing slope of Canoe Ridge is the source of grapes for Precept Wine's Canoe Ridge Vineyard winery in Walla Walla (a typical example of Washington's disregard for geographical precision) as well as many of the better reds of Chateau Ste. Michelle. It is also close enough to the broad Columbia River to be saved the worst extremes of summer weather and most winter freezes.

To the north and east of the Yakima Valley are some of the state's warmest vineyards

Piero Antinori of Italy is the most famous international investor in Washington wine. He opened his Red Mountain winery, Col Solare, as a joint venture with Chateau Ste. Michelle in 2006.

of all, including the famous **Wahluke Slope**, which runs down from the Saddle Mountains to the Columbia River, tilting vines southwards for maximum radiation in summer and encouraging cold air to drain away from them in winter. And it was from just north of the linked cities of Richland, Pasco, and Kennewick that in the 1970s the original vineyard of the now-vast Sagemoor group supplied grapes for some of the state's very first wines. Merlot and Syrah are widely planted here but the small, water-limited **Red Mountain** AVA has a well-deserved reputation for supple, long-lived Cabernet Sauvignon. The new (2011) **Naches Heights** AVA, northwest of the city of Yakima, has unique soils and claims the potential to produce distinctive wines, but only 37 acres (15ha) of vines have been planted.

Summers as far inland as **Walla Walla Valley** are also decidedly warm; winters are sunny but can turn dangerously cold, and rainfall on the slopes that ring Walla Walla is high enough for some vineyards to be dry-farmed. The genteel college town of Walla Walla is where a marked concentration of the state's most sought-after reds are made, if not grown. The AVA, pioneered in the early 1980s by Leonetti and Woodward Canyon, spills south into Oregon to include hundreds of acres of new plantings around the original Seven Hills vineyard on the northern flanks of the Blue Mountains. In the flatland

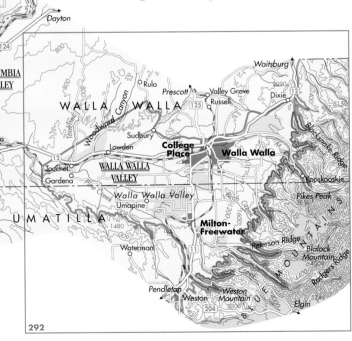

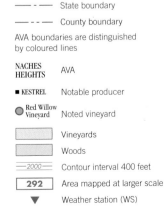

— · —	State boundary
— – —	County boundary

AVA boundaries are distinguished by coloured lines

NACHES HEIGHTS	AVA
■ KESTREL	Notable producer
● Red Willow Vineyard	Noted vineyard
▢	Vineyards
▢	Woods
—2000—	Contour interval 400 feet
292	Area mapped at larger scale
▼	Weather station (WS)

WASHINGTON: PROSSER ▼

Latitude / Altitude of WS
46.2° / 830ft (253m)

Average growing season temperature at WS
64.0°F (17.8°C)

Average annual rainfall at WS
8.9in (227mm)

Harvest month rainfall at WS
October: 0.8in (19mm)

Principal viticultural hazards
Winter freeze

Principal grape varieties
Riesling, Chardonnay, Cabernet Sauvignon, Merlot, Syrah, Pinot Gris

WALLA WALLA VALLEY

Walla Walla has the greatest concentration of renowned Washington wineries. But a substantial proportion of the grapes shipped in to the town's cellars are grown across the border in Oregon. The Walla Walla Valley AVA straddles the state line.

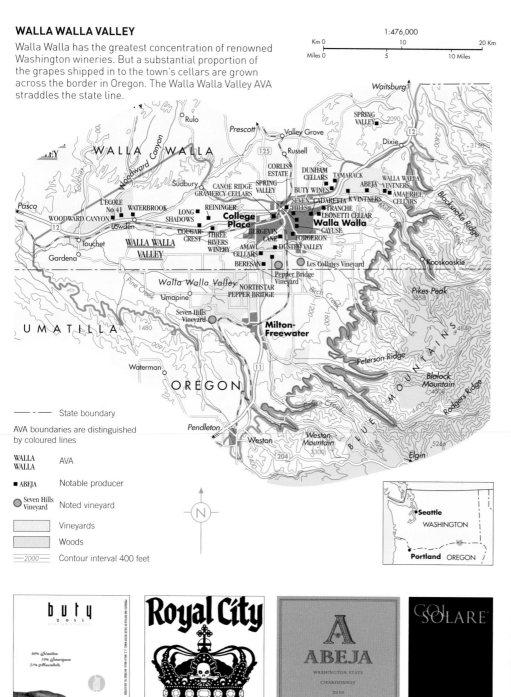

State boundary

AVA boundaries are distinguished by coloured lines

WALLA WALLA — AVA

■ ABEJA — Notable producer

⬤ Seven Hills Vineyard — Noted vineyard

Vineyards

Woods

—2000— Contour interval 400 feet

below, still on the Oregon side, are the stony vineyards known collectively as the Rocks.

The **Columbia Gorge** AVA in the southwest of the Columbia Valley (see map, p.287) also includes a good portion of Oregon and is particularly suitable for Chardonnay, aromatic white wine varieties, Pinot Noir, and Zinfandel. Lying in the northwest corner of the Columbia Valley, the **Lake Chelan** AVA is a promising and pretty area pioneered by the Sandidge family under the label CRS.

Rapid expansion

A new Washington winery is bonded almost weekly so that there were more than 700 by 2010 – double the number of grape-growers. This rapid growth means that many vines are young. They are planted on young, light soils, often from single clones. In the past most vines were grown, and yields decided, by fruit farmers rather than winemakers, but most of the state's expanding ranks of top-quality producers buy grapes by the acre, not the ton, and manage their own rows co-operatively with the grower. Yields are down, quality is up, the best wines sharing the deep colour, crisp acidity, and bright, frank flavours that typify Washington wine, as well as having admirable intensity of rich, soft fruit.

Only certain sites in this continental climate will ripen Cabernet Sauvignon fully, while Merlot, which has a much clearer identity here than in California, is more flexible, although it is inconveniently susceptible to winter freeze. Cabernet Franc has its followers, and not just because it is hardier. Petit Verdot, Malbec, Mourvèdre, Tempranillo, and Sangiovese are all grown successfully, albeit in small quantities, and are mostly used in blends.

Four decades ago, when Washington was believed to be suited only for cold-climate varieties, Riesling was widely planted. It fell out of favour only to find new popularity as a crisp, aromatic alternative to Chardonnay. As a result Ste. Michelle Wine Estates is now the world's largest Riesling producer. Furthermore, **Ancient Lakes** (north of Wahluke Slope), which has long grown many of the state's finest aromatic white wine grapes – Pinot Gris and Gewurztraminer as well as Riesling – now has its own AVA, and many established vineyards, if very few wineries. Sauvignon Blanc can be truly bracing, and Semillons such as L'Ecole 41's show that the grape can really shine when given the chance.

Grapes grown back west in the **Puget Sound** AVA around Seattle are completely different: early ripeners such as Müller-Thurgau, Madeleine Angevine, and Siegerrebe – a crew familiar to those who also live in a cool, rainy climate.

Old hands such as Quilceda Creek are now flanked by young bloods with funky labels. Eroica, a Chateau Ste. Michelle and Ernst Loosen project, put Riesling on the American wine map. The giant Banfi has since joined the Washington Riesling party by buying Pacific Rim from Randall Grahm of Bonny Doon.

Vines slope down to the Yakima River near Red Mountain. The irrigation lines are essential when average rainfall is only 6in (150mm) a year, but even this close to a river, piping water to them can add considerably to the cost of establishing a vineyard.

California

Ninety per cent of all American wine is grown in California: more wine than in any country outside Europe. And the planting goes on. Here at the vine's western limit there is a distinct shortage of geographical generalities and physical truisms. California's wine geography presents a series of surprises, and much more variety than outsiders give it credit for. The potential of a vineyard site is linked hardly at all to latitude but is crucially determined by what lies between it and the Pacific Ocean. The more mountains there are between the site and the sea, the less chance there is of marine air, often fog, reaching it to moderate the climate.

So cold is the inshore water of the Pacific here that it causes a perpetual fog bank all summer just off the coast. Each day that the temperatures approach 90°F (32°C) inland, the rising hot air draws the fog inland to fill its space. The Golden Gate Bridge in San Francisco straddles its most famous pathway, but everywhere up and down the coast where the Coast Ranges dip below about 1,500ft (460m), cold Pacific air spills over

and cools the land. Certain valleys that lie end-on to the ocean, particularly in Santa Barbara County, act as funnels that allow sea air to invade as far as 75 miles (120km) inland. So effectively are cool winds sucked off the Pacific over San Francisco Bay that they even have an effect on the climate in the Sierra Foothills, nearly 150 miles (240km) inland. Since foggy San Francisco Bay is northern California's chief air-conditioning unit, vineyards close to the waters of the bay, such as those of Carneros, skirting the south of Napa and Sonoma counties, can be rather cool, too. Within the inland Napa Valley, sheltered from Pacific influence by its almost unbroken ridge of western hills, it is those most southerly vineyards surrounding the town of Napa that are the coolest, due to the breezes off the bay, and those around Calistoga at the northern limit of the valley that are hottest. For similar reasons, if the result of different topography, the vineyards of the Santa Maria Valley way down the coast in Santa Barbara County, 140 miles (225km) northwest of Los Angeles, are some of the coolest in the state.

The Central (or San Joaquin) Valley on the other hand, the flat farmland that still makes agriculture California's most important economic activity (and grows three-quarters of the state's wine grapes), is too far inland to be directly influenced by the Pacific. It is one of the world's sunniest wine regions, with a hotter, drier climate than anywhere else in this book. Irrigation, increasingly expensive and controversial, is essential. Dry-farming is the dream of terroir-driven growers everywhere; it is a distant one in most of California.

The key facts panels show that summers are very much drier than those of most European wine regions. Total annual rainfall is not exceptionally low but it does tend to be concentrated in the first few months of the year, topping up reservoirs used throughout the summer for irrigation. In the warmth that is typical of a California September, atypical rain can wreak havoc. Autumn rains are very unusual, however, allowing growers to prolong the grapes' "hang time" almost as long as they like, or are asked to by the wine producers to whom they sell. This is just one important reason why California's wines have tended to be especially potent.

The most important of California's roughly 120 AVAs are mapped opposite and on the following pages, but even those marked should not be given too much significance. Some of the viticultural areas are so small that they affect only one winery, while North Coast, for example, encompasses much of Lake, Mendocino, Napa, and Sonoma counties.

Looking beyond the brand

There are excellent winemakers who still ignore AVAs, preferring to use good grapes from wherever they can get them, while others are as precise about individual sites as they can be. Hundreds of individual vineyard names are now in use on labels – powerful confirmation that California is moving on from the stage where it was only the grape variety and the brand name that counted. Geography has definitively entered the picture, although many producers use custom crush facilities and own little other than a label and the barrels they store there. They are not marked on these maps.

Fashion has always been important in California. Wine producers and consumers tend to act more uniformly than you would normally expect in a geographical unit roughly half as big as France. Recent vineyard trends have included better matching of grape variety to a specific site, more densely planted vines from a wider variety of clones, with much more controlled, less-dense foliage, more precise irrigation, and, this century, a new appreciation of freshness as opposed to super-ripeness.

THE CLIMATE REGIONS OF CALIFORNIA AND THE PACIFIC NORTHWEST

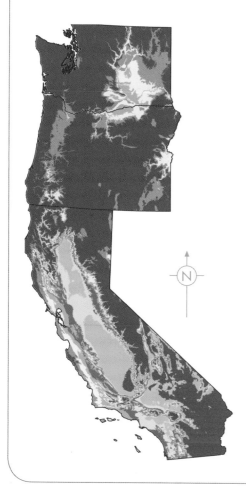

This climate classification scheme for viticulture was developed by UC Davis professors Amerine and Winkler for California and updated by Dr Gregory Jones for other cooler-climate regions. Wine regions are classed on a scale of "growing degree-days", which measures the heat accumulated over 50°F (10°C) between 1 April and 31 October (northern hemisphere). The classes broadly define grape-variety suitability (cool to hot) and wine style potential (light to full-bodied and fortified wines). For example, in Region Ia, only very early-ripening varieties, mostly hybrids, will produce high-quality, light-bodied table wines. Region III is suited to the production of high-quality, full-bodied wine, and Region V is typically suited to high-volume production, fortified wines, and table grapes.

- Too cool
- Region Ia: 1,500 to 2,000 degree days
- Region Ib: 2,000 to 2,500 degree days
- Region II: 2,500 to 3,000 degree days
- Region III: 3,000 to 3,500 degree days
- Region IV: 3,500 to 4,000 degree days
- Region V: 4,000 to 5,000 degree days
- Too hot

State boundary
County boundary
AVA boundaries not shown or not completed on larger-scale maps are distinguished by coloured lines
MADERA AVA
■ E & J GALLO Notable producer
296 Area mapped at larger scale on page shown

CALIFORNIA'S MAJOR WINE REGIONS

North Coast is a pretty extensive portion of a vast state. But an even larger area – from San Francisco all the way down to Santa Barbara – qualifies as Central Coast, and more and more of it is being planted with California's most valuable crop (after marijuana): grapes.

Bokisch (see p.310) is in Lodi, the most promising part of the vast Central Valley. South Coast Winery (see p.318) is near Los Angeles and Casey Flat Ranch is high above Lake Berryessa north of Napa.

Bokisch
VINEYARDS

Albariño   2011
TERRA ALTA VINEYARD
CLEMENTS HILLS=LODI   ALC 12.5% BY VOL.

SOUTH COAST WINERY

GVR
VINTAGE 2010   TEMECULA VALLEY
41% Viognier, 80% Grenache Blanc, 19% Roussanne

CfR
CASEY FLAT RANCH
2011 SAUVIGNON BLANC
CAPAY VALLEY

1:2,631,578

Km 0   50   100   150 Km
Miles 0   50   100 Miles

Mendocino and Lake

Mendocino County is California's northernmost outpost of the vine. Its most distinctive wine region is the Anderson Valley, where ocean fogs can drift in easily between the coastal hills to hang thick and low. The Navarro River tumbles down the valley through resin-scented redwoods. Long ago a few reclusive Italian families discovered that Zinfandel ripens splendidly on hillsides well above the fog line, but most of Anderson Valley has a super-cool ripening season – particularly in its lower reaches below the town of Philo. As Navarro Vineyards continues to prove, Riesling and Gewurztraminer are perfectly in tune with the climate. Roederer of Champagne has shown, from 1982, that the Anderson Valley can also yield fine fizz, while worthwhile still Pinot Noir has been emerging from the likes of Duckhorn's Goldeneye winery at Philo.

There is good natural acidity, too, in wines from **Yorkville Highlands** to the southeast, but the bulk of Mendocino's plantings are to be found in much warmer, drier conditions, well tucked in behind the coastal hills that rear up to 3,000ft (900m) north of Cloverdale and the Sonoma county line, protected from Pacific fogs. The fogs do not reach Ukiah, nor very often the Redwood Valley, and their wines (from some deep alluvial soils) are typically full-bodied, often rather soft, reds made from Cabernet, Petite Sirah, or, from particularly ancient vines above Ukiah, spicy Zinfandel. The distinctly cooler Potter Valley can also make very fine botrytised wines.

The oldest winery in Mendocino is Parducci. It was founded in 1932, a date that proclaims a visionary, for Prohibition was still in force (these days it is owned by the Mendocino Wine Co). Fetzer set down roots in 1968 to become justly celebrated as a source of dependable value and as one clear, confident voice in favour of organic wine production in a state so well suited to it. The winery is now owned by Chile's biggest wine company, Concha y Toro, while Fetzer family members grow increasing quantities of organic grapes for labels such as Ceàgo, Jeriko, Masut, Patianna, and Saracina.

Lake County to the east is as warm as the head of the Napa Valley and valued for its fruity Cabernet Sauvignon, Zinfandel, and Sauvignon Blanc at attractive prices, often bulking out wines labelled Napa. Brassfield, Obsidian Ridge, Steele, and Wildhurst are leading winery names.

Map legend:

- – – – County boundary
- AVA boundaries are distinguished by coloured lines
- CLEAR LAKE AVA
- ■ FREY Notable producer
- ⦿ The Narrows Vineyard Noted vineyard
- Vineyards
- Woods and chaparral
- —2500— Contour interval 500 feet
- ▼ Weather station (WS)

MENDOCINO: UKIAH ▼

Latitude / Altitude of WS
39.15° / 633ft (193m)

Average growing season temperature at WS
65.8°F (18.8°C)

Average annual rainfall at WS
39.9in (1,014mm)

Harvest month rainfall at WS
September: 0.4in (11mm)

Principal viticultural hazards
Over-winter drought, rain at harvest

Principal grape varieties
Chardonnay, Zinfandel, Cabernet Sauvignon, Merlot

Obsidian Ridge Vineyard, which lies at 2,650ft (800m), is named after the shiny black shards that litter the ground and release captured daytime warmth during nights that can be particularly cool at this elevation.

Northern Sonoma

According to the California Climate Rule – coast equals cool – Sonoma should be cooler than its inland neighbour, Napa. Overall it works. Sonoma County grows far more grapes than Napa County in more varied conditions, with much more potential for planting in cooler areas. Sonoma is also where fine wine started in California, early in the 19th century, even if in the late 20th century it was eclipsed by Napa's seminal role in the state's wine renaissance.

As elsewhere in California, climate is a function of the penetration of Pacific breezes, fogs, and the resultant cloud cover. Just south of the area mapped, there is a wide dip in the Coastal Ranges known as the Petaluma Gap. Thanks to this opening the vineyards in the south are the coolest, often being shrouded in mist until 11 in the morning and from 4 in the afternoon. The boundary of the **Russian River Valley** AVA, one of Sonoma's coolest, was extended southwards in 2005 to incorporate all those vineyards south of Sebastopol within the fog zone. (In 2011, the AVA grew yet again, at the behest of Gallo, to include the behemoth's Two Rock Vineyard in the southeast.) The Sebastopol Hills area, sometimes called southern Sebastopol, is slap-bang in the path of the fog that swirls in through the Petaluma Gap. It can be a struggle to ripen a commercial crop in the chilliest nooks of the Russian River Valley, particularly in its **Green Valley** sub-AVA, where Marimar Estate, Iron Horse, and Joseph Phelps' (of Napa Valley) Freestone winery are leading producers. The result can, however, be brilliantly lively wine. Both the Sebastopol Hills and Green Valley are on sandy Goldridge soil, while Laguna Ridge just east of Green Valley has the sandiest, fastest-draining soil of all.

Away from the Petaluma Gap, the Russian River Valley gradually warms up. Williams Selyem, Rochioli, and Gary Farrell, some of the first to draw attention to this characterful region, are clustered on Westside Road on the heavier soils

---

Morning fogs from the Pacific cling to Pinot Noir vines in Red Car Wines' La Bohème vineyard in the Russian River Valley. Nearby trees mean nearby birds – and the need to protect ripening grapes.

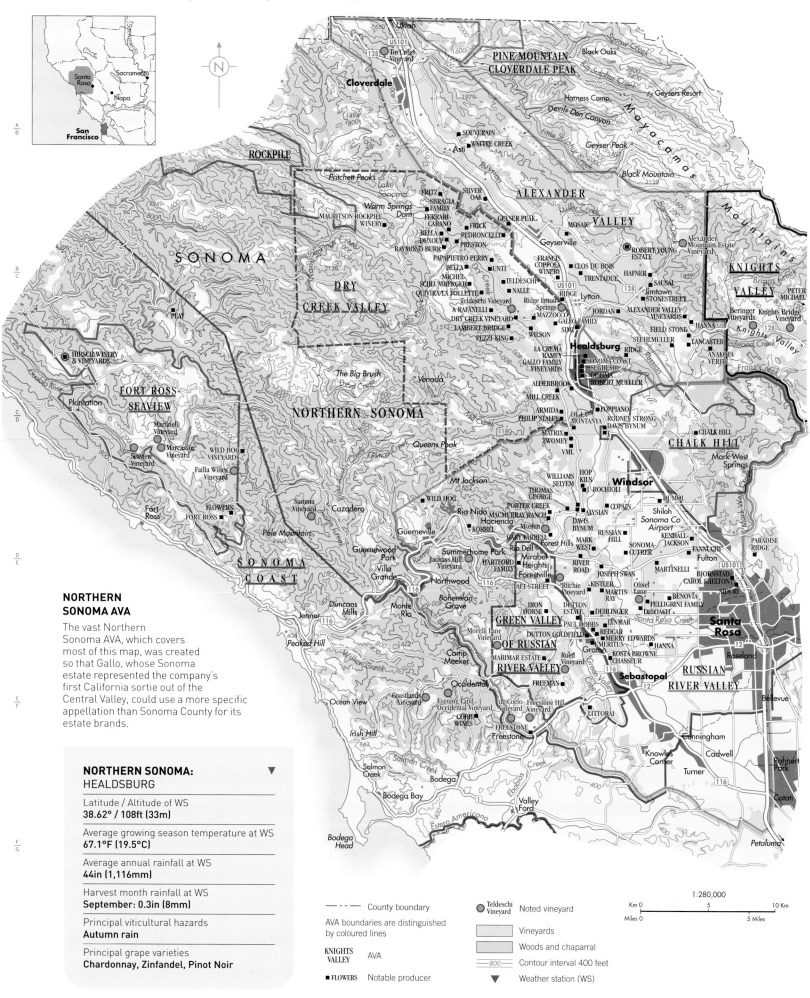

NORTHERN SONOMA AVA

The vast Northern Sonoma AVA, which covers most of this map, was created so that Gallo, whose Sonoma estate represented the company's first California sortie out of the Central Valley, could use a more specific appellation than Sonoma County for its estate brands.

NORTHERN SONOMA: HEALDSBURG

Latitude / Altitude of WS
38.62° / 108ft (33m)

Average growing season temperature at WS
67.1°F (19.5°C)

Average annual rainfall at WS
44in (1,116mm)

Harvest month rainfall at WS
September: 0.3in (8mm)

Principal viticultural hazards
Autumn rain

Principal grape varieties
Chardonnay, Zinfandel, Pinot Noir

--- County boundary

AVA boundaries are distinguished by coloured lines

KNIGHTS VALLEY   AVA

■ FLOWERS   Notable producer

● Teldeschi Vineyard   Noted vineyard

Vineyards

Woods and chaparral

—800— Contour interval 400 feet

▼ Weather station (WS)

1:280,000
Km 0 — 5 — 10 Km
Miles 0 — 5 Miles

of the banks of the Russian River itself in much warmer conditions than many of the newcomers. Grapes replaced apples as the principal crop along the winding roads of the valley with its old oaks and banks of flowers as recently as the 1990s.

Chardonnay, still by far Sonoma County's most planted grape, was initially the most celebrated variety here, planted in the white wine boom of the 1970s and 1980s, but it was the richness of Russian River Pinot Noir, with its red-berry flavours, that drew critical attention to the region. Thanks to the regular fog shroud, the levels of acidity usually remain notably and refreshingly high here – unless heat spikes in August and September rush ripening – so that Russian River can offer structured wines from both the Burgundy varieties. The lowest vineyards tend to be the coolest, because this is where the fog hangs longest. Vineyards above the fog line such as Martinelli's Jackass Hill and Dutton's Morelli Lane have long provided notable Zinfandel from vines originally planted by Italians who settled here after the Gold Rush. Higher-elevation vineyards are also showing promise with Syrah.

Chalk Hill to the northeast, southeast of Healdsburg, has its own AVA and is somewhat anomalously included in Russian River Valley, being much warmer and having volcanic soils. It is the fiefdom of Chalk Hill Estate, whose greatest strength is its particularly direct, medium-weight Chardonnay, although it has made some good Sauvignon Blanc, too, even if it is less zesty than Merry Edwards' version in the cooler reaches of the Russian River Valley. The inclusion in the Russian River AVA of the northern loop of the Russian River around Healdsburg, far from the cooling influence of fog, is equally difficult to justify climatologically.

Sonoma Coast
Between Russian River Valley and the ocean are some of the most exciting producers in the coolest reaches of the absurdly extensive **Sonoma Coast** AVA, which incorporates a total of half a million acres from Mendocino down to San Pablo Bay. The AVA was initially created to enable producers such as Sonoma-Cutrer, now owned by distiller Brown-Forman, to sell wines blended from their very varied holdings in this region as estate bottled, but there is now strong pressure to develop more geographically specific AVAs within it. The first, Fort Ross-Seaview AVA, was approved in 2012. Key producers in this particularly cool coastal region include Fort Ross, Wild Hog, Hirsch, and Flowers.

Site selection is critical here with exposure to marine influence, altitude, and orientation the crucial factors. Some of the finest fruit in the Russian River Valley inland comes from east-facing vineyards where the risk of raisining is minimal; south-facing sites, on the other hand, help to maximize ripening in the coolest local conditions. High-profile Sonoma Coast pioneers include Marcassin, Littorai, and Flowers. The Hirsch vineyard has long provided exceptional fruit for Russian River Valley producers and others.

North of the Russian River
The densely planted AVAs to the north of Russian River Valley are perceptibly warmer, even if, as in Chalk Hill, the floor of **Dry Creek Valley** is cooler than the hillsides. It can be positively damp at times, particularly at the southern end. (Compare Healdsburg's annual rainfall with that of somewhere as close as the town of Sonoma.) As in Russian River Valley, this encouraged 19th-century Italian settlers to plant the rot-prone Zinfandel above the fog-line and farm it without irrigation. Dry Creek Valley still has a reputation for some of the finest examples of this finicky variety. Throughout these northern California valleys, the east side, kept hotter for longer by the glow of the setting sun, tends to make fuller wines than the west. The best sites in the canyon enclosing Dry Creek Valley with substantial benchland benefit from a well-drained mixture of gravel and red clays known as Dry Creek Valley conglomerate. Zins and Cabernet thrive here, while the valley floor is left to white varieties, particularly Sauvignon Blanc. Dry Creek Vineyard showed the way as early as 1972, while more recently Quivira, an early convert to biodynamic viticulture, makes both good Sauvignon Blanc from valley floor vineyards and fine hillside Zinfandel. Rhône varieties have also been added to the mix, with Preston Vineyards leading the way. Some interesting Cabernet Sauvignon is made on the hillsides, too, particularly by A Rafanelli.

The broader, more open **Alexander Valley** north of Healdsburg is warmer still, thanks to some low hills that shelter it. On its alluvial soils Cabernet is consistently ripened to distinctive, almost chocolatey richness, while lower ground near the river can yield some appetizing Sauvignon Blanc and Chardonnay. There are even some old Zinfandel vines – including Ridge's ancient, mixed-variety Geyserville vineyard – and, much more unusual, Sangiovese vines in the northern Alexander Valley. Stonestreet's Alexander Mountain Estate, once known as Gauer Ranch, supplies some of California's most celebrated Chardonnay and has quite different, cooler conditions from the valley floor 450ft (140m) below. Local knowledge is everything in California; its terroirs are baffling to outsiders.

Knights Valley, southeast of Alexander Valley and almost an extension of the head of the Napa Valley, is warmer than Dry Creek Valley but cooler (because it is higher) than Alexander Valley. Peter Michael, owned by and named after an Englishman – a knight of the realm, no less – is a relatively unusual example of a hugely successful California winery owned by a foreign individual. The estate's vineyards of Chardonnay and Cabernet are on volcanic soils up to 2,000ft (600m) and 1,500ft (450m) above sea level, respectively. Beringer pioneered Knights Valley Cabernet and also makes a white and red Bordeaux blend from its Knights Valley vineyard called Alluvium, after the alluvial soils in this relatively warm site.

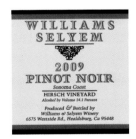

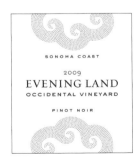

A glance at these, some of Northern Sonoma's finest, shows just how common it is now to cite the precise source of grapes – and even, in the case of Ridge, the precise proportions of each variety that went into this particular vintage. Geyserville is one of the warmer locations illustrated here.

Southern Sonoma and Carneros

This is where fine wine, or the first attempt at it, began in California, around the former mission, garrison town, and one-brief-time state capital of Sonoma. It was at Mission San Francisco de Solano, founded in 1823, that the Franciscan monks, moving up the Pacific coast, planted their last and most northerly vineyard, introducing the vine to one of its friendliest environments on earth.

The town of Sonoma has all the atmosphere of a little wine capital – in fact, of the capital of a very little republic: the original if short-lived Bear Flag Republic of California. Sonoma's tree-shaded square, with its old mission buildings and barracks, its stone-built city hall and ornate Sebastiani Theatre, is faintly Ruritanian in style and thickly layered with history.

The hills overlooking the town were the site of Agoston Haraszthy's famous pioneer estate of the 1850s and 1860s. Part of his Buena Vista cellars still stands in the side-valley to the east, and is being restored by its new owner, Burgundian Jean-Charles Boisset. Winemaking in northern California started here.

Like the Napa Valley, but in a smaller compass, the **Sonoma Valley** is cooled in the south by fogs and wind off San Pablo Bay and is progressively warmer towards the north, in this case into the lee of Sonoma Mountain, which shelters the valley from western storms and cooling sea breezes. The Mayacamas Mountains, Napa Valley's western edge, constitute the eastern boundary. There is plenty of evidence that this AVA can grow excellent Chardonnay, starting with Hanzell in the 1950s, the pioneer of oak-aging in California. Landmark Vineyard's local output, Kistler's Durell bottling, Durell Vineyard owner Bill Price's own wines, and Sonoma-Cutrer's Les Pierres vineyard (just west of Sonoma town) confirm it. Yet old-vine Zinfandels are Sonoma Valley's vinous heart and soul, with the standard-bearers being Kunde's Shaw Vineyard, the Old Hill Vineyard, and Pagani Ranch, all planted in the 1880s and, astoundingly, still producing.

Cabernet history

Evidence of excellent Cabernet Sauvignon first came in the 1940s from Louis Martini's famous Monte Rosso vineyard about 1,100ft (335m) up in the eastern hills, and more recently from the outstanding Laurel Glen Cabernets from **Sonoma Mountain**. This is a significant upland appellation in the west whose best wines seem to benefit from unusually thin, rocky soil, altitude, and long sunshine hours. The key to Cabernet and Zinfandel quality here again is to be above the fog line. Benziger is creating waves in Sonoma Mountain with its enthusiasm for biodynamic viticulture, and the nearby Richard Dinner Vineyard is the source of Paul Hobbs' opulent Chardonnays.

Adjoining the northwest boundary of Sonoma Mountain, the **Bennett Valley** AVA, whose best-known winery is Matanzas Creek, has similar soils to Sonoma Valley but much more cooling marine influence. The Crane Canyon wind gap (west of this map) is the secret. The area is too cool to ripen Cabernet Sauvignon reliably and Merlot has been the dominant variety, although the future may lie with Rhône varieties and Sauvignon Blanc.

At the southern end of Sonoma Valley, and included in the AVA, is the part of the relatively cool **Los Carneros** district (commonly known as Carneros) that lies in Sonoma County. Politically, Carneros straddles the Napa–Sonoma county line. Both Sonoma Carneros and Napa Carneros are mapped here as they have so much more in common with each other than with the rest of each county to the north.

On the low, rolling hills north of San Pablo Bay, Los Carneros (literally "the rams") is dairy country that was rapidly colonized by the vine in the late 1980s and 1990s. Winemakers Louis Martini and André Tchelistcheff had bought Carneros fruit as early as the 1930s, and Martini first planted Pinot Noir and Chardonnay there in the late 1940s. Shallow clay-loam soils, much less fertile than, for example, the Napa Valley and Sonoma Valley floors, help to regulate vine vigour and productivity. Strong winds off the Bay rattle the vine-leaves when hotter weather to the north sucks in cool air, particularly in the afternoons. They slow the ripening process to such an extent that Carneros produces some of California's most delicate wines, making them some of the state's better base wines for sparkling wine blends. Much hope and capital were invested here, particularly by Rene de Rosa in his Winery Lake vineyard in the 1960s, and later by champagne and Cava producers. With sparkling wine originally in mind, Pinot Noir and, especially, Chardonnay are the dominant varieties in vineyards regularly plundered by wineries in warmer country to the north.

The best still wines from Carneros can be delicious, the Chardonnays having more ageing potential than most in California with their crisp acidity and stone-fruit flavours. Carneros Pinot Noir, in transition between the old Martini and Swan clones and clones imported from Burgundy, is undoubtedly more transparent than that of Russian River Valley, tasting of herbs and cherries. Growers colonized Carneros long before wineries were constructed. Some of the most celebrated vineyards, whose names can be found on labels from top producers throughout Napa and Sonoma, are Hyde, Hudson, Sangiacomo, and Truchard. Syrah, Merlot, and Cabernet Franc can also shine here and Carneros is proving usefully versatile territory for those keen to try more adventurous varieties such as Tempranillo, Albariño, and Vermentino.

Yellow is the colour of a Carneros spring, thanks to the mustard that is encouraged to bloom between the contour-hugging rows of vines in the early months of the year. Cover crops encourage more organic matter in the soil and help to retain water.

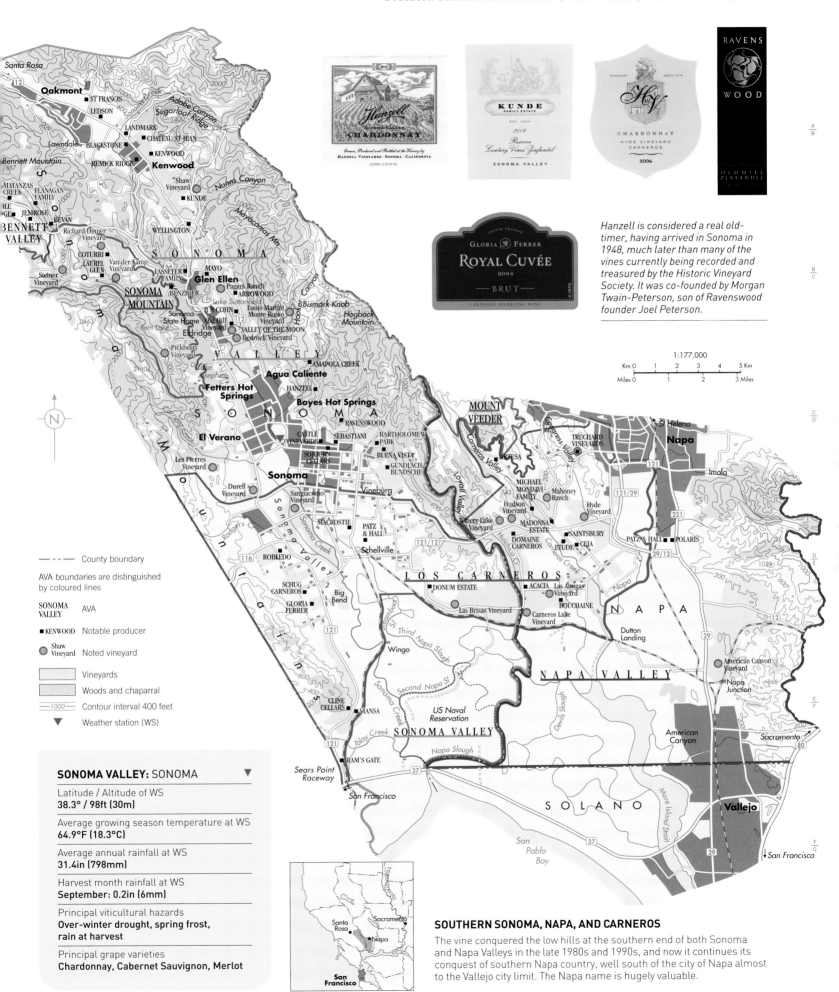

Hanzell is considered a real old-timer, having arrived in Sonoma in 1948, much later than many of the vines currently being recorded and treasured by the Historic Vineyard Society. It was co-founded by Morgan Twain-Peterson, son of Ravenswood founder Joel Peterson.

1:177,000

Km 0   1   2   3   4   5 Km
Miles 0   1   2   3 Miles

— · — · —   County boundary

AVA boundaries are distinguished by coloured lines

SONOMA VALLEY   AVA

■ **KENWOOD**   Notable producer

⬤ Shaw Vineyard   Noted vineyard

▢ Vineyards

▢ Woods and chaparral

═1000═   Contour interval 400 feet

▼   Weather station (WS)

SONOMA VALLEY: SONOMA ▼

Latitude / Altitude of WS
38.3° / 98ft (30m)

Average growing season temperature at WS
64.9°F (18.3°C)

Average annual rainfall at WS
31.4in (798mm)

Harvest month rainfall at WS
September: 0.2in (6mm)

Principal viticultural hazards
Over-winter drought, spring frost, rain at harvest

Principal grape varieties
Chardonnay, Cabernet Sauvignon, Merlot

SOUTHERN SONOMA, NAPA, AND CARNEROS

The vine conquered the low hills at the southern end of both Sonoma and Napa Valleys in the late 1980s and 1990s, and now it continues its conquest of southern Napa country, well south of the city of Napa almost to the Vallejo city limit. The Napa name is hugely valuable.

Napa Valley

Twenty per cent of the value of all California's wine comes from the Napa Valley – from only 4% of its volume. Such is the reputation of the world's most glamorous, most cosseted, and most heavily capitalized wine region. Its modern history starts in 1966, with the construction of the Robert Mondavi winery. The mission-style adobe arch and global ambitions of this iconic cellar signalled the start of the transformation of a sleepy farming community of walnut and prune orchards into a monoculture of 46,000 acres (18,620ha) of vines that is far more varied than most outsiders realize.

Half of the soil orders on earth (that is, fundamental species of soil, based on their creation) are to be found in the Napa Valley. In broad terms the valley is the result of the Napa River eroding its way between the Mayacamas Mountains on the west and the Vaca range on the east. Their respective peaks are the igneous outflows of Mount Veeder in the west and Atlas Peak and Mount George in the east, responsible at various times for a wide range of mineral deposits. Soils as a consequence are thinnest, oldest, and least fertile on the sides of the valley, while the valley floor is dominated by deep, fertile alluvial clays. There are some deep but well-drained soils on the benchlands on both sides of the valley.

As for climate, as elsewhere in northern California, the open (in this case southern) end of this narrow valley is much cooler than the northern end, by an average of at least 10°F (6.3°C) during the summer. In fact Carneros (see previous page) is almost at the coolest limit of fine wine production, with the new (2012) Coombsville AVA just 3 miles (5km) east of Napa city a close second. Coombsville's vines – both Bordeaux and Burgundy varieties – are planted as high as 1,200ft (370m), cooled by winds and fog from San Pablo Bay.

At the other end of the valley, Calistoga is as hot as any fine wine producer would care for, but much of the land in between is just right, especially for the late-ripening Cabernet Sauvignon. As the air heated by the long summer season rises, it draws in cooling draughts of ocean air, from Sonoma's Russian River Valley via the Chalk Hill Gap (see p.298) around Diamond Mountain and Spring Mountain or, more persistently, from Carneros.

Wines tend to taste progressively richer with riper tannins as you move north. As you move up into the hills, they have more structure and concentration than the valley floor counterparts they look directly down on. The less fertile hillsides have been colonized by the vine to a certain extent, despite problems with erosion and land use disputes. High-altitude vineyards both east and west of the valley often benefit from strong morning sunshine above a valley floor shrouded in fog. Then cool breezes bathe

Darioush winery was designed to evoke Persepolis, the ancient capital of Persia. Napa-style, the Iranian owner had the stone specially quarried near Persepolis and cut in Turkey and Italy.

the mountaintops in the late afternoon while the valley floor radiates heat trapped below an inversion layer.

This is the theory. What gets in the way of matching geography to bottle is less natural caprice – although vintages vary here far more than many wine drinkers realize – than how the Napa Valley is organized. To the millions of tourists attracted to "The Valley" each year, there seems to be an infinity of wineries flanking the traffic-jammed Highway 29 and its eastern counterpart, the quieter Silverado Trail. In fact, there are 420 wineries but around 700 grape-growers. The symbiotic functions of selling wine and growing vines have been more distinct here than in most fine wine districts, although an increasing proportion of wine is estate grown and, often, vineyard designated. Those wedded to expressing a specific terroir are likely to have spared no expense in analysing and understanding it.

Napa's own grape

Cabernet Sauvignon is the Napa Valley's grape. In fact, Napa's best Cabernets are incontrovertibly some of the world's most successful. They have unparalleled opulence and exuberance, yet the finest examples have rigour, too. Some of the more austere hillside examples apart, these are Cabernets that can be drunk with pleasure when only three or four years old, although the great mid-20th-century vintages from pioneers such as Beaulieu and Inglenook aged beautifully for 50 years. Most Napa-labelled Chardonnay now comes from the cooler climes of Carneros, but some good Sauvignon Blanc is produced just

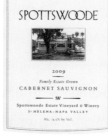

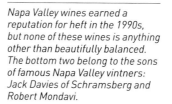

Napa Valley wines earned a reputation for heft in the 1990s, but none of these wines is anything other than beautifully balanced. The bottom two belong to the sons of famous Napa Valley vintners: Jack Davies of Schramsberg and Robert Mondavi.

THE HEART OF NAPA VALLEY

There is a world of difference between the flat, fertile valley floor swarming with tourists and the underpopulated mountain ranges on either side. Eastern slopes benefit from sunny afternoons, resulting in softer wines than those made on the west side of the valley (see diagrams overleaf).

1:175,000

Km 0   2   4   6 Km
Miles 0   2   4 Miles

NAPA VALLEY: ST HELENA ▼

Latitude / Altitude of WS
38.5° / 226ft (69m)

Average growing season temperature at WS
66.8°F (19.3°C)

Average annual rainfall at WS
36.6in (931mm)

Harvest month rainfall at WS
September: 0.3in (7mm)

Principal viticultural hazards
Over-winter drought, spring frost, heat spikes, autumn rain

Principal grape varieties
Cabernet Sauvignon, Merlot, Chardonnay, Zinfandel

north of Yountville. Syrah is being planted on some hillside sites, notably Mount Veeder, and some fine Zinfandel is produced in various Napa vineyards, particularly around Calistoga and on Mount Veeder, but Napa does not have a cohesive answer to Sonoma's Dry Creek Valley.

That said, Napa County has one of the more highly developed and cogent sets of AVAs – certainly more logical than Sonoma's. Napa Valley is the general AVA and includes not just the world-famous main valley, with its extraordinary concentration of modish restaurants, art galleries, and gift shops as well as wineries, but also a considerable area of quite separate land. The very warm Pope Valley to the northeast will surely be colonized by would-be vignerons, as the **Chiles Valley** AVA and American Canyon,

– – –   County boundary

AVA boundaries are distinguished by coloured lines

NAPA VALLEY   AVA

▪ LONG   Notable producer

⬤ Hudson Vineyard   Noted vineyard

   Vineyards

   Woods and chaparral

1000   Contour intervals: below 100 feet every 20 feet above 100 feet every 200 feet

305   Area mapped at larger scale on page shown

▼   Weather station (WS)

southeast of Napa city (mapped with Carneros on p.301), already have been. This southern territory towards the town of Vallejo has proved warm enough for extensive viticulture on land that is much more exposed and therefore cooler than most of the rest of the Napa Valley.

The valley floor

Rutherford, Oakville, and Stags Leap in the middle stretch of the valley are considered in detail overleaf. The **Oak Knoll District** AVA in the south has the distinction of being able to produce fine examples of both Riesling and long-lived Cabernet – as Trefethen can attest. **Yountville** immediately north of here is slightly warmer and, even if Dominus owes its fame to Cabernet, has a particular affinity with Merlot. This grape thrives on some of the clay-rich alluvial fans found in this AVA, characterized by massive blocks of intact rock that make up the area's distinctive knolls.

A little warmer than Rutherford, **St Helena** is not just the largest and busiest of the Napa Valley's wine towns, it is also the address of many of the valley's biggest wineries. Many ship in wine or grapes from well outside the area. The fortune of Sutter Home was built on palest pink "White" Zinfandel bought in from the Central Valley and Sierra Foothills. Beringer, for long a source of fine, geographically designated reds and whites, has endured a series of owners and is now a part of Treasury Wine Estates of Australia. V Sattui thrives on tourists, and so does the once-great

Louis Martini, making a comeback under Gallo ownership. St Helena also boasts the vineyards of some of the smallest, most cultish labels such as Grace Family, Vineyard 29, and Colgin Herb Lamb. Spottswoode and Corison are just some of those that show that this area can produce wines with real restraint and subtlety.

At the northern end of the valley, **Calistoga**, now with its own AVA, is all but surrounded by mountains – Mount St Helena to the north and the Mayacamas range to the west and east – which capture cold winter air at night and bring spring frosts, a perennial threat to all valley floor vineyards. Sprinkler systems and, particularly, wind machines are an eye-catching local feature of the vineyards on the volcanic soils around Calistoga. **Diamond Mountain District**, just southwest of the town, is best known for Diamond Creek Vineyard, an early exponent of occasionally impenetrable vineyard-designated bottlings from its extremely mixed soils.

Hillside vineyards

Mountain vineyards have become increasingly important in Napa Valley. All along the western ridge are single-minded individuals perceived, not least by themselves, as very different creatures from those on the valley floor below. **Spring Mountain District** benefits not just from altitude but from cool Pacific air. Stony Hill became the prototype for Napa Valley cult wines with its long-lived Chardonnays and Rieslings back in the 1960s and is still going strong. Today,

many of Spring Mountain's most supple wines carry the Pride Mountain label.

Mount Veeder to the south produces altogether tougher but highly distinctive wine from very thin, acid soils with a strong volcanic element not dissimilar to those found over the ridge in the Sonoma Valley (Monte Rosso, for example). The Hess Collection, with its exceptional art gallery, is Mount Veeder's foremost winery. On the east side of the valley, Dunn, La Jota, Liparita, O'Shaughnessy, and Robert Craig are some of the highest achievers on the cool, quiet, generally fog-free uplands of **Howell Mountain**. Just a few metres outside the Howell Mountain AVA, Delia Viader makes superb examples of Napa mountain Cabernet, Franc as well as Sauvignon.

The sheltered Conn Valley benefits from benchland soils and is clearly well suited to Cabernet. Pritchard Hill, pioneered in the 1960s by Donn Chappellet, is home to the profound Cabernets of Chappellet, Long, Colgin, Bryant, Ovid, and Continuum. **Atlas Peak** lies to the south, beyond Lake Hennessy and Pritchard Hill, on the heights above Stags Leap, relatively high and cool, with breezes straight from the bay. Its thin soils were planted with a slew of Italian grape varieties when Antinori of Italy arrived here in the 1990s. Cabernet, however, with particularly bright fruit and good natural acidity, is now the Atlas Peak speciality, with Antinori's renamed Antica Napa Valley the top producer. From edge to edge, Cabernet Sauvignon is Napa's own grape.

TEMPERATURE VARIATION IN THE NAPA VALLEY

The two diagrams below left and centre, supplied by California viticultural consultants Terra Spase, show actual morning and afternoon temperatures on one particular day, illustrating the typical variance between the two sides of the Napa Valley. Note how the south of the valley is consistently cooler than the north, and the land above the fog line is much warmer than the valley floor in the early morning.

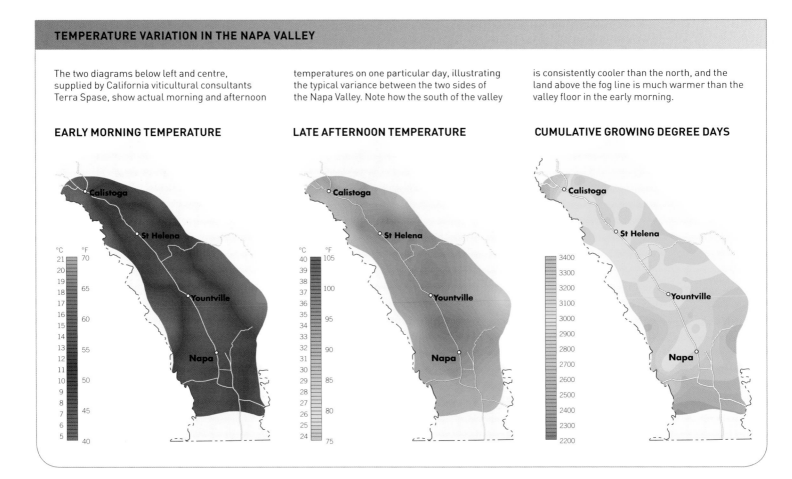

EARLY MORNING TEMPERATURE

LATE AFTERNOON TEMPERATURE

CUMULATIVE GROWING DEGREE DAYS

Rutherford

To explain Rutherford to a visitor schooled in French wine, you might describe it as the Pauillac of California. This is Cabernet country par excellence. Nearly two-thirds of the 3,500 acres (1,417ha) of vines here are Cabernet Sauvignon and most of the rest are other Bordeaux red grapes grown to complement it. Not that the Cabernet ripened in Rutherford's warm summers is left with any of the holes on the palate that in the Médoc may require Merlot and Cabernet Franc to fill them. Rutherford's is full-throttle Cabernet in terms of ripeness, even if it typically tends to have more structure, backbone, and longevity than almost any other California Cabernet.

Rutherford has produced great age-worthy Cabernet since the first half of the 20th century, when names such as Inglenook and Beaulieu carved California's reputation. The proof is still there, behind labels printed in the 1940s. Other famous specific vineyards include Bosché and Bella Oaks. Film director Francis Ford Coppola has revived Inglenook, once the district's most famous winery and vineyards, calling the property Niebaum Coppola, with its flagship wine Rubicon, until in 2011 he bought the Inglenook name and set about a lavish resoration of the 19th-century winery.

All of these are on the so-called Rutherford Bench on the west side of the valley, a slightly elevated stretch of sedimentary gravelly sand and alluvial fans carved out by the influential Napa River. Soils are deep and particularly well-drained, so conducive to lower crop loads, earlier ripening, and greater intensity of flavour than the valley norm. Many tasters detect a mineral element in wines produced here, known in shorthand as "Rutherford dust" – although the trend towards prolonged ripening or "hang time" has tended to blur Rutherford's distinction.

The Rutherford AVA is more homogeneous than most because elevation, up to 600ft (180m), is pretty uniform, although another notably successful district within Rutherford is on the east side between the Napa River and Conn Creek, where afternoon rays linger longest. Gravelly deposits washed down from the Vaca range have resulted in an especially well-drained cluster of vineyards, such as that used by Caymus to source its Special Selection Cabernet. Some cooling marine influence from San Pablo Bay reaches as far north as this, but not as much as in districts further south.

Many of the Napa Valley's greatest wines were made in the mid-20th century in the Inglenook winery. Then it was acquired, circuitously, by a mass market operation that sold it to winemaking neighbour and film director Francis Ford Coppola.

AVA boundaries are distinguished by coloured lines

RUTHERFORD AVA

- ■ CAYMUS   Notable producer
- ⬤ Bosché Vineyard   Noted vineyard
- ▢   Vineyards
- ▢   Woods and chaparral
- —500—   Contour interval 100 feet

The quality of wines made by André Tchelistcheff at Beaulieu in the mid-20th century provided more evidence of the greatness of Rutherford terroir. The Staglins bought 50 acres of Beaulieu vineyard in 1985, and as Beaulieu did, drafted in an oenologist from France, Michel Rolland.

Oakville

There may not be much more to Oakville than the Oakville Grocery store (one of the valley's best places to buy wine and food for picnics) and the Napa Wine Company (a popular custom crush facility). But it was in Oakville, in 1966, that the California wine revolution began when Robert Mondavi built his striking winery. Going north up the valley, Oakville is where really serious, meaty Cabernet begins. The wines may not have quite the weight and backbone of the best that Rutherford can offer but they certainly offer the Napa Valley's quintessential opulence. Oakville can also produce some vote-catching Chardonnay and Sauvignon Blanc, even some convincing Sangiovese, but Cabernet is its essence.

The AVA is far enough south to feel some marine influence from San Pablo Bay, although the knoll southeast of Cardinale has a bearing on exactly where those cooling fogs and breezes go.

As in Rutherford, there is a marked difference between the west and east sides of Oakville. Alluvial fans predominate in the west with, closest to the hillsides, large particles washed out of the Mayacamas Mountains providing relatively good drainage and not too high a level of fertility. Closer to the valley floor, the richer Bale loams predominate. Ripening grapes is easy here.

It is even easier on the eastern side – in fact, the warmth of afternoon sunshine on the lower slopes of the Vaca range in the east can be a threat to freshness of fruit. (The AVA boundary goes up to the 600ft/180m contour line, whereas much of the valley floor is at an altitude below 200ft/60m.) Soils here in the east are heavier and have more volcanic influence.

The To Kalon vineyard in the west was planted as long ago as 1868. Such is the sheer, exuberant quality of its Cabernet that its precise boundaries, ownership, and name have been fought over but are now shared by Robert Mondavi and the Napa Valley's dominant vineyard owner, Beckstoffer Vineyards. The first Napa Valley vineyard to achieve international fame in the modern era was Martha's Vineyard, bottled and label-designated by Joe Heitz, who consistently denied that its minty overlay had anything to do with the eucalyptus trees planted on its edge.

Today the name of Oakville is so potent that several of its producers allocate their wines rather than sell them, and donate a small proportion to America's charity auctions and marvel at the zeroes. Screaming Eagle, currently being replanted, in the east and the increasing range of wines from the Harlan estate on the opposite side of the valley are the most obvious, but by no means the only, examples.

Napa Valley is always beautiful, but never more so than in autumn. This is Far Niente's 100-acre (250ha) Martin Stelling vineyard behind the winery on the western side of Oakville.

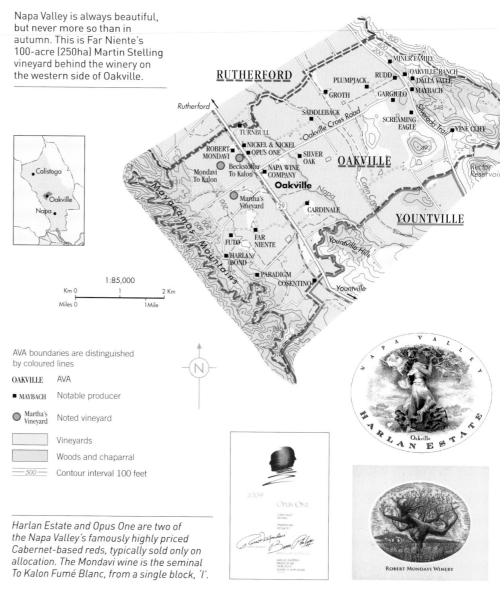

1:85,000

Km 0   1   2 Km
Miles 0   1 Mile

AVA boundaries are distinguished by coloured lines

OAKVILLE   AVA

■ MAYBACH   Notable producer

○ Martha's Vineyard   Noted vineyard

Vineyards

Woods and chaparral

—500—   Contour interval 100 feet

Harlan Estate and Opus One are two of the Napa Valley's famously highly priced Cabernet-based reds, typically sold only on allocation. The Mondavi wine is the seminal To Kalon Fumé Blanc, from a single block, 'I'.

ROBERT MONDAVI WINERY

Stags Leap

Stags Leap is the eastern opposite number to Yountville; the AVA for an enclave contained behind a high knoll on the valley floor and climbing the eastern hills of the Vaca range. Its reputation might make you expect something more imposing or extensive. Fame came overnight in 1976, when a Cabernet from Stag's Leap Wine Cellars came first in a Paris tasting that still makes the news four decades later. It pitted some of what were then California's better-known wines against some of the best of Bordeaux. Much to everyone's surprise, including the authors of this book, who were on the panel of judges, the California wines repeated the performance in a rerun exactly 30 years later. Of all Napa Cabernets, those of Stags Leap have arguably the most recognizable character: a silky texture, a certain aroma of violets or cherries, tannins that have always been supple, power with more delicacy than is usual in Napa Cabernet. Some make comparisons with St-Julien, others with Margaux.

The district, barely three miles by one, takes its name from a run of bare rocks, a basalt palisade, on the eastern edge of the valley, an afternoon suntrap from which warm air radiates. The heat is moderated by marine breezes, another afternoon phenomenon, which are funnelled through the Golden Gate, over San Pablo Bay and turned by the hills behind Berkeley straight up towards Chimney Rock and Clos du Val. The knoll above Stag's Leap Wine Cellars protects some vineyards from this cooling influence. Indeed, the AVA's rumpled series of hills and ridges makes generalizations more difficult than elsewhere in the Napa Valley. But the area is warm enough to see the vines start leafing a good two weeks ahead of more northerly areas, even though the ripening process is slower, with the result that harvest tends to be at about the same time as, say, Rutherford's.

Soils are moderately fertile volcanic, gravel-loams on the valley floor, with rockier, particularly well-drained terrain on the heavily protected hillsides. Shafer, another one of the district's top performers, benefits from its highly regarded hillside vineyard on a steep amphitheatre that was carved out of the eastern slopes before restrictions on the development of Napa Valley hillsides were put in place. Stags Leap Merlot is also notable, but the area is generally too hot for Chardonnay.

As early morning fog keeps temperatures down, while most tourists are still sleeping off last night's dinner, vineyard crews are hard at work, as here at Stags' Leap Winery. Without Mexican labour there would be no California wine industry.

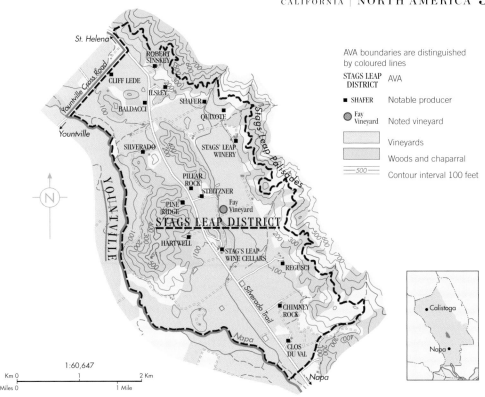

AVA boundaries are distinguished by coloured lines

STAGS LEAP DISTRICT — AVA

■ SHAFER — Notable producer

● Fay Vineyard — Noted vineyard

Vineyards

Woods and chaparral

—500— Contour interval 100 feet

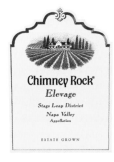

The Shafer family's Hillside Select is, like so many Napa Valley icons, made from 100% Cabernet Sauvignon. Ripeness is guaranteed on the rocky amphitheatre responsible for it; there is no need for the fleshier Merlot.

South of the Bay

The east side and the southern end of San Francisco Bay are nothing like the Napa and Sonoma valleys, either in terms of the wines they produce or their social history. To the east, the windswept, dry gravels of the **Livermore Valley** have been famous for white wine, especially Sauvignon Blanc with perhaps the most individual style in the state, ever since they were planted with cuttings from Château d'Yquem in 1869. The creative Wente family dominates the 4,000 acres (1,620ha) of vines under constant threat from urban development. Wente was also the first in California to bottle varietally labelled Chardonnay; indeed, the majority of Chardonnay vines in California can be traced to the original Wente clone.

The grey sprawl on the map has spread rapidly south of the Bay as Silicon Valley, whose original heart was Santa Clara, has flourished. High above it, the **Santa Cruz Mountains** AVA seems quite incongruous wine country, although it is older than Napa. Its isolated wineries are far fewer, and vineyards fewer still, but several of them are among California's most famous names.

In the 1950s, Martin Ray of Mount Eden was the first winemaker of the modern era to bring renown to these beautiful forested mountains. His eccentric, expensive wines, like those of his ex-cellarhand David Bruce, caused arguments and amusement in exactly the opposite proportion to those caused by their spiritual successor, Randall Grahm of Bonny Doon (whose ocean-cooled vineyards just northwest of the "alternative" town of Santa Cruz succumbed to Pierce's Disease in 1994). No matter. Grahm is a thoroughly benign agent provocateur and an inspired improviser.

The leader in the region is Ridge Vineyards, high above the fog line on a ridge overlooking the ocean one way and the Bay the other. Cabernet from the highest patch, Monte Bello vineyard, is one of the world's finest and longest-lived reds, thanks to old vine stock, infertile soils on steep slopes, and the inspirational conservatism of Paul Draper. Aged almost exclusively in seasoned American oak, with the bottle-age it demands, it can taste like Bordeaux. Ridge also vinifies grapes from ancient Zinfandel vines in Sonoma and Paso Robles at its Lytton Springs winery, near Healdsburg in Sonoma. Within sight of Ridge, Rhys has led a revival of refined, mountain-grown Pinot Noir.

Santa Clara Valley is a wine region almost squeezed out of existence by the digital revolution. Just a little further south, near "the garlic capital of the world", Gilroy, ancient Rhône vines persist. The local wineries can sell everything they make at the cellar door. As a result, few realize how good its wine can be, which makes the grey sprawl all the more of a threat.

Monterey County produces huge quantities of wine, mostly from vineyards on the valley floor that are a monument to 1970s corporate madness. The then large companies (several now defunct) and private investors pursuing tax breaks were encouraged by the University of California at Davis, preoccupied, if not obsessed, with its measure of degree days, to plant in what promised to be a wonderfully cool-climate zone. The Salinas Valley, with its mouth open to the ocean on Monterey Bay, forms a highly efficient funnel for a regular afternoon visitation of cold ocean air. The valley, with its short history of salad and vegetable growing and long history of exploitation (remember Steinbeck?), was enthusiastically turned over to vines in a planting spree that resulted in the current 70,000 acres (28,330ha) of vineyard – far more than Napa Valley's 46,000 planted acres (18,620ha). Unfortunately, the funnel proved all too efficient. On a hot day inland, clammy coastal air comes rushing up the valley with such force that it actually tears off vine shoots. The valley is extremely dry (with irrigation water aplenty from the underground Salinas River) but fiendishly cold. Vines regularly bud two weeks earlier than the California norm and are picked at least two weeks later, giving the Salinas Valley one of the longest growing seasons in the world of wine.

Monster vineyards

These huge vine farms stretch for miles between the bottom of the map opposite and the top of the one overleaf. The most notable is the record 11,000-acre (4,450ha) San Bernabe vineyard of which 5,500 acres (2,200ha) are planted; Scheid and Lockwood are two other monster vineyards. However, the **Santa Lucia Highlands**, on the east-facing slopes of Salinas Valley, has emerged as a grower of admirable Chardonnay and Pinot Noir. Its terraces sit well above the valley floor, with vines planted in low-vigour, well-drained granitic soils. Over-achievers include Morgan, with its Double L vineyard, Pisoni, and Gary Franscioni's ROAR Wines.

The excessively herbaceous wines that initially resulted, particularly Cabernets, sullied the name and reputation of Monterey. Even today, with viticultural practices much improved, a substantial amount of the production of Salinas Valley, now mainly white wine grapes and Pinot Noir, is sold in bulk, to be blended with wine from warmer regions and sold under the basic California appellation. **Arroyo Seco** has an even longer growing season, thanks to its notably low average daytime temperatures. The western section is more sheltered from the winds, and Riesling and Gewurztraminer vines on its pebbly vineyards can produce fine dry to off-dry wines, as well as botrytised wines with crystalline acidity.

There are vines as far south as hot **Hames Valley** near the San Luis Obispo county line (see p.295). Caymus of Napa Valley put its Mer Soleil vineyard here, but this is mainly vine-farming, not winemaking, country. **Chalone** Vineyard, with its own AVA, lies on a sun-scorched 2,000ft (600m) limestone hilltop on the road from Soledad to nowhere – except the Pinnacles National Monument. With varying degrees of success, Chalone has made Chardonnay and Pinot Noir with the conviction that Burgundy's Corton has somehow migrated west. Burgundy, or more precisely limestone, was the inspiration for Josh Jensen's Calera, founded in equally splendid, equally arid isolation to grow Pinot Noir just 20 miles (32km) north in **Mount Harlan**. The soil is right; the rainfall almost ruinously low. Calera's vineyard-designated estate wines are now supplemented by wines made from fruit bought in from Central Coast growers to the south. Since Chalone was acquired by Diageo in 2005 it has leaned heavily on cheaper fruit from Monterey.

The Monte Bello vineyard, originally planted in 1886, is so high on a ridge above the Pacific – up to 2,700ft (820m) – that there are views of both the ocean and Silicon Valley.

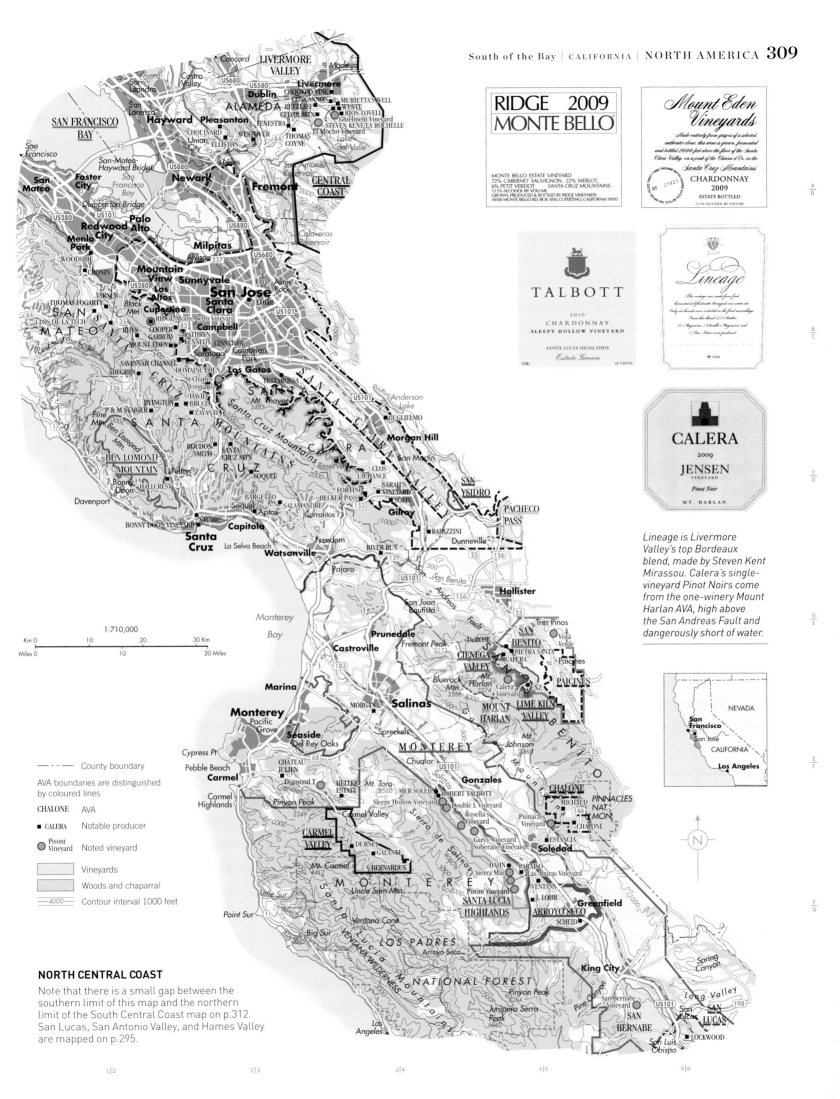

RIDGE 2009
MONTE BELLO

MONTE BELLO ESTATE VINEYARD
72% CABERNET SAUVIGNON, 22% MERLOT,
6% PETIT VERDOT   SANTA CRUZ MOUNTAINS
13.5% ALCOHOL BY VOLUME
GROWN, PRODUCED & BOTTLED BY RIDGE VINEYARDS
18100 MONTE BELLO RD, BOX 1810, CUPERTINO, CALIFORNIA 95015

Mount Eden
Vineyards
Made entirely from grapes of a selected,
authentic clone, this wine is grown, fermented
and bottled 2000 feet above the floor of the Santa
Clara Valley, on a peak of the Chaine d'Or, in the
Santa Cruz Mountains
CHARDONNAY
2009
ESTATE BOTTLED
13.5% ALCOHOL BY VOLUME

TALBOTT
2010
CHARDONNAY
SLEEPY HOLLOW VINEYARD
SANTA LUCIA HIGHLANDS
Estate Grown

Lineage

CALERA
2009
JENSEN
VINEYARD
Pinot Noir
MT. HARLAN

Lineage is Livermore Valley's top Bordeaux blend, made by Steven Kent Mirassou. Calera's single-vineyard Pinot Noirs come from the one-winery Mount Harlan AVA, high above the San Andreas Fault and dangerously short of water.

Km 0   10   20   30 Km
Miles 0   10   20 Miles
1:710,000

- - - - County boundary

AVA boundaries are distinguished by coloured lines

CHALONE   AVA

■ CALERA   Notable producer

● Pisoni   Noted vineyard
  Vineyard

Vineyards

Woods and chaparral

—4000— Contour interval 1000 feet

NORTH CENTRAL COAST

Note that there is a small gap between the southern limit of this map and the northern limit of the South Central Coast map on p.312. San Lucas, San Antonio Valley, and Hames Valley are mapped on p.295.

Sierra Foothills, Lodi, and the Delta

The Central Valley is a vast, flat, extremely fertile, heavily irrigated tract of industrial farmland, one of the planet's most important growers of citrus, orchard fruit, tomatoes, cotton, rice, nuts, and grapes. At its northern end the grapes become more interesting.

The Sacramento Delta has a very different character and style from the rest of the valley. The influence of nearby San Francisco Bay is felt in much cooler nights than are found either south or north of here. **Clarksburg** in the northwest portion of the Delta manages to produce particularly good honeyed Chenin Blanc.

Lodi lies on higher land, on soils washed down from the Sierras, both promising factors. Growers, many with a century-old history, have worked so hard on researching which district is best suited to which variety that no fewer than seven AVAs within Lodi were approved in 2006. Cabernet is good, but old-vine Zinfandel is Lodi's traditional strength.

Being coolish, fragmented, and distinctive, the **Sierra Foothills** AVA is precisely the opposite of the Central Valley. In the foothills of the Sierra, where the Gold Rush gave California its first notoriety, the wine industry that slaked the miners' thirst is quietly and determinedly being revived. In the late 19th century, there were more than 100 wineries in these hills that promised so much. During Prohibition, there was just one, and the vines, many of them Zinfandel, were all but abandoned. But the land was (and is still) of such relatively low value that it was not worth pulling many of the vines out. This is California's treasure chest of ancient Zinfandel stumps.

The wines of **El Dorado** County, its name a hopeful reference to the hills' most desirable natural resource, share a streak of natural acidity – not least because of the altitude of its expanding vineyards, which, at above 2,400ft (730m), are among the highest in California. Rain, and even snow, is commonplace, temperatures are low, and the wines from the thin soils tend to be relatively (mercifully, some think) light.

The vineyards of Amador County are at distinctly warmer, lower elevations of 1,000 to 1,600ft (300–490m) on a plateau where the altitude has little chance to temper the heat. This is especially true of **Shenandoah Valley**, west of Amador's other AVA, **Fiddletown**. About three-quarters of the county's vines are Zinfandel, some of them planted pre-Prohibition. Old or young, dry or rich, almost chewable, Amador Zinfandel tends to taste as rugged as (the experience of) the miners who made this region famous, and is none the worse for that. Syrah also works well here, as does Sangiovese and the occasional Sauvignon Blanc. Calaveras County vineyards to the south have an elevation, and therefore climate, somewhere in between those of El Dorado and Amador, although in some places its soils are more fertile than in either.

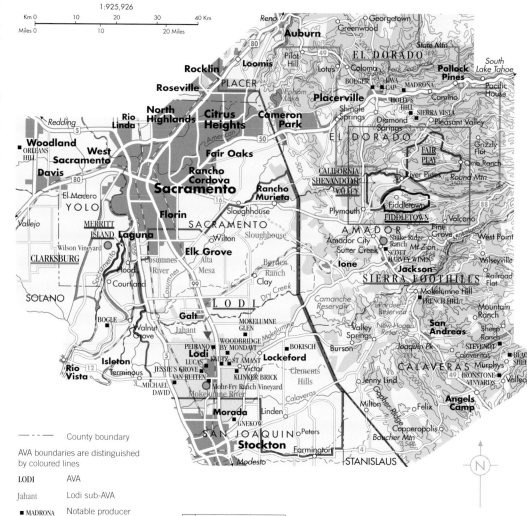

--- - --- County boundary

AVA boundaries are distinguished by coloured lines

LODI AVA

Jahant Lodi sub-AVA

■ MADRONA Notable producer

⬤ Shake Ridge Ranch Noted vineyard

Vineyards

Woods and chaparral

═2000═ Contour interval 500 feet

▼ Weather station (WS)

Area mapped at larger scale

LODI AND THE SIERRA FOOTHILLS

Conditions in Lodi, much flatter and lower, are quite different from those in the Sierra Foothills, but they share some soil deposits and some admirably senior vines. The heartland of the lively, often underestimated Sierra Foothills is mapped in detail below.

LODI: LODI ▼

Latitude / Altitude of WS
38.11° / 39ft (12m)

Average growing season temperature at WS
68.7°F (20.4°C)

Average annual rainfall at WS
19in (483mm)

Harvest month rainfall at WS
September: 0.3in (8mm)

Principal viticultural hazards
Botrytis, powdery mildew

Principal grape varieties
Zinfandel, Chardonnay, Cabernet Sauvignon

Central Coast

In less than 20 years the 100-plus miles of the Central Coast have spawned a clutch of California's most fashionable wine regions. It stretches all the way from the vineyards south of San Francisco Bay (see p.309) to the subtropical climate of greater Los Angeles (whose wine country is discussed on p.318). The two counties in between, San Luis Obispo and Santa Barbara, were transformed by the end of the 20th century from scrub oaks and cattle grazing to an undulating strip of vineyards that continues for tens of miles on end.

This part of California is geologically distinctive: the San Andreas Fault runs down the eastern side of the region; its vineyards are based on quite different, more marine-influenced, carbonate-infused soils, which, according to some authorities, is one of the reasons Central Coast wines have a certain voluptuousness. The climate here is primarily maritime, with mild winters (vines may not always get the chance of a restorative sleep) and summers much cooler than the California norm.

San Luis Obispo County has at least three distinct zones, two of them in the vast **Paso Robles** AVA. The rolling grassland east of Highway 101 is decidedly hot, with no direct access for cooling ocean breezes. Its deep, fertile soils produce supple, fruity, though hardly demanding varietals, some of which go to North Coast wineries and contract bottlers. The big companies Constellation (which includes Mondavi) and Treasury (which includes Beringer), as well as the locally based J Lohr, are major players in the district. Treasury's Meridian winery stands out for its hilltop site, a vantage point that dominates the ever-increasing vineyard landscape to the southeast.

The wooded hill terrain of the western section of Paso Robles on the other side of the highway has much more interesting soil – in some cases calcareous – and is usefully cooled by marine air (if rarely fog). The historic fame of Paso Robles, such as it is, comes largely from potent Zinfandels, many of which are dry-farmed, following Italian immigrant tradition and taste – not unlike Amador Foothill Zinfandel (see p.310). This was the area chosen by the Perrin family of Château de Beaucastel in Châteauneuf-du-Pape to plant a wide range of French clones of Rhône grapes at its Tablas Creek nursery and winery – with considerable success. Paso Robles has earned a reputation for its array of blended reds and blends of Rhône-ish whites (which are valued more highly than single varietals such as Syrah and Viognier).

No one could accuse the Santa Maria Valley of being overpopulated – not by people, anyway. Cambria's Chardonnay vineyard on rolling benchland dates from the early 1970s. Once called Tepusquet, it is now Katherine's Vineyard.

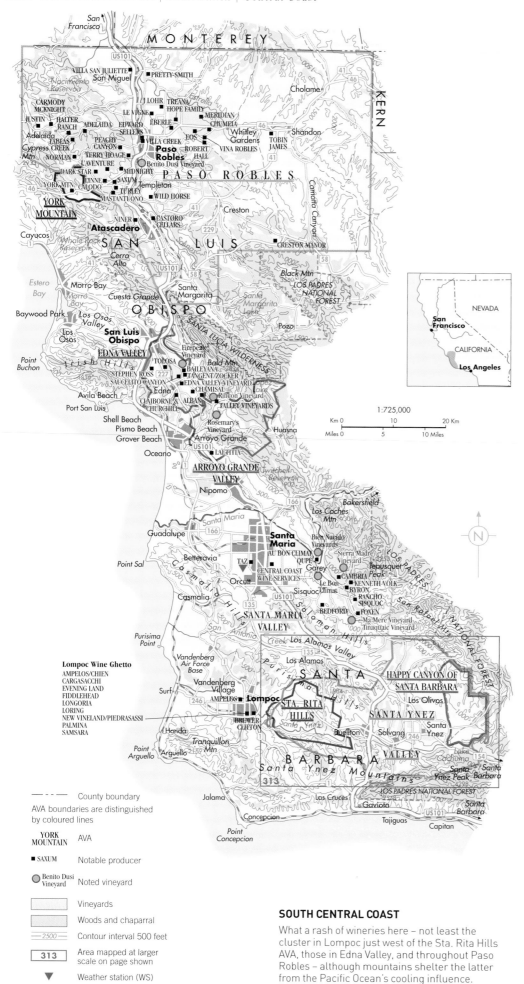

Edna Valley, over the Cuesta Pass to the south, is different again. Sea air swirls in from Morro Bay, making the valley as cool as any California wine region. It somehow manages to produce some quite luscious Chardonnays, albeit with a fine streak of lime to keep them lively. Alban, one of the Central Coast's most proficient exponents of red and white Rhône varieties, is a leader here, and manages, despite the sea air, to coax Syrah to ripeness levels unimaginable in the Rhône Valley.

To the immediate southeast, the more varied but generally even cooler **Arroyo Grande Valley** is gaining a name for fine Chardonnay and Pinot Noir from such producers as Talley and Laetitia.

Santa Barbara's Côte d'Or

Moving south again across the county line into Santa Barbara, the **Santa Maria Valley** is southern California's riposte to the Côte d'Or, providing conditions that are, if anything, cooler still. Its river runs out to sea in flat land that offers no opposition at all to the Pacific air. Some of its vineyard land is so low-lying that ocean fog moves in at midday and overabundant fruit can easily be underripe and over-acidic. This countryside is far from the stereotype of southern California – and indeed, from balmy, palmy Santa Barbara itself. Santa Barbara lies in the lee of the crucial mountains that run off the southeast corner of the map shown here, shielding it from the cold ocean fogs that invade the Santa Maria and Santa Ynez valleys.

What is common to all of Santa Barbara County, however, in contrast to Sonoma's Pinot country, is remarkably low rainfall (as the key facts panel shows). This means that there is no hurry to harvest before autumn rains. Santa Barbara's grapes, like those grown further north in Monterey and San Luis Obispo, benefit from an extremely long growing season, building flavour over months and months.

Most of the thousands of acres of grapes in Santa Maria Valley are owned by farmers rather than wineries, making vineyard names unusually prominent. Bien Nacido, for one, crops up on a range of different winery labels, while many of the region's wineries also buy grapes up and down the Central Coast. Cambria (part of the

---

Legend:

— · — County boundary

AVA boundaries are distinguished by coloured lines

YORK MOUNTAIN — AVA

■ SAXUM — Notable producer

◉ Benito Dusi Vineyard — Noted vineyard

▢ Vineyards

▢ Woods and chaparral

—2500— Contour interval 500 feet

▢ 313 — Area mapped at larger scale on page shown

▼ Weather station (WS)

SOUTH CENTRAL COAST

What a rash of wineries here – not least the cluster in Lompoc just west of the Sta. Rita Hills AVA, those in Edna Valley, and throughout Paso Robles – although mountains shelter the latter from the Pacific Ocean's cooling influence.

CENTRAL COAST: SANTA MARIA ▼

Latitude / Altitude of WS
34.55° / 253ft (77m)

Average growing season temperature at WS
60.7°F (16.0°C)

Average annual rainfall at WS
14in (354mm)

Harvest month rainfall at WS
September: 0.1in (4mm)

Principal viticultural hazards
Late ripening

Principal grape varieties
Chardonnay, Pinot Noir

Kendall-Jackson empire) is notably warmer than Bien Nacido because it is further from coastal influence. Rancho Sisquoc is the most sheltered, except for the positively secluded Foxen, which occupies its own canyon. The best grapes, Pinot Noir and Chardonnay in the main but Syrah, too, are grown on slopes high enough – 600ft-plus (180m) – above the valley floor to be on the fringe of the fog belt. Their naturally high acidity is offset by a fruity intensity which has something in common with the best of New Zealand. Much the most exciting winery in Santa Maria, informed by the sort of frenetic experimentation matched only by Bonny Doon in Santa Cruz, is Au Bon Climat and its partner in the same modest premises, Qupé. Heavily influenced by Burgundy, Jim Clendenen of Au Bon Climat has for three decades made a wide range of different styles of Chardonnay and Pinot Noir, but also Pinot Blanc, Pinot Gris, Viognier, Barbera, and Nebbiolo.

Just south of Santa Maria, in similarly cool, intensely rural conditions, is the (unofficial) Los Alamos region, where several thousand acres of vineyards produce lively Chardonnay. Conditions are a bit warmer and more stable over the Solomon Hills, particularly (as in Paso Robles) east of Highway 101. The **Santa Ynez Valley**, within easy reach of wine tourists and property developers from Los Angeles, has no obvious physical feature, but a sprawl of vineyards in rolling, oak-dotted hills around and to the north of Solvang, a town as peculiarly Danish as its name. East of the highway there are well-favoured sites with warm days and cold nights that can yield impressive red wines, both Syrah and the Bordeaux varieties, as well as such noted successes as Beckmen's Sauvignon Blanc and the Roussanne-Grenache Blanc blends of Andrew Murray.

Things get even better in the much cooler Santa Rita Hills appellation (officially **Sta. Rita Hills** AVA in deference to the powerful Chilean producer Santa Rita), a series of hills, some quite steep, in the far west of the Santa Ynez Valley between Lompoc and Buellton, where a bend in the Santa Ynez River marks the end of intense ocean influence. Soils are a patchwork of sand, silt, and clay. Pinot Noir, with Chardonnay as support, is the principal grape variety here and can be almost Burgundian. The AVA boundaries were established with Pinot Noir in mind, but the Babcock winery showed that the high acidities that are common here suit Sauvignon Blanc, Riesling, and Gewurztraminer, too. Kathy Joseph is another to do well with Pinot Noir under the name Fiddlehead, and Sauvignon Blanc from the relatively new **Happy Canyon of Santa Barbara** AVA in the east of the Santa Ynez Valley.

It was the Sanford & Benedict vineyard that first drew attention to the Santa Rita Hills. It lies in a sheltered north-facing niche that suits Pinot Noir perfectly. The Richard Sanford who lent it his name, a screwcap pioneer, now grows the Burgundian varieties organically at Alma Rosa nearby. Sea Smoke Cellars is the current darling of the critics.

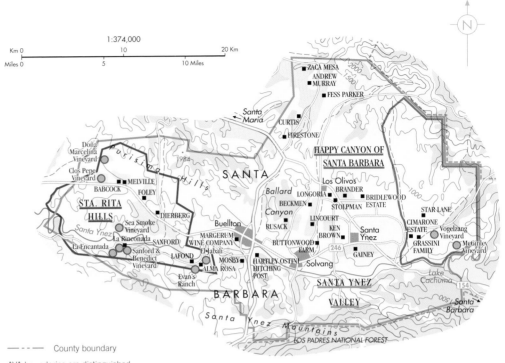

1:374,000

— - — - — County boundary

AVA boundaries are distinguished by coloured lines

STA. RITA HILLS   AVA

■ RUSACK   Notable producer

◉ Clos Pepe Vineyard   Noted vineyard

   Vineyards

   Woods and chaparral

— 2500 —   Contour interval 500 feet

NORTHWEST OF SANTA BARBARA

The potential of Sta. Rita Hills was clear in the early 1970s when the Sanford & Benedict Vineyard produced its first wines, even though the AVA was created as recently as 2001. And who could resist the 2009 AVA Happy Canyon of Santa Barbara?

Bob Lindquist of Qupé was making Rhône-ish wines in the 1980s and was instrumental in coining the term "Rhône Ranger" for those Californians looking for a change from the hegemony of Cabernet and Chardonnay. The Central Coast is now home to a refreshingly wide range of grape varieties.

Virginia

Between the Appalachians and Chesapeake Bay, its white-fenced grasslands in the lee of the Blue Ridge Mountains devoted to blue-blooded horses and dotted with pre-Civil War settlements of some of America's oldest stone houses, the sleepy southern state of Virginia seems a world away from the politics of Washington DC. Yet the northernmost vineyards of the Commonwealth state are well under an hour's drive from Capitol Hill. So it is not such a surprise that the most recent state governor determined to encourage a nascent wine industry. The hope is that it will sustain Virginia's rural attractions and provide an already steady influx of tourists with some additional stimulation.

Wine has been playing a more important part in the official vision of this US state than in any other. It had an unpromising start, as Thomas Jefferson found to his cost at Monticello, the spiritual home of the Virginia wine industry.

Jefferson was not only a connoisseur. He believed that "wine is, ... in truth, the only antidote to the bane of whiskey", introducing wine as a moral crusade. What no-one knew – that European vines need American rootstocks to protect them from the predations of the phylloxera louse – is now well known. And even today, vinifera vines in Virginia have to battle the climate: a relatively short growing season and a hot and humid summer, with few cool nights before September. Winters can be so cold in this continental climate that the soils take their time to warm up, and buds are rarely seen before late April, even in this era of climate change. Only quite recently have growers felt confident of vinifera vines surviving the harsh winters. In 1980, there were only five wineries in the state and they were growing mainly hybrid grapes. By 2012, there were closer to 200 and more than 80% of grapes were vinifera varieties.

Cabernet Sauvignon may not ripen until late September, when nights are cooler and days generally drier, but picking of early-ripening varieties usually begins in late August, when torrential summer downpours are by no means uncommon. Hurricanes and tropical storms are far from rare. Because many of the soils have a high clay content, ambitious growers have been seeking out slopes that drain quickly after summer downpours. The first wave of Virginia wines could be criticized for a lack of concentration, but more and more of them today have convincing grunt.

Most Virginia vineyards are in a belt about 30 miles (50km) east of the beautiful Blue Ridge Mountains, although the much less accessible **Shenandoah Valley** west of the mountains may well have more potential in the long run.

Since most Virginia wineries are small, many of them semi-hobbies, and tightly regulated, the great majority of them depend heavily on direct sales to passing tourists. Some are apparently driven more by attracting passers-by than by

---

Monticello, President Thomas Jefferson's model farm where the first known vinifera vines, imported from Europe, were planted – only to succumb to the American pests and diseases for which they are prey.

the quality of what they pour. With only about 3,200 acres (1,300ha) of vineyard, Virginia produces just a small proportion of all the wine drunk in the state, but the number of producers genuinely driven by a desire to make fine wine is growing fast.

Virginia's signature grape

Barboursville, owned by Zonin of Italy, is the granddaddy of them all, with the first vines having been planted in the late 1970s. As one might expect, it has persevered (successfully) with such grape varieties as Nebbiolo and Vermentino as well as the more usual range of varieties grown in Virginia. One of their most notable wines is a dense, sweet, lip-smacking "Malvaxia" Passito.

The four most planted varieties (see key facts panel) are unexceptional choices for modern American vine-growers. Cabernet Franc has shown the most affinity for the vineyards of northern and central Virginia – generally blended with various proportions of other Bordeaux grapes.

Less predictably, and led by innovator Dennis Horton, who established Horton Vineyards in the 1980s, Virginia's growers decided some years ago that Viognier would be their signature grape. While styles vary considerably from light and floral to heavy and sweetish, it seems to be a sensible choice, both from a marketing and viticultural point of view. Viognier's thick skins and loose bunches withstand humid summers better than most varieties. Petit Verdot and Petit Manseng are more recent Virginia specialities, the latter with particular success. But Horton also pioneered the all-American Norton grape that can make seriously appealing fruity red wine with no hint of the foxiness that puts so many noses off other American grapes. The Norton torch is now carried with particular enthusiasm by Jennifer McCloud at Chrysalis.

AVAs on the increase

Virginia already has seven AVAs, three of which, in northern and central Virginia, are mapped here. The most recent is **Middleburg Virginia**, which was steered through the approval process by Boxwood, one of the more sophisticated

operations, in 2012. Both Donald Trump and Jean and Steve Case of AOL acquired wineries in central Virginia in 2011. Will they drink their own wine?

Notable wineries outside our map include the substantial (60,000 cases filled a year) Château Morrisette in the **Rocky Knob** AVA of the Blue Ridge Region, which was established in the 1980s; Chatham, which makes a good Petit Verdot from a 17th-century farm on a spit of land between Chesapeake Bay and the Atlantic; and Rosemont in the warm far south of the state, which surprised everyone by winning a gold medal in the Virginia Governor's Cup competition at the first attempt with its Kilravock red Bordeaux blend.

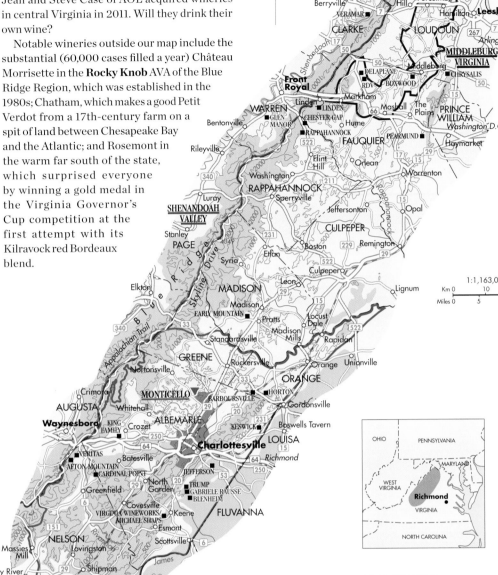

Arguably the most obvious omission here is Viognier, which has been adopted as Virginia's white wine grape speciality. Petit Manseng is waiting in the wings. But the labels shown here belong to wines that are world-class by any measure.

— · — State boundary

— · · — County boundary

AVA boundaries are distinguished by coloured lines

MONTICELLO AVA

■ CHRYSALIS Notable producer

▨ Woods

═2000═ Contour interval 1000 feet

▼ Weather station (WS)

NORTHERN AND CENTRAL VIRGINIA

This is only a portion of Virginia wine country but it is the most vibrant and shows the axis of the land, in the lee of the Blue Ridge Mountains. Monticello and Middleburg Virginia are the two most important of Virginia's seven AVAs.

VIRGINIA: CHARLOTTESVILLE ▼

Latitude / Altitude of WS
38.13° / 623ft (190m)

Average growing season temperature at WS
66.1°F (18.9°C)

Average annual rainfall at WS
42.7in (1,085mm)

Harvest month rainfall at WS
September: 4.5in (114mm)

Principal viticultural hazards
High summer rainfall

Principal grape varieties
Chardonnay, Merlot, Cabernet Franc, Cabernet Sauvignon, Viognier, Petit Verdot, Norton

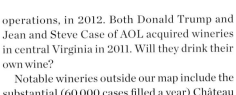

New York

New Yorkers tend to pride themselves on drinking the wines of the world, but their own state makes more wine than any other in the USA – other than California, which makes more than 12 times as much. Admittedly 20,000 (8,100ha) of its 34,000 acres (12,550ha) of vineyard are planted with American vines, typically *Vitis labrusca* producing grapes for grape juice and jelly. Most widely planted is the Concord grape, whose high-toned aroma, not unlike that of wild strawberries, is described as "foxy" and tends to disconcert traditional wine drinkers.

Juice and jelly are the raison d'être of the important grape belt along the south shore of **Lake Erie**, and fewer than 20 of the state's 320 wineries are to be found here. Climate change has provided growers with the confidence to try out some European vinifera plantings, but most of the wine made in the grape belt has so far been based on the sort of French hybrids described on p.282.

Like Ontario across the border, the rest of New York State is busy reinventing itself as a serious wine producer, however, and almost all of the state's new plantings are of vinifera. The majority of New York wineries are less than 20 years old, all of them small but ambitious operations, sprouting most noticeably in the Finger Lakes (about 100 wineries), Long Island (more than 50), and the Hudson River Region (more than 30).

Long Island, air-conditioned and occasionally battered by the Atlantic, is New York's youngest wine region and the state's answer to Bordeaux, both in terms of its maritime climate and the amiable and refreshing build of its wines. The ocean influence blurs the seasons and maintains the mild weather for so long that the growing season here is much longer than inland. The well-drained glacial soils have encouraged well-balanced vines and slow, steady ripening. Very creditable whites and sparkling wines have been making their appearance and we can expect more.

Long Island now has 3,000 acres (1,215ha) of vines, all vinifera (mainly Chardonnay, Merlot, and the Cabernets). The island has three AVAs: the original, most obviously agricultural, and quantitatively most significant North Fork; the cooler (and smaller) Hamptons or South Fork; and the over-arching Long Island. Being within easy reach of the financial ebb and flow of Manhattan means that Long Island wineries are a little better represented on lists and shelves there than their upstate counterparts, but the ebb in particular has also tended to generate regular changes of ownership.

The lake effect

Vines have been grown commercially in upper New York State around the **Finger Lakes** – deep glacial trenches carved by glaciers retreating from the great inland sea of Lake Ontario – since the 1850s. Indeed, the bucolic landscape, with its heavily wooded, low hills and boat-studded lakes, still looks remarkably like the Victorian playground it became once the colonizers managed to wrest this pretty region from the native Iroquois.

The lakes Ontario and particularly the "fingers" of Seneca, Cayuga, and Keuka – are crucial in moderating the climate, softening the sometimes fatal harshness of winter and storing the summer warmth. But the climate here is still extreme. In many parts of the region fewer than 200 days are frost-free. Winters are long, with temperatures down to -4°F (-20°C). As recently as 2003 many vines simply froze to death. Such harsh winters meant that American vines were the obvious choice initially, and even today vinifera varieties represent only about 15% of those grown on the region's 9,120 acres (3,700ha). French hybrids such as Seyval Blanc and Vignoles were introduced in the 1950s and, like the American labrusca varieties, produced sweet, rather bland wines aimed at tourists. Increasing efforts are being made to produce respectable, often dry wines from these hybrids. But the future of the region surely lies with European vinifera vines.

It was as long ago as the 1960s that Dr Konstantin Frank, a viticulturist from Ukraine and no stranger to cold winters, proved that relatively early-ripening vinifera vines such as Riesling and Chardonnay could thrive in the Finger Lakes, provided they were grafted onto the right rootstocks. Today, the Finger Lakes are slowly carving out a reputation for particularly fine, almost Saar-like dry, age-worthy Rieslings made by established producers such as Red Newt, Standing Stone, Hermann J Wiemer, and Dr Frank's Vinifera Wine Cellars. More recently they have been joined by producers with experience elsewhere, such as Heart & Hands and Ravines, which believe that there is potential for the Finger Lakes to establish themselves as an American Riesling counterpart to South Australia's Clare and Eden valleys.

Riesling, with its hard wood, can withstand low temperatures well and has proved a much better fit here than Chardonnay. Some red wines are produced, with early-ripening Pinot Noir so far the best bet in general, although some very fine Cabernet Franc is made in the most benign years.

LONG ISLAND

The map shows clearly how much more important the North Fork is for viticulture and winemaking. Land is much cheaper on the North Fork – no Hamptons here – and it is also more sheltered from Atlantic batterings.

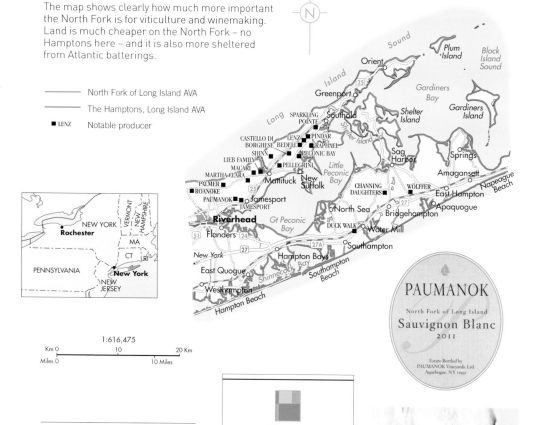

— North Fork of Long Island AVA

— The Hamptons, Long Island AVA

■ LENZ Notable producer

The maritime climate suits Bordeaux varieties in particular (the Sauvignon is superb), although Long Island, like virtually all American wine regions, has been tempted to try Chardonnay.

THE FINGER LAKES

The Cayuga Lake AVA is the region's oldest sub-AVA, having been established in 1988. Seneca Lake was awarded its AVA in 2003, and Keuka Lake will surely follow. This is prime vacation and touring country, so many wineries have depended on cellar-door sales of sweetish wines based on the productive hybrids and American vines that still proliferate.

County boundary

AVA boundaries are distinguished by coloured lines

FINGER LAKES AVA

■ RED NEWT Notable producer

Vineyards

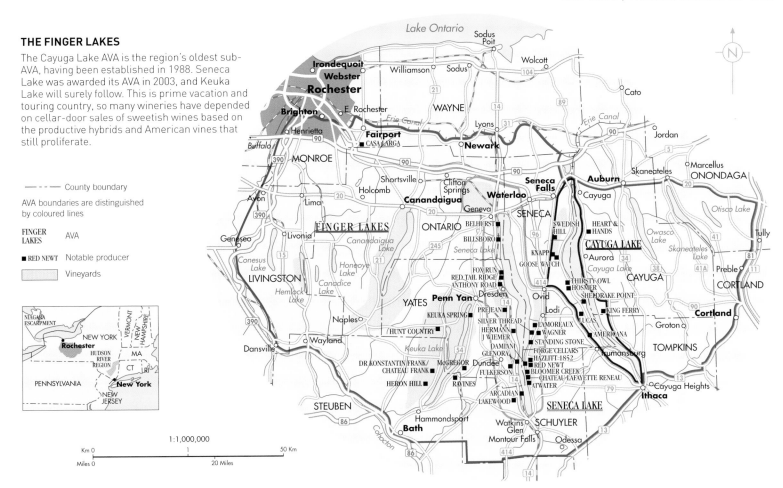

This satellite picture shows clearly the "lake effect" on both temperature and precipitation, whereby the lake shores are considerably less icy than the land between the Finger Lakes.

The research station at Geneva, the "fingertip" of Cayuga Lake, is known internationally for its work on vine-training and winter-hardy varieties, and the Finger Lakes wine region remains the commercial hub of the New York industry, not least thanks to the presence, since 1945, of the original headquarters of what is now the world's second-largest wine company, Constellation Brands.

The **Hudson River Region**, where New York's first recorded commercial vintage took place in 1839 at what is now the Brotherhood winery, is also an area of small wineries. Vinifera vines can be vulnerable here in a climate moderated only by the Hudson River, and until recently most of the planted 430 acres (175ha) were French hybrids. Operations such as Millbrook, however, have demonstrated that vinifera varieties such as Chardonnay, Cabernet Franc, and even Friulano can thrive in this pretty upstate region, too, while Clinton Vineyards has proved that diversification into other fruit wines can also pay.

Icewine made from the French hybrid Vidal is the most characteristic, and garlanded, produce of the eight wineries based in the **Niagara Escarpment** AVA, just over the border from Ontario's principal wine region (see p.285).

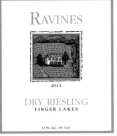

Finger Lakes is indubitably dry Riesling country and one of the most sought-after is Tierce, a joint production of three of the most admired producers: Fox Run, Anthony Road, and Red Newt.

Southwest States

Since 1650, and more than 100 years before the Mission grape reached California, its juice was being fermented for the needs of Spanish friars in Arizona, New Mexico, and near El Paso in Texas. Texas has a special place in the history of the vine, if not of wine. It is the botanical heart of America – and can boast more indigenous grapevine species than any other region on earth. Of 36 species of the genus *Vitis* scattered around the world, no fewer than 15 are Texas natives – a fact that was turned to important use during the phylloxera epidemic. Thomas V Munson of Denison, Texas, made hundreds of hybrids between *Vitis vinifera* and indigenous vines in his eventually successful search for immune rootstock. It was a Texan who saved not only France's but the whole world's wine industry.

That of Texas itself was killed by Prohibition. In 1920 the state had a score of wineries. Revival after repeal was slow and painful; 22 of the state's 254 counties are still "dry" today (although wine may now be made there if 75% is Texas-grown). In the early 1970s a new start was made with experimental plantings of vinifera and hybrid vines in the High Plains region at nearly 4,000ft (1,200m) near Lubbock, at what would become Llano Estacado and Pheasant Ridge wineries. They chose well. Despite the infinite exposure and dismal flatness of the region, its soil is deep, calcareous, and fertile, its sunshine brilliant, its nights cool (and its winters very cold). Abundant water from the Ogallala Aquifer feeds drip irrigation and helps offset extreme weather such as frost, hail, and high temperatures. Constant wind keeps disease at bay and helps cool the vineyards at night. Llano Estacado is now Texas's second-largest winery, making competent, bright-flavoured reds that have something in common with Washington State's best. Nearby CapRock has scored success with Roussanne.

Texas's biggest wine enterprise by far is 200 miles (320km) south near Fort Stockton, where the land-rich University of Texas planted an experimental vineyard in the late 1970s. The 1,000-acre (400ha) vineyard is now leased by a Texas company, Mesa Vineyards. Its inexpensive Ste. Genevieve varietals constitute more than half of all wine produced in the state. Peregrine Hill is its more ambitious label.

More promising for quality are the wineries in the Hill Country west of Austin in the heart of Texas, which has staked out three AVAs: Texas Hill Country, and Fredericksburg and Bell Mountain within it. These three AVAs include a staggering million acres (405,000ha), of which only about 500 (200ha) are planted, with a fluctuating roster of about 40 wineries operating there.

Although Pierce's Disease and humidity plague various parts of the state, Texas shows every symptom of wine-mania and now boasts more than 200 wineries. Many of them are clustered round the cities, processing grapes trucked from distant vineyards, and often wine produced even further away. It is the Rockies that allow **New Mexico** to even think of growing wine: elevation cools the climate down to the point where, in the north of the state, only French hybrid vines will survive. The Rio Grande Valley provides almost the only agricultural land, falling from over 7,000ft (2,000m) at Santa Fe to 4,500ft (1,300m) at Truth or Consequences. Insofar as New Mexico has any national reputation for wine, it is surprisingly (but quite justifiably) for the fine sparkling wine made by the Gruet winery.

Southeast **Arizona**, with the state's one AVA, Sonoita, shares much of the character of southern New Mexico, although the Sulphur Springs Valley/Willcox area about 50 miles (80km) east of Tucson is even warmer. The Callaghan winery in Sonoita has had some success with Cabernet and Merlot. A wine industry has also emerged near Sedona in central Arizona, with Caduceus and Page Spring Cellars the most promising producers.

To the north, wineries have been sprouting in **Colorado**, most of them in the shelter of the Grand Valley AVA on both sides of the Colorado River near Grand Junction at an elevation of 4,000ft (1,200m). Winter freeze and phylloxera threaten the mainly vinifera vines here, of which Chardonnay, Merlot, and Riesling are most common, although Viognier, Sangiovese, and Syrah are gaining ground.

Meanwhile, in **southern California** the vine is under greater threat than ever before from Pierce's Disease, although most remaining growers have upgraded clones and vineyard design to combat it. The most significant AVA, Temecula Valley, rises in bumps and hillocks to elevations of up to 1,500ft (450m), a mere 20-odd miles (32km) from the ocean and linked to it by the vital corridor known as Rainbow Gap. Every afternoon, ocean breezes cool this essentially subtropical area to temperatures no hotter than the upper Napa Valley. The cool nights help, too.

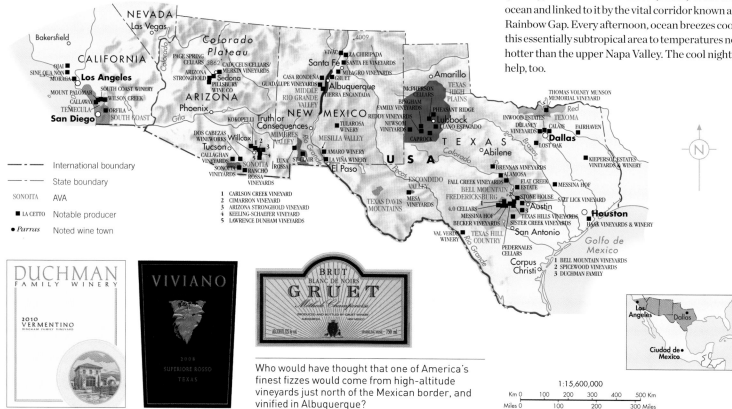

Who would have thought that one of America's finest fizzes would come from high-altitude vineyards just north of the Mexican border, and vinified in Albuquerque?

International boundary
State boundary
SONOITA AVA
■ LA CETTO Notable producer
● *Parras* Noted wine town

1 CARLSON CREEK VINEYARD
2 CIMARRON VINEYARD
3 ARIZONA STRONGHOLD VINEYARD
4 KEELING-SCHAEFER VINEYARD
5 LAWRENCE DUNHAM VINEYARDS

1 BELL MOUNTAIN VINEYARDS
2 SPICEWOOD VINEYARDS
3 DUCHMAN FAMILY

1:15,600,000

Mexico

Mexico has the oldest wine industry of the New World, founded in the 1530s when Governor Hernando Cortés decreed that all farmers plant 10 grapevines a year for every Indian slave on their estate, but it joined the modern wine era only very recently. In 1699, the king of Spain banned new vineyards in Mexico to protect the Spanish wine industry, thus setting back the development of a wine culture in Mexico for three centuries.

Veracruz, where the first vines were planted, proved too tropical for long-term viticulture, just as many of the higher-altitude sites assayed later were too wet to produce healthy grapes. In Parras Valley to the south, however, there were indigenous vines in abundance, and here Casa Madero, built in 1597, can claim to be the oldest winery of the Americas, while making thoroughly modern, Rhône-like reds and fresh white wines today. But it is an exception. Barely 10% of Mexico's 100,000 acres (40,000ha) of vines are dedicated to table wine; the great majority produces table grapes, raisins, and, especially, brandy.

In the 18th century, Basque immigrants brought grapes such as Grenache, Carignan, and Pedro Ximénez to Parras, and these, and other vinifera varieties, subsequently found their way to the northern end of the long finger of land, cooled by the Pacific, known as Baja California. Today it is responsible for a good 90% of all Mexican wine, produced from about 40 wineries. Although the first modern winery in Baja California was Santo Tomás, established in 1888, the pioneer of modern Mexican table wine was LA Cetto, begun by Italian immigrants in 1926. LA Cetto now owns 2,500 acres (1,000ha) of vineyards in the Guadalupe Valley, and notably imported Nebbiolo from the family's native Piemonte.

The **Guadalupe Valley**, just 60 miles (100km) south of the troubled border town of Tijuana, is the home of many of Mexico's new wave of ambitious vintners. Water is in very short supply so the wines from well-established vines, rarely troubled by pests and diseases, are remarkably intense. The vineyards are regularly cooled at night by Pacific fog and breezes blowing through Baja's east–west valleys, San Antonio de las Minas, Santo Tomás, and San Vicente, going south from Guadalupe. Relatively sandy soils help to keep phylloxera at bay on the valley floors, where low-vigour varieties such as Cabernet Sauvignon thrive.

LA Cetto was for many years a supplier to Pedro Domecq, Mexico's dominant brandy producer and once the country's second-biggest wine producer after Cetto. An important new direction was taken in 2005, when a consortium led by renowned winemaker Hugo D'Acosta acquired more than 450 acres (180ha), including 200 acres (80ha) of mature vines that once

supplied Domecq, becoming the second-largest vineyard owner in Mexico. Called Paralelo, the super-ecological operation's aim is to spread the wine gospel locally and to make quintessentially Mexican wines rather than copies of those made over the border in California. Mexico's fledgling wine producers are presumably particularly encouraged by the terroir-driven wines of Paralelo, the intense reds of Casa de Piedra (Hugo D'Acosta's first venture), Italian varietals

from Villa Montefiori, and particularly plush wines from Adobe Guadalupe.

In Querétaro province north of Mexico City, at altitudes of up to 6,500ft (2,000m), and in Zacatecas province to the immediate north, days are hot while nights are cool, but wines can suffer from heavy rains at vintage time. Oaked reds are the best so far in these provinces, but producers such as Freixenet are also making decent sparkling wine.

GUADALUPE VALLEY

The narrowness of the valley's opening to the ocean, chilled by the Humboldt Current, is important because it helps to funnel the cold air uphill – a bit like California's Edna Valley. Rainfall is wildly variable here and most vines are planted at 650–1,650ft (200–500m) although some producers are experimenting with even higher plantings.

1:225,000

Km 0   5   10 Km
Miles 0   5 Miles

- PARALELO   Notable producer
- El Porvenir   Wine centre
-    Vineyards
- —500—   Contour interval 100 metres

The Guadalupe norm is old vines and new wineries. Many of the winery labels are designed by Hugo D'Acosta's architect brother. Swiss oceanographer Antonio Badan's Bordeaux blend is widely admired.

KERUBIEL
ADOBE GUADALUPE
2008

Mogor-Badan
2008
PRODUCE OF MEXICO
750 ml. 13.5% Alc. Vol.

SOUTH AMERICA

Viña Tarapacá's hillside vineyard in the Maipo Valley, Chile

South America

Considering that South America possesses more vines and makes more wine than any continent except Europe, its entry into international trade is remarkably recent. Yet its settlers came in the main from countries with strong wine cultures – Spain, Portugal, and Italy – to lands where the vine is a perfect fit. They made large quantities of wine, but rarely up to international standards. This began to change in the last quarter of the 20th century. In the 2010s they are drawing level with the leaders.

Chile was first to export significant quantities. Argentina makes more wine. Brazil is the sleeper, third in quantity but only now showing its hand.

Brazil

If Brazil, until now, has made wine of local interest only it is because of where it was made: near centres of population, in areas of high humidity with fertile soils, by small farmers with rudimentary skills. Light, sweetish, often fizzy wine in the old Italian style was the norm.

The greatest spur to produce better quality came in the early 1990s, when Brazil opened its market to imported wines. It was immediately obvious, even to less discerning consumers, that many, though not all, the imports were of higher quality and better value. Producers have been investing in new vineyard areas and wineries and have shipped in respected foreign oenologists.

Traditionally, vine-growing was in the hands of thousands of small-scale farmers, mainly

Grapes are harvested for Bodegas Milcast's Vino Aranjuez in the brilliant sunlight of Tarija in the far south of Bolivia at around 6,500ft (2,000m) above sea level.

in the humid and mountainous Serra Gaúcha region in the state of Rio Grande do Sul, where rainfall is exceptionally and inconveniently high, with an average total of almost 69in (1,750mm) throughout the year, and soils tend to drain poorly. For this reason, hybrids, particularly Isabel (known as Isabella elsewhere), have been the common choice for their resistance to rot and mildew, and still comprise about 85% of all Brazil's grapevines. Yields here are generally too high to result in wine of exportable quality, and the grapes struggle to ripen fully. The Vale dos Vinhedos – "vineyard valley" – subregion does best and has been rewarded with its own DO for Merlot and Chardonnay, which usually ripen early enough to be harvested before the rains arrive at the end of March.

But the most important producers have been moving south, developing the Campanha (also known as Fronteira) region on the Uruguayan border and neighbouring Serra do Sudeste with their drier climate, longer days, and less fertile granite and limestone soils. This is currently the focus of fine wine development in Brazil, with particular attention now being paid to matching vine variety and soil type. The usual international varieties have proliferated, but some Portuguese grapes are also showing form. The cool, high plateau of Planalto Catarinense in the state of Santa Catarina, immediately north of Rio Grande do Sul, lies at elevations of 2,950–4,600ft (900–1,400m) above sea level. Its basalt-based soils have already demonstrated some potential for varieties such as Sauvignon Blanc and Pinot Noir.

The most dramatic of Brazil's new wine regions, however, is along the border of the states of Bahia and Pernambuco in the hot, dry Vale do

São Francisco in the northeast of the country, less than 10 degrees south of the equator. With at least two harvests a year using the full battery of tropical viticulture techniques, it has delivered reliable volumes of Cabernet, Shiraz, and Moscatel. Can wines of real interest be made under these conditions? It remains to be seen.

Uruguay

Unlike Brazilians, the people of Uruguay are some of South America's most dedicated wine drinkers (second only to the Argentines), making the country's unusual wine industry the continent's fourth largest. The modern era began in 1870 with Basque immigration and the import of superior European grape varieties such as Tannat, here called Harriague after its original promulgator. In a direct parallel to Malbec's softening transformation under the sunny skies of Argentina, the Tannat produced in Uruguay is much plumper and more velvety than in its homeland in southwest France, and can often be drunk when only a year or two old – most unlike the prototype Madiran.

Not that Uruguay's climate and topography have much in common with those of Argentina's wine regions. It is sunny but much wetter (making organic viticulture difficult), and nights in the southern, most important wine districts of Uruguay are cooled by the influence not of altitude – most of the country undulates only very gently – but by Antarctic currents in the south Atlantic. Evenings are often breezy and cool, ripening slow and gradual. Except in years when the autumn rains arrive early, acidity levels are attractively refreshing. This freshness of aromas and flavours is one of the welcome distinctions of well-balanced Uruguayan wines of all hues.

About 90% of Uruguay's wine is grown in the maritime climate of the southern coastal departments of Canelones, San José (in both of which there has been some French investment), Florida, and Montevideo, whose low hills offer a wide variety of different terroirs on generally loamy soils. Promising new plantings around the popular resort of Punta del Este are heavily influenced by the Atlantic. Garzón, in Maldonado, is one of the most ambitious new producers and is trialling a wide range of varieties on several hundred hectares.

In the developing Colonia department in the far southwest of the country, across the Río de la Plata estuary from Buenos Aires, the alluvial soils can be so fertile that vines are too vigorous to ripen grapes fully. International consultants have been hired to address this problem. A significant proportion of Uruguayan vineyards use the lyre trellis system to let the grapes see the sun, but maintaining the health and openness of such canopies in such a damp climate is time- and labour-consuming.

The original Harriague vines succumbed to viral disease and virtually all have been replaced by vines imported from France, called Tannat to distinguish them. However, Gabriel Pisano, a member of the

SOUTH AMERICA'S WINE REGIONS

Argentina makes far more wine than any other South American country, but Chile is catching up fast, and there are now serious wine industries in Uruguay, Brazil, Peru, and Bolivia.

youngest generation of this winemaking family, has developed a liqueur Tannat of rare intensity from surviving old-vine Harriague. There is also Viognier, Trebbiano, Torrontés, particularly promising Petit Verdot, and even Zinfandel – as well as the usual international suspects, including Chardonnay, Sauvignon Blanc, Cabernet, Syrah, and Merlot, which makes a juicy blending partner with the dominant Tannat.

In the Rivera department in the far northeast is a relatively new area that is viticulturally indistinguishable from Brazil's promising Campanha/Fronteira. The vine has also invaded sugar plantation country in the northwest and the centre of the country, where poor soils and good diurnal temperature variation may yield interesting results. In the hotter, drier, and less maritime climate of the department of Salto, where Harriague was first planted, H Stagniari produces a rich, rounded style of Tannat.

Wine companies of all sizes, not just the big Traversa, and a host of new, much smaller outfits, are now focusing on quality with an eye to the export market.

Bolivia, Venezuela, and Peru

Bolivia has been growing grapes since the 16th century, mainly for its domestic spirit, singani, and for eating. But recently, international wine varieties have been introduced to some of the world's highest vineyards, although they, too, can be plagued by summer rains. Wine production is concentrated in Tarija, high in the Andes in the south of the country, at altitudes of between 5,580 and 7,875ft (1,700–2,400m), although there are some plantings on the flatlands south of the city of Santa Cruz.

Venezuela deserves a marginal mention for at least one winery growing its own grapes. In Peru, on the other hand, Emile Peynaud, the Bordeaux professor, pioneered modern thinking about wine. The Tacama vineyards in Ica province benefit both from his advice and from the influence of the cold Pacific in much the same way as those of California's Central Coast, but there may be more potential at higher altitudes in the valleys close to Arequipa, where the vines today, like so many in Peru, are grown for pisco.

The two labels on the left are Bolivian, those on the right Uruguayan, and in the middle is Brazil's finest fizz from Cave Geisse. Even the label of Quinta do Seival's blend of Portuguese grapes grown in Brazil looks Portuguese.

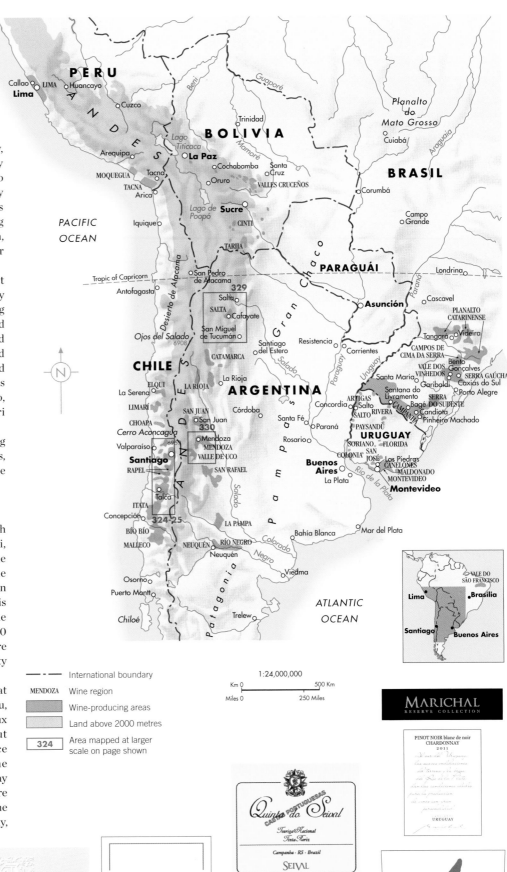

Chile

No other country has been sprouting new wine regions as rapidly as Chile. Chile made its reputation as a producer of low-cost, reliably fruity Cabernet and Merlot grown with enviable ease in the vine paradise that is the Central Valley, but now viticultural limits are being tested in all directions. Her wines are becoming more refined, and more regionally distinct. So great is the latitudinal variation of Chile's vineyards that

we are not able to map them all in this book, but have turned the map through a right angle for this edition (as in the Côte d'Or and Alsace) in order to show as much as possible.

Until recently the official Chilean wine map simply sliced the uniquely long, thin land mass – bounded by the chilly Pacific to the west and the soaring Andes to the east – horizontally into geopolitical valleys. But, in recognition of the huge significance of these two geographical influences (see panel overleaf), the map is now being sliced vertically, too. Since 2011, Chilean wine producers may use the terms Costa, Entre

Cordilleras, and Andes on their labels to indicate wines grown in the very different environments of coastal, central, and eastern hillside vineyards, respectively. Even within the fashionable Costa strip, though, there can be quite a difference between vine-growing conditions on the coastal sites most exposed to the ocean and those on the east-facing slopes of the Coastal Range.

And it is not just the climate that can vary enormously both laterally and longitudinally, but the soils and underlying rocks. Ancient granite, schist, and slate are found in the west of the country, while deep clay, loam, silt, and sand deposits are more common in the central plain between the Coastal Range and the Andes, where soils tend to be

*Data from 1971 to 2000

CHILE: CURICO ▼

Latitude / Altitude of WS
-34.97° / 748ft (228m)

Average growing season temperature at WS
63.4°F (17.4°C)

Average annual rainfall at WS
28in (724mm)

Harvest month rainfall at WS
March: 0.6in (14mm)

Principal viticultural hazards
Nematodes

Principal grape varieties
Cabernet Sauvignon, Sauvignon Blanc, Chardonnay, Merlot, Carmenère

- – · – Regional boundary
- Aconcagua
- Casablanca
- San Antonio
- Leyda
- Maipo
- Cachapoal (within Rapel)
- Colchagua (within Rapel)
- Curicó
- Maule
- Itata
- Lolol — Wine subregion
- ANAKENA — Notable producer
- 1200 — Contour interval 400 metres
- ▼ — Weather station (WS)

CENTRAL CHILE

Turned on its side to give maximum coverage (north is left), this map includes all four of the Central Valley's wine regions – from the hillside vineyards of Maipo around Santiago in the north through to the strikingly flat plain of Maule – together with some of the newer, cooler regions.

colluvial, presenting the would-be vine-grower with an extraordinary matrix of possible terroirs.

Chile is exceptionally well suited to vine growing. Its reliable Mediterranean climate results in day after day of cloudless sunlight in a dry, largely unpolluted atmosphere. If the country has any natural agricultural disadvantage it is that the summers are virtually rainless. Earlier (even Inca) farmers spotted this possible problem and dug an astonishing network of canals and gullies to flood the land with water from the snow that melts each year in the Andes (albeit less plentifully nowadays). This admirable, if imprecise, sort of irrigation is being replaced in newer vineyards by drip irrigation, which can both apply fertilizer (often needed in Chile's sandier soils) and respond more sensitively to the needs of each vine row. With light but generally fertile soil and complete control of the water supply, grape-growing is absurdly easy, even if the most quality-conscious producers are now actively seeking poorer soils for their best wines. And in some of the newer wine regions expensive boreholes are needed,

occasionally involving the politics of water rights. Rot and mildew are not unknown, but are much rarer than they are in most of Europe and even Argentina just across the Andes.

Chile has one more distinctive attribute as a wine producer that may well be a result of its geographical isolation: freedom from the predations of the phylloxera louse. Vines can safely grow on their own roots, which means that a new vineyard can be planted simply by sticking cuttings straight into the ground, without the time and expense of grafting on to resistant rootstock – although rootstocks are much more prevalent nowadays. They can be used to encourage even ripening, to adapt varieties to specific sites, for resistance to local problems such as nematodes, and just in case the recent influx of visitors from other wine regions should unwittingly import phylloxera.

Until the late 1990s, the most widely planted grape in Chile was the common País (Criolla Chica in Argentina, Mission in California), which is still widely grown for the tetrapak wine so popular within Chile. But Chile was also a rich repository of long-adapted Bordeaux grape varieties – from cuttings imported directly from Bordeaux before phylloxera ravaged the vineyards of Europe.

For at least a century, Chilean vineyards were dominated by País, Cabernet Sauvignon, "Sauvignon Blanc" (much of which was actually Sauvignon Vert or Sauvignonasse), and "Merlot" (much of which turned out to be Carmenère, the particularly vigorous historic Bordeaux variety that can yield grapes with a somewhat green streak and may be better as an ingredient in blends than in varietal form). But a late 20th and early 21st-century whirl of plantings of superior clones and new varieties dramatically widened the range of flavours available from these particularly healthy vineyards – not least because almost all of the new regions are cooler than the old. Today, although Cabernet still predominates, Chile produces fine examples of Syrah, Pinot Noir, Malbec, Sauvignons Blanc and Gris, Viognier, Chardonnay, Gewurztraminer, and Riesling.

Northern Chile

The rash of new wine regions are cooler than the Central Valley either because they are closer to the ocean, closer to Antarctica, and/or at higher altitudes. Possibly the most dramatic current extension of the Chilean wine map is in the far north (see p.323). Vines are now growing at 8,200ft (2,500m) above the Pacific in the middle of the Atacama Desert, as well as a full 1,100 miles (1,760km) north of the capital Santiago in the Andean resort of San Pedro de Atacama.

And vineyards are planned at the record-breaking altitude of 11,480ft (3,500m) in Talabre, high in the Andes, almost

1:1,100,000

Km 0   10   20   30   40 Km
Miles 0   10   20 Miles

THE CLIMATE OF THE CENTRAL VALLEY

The 870-mile (1,400km) spine of vineyards in the Central Valley is cooled by the chilly influence of the Humboldt Current, which originates in the Antarctic and steals inland from waters much colder than, say, California's at the same latitude. Another important cooling influence on the vineyards of Chile, particularly marked on the eastern half of the Central Valley, is the nightly descent of cool air from the Andes. Chilean winemakers need sweaters while their grapes ripen much more than their counterparts in, for example, France.

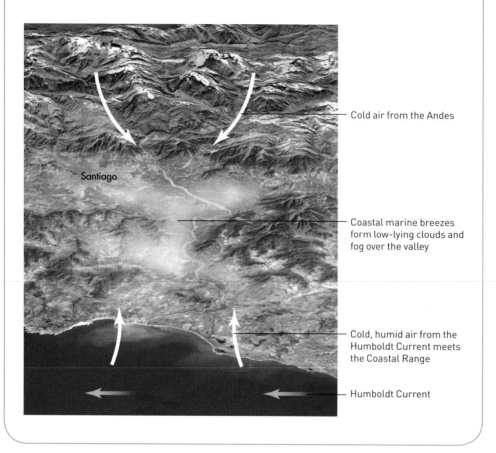

Cold air from the Andes

Santiago

Coastal marine breezes form low-lying clouds and fog over the valley

Cold, humid air from the Humboldt Current meets the Coastal Range

Humboldt Current

on the border with Bolivia. Even in Argentina no one has yet planted that high.

All these outposts are well north of Elqui and Limarí, which themselves are too far north to fit on to the map on the previous pages. The steep-sided **Elqui Valley** has been home to table grapes and grapes for pisco, Chile's curiously addictive Moscatel-based spirit, for years, but the Italian-owned Viña Falernia winery there has proved that the region is capable of producing award-winning wines, notably some particularly gutsy Syrah, at altitudes of over 6,600ft (2,000m). Granite and hillside vineyards bring to mind the northern Rhône – at the highest-possible volume.

Limarí to the south is a much more open valley, with its vineyards planted much closer to the coast being cooled by the Pacific because here, unusually for Chile, there is no Coastal Range to block the cold marine air. As a result, Tabalí, which has planted vines as close as 7.5 miles (12km) to the coast, has already shown that it can make world-class Sauvignon Blanc, Chardonnay, and some increasingly fine Pinot Noir. Like Elqui, this was pisco country originally, with an offshoot of the local pisco co-op being the one and only winery for

many years. It is a sign of national confidence in the region that the country's biggest wine producer by far, Concha y Toro, bought the winery in 2005 and renamed it Viña Maycas del Limarí.

Aconcagua

The northernmost (so leftmost) wine region that we map in detail is Aconcagua (named after the highest peak of the Andes, at 23,000ft/7,000m). It is made up of three contrasting subregions: the warm Aconcagua Valley itself and the notably cooler Casablanca and San Antonio valleys. The warmth of the broad, open Aconcagua Valley is tempered by winds that regularly sweep cool mountain air coastward in the early afternoons and funnel ocean air up from the river mouth most evenings, to cool the west-facing foothills of the Andes. In the late 19th century, the Errázuriz family's property at Panquehue (see p.32) was reputed to be the single biggest wine estate in the world. Today, about 2,500 acres (1,000ha) of wine grapes are grown in the Aconcagua Valley, and the hillsides are being converted to vineyards under Errázuriz's auspices. There are also notable new plantings west of Colmo, just 10

miles (16km) from the ocean (and about as cool as Marlborough in New Zealand).

The **Casablanca Valley**, developed at a rapid rate in the 1990s, was the first of Chile's coastal-influenced wine regions and added fresh Sauvignon Blanc, Chardonnay, and Pinot Noir to the country's wine palette. Dozens of bodegas, and almost all of the big ones, buy or grow fruit here. The valley is too far from the Andes for the regular evening dose of cooling mountain air that refreshes vines further inland, or even for access to meltwater for irrigation. Although the far east is warm enough for Veramonte to make fine, full-bodied reds here, much of Casablanca is so close to the sea that cool breezes can be relied upon to lower afternoon temperatures by as much as 18°F (10°C), which, with the valley's mild winters, makes Casablanca's growing season up to a month longer than that of most Central Valley vineyards. Spring frost is a perennial and inconvenient threat, and it is not unknown for vineyards on the frost-prone open valley floor to suffer frost a week before harvest. The water shortage makes anti-frost sprinklers a luxury, however. The naturally low-vigour vines are also prey to nematodes, so vines have to be grafted on to resistant rootstocks. Growing costs are higher here than elsewhere.

The success of Casablanca encouraged the development of the rolling coastal hills of the **San Antonio Valley**, first planted in 1997 by Viña Leyda and officially recognized in 2002. The varied topography makes San Antonio even more subject to cool, damp ocean influence than western Casablanca. Along with Viña Leyda, the most important pioneers were Casa Marin, Matetic, and Amayna, but many other producers source grapes here, particularly Sauvignon Blanc, Chardonnay, Pinot Noir, and more recently Syrah, which has emerged as one of modern Chile's strongest suits. The infertile soils consist mainly of thin layers of red clay on granite, as in the westernmost part of Casablanca, and irrigation water is just as scarce. The **Leyda Valley** is an officially recognized zone in the south of the San Antonio Valley.

The Central Valley

Our map shows the Central Valley's four subregions: Curicó, and the three named after the Maipo, Rapel, and Maule rivers that cross the central plain, like gradations on a thermometer, to pierce the low Coastal Range and find the sea. **Maipo** has the hottest climate, an atmosphere occasionally polluted by the smogs of Santiago, and the smallest vineyard area of the Central Valley's regions, but a high concentration of bodegas. Its proximity to the capital spawned a tradition of grand plantations and extensive homesteads belonging to Chile's 19th-century gentlemen-farmers, some of whom established the country's grandfather wine companies Concha y Toro, Santa Rita, and Santa Carolina. It was here, a convenient ride south of Santiago, that Chile's first generation of serious wine was made. Maipo is essentially red wine country and when yields are restricted the Bordeaux varieties can produce world-class wines vaguely reminiscent of Napa Valley Cabernets. Puente Alto is where vineyards creep up the Andean foothills and the mountain influence is most keenly felt. Its relatively chilly mornings and poor soils have already resulted in some of Chile's most admired Cabernets such as Almaviva, Domus Aurea, Casa Real (Santa Rita's top bottling), and those of Haras de Pirque and Viñedo Chadwick. Vines have been creeping uphill throughout the long Central Valley in fact, both towards the Coastal Range in the west but particularly on the drier, cooler eastern slopes of the foothills of the Andes with their long hours of sunshine.

The burgeoning and varied region of **Rapel** to the immediate south of Maipo encompasses the valleys of **Cachapoal** in the north (including the Rancagua, Requinoa, and Rengo areas – all names occasionally found on labels), and fashionable **Colchagua** to the south, including San Fernando, Nancagua, Chimbarongo, and Marchigüe (Marchihue), and Apalta, where Montes and Lapostolle are based. Cachapoal and, especially, Colchagua are names more often found on labels than Rapel, which tends to be reserved for blends from both subregions. Colchagua, where Luis Felipe Edwards has planted vines as high as 3,300ft (1,000m), has earned itself a reputation for Chile's most succulent and concentrated Merlot (or is it Carmenère?). As throughout Chile, soils vary enormously, even within small zones such as Colchagua, but there is some of Merlot's classic partner clay here as well as the usual Chilean cocktail of silty loam and sand, and some volcanic areas. Red and white blends such as those from Altaïr and Calyptra are becoming some of Cachapoal's most respected wines.

Quite a way down the Pan-American Highway, with its ancient trucks and unpredictable fauna, are the vineyards of **Curicó**, including the Lontué zone, which is also often specified on wine labels. Here the climate becomes slightly more temperate and irrigation is less likely to be a necessity. Average rainfall is 10 times higher than in the Elqui Valley, the frost risk is very much higher, and the Coastal Range extends far enough east to effectively block any Pacific influence. Miguel Torres of Catalunya famously invested in a winery here in 1979 (the same year that Baron Philippe de Rothschild struck another seminal transatlantic deal with Robert Mondavi of California), and this act of faith in wine country once thought of as being impossibly far south was followed by many others. The San Pedro winery at Molina is surrounded by South America's largest block of vines (3,000 acres/1,200ha), which is run, like much in the Chilean wine industry, with a technical precision far from any Latin American stereotype.

The southernmost subregion of the Central Valley and Chile's oldest wine region, **Maule** has three times the rainfall of Santiago (although the same dry summers) and Chile's greatest area of vines on substantially volcanic soils. Many of them are basic País, and mixed plantings of varieties such as Malbec, Tannat, and Carmenère. Cabernet Sauvignon has been widely planted, but the old Carignan vines dry-farmed on smallholdings in the west of the region are increasingly valued. Until recently, most Maule grapes disappeared into big company blends labelled Central Valley, but Vigno is an admirable initiative, an informal appellation designed to showcase old-vine Maule Carignan voluntarily adopted by a group of small-scale producers. Torres has been experimenting with a Pinot Noir grown on slate-dominated terroir in Empedrado in western Maule.

Southern Chile

The three subregions of the Sur (Spanish for South), **Itata**, **Bío Bío**, and **Malleco**, have less protection from the Coastal Range and even cooler, wetter conditions than Maule (which favour grapes such as Riesling, Gewurztraminer, Sauvignon Blanc, Chardonnay, and Pinot Noir). They are still dominated by País and (especially in Itata) Moscatel, but there has been serious pioneering work on the part of producers such as Viñedos Córpora and Concha y Toro at Mulchén. The quality of Viña Aquitania's Sol de Sol Chardonnay from Malleco was the first internationally recognized wine that encouraged others to extend the Chilean wine map even further south. The southernmost plantings at the time of writing are more than 200 miles (320km) south of the Malleco Valley in Coihaique.

Precision viticulture

Since the early, well-publicized incursions of Torres and the Lafite-Rothschilds (who have since extricated themselves from the Peralillo estate of Los Vascos), dozens of foreigners have invested in Chilean wine production. But the most heartening aspect of Chile's recent wine history is the country's own, often peripatetic, viticulturists and oenologists, who are admirably well-qualified, well-travelled, and competent, and are often backed by well-funded operators with experience in general fruit farming.

Those responsible for the rash of new plantings have generally been much more fastidious about the precise location and design of their vineyards than the old-timers. In the old days, the temptation was to overuse fertilizers and irrigation, but this has become rarer – not least for vines weighed down by Chile's naturally dense canopy. Too many grapes have a nasty habit of failing to ripen properly – a common criticism of Chilean wine. Encouraged by the unusually benign climate, an increasing proportion of Chilean vines are cultivated organically, even if relatively few growers take the trouble to gain certification. Concha y Toro can afford the necessary time and money, however, and its subsidiary Emiliana Orgánico operates the world's largest single biodynamic vineyard, Los Robles estate in Colchagua, run by Chile's organic pioneer Alvaro Espinoza.

In the cellars, since the emergence of an export-oriented economy – Chile exports an even bigger percentage of its production than Australia (about 70%) – there has been extraordinary investment in winery hardware, and oak is now more likely to be harnessed than flaunted. As Chilean winemakers strive to tame nature and make increasingly complex wines, average yields have declined, and grape prices have risen – not helped on export markets by the copper-bottomed strength of the peso.

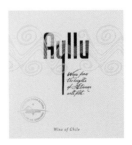

Chilean labels can be particularly colourful and inventive. Montes draws on the imagination of self-styled "Gonzo artist" Ralph Steadman for Montes Folly, grown on 45° slopes in Apalta, for example. Luyt's wine is one of the new breed of Maule old-vine Carignans.

Argentina

The altitude of vineyards always deserves a mention, for its effects on climate and hence the style and quality of every wine. In Argentina it makes the headline. Chile takes differences of latitude to extremes; Argentina, extremes of altitude. But Argentina's appearance on the international wine map is a remarkably recent story. Blessed with an enviable diversity of grape varieties, thanks to mid-19th century immigration from Spain and Italy, Argentina had little or no export aspirations before the mid-1990s, which saw a rapid change of pace for what is now the world's fifth-biggest wine producer. After a long period of economic chaos, old cellars were rejuvenated, glamorous new ones built by investors from all over the world, and new vineyards planted at a

furious rate at ever-higher altitudes. Argentines themselves began to drink less but fruitier wine, and abroad, Argentina's intensely flavoured, full-bodied reds, and some whites, became first more familiar and then actively admired, particularly in the USA.

The tree-lined city of Mendoza is only 50 minutes by air from the Chilean capital Santiago – so close that shopping bags are a common sight on the crowded flights. Yet the plane has to clear the highest ridge of the Andes, a 20,000ft (6,000m) serrated blade of rock and ice. The centres of Argentine and Chilean wine may be cheek by jowl, yet they are poles apart in terms of natural conditions. Both lie in the low latitudes for wine-growing, but while Chile's wine regions owe their ideal growing conditions to their isolation (they are sandwiched between the cold Andes and the cold Pacific), Argentine vineyards, typically oases of green set in uncompromisingly arid semi-desert, exist because of altitude.

Reaching for the skies

At the heights that are typical of Argentine wine-growing, overnight temperatures are low enough to give well-flavoured, deeply coloured grapes for red wine, and in the cooler areas, especially in the north, aromatic whites. With little or no disease in the dry mountain air, provided there is abundant water, crops can reach yields virtually unknown elsewhere. The current challenge in Argentine viticulture is to harness irrigation so as to deliver quality before quantity. Traditional vineyards and irrigation channels were sited so that the vines were routinely flooded with meltwater off the Andes. Today, as less and less snow seems to fall on the mountains, and so many

Catena Zapata, arguably Argentina's best-known wine producer internationally, has been pushing ever further up into the Andes and was one of the first to cite vineyard altitudes on wine labels.

vineyards are sited in completely new districts, supplies of water are very much more restricted. As elsewhere, this is becoming a key factor in the economics, even viability, of a wine operation.

New plantings of the more phylloxera-sensitive varieties such as Chardonnay may be grafted on to rootstocks, for the louse is not absent. This is a worry for Chileans now that all of Chile's major wine companies have invested in Argentina's vineyard land, bought at less expensive prices than in Chile, but phylloxera has so far posed no great threat. That flood irrigation was so common and soils are relatively sandy may be pertinent. As in Chile, nematodes in the soil are generally a greater threat, but otherwise, thanks to almost constant dry winds blowing from the Andes, Argentine vines are remarkably healthy.

The weather, though, is far from predictable and conditions are not perfect. At these altitudes winters are cold (importantly, cold enough for vine dormancy), but spring and sometimes autumn frosts present real danger to a significant proportion of vineyards. Summers in some of the lower-altitude, lower-latitude regions such as parts of San Juan and La Rioja provinces, and eastern San Rafael in the south of Mendoza (see map, p.323) can be just too hot for fine wine production. And as the key facts panel shows, Argentina's annual precipitation may be very low (even in El Niño years) but is concentrated in the growing season. In some areas, particularly in the province of Mendoza, where almost 70% of Argentina's vines are planted, it has a nasty tendency to fall as very localized hail, which can devastate an entire year's crop. Some growers have invested in special hail nets, which can also usefully reduce the risk of sunburn in Argentina's intense sunlight. The zonda, a fearsome hot, dry wind from the northeast, is another liability, particularly at high altitudes, and particularly at flowering.

Soils tend to be relatively young and alluvial with quite a high proportion of sand in many areas. The intensity of flavour that the best wines demonstrate comes not from below but from above, from the intense sunlight, the dry air, and temperature differences at these altitudes. At up to 36°F (20°C) the diurnal temperature variation is higher in Argentine vineyards than practically anywhere else in the world. This is often because of altitude, but in Patagonia in the south it is because of the high latitude. Apart from in the most southerly vineyards of Patagonia, in

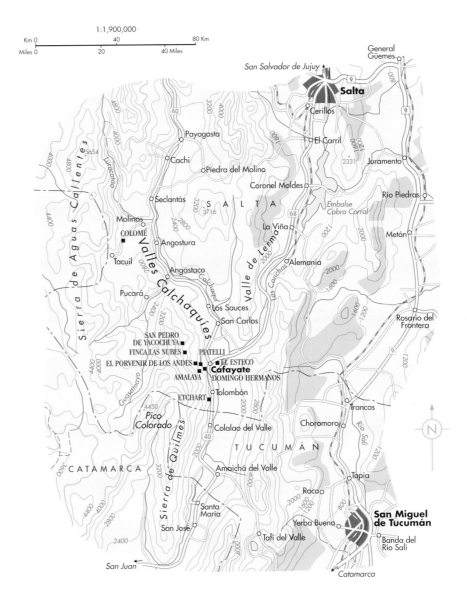

CALCHAQUI VALLEY

This is the world's epicentre of the growing and making of Argentina's characteristic white wine grape Torrontés, although some fine red is made here, too. Wine adds considerably to the appeal of the holiday town of Cafayate in the province of Salta.

— · — · —	Province boundary
■ ETCHART	Notable producer
▨	Woods
‒2000‒	Contour interval 400 metres

This collection of labels from the Calchaquí Valley includes Amalaya, an accessible Torrontés-dominated blend, which is a sister company of Colomé – the dizzyingly high winery owned by Swiss art collector Donald Hess. Yacochuya is made by Pomerol oenologist Michel Rolland and is just one of his Argentine projects.

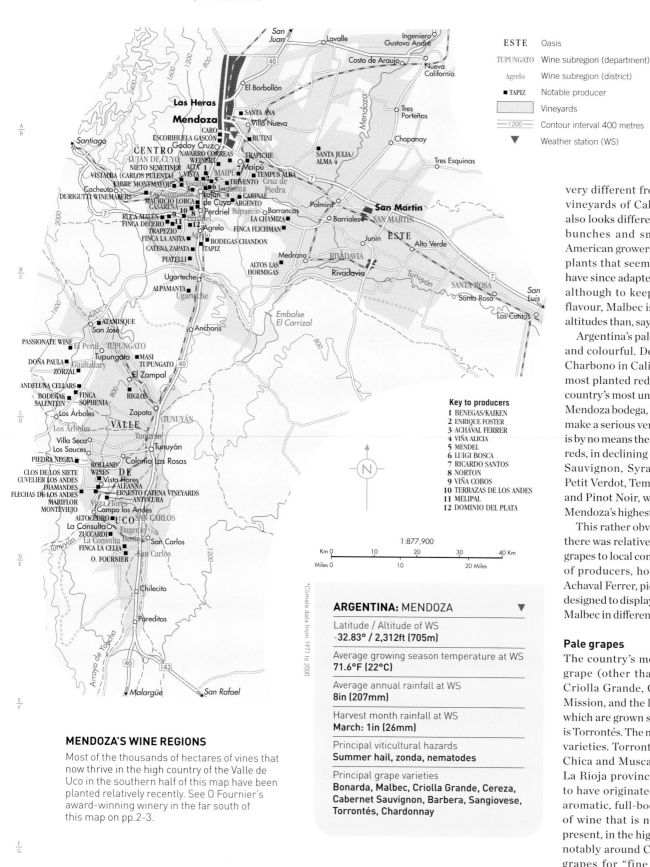

ESTE — Oasis
TUPUNGATO — Wine subregion (department)
Agrelo — Wine subregion (district)
■ TAPIZ — Notable producer
Vineyards
1200 — Contour interval 400 metres
▼ — Weather station (WS)

Key to producers
1 BENEGAS/KAIKEN
2 ENRIQUE FOSTER
3 ACHÁVAL FERRER
4 VIÑA ALICIA
5 MENDEL
6 LUIGI BOSCA
7 RICARDO SANTOS
8 NORTON
9 VIÑA COBOS
10 TERRAZAS DE LOS ANDES
11 MELIPAL
12 DOMINIO DEL PLATA

1:877,900

Km 0 | 10 | 20 | 30 | 40 Km
Miles 0 | 10 | 20 Miles

*Climate data from 1971 to 2000

ARGENTINA: MENDOZA ▼

Latitude / Altitude of WS
-32.83° / 2,312ft (705m)

Average growing season temperature at WS
71.6°F (22°C)

Average annual rainfall at WS
8in (207mm)

Harvest month rainfall at WS
March: 1in (26mm)

Principal viticultural hazards
Summer hail, zonda, nematodes

Principal grape varieties
Bonarda, Malbec, Criolla Grande, Cereza, Cabernet Sauvignon, Barbera, Sangiovese, Torrontés, Chardonnay

MENDOZA'S WINE REGIONS

Most of the thousands of hectares of vines that now thrive in the high country of the Valle de Uco in the southern half of this map have been planted relatively recently. See O Fournier's award-winning winery in the far south of this map on pp.2-3.

Neuquén and Río Negro, full ripeness is easy to achieve. Argentina's high temperatures can be tasted in particularly soft tannins and sometimes high alcohols in the red wines, although dedicated growers try to delay the accumulation of sugar by controlling the water supply or using hail nets to slow ripening. Alcohol levels in white wines may be moderated by blending grapes picked

on different dates, but acid has to be added to most Argentine wines of any colour.

The country's wine reputation abroad was built largely on its most-planted red wine grape, Malbec, introduced to Argentina in 1868 at the request of the then president by the French agronomist Michel Pouget. The opulent Malbec grown today in Argentina not only tastes

very different from that which dominates the vineyards of Cahors in Southwest France, it also looks different, with much smaller, tighter bunches and smaller berries. Early South American growers must have selected particular plants that seemed to perform well and these have since adapted perfectly to local conditions, although to keep its acidity and intensity of flavour, Malbec is best grown at slightly higher altitudes than, say, Cabernet Sauvignon.

Argentina's palette of grape varieties is varied and colourful. Deep-coloured Bonarda, called Charbono in California, is Argentina's second-most planted red wine grape, and arguably the country's most underdeveloped wine resource. A Mendoza bodega, Nieto Senetiner, was the first to make a serious version of this fruity variety but it is by no means the only one now. Other significant reds, in declining order of acreage, are Cabernet Sauvignon, Syrah, Merlot, Cabernet Franc, Petit Verdot, Tempranillo, Barbera, Sangiovese, and Pinot Noir, which is best in Patagonia or in Mendoza's highest vineyards.

This rather obvious case apart, for a long time there was relatively little discipline in matching grapes to local conditions. An increasing number of producers, however, led by Alta Vista and Achaval Ferrer, pioneered single-vineyard wines designed to display the characteristics of, usually, Malbec in different areas.

Pale grapes

The country's most distinctive light-skinned grape (other than the coarse, pink-skinned Criolla Grande, Cereza, and Criolla Chica or Mission, and the light-skinned Pedro Giménez, which are grown strictly for local consumption) is Torrontés. The name is applied to three distinct varieties. Torrontés Riojano, a cross of Criolla Chica and Muscat of Alexandria named after La Rioja province where it was long thought to have originated, is the finest. It reaches its aromatic, full-bodied apogee, albeit in a style of wine that is not especially fashionable at present, in the high vineyards of Salta province, notably around Cafayete. Other widely grown grapes for "fine white wine", as Argentine authorities call anything pale and conceivably exportable, are Chardonnay (planted with particular enthusiasm and considerable success), Chenin Blanc, Ugni Blanc, Pinot Gris (from cuttings brought in from Alsace by Lurton), and an increasing acreage of Sauvignon Blanc – a sign perhaps of just how high and therefore cool some of the new plantings are. The odd Viognier has also emerged and Sémillon, (pronounced *Semijon*) Mendoza's relatively common and emblematic white, is enjoying a renaissance.

North and Central Argentina

Argentina's most northerly vines are grown, at around 7,900ft (2,400m), by Fernando Dupont close to the border with Bolivia. To the immediate south, **Salta** is home to what are claimed to be the highest vineyards in the world, grown for Donald Hess's Colomé mountain wine in the Calchaquí Valley. At rather lower altitudes, the holiday country of Cafayete has a reputation for aromatic white Torrontés, and San Pedro de Yacochuya has shown that old vines and low yields are the key to red wine quality here. Respectable wine is also now being made in Tucumán very near the border with Salta. Just to the south, **Catamarca** province is better known for table grapes than wine but Santa María has proved that good wine can be made, even if it is misleadingly labelled Valles Calchaquíes. **La Rioja** province is best known for, logically, Torrontés Riojano, which is typically trained on pergolas and vinified by the local co-op, Chilecito, in the dry, windy Famatina Valley, its best-known wine region.

The only province that makes wine in any quantity to rival that of Mendoza is **San Juan**, which is even hotter and drier (just 3.5in/90mm of rain in an average year) than Mendoza to the immediate south. Almost a quarter of all Argentine wine is made here, much of it based on Moscatel de Alejandría or Muscat of Alexandria, the predominant Muscat in Argentina. Syrah is increasingly popular here, although much of the land is too hot to yield wines with much varietal definition. There is also a little promising Viognier, Chardonnay, Petit Verdot, and Tannat. Just as in Mendoza, quality-conscious producers are developing vineyards at ever-higher altitudes in the Zonda, Calingasta, and Pedernal valleys.

Mendoza, centred on the vibrant city of the same name, is by far the dominant Argentine wine province, with many very different regions within it. Central Mendoza has the longest tradition of fine wine, and a high proportion of Argentina's most famous producers are based here. Vineyards on either side of the avenues that radiate from the city, in the Luján de Cuyo department, have developed a reputation for especially fine Malbec. Vineyard districts within this area that have carved out their own reputations for Malbec include Vistalba, Perdriel, Agrelo, and Las Compuertas, where soils are particularly poor. The average age of vines here, many of which escaped being pulled out in favour of housing developments in the 1970s and 1980s, has contributed to wine quality. The department of Maipú may be better for Cabernet Sauvignon and Syrah than Malbec, as it is slightly lower and warmer.

Central Mendoza's climate is temperate (almost cool in Agrelo) and the soils unusually gravelly for Argentina (especially in Maipú) when elsewhere in Mendoza soils are typically alluvial and sandy. And there are few of the salinity problems that plague some parts of Luján de Cuyo and parts of the eastern districts, which churn out oceans of table wine from Cereza, the Criollas, Pedro Giménez, Moscatel Alejandría, and the high-yielding Bonarda.

East Mendoza is better known for quantity than quality, although the innovative Zuccardi family provides an exception. Vineyards here are at lower altitudes, where the cooling influence of the Andes is at its weakest. The Mendoza and Tunuyán rivers traditionally provided ample, grape-swelling irrigation for the pergola vines that spew forth wine for the local market.

About 130 miles (235km) southeast of Mendoza city, San Rafael is lower, with its vineyards between the Diamante and Atuel rivers generally ranging between 1,475 and 2,625ft (450–800m) above sea level. Being further south it is cooler than anywhere else in Mendoza province, apart from the Uco Valley. It has the country's most extensive plantings of Chenin Blanc and Sauvignonasse (called Tocai Friulano here). San Rafael would make even more fine wine were it not so prone to hail.

The most exciting part of Mendoza from the fine wine lover's point of view is the Uco Valley, named not after a river but after a pre-Columbian Indian chief reputed to have introduced irrigation here. There are now well over 40,000 acres (16,500ha) of vineyard, much of it notably youthful, at altitudes of 2,950–4,900ft (900–1,500m). Producers such as Catena and the LVMH-owned Terrazas de los Andes specify precise altitudes on their front labels.

The highest vineyards are in Tupungato, the northernmost department, where much of Argentina's surprisingly fine Chardonnay is grown. Tupungato has been the focus of sophisticated modern vineyard development, and some of the older wineries are at quite a distance from the vineyards. Nights are cool enough to produce delicate fruit flavours, and acidity levels are high enough to make malolactic fermentation desirable. The frost-free period lasts no longer than in New York's Finger Lakes region, however, and late frosts are a particular threat in the east of the Uco Valley on the slightly lower slopes of the department of San Carlos.

Other notable vineyards include Clos de los Siete, near Vista Flores in Tunuyán, a group of red wine estates at slightly lower altitudes than Tupungato designed by Michel Rolland of Pomerol with fellow investors. The upper limits of vine cultivation in Mendoza are still being tested, but a shortage of irrigation water is another potential constraint. To compensate, however, much is made of the intensity of sunlight in this unpolluted area high in the Andes, which seems to act as a spur to photosynthesis and naturally ripens phenolics such as colour, flavour, and tannins. It is a rare Argentine wine, however young, that is uncomfortably astringent. The prevailing texture of Mendoza red is velvet.

Patagonia

The wines of Patagonia in the south of the country, in the provinces of **Neuquén** and especially **Río Negro**, in what were once vast irrigated pear orchards, tend to have their own distinctive character – chewier and drier if no less intense than Mendoza's wines. Antarctic influences keep temperatures down, and dry weather and strong, persistent winds keep vine disease at bay. These are bright, distinctively sculpted wines, strong on structure and character. Several of the relatively few wineries in Patagonia have some non-Argentine connection: Bordeaux-inspired Fabre Montmayou has Infinitus; Noemia is made by Dane Hans Vinding-Diers, who co-owns the winery with Italian Countess Noemi Marone Cinzano; Bodega Familia Schroeder has its origins in Europe; and Bodega Chacra, which makes wines from an old, once-abandoned Pinot Noir vineyard in Río Negro, is owned by the Tuscan Piero Incisa della Rocchetta.

Early offerings from the southernmost wine vines in the province of Chubut manage to combine razor-sharp natural acidity with alcohol levels of only about 12%. Argentina keeps on surprising us.

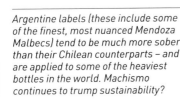

Argentine labels (these include some of the finest, most nuanced Mendoza Malbecs) tend to be much more sober than their Chilean counterparts – and are applied to some of the heaviest bottles in the world. Machismo continues to trump sustainability?

AUSTRALIA & NEW ZEALAND

Schubert Wines' Dakins Road Vineyard in the Gladstone subregion of Wairarapa, New Zealand

Australia

The first European settlers proved in the late 18th century that imported vines thrived in Australia, and by the late 19th century it was a substantial producer of strapping wine, routinely treated with disdain in Britain, its only export market. Most of it was fortified and called port or sherry; a small fraction earned an almost mystical reputation as table wine of original character and legendary lasting power. The 1970s saw a radical change. Fortified wine sales slumped; table wines took off – and found an eager export market. Such thrusting salesmen as Wolf Blass formulated sweet, oaky, concentrated wines that collected gold medals and high reputations. More sensitive wine-growers (there were many) made less money and were soon gobbled up by big breweries.

In the 1990s and early 2000s, Australian wine exports soared, but this encouraged a frenzy of planting, some of it misguidedly encouraged by tax breaks. A grape glut, perhaps inevitably, followed, exacerbated by deep discounting on the domestic market and a strengthening of the Australian dollar, thanks to Asian demand for the country's rich mineral deposits. By 2012, Australia's 6,250 vine-growers (down from 8,570 in 2004) were facing serious challenges in an era of changing climate and changing tastes.

Australia is strongly affected by the El Niño and La Niña weather systems, leading to testing extremes. Since 2006 they have really hurt. Drought plagued many wine regions between 2007 and 2010, with grapes picked weeks earlier than usual. The Victorian bush fires of 2009 cost lives as well as destroying about 3% of the Yarra Valley's vineyards and wineries. Then, from 2011, La Niña inflicted some of the wettest growing seasons ever on South Eastern Australian farmers. Meanwhile Western Australian vineyards experienced a sublime run of vintages from 2006 – which emphasizes just how enormous Australia is: Perth to Brisbane by road is nearly 2,800 miles (4,500km).

The world's largest island is very far from any but its domestic consumers. They do their best, drinking more than five times as much wine per head as they did in 1960. But they only soak up about a third of all the wine their country produces. As the surface temperature map on p.336 shows, most of this vast country is too hot and/or too dry even for the hardy vine, and most wine regions hug the coast, mainly the coolest, most heavily populated southeast coast, plus Tasmania and the far southwest.

There are two paths to cooler conditions: further south or uphill. The Great Dividing Range is flanked by wine regions all the way. At its northern limit is the wine country of Queensland, focused on two relatively high-altitude wine regions known as Geographical Indications (inevitably abbreviated to GIs). Both the Granite Belt and South Burnett depend on altitude to keep cool. **Queensland** has twice as much vineyard in total as the much cooler state of Tasmania, but low rainfall limits its normal crop to under half of Tasmania's. The Granite Belt, responsible for two-thirds of all Queensland wines, has one of the country's most dramatic landscapes, scattered with giant granite boulders. It cleverly differentiated itself as early as 2007 by specializing in grapes other than the usual suspects – known in Australia as "alternative varieties".

Great grape changes

One of the most obvious changes in the last few years has been the rise of these alternative varieties. The first to achieve commercial success was Pinot Gris/Grigio, pioneered on Victoria's Mornington Peninsula. It now produces more wine than Riesling, Australia's classic white grape, and was outlawed from the annual Australian Alternative Variety Show in 2010 on the basis that it made up 2.4% of the total national crush. It is surpassed in premium whites only by Chardonnay, Sauvignon Blanc, and Semillon.

Although slowed by Australia's painstaking plant quarantine, the range of varieties is rapidly growing. By 2010, Viognier had almost overtaken the historic Verdelho, there was more Tempranillo and Sangiovese in the ground than Cabernet Franc, and well over 250 acres (100ha) of, in declining order, Arneis, Dolcetto, Zinfandel, Barbera, Nebbiolo, and Savagnin (Traminer), this last having originally been sold as Albariño as the result of a mix-up in a Spanish nursery.

As for the major varieties, Shiraz continues to be the signature grape of Australia: almost one vine in every four. Its wines vary enormously but, mirroring a general trend, there has been a swing away from super-concentrated, heavily oaked wines made from often overripe grapes to styles that speak more of the vineyard than wizardry in the cellar. A fashion for co-fermenting Shiraz with Viognier has waned, and some of the fresher-style wines are labelled "Syrah" rather than "Shiraz" as a nod to France. In 2011, the famous Jimmy Watson Trophy for the best young red of the Melbourne Show went to Glaetzer-Dixon's distinctly transparent Shiraz from... Tasmania. Even Australia's agenda-setting wine shows have been changing.

But if Shiraz has evolved, Chardonnay (now the country's second most planted variety, having overtaken Cabernet Sauvignon) has had a complete personality change. (Changes that would take generations in Europe seem to take Australians no more than a couple of years.) It was plump, rich oakiness that first sold Australian Chardonnay in the 1990s. But the minute Australian exporters sensed that their major markets, the UK and US, were tired of this style, winemakers throughout Australia put their Chardonnays on the strictest of diets. Today, Australian Chardonnay is lean, occasionally mean, but more often a hugely appetizing, well-made, well-priced answer to white burgundy.

For all varieties, and the increasing number of blends, there has been a real shift away from pride in technical prowess towards more artisanal methods. Good producers want to express geography more than technique.

Selling Wine Australia

Australian wine producers listen carefully to their customers abroad because they are so dependent on them. At home, imports, helped by the mighty Australian dollar, are stiff competition. A glut of New Zealand's most famous wine resulted in such

a flood of Marlborough Sauvignon Blanc that it was nicknamed a "Savalanche". It became a sore point that the single biggest-selling wine brand in Australia was from New Zealand.

At the same time, Australia's two most important export markets wobbled. In the US, there had been a flurry of interest in turbo-charged Shiraz, fuelled by wine guru Robert Parker. Many American wine collectors expected them to age beautifully and were disappointed. At the other end of the market, the Casella family of New South Wales had seen a sales boom for the Yellow Tail brand designed expressly for the US, but it and its imitators did little for the image of Australian wine in general and came to be dismissed, along with its many imitators, as unsophisticated "critter brands".

At more or less the same time the handful of supermarket retailers that rule the British mass market decided that Australian brands in bottle

were becoming too expensive and switched to importing in bulk wine bought to a price for their own-label brands. For the first time, in 2008, total exports of Australian wine were less than the year before, and by early 2012, Australia was exporting more wine in bulk than in bottle. This was despite the huge success that Australian exporters have had in China, now the country's third most important market and worth almost half as much as the UK.

The wine factories

Much of the wine exported in bulk, indeed 60% of the country's entire crop, comes from Australia's vast inland vineyard, in declining order of the amount of wine produced, **Riverland** in South Australia, **Murray Darling** straddling the Victoria–New South Wales border, and **Riverina** in New South Wales. Riverina is not all about bulk; there is some rich botrytised Semillon

SOUTH EASTERN AUSTRALIA'S GIs

There is a marked contrast between most of these wine regions ("GIs" in Strine) and the heavily and increasingly expensively irrigated inland regions on the Murray, Darling, Murrumbidgee, and Lachlan rivers. The economics of Riverland, Murray Darling, and Riverina are under threat.

1:5,300,000

| Km 0 | 50 | 100 | 150 Km |
| Miles 0 | | 50 | 100 Miles |

- - - State boundary

● Penola Notable wine town

HUNTER Geographical Indication (GI)

Land 500-1000 metres

Land above 1000 metres

340 Area mapped at larger scale on page shown

Western Australia map p.337

Tasmania map p.353

from Griffith. These are regions that would not exist without irrigation from the Murray, Darling, or Murrumbidgee rivers and are run with staggering efficiency, if dangerously depleting reserves of water. Some of the red wines need bolstering with ingredients from cooler regions, and these vast wine factories in the desert will undoubtedly shrink further if there is another run of drought years. (One of the few benefits of the drought years has been to impose much greater discipline on water use and re-use.) As it is, Australia's total area under vine had shrunk to barely 370,700 acres (150,000ha) by 2012 and the average value of a tonne of wine grapes in Australia plummeted from A$880 for the 2007 harvest to just A$410 five years later.

Wines from the inland river regions are labelled **South Eastern Australia**, a GI used liberally for many a wine made from the blended produce of virtually anywhere other than Western Australia. Australia has a long tradition of blending between different regions. Indeed some of the greatest Australian wines the authors have ever tasted qualify as "inter-regional blends". They are unlikely to disappear, however unfashionable they may be currently with geographical purists.

Australia was the first major wine country to embrace screw caps, for red wines as well as whites, spurred on initially by the much smaller New Zealand wine industry. Exporters may offer the choice of traditional cork or screw cap but the great majority of Australian producers, and the all-important show judges, are completely converted to the virtues of Stelvin, referring to it by the name of the dominant brand.

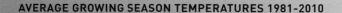

AVERAGE GROWING SEASON TEMPERATURES 1981-2010

These average temperatures, from 1 October to 30 April, broadly correlate to the maturity potential for wine grape varieties (see p.20). The cool limit for viticulture is found in much of Tasmania, in the south of Victoria, and in elevated parts of eastern New South Wales, making them the focus for cool-climate viticulture. The upper limit is roughly 70°F (21°C), so that much of Australia is unsuited to wine-growing. (Data source: Australian Bureau of Meteorology.)

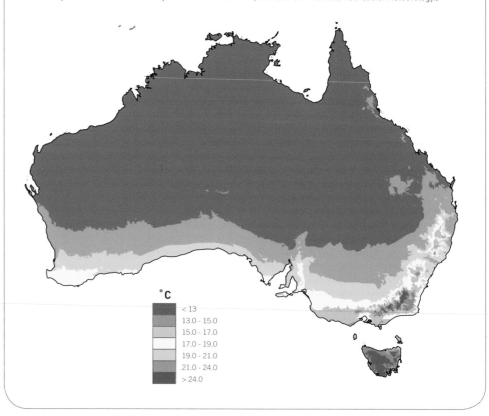

°C
- < 13
- 13.0 - 15.0
- 15.0 - 17.0
- 17.0 - 19.0
- 19.0 - 21.0
- 21.0 - 24.0
- > 24.0

Limestone Coast

One relatively important wine region not mapped in detail on the following pages is South Australia's **Limestone Coast**. The most important of the official regions within this geometrically drawn GI are Coonawarra (considered in detail on p.347), then Padthaway and Wrattonbully, with Mount Benson, Robe, and Mount Gambier much smaller, and Bordertown yet to seek individual recognition.

Padthaway was the first limestone-rich alternative to Coonawarra to be scouted out in this remote corner of Australia's wine state. While the soils are not dissimilar to Coonawarra's, the climate is usefully warmer, although it took the big companies that dominated vineyard ownership here some time to work out that the region is best at Chardonnay and Shiraz. Most of the grapes are shipped north to be vinified in big company cellars.

Wrattonbully, just north of Coonawarra, is cooler and more homogeneous than Padthaway and, not least thanks to its terra rossa soils, is likely to prove the most interesting, although it has only about a third the vineyard area of Coonawarra and half that of the more established Padthaway. Several high-profile family companies have invested here. A few plantings around **Mount Gambier**, the newest GI, suggest that this southern outpost of mixed farming is too cool to ripen Bordeaux grapes but shows potential for Pinot Noir.

Mount Benson has almost a score of individual growers, while **Robe**, the remarkably similar region to the south, has been virtually colonized by Treasury Wine Estates. Wine made from fruit grown right on the coast here is juicier, less concentrated, than the sinewy ferments of Coonawarra. Sea breezes cool the vineyards almost constantly, although they can be dangerously salty this close to the sea. At least the underground water table is free of salinity (a common problem in parts of Australia), and the prospects, give or take a frost or two, look good.

There are several extensive vineyards, the warmest at Limestone Coast, just west of Bordertown, to the northeast of Padthaway, and at Elgin near the coast, due west of Coonawarra, as well as scattered plantings at Mundulla and Lucindale.

Chandon's fizz is based on grapes grown in more than one state, a classic Oz ploy. Boireann is one of Queensland's best, and the other two are thoroughly modern wines from Wrattonbully on the Limestone Coast.

Western Australia

West to east is the way this Atlas travels. "WA" is our landfall; not the first in importance of Australia's wine regions, with less than 5% of the country's wine output, but in quality terms very near the top, with a distinctive lightness of touch combined with ripeness of fruit – an unusual combination in Australia. Margaret River, its single most important region, is mapped overleaf.

The first colonists of Western Australia were almost as quick to start winemaking as those of New South Wales. The Swan Valley, just upstream from the state capital, Perth, saw its first vintage in 1834. From the searing heat of the summer, with dry winds from the interior keeping temperatures close to 100°F (38°C) for weeks, the early vintners realized that their forte for many decades would be dessert wines. It says much for their skill and ingenuity that the pioneer, Houghton, nonetheless made what for years was the whole country's best-selling dry white: its "White Burgundy", based on Chenin Blanc and perfumed with who-knows-what, in the baking heat of vineyards around Perth. It was not until the late 1960s that Western Australians realized that the real potential lay further south, in the cooler parts of this vast, almost empty, state where Antarctic currents and onshore westerlies cool things down considerably.

Great Southern

The **Great Southern** region, first staked out at Mount Barker in the 1960s and progressively extended, offers some of the coolest, wettest terrain in Australia with some grapes still on the vine well into May. Plantagenet was the pre-eminent pioneer, but the region has since been invaded by an army of small growers. Some of them rely on one of several sizeable contract winemaking operations, but more and more of them are pursuing their own small-scale independent projects. Unusually for Australia, Great Southern has been divided into subregions: Albany, Denmark, Frankland River, Mount Barker, and Porongurup.

The most obvious strengths of **Mount Barker** (not to be confused with the Mount Barker of Adelaide Hills) have so far been fine Riesling, Cabernet Sauvignon, and some attractively peppery Shiraz. Forest Hill vineyard, planted in 1966, recently revived, and supplying the winery of the same name in Denmark, qualifies as one of the Western Australian wine industry's historic landmarks. **Denmark** on the coast is even wetter but often warmer. It can be a challenge to ripen Bordeaux varieties and keep thinner-skinned Shiraz healthy, so early-maturing Pinot Noir and Chardonnay work best.

Albany is the region's principal population centre, and Western Australia's first European settlement. Shiraz and Pinot Noir both seem at home here. Higher and further inland, a string of vineyards along the Porongurup's striking granite range produce fine, particularly mineral, taut Riesling, while Chardonnay and Pinot Noir go from strength to strength.

Boom-time arrived at the **Frankland River** in the late 1990s, largely driven by tax incentives. This subregion, inland and west of Mount Barker, now has Great Southern's greatest concentration of vineyards (and a 1,000-acre/400ha olive estate), though few wineries. Ferngrove is by far the biggest operation; Alkoomi has an established reputation for Sauvignon Blanc (and olive oil). Frankland Estate's strength is single-vineyard Riesling and a Bordeaux blend known as Olmo's Reward in recognition of the California professor who first suggested back in the 1950s that the area would be suitable for viticulture. The Westfield vineyard has long provided fruit for Houghton's superlative red blend named after Jack Mann, even if, as so often, Great Southern is not acknowledged on the label.

Towards the Indian Ocean

Most significant of the many vineyards between here and the Indian Ocean coast are the plantings in truffle capital Manjimup and Pemberton.

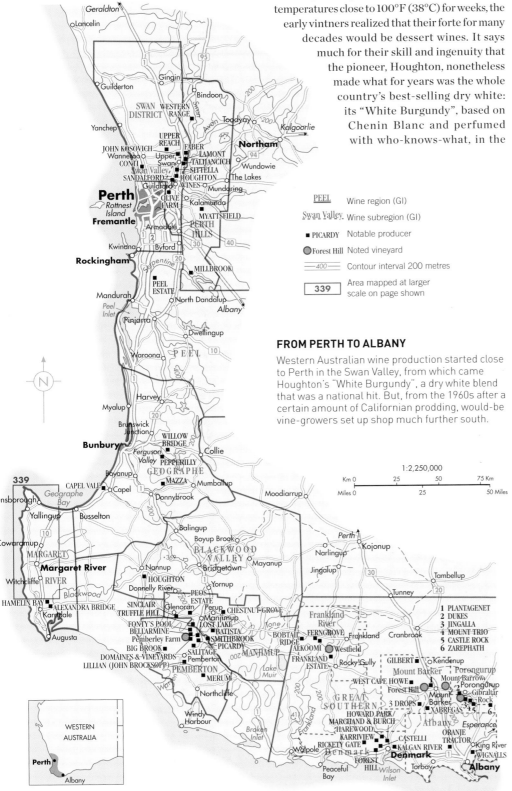

FROM PERTH TO ALBANY

Western Australian wine production started close to Perth in the Swan Valley, from which came Houghton's "White Burgundy", a dry white blend that was a national hit. But, from the 1960s after a certain amount of Californian prodding, would-be vine-growers set up shop much further south.

PEEL — Wine region (GI)
Swan Valley — Wine subregion (GI)
■ PICARDY — Notable producer
⬤ Forest Hill — Noted vineyard
400 — Contour interval 200 metres
339 — Area mapped at larger scale on page shown

1 PLANTAGENET
2 DUKES
3 JINGALLA
4 MOUNT TRIO
5 CASTLE ROCK
6 ZAREPHATH

The proximity of the Indian Ocean and its underpopulated coastline is a key feature of Margaret River's appeal to tourists, wine drinkers, and winemakers with a love of surfing.

Being further from the cooling influence of Antarctic currents on the coast, **Manjimup** has a slightly more continental climate, and a higher proportion of gravelly loam soils. But although

Manjimup's potential shines through in Batista Pinot Noirs, **Pemberton** has the higher profile. Producers such as Picardy and Salitage are concentrating on Burgundy varieties with some fine results, and Pemberton's Sauvignon Blanc is among the state's best. Pemberley Farms grows fruit for many of the state's benchmark examples. Bellarmine's German founders make great Riesling, while Leeuwin Estate's former

viticulturist, John Brocksopp of Lillian, has a winning way with white Rhône varieties.

As in Margaret River to the south, it was men of medicine – Dr Peter Pratten (of Capel Vale) and Dr Barry Killerby – who, in the 1970s, established the **Geographe** wine region. Both planted vineyards on the southern coastal strip between Bunbury and Busselton known as Capel. Geographe's climate, like Margaret River's, is thoroughly influenced by the Indian Ocean, but the soils are more varied, ranging from sandy coastal plains (the so-called Tuart Sands) to alluvial soils and, in the hillier country away from the coast, granite. There has been considerable growth, especially inland in the Ferguson Valley, Donnybrook, and Harvey. A wide range of grape varieties can thrive here. In addition to traditional strengths Chardonnay and the Bordeaux varieties, Tempranillo shows promise, as do some Italian varieties. Rhôneish red blends are becoming a signature strength of the Ferguson Valley. **Blackwood Valley** is essentially the land between Geographe and Manjimup. The region has grown significantly in the last 15 years, but has been slower to raise its profile, although Barwick Estates' The Collectables Cabernet Sauvignon demonstrates just how well suited the variety is to this beautiful corner of the world.

Some of Great Southern's most exciting expressions of the two Burgundy grapes are to be found under the Marchand & Burch label, a joint venture between French Canadian winemaker Pascal Marchand and Howard Park's owners, Jeff and Amy Burch.

Margaret River

Australia has few landscapes as green or forests as splendid as the soaring karri and jarrah woods of Western Australia's most famous wine region, dotted with brilliantly coloured birds and lolloping kangaroos. Surf reliably breaks on the rocky, deserted coastline and the introduction of vineyards surely tilted the whole package slap-bang into paradise. Today, tourists can choose from no fewer than 80 cellar doors to encourage the illusion.

The first wines here emerged in the early 1970s, from Vasse Felix, followed by Moss Wood and then Cullen – all of them, true to Australian wine history form, created by doctors. Critics immediately recognized a quite remarkable quality in the wines, particularly in the Cabernets. Sandalford, Houghton's neighbour and rival in the Swan Valley, rapidly moved in with a large plantation. Robert Mondavi of California became enthused and encouraged Denis Horgan to develop the ambitious Leeuwin Estate, which rapidly became as famous for its creamily authoritative Chardonnay as for its world-class outdoor concerts.

Today, Margaret River has more than 150 producers, on wildly varying soils, of which free-draining ironstone gravels are most prized for the region's exceptionally fine reds. Spring can be so windy as to affect flowering and reduce the crop, especially of the millerandage-prone Gingin clone of Chardonnay that predominates here. Yet, this is one of the reasons for the concentration of flavour in many wines from the heartland of Margaret River. Summers are dry and warm and, because the region is less than 19 miles (30km) wide, it is tempered by winds off the Indian Ocean. Grapes may be picked as early as January.

The Cabernet heartland of the Wilyabrup Valley is most heavily planted, but the vine extends the whole length of the region – from milder Yallingup in the north (which benefits from the tempering influence of Geographe Bay) all the way to Augusta on the Southern Ocean coast. Here, the dominant influence is Antarctica rather than the Indian Ocean. This is classic white wine country, although Suckfizzle, McHenry Hohnen, and others have demonstrated that fine reds can also be produced in the southern half of this map.

Margaret River's reputation has been built on Cabernet Sauvignon. It joins such other west coast wine regions as Bordeaux, Bolgheri, Napa Valley, and the Limestone Coast (see p.336) in its propensity to turn the rays of the setting sun into some of the most satisfying, and age-worthy, red wine in the world. There is both finesse and ripeness in Margaret River's best Cabernets, although most producers also make a Bordeaux blend, usually Cabernet/Merlot (of which Cullen is the prime exponent). Malbec and Petit Verdot are increasingly grown, too.

Nor has the region's obvious affinity with Cabernet hindered plantings of Shiraz, which is almost as important and typically reaches an appetizing halfway house of ripeness between Barossa heft and white pepper. Chardonnay shines here too, not just at Leeuwin Estate but notably at Pierro, Voyager Estate, Cape Mentelle, Xanadu, Cullen, and others. The region has also established a national if not international reputation for its very own vibrant, tropical fruit-flavoured blend of Semillon and Sauvignon Blanc. The range of grape varieties planted and taken seriously has been expanding as rapidly in Margaret River as elsewhere.

NORTHERN AND CENTRAL MARGARET RIVER

Most of Margaret River's finest wines have so far been produced in a remarkably small area in the north of the region, but the southern sector is being developed by increasingly ambitious producers.

MARGARET RIVER: ▼
MARGARET RIVER

Latitude / Altitude of WS
-33.53° / 358ft (109m)

Average growing season temperature at WS
66.2°F (19.0°C)

Average annual rainfall at WS
30in (759mm)

Harvest month rainfall at WS
March: 1.4in (21mm)

Principal viticultural hazards
Wind, birds

Principal grape varieties
Cabernet Sauvignon, Shiraz, Semillon, Chardonnay, Sauvignon Blanc

Cabernet blends are Margaret River's most obvious forte, but the whites can be very good, too. Sauvignon/Semillon blends are another Margaret River speciality, and Stella Bella's Suckfizzle is given a Graves-like twist by being partially barrel-fermented.

■ CULLEN   Notable producer
    Vineyards
─ 100 ─   Contour interval 50 metres
▼   Weather station (WS)

South Australia: Barossa Valley

South Australia is to Australia what California is to the USA: the wine state. It crushes an increasing proportion, already almost half, of every vintage and houses all the most important wine and vine research organizations. Adelaide, the state capital, is fittingly surrounded by vineyards. The landscape on the 35-mile (55km) drive northeast to South Australia's answer to the Napa Valley, Barossa Valley, is filled with vines. Founded by German-speaking immigrants from Silesia in what is now Poland, much in the Barossa Valley, including a sense of community and an appetite for hard work and Wurst, is still Germanic to this day.

Barossa is Australia's biggest quality wine district. It follows the North Para River for almost 20 closely planted miles (nearly 30km), and spreads eastwards into the next valley, Eden Valley (see overleaf), from the 750ft (230m) altitude of Lyndoch to 1,800ft (550m) in the east Barossa Ranges. The Barossa Zone encompasses these two contiguous wine regions, so a wine labelled just "Barossa" may be made from a blend of Eden Valley and Barossa Valley grapes.

Although nights are cool (much cooler than McLaren Vale, for instance), Barossa summers are hot and dry. But the region's rich legacy of

mature, deep-rooted, unirrigated bush-vines – of which around 200 acres (80ha) are over 100 years old – are well-adapted to this climate. Because there is a stringently imposed quarantine, South Australia is yet to be invaded by the phylloxera louse, so most vines are ungrafted and are planted directly into the soil, many of them cuttings from older vines.

Such vines can produce the most concentrated form of what has become one of the world's most distinctive wine styles, Barossa Shiraz. Rich and chocolaty, spicy and never shy,

these wines can range from unctuously alcoholic elixirs to a more modern idea: earlier picked wines designed to showcase the valley's many different terroirs. Some Barossa winemakers add tannins as well as acid, however, so the typical Barossa Shiraz is a demanding mouthful, especially in youth. Instead of the long post-fermentation maceration that Bordeaux producers give their wines while extracting colour and tannins, Barossa

BAROSSA'S WINE COUNTRY

It is quite possible that when this map is updated for the next edition the names of some of the noted vineyards will have become official subregions.

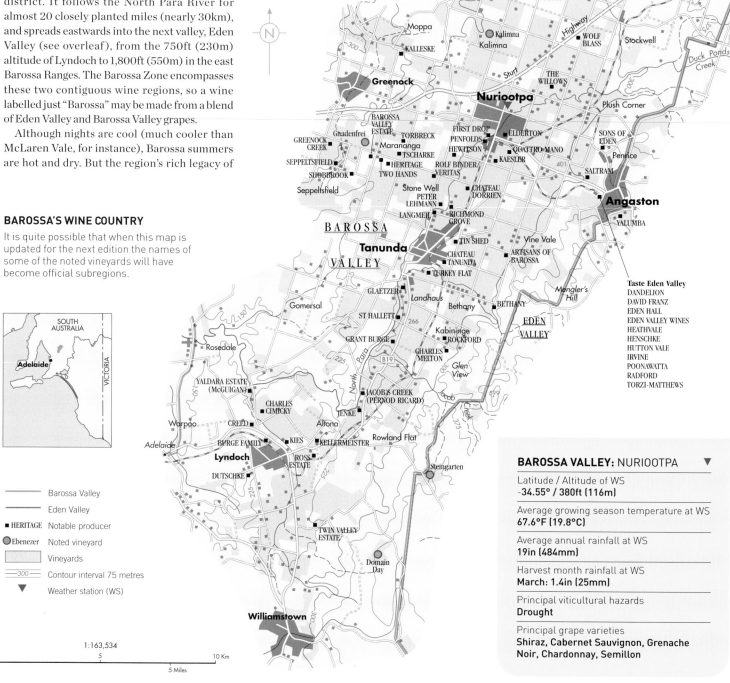

Barossa Valley
Eden Valley
■ HERITAGE   Notable producer
◉ Ebenezer   Noted vineyard
▭   Vineyards
═300═   Contour interval 75 metres
▼   Weather station (WS)

1:163,534
Km 0   5   10 Km
Miles 0   5 Miles

Taste Eden Valley
DANDELION
DAVID FRANZ
EDEN HALL
EDEN VALLEY WINES
HEATHVALE
HENSCHKE
HUTTON VALE
IRVINE
POONAWATTA
RADFORD
TORZI-MATTHEWS

BAROSSA VALLEY: NURIOOTPA ▼

Latitude / Altitude of WS
-34.55° / 380ft (116m)

Average growing season temperature at WS
67.6°F (19.8°C)

Average annual rainfall at WS
19in (484mm)

Harvest month rainfall at WS
March: 1.4in (25mm)

Principal viticultural hazards
Drought

Principal grape varieties
Shiraz, Cabernet Sauvignon, Grenache Noir, Chardonnay, Semillon

reds are typically encouraged to finish their fermentation in American oak barrels, imbuing them with a heady Bourbon sweetness and smoothness. Although here again, the Australian winemaker's constant quest for evolution can be seen in the increasing use of more carefully coopered barrels of both American and, in some cases, French oak. Blends, whether inspired by the Rhône or Iberia, are increasingly popular.

Big business

In sheer volume, Barossa is dominated by the large subsidiaries of even larger global corporations. Treasury Wine Estates, for example, owns Penfolds (which blends its flagship Grange here from wines produced all over South Australia), Wolf Blass, and a host of other brands. French pastis maker Pernod Ricard owns the old Orlando, whose most famous brand by far is Jacob's Creek, named after a trickle near Rowland Flat. The biggest family-owned company, Yalumba, is based in Angaston on the border between Barossa and Eden valleys, but there are many others, of varying sizes. These range from Peter Lehmann, who virtually rescued the reputation of old-vine Barossa Shiraz single-handedly in the late 1980s when Cabernet was much more fashionable (but whose company was eventually taken over by Donald Hess of Switzerland in 2003), down to a host of ambitious winemakers keen to exploit the region's pockets of old vines, and also to play with alternative grape varieties.

There are old Grenache vines, too (capable of even higher alcohols) and old Mourvèdre, long called Mataro. "GSM" blends of both grapes with the ubiquitous Shiraz are popular. Semillon, some of it Barossa's very own pink-skinned clone, was

until recently more common than Chardonnay and can produce stunningly rich white wines. Cabernet Sauvignon can shine when planted on the most favoured dark grey-brown soils but Shiraz is more dependable, summer in and summer out, especially on the clay and limestone soils of the valley.

Some of the most admired Shirazes come from the valley's northwest and central reaches around Ebenezer, Tanunda, Moppa, Kalimna, Greenock, Marananga, and Stonewell, where ancient stocks of dry-farmed Shiraz can yield wines of real complexity. However, such a high proportion of vines is owned by growers, rather than winemakers, that there is a delicate tension between grape prices and quality. Most of these ancient vines have been farmed all their lives by the same family, and many are hidden from view

Seppeltsfield, built of course by the Seppelt family, was Australia's biggest winery in 1900. It has been restored as the home of Barossa Valley's leading collection of fortified wines, many of them delicious antiques. This is the only producer in the world able to release a 100-year-old wine every year – albeit by the individual thimbleful.

of the thousands of tourists who flood the valley every week. Increasingly, the names of districts or subregions and even growers are cited on labels as producers seek to tease out the geographical distinctions within the valley and articulate the history and heritage behind the vines. In time, the Barossa Grape and Wine Association's Barossa Grounds project may result in these distinctions being formally recognized as subregions, as High Eden in the Eden Valley already is (see overleaf).

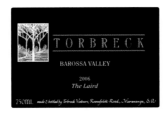

Some of the Barossa's finest from names old (Lehmann and Kalleske), new (First Drop's 2% of Tempranillo in the Shiraz) and middle-aged (Torbreck and John Duval, who made the iconic Penfolds Grange before going solo).

Eden Valley

The Eden Valley is in higher, prettier country than the Barossa Valley. Its vineyards, planted up to 1,640ft (500m) but much more sporadically than on the valley floor, are scattered among rocky hills, dusty lanes, country estates, and eucalyptus groves. Historically, though, it is an eastern extension of the Barossa Valley. Captain Joseph Gilbert established the Pewsey Vale vineyard as early as 1847; the site now belongs to Yalumba of Angaston, the family company that has played such a large part in developing Eden Valley's potential for Riesling.

When modern times called for table wines rather than the fortified dessert wines, it was Riesling, strangely enough, that Barossa did best. With the Silesian settlers came a fondness for the grape, and growers found that the higher they went into the hills to the east, the finer and more crisply fruity the wine became. In the early 1960s, Colin Gramp (whose family owned Orlando until 1971) was inspired by a trip to Germany to devote a patch of schistous hilltop that a sheep would scarcely pause on to Riesling and called it Steingarten, thereby giving Australian Riesling a new dimension and proving its longevity.

Eden Valley Riesling at its best has a floral, sometimes mineral, top note to it when young. Like the Clare Valley Riesling with which it is inevitably compared, it becomes increasingly toasty after time in the bottle. Eden Valley Riesling loses its acidity faster and tends towards grapefruit whereas Clare Valley Riesling is characterized more by piercing lime.

Riesling may be important, but Shiraz is the region's leading grape, however, and Henschke grows some of Australia's very best examples: Mount Edelstone, well up in the hills, and above all from the Hill of Grace vineyard originally planted in 1860. The first single-vineyard bottling from the Shiraz vines grown on half of this historic, actually rather flat 19 acre (8ha) site was the 1958 vintage. Today, its price on release rivals that of the iconic, and notably more concentrated, South Australian blend Penfolds Grange. A new generation – Hobbs, Radford, Shobbrook, Torzi Matthews, Tin Shed, and their like – are demonstrating the finesse of which this high country is capable in single-vineyard wines, while many a wine labelled simply "Barossa" (as opposed to "Barossa Valley") owes its vivaciousness to the addition of an Eden Valley component.

Fingers over a hose help to aerate must at Henschke, the most revered wine family of Eden Valley. No shortage of colour here. Note the characteristic architecture in the background. The Henschke family has been making wine for six generations – although this is not exceptional in the South Australian wine industry.

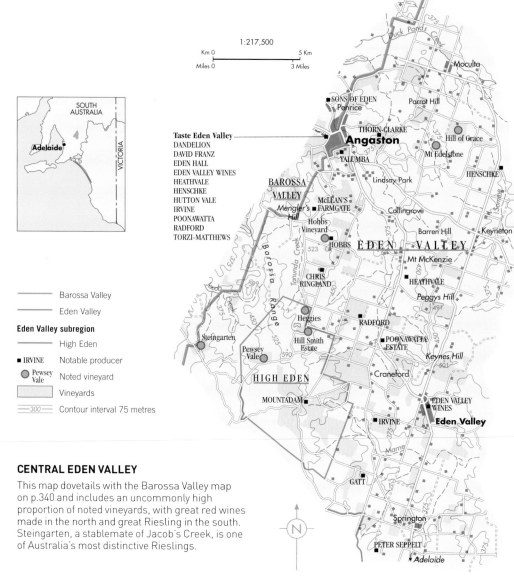

Taste Eden Valley
DANDELION
DAVID FRANZ
EDEN HALL
EDEN VALLEY WINES
HEATHVALE
HENSCHKE
HUTTON VALE
IRVINE
POONAWATTA
RADFORD
TORZI-MATTHEWS

— Barossa Valley
— Eden Valley
Eden Valley subregion
— High Eden
■ IRVINE Notable producer
◉ Pewsey Vale Noted vineyard
▨ Vineyards
═300═ Contour interval 75 metres

CENTRAL EDEN VALLEY

This map dovetails with the Barossa Valley map on p.340 and includes an uncommonly high proportion of noted vineyards, with great red wines made in the north and great Riesling in the south. Steingarten, a stablemate of Jacob's Creek, is one of Australia's most distinctive Rieslings.

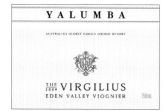

Yalumba was a pioneer of Australia's now well-established Viognier production, The Virgilius its top bottling. Torzi Matthews' brand name acknowledges the frost pocket on Mount McKenzie, where its low-yielding Shiraz is planted at 1,240ft (380m) altitude.

Clare Valley

Riesling is even better entrenched in the prettily pastoral Clare Valley than in the Eden Valley. Clare lies well north of the northernmost limit of Barossa, isolated and rural but multi-talented. It has the unique distinction of making world-class Shiraz and Cabernet as well as one of Riesling's great archetypes.

Clare Valley is in fact a series of narrow, mainly north–south valleys on an elevated plateau with very different soil types in each. In the southern heartland of the region between Watervale and Auburn, considered classic Riesling country, is some of the famous limestone-based terra rossa (see p.347), which yields perfumed, highly expressive Rieslings. A few miles north around Polish Hill River, notably at Jeffrey Grosset's revered Polish Hill vineyard, vines struggle in the hard slate soils and the wines are more austere. The northern, more open part of the Clare Valley feels warm westerlies blowing in from the Spencer Gulf, whereas the southern part, from Watervale south, enjoys cooler breezes from Gulf St Vincent. Clare is only about a third of the size of Barossa Valley, but with its higher altitude has a more extreme climate. The cool

nights help to preserve acidity; in many vintages routine acid addition is unnecessary.

Clare feels remote. Its producers are proud to be distant from the influence of fashion and big company politics. Only Knappstein and Petaluma, part of Lion Nathan, and Annie's Lane and Leo Buring, owned by Treasury Wine Estates, have any connection with large corporations. This is farming country in the hands of small farmers in the main, who form an unusually cohesive group. They were the first in Australia to agree to move to screw caps to preserve the steely purity of their Rieslings.

In the hands of literally dozens of Riesling producers as capable as Grosset, Kilikanoon, Jim Barry, and Petaluma, Clare Riesling has established itself as Australia's most distinctive:

NORTHERN AND CENTRAL CLARE VALLEY

Given its latitude, this strip shouldn't really make some of the world's more thrilling Riesling – but it does. Altitude helps, as vineyards are at 1,300–1,870ft (400–570m), but so do breezes off the gulfs to the south.

Netting as grapes register alluring (to birds) levels of sugar is essential at Sevenhills winery, the oldest in Clare Valley and established in 1851 by Jesuits to provide sacramental wine.

firm and dry, sometimes eye-watering in youth, but usually with a rich undertow of lime that can mature to toastiness after years in bottle. These are the wines for which Australia's famous fusion food has surely been designed. More recently, a trickle of slightly sweeter styles of Riesling has emerged to please those of less masochistic tendencies.

Great, plummy reds with excellent acidity and structure are also made, provoking discussion as to whether Shiraz or Cabernet is Clare's most eloquent dark expression. Particularly smooth-talking Cabernets and Shirazes come from Jim Barry, Kilikanoon, Taylors, and Skillogalee. From the region's highest vineyard (at 1,870ft/570m), Grosset's perfumed Gaia Bordeaux blend is a little more elegant than most, while the reds of pioneer Wendouree continue to be positively and distinctively chewable.

■ GROSSET Notable producer
⬤ Clos Clare Noted vineyard
▢ Vineyards
〜300〜 Contour interval 75 metres

1:250,000

Km 0 —— 5 —— 10 Km
Miles 0 —— 5 Miles

SOUTH AUSTRALIA

Adelaide

VICTORIA

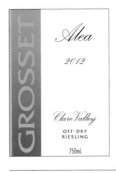

Grosset led the march into bone-dry, almost austere Oz Rieslings, but Alea suggests that a little bit of sweetness may not be totally evil. Kilikanoon is another Clare Valley star, with a particularly wide range of accomplishments.

McLaren Vale and Beyond

The Fleurieu Zone, named after the Fleurieu Peninsula, points southwest from Adelaide, through McLaren Vale and Southern Fleurieu to Kangaroo Island, now a fashionable resort. It also extends southeast to include Langhorne Creek and Currency Creek (see map, p.334). Jacques Lurton from Bordeaux has reversed the usual flying winemaker pattern here, commuting to **Kangaroo Island**, while at the highest point in **Southern Fleurieu** Brian Croser, founder of Petaluma, is making some pretty impressive Pinot Noir.

But for the moment by far the most prominent and historic wine region in the Fleurieu Zone is McLaren Vale, a popular tourist destination, but unfortunately a victim of Adelaide's urban sprawl. John Reynell, who gave his name to Chateau Reynella, planted South Australia's first vines in 1838, and McLaren Vale can still boast many old vines, some more than 100 years old. [For most of the intervening decades, Reynella claret and fortified wines were respected names, and the original underground cellar that Reynell built is one of the historic landmarks of Australian wine. Today, it is the headquarters of the almost equally ancient firm of Thomas Hardy & Sons (now part of the giant Accolade company) along with the Tintara winery bought by the original Thomas Hardy in 1876.

In the cooler northern area around Blewitt Springs, deep sandy soils over clay produce good, aromatic, spicy Grenache and Shiraz. With its greater diurnal range, Kangarilla to the east produces more "elegant", tarter Shiraz than the McLaren Vale norm. The area north of the township of **McLaren Vale** has some of the thinnest topsoil, resulting in low yields and intense flavours. Willunga, lying to the south of the town, feels less of the ocean and seems to ripen its grapes later.

Recent plantings, many of which are in the flat southeastern sector of the region (although some nudge up into the Sellicks foothills that overlook the coast) tend to ripen faster than the norm and often have a herbal note. Overall, harvesting begins in February and may continue well into April for some of the classic Grenache and Mourvèdre vines.

The local climate could hardly be better for the vine than in this coastal zone, a narrow band between the heights of Mount Lofty Ranges and the temperate sea. There is a long, warm growing season, good air drainage to prevent frosts, and about 20% of vineyards survive without the irrigation water that is in increasingly short supply. The ocean supplies some cooling influence, particularly in the form of afternoon breezes, which help to retain acidity. Nonetheless, white grapes are very much in the minority and the region has yet to develop a clear varietal strength, though not for want of experimentation. Vermentino, Fiano,

The dramatic distinction between the dry hills and the verdant, nay luxuriant, vineyards suggests that added water is a factor here. McLaren Vale now represents a model of waste water recovery and re-use for other Australian wine regions to copy.

Viognier, and Roussanne all show promise. As for Chardonnay and Sauvignon Blanc, the cooler neighbouring Adelaide Hills is much more suitable. And why try to grow everything?

There is a confidence in McLaren Vale's glossily seductive reds, with old-vine Shiraz, Cabernet Sauvignon, and then Grenache clear varietal strengths. Chapel Hill, d'Arenberg, Hugh Hamilton, Paxton, Samuel's Gorge, SC Pannell, Ulithorne, Wirra Wirra, and Yangarra Estate all make good examples. And Coriole, Kangarilla Road, and Primo Estate demonstrated quite some time ago that the palette of varieties could be widened to include at least Sangiovese, Nebbiolo, and Primitivo (also known as Zinfandel). Iberian grapes are showing great promise, especially Tempranillo at Cascabel and Gemtree Estate, while Georgia's Saperavi and Italy's Sagrantino are especially valued for their high acidity. At least 80 wineries are based in McLaren Vale, although more than half the fruit grown here is plundered by others – some located as far afield as the Hunter Valley – to add plump ballast to blends. McLaren Vale's Shiraz is said to contribute a mocha and warm-earth character; others detect savoury black olive and leather notes.

South Australia's big secret

Langhorne Creek, it could be argued, is South Australian wine's big secret. Less than a fifth of the wine made here is sold with the region's name on the label, even though it is as productive as McLaren Vale. Most wine disappears into the blends put together by the big companies keen to take advantage of the region's dominant strengths: soft, gentle, mouth-filling Shiraz and succulent Cabernet Sauvignon. Originally, this fertile bed of deep alluvium was irrigated by deliberate late-winter flooding from the diverted Bremer and Angas rivers, an unreliable water supply that limited expansion. It has only been since the early 1990s, when licences were granted to transport irrigation water from Lake Alexandrina at the mouth of the mighty Murray River, that Langhorne Creek has seen rapid development.

The older vines tend to be close to the riverbanks. They include the famous Metala vineyard owned by the Adams family, of Brothers in Arms, since 1891, and those planted by Frank Potts at Bleasdale once he had felled the titanic red gums growing by the Bremer River. But ambitious new plantings such as those of Angas Vineyards pipe water to their high-tech irrigation systems via a complex network of ditches on the pancake flat-land.

The so-called Lake Doctor, a reliable afternoon breeze off the lake, slows ripening here so that grapes are usually picked two weeks later than those of McLaren Vale.

Currency Creek to the immediate west also depends crucially on irrigation, but is so far the domain of small, relatively low-profile wineries. It is slightly warmer than Langhorne Creek, but even more maritime.

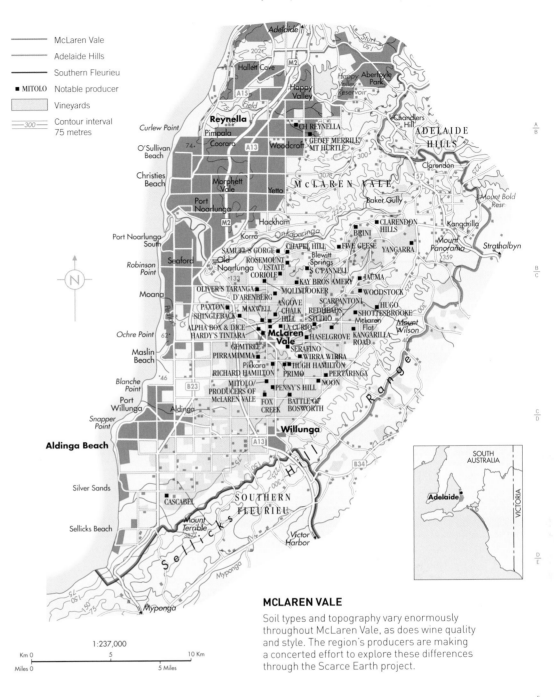

Legend:
- McLaren Vale
- Adelaide Hills
- Southern Fleurieu
- ■ MITOLO Notable producer
- Vineyards
- —300— Contour interval 75 metres

1:237,000
Km 0 — 5 — 10 Km
Miles 0 — 5 Miles

MCLAREN VALE

Soil types and topography vary enormously throughout McLaren Vale, as does wine quality and style. The region's producers are making a concerted effort to explore these differences through the Scarce Earth project.

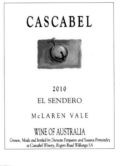

First Shiraz, then GSMs (blends of Grenache, Mourvèdre, and Shiraz) became commonplace. But now, all-Grenaches such as Steve Pannell's are gaining respect, especially in McLaren Vale, where the best wines really do taste like sunshine in a bottle.

Adelaide Hills

When Adelaide warms up in the summer there is always somewhere nearby to cool off: the Mount Lofty Ranges just east of the city. Clouds from the west collect here over green hills. The southern tip of the Adelaide Hills region may skirt the northeastern boundary of McLaren Vale but they are worlds apart. **Adelaide Hills** was the first Australian region to establish a reputation for reliably citrus-fresh Sauvignon Blanc – now the area's lead variety, closely followed by Chardonnay. The 1,300ft (400m) contour line provides the boundary of the appellation, except to the north. At altitudes above this, grey mist is common, as is spring frost, and chilly nights, even in summer. Rainfall is relatively high, but concentrated in winter. Generalizations are difficult, however, about a wine region that stretches 50 miles (80km) from northeast to southwest.

The **Piccadilly Valley** on Mount Lofty was originally staked out in the 1970s by Brian Croser, founder of Petaluma, as a defiantly cool area for Chardonnay vines, then a novelty in Australia. Since then, the area under vine has substantially increased. Everyone wants cool-climate fruit. These days, the region has around 90 wineries, and many more growers who supply producers big and small.

While Shiraz plantings have almost doubled over the last decade, Cabernet and, especially Merlot have declined in importance. Perhaps unsurprisingly, given that the region also makes fine sparkling wines, Pinot Noir is the lead red variety, and producers such as Ashton Hills, Barratt Wines, Jeffrey Grosset, Henschke, Leabrook Estate, Lucy Margaux Vineyards, and Nepenthe have made competent still versions. Tempranillo and Italian varieties, especially Nebbiolo, show promise.

Even Chardonnay can be Sauvignon-like with brisk nectarine flavours and real precision. Such producers as Nepenthe and The Lane make equally precise aromatic wines from Viognier and Pinot Gris. Riesling clearly thrives here, too.

Piccadilly Valley and **Lenswood** are the only two official subregions to date, but many locals consider that Basket Range, Birdwood, Charleston, Echunga, Hahndorf, Kuitpo, Macclesfield, Mount Barker, Paracombe, and Woodside all have discernible and distinctive characteristics.

SOUTHWEST ADELAIDE HILLS

Only the southwestern corner of the Adelaide Hills is mapped in detail here. To the north, vineyards around Gumeracha are warm enough to ripen Cabernet Sauvignon, and some particularly Rhône-like Shiraz comes from Mount Barker, southeast of Stirling.

For a long time, Adelaide Hills was regarded as a white wine region, but Australia's newfound enthusiasm for (relatively) cool-climate Shiraz has changed perceptions of some of the region's reds.

ADELAIDE HILLS: LENSWOOD ▼

Latitude / Altitude of WS
-35.06° / 1,191ft (363m)

Average growing season temperature at WS
63.2°F (17.3°C)

Average annual rainfall at WS
28in (717mm)

Harvest month rainfall at WS
April: 1.9in (49mm)

Principal viticultural hazards
Poor fruit set, spring frost

Principal grape varieties
Sauvignon Blanc, Chardonnay, Pinot Noir, Shiraz, Pinot Gris/Grigio, Riesling.

Coonawarra

The story of Coonawarra is to a large extent the story of terra rossa. Indeed, it has defined the region's hotly contested borders. As far back as the 1860s, early settlers became aware of a very odd patch of ground 250 miles (400km) south of Adelaide and its essentially Mediterranean climate. Just north of the village of Penola, a long, narrow rectangle, only 9 miles by less than one (15 by 1.5km), of completely level soil is distinctively red in colour and crumbly to touch. Below lies pure, free-draining limestone and, beneath that, a permanent table of relatively pure water. No land could be better designed for fruit growing. The entrepreneur John Riddoch started the Penola Fruit Colony, and by 1900 the area, under the name of Coonawarra, was producing large quantities of an unfamiliar kind of wine, largely Shiraz, but brisk and fruity with moderate alcohol: not unlike Bordeaux, in fact.

This great resource, an Australian vineyard producing wines with a structure quite different from most, was for a long time appreciated by very few. Only with the table wine boom in the 1960s was its potential fully realized, and the big names of the wine industry began to move in. Wynns is by far the single largest winemaking landowner, although its owner, Treasury Wine Estates, controls a good half of all the vineyard through its other labels Penfolds, Lindeman's, and Jamiesons Run as well. Partly because of this, considerable amounts of Coonawarra fruit end up in wines blended and bottled many miles away. Such producers as Balnaves, Bowen, Hollick, Katnook, Leconfield, Majella, Parker, Penley, Petaluma, Rymill, and Zema on the other hand offer something much closer to the estate model.

Made in heaven

Shiraz may have been the original Coonawarra speciality, but since Mildara demonstrated in the early 1960s that conditions were close to ideal for Cabernet Sauvignon, Coonawarra Cabernet has been one of Australia's remarkably few

Yalumba's vineyard for its The Menzies Coonawarra Cabernet illustrates terra rossa ("red earth") nicely. Note those carefully orientated rows.

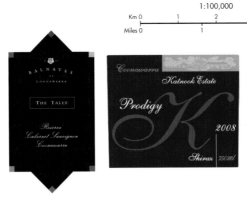
For decades, much of Coonawarra's vineyard has been dictated by head offices hundreds of miles away (Katnook is owned by Freixenet of Catalunya in Spain) but there are family companies here, too, such as Balnaves.

touchstone combinations of variety and place. Since almost six vines in every 10 in Coonawarra are Cabernet Sauvignon, the fortunes of Coonawarra have tended to rise and fall with the popularity of Australian Cabernet.

Coonawarra's soil was not the only reason for this marriage apparently made in heaven. The area is considerably further south, hence cooler, than any other South Australian wine region, and only 50 miles (80km) from an exposed coast, washed by the Antarctic currents and fanned by westerlies all summer. Frost is a problem in spring and rain at vintage time – enough to make a French grower quite nostalgic. Indeed, Coonawarra is cooler than Bordeaux, and sprinkler irrigation is used to counter the threat of frost. That said, in the last, relatively dry decade most producers have had to introduce some form of supplementary irrigation. If the will is there, vigour can be fine-tuned on terra rossa, unlike the darker and naturally damper rendzina soils to the west.

In the 1990s, Coonawarra's total vineyard area more than doubled and the region's isolation and sparse population meant that many vines were pruned, or at least pre-pruned, and picked mechanically. While Cabernet remains by far the most planted variety, Shiraz and various clones of Malbec are now rather more common. More than 25 cellar doors are valiantly aimed at such tourists as make it this far south – quite a feat considering that there are only 15 working wineries.

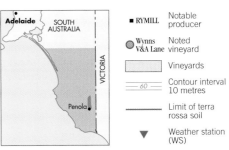

COONAWARRA: COONAWARRA ▼

Latitude / Altitude of WS
-37.75° / 207ft (63m)

Average growing season temperature at WS
61.9°F (16.6°C)

Average annual rainfall at WS
23in (576mm)

Harvest month rainfall at WS
April: 1.4in (35mm)

Principal viticultural hazards
Underripeness, spring frost, harvest rainfall

Principal grape varieties
Cabernet Sauvignon, Shiraz, Chardonnay, Merlot

Victoria

In many ways Victoria is the most interesting, the most dynamic, and certainly the most varied of Australia's wine states, even if today it is nowhere near as quantitatively important as it was at the end of the 19th century, when it had as much vineyard as New South Wales and South Australia put together. The gold rush of the mid-19th century helped to establish a wine industry (just as it had done in California), but then phylloxera arrived in the 1870s and was fatally destructive. Today Victoria produces less than half as much wine as South Australia, which has never known phylloxera, even if Victoria has almost twice as many wineries: 600, the majority relatively small scale.

No state makes a wider range of wine styles than Victoria. And because it is not associated with one or two particular wines, Victorian producers have long been some of the most idiosyncratic and experimental. The mysterious trees belong to new overachiever William Downie, who is making both Pinot Noir and Petit Manseng in a range of locations.

The state is the smallest and coolest on the Australian mainland, but it can boast the most diverse conditions for vine-growing, as you can see from the 19 official wine zones mapped opposite. They range from the arid, heavily irrigated inland Murray Darling region around Mildura, which straddles the Victoria–New South Wales border and grows 75% of all Victorian grapes by volume, to the mainland's coolest wine regions.

North East Victoria

The most important survivor of phylloxera, however, was the incontrovertibly hot North East Victoria Zone, which continues to specialize in fortified dessert wines unlike anything produced anywhere else. Marked differences between day- and night-time temperatures and long, dry autumns are the secret to **Rutherglen**'s famous "stickies", which benefit from Australia's longest

Brown Brothers' snow-covered Whitlands Vineyard leaves little doubt that King Valley is cool. A host of Melbourne wine lovers are introduced to some of Victoria's most interesting wine regions on their way to and from the ski slopes.

harvest. They are based on raisined dark-skinned Muscat and the more caramelized "Topaque": the new name for the Muscadelle of Sauternes and Bergerac also grown here. After years of ageing in old wooden casks they can achieve astonishingly silky richness, none more so than Rutherglen's Rare Muscats. Some truly boot-strapping reds are also made around Rutherglen and **Glenrowan**, the Jerez and Oporto of Australia, with the ancient Rhône Durif variety a speciality of Rutherglen.

Also in this corner of the state are three much higher, cooler wine regions: King Valley, Alpine Valleys, and Beechworth – all of potential interest to skiers as they head hopefully towards the snowfields of the Great Dividing Range. The family-owned Brown Brothers of Milawa is by far the dominant company of **King Valley**. Its flagship sparkling wine, Patricia, a blend of Pinot Noir and Chardonnay, is based on one of the company's highest vineyards, Whitlands at 2,600ft (800m). Brown Brothers was also one of the first in Australia to experiment with alternative grape varieties. Italian grapes have become a particular speciality here, not least

Key to producers
1 MUNARI
2 PAUL OSICKA
3 JASPER HILL/OCCAM'S RAZOR
4 DOWNING ESTATE
5 DOM TERLATO & M CHAPOUTIER
6 HEATHCOTE WINERY
7 HEATHCOTE ESTATE
8 DOM TOURNON (CHAPOUTIER)
9 WILD DUCK CREEK
10 REDESDALE ESTATE

State boundary

BENDIGO Geographical Indication (GI)

■ TAHBILK Notable producer

● Mt Ida Noted vineyard

Vineyards

Land above 600 metres

351 Area mapped at larger scale on page shown

1:2,000,000
Km 0   25   50   75   100 Km
Miles 0   25   50 Miles

CENTRAL VICTORIA

Just the look of all these wine regions is exciting enough. This is clearly a state with great variation today, but it also has a glorious wine-producing past. Partly thanks to the 19th-century gold rush, it was at one time Australia's leading wine state. But phylloxera did not help...

thanks to the pioneering work of the Pizzini family. Prosecco pioneer Dal Zotto has a similar Italian heritage, as does De Bortoli which sources its BellaRiva wines from a single vineyard here.

Many of these producers source grapes in the **Alpine Valleys** region, whose vineyards range between 180 to 600m. It, too, has more than a smattering of Italian and other alternative varieties. Gapsted is the label of the Victorian Alps Wine Company, a contract winery much used by companies outside the region – not least because this region is still plagued by phylloxera.

At rather lower altitudes around the historic gold-mining town of **Beechworth** some superlative, California-influenced Chardonnay is made by Giaconda, famous, too, for Roussanne and

its reds, while some markedly transparent Shiraz and Italian varieties are Castagna's speciality. Some gloriously intense grapes, including some unusual Gamay, are grown at Sorrenberg, one of the first of the modern wave of vineyards, which still cover just a tiny fraction of the area planted in the early 19th century. Savaterre has swiftly built a reputation for its muscular Pinot Noirs and Chardonnays. Unsurprisingly, the region's fruit draws top winemaking talent from afar; Brokenwood and Gary Mills of Jamsheed both produce Beechworth wines.

Western Victoria

Like the North East wine country, Great Western, the district made famous by Seppelt's

"champagne", never gave up, either. Now called **Grampians**, the region lies 1,100ft (335m) up at the westernmost end of the Great Dividing Range, on lime-rich soil. Seppelt and Best's, a miniature by comparison, have a long record of producing good still and sparkling wines in deep, cool caves here. Grapes for the oceans of fizz made at Seppelt Great Western come partly from Padthaway over the heavily patrolled (for phylloxera) border in South Australia and partly from irrigated vineyards along the Murray, but those for its extraordinary and deservedly celebrated sparkling Shiraz are grown locally. Mount Langi Ghiran's authoritatively peppery Shiraz eloquently explains why.

Pyrenees is the (ironic?) name of the rolling landscape to the east of the Grampians. This

country to the east, especially on its own special red Cambrian soils. The region is renowned for hauntingly rich but juicy Shiraz, although, with the benefit of specially selected Tuscan clones, Greenstone has shown that Heathcote Sangiovese can be remarkably refined. Also in this zone is **Goulbourn Valley**, where David Traeger, Mitchelton, and Tahbilk, once the sole survivor of the region, cluster in the far south. The special qualities here have earned it the status of a subregion called **Nagambie Lakes**, where, belying its name, a shortage of water is perennial. Rhône grapes thrive at Mitchelton and at Tahbilk, which is old enough to be classed a national monument. It still has Shiraz planted in 1860 and what are reputedly the world's oldest Marsanne vines.

Upper Goulburn is another wine region overlooked by ski country. Its higher altitudes (at Delatite, for example) can make wines with unusually fine definition, including an impressive range of vivid Rieslings. The memorably named **Strathbogie Ranges** lies between the two Goulburn regions and also makes some fine, taut Rieslings. It includes some extensive vineyards at up to 1,970ft (600m), where acidities are so high that Domaine Chandon grows Pinot Noir and Chardonnay as base wines for fizz.

Port Phillip and Gippsland

The Port Phillip Zone is now the name for the regions clustered around the epicurean city of Melbourne. The Mornington Peninsula and Yarra Valley are considered separately overleaf, but the long-established **Sunbury**, on the plains just north of Melbourne airport, is even closer to the city centre. Its standard-bearer has long been Craiglee, whose particular style of defiantly dry Shiraz has for decades remained admirably constant, savoury, and long-lived.

North of Sunbury, towards Bendigo, lies the **Macedon Ranges**, which encompasses some of Australia's coolest, not to say postively chilly, vine-growing conditions. Bindi's efforts near Gisborne and Curly Flat's near Lancefield show that this is fine Chardonnay and Pinot Noir country.

Pinot Noir is also the grape of choice for many growers in Victoria's new coastal wine regions, particularly in the barren, windy wine country of **Geelong**, where maritime influence is paramount, and By Farr, Bannockburn, and Scotchmans Hill ripen bumptious Pinot. Shadowfax is another ambitious winery on the western edge of Melbourne which buys fruit in this district.

Finally **Gippsland**, so big it's both a zone and a region that stretches far off this map to the east (see p.335), contains another vast array of different environments – so many that the region is ripe for subdivision. The wine with the longest track record is Bass Phillip's idiosyncratic Pinot Noir, grown just south of Leongatha, but William (Bill) Downie is proving definitively that this is Pinot country.

region is not notably cool (except sometimes at night) and its showpiece wines are big reds from Redbank and Dalwhinnie, which has also made a fine Chardonnay.

Henty, the third region of the Western Victoria Zone, has forged its reputation on wines from the cool, marginal south. Seppelt pioneered the region, calling it Drumborg, and was at times tempted to give up, but climate change has worked in Henty's favour. Crawford River, planted in 1975 by an ex-grazier, has shown that exceptionally fine, age-worthy Riesling can be produced here Further north and warmer – some 60 miles (100km) inland around Hamilton/Tarrington and a cluster of boutique wineries are becoming known for their cool-climate Shiraz. Tarrington

The modern face of Victorian wine production. Yering Station in Yarra Valley includes a modern bar and restaurant, art gallery, occasional farmers' market, and of course a cellar door for sales direct to all those visitors.

Vineyards has demonstrated extraordinary devotion to duty with Burgundian varieties.

Central Victoria

Inland, **Bendigo** in the Central Victorian Zone is even warmer. Its wines are epitomized (and were launched) by Balgownie's sumptuous reds. Then Jasper Hill and others showed what could be done in Heathcote's slightly cooler

Mornington Peninsula

Every other year the Mornington Peninsula, south of Melbourne, hosts an International Pinot Noir Celebration. For obvious reasons several of Burgundy's better wine producers are usually invited. They tend to arrive in Australia's greatest concentration of Pinot Noir vineyards sceptical and leave impressed.

It is difficult to think of any of the world's mushrooming hotbeds of Pinot Noir production that are quite as maritime as the Mornington Peninsula. It enjoys almost constant breezes, whether from the northwest over Port Phillip Bay or cooler winds from the southeast off the Southern Ocean. But these seem to serve merely as heat moderators rather than imbuing the wines with any obviously marine flavours. Indeed, the locals say that what determines ripeness and picking dates is much less likely to be the elevation of a specific vineyard but the prevailing winds to which it is exposed.

Summers are (usually) mild with mean January temperatures less than 68°F (20°C) – cooler than mean July temperatures in Burgundy – although there are occasional heat spikes that can inflict sunburn on the delicate Pinot grapes.

Vines have been grown on the peninsula since 1886, and in 1891, 14 grape-growers were mentioned in a royal commission into the fruit and vegetable industry. The modern wine scene dates from the early 1970s and the modern pioneers include Main Ridge, Moorooduc, Paringa, and Stonier, now part of Lion Nathan. Other old hands, all intensely involved in improving quality and promoting the region, include Eldridge, Kooyong, and Ten Minutes by Tractor, but there has been no shortage of new talent.

Fine food, fine art, fine wine

Unusually for Australia, there is no contract winery in this lush pastoral landscape, dotted with grand houses and estates built by well-heeled Melbournites. Instead, a good 60 of the 200-plus growers follow the Burgundy model of growing their own vines and making their own wine. An intense level of hands-on involvement is encouraged by the fact that two-thirds of wine estates are less than 10 acres (4ha). Because the area is so close to Melbourne, there are more than 50 cellar doors and, in line with Melbournian culture, many of these wineries have fine restaurants and/or art galleries attached. About a third of all Mornington Peninsula wine is sold at the cellar door. Too little of it is exported.

Mornington's signature grape

Although they have slowed because of the high cost of land here, total plantings of the vine doubled between 1996 and 2008. Pinot Noir has definitely been crowned the signature grape of Mornington, and accounts for about half of all plantings with more than 1,060 acres (430ha) in 2008, but the region is not quite as dependent on Pinot Noir as, say, Central Otago in New Zealand is. Chardonnay (some of which is very fine) has fallen to about 25% of all vines, while fashionable Pinot Gris/Grigio is now more than 10%. (The Yarra Valley has almost twice as much Pinot Noir in the ground as Mornington but it represents less than a quarter of all vines planted.) Soils vary considerably and include the red volcanic soils of Red Hill, the sedimentary yellow duplex of Tuerong, brown duplex of Merricks, and the sandier clay loam of Moorooduc.

The MV6 clone of Pinot Noir, Australia's most common, thought to have been brought from Clos Vougeot by James Busby in the early 19th century, has played an important part in the Mornington Peninsula, although Burgundian clones are now increasingly planted.

The most notable feature of Mornington Peninsula Pinot Noir is its refreshing acidity and purity. Very few wines are especially deep coloured nor particularly potent, but they are generally very pretty without being light. Wines, whether Pinot Noir, Pinot Gris (T'Gallant pioneered this variety in Australia here), or Chardonnay have crystalline, well-defined structure and no excess of body. For much of the late 20th century, Mornington Peninsula was a sort of playground for Melbournites who liked to get their fingers sticky with grape juice, but as vines have matured and the people growing them have been sucked into the absorbing minutiae of wine culture, quality has perceptibly risen so that this is one of Australia's most rewarding sources of handcrafted wine.

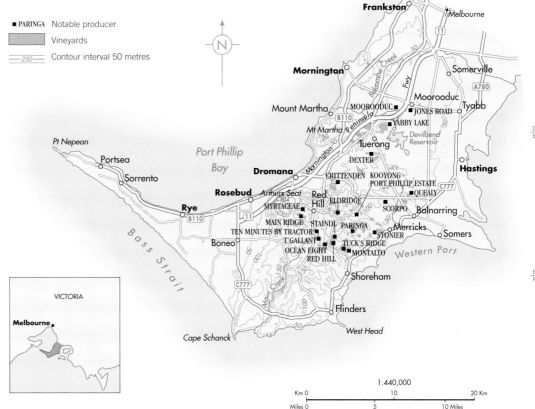

Paringa Estate and Main Ridge are two of the old-timers, meaning their first vines went into the ground in the 1970s, while 2000 was the inaugural vintage of the memorably named Ten Minutes by Tractor, a three-family co-operative. Kooyong's first vintage was made in 2001.

Yarra Valley

The Yarra Valley is on Melbourne's doorstep and can offer its famous restaurants and wine bars a dazzling array of food-friendly wines. The valley's topography is complex, with steep, shallow slopes at altitudes of 160–1,540ft (50–470m) facing all points of the compass. The upper slopes are cool and most of the valley enjoys cool nights, however warm the days. Rainfall is also relatively high, although a recent run of drought years have been drier than these figures suggest. Soils range from grey sandy or clay loam to vivid red volcanic earth so fertile that enormous "mountain ashes" (*Eucalyptus regnans*) tower above the blue-leaved wattle along the creeks.

The rebirth of the valley dates from the 1960s, when the customary clutch of doctors fanatical about wine arrived. Drs Carrodus at Yarra Yering, Middleton at Mount Mary, and McMahon at Seville Estate set impeccable standards, albeit on a tiny scale, and until the 1980s the valley's reputation rested on its deceptively silky, age-worthy Bordeaux blends. Those who followed included Dr Lance at Diamond Valley (whose vineyard is now run by his son James) and the wine writer James Halliday at Coldstream Hills (now owned by Treasury Wine Estates), both fired with the desire to grow Australia's first great Pinot Noir.

Pinot Noir is clearly one of the Yarra Valley's strongest suits, although today the valley is even better known for its Chardonnays, having pioneered Australia's more refined, occasionally austere, styles thanks to the naturally cool conditions in the elevated, southern end of the valley south of "the Warbie" (the Warburton Highway). Top wines today may be varied but are much more likely to express exactly where they were grown in place of the barrel selections of the 1990s. Yarra Shiraz has benefited from the Australians' newfound enthusiasm for cooler-climate Shiraz (though, like Cabernet, it tends to be grown on the warmer valley floor), and the use of Burgundian winemaking techniques has opened a new chapter for it.

When Moët & Chandon decided to make a fair copy of champagne in Australia, it chose to establish Domaine Chandon here. Today, Chandon also produces Green Point still wine, but nearly 70% of the fruit for its sparkling wines is still grown in the valley's cool upper reaches. Fizz fanatics can now choose from a range of artisanally made Yarra sparkling wines. Virtually all of the big companies have bought a slice of Yarra's relatively cool vineyard, with family-owned De Bortoli widely acknowledged as a seedbed of new talent.

■ OAKRIDGE Notable producer

● Lance's Vineyard Noted vineyard

▢ Vineyards

— *500* — Contour interval 100 metres

▼ Weather station (WS)

The family-owned De Bortoli operation, with roots in Riverina in the interior, is widely acknowledged as a seedbed of new talent such as those producers represented here. Luke Lambert is trying his hand at Nebbiolo as well as Syrah.

YARRA VALLEY: HEALESVILLE ▼

Latitude / Altitude of WS
-37.81° / 426ft (130m)

Average growing season temperature at WS
65.5°F (18.6°C)

Average annual rainfall at WS
24in (603mm)

Harvest month rainfall at WS
March: 2in (41mm)

Principal viticultural hazards
Underripeness, fungal disease, frost

Principal grape varieties
Pinot Noir, Chardonnay, Cabernet Sauvignon, Shiraz

Tasmania

The continuing search for cooler climates in Australia is leading to its southernmost, and sea-girt, state: Tasmania. Its high latitudes (the same as New Zealand's South Island) have made it the envy of many mainland winemakers. Hardys long relied on Tasmania for fruit for its top House of Arras fizz. Yalumba did the same for Jansz and recently acquired the admired Dalrymple operation. Goelet Wine Estates, owner of Taltarni in Victoria, now depends on Tasmania for its Clover Hill and Lalla Gully wines. Shaw + Smith's 2011 acquisition of the renowned Tolpuddle vineyard was its first foray outside the Adelaide Hills. And Brown Bros of Victoria made the boldest move into Tasmania of all: having acquired interests including Tamar Ridge, Pirie, and Devil's Corner, it is now the island's leading

producer. Its nearest rival, making Pipers Brook and Ninth Island wines, is Flemish-owned Kreglinger Wine Estates.

Even as recently a 2013 the island's grand total of 230 vineyards accounted for a mere 3,741 acres (1,514 ha), limited in many cases by the availability of irrigation water. For although the island's west coast is one of Australia's wettest areas, Hobart vies with Adelaide as the driest state capital. So far, vineyards are confined to the eastern third of the island, in unofficial regions (all wines are labelled simply Tasmania) with very distinct characters. The sheltered **Tamar Valley** and the wooded, wetter, later-ripening **Pipers River** regions in the northeast of the island are reckoned to be some of Australia's most propitious areas for cool-climate wine production. The river helps moderate temperatures, and valley slopes ward off dangerous frosts. But there are sites on the southeast coast so sheltered by the principal mountains that the fact that there is no land

between them and the Antarctic seems hardly relevant. The natural amphitheatre around Freycinet seems pre-ordained for viticulture and has yielded some exceptionally pretty Pinot Noir when summers are not too hot.

Even **Huon Valley**, Australia's southernmost wine region, has produced some fully ripe medal-winners. **Derwent Valley** and **Coal River**, to the north and northeast of Hobart, respectively, are notably dry, being in the rain shadow of Mount Wellington, although Coal River at least now has good acccess to irrigation water. They are probably best at Chardonnay, Pinot Noir, and Riesling (dry to very sweet), but carefully chosen and managed sites can be warm enough to ripen Cabernet Sauvignon, as the fanatical owners of Domaine A have proved.

No one now doubts that, as well as being a prime source of base wine for Australian sparkling wine, the island can also make exceptionally fine still wines. All of the Pinot Noir and a great deal of the Chardonnay that goes into Hardys' top Eileen Hardy wines is Tasmanian. Penfolds has been steadily increasing the Tasmanian proportion in its "icon" Chardonnay, Yattarna. The island's history as a supplier of base wine for fizz means that Pinot Noir, then Chardonnay, are the most important varieties by far, but it was the quality of the island's unusually fresh, well-balanced still Pinots that attracted Brown Bros.

The coastal winds provide a natural limit to yields in the vineyards carved out of Tasmania's rich and floriferous bush. Screens are necessary in some places to preserve the vine leaves on the seaward slope. But ripening is as slow and sure as any vintner could hope for, and flavour correspondingly intense.

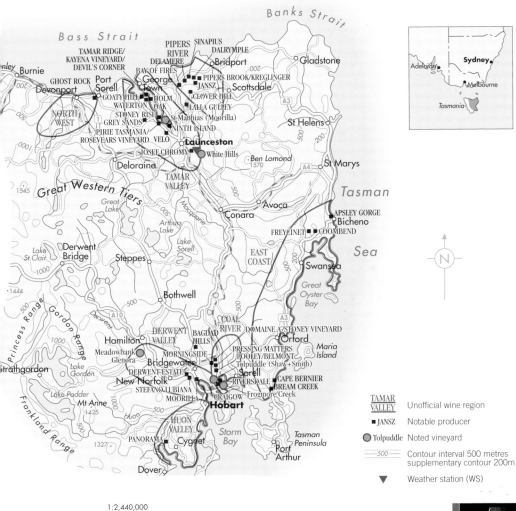

TASMANIA: LAUNCESTON ▼
Latitude / Altitude of WS
-41.54° / 544ft (166m)
Average growing season temperature at WS
58.0°F (14.4°C)
Average annual rainfall at WS
24in (620mm)
Harvest month rainfall at WS
April: 1.9in (47mm)
Principal viticultural hazards
Botrytis, coulure
Principal grape varieties
Pinot Noir, Chardonnay, Sauvignon Blanc, Riesling

TAMAR VALLEY — Unofficial wine region
■ JANSZ — Notable producer
◉ Tolpuddle — Noted vineyard
500 — Contour interval 500 metres supplementary contour 200m
▼ — Weather station (WS)

1:2,440,000
Km 0   50   100 Km
Miles 0   50 Miles

The Tasmanian component in Yattarna, Penfolds' flagship "white Grange", has increased dramatically in recent vintages, just as it has in its competitor's Eileen Hardy Chardonnay. But the island also makes some stunning Riesling, at all sweetness levels.

New South Wales

New South Wales, Australian wine's birthplace, has long since been overtaken by South Australia as the nucleus of the industry. But there remains one district 100 miles (160km) north of Sydney as famous as any in the country, even if it is progressively being overtaken by the state's swelling roster of new wine regions. The Lower Hunter Valley around Branxton and the mining town of Cessnock represent a triumph of proximity over suitability. The **Hunter**, as it is known, is a far from ideal place to grow grapes. It is subtropical; the most northerly of Australia's traditional wine regions: summers are invariably very hot and autumns can be vexingly wet. The prevailing northeast winds from the Pacific counter the extreme heat to some extent, and summer skies are often cloud-covered so the direct sun is diffused. More than two-thirds of the region's relatively high annual rainfall of 29in (750mm) falls in the crucial first four months of the year, harvest time. There is plenty for the farmer to curse: vintages are as uneven as they are in France.

The reason for the rash of wineries on the map is not so much a natural affinity with the vine as the fact that they are just two hours' drive from Sydney and a mecca for wine tourists and investors. No other Australian wine region sets its cap so obviously at the casual visitor. Restaurants, guesthouses, golf courses, and, of course, cellar doors proliferate.

The soil that gave the Hunter Valley its reputation is found to the south in the foothills of the Brokenback Range. Around the east side of the hills there is a strip of weathered basalt, the sign of ancient volcanic activity, that restricts vine vigour and concentrates often distinctly mineral flavour into the grapes. The red volcanic soils on higher ground, such as those of Pokolbin subregion, are particularly suitable for Shiraz, the classic red grape of the Hunter, based on some particularly old clones. Semillon grown on the white sands and loams – alluvial creek beds – on lower ground is the traditional white, even if it has been overtaken quantitatively by Chardonnay. No more than medium-bodied, Hunter Shiraz is sometimes beefed up with stronger stuff imported from South Australia, up to the permitted maximum of 15%, although winemakers are increasingly keen to show off the Hunter's uniquely "Burgundian" style. Soft and earthy but long and spicy, Hunter Shiraz from a successful vintage may ripen relatively early, but lasts well and grows complex and leathery with time.

Hunter Semillon is one of Australia's classic, if underappreciated, wine styles. The grapes are picked at low sugar levels, fermented in vat, and bottled fairly early at around 11% alcohol without any softening (and accelerating) malolactic fermentation. These grassy or citrus,

relatively austere young wines age in bottle quite magnificently into green-gold, toasty, mineral-laden bombs packed with explosive layers of flavour, although the style is not for neophytes. Verdelho also has a long history in the Hunter.

The Hunter was in the forefront of Australia's love affair with imported French grapes. In the early 1970s, Murray Tyrrell, inspired by Len Evans, the impresario not only of the Hunter but of modern Australian wine in general, did with Chardonnay what Max Lake had done in the 1960s with Cabernet: put down a marker no winemaker could ignore, his Vat 47. It launched a thousand – make that a million? – Australian Chardonnays.

Chardonnay is also by far the principal, some might say only, grape variety in the Upper Hunter subregion put resoundingly on the map in the 1970s by Rosemount. It lies 40 miles (60km) to the northwest on higher ground around Denman and Muswellbrook. Rainfall is lower and irrigation freely practised. The Broke Fordwich subregion half an hour's drive west of the area mapped here is currently much more dynamic, producing distinctive Semillons on sandy, alluvial soils.

Beyond the Hunter

To the west of the Hunter, about 1,500ft (450m) up on the western slopes of the Great Dividing Range, **Mudgee** has also made its mark since the 1970s (see p.335 for the location of all New South Wales wine regions). Its origins are almost as old as those of the Hunter Valley, but Mudgee dwelt in obscurity until the hunt began for cooler districts. Intense, long-established Chardonnay and Cabernet (especially from Huntingdon Estate) are its traditional strengths; Riesling and Shiraz can be very good, too. Having added Poet's Corner and the historic Montrose to the Oatley family's existing vineyards retained after the sale of Rosemount, Rosemount founder Robert Oatley's eponymous new venture is easily the region's dominant force.

New South Wales has seen a sustained and vigorous quest for new wine regions, all of them in cooler, often higher, pockets of the state. The latest addition is New England, Australia's highest wine region, which rises to 4,330ft (1,320m). **Orange**, on the slopes of the extinct volcano Mount Canobolas, is defined by altitude. Its vineyards, above 1,970ft (600m) and sometimes much higher, are distinguished from the rolling hills of the Central Ranges wine zone. The range of varieties that can be grown at such heights is wide, but a common thread of Orange wines is notably pure natural acidity. Riesling, Sauvignon Blanc, and Chardonnay thrive. In the higher reaches, beneficial aspect, rigorous

Tourism is all-important in the Hunter Valley in Sydney's backyard. Golf sometimes seems more important than wine. At least the hot-air balloon rides are designed with vineyard viewing in mind.

HUNTER VALLEY

The part of the Hunter Valley mapped in detail here includes the nucleus of wineries and vineyards that constituted such a vibrant part of Australian wine culture in the mid-20th century.

canopy management, and ruthless yields are hallmarks of the best reds.

Cowra has a much longer history for lush, fulsome, exuberant Chardonnays grown at fairly high yields and much lower altitudes: on average only about 1,150ft (350m). **Hilltops**, a little to the south, around the town of Young, and higher than Cowra, is much more recent and, like most of these relatively obscure New South Wales wine regions, tends to grow fruit – notably red grapes, Chardonnay, and Semillon – for wineries outside the region. There are half a dozen small enterprises, by far the most important being McWilliam's Barwang. The great surprise about **Canberra District**, the cluster of vineyards around the nation's capital, is firstly that there are so many of them, secondly that almost all are actually in New South Wales, and thirdly that they have been in existence for so long. Research doctors John Kirk of Clonakilla and Edgar Riek of Lake George planted the first vines as long ago as 1971. The former's son Tim virtually pioneered Australia's popular Shiraz/Viognier blend modelled on Côte-Rôtie. The highest vineyards such as Lark Hill's, now biodynamic, are not just cool but cold (frost can strike), and the result can be some of Australia's most delicate Pinot Noir, Riesling, and even Grüner Veltliner.

Shoalhaven Coast is also developing fast, although, like **Hastings River** around Port Macquarie to the north, it suffers from high humidity. Hybrids such as Chambourcin offer a solution of a sort. **Tumbarumba** is another extremely cool, high-altitude region, of particular interest to blenders of refined Chardonnays and sparkling wine. And an increasing number of Tumbarumba-labelled whites are being bottled by producers in nearby Hilltops and Canberra District.

Key to producers
1 CONSTABLE & HERSHON
2 HONEYTREE
3 GLENGUIN
4 McGUIGAN
5 TEMPUS TWO
6 SMALL WINEMAKERS CENTRE
7 TAMBURLAINE
8 PEPPER TREE
9 TOWER
10 HUNGERFORD HILL

1:250,000

Km 0   5   10 Km
Miles 0   5 Miles

POKOLBIN   Wine subregion (GI)
LOVEDALE   Unofficial wine subregion
■ ADINA   Notable producer
● Mount View   Noted vineyard
  Vineyards
300   Contour interval 75 metres
▼   Weather station (WS)

These labels represent some of the best wines from all New South Wales vineyards, not just those that can be labelled "Proudly Hunter Valley". Helm of Canberra has long been one of Australia's prime exponents of Riesling, while the extensively be-medalled 842 is grown on one of Tumbarumba's finest vineyards. Ross Hill represents Orange, while Moppity is a Hilltops ambassador, and Montrose is produced in historic Mudgee.

New Zealand

Few wine countries have quite so sharp an image as New Zealand. The word "sharp" is apt, for the wines speak in a Kiwi accent that is hard to mistake, characterized by piercingly crystalline flavours and bracing acidity. But then many of the world's wine drinkers have never experienced proof of this, for New Zealand is not just one of the most isolated countries on earth (three hours' flight from its nearest neighbour Australia), but it is a relative newcomer to wine. And it is small, producing less than 1% of the world's crop. New Zealand has colonized as much space in this book as it has because it is a serious exporter – two-thirds of its wine is now sold abroad – and because so many of those who try the wines, even including Australians, fall madly in love with their unusually powerful, direct flavours.

The first (1971) edition of this book hardly mentioned New Zealand. It had few vines, too many of them hybrids. By 1980 there were 14,000 acres (5,600ha), 2,000 (800) of which were in the brand-new Marlborough region on the South Island. Since the 1990s it has seemed as though anyone with a few acres has tried their hand at vine-growing. By 2012, the total area in production was 84,730 acres (34,290ha). It was New Zealanders who coined the term "lifestyle winery": a bucolic way of life whereby, typically, a fine education is focused on producing, in the most pleasing environment, one of life's more delicious commodities from the earth. An extraordinary bumper crop in 2008 jolted the industry, however. For the first time in the modern era wine firms had to grapple with a serious glut of grapes – so much so that many remained unpicked on the vines. The number of grape-growers fell from 1,060 in 2008 to barely 800 in 2012. Meanwhile, the number of wine producers has grown steadily and had reached 700 by 2012. Contract winemaking is big business; a high proportion of growers have a label but no winery of their own.

New Zealand had some natural problems to contend with before its wine-mania could take practical and fruitful form. Only 150 years ago much of this long, thin country was covered with rainforest. Soils here can be so rich in nutrients that vines, like everything else, grow too vigorously for their own good, a phenomenon exacerbated by the country's generous rainfall. Canopy management techniques were sorely needed, and were introduced in the 1980s, most notably by the then state viticulturist Dr Richard Smart, allowing light to shine both literally and figuratively on New Zealand's unique style of wine.

Wine-growing New Zealand lies, in terms of the northern hemisphere, on latitudes between those of Lebanon and Bordeaux. The effects of latitude are countered, though, by the Pacific, by strong

Wine regions

- Northland
- Auckland
- Waikato
- Bay of Plenty
- Gisborne
- Hawke's Bay
- Wairarapa
- Nelson
- Marlborough
- Canterbury
- Otago

Region boundary

Kumeu — Wine subregion

358 — Area mapped at larger scale on page shown

NEW ZEALAND'S WINE REGIONS

Most of the west and south coast is too wet for wine production, and the far north of Northland is almost tropical, but much of the rest of the country is suitable for viticulture. Subregions marked are unofficial, but the most significant.

1:7,895,000

prevailing westerlies, and by the effects of the mountains on their rain-clouds: factors that give the two islands a wide range of growing conditions – almost all cooler than the statistics suggest.

New Zealand's calling card

It was Sauvignon Blanc that made the world take notice of New Zealand. After all, a cool climate is needed if the wine is to be lively, and the cool, bright, sunny, and windy northern tip of the South Island seems to have been designed to intensify the scarcely subtle twang of Sauvignon. Early

examples of Marlborough Sauvignon in the 1980s opened a Pandora's box of flavour that no one could ignore and, most importantly, no other part of the world seemed able to replicate. Today, Sauvignon Blanc is the country's most important grape by far, accounting for a staggering 70% of the 2011 harvest.

And yet only towards the end of 2008 did supply finally match demand – just after New Zealand wine was paid the compliment of more interest from multinational corporations than ever before. In 2005, Pernod Ricard New Zealand acquired the country's dominant producer, now known as Brancott Estate. Other substantial producers include Constellation NZ (formerly Nobilo); Delegat's/Oyster Bay; Saint Clair; Mud House; Treasury Wine Estates (Matua); Villa Maria (including Esk Valley and Vidal); Wither Hills; and the relatively new

Yealands operation. All of them put many eggs in the Sauvignon Blanc basket.

Chardonnay, enlivened by the country's trademark zestiness, was initially New Zealand's other calling card, but by 2006 it had definitively been overtaken in terms of vineyard area, and certainly in terms of reputation, by Pinot Noir. The country's second-most planted variety has enjoyed success for much the same reason as Sauvignon Blanc: New Zealand's cool climate and bright sun. In a surprisingly wide range of wine regions, this finicky grape provided Kiwi growers with another chance of succeeding where so many other regions (most importantly, most of Australia) had so far struggled.

Merlot overtook the inconveniently late-ripening Cabernet Sauvignon in 2000 and Syrah is becoming increasingly popular. Bordeaux blends are in general more popular with Kiwis themselves than outside in the big, wide, Cabernet-saturated world. Other significant grapes include Riesling, both dry and sweet, which can be very fine here, and a significant number of producers and growers are now investing their hopes in other aromatic varieties such as Pinot Gris (which accounted for nearly 7% of all plantings in 2012) and Gewurztraminer. Isolation has proved no defence against vine pests and diseases, however; most vines are grafted on to phylloxera-resistant rootstocks.

North Island

New Zealand wine has come a long way since it was known locally as "Dally plonk", a reference to settlers from Dalmatia, lured from the kauri gum forests of the far north to plant vineyards near **Auckland** in the early 20th century. They persisted despite a rainy subtropical climate; several of the families in what is now a surprisingly good red wine area have Croatian names. As in Australia's Hunter Valley, cloud cover moderates what could be too much sunshine and gives steady ripening conditions. Vintage-time rain and rot are problems, although Waiheke Island to the east misses some of the mainland rain. Stonyridge long ago showed the island's potential with Bordeaux grapes, but prospects for Syrah look even brighter if anything. In the subtropical far north, **Northland** growers produce a trickle of impressive Syrah, Pinot Gris, and Chardonnay in drier seasons.

Gisborne on the east coast of the North Island (like so many of New Zealand's wine regions it has another name, Poverty Bay) with its relatively few wineries is a good example of a region plundered, and now abandoned, by the bottlers. In terms of vineyard area, it is no longer in third place after Marlborough and Hawke's Bay, having been overtaken by Otago. Its signature variety, Chardonnay, is now less sought after than Sauvignon Blanc and Pinot Gris grown in cooler regions to the south. Warmer but wetter than Hawke's Bay, especially in autumn, Gisborne grows almost exclusively white grapes on relatively fertile loamy soils generally

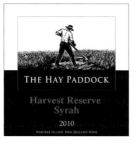

The two wines on the far left are some of Auckland's best. Man O'War is making waves for its robustly named wines grown on Waiheke Island, a short ferry ride from Auckland. Neudorf and Seifried have some of Nelson's most admirable track records.

picked two to three weeks before Hawke's Bay and Marlborough. It also produces some rich, varietally true Gewurztraminer as well as floral, intense Semillon. Merlot and Malbec are notably approachable, too.

South of Auckland, the **Waikato** and **Bay of Plenty** regions are low-profile sources of sound whites and reds. **Ohau**, a new wine-growing district on the east coast, north of Wellington, is yielding crisp, punchy Sauvignon Blanc and Pinot Gris.

South Island

Just across the notoriously windy Cook Strait on the South Island and to the west of Marlborough, **Nelson** has about the same area of vines planted as Wairarapa in the North Island (see p.359),

but it has a higher rainfall, and hardly any big company influence. The vineyards are clustered on the southwest coast of Tasman Bay, both on the clay soils of the rolling Moutere Hills and on the richer, more alluvial soils of the Waimea Plains. A versatile region, producing freshly herbaceous Sauvignon Blanc and sturdy, rich Chardonnay and Pinot Noir, it also has a strong reputation for aromatic whites, especially Riesling and the increasingly popular Pinot Gris.

Looking up the Tukituki River towards Te Mata Peak, which lent its name to one of Hawke's Bay's first internationally admired wineries. New Zealand's landscape does look relatively recently formed somehow.

Hawke's Bay

In New Zealand terms, Hawke's Bay is an historic wine region, having been planted by Marist missionaries in the mid-19th century. But it was Cabernets made here in the 1960s for the Australian company McWilliam's that hinted at the long-term promise of the area. When serious planting began in the 1970s, Hawke's Bay was a logical place to expand, especially with the Cabernet Sauvignon that was then de rigueur. Hawke's Bay has been the Kiwi standard-bearer for claret-style reds ever since, but it was only in the late 1990s that the region began to make wines that demanded attention. The 1998 vintage, so hot and dry that Hawke's Bay's sheep had to be trucked west over the mountains to greener pastures, produced wines that were obviously made from fully ripe grapes, and had the gentle but insistent tannins to suggest a serious future. Later vintages, such as 2007 and 2009, suggested that the region's Bordeaux blends can stand comparison with the archetypes. They may evolve more rapidly, but cost very much less.

It was also in the late 1990s that growers began fully to understand and take advantage of the complexities of Hawke's Bay soils. It had long been obvious that the maritime climate of this wide bay on the east coast of the North Island, sheltered from the westerlies by the Ruahine and Kaweka ranges, could offer one of the country's most favourable combinations of relatively low rainfall and high temperatures (albeit lower than Bordeaux's – see panel, right). What happened underground took longer to understand.

Poorest soils, ripest grapes

An aerial view of Hawke's Bay vividly shows the remarkable variety of rich alluvial and less fertile, gravelly soils and their distribution in a pattern flowing from mountain to sea. Silt, loams, and gravel have very different water-holding capacities; one vineyard can be at saturation point, shooting forth vegetation at a furious rate, while another will perish if not irrigated. It became clear that the ripest grapes were grown on the poorest soils, which limited vine growth and on which irrigation could carefully control just how much water each vine received (even if summers seem now to be getting hotter and red grape ripening more reliable). There are no soils poorer than the 2,000 acres (800ha) of deep, warm shingle that remain where the Gimblett Road now runs, northwest of Hastings, along what was the course of the Ngaruroro River until a dramatic flood in 1870. The late 1990s saw a viticultural land grab on this area craftily called Gimblett Gravels, a frenzy during which the last three-quarters of available land was bought and planted in readiness for virtually hydroponic cultivation.

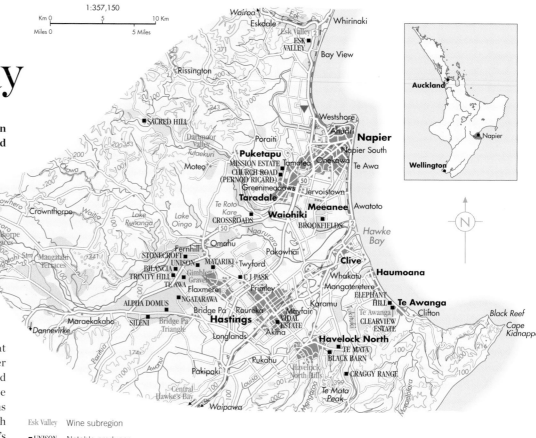

Esk Valley — Wine subregion
■ UNISON — Notable producer
▢ — Vineyards
—200— — Contour interval 100 metres
▼ — Weather station (WS)

AROUND HAWKE BAY

The weather station in Napier is likely to be a little more temperate than some of Hawke's Bay's most famous vineyards further from the coast. Note the principal subregions, of which Gimblett Gravels has made the most noise.

Other fine areas for ripening red grapes include the Bridge Pa Triangle just south of and slightly cooler than here, selected sites on the limestone hills of Havelock North, such as that colonized by Te Mata many years earlier, and a cool, late-ripening strip of shingle along the coast between Haumoana and Te Awanga.

Like everywhere else, New Zealand suffered excessive Cabernet Sauvignon worship in the 1980s, but even in Hawke's Bay this variety does not always ripen fully, and plantings of the much more reliable, earlier-ripening Merlot are now more than double those of Cabernet Sauvignon. Early ripening Malbec also thrives here and is popular in blends, although it is prone to poor

HAWKE'S BAY: NAPIER ▼

Latitude / Altitude of WS
-39.50° / 7ft (2m)

Average growing season temperature at WS
62.9°F (17.2°C)

Average annual rainfall at WS
31in (786mm)

Harvest month rainfall at WS
March: 2.6in (67mm)

Principal viticultural hazards
Autumn rain, fungal diseases

Principal grape varieties
Merlot, Sauvignon Blanc, Chardonnay

fruit set. Syrah undoubtedly has a bright future here, too. Two in every three of the country's Syrah vines are planted in Hawke's Bay's poor soils, ripening satisfactorily most years. There can be considerable vintage variation, but then there can be on the Rhône. Even warmish Hawke's Bay is not immune to Sauvignon Blanc fever (see panel).

Many of Hawke's Bay's most admired wines are red Bordeaux blends, but Bilancia's La Collina is recognized as one of the country's finest Syrahs. Some pretty lip-smacking Chardonnay is made, too.

Wairarapa

The North Island's most exciting area for Pinot Noir, and the first in New Zealand to establish a reputation for it, is Wairarapa. It includes Martinborough, a southern subregion named after Wairarapa's wine capital, a small town apparently devoted to food and wine, and Gladstone, off our map to the north. An hour's drive northeast of the nation's capital, over the mountains and into the island's eastern rain shadow, Wairarapa has such low temperatures that ex-research scientist Dr Neil McCallum, the founder of Dry River, is able to observe drily: "We're very like Edinburgh in terms of our heat summation." Thanks to the mountains to the west, however, Martinborough's autumns are the North Island's most reliably dry, giving Wairarapa's 60-plus wineries the chance to make some of the most vivid and Burgundian Pinot Noir, the region's dominant vine. It ranges from potently plummy to lean, dry, and earthy – but then so does burgundy.

The Burgundian parallel extends to the structure of the wine business here, with wines typically made by the same people who grew the grapes. Grape farmers would be more likely to be attracted to the predictably generous yields of Marlborough than the Martinborough average of barely 2 tonnes/acre. The region has thin, poor soils on free-draining deep gravels, silts, and clay, and the prevailing westerlies in this windy area are particularly persistent at flowering time, generally after a cool spring during which frosts are a perennial threat. Grapes are routinely treated to a particularly long growing season, however, thanks to the long autumns and because Martinborough enjoys one of New Zealand's greatest diurnal temperature variations. Many of the leading wineries, Ata Rangi, Martinborough Vineyard, and Dry River, were established in the early 1980s. The individuals behind them have built consistent and very personal reputations, although Larry McKenna, once of Martinborough Vineyard, has now established a second-generation operation in Escarpment and Neil McCallum is no longer the owner of Dry River.

The region has also shown real proficiency in New Zealand's latest varietal darling, Pinot Gris, especially those wines based on the original clone imported for the Mission winery of Hawke's Bay in the 1880s, even though Sauvignon Blanc is Wairarapa's second-most planted variety. In the hugely self-conscious world of New Zealand Pinot Noir, there is considerable rivalry between Martinborough and Central Otago, each organizing major international events to celebrate the variety, according to alternating cycles.

Two of Martinborough's established classics flank a more recent arrival. Hiroyuki Kusuda gave up his career in the Japanese diplomatic service after falling in love with Martinborough's potential for Pinot Noir and Syrah.

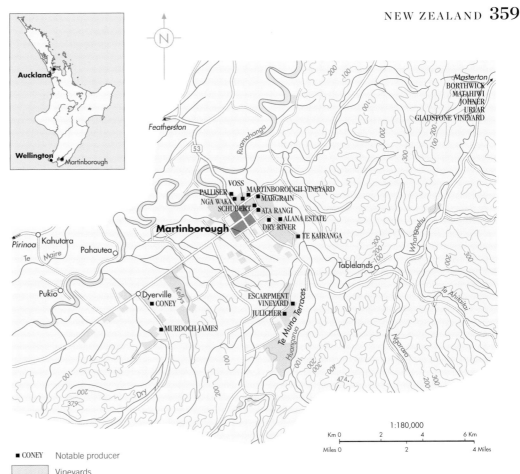

■ CONEY   Notable producer

▨   Vineyards

〰500〰   Contour interval 100 metres

The town of Martinborough has developed into a particularly concentrated collection of wine bars, restaurants, and tourist accommodation such as the Martinborough Hotel, built in 1882 and with few changes since.

MARTINBOROUGH

Over the mountains from Wellington, and in the lee of the hills to the east, Martinborough's tight cluster of wineries and vineyards enjoys a relatively cool, dry growing season most years – propitious for Pinot Noir.

Marlborough

At the northeastern tip of the South Island, Marlborough has seen such feverish vine planting in recent years that it has pulled far ahead of all other regions. You could say it epitomizes New Zealand wine. Around 60% of all the country's vineyards lie in this very particular corner of the wine world – quite an achievement given that, apart from one settler who planted vines at Meadowbank Farm (today the site of Auntsfield Estate) around 1873, the vine was almost unknown here until 1973, the year when Montana (the country's dominant wine producer, now called Brancott) planted the first commercial vineyard of 500 acres (200ha).

Lack of irrigation caused teething problems, but in 1975 the first Sauvignon Blanc vines were planted. By 1979, the first vintage of Montana

WAIRAU VALLEY

What a roller coaster this small valley and quiet town has known: from sheep to vine bonanza to glut in barely more than two decades. The potential is indubitable but not unlimited. Viticultural details and evolving subregions can make all the difference to wine quality.

Marlborough Sauvignon Blanc was bottled and the special intensity from this region was too obvious to ignore. Such an exhilarating, easy-to-understand wine clearly had extraordinary potential, and this was rapidly realized by, among others, David Hohnen of Cape Mentelle in Western Australia. In 1985, he launched Cloudy Bay, whose name, evocative label, and smoky, almost chokingly pungent flavour have since become legendary.

By 2012, Marlborough had close to 50,000 acres (nearly 20,000ha) under vine, nearly four – yes, four – times the area planted at the turn of the century. The number of wine producers passed 150 in 2012. The proportion of fruit leaving the region in bulk, to be shipped across Cook Strait for processing in the North Island, has consequently plummeted – much to the benefit of the resultant wine. Today an increasing proportion of the growers who once sold their

grapes to one of the big companies have their own label, which may well be applied at one of the region's busy contract wineries.

What makes Marlborough special

The wide, flat **Wairau Valley** was, until the 2008 glut, a magnet for investors and those who simply liked the idea of making wine their life. Some in their enthusiasm planted so far inland that grapes don't ripen every year, on land where the valley's precious water supply is scarce. Since 2008, the price of land has plummeted, and the need for frost protection on the wide, flat valley floor has proved another stumbling block. Boom-time had its usual victims.

What makes Marlborough special as a wine region is its unusual combination of long days, cold nights, bright sunshine, and, in good years, dryish autumns. In such relatively low temperatures (see key facts panel), rainy autumns are fatal, but here grapes can usually (but not always) be left on the vine to ripen slowly, building high sugars without, thanks to the cold nights, sacrificing the acidity that delineates New Zealand's wines.

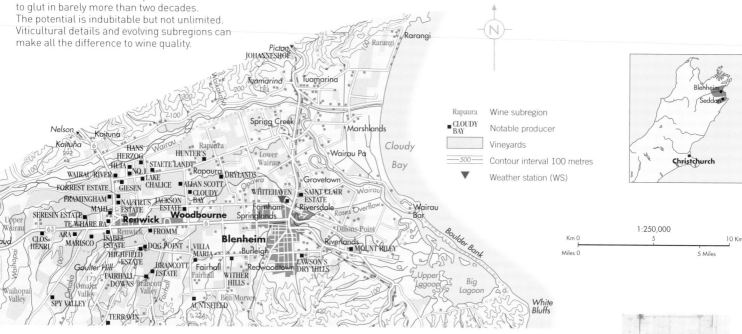

MARLBOROUGH: BLENHEIM ▼
Latitude / Altitude of WS -41.50° / 115ft (35m)
Average growing season temperature at WS 59.7°F (15.4°C)
Average annual rainfall at WS 28in (711mm)
Harvest month rainfall at WS April: 2.1in (53mm)
Principal viticultural hazards Autumn rain
Principal grape varieties Sauvignon Blanc, Pinot Noir, Chardonnay

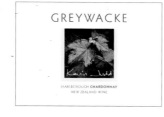

Greywacke is the label of Kevin Judd, who made wine at Cloudy Bay throughout the time that particular Sauvignon Blanc was making worldwide waves. But Marlborough also produces some fine Pinot Noir and exceptional Riesling.

Only the hat and sunglasses give the location away. The vineyard owner, cinematographer Michael Seresin, is one of New Zealand's most enthusiastic coverts to biodynamic viticulture. His winemaker is British.

This diurnal temperature variation is most marked in the slightly drier, cooler, and windier **Awatere Valley**. It was pioneered by Vavasour in 1986 and has expanded enormously in recent years, thanks to irrigation schemes and the enthusiastic vineyard planting of, in particular, Yealands Estate.

If the Awatere Valley were treated as a region in its own right – rather than as a subregion of Marlborough – it would rank as the second-largest in the country, behind only the Wairau Valley and ahead of Hawke's Bay. Both budbreak and harvest tend to be later in the Awatere Valley than on the Wairau Valley floor, but summers are long and hot – certainly warm enough to ripen most white wine varieties (especially Sauvignon Blanc, Riesling, Chardonnay, and Pinot Gris) and Pinot Noir. Vines have also been planted with some success in the Ure Valley and at Kekerengu, well south of the Awatere Valley. But perhaps the most significant variation in Marlborough is that of soils. North of Highways 6 and 63 which run east–west through the Wairau Valley, with a few exceptions around Woodbourne, soils are very much younger than those to the south. In places, the water table can be dangerously high and the best vineyards on these young, stony soils are the best-drained on light loams over the shingle that was once the river bed. Mature vines develop deep root systems, although young vines need irrigation to survive the dry summers.

South of Highway 63, the lowest-lying older soils are too poorly drained for fine wine production, but higher-altitude vineyards on the exposed, barren southern edge of the valley can produce interesting fruit from much drier soils. Pinot Noir yields its most floral, rich and supple wines in elevated, clay-based sites on this southern side.

Standing out from the crowd
The bigger producers of Sauvignon Blanc typically blend fruit grown on different soils in slightly different climatic conditions in an attempt to differentiate their produce in what risks being a rather monotone category. Restrained use of French oak and malolactic fermentation can help, and a growing number of single-vineyard Sauvignons are emerging.

Marlborough has produced some fine Pinot Gris – a variety that has become as popular with Kiwi drinkers as it seems to be everywhere else – and Riesling, including some inspiring late-harvest examples. Pinot Noir, though, and Chardonnay are still quantitatively more important. They are both grown for sparkling as well as still wine, and the fruity Marlborough Pinots have grown considerably in stature as the vines have aged.

AWATERE VALLEY
Vavasour (see label opposite) pioneered vine-growing in the Awatere Valley to the south of the Wairau Valley. The vast Yealands Estate uses Babydoll miniature sheep, too short to reach the grapes, for mowing, weed- and pest-control – and fertilizer.

Upper Awatere — Wine subregion
■ VAVASOUR — Notable producer
☐ — Vineyards
⎼500⎼ — Contour interval 100 metres

1:250,000
Km 0 — 5 — 10 Km
Miles 0 — 5 Miles

Canterbury

Canterbury is the name given to the extensive hinterland of South Island's capital, Christchurch. As a wine region it shapes a different course from most of New Zealand, making some of the most burgundian of the country's Pinots and Chardonnays, believing in its Riesling (with justification, however hard it is to sell), and leaving Sauvignon Blanc trailing in fourth place. Vines were first planted here in the mid-19th century, on the Banks Peninsula, but commercial wine production waited more than a century. The whole region is cool: too cool to ripen red Bordeaux grapes. Long, dry summers and fairly constant winds – whether the hot, dry nor'wester that can be so strong it can damage vines, or the much cooler wind from the south – are its advantages. They keep grapes healthy. But water is scarce. Irrigation, from artesian wells, is generally essential.

The plains around and to the south of Christchurch are extremely windy and exposed, but the more undulating terrain of **Waipara**, an hour's drive north of the city, is protected from east winds by the low range of the Teviotdale Hills. The Southern Alps to the west contribute their shelter, too. The plains are generally silty over gravel, sometimes covered with thin loess. Waipara's soil is calcareous loam with clay and limestone deposits. The pioneer Pegasus Bay, founded by a Christchurch doctor, soon built a reputation for fine Rieslings – excellent dry, easier sweet – but most other producers concentrate on Chardonnay, not lacking in structure, and Pinot Noir that ranges from disappointingly herbal to extremely promising. The best wines have a subtlety that is rare to the immediate south and north of Canterbury.

Two of the most significant producers struck out west, over the Weka Pass; their wines must be sold as Canterbury rather than Waipara. Both Bell Hill, established in 1997, and Pyramid Valley, from 2000, have scouted out limestone, and the burgundian connection is evident in their best bottles – both red and white.

Wineries cluster along the main road northwest of Amberley, but this is not a densely planted region. The isolation of most vineyards, the reasonably dry climate, and persistent winds make organic viticulture relatively easy here.

The country's leading producer, Brancott Estate, has planted several hundred hectares of vineyard in Canterbury; land is cheaper and diurnal temperature variation greater than in Marlborough. Frost is a perennial threat between late September and early November and yields suffer. Most producers are relatively small and wines tend to be more handcrafted than in, for example, Marlborough. As yet more evidence of an affinity with Burgundy, Canterbury's most obvious sign of climate change is that the region is now too frequently struck by hail.

WAIPARA

Below is Canterbury's biggest concentration of wineries and vineyards, just north of earthquake-damaged Christchurch. Cellar door sales are important, judging by their roadside locations.

The country's biggest producer, Brancott Estate, has planted several hundred hectares of baby vines in Waipara. The plastic tubes protect the growing vines from greedy animals.

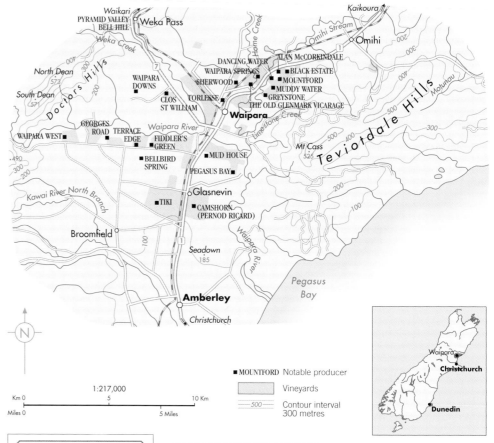

■ MOUNTFORD Notable producer

Vineyards

—500— Contour interval 300 metres

1:217,000

Km 0   5   10 Km
Miles 0   5 Miles

Some of Canterbury's most exciting wines are being made west of the area shown on the map above, on a very small scale but using meticulous, traditional techniques. North Canterbury is the appellation.

Central Otago

Central Otago (or "Central", as the locals call it) is the world's southernmost wine region and one of its most wildly beautiful. Brilliant turquoise rivers tumble through wild thyme-scented gorges, overlooked by snowcapped mountains even in summer. In 1997, there were just 14 wine producers and fewer than 500 acres (200ha) of vines. By 2012, official figures saw the number of producers rise to 118, drawing on 3,812 acres (1,543ha) of vineyards planted mainly with youthful Pinot Noir vines, much of whose grapes become wine at contract wineries.

Unlike the rest of New Zealand, Central Otago has a dramatically continental rather than maritime climate, which makes summers sunny and dry but short. Frosts are a threat throughout the year, and in cooler areas, such as Gibbston, even the early-ripening Pinot occasionally has difficulty reaching full maturity before the advent of winter.

On the other hand the summer sunlight is blinding. The hole in the ozone layer over this isolated part of the world may account for this high solar radiation (schoolchildren are obliged to wear hats), but reliably cold nights preserve the acidity the grapes need for quality. The result is dazzlingly bright fruit flavours, and such ripeness that wines with less than 14% alcohol are relatively rare. Central Otago Pinot Noir, like Marlborough Sauvignon Blanc, may not be the subtlest wine in the world but it is easy to like almost as soon as it's bottled.

The region's summers and early autumns are so dry that even the rot-prone Pinot Noir rarely suffers fungal diseases, and there is no shortage of irrigation water. The soils' water-holding capacity is very limited, however; typical soils are light, fast-draining loess with some gravel over schist.

The southernmost subregion is relatively cool Alexandra, originally planted in the 1860s, and then in 1973. Gibbston, slightly northwest of here, is even cooler, but the vines are planted on north-facing slopes of the stunning Kawarau Gorge. In longer growing seasons wines from here can have some of the most complex flavours of all. Bannockburn, where the gorge meets the Cromwell Valley, is one of the most intensively planted subregions. Like so many fine wine areas, this was once gold-mining country. Bendigo to the north, also relatively warm, is rapidly being planted with vines, though there are no wineries here yet. There is also great potential at Lowburn, and on the Pisa Flats, warm districts on flat land on the western shores of Lake Dunstan.

The most northerly subregion of all, Wanaka, was one of the first to be developed, in the 1980s. Rippon's vineyards (now biodyamic) are right on the lake, which usefully reduces the risk of frost. Vines, blue water, golden autumn trees, and distant snow add up to a picture photographers don't try to resist. North Otago now has its own

wine region, Waitaki Valley, where prospectors are banking on the limestone, unknown in "Central", to match Burgundy's – although they, too, have to cope with the perennial risk of frost, cold winds during flowering, and, of course,

young vines. Pinot Noir, Pinot Gris, and Riesling are all promising. The Pasquale winery, which has vineyards in the Waitaki Valley, is also producing wines from the Hakataramea Valley, on the north side of the Waitaki River in South Canterbury.

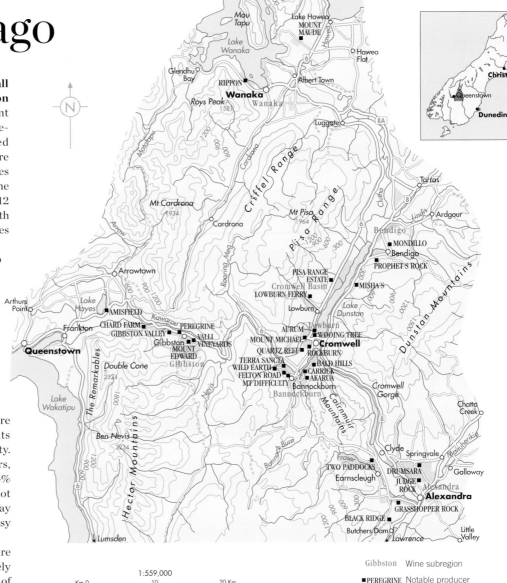

1:559,000

Km 0 — 10 — 20 Km

Miles 0 — 5 — 10 Miles

Gibbston — Wine subregion
■ PEREGRINE — Notable producer
▢ — Vineyards
〰 600 — Contour interval 300 metres

Central Otago's wine producers are some of the most cohesive and co-operative in the world. Many of them share a (contract) winemaker, but these wines are all vinified on individual estates. Like Kusuda in Martinborough, Sato is a newcomer from Japan.

SOUTH AFRICA

Simonsberg mountain range overlooking the Stellenbosch and Franschhoek wine districts, Western Cape.

South Africa

There are many contestants in the world's vineyard beauty contest, but South Africa is always in the finals. Blue-shadowed stacks of Table Mountain sandstone and decomposed granite rise from vivid green pastures dotted with the brilliant white façades of 300-year-old Cape Dutch homesteads. To the casual observer the Cape winelands may look just as they did in the decades leading up to 1994, but in reality the people, the vineyards, the cellars, the wine map, and the wines have changed out of all recognition.

South African vines thrive in a climate cooler than latitudes suggest, thanks to the cold Benguela Current from Antarctica that washes the western Atlantic coast. Rain here is usually concentrated in the winter months; where and how it falls depends on the Cape's extremely diverse topography. Prevailing winter westerlies temper the climate; the further south and west, and nearer the sea, the cooler and better supplied with rain. Rainfall can be heavy on either side of such mountain chains as the Drakenstein, Hottentots Holland, and Langeberg ranges, yet dwindle to as little as 8in (200mm) a year within only a few miles. The mountains also play a part in funnelling the famous Cape Doctor, a powerful southeaster that can ward off rot and mildew but can also batter young vines.

The Wine of Origin scheme first gave official recognition to regions, districts, and wards (the smallest geographical entities) in 1973 and continues to develop. The most significant ones are mapped here and on the following pages.

Biodiversity and sustainability

The Cape boasts the oldest geology in the wine-growing world: ancient weathered soils, typically based on either granite, Table Mountain sandstone, or shale, which naturally curtail the vigour of the wines. Much is now also made of the fact that these soils nurture the richest floral kingdom on the planet; biodiversity has become the mantra of the South African wine industry. Wine producers are encouraged to preserve natural vegetation and add features of interest to ecotourists to their land. Registration of single vineyards, which must be smaller than 15 acres (6ha) and planted with a single vine variety, is encouraged, and official study of their individual characteristics and favoured grape varieties is underway. (Vineyard names first appeared on wine labels in 2005.) By 2012, nearly 90% of Wine of Origin wine also qualified for the official sustainability seal. Lacking the equivalent of, for example, Australia's vast mechanized inland wine regions, South African wine producers are all too aware of the need to deliver something more valuable than low prices to survive. Eighty per cent of the South African grape harvest is now sold as wine, the rest being either low-grade stuff made into grape-juice concentrate, of which South Africa is a major producer, or distilled into brandy.

The structure of the South African wine industry today is very different from the stifling regime that governed wine-growers for most of the 20th century, although co-ops and former co-ops are still important. As soon as apartheid and isolationism were abandoned, a new generation of young wine producers travelled the world, soaking up techniques and inspiration with unparalleled curiosity. Considerable new capital has been invested in the Cape's wine industry, so that today there are nearly 600 wineries, of which almost half crush fewer than 100 tons of grapes. Freedom was palpably celebrated in the 1990s by a rash of experimental planting in new, typically cooler, regions. Just as significantly, some of the older wine regions have been re-evaluated, notably Swartland and Olifants River.

Regions, districts, and wards

The ward of Durbanville is practically in the Cape Town suburbs and can easily be underestimated, but the nearby ocean brings nights cool enough to yield truly refreshing whites and well-defined Cabernet and Merlot. Philadelphia too, another ward of the **Tygerberg** district, with dramatic views over the city, may have a bright future.

Tulbagh, to the immediate east of Swartland, hemmed in on three sides by the Winterhoek Mountains, is another rediscovered and most distinctive wine district. Soils as well as exposures and elevations vary enormously, but diurnal temperature variation is reliably high; mornings can be exceptionally cool as cold overnight air sits trapped in the amphitheatre formed by the mountains.

Further north, Namaqua at Vredendal, with nearly 12,400 acres (5,000ha) of vines, has shown that lower latitude need not mean lower quality. Much of the crisp Chenin and Colombard that can make South Africa seem the world's best source of bargain white wines comes from up here in the **Olifants River** region, especially its **Citrusdal** and **Lutzville** districts. Bamboes Bay, a ward on the west coast, produces much finer Sauvignon Blanc than might be expected at this latitude. Altitude is the advantage of the separate Cederberg ward, just east of Olifants River, as it is of one of the most interesting recent expansions: vineyards in the Sutherland-Karoo district off the map to the north. These new vineyards, in the Northern Cape rather than Western Cape Province, are the highest, most continental vineyards in all of South Africa. **Lower Orange**, also off the map to the north, is even hotter in summer and depends heavily on irrigation from the Orange River. Much work has gone into vine trellising to protect the grapes from the relentless sunlight here.

Summer temperatures in **Klein Karoo**, the great eastern sweep of arid inland scrub, are so high that fortified wines, made possible only by irrigation, are the local speciality, along with some red table wines, and ostriches (for their meat and feathers). Muscats and Douro Valley grapes such as Tinta Barocca (Barroca in Portugal), Touriga Nacional, and Souzão thrive here. Portugal's port producers have been keeping a wary but respectful eye on developments, notably in the **Calitzdorp** district, which routinely produces the trophy-winners in South Africa's fortified wine classes.

A little closer to the gentle influence of the Atlantic, but still so warm and dry that irrigation is de rigueur, are **Worcester** and **Breedekloof** in the **Breede River Valley** region. More wine is made here than in any other Cape region: more than a quarter of the country's entire wine output. Much of it ends up as brandy, but this is the source of some well-made commercial red and white, too.

Robertson, further down the Breede River Valley towards the Indian Ocean, can boast good co-op wines and one or two fine estates. Add to this enough limestone to support substantial stud farming and you have a district that is useful

The only classics here are the commendably port-like wine made by De Krans in the heat of Klein Karoo (the p-word would not be allowed in the EU) and the Chenin Blanc that has been made in remote Cederberg since the 1970s. The rest are newcomers.

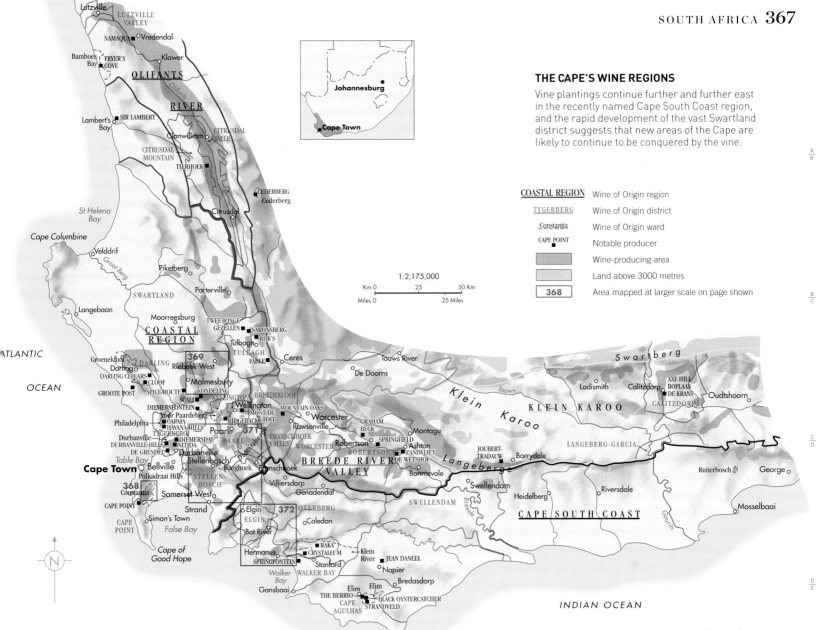

A/B
B/C
C/D
D/E
E/F
F/G

THE CAPE'S WINE REGIONS

Vine plantings continue further and further east in the recently named Cape South Coast region, and the rapid development of the vast Swartland district suggests that new areas of the Cape are likely to continue to be conquered by the vine.

COASTAL REGION	Wine of Origin region
TYGERBERG	Wine of Origin district
Constantia	Wine of Origin ward
CAPE POINT ■	Notable producer
	Wine-producing area
	Land above 3000 metres
368	Area mapped at larger scale on page shown

1:2,175,000

Km 0 · · · 25 · · · 50 Km
Miles 0 · · · 25 Miles

for white wine, particularly juicy Chardonnay, with a growing reputation for reds. Rainfall is low, summers are hot, but southeasterlies help to funnel cooling marine air off the Indian Ocean into the valley.

Grapes of the Cape

The most noticeable trend in Cape grapes has been the wholesale substitution of red for white, especially of the Chenin Blanc vines that once dominated South African vineyards. Chenin is still the most-planted variety, but now represents fewer than one vine in five. To pull up more would be a mistake; old bush-vine Chenin is still the Cape's most original contribution: wine of real style and substance at a relatively bargain price. Chenin generally does best where coastal influence helps maintain its high natural acidity, although old bush-vines in Olifants River make good examples, too – probably from clones well adapted to local conditions. Ken Forrester, Rudera, and De Trafford make some of the finest examples in Stellenbosch, while the Sadie Family's Palladius blend, based on old bush-vines in Paardeberg in Swartland, set a new standard. It inspired a new generation of varietal Chenins and

white blends from Swartland as well as Olifants River and Stellenbosch.

Colombard is the Cape's fourth-most planted variety, much used for distillation. Sauvignon Blanc has its own distinct style in South Africa, not lacking natural acidity, and has overtaken Chardonnay – a pity because in all but the hottest vineyards Chardonnay can achieve a finesse, and in some cases ageing potential, rare outside Burgundy. Cabernet Sauvignon is the most-planted red wine grape but Shiraz (sic) has been catching up fast, so popular are South African variations on this theme, from the determinedly peppery northern Rhône-style "Syrahs" of Boekenhoutskloof and Mullineux to the much richer, brighter, sweeter style favoured by Haskell, Saxenburg, and Fairview.

The pungent Pinotage, South Africa's own crossing of Pinot Noir and Cinsaut, can be found either as an answer to Beaujolais or as a more seriously oaked, if still fleshy, mouthful. The debate as to which works better continues.The

country's red wine production, with Merlot in fourth place, was long plagued by leafroll virus in the vineyards, which stops grapes ripening fully. One of the greatest challenges for South African viticulture will be to ensure that the heavily quarantined plant material that has been widely planted proves robust and healthy.

But without doubt the potentially greatest evolutionary step in South Africa is social. It has not proved easy to share more equitably ownership and management of an industry run for so long by the white minority. There have been plenty of setbacks, but the introduction of an ethical seal (encouraged by some major importers of South African wine) may help. Some people hope that eventually the black majority of South Africans will become a significant market for South African wine. Black empowerment schemes and joint ventures are under way, albeit sometimes developing slowly. Mentoring and training schemes are specifically designed to encourage wider participation in the wine industry, while more winery funds are being directed at better housing, conditions, wages, and general social upliftment, as they call it. Nevertheless, impatience is understandable.

Constantia

Historically, the most famous wine name of South Africa is Constantia, a legendary dessert wine which, by the late 18th century, was recognized as one of the greatest wines in the world. Constantia is now a suburb, a particularly pretty southern suburb, of Cape Town. Land prices are consequently high. Expansion is limited and has been confined to the steeper eastern, southeastern, and northeastern slopes of Constantiaberg, which is effectively the eastern tail of Table Mountain.

But this corner of the Cape, effectively a mountain amphitheatre that opens directly on to False Bay, produces some of its most distinctive wines. It is constantly cooled by the Cape Doctor, the southeaster that blows in from the ocean. Fungal problems are a risk in the warm climate and relatively high rainfall. The Doctor helps.

The grape of choice today in Constantia's 1,100 acres (445ha) of vineyard is Sauvignon Blanc. It represents a third of all the region's vines, with Cabernet Sauvignon, Merlot, and Chardonnay a long way behind. The relatively low temperatures encourage the retention of pyrazine, which is responsible for the grassy range of aromas associated with Sauvignon. Perhaps the most dramatic example of Constantia Sauvignon is at Steenberg, a particularly windswept site. Semillon, which in the early 19th century was by far the most planted grape variety in South Africa, can be outstanding. Excellent examples are made by both Steenberg and Constantia Uitsig. Soils here are deeply weathered, acid, and reddish brown with a high clay content, except around Uitsig, where sand predominates. It is vines in these soils, the warmest and lowest in Constantia, that ripen their grapes first.

Despite the pressures of encroaching urban development (and the occasional marauding baboon from the mountainous nature reserves nearby), several new wineries opened in Constantia in the early 21st century, bringing the total to 10. This total excludes the exemplary **Cape Point** just to the southwest, (see map, p.367) a one-winery district even cooler than Constantia but outstanding for its Sauvignon and Semillon.

In Constantia, both Klein Constantia and Groot Constantia continue the dessert wine tradition with, respectively, their Vin de Constance and Grand Constance, made from small-berried Muscat grapes picked late enough to notch up serious sugar levels and a resultant suggestion of 18th- and 19th-century decadence.

Small-berried pale Muscat grapes are allowed to shrivel on the vine before they are picked and pressed to produce a sweet Constantia wine, in the image of one that was famous around the world in the 18th century. Napoleon ordered Constantia from exile on St Helena.

——	Constantia Wine of Origin ward
■STEENBERG	Notable producer
	Vineyards
	Woods
—500—	Contour interval 100 metres
– – –	National Park boundary

1:77,400

The cool, windswept area of Constantia, overlooked by Table Mountain, is particularly suitable for South Africa's most fashionable white wine grape, Sauvignon Blanc. These are the top two bottlings from two of the finest producers.

Swartland

On the decidedly fluid South African wine scene, it is the Swartland district that has undergone the most dramatic transformation of all. For years it was a name visitors to the Cape seldom heard, and locally was associated with nothing more distinguished than robust ingredients for the co-ops. It still produces plenty of pretty ordinary stuff, but recently this swathe of land north of Cape Town has become the source of some of South Africa's most admired wines. The Swartland Revolution festival every November is the rallying point of a younger generation determined to put Swartland on the international map. Most of this vast area is undulating wheatland, green in winter and burnished gold in summer. But in certain key areas the ochre is punctuated by the green of vines, most of them unirrigated old Chenin bushvines planted in the 1960s to feed the white wine boom, but also red wine vines: Cabernet for quantity, Shiraz/Syrah for some stunning quality.

Re-evaluation of Swartland began in the late 1990s when Charles Back of Fairview set up the Spice Route estate. Its first winemaker, Eben Sadie, was quick to realize the potential of the region's old vines and in 2000 produced the first vintage of his groundbreaking Syrah/Mouvèdre blend Columella. This was followed in 2002 by Palladius, based on Chenin Blanc. Both blends, the produce of several different vineyards managed but not owned, have been much emulated, and Syrah and Chenin continue to demonstrate their affinity with Swartland.

Initially, most attention was focused on the foothills of the granitic Perdeberg (Afrikaans), which attracts more cooling Atlantic air than most of Swartland. Voor Paardeberg (Dutch), the eastward extension of Perdeberg, is technically a ward of Paarl. But the shale and clay Riebeek mountains have subsequently been developed and the pretty little town of Riebeek-Kasteel has become an unofficial wine capital. Johann Rupert of Anthonij Rupert acquired vineyards here to supply raw material for his well-funded winery in Franschhoek. A parallel development is that of Porseleinberg, a wine farm on a Riebeek hillside established by Boekenhoutskloof of Franschhoek, famous for its fine Syrah, to produce its own biodynamic wines. Mullineux Family Wines of Riebeek-Kasteel meanwhile created a stir with their single-terroir Syrahs grown respectively on granite and schist. The young bloods of Swartland are showing distinctly "natural" wine tendencies.

Darling wine district is off this map to the southwest, but is an enclave within Swartland. Its ward Groenekloof is well exposed to cool breezes from the Atlantic and has built up quite a reputation for its crystalline Sauvignon Blanc, pioneered by Neil Ellis. Darling is virtually on Cape Town's doorstep, making this beautiful part of South Africa an easy trip for wine tourists.

THE HEART OF SWARTLAND

The map on p.367 shows just how small a proportion of Swartland is mapped here, but for the moment this is where the new wave of ambitious producers are clustered. The annual Swartland Revolution wine festival is centred on Riebeek-Kasteel.

MALMESBURY — Wine of Origin ward

■ MEERHOF — Notable producer

     Vineyards

     Woods

—500— Contour interval 100 metres

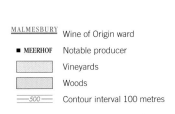

Eben Sadie's Columella arguably kicked off the Swartland revolution, while Boekenhoutskloof's investment in Porseleinberg pays it a major compliment. Testalonga's El Bandito is made by Lammershoek's winemaker Craig Hawkins.

The Stellenbosch Area

South African wine has historically been focused on the area mapped opposite, its centre Stellenbosch a leafy university town surrounded by Arcadian countryside whose curling white Cape Dutch gables are the beautiful cliché of the Cape. South African wine academe lives here, now with students of all backgrounds and including the important Nietvoorbij Agricultural Research Centre.

Stellenbosch

The soils of Stellenbosch vary from light and sandy on the western valley floor (historically Chenin Blanc country) to heavier soils on mountain slopes and decomposed granite at the foot of the Simonsberg, Stellenbosch, Drakenstein, and Franschhoek mountains in the east (the last two ranges being in Franschhoek rather than Stellenbosch). The contour lines and distribution of blue on the map opposite are enough to hint at just how varied a range of terroirs can be found here. At this stage in South African wine evolution, however, it can be dangerous to associate a winery's location too closely with a likely terroir effect, since so many producers vinify fruit from scattered vineyards, often blending so that Coastal Region and the even vaguer Western Cape appellation are common on labels, especially in export markets.

In the north, further from the sea, temperatures tend to be higher, but the climate is in general pretty perfect for wine grapes. Rainfall is just about right, and concentrated in the winter months; summers are just slightly warmer than Bordeaux. Chenin Blanc, once overwhelmingly dominant, has long been overtaken by Cabernet Sauvignon (definitively), Shiraz, and Merlot in terms of total acreage here, while in 2012 Sauvignon Blanc was the area's second-most planted grape. Blends have long been important too, whites as well as reds.

So established and varied are the vineyards of Stellenbosch that there has been time to subdivide what is, according to official South African wine nomenclature, a district in the Coastal Region into several wards. The first ward to gain official recognition was Simonsberg-Stellenbosch, including all the cooler, well-drained southern flanks of the imposing Simonsberg Mountain (the heavy-hitting Thelema estate, not a wine farm when the boundaries were drawn up in 1980, is excluded). Jonkershoek Valley is a small but long-recognized area in the eponymous mountains east of Stellenbosch, while the equally minute Papegaaiberg sits on the opposite side of the town, buffering it from the thriving ward based on the sheltered Devon Valley. The much larger, flatter, and more recent Bottelary ward to the north borrows its name from the hills in its far southwest corner. Banghoek was the newest ward until Polkadraai Hills to the west gained recognition in 2006 (see map, p.367).

On the whole the best wines come from estates on land open to southerly breezes from False Bay and/or high enough in the hills for altitude and cooling winds to slow down the ripening process. The imposing Helderberg mountain running northeast of Somerset West is an obvious factor in local wine geography, for example, and on their western flanks are many winemaking high-flyers. Anglo American's historic and much-garlanded Vergelegen winery lies at the southeastern foot of the range, spectacularly sited above Somerset West.

Franschhoek and Paarl

Paarl, further from the cooling influence of False Bay, may not be the focus of the Cape wine scene that it was in the fortified wine era, but fine table wines are made here by such producers such as Fairview, Glen Carlou and Rupert & Rothschild. Vilafonté, an ambitious American-owned winery in Stellenbosch, also grows its grapes in Paarl.

Franschhoek Valley to the east (only partly mapped here) is now recognized as a wine district in its own right. It was once farmed by Huguenots and is still distinguished by its French place names. The valley, enclosed on three sides by mountains, has more than its fair share of fine restaurants and hotels and pretty scenery, but it can boast a handful of top performers, of which Chamonix is outstanding and makes wine exclusively from Franschhoek vineyards. The valley's other obvious over-performer, Boekenhoutskloof, grows grapes elsewhere, too, not least in an exciting new development in Swartland (see p.369). For long, Boekenhoutskloof bought its Syrah (sic) grapes from one of the cooler corners of Wellington, a less fashionable district to the north of Paarl. Wellington, with greater diurnal temperature variation than areas closer to the coast, is made up of a varied mixture of alluvial terraces, stretching towards Swartland's rolling cereal country, and some more dramatic sites in the foothills of the Hawequa Mountains.

Classic Cape Dutch gables at the 170-year-old Longridge wine estate beneath the crags of the Helderberg. Tourism is, understandably, important to the South African wine scene. Longridge has its own smart restaurant.

In the top row, Vilafonté is the Paarl-grown joint venture between Californians Zelma Long and Phil Freese with Michael Ratcliffe of Warwick Estate. It is flanked by two great white wines grown in Franschhoek. The rest are all grown in Stellenbosch, both Quoin Rock's and Haskell's being fashionable Syrahs.

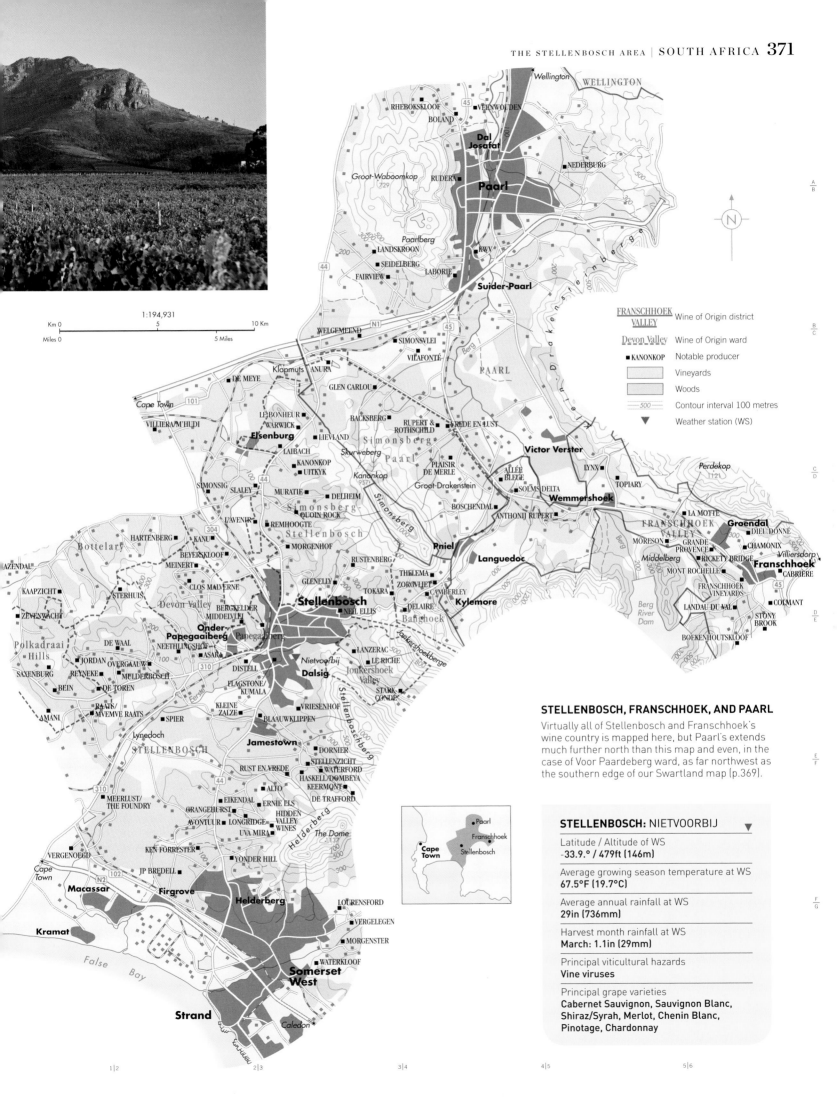

WELLINGTON

Wellington

RHEBOKSKLOOF
BOLAND
VERNWOUDEN

Dal Josafat

NEDERBURG

Groot-Waboomkop RUDERA

Paarl

KWV

Paarlberg

LANDSKROON

SEIDELBERG
FAIRVIEW LABORIE

Suider-Paarl

WELGEMEEND

SIMONSVLEI

VILAFONTÉ

Berg

PAARL

DE MEYE
Klapmuts ANURA

GLEN CARLOU

Cape Town

VILLIERA/M'HUDI

LE BONHEUR
WARWICK
BACKSBERG
RUPERT & ROTHSCHILD
VREDE EN LUST

Elsenburg

LIEVLAND

LAIBACH

Simonsberg
Skurweberg *Paarl*

KANONKOP
UITKYK

PLAISIR DE MERLE

ALLÉE BLEUE

SIMONSIG SLALEY

Victor Verster

LYNX
TOPIARY

Perdekop

MURATIE
DELHEIM

Kanonkop

SOLMS DELTA

Wemmershoek

L'AVENIR
QUOIN ROCK

Simonsberg-
Stellenbosch

BOSCHENDAL

ANTHONIJ RUPERT

LA MOTTE

Groendal
DIEU DONNÉ

REMHOOGTE
MORGENHOF

Groot-Drakenstein

MORESON
GRANDE PROVENCE

CHAMONIX

HARTENBERG KANU

RUSTENBERG

Rniel

FRANSCHHOEK VALLEY

RICKETY BRIDGE

Villiersdorp

Bottelary

BEYERSKLOOF
MEINERT

THELEMA
ZORGVLIET

Languedoc

MONT ROCHELLE

Franschhoek
CABRIÈRE

AZENDAL

CLOS MALVERNE

GLENELLY

TOKARA

CAMBERLEY

KYLEMORE

FRANSCHHOEK VINEYARDS

KAAPZICHT
STERHUIS

Devon Valley
BERGKELDER
MIDDELVLEI

Stellenbosch

DELAIRE

Kylemore

LANDAU DU VAL

COLMANT

ZEVENWACHT

NEIL ELLIS

Banghoek

Berg River Dam

Middelberg

STONY BROOK

Onder-Papegaaiberg
Papegaaiberg

NEETHLINGSHOF
ASARA

LANZERAC
LE RICHE

BOEKENHOUTSKLOOF

Polkadraai Hills

DE WAAL

JORDAN
OVERGAAUW

Nietvoorbij

Jonkershoek Valley

SAXENBURG
REYNEKE
DE TOREN

MULDERBOSCH

DISTELL

Dalsig

STARK-CONDÉ

BEIN

RAATS/
MVEMVE RAATS

FLAGSTONE/
KUMALA

KLEINE ZALZE

VRIESENHOF

AMANI
SPIER

BLAAUWKLIPPEN

Stellenboschberg

Lynedoch

STELLENBOSCH

Jamestown

DORNIER

STELLENZICHT

RUST EN VREDE
WATERFORD

MEERLUST/
THE FOUNDRY

HASKELL/DOMBEYA
KEERMONT

ALTO

DE TRAFFORD

EIKENDAL
ERNIE ELS

GRANGEHURST

HIDDEN VALLEY WINES

AVONTUUR LONGRIDGE
UVA MIRA

The Dome

KEN FORRESTER

Helderberg

YONDER HILL

VERGENOEGD

JP BREDELL

Cape Town

Macassar
Firgrove

LOURENSFORD

VERGELEGEN

Kramat

Helderberg

MORGENSTER

WATERKLOOF

Somerset West

False Bay

Strand

Caledon

FRANSCHHOEK VALLEY Wine of Origin district

Devon Valley Wine of Origin ward

■ KANONKOP Notable producer

Vineyards

Woods

—500— Contour interval 100 metres

▼ Weather station (WS)

STELLENBOSCH, FRANSCHHOEK, AND PAARL

Virtually all of Stellenbosch and Franschhoek's wine country is mapped here, but Paarl's extends much further north than this map and even, in the case of Voor Paardeberg ward, as far northwest as the southern edge of our Swartland map (p.369).

Paarl
Franschhoek
Cape Town
Stellenbosch

STELLENBOSCH: NIETVOORBIJ ▼

Latitude / Altitude of WS
-33.9.° / 479ft (146m)

Average growing season temperature at WS
67.5°F (19.7°C)

Average annual rainfall at WS
29in (736mm)

Harvest month rainfall at WS
March: 1.1in (29mm)

Principal viticultural hazards
Vine viruses

Principal grape varieties
Cabernet Sauvignon, Sauvignon Blanc, Shiraz/Syrah, Merlot, Chenin Blanc, Pinotage, Chardonnay

1:194,931

Km 0 — 5 — 10 Km
Miles 0 — 5 Miles

Cape South Coast

Cooler climates beckon winemakers around the world. Until the 1970s no one grew grapes this close to the cool Cape coast, but in 1975 a retired advertising man, Tim Hamilton-Russell, took a chance with Pinot Noir in the Hemel-en-Aarde Valley above the whale-watching resort of Hermanus. Nothing so close to France in style had ever been made in South Africa. His Chardonnay was even better. It was not until 1989 that the area's second winery was established, by Hamilton Russell's ex-winemaker Peter Finlayson. It was still a tentative zone. Newton Johnson came next, in 2000. Now the region is called **Walker Bay** and has 15 wineries whose aromatic, balanced wines make a distinct and exciting contribution to the Cape wine scene.

The chain of Hemel-en-Aarde valleys, cooled by the Atlantic, still feels remote and wild. Its climate grows more continental as one ventures inland, with summers hottest and winters coldest in Hemel-en-Aarde Ridge. Although average rainfall is 29.5in (750mm) a year, supplementary irrigation is needed in some inland sites, especially those on weathered shale and sandstone. Happily there is enough clay in places to allow dry-farming of Burgundy's grapes. The area has the Cape's highest proportion of Pinot Noir planted and grows excellent Chardonnay, but the easily sold Sauvignon Blanc has become increasingly popular with growers.

Between here and Stellenbosch to the northwest, the old apple-growing district of **Elgin** has had experimental vine plantings since the 1980s, but at the turn of the century the Paul Cluver estate was the only winery. The debut 2001 vintage of Andrew Gunn's Iona Elgin Savignon Blanc inspired a wave of investment. Longstanding grape-grower Oak Valley now makes wine under its own label, and many other apple growers have planted vines. Producers such as Tokara and Thelema vinify their Elgin grapes at their Stellenbosch wineries while other incomers have built their own cellars.

Vineyards are as high as 650–1,380ft (200–420m) and, thanks to prevailing winds off the Atlantic, the average February temperature is below 68°F (20°C). Harvest here is one of the latest on the Cape. Annual rainfall can be as high as 39in (1,000mm), but low-vigour shale and sandstone soils help ward off fungal diseases. Racy whites are Elgin's speciality, but some fine Pinots and even the odd Bordeaux-inspired red have been made.

Other optimists planted the Cape's most southerly vineyards, in the teeth of salt-laden winds east of the village of Elim in the hinterland of **Cape Agulhas**, the very tip of Africa (see map, p.367). Bracing Sauvignon Blanc was Elim's original calling card, but the Cape's other fashionable variety, Shiraz, seems to ripen well.

FROM ELGIN TO WALKER BAY

The most significant parts of the cool Elgin district have been transformed from orchards to vineyards. The dynamic Walker Bay district has been divided into five wards, three of which are shown here.

The Newton Johnson vineyards are surrounded by swathes of fynbos, the Cape's unique flora. The family's farming methods are environmentally friendly, in keeping with the location, and their Chardonnay is especially fine.

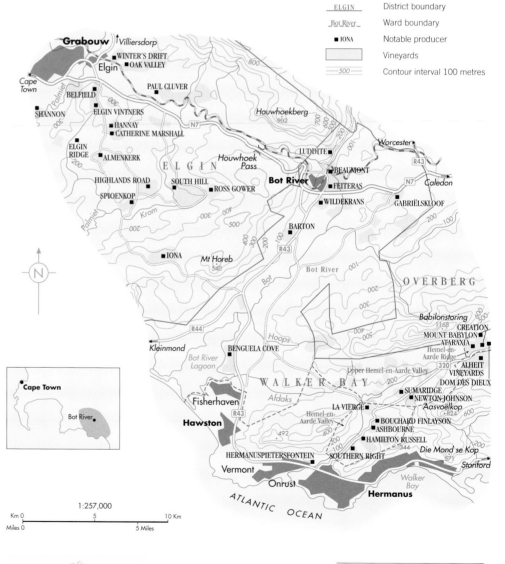

ELGIN	District boundary
Bot River	Ward boundary
∎ IONA	Notable producer
	Vineyards
—500—	Contour interval 100 metres

1:257,000

Km 0 ___ 5 ___ 10 Km
Miles 0 ___ 5 Miles

SHANNON
vineyards
Rockview Ridge
PINOT NOIR 2011
ELGIN VALLEY · SOUTH AFRICA

Jean Daneel

Jean Daneel grows exceptional Chenin Blanc in isolation, well east of Hermanus on the area mapped above (see map p.367), while Shannon of Elgin has benefited enormously from the work of South Africa's top viticulturist, Rosa Kruger.

Asia

Asia, not long ago regarded as the one continent of no relevance to the world of wine, has become pivotal to its future. China, discussed in detail overleaf, has not only become one of the world's most significant wine producers, it is also seen as a market with vast and irresistible potential by wine producers the world over. But they have also been encouraged by how quickly wine consumption has established itself in so much of the rest of Asia as a cultural signifier and general marker of westernization.

Japan, considered in detail on pp.376–77, was the first Asian country to develop a wine culture, including sometimes historic vineyards and wines of its own. But today, wine is produced not just in the Central Asian republics, the "-stans", which have a long history of growing vines and making (traditionally rather syrupy) wines, but in such unlikely countries as India, Thailand, Vietnam, Taiwan, Indonesia (Bali), Burma (Shan state), Cambodia (near Battambang), and Korea (near Gyeongju). Each of these, and possibly even more very recent converts to vine-growing, has a fledgling wine industry, usually based on tropical or near-tropical viticulture. Vines here would naturally produce several rather vapid crops a year, but in most cases are persuaded to produce less often but better quality by judicious pruning, trimming, watering, withholding water and/or the application of various chemicals and hormones.

India's swelling, increasingly westernized, and increasingly prosperous middle class is encouragement enough for the local wine industry. The imposition of heavy duties on imported wines in 2005 provided another spur to the domestic wine industry, which by 2013 comprised more than 70 wineries, although some are dormant or exist simply to sell fruit to other producers. From 2001, the state of Maharashtra actively encouraged vine-growing and wine production via various financial incentives and now grows about two-thirds of all Indian wine. A substantial proportion of Maharashtra's wineries are in the Nashik district, where relatively high altitudes offset the low latitude.

The 2008 Mumbai bombings and resultant fall in tourist numbers temporarily slowed growth, but wine has become a serious interest for many well-heeled, younger Indians, particularly (but not exclusively) those with experience of western cultures. Rajeev Samant, for instance, returned to India from Silicon Valley in the mid-1990s with California wine sensibilities and set about making fresh, fruity, dry white wines, most notably Sula Sauvignon Blanc. Sula's debut vintage was 2000, producing 5,000 cases, but by 2012 annual production was 4.5 million bottles, making it the country's dominant wine company.

The Grover family's highly successful wine operation is older and was established in the Nandi Hills above Bangalore in the state of Karnataka (although they have invested in Maharashtra for a second line of wines). As long ago as the mid-1990s they hired Michel Rolland of Pomerol as winemaking consultant, and the result was La Réserve, a red that would not look remotely out of place on a Bordeaux merchant's tasting bench. The vines are never dormant but careful pruning results in just one harvest each year in March or April.

French colonists introduced viticulture to the highlands of southern **Vietnam** and this continues to a limited extent today. **Thailand**'s wine industry is also much smaller than India's, producing only about 800,000 bottles of wine a year targeted more at tourists than locals. But the six winery members of the Thai Wine Association in three Thai regions form a cohesive whole – as well they might in a country with some powerful forces dedicated to banning alcohol altogether. Its roots go back to the 1960s when vines were planted, mainly for table grapes, in the Chao

Is it the headgear that makes this vineyard, one of Grover's in the Nandi Hills above Bangalore, look so different? Grover's strength is red wine, but transport and storage conditions present a constant challenge for producers of Indian wine.

Praya Delta just west of Bangkok. Today, there are vineyards in the Khao Yai region northeast of Bangkok at altitudes up to 1,800ft (550m). And Siam Winery also has some vineyards and a wine centre for tourists in the hinterland of the resort of Hua Hin, in the south of the country, at only 10 degrees north of the equator. Wines are certainly competently made, and the most conscientious producers try to harvest just once every 12 months, even though it is quite possible to pick five crops every two years.

It is common practice throughout Asia to supplement locally grown grapes with imported wine or grape concentrate, but the Thai Wine Association insists that its members label wines clearly as non-Thai if the imported component is above 10% – welcome rigour in wine's newest territory.

India makes far more wine, including the Sula and Italian-influenced Fratelli labels, than any Asian country other than China and Japan. Thai producers have a will to improve; Monsoon Valley belongs to the same owner as the Red Bull energy drink.

China

One of the more potent symbols of the westernization of China has been the extent to which the staggeringly numerous Chinese have taken to wine. Consumption is rising at such a rate, estimated at 15% a year, that not just Shanghai and Beijing but the so-called second-tier Chinese cities have become even more popular destinations for French wine exporters than New York and London. So effective has the Bordeaux sales machine been that a considerable proportion of the fortunes recently made in China have been spent on red Bordeaux – especially the grandest names and particularly, for a while, the first growth Château Lafite – with a direct inflationary effect on global wine prices. Then, as the Chinese discovered France's second most famous red wine, burgundy prices rose, too. China's new connoisseurs have even begun to invest in foreign wine estates themselves, typically for hard-nosed commercial reasons.

The vine was known to gardeners in far western China at least as early as the 2nd century AD when wine, very possibly grape wine, was certainly made and consumed. European grape varieties were introduced to eastern China at the end of the 19th century, but it was only in the late 20th century that grape-based wine insinuated itself into Chinese (urban) society.

China's love affair with grape wine – *putaojiu* as opposed to mere *jiu*, meaning any alcoholic drink – was so effectively encouraged by the state, partly in an effort to reduce cereal imports, that according to the most recent OIV figures, China's total vineyard area (including those devoted to fresh and dried grape production) nearly doubled to an estimated 1,384,000 acres (560,000ha) between 2000 and 2011. Those same figures suggest that China has been the world's sixth most important wine producer since the turn of the century. Independently verified Chinese statistics are hard to come by, however, and Chinese wine bottlers have notoriously bumped up production with imported wine, grape must, grape concentrate, and even liquids completely unrelated to grapes.

Throughout the early years of this century, it was difficult to find wines labelled as Chinese of any real quality. So fashionable was anything presented to Chinese consumers as a fair copy of red Bordeaux (for linguistic and cultural reasons, the average Chinese consumer insists wine must be red) that there was little incentive to try very hard. Cabernet Sauvignon, and to a lesser extent Merlot and Cabernet Gernischt (Carmenère),

HEBEI AND SHANDONG

This lower map shows that part of China first colonized by the wine grape vine, with wineries owned by such giants as Changyu and three by the government-owned COFCO, including its showcase Château Junding on the coast northwest of Yantai.

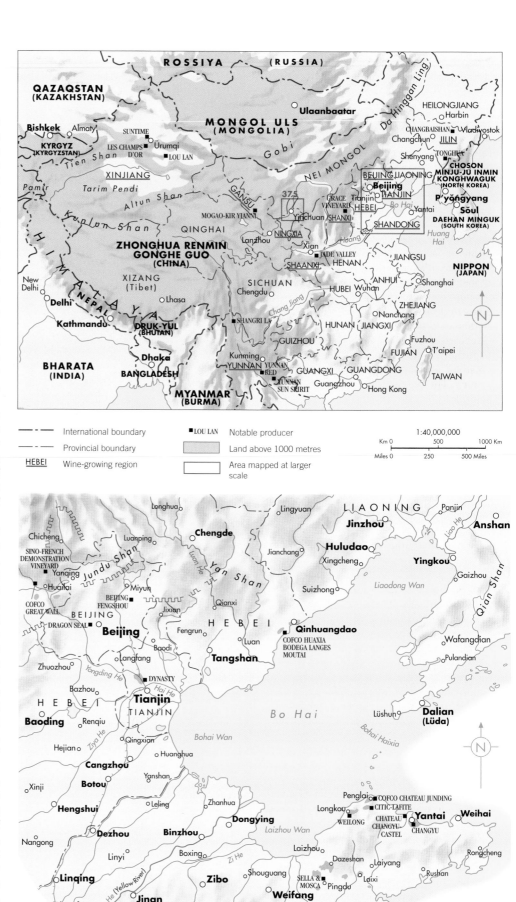

– · – · – International boundary	■ LOU LAN Notable producer	1:40,000,000
– · · – · · – Provincial boundary	▨ Land above 1000 metres	Km 0 500 1000 Km
HEBEI Wine-growing region	☐ Area mapped at larger scale	Miles 0 250 500 Miles

1:5,128,000
Km 0   50   100   150 Km
Miles 0   50   100 Miles

—— Province boundary	
■ QINGDAO Notable producer	
▨ Vineyards	

dominated plantings, but wines were typically under ripe and over-oaked. By about 2010, however, a small elite of carefully made, truly Chinese-grown wines finally emerged.

Extreme weather

China's vastness can offer a staggering range of soils and latitudes. Climate is more problematical. Inland China suffers typical continental extremes so that most vines have to be painstakingly banked up every autumn to protect them from fatally freezing temperatures in winter. This adds considerably to production costs, not least because a certain proportion of vines are lost each year as a consequence of being manhandled, but is currently just about affordable. The continued movement of the Chinese from countryside to cities, however, means that increased mechanization of this laborious operation is surely likely.

Meanwhile, much of the coast, especially in southern and central areas, is subject to monsoons at inconvenient times for grape-growing. On the face of it the **Shandong** Peninsula in eastern China looks one of the more likely places to grow European grapes. With a truly maritime climate that requires no winter protection of vines, it offers well-drained, south-facing slopes. The first wineries and vineyards of the modern era were established there. Storms can strike inconveniently at any time between flowering and harvest but winters are mild. This is where about a quarter of China's hundreds of wineries are now based, but fungal diseases in late summer and autumn are the main drawback. Changyu was the pioneer and is still by far the dominant producer while Chateau Changyu-Castel is a separate joint venture with the Castel family of Bordeaux. When, in 2009, the owner of Château Lafite decided to establish a serious winery in China, in conjunction with the Chinese giant company CITIC, rather to the surprise of industry observers, its chose Shandong's Penglai Peninsula. Further inland, **Hebei** province has the advantage of being even closer to Beijing, and its viticultural potential is probably not yet fully unlocked, but ambitious wine producers have been moving systematically west.

Grace Vineyard was established in **Shanxi** province in 1997. By 2004, it was producing some of the finest wines in China but has since, like many others, been exploring **Ningxia**, **Shaanxi**, and **Gansu** provinces further west. Indeed, Ningxia's local government is determined to make its reclaimed land – at around 3,300ft (1,000m) altitude on the gravelly east-facing banks of the Yellow River – China's most important wine province. Pernod Ricard and LVMH (for sparkling wine production) have already been lured to set down roots here, and both the tentacular giant COFCO and Changyu, originally based in Shandong, are becoming significant producers in Ningxia. Lack of labour and warmth has dogged some Shaanxi trials. Boutari of Greece has invested in Gansu, although soils can be less well-drained here.

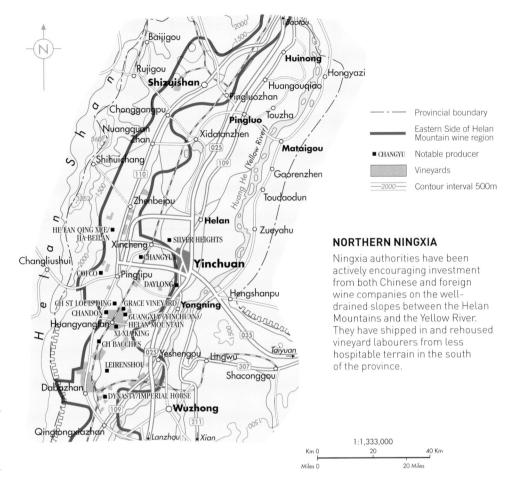

NORTHERN NINGXIA

Ningxia authorities have been actively encouraging investment from both Chinese and foreign wine companies on the well-drained slopes between the Helan Mountains and the Yellow River. They have shipped in and rehoused vineyard labourers from less hospitable terrain in the south of the province.

1:1,333,000

Much to everyone's surprise, a Jiabeilan 2009 waltzed off with an important international trophy at the Decanter World Wine Awards 2011. This bottling shows the footprints of the winemaker's baby girl. The Chardonnay and Silver Heights are also from Ningxia, while Jade Valley, maker of the Pinot, is in Shaanxi and Grace Vineyard is in Shanxi.

In **Xinjiang** province in the far northwest, where much of the population is Muslim, ingenious irrigation systems harness meltwater from some of the highest mountains in the world, but the growing season is short – sometimes too short for wine grapes to ripen properly (many of the vines planted are for table and drying grapes) and the vineyards are thousands of miles from most consumers.

Hunnan/Yunnan province in the far south near Tibet is almost as far away, but its latitude means that winters are much milder. The privately owned Shangri-la winery is producing premium Cabernet Sauvignon, with both Chinese and Australian expertise, at well over 9,800ft (3,000m) altitude on the Diqing Plateau. A new frontier indeed.

Japan

The Japanese palate is famously refined. No other country has an association of sommeliers thousands-strong. Japanese sake in all its nuances is increasingly fashionable and appreciated around the globe. Japanese winemaking is becoming almost as polished. But in constructing Japan, nature seems to have had almost every form of pleasure and enterprise in view except wine. Although the latitude of Honshū, the main island of the Japanese archipelago, coincides with that of the Mediterranean, its climate does not. Like the eastern USA (lying in the same latitudes), it suffers from having a vast continent to the west. Caught between Asia and the Pacific, the greatest land and sea masses in the world, its predictably extreme climate is peculiar to itself. Winds from Siberia freeze its winters; monsoons from the Pacific and the Sea of Japan drench its springs and summers. At the precise moments when the vines most need sunshine they are often lashed by typhoons. Viticulture is a continuous struggle against high humidity during the growing season, with the rainy season in June and July, and typhoons that typically make landfall between July and October.

The land the typhoons lash is hard-boned and mountainous, almost two-thirds of it so steep that only the forests prevent the volcanic, acid soil from being washed into the short, turbulent rivers. The plains have alluvial soils, washed from the hills, poor-draining and good for rice, not vines. Such little gently sloping arable land as exists is consequently extremely valuable and demands a high return.

Ancient and modern

It is not surprising, therefore, that Japan has hesitated about wine; hesitated, that is, for about 1,300 years. History is exact. Grapes were grown in the 8th century AD at the court of Nara. Buddhist missionaries spread the grapevine around the country – although not necessarily with wine in mind.

A wine industry, in the modern sense, has existed since 1874: much longer than any other in Asia. Japan's first outward-looking government sent researchers to Europe in the 1870s to study methods and to bring back vines. The roots of the country's biggest wine producers Mercian and Suntory, for example, date back to 1877 and 1909 respectively. And they are far from the only wineries in Yamanashi prefecture, the most important for wine production, that date back to the late 19th century.

In Japan, the most widely planted vine varieties are the hardy American grapes Delaware and Niagara and the Japanese Kyoho. Indeed, Delaware accounts for 20% of the total area of vines grown but, like Kyoho, it is now used relatively rarely for winemaking.

Muscat Bailey A is a Japanese speciality for red wine, but the most distinctive grape used for wine and the one most readily associated with Japan by foreigners, is the pink-skinned Koshu. This vinifera variety of mysterious origin seems to have been grown in Japan for several centuries. It was originally a table grape but may well be the variety best-suited to winemaking in Japanese conditions. Its thick skins withstand damp well and it can make confident, delicate but well-balanced whites, both oaked and non-oaked, sweet and dry. With each succeeding vintage Koshu producers seem to become more familiar with the variety and more accomplished at turning it into interesting wine, although chaptalization is often necessary.

Today, the Japanese wine market, which is blessed by considerable expertise and some refined palates, is dominated by Mercian, Suntory (which has wine holdings elsewhere, notably the Bordeaux classed growth Château Lagrange), Manns, Sapporo, and Asahi. These five account for more than 80% of all domestic production. All have access to the best Japanese-grown European grapes, from some of the world's most manicured vines. Most vineyards are relatively small by international standards and even some of the well-known wine producers may own as few as 5 acres (2ha) of vines themselves.

Japan is an enthusiastic importer of bulk wine and grape must, although imported content must now be specified on labels. About three-quarters of the wine bottled by Japanese producers relies on some addition of imported bulk wine and grape concentrate.

JAPAN'S WINE PRODUCERS

Japan's thousands of islands extend from latitude 24 to 46 degrees north, so there is enormous variation in local conditions for vine-growing, but the main challenge in the central prefectures, which have the most vineyards, is humidity and fungal diseases in summer.

Even thick-skinned Koshu grapes, a Japanese speciality, are sometimes treated to individual protection, little "rain hats" painstakingly applied by hand to each bunch. A pergola system encourages aeration and can be useful in a monsoon.

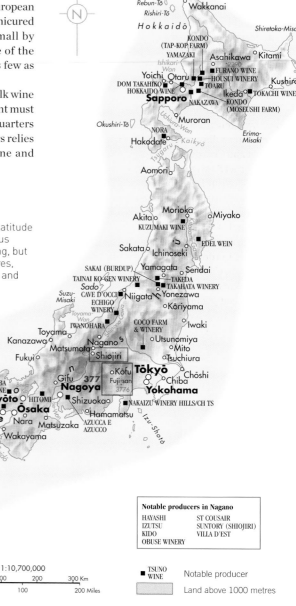

Notable producers in Nagano	
HAYASHI	ST COUSAIR
IZUTSU	SUNTORY (SHIOJIRI)
KIDO	VILLA D'EST
OBUSE WINERY	

■ TSUNO WINE — Notable producer

▢ Land above 1000 metres

1:10,700,000

Wine is now made in 36 of Japan's 47 prefectures. Historically most important among them, however, are those with lowest rainfall – not just Yamanashi but also Nagano, Hokkaidō, and Yamagata.

The wine industry was based from the start in the hills around the Kōfu Basin in Yamanashi prefecture – within view of spectacular Mount Fuji and convenient for the capital. Yamanashi also has the highest average temperatures and the earliest budbreak, flowering, and vintage. Average growing seasons in Yamanashi can vary from about 1,220 hours in Katsunuma to almost 1,600 hours in Akeno. (Comparable figures are under 1,200 hours in Yoichi in Hokkaidō and as opposed to about 1,400 hours in Matsumoto in Nagano.) Forty per cent of Japan's 185 wineries (as opposed to blending and bottling plants, or production centres for rice-based sake) are here.

Nagano is less prone to monsoons than Yamanashi, grows some of the finest Japanese wine, and can now boast 20 wineries. Among others, Shiojiri district, located at an altitude of 2,300ft (700m) in a cool region, produces high-quality Merlot and Chardonnay. Hokushin district is also promising.

In recent years, **Hokkaidō**, the coolest, northernmost part of Japan, rarely influenced by rainy seasons or typhoons and perhaps helped by global warming, has begun to make some interesting wine, notably from Kerner and Zweigelt grapes. **Yamagata** prefecture, also in northern Japan, has made some promising Merlot and Chardonnay.

Cabernet Sauvignon needs kid-glove treatment to ripen fully in Japan, but some decent examples have emerged from the most manicured vineyards of Yamanashi and from **Hyōgo** prefecture in the hinterland of Kōbe.

In the south of Japan, **Kyūshū** is known for refined Chardonnays and light, sweetish rosé made from Campbell Early grapes. All of them are titillating one of Asia's most discerning, experienced, yet fast-evolving wine markets.

YAMANASHI

Yamanashi prefecture is the cradle of the modern Japanese wine industry. It is conveniently close to major cities, inconveniently densely populated – so many vineyards are relatively small, and shoehorned into a basin overlooked by serene, snow-covered Mount Fuji.

Key to producers
1 SAPPORO (KATSUNUMA)
2 ASAYA
3 L'ORIENT
4 CH LUMIÈRE
5 MARS
6 KATSUNUMA JYOZO (ARUGABRANCA)
7 SORYU
8 RUBAIYAT (MARUFUJI)
9 MARQUIS
10 FUJICLAIR

1:700,000

Grace (no relation to the Chinese one) and Arugabranca make some of the most admired Koshus. Domaine Sogga's "natural" Merlot is keenly sought after; Takahiko's Pinot Noir, grown on Hokkaido, is an insider's wine. Mercian is big, but makes fine wine.

JAPAN: KOFU ▼

Latitude / Altitude of WS
35.67° / 922ft (281m)

Average growing season temperature at WS
69.3°F (20.7°C)

Average annual rainfall at WS
45in (1,136mm)

Harvest month rainfall at WS
September: 7.2in (183mm)

Principal viticultural hazards
Rain, summer typhoons, fungal diseases

Principal grape varieties
Koshu, Merlot, Chardonnay, Cabernet Sauvignon, Delaware, Kyoho, Niagara

Index

Châteaux, domaines, etc. appear under their individual names. Main treatments are indicated in **bold**, page numbers in *italics* refer to illustration captions.

Gazetteer

This gazetteer includes place name references of vineyards, châteaux, quintas, general wine areas, and other information appearing on the maps in the Atlas, with the exception of minor place names and geographical features that appear as background information in sans serif type. All châteaux are listed under C (eg château Yquem, d') and quintas under Q (eg quinta Noval, do) in the gazetteer. Domaines, wineries, etc appear under their individual name. The alphanumeric before the page number refers to the grid reference system on the map pages. Vineyards, etc are indexed under their main name (eg Perrières, les). Identical names are distinguished by either the country or region being indicated in *italic* type. Alternative names are shown in brackets: Praha (Prague), etc. Wine producers whose names appear on the maps are also listed.

Freedom Hill Vineyard E3 289
Freeman E4 298
Freemark Abbey B3 303
Freestone F4 298
Freestone Hill Vineyard F4 298
Frégate, Dom de E3 142
Freinsheim B4 236
Freisa d'Asti D3 151
Freisa di Chieri D3 151
Freixenet E4 195
Freixo de Espada à Cinta C6 208
Frelonnerie, la D3 115
Fremières, les C3 C4 60
Fremiers, les F5 55
Frémiets F5 55
Fremont C3 295, A3 309
French Hill C5 310
Frères Couillard F3 111
Freundstück E3 237
Frey A3 296
Freycinet E3 353
Frick B4 298
Frickenhausen C4 241
Friedelsheim B4 236
Friesenheim E3 234
Frionnes, les D3 54
Fritz B4 298
Friuli Aquileia D5 159
Friuli Colli Orientali C4 165
Friuli Grave D5 159
Friuli Isonzo D6 159, E4 165
Friuli Latisana D5 159
Froehn C3 121
Frog's Leap E5 305
Frogmore Creek F2 353
Froichots, les C4 60
Fromm E2 360
Fronhof C3 237
Fronsac D4 77, B5 98, C5 79
Frontignan F5 136
Frühlingsplätzchen F4 G5 228
Fruška Gora E5 261
Frutos Villar E3 190
Fryer's Cove A1 367
Fuchs E2 223
Fuchsberg F6 230
Fuchsmantel C3 237
Fuées, les B3 60
Fuentecén D4 189
Fuentespina D4 189
Fuerteventura G4 185
Fuissé F5 49, F3 64, D4 65
Fujiclair C5 377
Fuligni B5 173
Fulkerson C4 317
Fully G2 247
Funchal D3 215
Furano Wine D6 376
Furleigh G4 243
Furstentum B3 121
Furth-bei Göttweig F4 252
Futo E4 306

Gabbas B4 180
Gabriel's Paddock B4 355
Gabriele Rausse D4 315
Gabriëlskloof D5 372
Gadais Père & Fils F3 111
Gageac-et-Rouillac B5 109
Gaia D5 275, E4 276
Gaia Principe C3 155
Gainey C5 313
Gaisberg, *Kamptal* B1 253
Gaisberg, *Kremstal* E3 252, A5 251
Gaisböhl G4 237
Gaispfad D6 227
Galambos F3 259
Galante F3 309
Galantin, Dom le E5 142
Galardi D2 176
Galatás E4 276
Galatina C6 177
Galet des Papes, Dom du E4 133
Galgenberg B1 253
Gali A3 277
Galil Mountain D5 279
Galilee D3 279
Galippe, la G6 114
Galiziberg B4 251
Gallina B3 155
Gallo Family C4 298
Gallo Family Vineyards C5 298
Gallo, E & J C4 295
Galuches, les D2 114
Gamache F4 290
Gamaires, les C3 60
Gamay, sur E3 54
Gambellara E3 159, G4 163
Gambino B5 179
Gamets, les E2 55
Gamlitz F3 249
Gamot, Clos de C4 107
Gancia C4 157
Ganevat, Dom G2 144
Gänserndorf B5 249
Gansu B4 374
Gapsted B6 349
Garance, Dom de la F3 136
Garanza F3 190
Garbutti-Parafada D5 157
Garda E2 159, E3 E5 G4 162, F2 163
Garda Classico F3 162
Gardière, la C1 114
Gardiés, Dom A3 139
Gárdony F1 259
Garenne ou sur la Garenne, la F4 54
Garenne, Clos de la F4 54
Gargaliáni F3 276
Gargiulo D5 306
Gargouillot, en G3 55
Gärkammer E3 220
Garrigue, Dom la D4 131
Gärtchen C4 225
Gartenäcker C4 255
Gartl C3 252
Gärtling C3 252
Gary Farrell D4 298
Garys' Vineyard F4 309
Gat, Clos de F5 279
Gatt D5 342
Gattera B4 157
Gattinara B3 151
Gau-Algesheim D2 234
Gau-Odernheim F3 234
Gauby, Dom B4 139
Gaudichots, les F1 F2 59
Gaudichots ou la Tâche, les F2 59
Gaudrelle, la B3 115
Gaujal F3 136
Gauthey, le Clos E3 55
Gavalas D5 275
Gavarini E5 157
Gavi D4 151
Gavoty, Dom C2 141
Gaziantep B6 277
Gebling D4 252
Gebling, im D5 252
Gedersdorf B4 249, C6 252
Geelong G2 335, D3 349
Gehrn E4 232
Geierslay D5 225
Geisberg C4 121
Geisenheim D4 G6 230
Gembrook Hill E5 352
Gemtree C4 345
Genaivrières, aux G1 59
Genavrières, les B4 60
Genet, Clos E2 53
Genêt, en C6 56
Geneva B4 317
Genève C1 245, F4 246
Genevrières Dessous, les G6 54
Genevrières Dessus, les F6 54
Genevrières et le Suchot, les C3 57
Gentilini C2 275
Geoff Merrill B5 345
Geoff Weaver B5 346
Geographe E2 337
Georgakopoulos Estate B3 275
Georgas C4 275
Georges Duboeuf C6 68
Georges Road E3 362
Georgia C5 283
Gérard Charvet, Dom C6 68
Gérard Mouton, Dom D5 62
Gérard Parize, Dom D6 62
Gerla, la B5 173
Gerovassiliou A3 275
Gerümpel E4 237
Gestühl B2 239
Getariako Txakolina C4 182
Gevegelija-Valandovo F6 261
Gevrey-Chambertin C6 49, B1 61
Geyersberg A4 A5 235
Geyser Peak B4 298
Gfanger C4 255
Ghemme B4 151
Ghielmetti Vineyard A3 309
Ghioroc C2 269
Ghost Rock D1 353
Giachini C4 157
Giachino, Dom C4 145
Giaconda A6 349
Giacosa E3 155
Giant Steps D5 352
Giarre C6 179
Gibassier, les B4 61
Gibbston C4 363
Gibbston Valley C4 363
Gibraltar Rock G4 337
Giesen E2 360
Gigondas C3 129, C5 131
Gigotte, la F4 55
Gilbert G4 337
Gilles Berlioz C4 145
Gillmore Estate F3 325
Gimblett Gravels B4 358
Gimmeldingen C4 236
Gimnó E4 276
Ginestet B5 109
Ginestra E5 157
Gioia del Colle B4 177
Giovanni Battista Columbu B3 180
Gippsland G3 335
Girardières, les B4 115
Girolamo Dorigo C3 165
Girolate A3 93
Gisborne B6 356
Givry D5 49, D6 62
Gizeux B6 110
Gladstone C5 356
Gladstone Vineyard A6 359
Glaetzer E4 340
Glarus B5 245
Glen Carlou C3 371
Glen Ellen C2 301
Glen Manor B5 315
Glenelly D3 371
Glenguin C4 355
Glenmore C5 339
Glenora C4 317
Glénouze C5 110
Glenrowan F2 F3 335, A5 349
Glinavos B2 275
Gloeckelberg C5 121
Gloggnitz D4 249
Gloria Ferrer E3 301
Gnadenfrei D3 340
Gnekow D4 310
Goaty Hill D2 353
Gobelsberger Haide C6 252
Göcklingen D3 236
Godeaux, les B2 57
Godeval F4 187
Goisses, Clos des D4 75
Golan Heights D5 279
Goldatzel E1 E2 F2 231
Goldbächel D4 237
Goldberg, *Burgenland* C6 255
Goldberg, *Kremstal* C3 252
Goldberg, *Neusiedlersee* E4 254
Goldberg, *Rheingau* E3 231
Goldberg, *Rheinhessen* A4 B2 B5 C3 D5 235
Goldberg, *Saar* C1 223
Goldberg Danzern D3 252
Goldbühel F5 252
Goldeneye B2 296
Goldert B4 120
Goldgrube B5 227
Goldkaul E2 220
Goldschatz G2 227
Goldtröpfchen C2 C3 225
Goldwingert B2 227
Gollot, en B1 55
Golop E1 259
Gols C6 249, E4 254
Gomera, la G2 185
Gönnheim B4 236
Goose Watch B5 317
Goosecross Cellars D5 303
Görbe-Baksó G3 259
Gordon Estate E1 291
Gorelli C5 173
Gorges de Narvaux, les F6 54
Goriška Brda C5 165, D4 264
Gorizia D6 159, D6 165
Gorman A3 287
Gössenheim B3 241
Gottardi E5 161
Gottesacker F6 232
Gottesfuss B3 223
Göttlesbrunn C5 249
Gottschelle F3 252
Götzenfels F5 229
Goubert, Dom les C4 131
Gouin, en D3 54
Goujonne, la G6 53, G1 54
Goulburn Valley F2 335, A4 349
Goulots, les A2 61
Goulotte, la D3 55
Gouménissa A3 275
Gourt de Mautens, Dom B4 131
Gouttes d'Or, les F1 55
Goyo García Viadero (Bodegas Valduero) C4 189
Graach a.d. Mosel E4 227
Graben F4 227
Grace Family C3 303
Grace Vineyard, *Ningxia* C3 375
Grace Vineyard, *Shanxi* B5 374
Grace Wine C5 377
Graci A5 179
Gracia 1 E2 103
Gracia 2 C3 99
Gracin (Suha Punta) D4 263
Gradis'ciutta D5 165
Grafenberg, *Mosel* D2 225
Gräfenberg, *Rheingau* E3 232
Grafschafter Sonnenberg G1 227
Graham Beck C3 367
Grain d'Orient, Dom A1 139
Grainhübel F4 237
Gralyn D5 339
Gramenon, Dom A3 129
Gramolere D4 157
Gramona E4 195
Grampians G1 335, C1 349
Grampians Estate C1 349
Gran Canaria G3 185
Gran Clos D4 196
Grand Clos Rousseau D1 53
Grand Crès, Dom du C2 135
Grand Enclos B5 87
Grand Mayne, Dom du C4 109
Grand Mont C3 114
Grand Mouton, Dom du F3 111
Grande Borne, la G4 53
Grande Côte, la B3 117
Grande Montagne, la F5 F6 53, F1 54
Grande Provence D6 371
Grande Rue, la F2 59
Grandes Bastes, les A5 115
Grandes Places, les A5 125
Grandes Ruchottes F5 53
Grandes Vignes, les E1 55
Grandmaison, Dom de E4 95
Grands Champs, les, *Puligny-Montrachet* G4 54
Grands Champs, les, *Volnay* F4 55
Grands Charrons, les F1 55
Grands Clos, les F5 53
Grands Devers, Dom des A3 129
Grands Echézeaux, les F3 59
Grands Epenots, les C1 56
Grands Liards, aux B2 57
Grands Murs, les C2 60
Grands Picotins C1 57
Grands Poisots, les F5 55
Grands Terres, les G5 53
Grands Vignes, les F2 58
Grands-Champs, les E2 55
Grange de Quatre Sous, la A3 135
Grange des Pères, Dom de la D4 136
Grangehurst F2 371
Grangeneuve, Dom de A2 129
Granite Belt B5 335
Granite Springs F4 310
Granja-Amareleja E4 213
Grant Burge E4 340
Grapillon d'Or, Dom du C4 131
Grassa, Dom E2 107
Grasshopper Rock D5 363
Grassini Family B6 313
Grasweg C5 121
Gratallops C4 196
Gratien & Meyer B4 113
Grattamacco B5 169
Graubünden E5 245
Grauves F3 75
Gravains, aux B2 57
Graves E3 77, D5 92, D4 79
Gravières, les F4 53
Gravillas, Clos du B3 135
Gravina B3 177
Gravner D6 165
Gray Monk D6 284
Graz E3 249
Graziano Family C4 296
Great Southern G3 337
Grécaux, Dom des D4 136
Greco di Bianco G4 176
Greco di Tufo D2 176
Greek Wine Cellars C4 275
Green & Red B5 303
Green Valley F6 339
Green Valley of Russian River Valley E4 298
Greenock Creek D3 340
Greenstone B4 349
Greenwood Ridge B2 296
Gréffieux, les B4 127
Gregory Graham C5 296
Grendel, de D2 367
Grenouilles D4 71
Greppone Mazzi C5 173
Grés de Montpellier D5 E4 136
Grèves, les C5 56, C4 57
Grèves, sur les C4 56
Grevilly A5 64
Grey Sands D2 353
Greystone D4 362
Grgich Hills E5 305
Griffith E3 335
Grignan-les-Adhémar C5 123
Grignolino d'Asti C4 153
Grignolino del Monferrato Casalese C3 151, B4 153
Grille, la F3 114
Grillenparz E3 252
Grinzane Cavour A5 157
Grinzing B5 249
Griotte-Chambertin C6 60
Groenekloof C1 367
Gróf Degenfeld G3 259
Groot Constantia B4 368
Groote Post C2 367
Gros des Vignes, le B4 127
Gros Noré, Dom du E4 142
Groseilles, les C2 60
Gross Gebirg F4 252
Gross-Bottwar D4 238
Grosser Hengelberg E2 225
Grosser Herrgott C5 D5 225
Grosset G2 343
Grosset Gaia F2 343
Grosset Polish Hill E2 343
Grosset Watervale F2 343
Grossfeld E3 254
Grosshöflein C5 249
Grosskarlbach B4 236
Grosslangheim C4 241
Grossostheim B1 241
Grosswallstadt C1 241
Groth D5 306
Grub A1 253
Grübeläcker C5 255
Gruenchers, les B2 C4 60
Gruet E3 318
Grünstadt B4 236
Gruyaches, les G5 54
Guadalupe B5 319
Guadalupe Vineyards E3 318
Guadalupe, Valle de C4 319
Gualdo del Re E5 169
Gualtallary C1 330
Guangxia (Yinchuan) C3 375
Guardiola A4 179
Gueberschwihr E4 119, B4 120
Guebwiller F3 119, A1 120
Guenoc Valley D6 296
Guerchère G5 53
Guérets, les C3 57
Guerila F3 264
Guéripes, les B2 60
Gués d'Amant, les B3 115
Guetottes A1 57
Guettes, aux A2 57
Gueulepines, les B2 61
Guffens-Heynen, Dom A3 65
Guglielmo C3 309
Guicciardini Strozzi F1 171
Guilhémas, Dom F6 106
Guilliams B2 303
Guillot-Broux, Dom C5 64
Guimaro F3 187
Guirouilh, Clos G1 107
Gulfi F5 178
Gülor A3 277
Gumiel de Izán C4 189
Gumiel de Mercado C4 189
Gumpoldskirchen C5 249
Gundagai E3 335
Gundelsheim C4 238
Gundheim G3 234, C4 235
Gundlach-Bundschu D3 301
Guntersblay D4 225
Guntramsdorf C5 249
Gurjaani G5 270, C4 273
Gurrida A4 179
Gusbourne G6 243
Gutenberg F2 F3 G2 231
Gutenhölle F4 229
Gutturnio D5 151
Gyöngyös B4 257
Gyopáros D4 259

Haak Vineyards & Winery F5 318
Haardt C4 236
Hacienda Araucano E1 325
Hacienda Monasterio D3 189
Hadratstall Hohenäcker F3 252
Hadres A4 249
Hafner C5 298
Hagafen E5 303
Hahn F4 309
Hahndorf Hill C5 346
Haid, auf der D4 252
Haideboden E3 254
Haie Martel, la G5 114
Hainburg B6 249
Hajós C3 257
Hajós-Baja C3 257
Halandrítsa D3 276
Halbjoch E2 254
Halbturn C6 249
Halenberg G5 228
Halewood D4 269
Halfpenny Green E4 243
Hall C3 303
Hallcrest D2 309
Hallebühl E3 254
Halter Ranch B1 312
Haltingen G1 238
Hambach C4 236
Hameau de Blagny F4 54
Hamelin Bay F1 337
Hames Valley E4 295
Hamilton Russell F5 372
Hamptons, The E1 316
Handley B2 296
Hanging Rock C3 349
Haniá E4 275
Hanna C5 298
Hannay D3 372
Hannersdorf E5 249
Hans Herzog E2 360
Hansenberg E2 231
Hanzell C3 301
Happs C6 339
Happy Canyon of Santa Barbara E3 312, B5 313
Haramo C5 377
Haras de Pirque C4 324
Hard Row to Hoe A5 287
Hardtberg E2 F2 220
Hardy's Tintara C4 345
Harewood G3 337
Harlaftis C4 275, E4 276
Harlan E4 306
Haro D3 182, A6 192, F3 193
Harrison C5 303
Harrison Hill Vineyard E3 290
Harsovo F2 266
Hartberg C6 250
Hartenberg D2 371
Hartford Family E4 298
Hartley Ostini Hitching Post C4 313
Hartwell B4 307
Häschen E2 225
Hasel B2 253
Haselgrove C5 345
Haseln A6 252
Hasenberg & Steingruble B2 239
Hasenbiss B5 235
Hasenlauf C3 235
Hasensprung, *Rheingau* F2 F3 G2 231
Hasensprung, *Rheinhessen* A4 235
Haskell F3 371
Haskovo E3 266
Hassel F1 232
Hastings River D6 335
Hastings, *Australia* D4 349, E6 351
Hastings, *New Zealand* C5 356, C4 358
Hatalos F3 259
Hâtes, les F3 53
Hatschbourg B4 120
Hattenheim F6 231, F1 232
Hattingley Valley F5 243
Hattstatt E4 119, B4 120
Hatzi A2 275
Hatzidakis D5 275
Hatzimichalis C3 275
Haugsdorf A4 249
Hauner D5 178
Hausbergen C3 252
Hauserer, Clos B6 120
Haussatz F1 254
Haut Cousse, le A4 115
Haut Lieu, le B3 115
Haut-Pécharmant, Dom du B5 109
Haut-Peyraguey, Clos F2 97
Haut-Poitou D2 47
Haut-Valais E5 247
Haute Perche, Dom de D4 112
Haute Vallée de l'Aude G3 47
Haute Vallée de l'Orb G3 47
Haute-Combe, Clos de A5 68
Haute-Févrie, Dom de la G3 111
Hautés, les E1 55
Hautes Cances, Dom les B3 131
Hautes Collines de la Côte d'Azur, Dom des A5 141
Hautes Maizières F2 59
Hautes Noëlles, Dom les E3 111
Hautes Terres, Dom les D6 134
Hautes-Côtes de Beaune F2 50
Hautes-Côtes de Nuits D4 50
Hauts Beaux Monts, les E2 59
Hauts Brins, les E4 55
Hauts Champs, les C3 114
Hauts de Caillevel, les B5 109
Hauts Doix, les C2 60
Hauts Jarrons B1 57
Hauts Marconnets, les B6 56
Hauts Poirets, les F4 58
Hauts Pruliers, les F4 58
Hauvette, Dom A3 140
Havana Hills C2 367
Havelock North Hills C5 358
Hawk & Horse C5 296
Hay Shed Hill D5 339
Hayashi F5 376
Hayastan (Armenia) G5 270
Hazendal D1 371
Hazlitt 1852 C5 317
HdV F6 303
Healdsburg C5 298
Healesville G2 335, C5 349, D5 352
Heart & Hands B5 317
Heathcote F2 335, B3 349
Heathcote Estate B4 349
Heathcote II B4 349
Heathcote Winery B4 349
Heathvale D5 340, B5 342
Hebei B5 374
Hecker Pass D3 309
Hecklingen A5 239
Hedges Family Estate F2 290
Heggies C5 342
Heil A4 235
Heilbronn D4 238
Heiligen Häuschen, am E5 235
Heiligenberg D6 231, F1 232
Heiligenstein A6 252
Heiligkreuz B4 235
Heimbach A5 239
Heimberg F1 229
Heimbourg B1 121
Heimersheim F2 234
Heitz Wine Cellars C3 303
Heizenleithen B1 251
Helan Mountain C3 375
Helan Qing Xue B3 375
Held F1 225
Helenenkloster G2 227
Helios, Dom D4 276
Heller Estate F3 309
Helvécia C4 257
Hemel-en-Aarde Ridge E6 372
Hemel-en-Aarde Valley F5 372
Hendelberg D5 231
Hendry F5 303
Hengst B6 120
Henkenberg C2 239
Henri Bonneau, Dom E3 133
Henri Bourgeois B3 117
Henri et Paul Jacqueson, Dom B6 62
Henri Natter, Dom D2 117
Henri, Clos E1 360
Henriques & Henriques C2 215
Henry, Dom E5 136
Henry Estate F2 287
Henry of Pelham F5 285
Henschke B5 B6 342, D5 340
Henschke Lenswood B5 346
Henty G1 335, D1 349
Heppingen D5 220
Heptures, les D1 55
Herbues, aux, *Gevrey-Chambertin* B3 61
Herbues, aux, *Nuits-St-Georges* G6 58
Herbues, les C3 60
Herbuottes, les C4 60
Hercegkút D5 259
Herdade da Malhadhina Nova F2 213
Herdade da Perescuma D3 213
Herdade da Pimenta D3 213
Herdade de São Miguel D3 213
Herdade do Esporão D3 213
Herdade do Peso E3 213
Herdade do Rocim E2 213
Herdade dos Coelheiros D3 213
Herdade dos Grous F2 213
Herder F5 284
Heritage, *Australia* D4 340
Heritage, *Lebanon* C6 279
Héritiers du Comte Lafon, Dom des E3 64
Hermann J Wiemer C4 317
Hermannsberg G3 229
Hermannshöhle G3 229
Hermanos Sastre C4 189
Hermanus D3 367, F5 372
Hermanuspietersfontein F5 372
Hermitage B5 123
Hermitage, Dom de l' D5 142
Hermite, l' B4 127
Heron Hill C4 317
Herrenberg, *Ahr* F2 220

Acknowledgments

We would like to thank the following for their invaluable specialist expertise, and particularly apologize to those we may have overlooked.

Introduction Key Facts Climate Data, *Wine and Weather* Dr Gregory Jones; *Terroir* Pedro Parra; Cornelis van Leeuwen; Rob Bramley

France *Burgundy* Jasper Morris MW; *Beaujolais* Michel Bettane; *Chablis* Rosemary George MW; *Champagne* Peter Liem; *Bordeaux* James Lawther MW; Alessandro Masnaghetti; Cornelis van Leeuwen; Christian Seely; *Southwest France* Jérôme Perez; *Loire* Richard Kelley MW; *Alsace* Thierry Fritsch; *Rhône* John Livingstone Learmonth; Michel Blanc; *Languedoc* Rosemary George MW; *Roussillon* Tom Lubbe; *Provence* Elizabeth Gabay MW; *Corsica* Lance Foyster MW; *Jura, Savoie, Bugey* Wink Lorch

Italy Walter Speller; Alessandro Masnaghetti; *Etna* Salvo Foti

Spain Victor de la Serna; Luis Gutiérrez; *Catalunya* Ferran Centelles; *Priorat* Rachel Ritchie

Portugal Sarah Ahmed; *Northern Vinho Verde* Luis Cedira; *Douro* Paul Symington, Pedro Leal da Costa; Francisco Javier de Olazabal, Luisa Olazabal; *Bairrada* Filipa Pato; *Lisboa* Sandra Tavares

Germany Michael Schmidt

England and Wales Stephen Skelton MW

Switzerland José Vouillamoz; Gabriel Tinguely

Austria Luzia Schrampf

Hungary Richard Nemes; Alder Yarrow

Czech Republic Richard Stavek; Marie Pazourova

Slovakia Fedor Malik

Western Balkans Caroline Gilby MW

Croatia Caroline Gilby MW; Leo Gracin; Edi Maletić

Slovenia Robert Gorjak

Bulgaria Caroline Gilby MW

Romania Caroline Gilby MW

Russia Volodymyr Pukish

Ukraine Igor Nykolyn

Georgia John Wurdeman; Tina Kezeli

Greece Konstantinos Lazarakis MW

Turkey Umay Çeviker

Eastern Mediterranean *Cyprus* Caroline Gilby MW; Akis Zambartas; *Israel* Adam Montefiore; *Lebanon* Michael Karam

North America *Canada* Janet Dorozynski; *Quebec* François Chartier; *USA and California* Linda Murphy; *Pacific Northwest* Paul Gregutt; *Virginia* Jim Linden; *Mexico* Wyatt Peabody

South America *Bolivia* Francisco Roig; *Brazil* Luiz Horta; *Uruguay* Fabiana Bracco; *Chile* Peter Richards MW; *Argentina* Andres Rosberg

Australia Sarah Ahmed; *Western Australia* Vanya Cullen; Andrew Hoadley; *Barossa Valley, Eden Valley* Troy Kalleske; *Adelaide Hills* Michael Hill-Smith MW, David LeMire MW; *Victoria* Colin Campbell; *Yarra Valley* Steve Webber

New Zealand Michael Cooper; Matt Thompson

South Africa Tim James; Eben Sadie; Dave Johnson; James Downes

Asia *India* Reva K Singh

China Fongyee Walker, Edward Ragg, Gus Zhu; Jim Boyce; *Ningxia* Demei Li; Huang Shan

Japan Ken Ohashi; Yoshiji Sato

Photographs

Mitchell Beazley would like to acknowledge and thank all those who have kindly supplied both help and photographs for use in this book.

Courtesy **Amorim & Irmãos SA** 31 above; **Chris Terry** 7; **4Corners Images** Giovanni Simeone/SIME 216; Günter Gräfenhain/Huber 48; Justin Foulkes 364-5; Livio Piatta/SIME 150; Maurizio Rellini/SIME 172; Michael Howard 202; Stefano Scatà/SIME 350; **Alamy** Armin Faber/Bon Appetit 268; Bon Appetit 118, 220, 236, 253; Camilla Watson/John Warburton Lee Photography 200-201; Dario Fusaro/Cephas 152; David Noton Photography 44-45; GoPlaces 343; Hans-Peter Siffert/Bon Appetit 90; Hemis 302; Imagebroker 240, 251; Lourens Smak 113; Nigel Cattlin 70; Per Karlsson – BKWine.com 80; Prisma Bildagentur AG 244; Tips Italia Srl a socio unico 164; Travel Pictures 209; Wildlife GmbH 15 left; Will Steeley 354; courtesy of the Alaverdi Monastery Archive 272; **Andreas Durst** www.ikonodule. de 224; **Armin Faber** 229; **Austrian Wine Marketing Board** Anna Stöcher 248-249, Armin Faber 255; photo Bob Campbell MW 25 above right; **Brent Winebrenner** 311; courtesy **Bret Brothers** 63; **Bridgeman Art Library** AISA 10; **British Columbia Wine Institute** 28; courtesy **Brown Brothers Whitlands Vineyard**, King Valley 348; **Cephas Picture Library** Diane Mewes 130; Janis Miglavs 8; Jean-Bernard Nadeau 76; Kevin Judd 332-333; Matt Wilson 2-3;

Mick Rock 15 centre right & right, 25 above left, 74, 82-83, 84, 86, 168, 197; Ted Stefanski 300; courtesy **Château Cheval Blanc** photo Erick Saillet **104**; **Claes Lofgren** www.winepictures.com 320-321; courtesy **Col Solare** photo Kevin Cruff 291; **Corbis** Arcangelo Piai/SOPA 158; Eduardo Longoni 328; **Daniel d'Agostini** 280-281; **Dragan Radocaj** 342; courtesy **Errázuriz** 32-3; courtesy **Fanagoria Estate Winery** 30; **Getty Images** Andrew Watson 338; Clay McLachlan 177; Digitaler Lumpensammler 146-147; Frans Lemmens 370-371; Gerard Labriet/Photononstop 120; Jean-Daniel Sudres/Hemis 140; Justin Sullivan 307; Leanna Rathkelly 166; Michael Busselle 73; Milton Wordley 347; Oliver Strewe/Lonely Planet 359; Paolo Negri 156; Paul Kennedy 362; Peter Walton Photography 344; Slow Images 163; Wes Walker 306; Westend61 264; courtesy **Gimblett Gravels Winegrowers Association** photo Richard Brimer 357; courtesy **Grover Vineyards** 373; courtesy **Institut Français de la Vigne et du Vin** 15 centre left; photo **István Balassa** 259; **Janis Miglavs** 184, 286; **Jerry Dodrill** 297; **Jon Wyand** 122, 148, 305; courtesy **José Vouillamoz** 31 centre; **Kameraphoto** Valter Vinagre 210; courtesy **Klein Constantia** 368; courtesy **Kloster Eberbach** 233; courtesy **Marc Chatelain** 145; **Maureen Downey** 37; **Mauricio Abreu** 214, 205; courtesy **Viñedos y Bodegas Milcast** 322; courtesy **Château La Mission Haut-Brion** 94; **NASA** 317; courtesy **Newton Johnson** photo Bernard Jordaan 372; **Octopus Publishing Group** 31 below except right; Russell Sadur 41 above; **Olga and Igor Ulka** 4-5; courtesy **DOQ Priorat** 181;

Philippe Roy 100; **Richard Hemming MW** 20, 25 below; **Robert Harding Picture Library** Julian Elliott 116; **Robert Holmes** 361, 308; **Sara Janini** 188; **Scope Image** Noel Hautemanière 138, Jacques Guillard 57, 61, Jean-Luc Barde 59, 96, 126, Michel Guillard 88, Sara Matthews 154; courtesy **Seppeltsfield Winery** 13, 341; **SuperStock** age fotostock 293; Iain Masterton/age fotostock 226; Funkystock 262; Photononstop 66, 108, 128; Robert Harding Picture Library 198, 218; courtesy **DO Terra Alta** 195; **Thinkstock** iStockphoto 267; **Thomas Jefferson Foundation at Monticello** photo Leonard Phillips 314; courtesy **Vereinigte Hospitien, Trier** 222; courtesy **Vino-Lok** 31 below right; www.weinlandschweiz.ch 247; courtesy **Xavier Choné** 23; courtesy **Yamajin Co Ltd** 376; **Zoltán Szabó** 256

Illustrations

Grade Design Jacket Design; **Fiona Bell Currie** Jacket Illustration, 16b, 17; **Lisa Alderson/Advocate** 14, 16t, 18–19 (19tr based on a photograph by Peter Oberleithner); **Stantiall's Studio Ltd** 34–35; **Grace Helmer** 38, 40

Every effort has been made to trace the owners of copyright photographs. Anyone who may have been inadvertently omitted from this list is invited to write to the publishers who will be pleased to make any necessary amendments to future printings of this publication.